PEARSON CUSTOM
BUSINESS RESOURCES

Introduction to Business
BusAd 250
Iowa State University

PEARSON

ISBN 10: 1-269-10190-0
ISBN 13: 978-1-269-10190-5

PEARSON

Table of Contents

Developing a Business Mindset

From Chapter 1 of *Business in Action*, Sixth Edition. Courtland L. Bovée, John V. Thill. Copyright © 2013 by Pearson Education, Inc. Published by Pearson Business. All rights reserved.

Developing a Business Mindset

LEARNING OBJECTIVES   After studying this chapter, you will be able to

1 Explain the concept of adding value in a business and identify the major types of businesses

2 List three steps you can take to help make the leap from consumer to business professional

3 Discuss the five major environments in which every business operates

4 Explain the purpose of the six major functional areas in a business enterprise

5 Summarize seven of the most important business professions

6 Identify seven components of professionalism

MyBizLab

Where you see MyBizLab in this chapter, go to www.mybizlab.com for additional activities on the topic being discussed.

BEHIND THE SCENES   ENTER THE HAGGIS ENTERS THE MUSIC BUSINESS ON ITS OWN TERMS

Courtesy of Enter the Haggis

The five members of Enter the Haggis need to treat their music as a business to ensure a long and healthy career in the music industry.

www.enterthehaggis.com

Chances are Trevor Lewington, Brian Buchanan, Craig Downie, Mark Abraham, and James Campbell don't wake up every morning and head off to work thinking of themselves as businesspeople. They are musicians first and foremost, members of Enter the Haggis (ETH), a Toronto-based Celtic rock band that has been steadily building a fan base across North America since the lads met in college in the early 2000s.

They're musicians, but they can't help being businesspeople as well. Being a musician can be a lifetime calling and a consuming passion, but earning a living as a professional musician requires much more than artistic inspiration and talent. Musicians who want to survive and thrive in today's fragmented media landscape are increasingly taking control and managing their careers as business operations.

Any music fan who has been purchasing music over the past decade or so knows that the music industry has been undergoing some profound changes. Sales of compact discs have dropped in half since their peak in 2000, as online sales through digital downloads and digital streaming services have grown rapidly. Legal sales of digital music are increasing, although the vast majority of downloads are illegal. However, not all musicians are dead-set against unauthorized downloading, and many openly encourage it as a way to build audiences for their music and increase demand for concert ticket sales.

As revolutionary as it has been, the transition to digital song files is not the only seismic shake-up affecting the music industry. Behind the scenes, a battle is raging between a handful of large record labels (companies that produce and promote recorded music) and hundreds of smaller independent companies, usually known as the "indies." Musicians who can't get signed by one of the majors—or who don't care for the terms of a major label contract—can try to find a home at an indie label instead.

If you were a member of ETH, what path would you like the group to take? Would you try to sign with a major label or go with an indie? What stance would you take on unauthorized music downloads? How would you build a business to support your dreams of a successful career in music?[1]

INTRODUCTION

Like all other professional bands, Enter the Haggis (profiled in the chapter-opening Behind the Scenes) is more than just an artistic endeavor. It is also a business—with customers, suppliers, payroll, production costs, taxes, legal issues, and almost everything else that comes with being in business. And like all other businesses, it is affected by external forces, from population trends to new technologies. This chapter gets you ready for the whirlwind tour of the business world you'll get in this course, starting with a quick overview of what businesses do and then some advice on making the leap from consumer to business professional.

Understanding What Businesses Do

1 **LEARNING OBJECTIVE**

Explain the concept of adding value in a business, and identify the major types of businesses.

The term *business* is used in a number of ways:

- As a label for the overall field of business concepts, as in "I plan to major in business."
- As a collective label for the activities of many companies, as in "This legislation is viewed as harmful to American business."
- As a way to indicate specific activities or efforts, as in "Our furniture business earned record profits last year, but our housewares business has lost money for the third year in a row."
- As a synonym for *company*, as in "Apple is a successful business." Other common synonyms here are *firm* and *enterprise*.

In this last sense, a **business** is any profit-seeking organization that provides goods and services designed to satisfy customers' needs. Enter the Haggis, for example, satisfies an important aspect of consumers' entertainment needs. Although the band is not in it primarily for the money, generating positive financial outcomes is essential to the group's survival in the music industry.

business Any profit-seeking organization that provides goods and services designed to satisfy customers' needs

ADDING VALUE: THE BUSINESS OF BUSINESS

A good way to understand what any business does is to view it as a system for satisfying customers by transforming lower-value inputs into higher-value outputs (see Exhibit 1). If you want a loaf of bread, for instance, a silo full of wheat isn't of much value to you. After that wheat has been milled into flour, it gets one step closer but is valuable only if you want to bake your own bread. A bakery can take care of the baking, but that helps only if you're willing to travel to the bakery instead of go to the supermarket where you normally shop. At every stage, a company adds value to create the product in a way that makes it appealing to the next customer in the chain.

EXHIBIT 1	**Adding Value to Satisfy Customers**

Every company in this chain adds value for the next customer and for the ultimate consumer.

| Wheat farm | Converts soil, seed, and time to wheat | Flour mill | Converts wheat to flour | Bakery | Converts flour to bread | Grocery store | Makes bread easier to purchase | Consumer | Benefits from value added at every stage |

revenue Money a company brings in through the sale of goods and services

business model A concise description of how a business intends to generate revenue

profit Money left over after all the costs involved in doing business have been deducted from revenue

Each company in this chain has made certain choices about what it will do to generate **revenue**, money the company brings in through the sale of goods and services. The result of these decisions is a company's **business model**, a clear, simple outline of how the business intends to generate revenue. Of course, generating revenue isn't enough; the business model must also indicate how the company is going to realize **profit**, the amount of money left over after *expenses*—all the costs involved in doing business—have been deducted from revenue.

Competing to Attract and Satisfy Customers

As businesses create their value-added products and offer them for sale to customers, they obviously don't do so in a vacuum. Other companies are also trying to sell their products to those same customers, and the result is competition. Competition gives customers a wider range of options, and it tends to increase quality, improve customer service, and lower prices.

One of the beauties of a free-market economy is that companies generally have considerable freedom in deciding which customers they want to focus on and how they want to compete. For instance, one bakery might decide to compete on price and structure its business model in such a way as to mass-produce bread at the lowest possible cost. Another might decide to compete on quality or uniqueness and structure its business model around handcrafted "artisan" bread that costs two or three times as much as the mass-produced bread. Each company seeks a **competitive advantage** that makes its products or the company as a whole more appealing to its chosen customers. Consumers benefit from better products and more choices, and companies get to focus on what they do best.

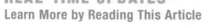

REAL-TIME UPDATES
Learn More by Reading This Article

Ten technology trends that are turning business models upside down

See whether these developments have the potential to enable entirely new business models or knock over old models. Go to http://real-timeupdates.com/bia6 and click on Learn More. If you are using MyBizLab, you can access Real-Time Updates within the chapter or under Student Study Tools.

competitive advantage Some aspect of a product or company that makes it more appealing to target customers

Accepting Risks in the Pursuit of Rewards

Take another look at Exhibit 1. Notice how every company from the farmer to the grocery store must accept some level of risk in order to conduct its business. Bad weather or disease could destroy the wheat crop. A shift in consumer behavior, such as cash-strapped families in a recession switching to bakery-outlet stores instead of regular grocery stores, could leave some bakers, distributors, and retailers with bread nobody wants to buy. Businesses take these risks in anticipation of future rewards.

This linking of risk and reward is critical for two reasons. The first and more obvious reason is that without the promise of rewards, businesses would have no incentive to take on the risks. And without entrepreneurs and companies willing to accept risk, very little would get done in the economy. The second reason that the risk associated with business decisions needs to "stay attached" to those decisions is to encourage smart and responsible decision making. If individuals and companies believe they can pursue rewards without facing the risks that should be attached to those pursuits, they are more likely to engage in irresponsible and even unethical behavior—a situation known as *moral hazard* (see Exhibit 2).

IDENTIFYING MAJOR TYPES OF BUSINESSES

not-for-profit organizations Organizations that provide goods and services without having a profit motive; also called *nonprofit organizations*

goods-producing businesses Companies that create value by making "things," most of which are tangible (digital products such as software are a notable exception)

service businesses Companies that create value by performing activities that deliver some benefit to customers

The driving forces behind most businesses are the prospects of earning profits and building *assets*, which are anything of meaningful value, from patents and brand names to real estate and company stock. In contrast, **not-for-profit organizations** (also known as *nonprofit organizations*) such as museums, most universities, and charities do not have a profit motive. However, they must operate efficiently and effectively to achieve their goals, and successful nonprofits apply many of the business-management principles you'll learn in this course.

Businesses can be classified into two broad categories. **Goods-producing businesses** create value by making "things," from Pop-Tarts to school furniture to spacecraft. Most goods are *tangible*, meaning they have a physical presence, although software, music downloads, and other digital products are intangible. **Service businesses** create value by performing activities that deliver some benefit to the customer, such

EXHIBIT 2	Risk, Reward, and the Problem of Moral Hazard

The relationship between risk and reward is fundamental to every modern economy. A company needs to see some promise of reward before it will decide to accept the risks involved in creating and selling products. However, to ensure responsible behavior, these risks need to stay attached to those decisions, meaning if a decision turns out bad, that company should suffer the consequences. If the risk gets disconnected from the decision—meaning someone else will suffer if the decision turns out bad—a situation known as *moral hazard* is created. A significant recent example of this problem involved home-mortgage companies lending money to homeowners who were practically guaranteed to default on their loans but then selling those loans as investments and thereby transferring the risk of nonpayment to someone else.

Proper connection between risk and reward

Moral hazard: Link between risk and reward is broken

as finance, insurance, transportation, construction, utilities, wholesale and retail trade, banking, entertainment, health care, maintenance and repair, and information. Twitter, Jiffy Lube, HBO, and Verizon Wireless are examples of service businesses. Many companies are both goods-producing and service businesses.

Over the past few decades, the U.S. economy has undergone a profound transformation from being dominated by manufacturing to being dominated by services. The service sector now accounts for roughly three-quarters of the nation's economic output.[2] Although the United States remains one of the world's manufacturing powerhouses, more than half of the 100 largest U.S. companies are now primarily service providers.[3]

Because they require large amounts of money, equipment, land, and other resources to get started and to operate,

Capital-intensive businesses often have high barriers to entry, given the amount of money needed to start operations.

barrier to entry Any resource or capability a company must have before it can start competing in a given market

goods-producing businesses are often *capital-intensive businesses*. The capital needed to compete in these industries is a **barrier to entry**, a resource or capability a company must have before it can start competing in a given market. Other barriers to entry include government testing and approval, tightly controlled markets, strict licensing procedures, limited supplies of raw materials, and the need for highly skilled employees. Service businesses tend to be *labor-intensive businesses*, in that they rely more on human resources than on buildings, machinery, and equipment to prosper. However, the Internet and other technologies have reduced the labor required to operate many types of service businesses.

✔ Checkpoint

LEARNING OBJECTIVE 1: Explain the concept of adding value in a business, and identify the major types of businesses.

SUMMARY: Businesses add value by transforming lower-value inputs to higher-value outputs. In other words, they make goods and services more attractive from the buyer's perspective, whether it's creating products that are more useful or simply making them more convenient to purchase. Companies fall into two general categories: goods-producing businesses, which create tangible things (except in the case of digital goods), and service businesses, which perform various activities of value to customers. Many companies are both goods-producing and service businesses. Businesses can also be categorized as capital intensive or labor intensive.

CRITICAL THINKING: (1) What inputs does a musical group use to create its outputs? (2) Can not-for-profit organizations benefit from practices used by for-profit companies? Why or why not?

IT'S YOUR BUSINESS: (1) Think back to the last product you purchased; how did the companies involved in its manufacture and sale add value in a way that benefited you personally? (2) Can you see yourself working for a not-for-profit organization after you graduate? Why or why not?

KEY TERMS TO KNOW: business, revenue, business model, profit, competitive advantage, not-for-profit organizations, goods-producing businesses, service businesses, barrier to entry

2 **LEARNING OBJECTIVE**

List three steps you can take to help make the leap from consumer to business professional.

Making the Leap from Buyer to Seller

Even if this course is your first formal exposure to the business world, you already know a lot about business, thanks to your experiences as a consumer. You understand the impact of poor customer service, for example. You have a sense for product value and why some products meet your needs and others don't. In fact, you're an expert in the entire experience of searching for, purchasing, and owning products.

SEEING BUSINESS FROM THE INSIDE OUT

business mindset A view of business that considers the myriad decisions that must be made and the many problems that must be overcome before companies can deliver the products that satisfy customer needs

As you progress through this course, you'll begin to look at things through the eyes of a business professional rather than those of a consumer. Instead of thinking about the cost of buying a particular product, you'll start to think about the cost of making it, promoting it, and distributing it. You'll think about what it takes to make a product stand out from the crowd and recognize the importance of finding opportunities in the marketplace. You'll begin to see business as an integrated system of inputs, processes, and outputs. You'll start to develop a **business mindset** as you gain an appreciation for the many decisions that must

EXHIBIT 3	The Business Mindset

Your experiences as a consumer have taught you a great deal about business already. Now the challenge is to turn those experiences around and view the world from a manager's perspective. Here are a few examples of how a business professional approaches some of the questions you've asked as a consumer.

The Consumer's Perspective

Which product will meet my needs?

How can I learn more about this product?

How will it make me feel about myself?

Can I afford it?

Where can I buy it?

Can I get support after the sale?

The Manager's Perspective

What products should we make?
How should we make them?
Can we make them ourselves?
Are there any safety issues?

How can we reach potential buyers?
What should we say?
How can we rise above the noise?
Do we need our own salesforce?

What is our brand image?
Do we need to change or improve it?
Do we need more than one brand?
How do we protect our brand?

How much will it cost to produce?
What price will the market accept?
How much do competitors charge?
Can we turn a profit? At what volume?

Which are the best retail channels?
Will they carry our products?
How much do these channels cost?
Will they support our brand image?

What support services do they expect?
How much can we afford to offer?
Will they pay for some services?
What do our competitors offer?

be made and the many challenges that must be overcome before companies can deliver the products that satisfy customer needs (see Exhibit 3).

APPRECIATING THE ROLE OF BUSINESS IN SOCIETY

Your experiences as a consumer, an employee, and a taxpayer have also given you some insights into the complex relationship between business and society. For now, just consider some of the major elements of this relationship. Business has the potential to contribute to society in many useful ways, including the following (see Exhibit 4 on the next page):

- **Offering valuable goods and services.** If you look around in your daily life, you'll probably realize that most of the goods and services you consider essential to your quality of life were made possible by someone with a profit motive.
- **Providing employment.** U.S. businesses pay out more than $2 trillion in salaries and wages every year, giving millions of employees the means to provide for themselves and their families.[4] In addition, many companies help their employees meet the costs of health care, child care, insurance, retirement, and other living expenses.
- **Paying taxes.** U.S. businesses pay roughly $500 billion dollars in taxes every year,[5] money that helps build highways, fund education, further scientific research, enhance public safety and national defense, and support other vital functions of government.

EXHIBIT 4 Positive and Negative Effects of Business

The relationship between business and society is complex and far reaching. Individuals, communities, and entire nations benefit in multiple ways from the efforts of businesses, but even responsibly managed companies can at times have negative impacts on society in return.

Potential contributions	Potential negative effects
Offering valuable goods and services	Generating pollution and creating waste
Providing employment	Creating health and safety risks
Paying taxes	Disrupting communities
Contributing to growth, stability, and security	Causing financial instability

- **Contributing to national growth, stability, and security.** Beyond the mere dollars of taxes paid, a strong economy helps ensure a strong country. As one example, by providing job opportunities to the vast majority of people who want to work, businesses help the country avoid the social unrest and family disruptions that often result from high unemployment.

Unfortunately, businesses don't always operate in ways that benefit society. As you progress into positions of increasing responsibility in your career, be aware of the potentially negative effects that business can have on society:

- **Generating pollution and creating waste.** Just like all individuals, all companies consume resources and produce waste and therefore have an impact on the natural environment and the soil, air, and water upon which all living creatures depend.
- **Creating health and safety risks.** Many business operations involve an element of risk to the health and safety of employees and surrounding communities. For instance, some of the products you use every day, from your digital music player to your laptop computer, contain many toxic materials. If these materials are not created, handled, and disposed of properly, they can cause serious illness or death.
- **Disrupting communities.** From occupying land to displacing existing businesses to overloading schools and roads with employees and their children, growing businesses can disrupt communities even as they provide employment and other benefits. And when businesses fall into decline, they can leave behind everything from abandoned buildings to laid-off workers.
- **Causing financial instability.** Irresponsible or poorly managed companies can become a liability to society if they are unable to meet their financial obligations and need assistance from the government, for example.

The potential negative effects of business are serious matters, but the good news is that you have a say in how business operates. Even as an employee early in your career, you can conduct yourself in ways that balance the profit motive with society's shared interests. And as you climb the corporate ladder or perhaps launch your own business, you'll be in a position to make decisions that help your company prosper in an ethical and sustainable manner.

USING THIS COURSE TO JUMP-START YOUR CAREER

No matter where your career plans take you, the dynamics of business will affect your work and life in innumerable ways. If you aspire to be a manager or an entrepreneur, knowing how to run a business is vital, of course. If you plan a career in a professional specialty such as law, engineering, or finance, knowing how businesses operate will help you interact with clients and colleagues more effectively. Even if you plan to work in government, education, or some other noncommercial setting, business awareness can help you; many of these organizations look to business for new ideas and leadership techniques. *Social entrepreneurs*, people who apply entrepreneurial strategies to enable large-scale social change, use business concepts as well.

As you progress through this course, you'll develop a fundamental business vocabulary that will help you keep up with the latest news and make better-informed decisions. By participating in classroom discussions and completing the chapter exercises, you'll gain some valuable critical-thinking, problem-solving, team-building, and communication skills that you can use on the job and throughout your life.

This course will also introduce you to a variety of jobs in business fields such as accounting, economics, human resources, management, finance, and marketing. You'll see how people who work in these fields contribute to the success of a company as a whole. You'll gain insight into the types of skills and knowledge these jobs require—and you'll discover that a career in business today is fascinating, challenging, and often quite rewarding.

In addition, a study of business management will help you appreciate the larger context in which businesses operate and the many legal and ethical questions managers must consider as they make business decisions. Government regulators and society as a whole have numerous expectations regarding the ways businesses treat employees, shareholders, the environment, other businesses, and the communities in which they operate.

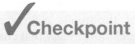 Checkpoint

LEARNING OBJECTIVE 2: List three steps you can take to help make the leap from consumer to business professional.

SUMMARY: To accelerate your transition from consumer to professional, develop a business mindset that views business from the inside out rather than the outside in, recognize the positive and negative effects that business can have on society, and use this course to develop a business vocabulary and explore the wide variety of jobs in the field of business.

CRITICAL THINKING: (1) How can consumer experiences help a business professional excel on the job? (2) If organized businesses didn't exist and the economy were composed of individual craftspeople, would the result be more or less pollution? Explain your answer.

IT'S YOUR BUSINESS: (1) Have you thought about how you might contribute to society as a business professional? (2) What is your view of business at this point in your life? Negative? Positive? A mixture of both?

KEY TERM TO KNOW: business mindset

Recognizing the Multiple Environments of Business

 LEARNING OBJECTIVE

Discuss the five major environments in which every business operates.

The potential effects of business, both positive and negative, highlight the fact that no business operates in a vacuum. Every company operates within a number of interrelated environments that affect and are affected by business (see Exhibit 5 on the next page).

EXHIBIT 5	The Multiple Environments of Business

Every business operates in an overlapping mix of dynamic environments that continuously create both opportunities and constraints.

Company

Market environment:
Target customers, the buying influences that shape the behavior of those customers, and competitors that market similar products to those customers

Legal and regulatory environment:
Laws and regulations that restrain, support, and protect businesses at local, state, national, and international levels

Economic environment:
Conditions and forces (both managed and unmanaged) that affect the cost and availability of goods, services, and labor and thereby shape the behavior of buyers and sellers

Technological environment:
Forces resulting from the practical application of science to innovations, products, and processes; can create and destroy business opportunities

Social environment:
Population trends, social values, relationship of society and business

THE SOCIAL ENVIRONMENT

social environment Trends and forces in society at large

Every business operates within the broad **social environment**, the trends and forces in society at large. For instance, all companies are affected by population trends that change the composition of consumer markets and the workforce. One great example of this is the so-called Baby Boom generation, a generational "bulge" in the population made up of people born between 1946 and 1964. This large group of people has affected business in numerous ways as it has moved through childhood, then into adulthood as consumers and workers, and finally back out of the workforce now that the first wave of boomers has reached retirement age. This population bulge has occupied a large number of middle- and upper-management positions, frustrating younger professionals who would like to climb the company ladder and causing many to leave and start their own companies.[6]

stakeholders Internal and external groups affected by a company's decisions and activities

In addition to aggregate numbers of consumers and employees, various segments of society also have expectations about the appropriate relationship of business and society. The responsibility of a company to its **stakeholders**, all those groups affected by its activities, from employees to local communities to advocacy groups, is a subject of ongoing controversy.

THE TECHNOLOGICAL ENVIRONMENT

technological environment Forces resulting from the practical application of science to innovations, products, and processes

The story of ETH highlights the influence of the **technological environment**, forces resulting from the practical application of science to innovations, products, and processes. Technological changes have the potential to change every facet of business, from altering internal processes to creating or destroying market opportunities. *Disruptive technologies*, those that fundamentally change the nature of an industry, can be powerful enough to create or destroy entire companies.

The fact that music can even be recorded and played back in a different time and place is a profound advance made possible by technology. (Imagine how different your life would sound if the only way to hear music were for it to be played live.) In the 130 years or so that recorded music has been around, it has been available on numerous technological platforms, from wax cylinders and wire recorders to vinyl discs, a variety of tape formats, compact discs, and finally digital formats such as MP3. And each new technology has created opportunities for some businesses and destroyed opportunities for others. For example, if music weren't available as individual digital files, Apple might still be just a computer company and not the biggest music retailer in the United States (through its iTunes store).[7]

Speaking of media, social media might turn out to be some of the most disruptive technologies that ever hit the business world. In addition to redefining the relationships between businesses and their stakeholders, social media are redefining companies themselves by redistributing power from vertical hierarchies to horizontal networks.[8]

THE ECONOMIC ENVIRONMENT

Directly or indirectly, virtually every decision a company makes is influenced by the **economic environment**, the conditions and forces that (1) affect the cost and availability of goods, services, and labor and (2) thereby shape the behavior of buyers and sellers. For example, a growing economy can help companies by increasing demand and supporting higher prices for their products, but it can also raise the costs of labor and the materials the companies need to do business. A strong economy can also prompt managers to make decisions that turn out to be unwise in the long term, such as adding costly facilities or employee benefits that the company can't afford when the economy slows down again. A shrinking economy, on the other hand, can damage even well-run, financially healthy companies by limiting demand for their products or the availability of loans or investments needed to expand operations.

economic environment The conditions and forces that affect the cost and availability of goods, services, and labor and thereby shape the behavior of buyers and sellers

THE LEGAL AND REGULATORY ENVIRONMENT

Every business is affected by the **legal and regulatory environment**, the sum of laws and regulations at local, state, national, and even international levels. Some businesses, such as electricity and other basic utilities, are heavily regulated, even to the point of government agencies determining how much such companies can charge for their services. The degree to which various industries should be regulated remains a point of contention, year in and year out.

The policies and practices of government bodies also establish an overall level of support for businesses operating within their jurisdictions. Taxation, fees, efforts to coordinate multiple regulatory agencies, the speed of granting permits and licenses, labor rules, environmental restrictions, protection for assets such as patents and brand names, roads and other infrastructure, and the transparency and consistency of decision making all affect this level of support. Not surprisingly, businesses prefer to locate and do business in jurisdictions that offer lower costs, lower complexity, and greater stability and predictability.

legal and regulatory environment Laws and regulations at local, state, national, and even international levels

THE MARKET ENVIRONMENT

Within the various other environments just discussed, every company operates within a specific **market environment** composed of three important groups: (1) its *target customers*, (2) *buying influences* that shape the behavior of those customers, and (3) *competitors*—other companies that market similar products to those customers. The nature and behavior of these groups and their effect on business strategy vary widely from industry to industry.

In commercial air travel, for instance, airlines have two choices for purchasing large passenger planes: the U.S. company Boeing and the European consortium Airbus. The barriers to entry in commercial aviation are extremely high, and the customer decision-making process is lengthy and driven almost entirely by financial considerations. So while Boeing and Airbus have to make major investment decisions years in advance of launching new products, they can do so with the reasonable assumption that a new competitor isn't going to pop up overnight and that their target customers will behave in fairly predictable ways.

In sharp contrast, clothing fashions and fads can change in a matter of weeks or days, and the behavior of celebrities and other buying influences can have a major impact on consumer choices. Moreover, because it is much easier to launch a new line of clothing than a new airplane, competitors can appear almost literally overnight.

market environment A company's target customers, the buying influences that shape the behavior of those customers, and competitors that market similar products to those customers

✓ Checkpoint

LEARNING OBJECTIVE 3: Discuss the five major environments in which every business operates.

SUMMARY: Business influences and is influenced by (1) the social environment, trends and forces in society at large; (2) the technological environment and its ability to create and destroy markets and alter business processes; (3) the economic environment, the conditions and forces that affect the cost and availability of goods, services, and labor and thereby shape the behavior of buyers and sellers; (4) the legal and regulatory environment, comprising all the rules and regulations relating to business activities; and (5) the market environment, composed of target customers, buying influences, and competitors.

CRITICAL THINKING: (1) Is it wise for cities and states to compete with each other to be more business friendly, specifically with regard to lower tax rates on businesses? Why or why not? (2) Even though it never sells directly to consumers, does a company such as Boeing need to pay attention to population trends? Why or why not?

IT'S YOUR BUSINESS: (1) How has technology made your educational experience in college different from your experience in high school? (2) Have current economic conditions affected your career-planning decisions in any way?

KEY TERMS TO KNOW: social environment, stakeholders, technological environment, economic environment, legal and regulatory environment, market environment

---

4 **LEARNING OBJECTIVE**

Explain the purpose of the six major functional areas in a business enterprise.

Identifying the Major Functional Areas in a Business Enterprise

Throughout this course, you'll have the opportunity to learn more about the major functional areas within a business enterprise. In the meantime, the following sections offer a brief overview to help you see how all the pieces work together (see Exhibit 6).

RESEARCH AND DEVELOPMENT

research and development (R&D)
Functional area responsible for conceiving and designing new products

Products are conceived and designed through **research and development (R&D)**, sometimes known as *product design* or *engineering*. Of course, not all companies have an R&D function; many companies simply resell products that other firms make, for example. However, for companies that do develop products, R&D is essential to their survival because it provides the ideas and designs that allow these firms to meet customer needs in competitive markets.

information technology (IT)
Systems that promote communication and information usage through the company or that allow companies to offer new services to their customers

Companies can also engage in *process* R&D to design new and better ways to run their operations. Much of this effort goes into **information technology (IT)** systems that promote communication and information usage through the company or allow companies to offer new services to their customers.

MANUFACTURING, PRODUCTION, AND OPERATIONS

Variously called *manufacturing*, *production*, or *operations*, this area is where the company makes whatever it makes (for goods-producing businesses) or does whatever it does (for service businesses). In addition to supervising the actual production activity, operations managers are responsible for a wide range of other strategies and decisions, including *purchasing* (arranging to buy the necessary materials for manufacturing), *logistics* (coordinating the incoming flow of materials and the outgoing flow of finished products), and *facilities management* (everything from planning new buildings to maintaining them).

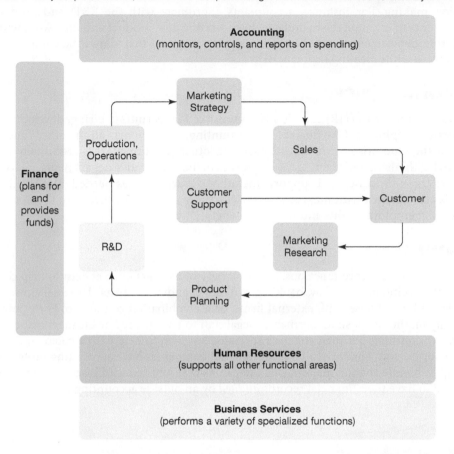

EXHIBIT 6 — **Major Functional Areas in a Business Enterprise**

The functional areas in a business coordinate their efforts to understand and satisfy customer needs. Note that this is a vastly simplified model, and various companies organize their activities in different ways.

MARKETING, SALES, DISTRIBUTION, AND CUSTOMER SUPPORT

Your experience as a consumer probably gives you more insight into marketing, sales, distribution, and customer support than any other functional area in business. Although the lines separating these three activities are often blurry, generally speaking, *marketing* is charged with identifying opportunities in the marketplace, working with R&D to develop the products to address those opportunities, creating branding and advertising strategies to communicate with potential customers, and setting prices. The *sales* function develops relationships with potential customers and persuades customers, transaction by transaction, to buy the company's goods and services. Depending on the type of product, a *distribution* function can be involved both before the sale (helping to promote products to retailers, for example) and after (to physically deliver products). After products are in buyers' hands, *customer support* then goes to work after the sale, making sure customers have the support and information they need.

Perhaps no aspect of business has been changed as dramatically by recent technological advances as these marketing, sales, distribution, and customer support activities. The advent of *social media* has enabled customers to participate in a multidirectional conversation with companies and with each other rather than being passive recipients of broadcast advertising messages. The result is a profound power shift that puts buyers on much more equal footing with sellers.

FINANCE AND ACCOUNTING

The finance and accounting functions are responsible for virtually every aspect of a firm's finances, including ensuring that the company has the funds it needs to operate, monitoring and controlling how those funds are spent, and drafting reports for company management and outside audiences such as investors and government regulators. Roughly speaking, *financial managers* are responsible for planning, while *accounting managers* are responsible for monitoring and reporting.

Accounting specialists work closely with other functional areas to ensure profitable decision making. For instance, accountants coordinate with the R&D and production departments to estimate the manufacturing costs of a new product and then work with the marketing department to set the product's price at a level that allows the company to be competitive while meeting its financial goals.

HUMAN RESOURCES

The human resources (HR) function is responsible for recruiting, hiring, developing, and supporting employees. Like finance and accounting, HR supports all the other functional areas in the enterprise. Although managers in other functional areas are usually closely involved with hiring and training the employees in their respective departments, HR usually oversees these processes and supports the other departments as needed. The HR department is also charged with making sure the company is in compliance with the many laws concerning employee rights and workplace safety.

BUSINESS SERVICES

In addition to these core functions, a wide variety of *business services* exist to help companies with specific needs in law, banking, real estate, and other areas. These services can be performed by in-house staff, external firms, or a combination of the two. For example, a company might have a small permanent legal staff to handle routine business matters such as writing contracts but then engage a specialist law firm to help with a patent application or a major lawsuit. Similarly, all but the smallest companies have accounting professionals on staff to handle routine matters, but companies that sell shares of stock to the public are required to have their financial records *audited* by an outside accounting firm.

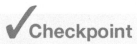 **Checkpoint**

LEARNING OBJECTIVE 4: Explain the purpose of the six major functional areas in a business enterprise.

SUMMARY: (1) Research and development (R&D) creates the goods and services that a company can manufacture or perform for its customers. (2) Manufacturing, production, or operations is the part of the company where the firm makes whatever it makes or performs whatever services it performs. (3) The related group of functions in marketing, sales, distribution, and customer support are responsible for identifying market opportunities, crafting promotional strategies, and making sure customers are supplied and satisfied with their purchases. (4) Finance and accounting plan for the company's financial needs, control spending, and report on financial matters. (5) Human resources recruits, hires, develops, and supports employees. (6) A variety of business services provide expertise in law, real estate, and other areas.

CRITICAL THINKING: (1) Do service companies ever need to engage in research and development, since they're not creating tangible products? Why or why not? (2) Why is good customer support essential to the success of marketing and sales activities?

IT'S YOUR BUSINESS: (1) Think of a strongly positive or strongly negative experience you've had with a product or company. What feedback would you like to give the company, and to which functional area would you direct your feedback? (2) Have you already chosen the functional area where you want to work after graduation? If so, what led you to that choice?

KEY TERMS TO KNOW: research and development (R&D), information technology (IT)

Exploring Careers in Business

Whether you're getting ready to start your career or you've been in the workforce for a while, use this course as an opportunity to explore the many career track options in the world of business. To help stimulate your thinking, this section offers a quick overview of six major business fields.[9] However, don't limit yourself to these six by any means. For just about any professional interest you might have, you can probably find a business-related career to pursue, from entertainment and sports to health care and sciences and everything in between. Also, pay attention to employment trends; as the business environment evolves, employment opportunities in various fields grow and shrink at different rates (see Exhibit 7).

5	LEARNING OBJECTIVE

Summarize seven of the most important business professions.

EXHIBIT 7	Business Occupations: Where the Opportunities Are

As conditions in the various business environments change, employment outlook rises and falls in specific professions. This chart shows projected gains and losses among selected business occupations.

Career Opportunities
% Change in U.S. Employment, 2008–2018

Source: Adapted from T. Alan Lacey and Benjamin Wright, "Occupational Employment Projections to 2018," *Monthly Labor Review*, November 2009 (revised 22 December 2010), 3–10.

OPERATIONS MANAGER

operations management
Management of the people and processes involved in creating goods and services

Operations management encompasses all the people and processes used to create the goods and perform the services that a company sells. The work can involve a wide range of tasks and disciplines, including production engineering, assembly, testing, scheduling, quality assurance, information technology, forecasting, finance, logistics, and customer support. Some degree of technical acumen is always required, and many managers begin their careers in technical positions such as industrial engineering.

The work can be stressful as the organization deals with fluctuating demand levels and process and supply problems. On the other hand, if you want to balance your business interests with being involved in creating a company's products, one of these management positions might be perfect for you.

HUMAN RESOURCES SPECIALIST

HR specialists and managers plan and direct human resources activities that include recruiting, training and development, compensation and benefits, employee and labor relations, and health and safety. In addition, HR managers develop and implement human resources systems and practices to accommodate a firm's strategy and to motivate and manage diverse workforces. In the past, top executives and professionals in other functional areas sometimes viewed HR as a tactical function concerned mostly with processing employee records and other non-strategic duties. However, in many companies, the HR function is becoming more strategic and focused on the global competition to find, attract, and keep the best talent on the market.[10]

INFORMATION TECHNOLOGY MANAGER

Like HR, information technology (IT) is evolving from a tactical support function to a critical strategic component. Reflecting IT's strategic importance, many midsize and large companies now have a *chief information officer* (CIO) position at the executive level to plot IT strategy. IT specialists design, implement, and maintain systems that help deliver the right information at the right time to the right people in the organization. Jobs in IT typically require a degree in a technical field, but an understanding of business processes, finance, and management is also important—particularly as you progress up through the ranks of IT management. Many IT managers and executives also have a business degree, although not all companies require one.[11]

MARKETING SPECIALIST

A wide range of career opportunities exist in the interrelated tasks of identifying and understanding market opportunities and shaping the product, pricing, and communication strategies needed to pursue those opportunities. Whether your interests lie in branding strategy, electronic commerce, advertising, public relations, creative communication, interpersonal relations, or social media, chances are you can find a good fit somewhere in the world of marketing.

Many small companies and virtually all midsize and large companies have a variety of marketing positions, but many of these jobs are also found in advertising agencies, public relations (PR) firms, and other companies that offer specialized services to clients. Some marketing jobs are highly specialized (advertising copywriter and e-commerce architect, for instance), whereas others encompass many different aspects of marketing (brand managers, for example, deal with multiple aspects of the marketing and sales functions).

SALES PROFESSIONAL

If you thrive on competition, enjoy solving problems, and get energized by working with a wide range of people, you should definitely consider a career in sales, becoming one of the professionals responsible for building relationships with customers and helping them make purchase decisions. As a consumer, your exposure to sales might be limited to the retail sector of professional selling, but the field is much more diverse. Salespeople sell everything from design services to pharmaceuticals to airliners.

Many salespeople enjoy a degree of day-to-day freedom and flexibility not usually found in office-bound jobs. On the other hand, the pressure is usually intense; few jobs have the immediate indicators of success or failure that sales has, and most salespeople have specific targets, or *quotas*, they are expected to meet.

The qualifications for professional selling depend on the industry and the types of goods and services being sold. Personal characteristics are of the utmost importance in a sales professional as well, including the ability to listen carefully to customers' needs and communicate information about solutions clearly and persuasively.

ACCOUNTANT

If working at the intersection of mathematics and business sounds appealing, a career in accounting or finance could be just right for you. Accounting tasks vary by job and industry, but in general, *management accountants* are responsible for collecting, analyzing, and reporting on financial matters—such as analyzing budgets, assessing the manufacturing costs of new products, and preparing state and federal tax returns. *Internal auditors* verify the work of the company's accounting effort and look for opportunities to improve efficiency and cost-effectiveness. *Public accountants* offer accounting, tax preparation, and investment advice to individuals, companies, and other organizations. *External auditors* verify the financial reports of public companies as required by law, and *forensic accountants* investigate financial crimes.

Accounting professionals need to have an affinity for numbers, analytical minds, and attention to detail. Their work can have wide-ranging effects on investors, employees, and executives, so accuracy and timeliness are critical. Communication skills are important in virtually every accounting function. Computer skills are also increasingly important, particularly for accountants closely involved with the design or operation of accounting systems.

FINANCIAL MANAGER

Financial managers perform a variety of leadership and strategic functions. *Controllers* oversee the preparation of income statements, balance sheets, and other financial reports; they frequently manage accounting departments as well. *Treasurers* and *finance officers* have a more strategic role, establishing long-term financial goals and budgets, investing the firm's funds, and raising capital as needed. Other financial management positions include *credit managers*, who supervise credit accounts established for customers, and *cash managers*, who monitor and control cash flow.

Unlike accounting tasks, for which there is a long tradition of outsourcing, the work of financial managers is generally kept in-house, particularly in midsize and large companies. The work of a financial manager touches every part of the company, so a broad understanding of the various functional areas in business is a key attribute for this position. The ability to communicate with people who aren't financial experts is also vital. Moreover, awareness of information technology developments is important for chief financial officers (CFOs) and other top financial managers, so that they can direct their companies' investments in new or improved accounting systems as needed.

 Checkpoint

LEARNING OBJECTIVE 5: Summarize seven of the most important business professions.

SUMMARY: (1) Operations managers oversee all the people and processes involved in creating the goods and services that a company sells. (2) HR specialists and managers plan and direct human resources activities such as recruiting, training and development, compensation and benefits, employee and labor relations, and health and safety. (3) IT managers oversee the design, implementation, and maintenance of systems that help deliver the right information at the right time to the right people in the organization. (4) Marketing specialists perform one or more tasks involved in identifying and understanding market opportunities and shaping the product, pricing, and promotional strategies needed to pursue those opportunities. (5) Sales professionals build relationships with customers and help them make purchase decisions. (6) Accountants collect, analyze, and report on financial matters; they also perform audits to verify financial reports or find ways to lower costs. (7) Financial managers plan for the company's financial needs, invest funds, and raise capital.

CRITICAL THINKING: (1) Why are communication skills essential in all seven of the functional areas discussed in this section? (2) Why would financial managers be in a good position to rise up the company ladder?

IT'S YOUR BUSINESS: (1) Which of these seven general career areas appeals to you the most? Why? (2) What is your view of the sales profession? If it is not entirely positive, what would you do as a sales professional to change that public image?

KEY TERM TO KNOW: operations management

6 LEARNING OBJECTIVE

Identify seven components of professionalism.

professionalism The quality of performing at a high level and conducting oneself with purpose and pride

Achieving Professionalism

As you map out your career, think about what kind of businessperson you want to be. Will you be someone who just puts in the hours and collects a paycheck? Or will you be someone who performs on a higher plane, someone who wants to make a meaningful contribution and be viewed as a true professional? **Professionalism** is the quality of performing at a high level and conducting oneself with purpose and pride. True professionals exhibit seven distinct traits: striving to excel, being dependable and accountable, being a team player, communicating effectively, demonstrating a sense of etiquette, making ethical decisions, and maintaining a positive outlook (see Exhibit 8).

STRIVING TO EXCEL

Pros are good at what they do, and they never stop improving. No matter what your job might be at any given time—even if it is far from where you aspire to be—strive to perform at the highest possible level. Not only do you have an ethical obligation to give your employer and your customers your best effort, but excelling at each level in your career is the best way to keep climbing up to new positions of responsibility. Plus, being good at what you do delivers a sense of satisfaction that is hard to beat.

In many jobs and in many industries, performing at a high level requires a commitment to continuous learning and improvement. The nature of the work often changes as markets and technologies evolve, and expectations of quality tend to increase over time as well. View this constant change as a positive thing, as a way to avoid stagnation and boredom.

BEING DEPENDABLE AND ACCOUNTABLE

Develop a reputation as somebody people can count on. This means meeting your commitments, including staying on schedule and staying within budgets. These are skills that take some time to develop as you gain experience with how much time and money are required to accomplish various tasks and projects. With experience, you'll learn to be conservative with your commitments. You don't want to be known as someone who overpromises and underdelivers.

EXHIBIT 8   **Elements of Professionalism**

To develop a reputation as a true professional, develop these seven attributes—and keep improving all the way through your career.

Be the best	• Pros strive to excel, to be the best they can be at everything they do. • Excelling at every level is how you build a great career.
Be dependable	• Pros keep their promises and meet their commitments. • Pros learn from their mistakes and take responsiblity for their errors.
Be a team player	• Pros know how to contribute to a larger cause. • Team players make others around them better.
Be clear	• Communication is the single most important skill you can develop. • Learn to listen as well as you speak and write.
Be respectful	• Good business etiquette is a sign of respect for those around you. • Respecting others is not only good, it's good for your career.
Be ethical	• Responsible professionals work to avoid ethical lapses. • Pros weigh their options carefully when facing ethical dilemmas.
Be positive	• Successful people believe in what they're doing and in themselves. • Pros don't complain about problems; they find them and fix them.

Being accountable also means owning up to your mistakes and learning from failure so that you can continue to improve. Pros don't make excuses or blame others. When they make mistakes—and everybody does—they face the situation head on, make amends, and move on.

BEING A TEAM PLAYER

Professionals know that they are contributors to a larger cause, that it's not all about them. Just as in athletics and other team efforts, being a team player in business is something of a balancing act. On the one hand, you need to pay enough attention to your own efforts and skills to make sure you're pulling your own weight. On the other hand, you need to pay attention to the overall team effort to make sure the team succeeds. Remember that if the team fails, you fail, too.

Great team players know how to make those around them more effective, whether it's lending a hand during crunch time, sharing resources, removing obstacles, making introductions, or offering expertise. In fact, the ability to help others improve their performance is one of the key attributes executives look for when they want to promote people into management.

Being a team player also means showing loyalty to your organization and protecting your employer's reputation—one of the most important assets any company has. Pros don't trash their employers in front of customers or in their personal blogs. When they have a problem, they solve it; they don't share it.

COMMUNICATING EFFECTIVELY

If you're looking for a surefire way to stand out from your competition and establish yourself as a competent professional, improving your communication skills may be the most important step you can take. Follow these guidelines to improve your effectiveness as a communicator:

- **Listen actively.** Active listening means making a conscious effort to turn off your own filters and biases to truly hear and understand what someone else is saying.
- **Provide practical information.** Give people useful information that is adapted to their specific needs.
- **Give facts rather than vague impressions.** Use concrete language, specific detail, and supporting information that is clear, convincing, accurate, and ethical.
- **Don't present opinions as facts.** If you are offering an opinion, make sure the audience understands that.
- **Present information in a concise, efficient manner.** Audiences appreciate—and respond more positively to—high-efficiency messages.
- **Clarify expectations and responsibilities.** Clearly state what you expect from your readers or listeners and what you can do for them.
- **Offer compelling, persuasive arguments and recommendations.** Make it clear to people how they will benefit from responding to your messages the way you want them to.

DEMONSTRATING ETIQUETTE

etiquette The expected norms of behavior in any particular situation

A vital element of professionalism is **etiquette**, the expected norms of behavior in any particular situation. The way you conduct yourself, interact with others, and handle conflict can have a profound influence on your company's success and on your career. Etiquette blunders can have serious financial costs through lower productivity and lost business opportunities.[12] When executives hire and promote you, they expect your behavior to protect the company's reputation. The more you understand such expectations, the better chance you have of avoiding career-damaging mistakes. Moreover, etiquette is an important way to show respect for others and contribute to a smooth-running workplace.

Long lists of etiquette "rules" can be overwhelming, and you'll never be able to memorize all of them. Fortunately, you can count on three principles to get you through any situation: respect, courtesy, and common sense. Moreover, following these principles will encourage forgiveness if you do happen to make a mistake. As you prepare to encounter new situations, take some time to learn the expectations of the other people involved. Travel guidebooks are a great source of information about norms and customs in other countries. Check to see if your library has online access to the Culture-Grams database or review the country etiquette guides available through the Real-Time Updates Learn More item on this page. Don't be afraid to ask questions, either. People will respect your concern and curiosity. You will gradually accumulate considerable knowledge, which will help you feel comfortable and be effective in a wide range of business situations.

MAKING ETHICAL DECISIONS

True professionals conduct themselves with a clear sense of right and wrong. They avoid committing *ethical lapses*, and they carefully weigh all the options when confronted with *ethical dilemmas*.

REAL-TIME UPDATES
Learn More by Reading This Article

Doing business globally with local sensitivity

Get insider tips on how to get along in business cultures around the world. Go to http://real-timeupdates.com/bia6 and click on Learn More. If you are using MyBizLab, you can access Real-Time Updates within the chapter or under Student Study Tools.

MAINTAINING A CONFIDENT, POSITIVE OUTLOOK

Spend a few minutes around successful people in any field, and chances are you'll notice how optimistic they are. They believe in what they're doing, and they believe in themselves and their ability to solve problems and overcome obstacles.

Being positive doesn't mean displaying mindless optimism or spewing happy talk all the time. It means acknowledging that things may be difficult but then buckling down and getting the job done anyway. It means no whining and no slacking off, even when the going gets tough. We live in an imperfect world, no question—jobs can be boring or difficult, customers can be unpleasant, and bosses can be unreasonable. But when you're a pro, you find a way to power through.

Your energy, positive or negative, is also contagious. Both in-person and online, you'll spend as much time with your colleagues as you spend with family and friends. Personal demeanor is therefore a vital element of workplace harmony. No one expects (or wants) you to be artificially upbeat and bubbly every second of the day, but one negative personality can make an entire office miserable and unproductive. Every person in a company has a responsibility to contribute to a positive, energetic work environment.

For the latest information on developing a business mindset and becoming a successful professional, visit http://real-timeupdates.com/bia6.

 Checkpoint

LEARNING OBJECTIVE 6: Identify seven components of professionalism.

SUMMARY: Professionalism is the quality of performing at a high level and conducting yourself with purpose and pride. Seven key traits of professionalism are striving to excel, being dependable and accountable, being a team player, communicating effectively, demonstrating a sense of etiquette, making ethical decisions, and maintaining a positive outlook.

CRITICAL THINKING: (1) How much loyalty do employees owe to their employers? Explain your answer. (2) Would it be unethical to maintain a positive public persona if you have private doubts about the path your company is pursuing? Why or why not?

IT'S YOUR BUSINESS: (1) In what ways do you exhibit professionalism as a student? (2) You can see plenty of examples of unprofessional business behavior in the news media and in your own consumer and employee experiences. Why should you bother being professional yourself?

KEY TERMS TO KNOW: professionalism, etiquette

BEHIND THE SCENES

BUILD A BAND, THEN BUILD A BUSINESS

MyBizLab

The beginnings of the Celtic rock band Enter the Haggis (ETH) coincided with the beginning of the revolution in the music industry. Millions of music listeners were fed up with the business model that had been in place for decades, in which record labels forced customers to purchase entire albums for $15 to $20, even when they might want only one or two songs on an album—and usually without the opportunity to listen to the rest of the album first.

Within the music business, thousands of musicians were fed up with the mainstream business model as well. The industry was dominated by a small number of large record companies, also known as *record labels*. These labels made major

investments in the careers of a small number of musicians, from paying for recording sessions to promoting the music to radio stations, which to a large degree dictated the music the public got to hear.

This business model worked out nicely for those musicians lucky enough to get signed by one of the major labels, lucky enough to get significant radio airplay, lucky enough to get significant album and concert sales as a result of that radio exposure, and lucky or smart enough to sign a contract that actually passed some of the resulting profits back to the musicians.

However, the dominant business model was far less satisfying for thousands of other musical acts. With a business model built around big investments made in the hope of big paybacks, the big labels focused on acts with the best chance of appealing to a wide audience. Musicians and groups without a mainstream sound usually needed to look elsewhere. And when the major labels did sign an act, they often exerted a lot of creative and financial control, influencing the sound, the public image, and the career track of the artists in which they invested. Moreover, they recouped their costs before the artist saw any money from album sales, meaning an artist usually had to sell a huge pile of albums to start seeing any money at all from a recording contract. In other words, for many artists, the chances of getting a major label contract were slim, and the chances of being satisfied with such a contract were even slimmer.

Against this backdrop of widespread dissatisfaction on the part of both consumers and creators, a number of forces in the technological environment were turning the industry upside down. The compact disc (CD) gradually replaced most sales of vinyl albums, but it triggered something much more disruptive than simply replacing one album format with another. CDs, of course, store music in digital format, which means the music can be transferred to and played on computers and other digital devices—and distributed over computer networks. The introduction of widely accepted standard file formats, most notably MP3, made it easy to copy and share song files from one device to another. The rapid spread of high-speed Internet connections, low-cost digital music players such as the iPod, and social media such as MySpace and Last.fm added the final pieces of the puzzle. The music industry would never be the same again.

ETH stepped right into this upheaval and embraced a new way of thinking. The group signed with United for Opportunity (UFO), which describes itself as "an organization of experienced, independent-thinking music industry activists that have come together to create a new model for a record label/music distribution company." Not only does UFO support the band's philosophy of giving musicians and their fans more control, but signing with an indie makes more financial sense, too. According to ETH's Brian Buchanan, "The average independent musician sees more real cash from 10,000 independent sales than many major artists see from a million sales."

Will ETH ever become filthy rich playing Celtic-influenced music? Probably not. However, as Buchanan puts it, "Success is making any kind of a living doing the thing you love." By meshing their business model with the changing business environment and working tirelessly to connect with their customers, ETH stands a good chance of making enough money to keep doing what they love for as long as they love doing it.

Critical Thinking Questions

1. Assume that ETH really were in it for the money and not the music. Would it still make sense to stick with an indie label, or should the band pursue a major label contract and all the potential marketing exposure that comes with it? Explain your answer.
2. Search online for "Enter the Haggis" and identify how many ways you can listen to the band's music for free. Why is it in the group's long-term interest to make its music available for free like this?
3. If the band had begun its professional existence 10 years earlier, how might its business strategy be different from the path it took?

LEARN MORE ONLINE

Explore the band's website, at **www.enterthehaggis.com**, and its presence on Facebook, YouTube, MySpace, Twitter, and iLike. How does the band use its online presence to build a relationship with fans?

MyBizLab

Log on to www.mybizlab.com to access study and assessment aids associated with this chapter.

KEY TERMS

barrier to entry
business
business mindset
business model
competitive advantage
economic environment
etiquette
goods-producing businesses
information technology (IT)
legal and regulatory environment
market environment

not-for-profit organizations
operations management
professionalism
profit
research and development (R&D)
revenue
service businesses
social environment
stakeholders
technological environment

TEST YOUR KNOWLEDGE

Questions for Review

1. What is a business model?
2. What are four ways that business can benefit society?
3. Do all companies have an R&D function? Explain your answer.
4. How does the role of a financial manager differ from the role of an accountant?
5. What is professionalism?

Questions for Analysis

6. Why is it often easier to start a service business than a goods-producing business?
7. Does a downturn in the economy hurt all companies equally? Provide several examples to support your answer.
8. Do laws and regulations always restrict or impede the efforts of business professionals, or can they actually help businesses? Explain you answer.

9. Why is it important for IT specialists and managers to understand business in addition to information technology?
10. **Ethical Considerations.** Is managing a business in ways that reflect society's core values always ethical? Explain your answer.

Questions for Application

11. How will you be able to apply your experience as a consumer of educational services to the challenges you'll face in your career after graduation?
12. What are some of the ways a company in the health-care industry could improve its long-term planning by studying population trends?
13. Identify at least five ways in which your life would be different without digital technology. Would it be more or less enjoyable? More or less productive?
14. Identify three ways in which the principles of professionalism described in this chapter can make you a more successful student.

EXPAND YOUR KNOWLEDGE

Discovering Career Opportunities

Your college's career center offers numerous resources to help you launch your career. Imagine that you write a blog for students at your college, and you want to introduce them to the center's services. Write a blog post of 300 to 400 words, summarizing what the center can do for students.

Improving Your Tech Insights: Digital Products

The category of digital products encompasses an extremely broad range of product types, from e-books to music and movie files to software and instruction sets for automated machinery. Digital products are commonplace these days, but the ability to remotely deliver product value is quite a staggering concept when you think about it. (As just one example, consider that a single iPod or other digital music players can carry the equivalent of several thousand tapes or CDs.)

Supplying music over the Internet is amazing enough, but today even *tangible* products can be delivered electronically: The technology that deposits layers of ink in inkjet printers is being adapted to deposit layers of other liquefied materials, including plastics and metals. Called *3D printing*, *inkjet fabrication*, or *additive fabrication*, this technology is already being used to "print" product prototypes, architectural models, and a variety of electronic and mechanical components. As the price of the technology continues to drop, don't be surprised if one day you'll be able to download product description files from the Internet and fabricate physical items right on your own home "printer." For more about this technology, visit Dimension 3D Printing (www.dimensionprinting.com), Stratasys (www.stratasys.com), or Z Corporation (www.zcorp.com).

Choose a category of products that has been changed dramatically by the ability to deliver value digitally. In a brief email message to your instructor, explain how digital technology revolutionized this market segment.[13]

PRACTICE YOUR SKILLS

Sharpening Your Communication Skills

Select a local service business where you have been a customer. How does that business try to gain a competitive advantage in the marketplace? Write a brief summary describing whether the company competes on speed, quality, price, innovation, service, or a combination of those attributes. Be prepared to present your analysis to your classmates.

Building Your Team Skills

In teams assigned by your instructor, each member should first identify one career path (such as marketing or accounting) that he or she might like to pursue after graduation and share that choice with the rest of the team. Each team member should then research the others' career options to find at least one significant factor, positive or negative, that could affect someone entering that career. For example, if there are four people on your team, you will research the three careers identified by your three teammates. After the research is complete, convene an in-person or online meeting to give each member of the team an informal career counseling session based on the research findings.

Developing Your Research Skills

Gaining a competitive advantage in today's marketplace is critical to a company's success. Research any company that sounds interesting to you and identify the steps it has taken to create competitive advantages for individual products or the company as a whole.

1. What goods or services does the company manufacture or sell?
2. How does the company set its goods or services apart from those of its competitors? Does the company compete on price, quality, service, innovation, or some other attribute?
3. How do the company's customer communication efforts convey those competitive advantages?

REFERENCES

1. Adapted from Enter the Haggis website, accessed 28 July 2011, www.enterthehaggis.com; United for Opportunity website, accessed 28 July 2011, www.ufomusic.com; Bill Palladino, "Music Business Economics 101," Claudia Schmidt website, accessed 10 May 2009, www.claudiaschmidt.com; Brian Buchanan, "21st Century Rockstardom," blog post, 7 April 2008, www.enterthe-haggis.com; Christopher Knab, "Oh, How the Music Business Keeps Changing," Music Biz Academy.com, January 2009, www .musicbizacademy.com; Ethan Smith, "Can He Save Rock 'n' Roll?" *Wall Street Journal*, 21 February 2009, http://online.wsj .com.
2. "Gross-Domestic-Product-by-Industry Accounts," U.S. Bureau of Economic Analysis website, Release Date: 26 April 2011, www .bea.gov.
3. "The 2011 Fortune 500," *Fortune*, accessed 27 July 2011, http:// money.cnn.com.
4. "SOI Tax Stats–Integrated Business Data," IRS website, accessed 27 July 2011, www.irs.gov.
5. "SOI Tax Stats–Integrated Business Data."
6. Cheryl Winokur Munk, "4 Generations," *Community Banker*, January 2009, 30–33.
7. Ed Christman, "Digital Divide," *Billboard*, 22 May 2010, www .billboard.biz.
8. David Kirkpatrick, "Social Power and the Coming Corporate Revolutions," *Forbes*, 7 September 2011, www.forbes.com.
9. Career profiles in this section adapted from U.S. Bureau of Labor Statistics, *Occupational Outlook Handbook, 2008–2009 Edition*, www.bls.gov/oco.
10. Kris Dunn, "The Five Sweetest Jobs in HR and Talent Management," *Workforce*, July 2008, www.workforce.com.
11. Meredith Levinson, "Should You Get an MBA?" *CIO*, 5 July 2007, www.cio.com.
12. Susan G. Hauser, "The Degeneration of Decorum," *Workforce Management*, January 2011, 16–18, 20–21.
13. Adapted from Dimension 3D Printing website, accessed 28 July 2011, www.dimensionprinting.com; Stratasys website, accessed 28 July 2011, www.stratasys.com; Z Corporation, accessed 28 July 2011, www.zcorp.com.

GLOSSARY

barrier to entry Any resource or capability a company must have before it can start competing in a given market

business Any profit-seeking organization that provides goods and services designed to satisfy customers' needs

business mindset A view of business that considers the myriad decisions that must be made and the many problems that must be overcome before companies can deliver the products that satisfy customer needs

business model A concise description of how a business intends to generate revenue

competitive advantage Some aspect of a product or company that makes it more appealing to target customers

economic environment The conditions and forces that affect the cost and availability of goods, services, and labor and thereby shape the behavior of buyers and sellers

etiquette The expected norms of behavior in any particular situation

goods-producing businesses Companies that create value by making "things," most of which are tangible (digital products such as software are a notable exception)

information technology (IT) Systems that promote communication and information usage through the company or that allow companies to offer new services to their customers

legal and regulatory environment Laws and regulations at local, state, national, and even international levels

market environment A company's target customers, the buying influences that shape the behavior of those customers, and competitors that market similar products to those customers

not-for-profit organizations Organizations that provide goods and services without having a profit motive; also called nonprofit organizations

operations management Management of the people and processes involved in creating goods and services

professionalism The quality of performing at a high level and conducting oneself with purpose and pride

profit Money left over after all the costs involved in doing business have been deducted from revenue

research and development (R&D) Functional area responsible for conceiving and designing new products

revenue Money a company brings in through the sale of goods and services

service businesses Companies that create value by performing activities that deliver some benefit to customers

social environment Trends and forces in society at large

stakeholders Internal and external groups affected by a company's decisions and activities

technological environment Forces resulting from the practical application of science to innovations, products, and processes

Understanding Basic Economics

1 Define *economics* and explain why scarcity is central to economic decision making

2 Differentiate among the major types of economic systems

3 Explain the interaction between demand and supply

4 Identify four macroeconomic issues that are essential to understanding the behavior of the economy

5 Outline the debate over deregulation and identify four key roles that governments play in the economy

6 Identify the major ways of measuring economic activity

MyBizLab

Where you see MyBizLab in this chapter, go to www.mybizlab.com for additional activities on the topic being discussed.

BEHIND THE SCENES WILL THE SUN KEEP SHINING ON SUNTECH POWER?

AP Photo

As a worldwide leader in solar energy products, Suntech Power influences—and is influenced by—the economies of many countries.

www.suntech-power.com

The sun sustains life on Earth, but can it power a modern economy?

Solar energy technologists have been working for decades to create photovoltaic panels that can generate electricity cheaply enough to compete with coal, nuclear, natural gas, and hydroelectric power, which currently supply the vast majority of U.S. electricity needs. (Photovoltaic panels, which convert sunlight into electricity directly, are one of two main solar electricity methods. An alternative method uses mirrors to concentrate sunlight to boil water for steam generators.)

Renewable energy sources such as solar, which don't require a continuous source of fuel, could have tremendous benefits in a modern economy. Moreover, because solar energy doesn't involve burning some kind of fuel or impeding the flow of a river, it doesn't present the same environmental challenges as other energy sources. (That is not to say that solar is an absolutely "clean" energy; the manufacture of photovoltaic panels requires both energy and nonrenewable resources, for example.)

However, for any energy source to have an important role in powering the economy, it has to be cost-competitive with existing sources before a significant number of energy consumers will switch. In the electricity business, cost-competitiveness goes by the name of *grid parity*, which means costing the same as the energy sources that currently power the "grid," the electricity transmission network.

While photovoltaic energy doesn't require a fuel supply, it does require the manufacture of technologically sophisticated solar panels. If solar power is to reach grid parity, photovoltaics manufacturers must be able to sell panels at a cost that is low enough to compete with other sources but high enough to cover their costs.

Is this an achievable dream? Can solar power become an economically viable alternative to conventional sources, all of which have significant disadvantages? And can a company providing solar energy equipment be both cost-competitive and profitable?

Zhengrong Shi's answer to all these questions is a resounding yes. Shi is founder and CEO of the Chinese company Suntech Power, one of the world's largest suppliers of photovoltaic modules. After its founding in 2001, Suntech quickly shot past $1 billion in revenue and made China a major player in solar energy. Shi is a brilliant engineer and an astute manager, but the challenges Suntech faces are formidable. Is grid parity a realistic goal? Can Shi oversee the necessary technical advances while guiding the company through a turbulent economy with costs, demand levels, and material supplies bouncing all over the place? If you were in Shi's place, how would you apply the principles of economics to achieve grid parity while maintaining Suntech's profitability?[1]

INTRODUCTION

The experience of Suntech Power (profiled in the chapter-opening Behind the Scenes) is a clear reminder of how economic forces affect every aspect of business. This chapter offers a brief introduction to economics from a business professional's perspective, starting with a high-level look at the study of economics and the all-important concept of scarcity. Understanding basic economic principles is essential to successful business management, and this knowledge can make you a more satisfied consumer and a more successful investor, too.

1 LEARNING OBJECTIVE

Define *economics,* and explain why scarcity is central to economic decision making.

economy The sum total of all the economic activity within a given region

economics The study of how a society uses its scarce resources to produce and distribute goods and services

microeconomics The study of how consumers, businesses, and industries collectively determine the quantity of goods and services demanded and supplied at different prices

macroeconomics The study of "big picture" issues in an economy, including competitive behavior among firms, the effect of government policies, and overall resource allocation issues

natural resources Land, forests, minerals, water, and other tangible assets usable in their natural state

human resources All the people who work in an organization or on its behalf

capital The funds that finance the operations of a business as well as the physical, human-made elements used to produce goods and services, such as factories and computers

What Is This Thing Called the Economy?

The **economy** is the sum total of all the economic activity within a given region, from a single city to a whole country to the entire world. The economy can be a difficult thing to get your mind wrapped around because it is so complex, constantly in motion, and at times hard to see—even though it's everywhere around us. People who devote their lives to studying it can have a hard time agreeing on how the economy works, when it might be "broken," or how to fix it if it is broken, but business leaders need to understand and pay attention to some key principles. **Economics** is the study of how a society uses its scarce resources to produce and distribute goods and services.

Economics is roughly divided into a small-scale perspective and a large-scale perspective. The study of economic behavior among consumers, businesses, and industries that collectively determine the quantity of goods and services demanded and supplied at different prices is termed **microeconomics**. The study of a country's larger economic issues, such as how firms compete, the effect of government policies, and how an economy maintains and allocates its scarce resources, is termed **macroeconomics**.

While microeconomics looks at the small picture and macroeconomics looks at the big picture, understanding the economy at either scale requires an understanding of how the small and large forces interact. For instance, a number of macro forces and policies determine whether homeowners can afford to install solar energy systems. In turn, the aggregate behavior of all those homeowners at the micro level affects the vitality and direction of the overall economy.

FACTORS OF PRODUCTION

Each society must decide how to use its economic resources, or *factors of production* (see Exhibit 1). **Natural resources** are things that are useful in their natural state, such as land, forests, minerals, and water. **Human resources** are people and their individual talents and capacities. **Capital** includes money, computers, machines, tools, and buildings that

EXHIBIT 1 | Factors of Production

Every good or service is created from some combination of these five factors of production.

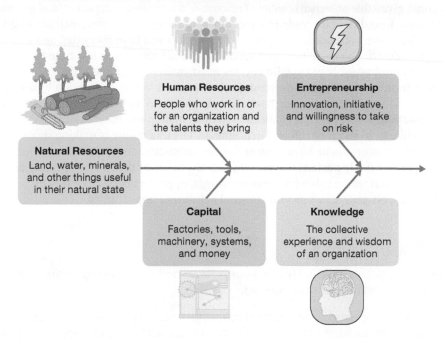

Human Resources
People who work in or for an organization and the talents they bring

Entrepreneurship
Innovation, initiative, and willingness to take on risk

Natural Resources
Land, water, minerals, and other things useful in their natural state

Capital
Factories, tools, machinery, systems, and money

Knowledge
The collective experience and wisdom of an organization

a business needs in order to produce goods and services. **Entrepreneurship** is the spirit of innovation, the initiative, and the willingness to take the risks involved in creating and operating businesses. **Knowledge** is the collective intelligence of an organization. *Knowledge workers,* employees whose primary contribution is the acquisition and application of business knowledge, are a key economic resource for businesses in the 21st century.

Traditionally, a business or a country was considered to have an advantage if its location offered plentiful supplies of natural resources, human resources, capital, and entrepreneurs. In today's global marketplace, however, intellectual assets are often the key. Companies can now obtain capital from one part of the world, purchase supplies from another, and locate production facilities in still another. They can relocate some of their operations to wherever they find a steady supply of affordable workers, or they can assemble virtual teams of knowledge workers from anywhere on the planet.

entrepreneurship The combination of innovation, initiative, and willingness to take the risks required to create and operate new businesses

knowledge Expertise gained through experience or association

THE ECONOMIC IMPACT OF SCARCITY

The impact of scarcity is fundamental to understanding economics. Looking back over the factors of production, you can see that the supply of all these resources is limited. Even entrepreneurial energy is limited in the sense that there are only so many entrepreneurs in the economy, and each entrepreneur can accomplish only so much during a given time span. (Note that "scarcity" doesn't mean a shortage of a particular resource; rather, it means that the resource has a finite supply.[2])

Scarcity has two powerful effects: It creates competition for resources, and it forces trade-offs on the part of every participant in the economy. First, at every stage of economic activity, people and organizations compete for the resources they need. Businesses and industries compete with each other for materials, employees, and customers. Suntech Power competes with other photovoltaics manufacturers for supplies of semiconductor-grade silicon, and the entire photovoltaic industry also competes with the computer industry for silicon. As a consumer, you compete with other consumers. If you were the only person in town who needed a loaf of

REAL-TIME UPDATES
Learn More by Reading This PDF

Take a closer look at economics

Dig a little deeper into essential economics with this handy tutorial from Investopedia.com. Go to http://real-timeupdates.com/bia6 and click on Learn More. If you are using MyBizLab, you can access Real-Time Updates within the chapter or under Student Study Tools.

bread, you would have tremendous power over the bakeries and grocery stores as the only customer in town. However, because you compete with thousands of other consumers for a limited supply of bread, you have far less control over the bread market.

Second, given this universal scarcity of resources, consumers, companies, and governments are constantly forced to make *trade-offs*, meaning they have to give up something to get something else. You have to decide how to spend the 24 hours you have every day, and every choice involves a trade-off: The more time you spend on one activity means less time for every other activity you could possibly pursue. Businesses must make similar trade-offs, such as deciding how much money to spend on advertising a new product versus how much to spend on the materials used to make it, or deciding how many employees to have in sales versus customer support. Just like you, businesses never have enough time, money, and other resources to accomplish what they'd like to, so success in life and in business is largely a matter of making smart trade-offs.

By the way, economists have a name for the most-attractive option not selected when making a trade-off. **Opportunity cost** refers to the value of the most appealing alternative from all those that weren't chosen.[3] In other words, opportunity cost is a way to measure the value of what you gave up when you pursued a different opportunity.

MyBizLab

For an interactive, real-world example of this topic, access this chapter's simulation entitled Adapting to the Economic Environment, located at **www.mybizlab.com**.

opportunity cost The value of the most appealing alternative not chosen

✔ Checkpoint

LEARNING OBJECTIVE 1: Define *economics*, and explain why scarcity is central to economic decision making.

SUMMARY: Economics is the study of how individuals, companies, and governments use scarce resources to produce the goods and services that meet a society's needs. Scarcity is a crucial concept in economics because it creates competition for resources and forces everyone to make trade-offs.

CRITICAL THINKING: (1) Why is entrepreneurship considered a factor of production? (2) If you had an unlimited amount of money, would you ever need to make trade-offs again? Why or why not?

IT'S YOUR BUSINESS: (1) Did you consider opportunity cost when you chose the college or university you are currently attending? (2) What trade-offs did you make in order to read this chapter at this exact moment in your life? (Think about the decisions you made to get to a point in your life where you're taking a business course.)

KEY TERMS TO KNOW: economy, economics, microeconomics, macroeconomics, natural resources, human resources, capital, entrepreneurship, knowledge, opportunity cost

2 LEARNING OBJECTIVE

Differentiate among the major types of economic systems.

economic system The policies that define a society's particular economic structure; the rules by which a society allocates economic resources

free-market system Economic system in which decisions about what to produce and in what quantities are decided by the market's buyers and sellers

capitalism Economic system based on economic freedom and competition

Economic Systems

The roles that individuals, businesses, and the government play in allocating a society's resources depend on the society's **economic system**, the basic set of rules for allocating resources to satisfy its citizens' needs (see Exhibit 2). Economic systems are generally categorized as either *free-market systems* or *planned systems*, although these are really theoretical extremes; every economy exhibits aspects of both approaches.

FREE-MARKET SYSTEMS

In a **free-market system**, individuals and companies are largely free to decide what products to produce, how to produce them, whom to sell them to, and at what price to sell them. In other words, they have the chance to succeed—or fail—by their own efforts. **Capitalism** and *private enterprise* are the terms most often used to describe the free-market system, one in which private parties (individuals, partnerships, or corporations) own and operate the majority of businesses and where competition, supply, and demand determine which goods and services are produced.

EXHIBIT 2   Economic Systems

All economic systems are based on certain fundamental principles about how a country should allocate its resources to satisfy the needs of its citizens. Except at the theoretical extremes, the distinctions between systems tend to be blurry, and arguments continue over the precise definition of each system. Most modern economies exhibit a combination of capitalism and socialism. Here are a few of the characteristics that distinguish the three major systems.

Public/government ownership of productive resources; centralized economic planning and control

Communism
- State ownership of all major productive resources
- Absence of economic classes
- Few opportunities for entrepreneurship

Socialism
- State ownership of certain productive resources
- Managed efforts to minimize dramatic differences between economic classes
- Opportunities for entrepreneurship, with varying degrees of restrictions

Capitalism
- Private ownership of most productive resources
- Few efforts to minimize differences between economic classes
- Government policies actively support entrepreneurship

Private ownership of productive resources; free-market economic principles

In practice, however, no economy is truly "free" in the sense that anyone can do whatever he or she wants to do. Local, state, national, and even international governments such as the European Community intervene in the economy to accomplish goals that leaders deem socially or economically desirable. This practice of limited intervention is characteristic of a *mixed economy* or *mixed capitalism,* which is the economic system of the United States and most other countries. For example, government bodies intervene in the U.S. economy in a variety of ways, such as influencing particular allocations of resources through tax incentives, prohibiting or restricting the sale of certain goods and services, or setting *price controls.* Price controls can involve maximum allowable prices (such as limiting rent increases) and minimum allowable prices (such as supplementing the prices of agricultural goods to ensure producers a minimum level of income or establishing minimum wage levels).[4]

PLANNED SYSTEMS

In a **planned system**, governments largely control the allocation of resources and limit freedom of choice in order to accomplish government goals. Because social equality is a major goal of planned systems, private enterprise and the pursuit of private gain are generally regarded as wasteful and exploitive. The planned system that allows individuals the least degree of economic freedom is *communism,* which still exists in a few countries, most notably North Korea and China. As an economic system, communism can't be regarded as anything but a dismal failure. In fact, even as its government remains strongly communist from a political perspective, China has embraced many concepts of capitalism in recent years and has become one of the world's most powerful and important economies as a result.

Socialism lies somewhere between capitalism and communism, with a fairly high degree of government planning and some government ownership of capital resources. However, government ownership tends to be focused on industries considered vital to the common welfare, such as transportation, health care, and communications. Private ownership is permitted in other industries.

Although "socialism" is sometimes used as a pejorative term in today's heated political and economic dialogues, and many people believe capitalism is inherently superior to socialism, that opinion is not universal. For example, many European countries, including

planned system Economic system in which the government controls most of the factors of production and regulates their allocation

socialism Economic system characterized by public ownership and operation of key industries combined with private ownership and operation of less-vital industries economic heavyweights France and Germany, incorporate varying degrees of socialism. Norway is strongly socialist; while most of the world's economies sank into a deep recession after the collapse of the U.S. housing and credit markets in 2008, Norway's economy remained stable.[5]

Moreover, while free-market capitalism remains the foundation of the U.S. economy, some important elements of the U.S. economy are socialized and have been for many years. Public schools, the postal service, much of the transportation infrastructure, various local and regional utilities, and several major health care programs all fit the economic definition of socialism. Socialism and capitalism are competing philosophies, but they are not mutually exclusive, and each approach has strengths and weaknesses, which is why most modern economies combine aspects of both.

NATIONALIZATION AND PRIVATIZATION

nationalizing A government's takeover of selected companies or industries

privatizing Turning over services once performed by the government and allowing private businesses to perform them instead

The line between socialism and capitalism isn't always easy to define, and it doesn't always stay in the same place, either. Governments can change the structure of the economy by **nationalizing**—assuming ownership of—selected companies or in extreme cases even entire industries. They can also move in the opposite direction, **privatizing** services once performed by the government by allowing private businesses to perform them instead.

In recent years, governments of various countries have done both, for different reasons and in different industries. In the United States, private companies now own or operate a number of highways, bridges, ports, prisons, and other infrastructure elements, providing services once provided by the government. The primary reason for this trend is the belief that private firms motivated by the profit incentive can do a more efficient job of running these facilities.[6] Nationalization is less common and more drastic, but it has happened in recent years, most notably during the recent global banking crisis. For example, the second-largest bank in Britain, the Royal Bank of Scotland, was effectively nationalized after the British government became the majority owner in an attempt to prevent the bank from collapsing.[7]

 Checkpoint

LEARNING OBJECTIVE 2: Differentiate among the major types of economic systems.

SUMMARY: The two basic types of economic systems are free-market systems, in which individuals and companies are largely free to make economic decisions, and planned systems, in which government administrators make all major decisions. The terms *capitalism* and *private enterprise* are often used to describe free-market systems. Communism is the most extreme type of planned system; socialism lies somewhere between capitalism and communism and generally refers to government ownership of fundamental services. The U.S. economy, like virtually all other economies, blends elements of free-market capitalism and government control.

CRITICAL THINKING: (1) Why are no economies truly free, in the sense of having no controls or restrictions? (2) What are some possible risks of privatizing basic services such as the transportation infrastructure?

IT'S YOUR BUSINESS: (1) What is your emotional reaction to the terms *capitalism* and *socialism*? Explain why you feel the way you do. (2) Would you rather pay lower taxes and accept the fact that you need to pay for many services such as health care and education or pay higher taxes with the assurance that the government will provide many basic services for you? Why?

KEY TERMS TO KNOW: economic system, free-market system, capitalism, planned system, socialism, nationalizing, privatizing

The Forces of Demand and Supply

3 **LEARNING OBJECTIVE**

Explain the interaction between demand and supply.

At the heart of every business transaction is an exchange between a buyer and a seller. The buyer wants or needs a particular service or good and is willing to pay the seller in order to obtain it. The seller is willing to participate in the transaction because of the anticipated financial gains. In a free-market system, the marketplace (composed of individuals, firms, and industries) and the forces of demand and supply determine the quantity of goods and services produced and the prices at which they are sold. **Demand** refers to the amount of a good or service that customers will buy at a given time at various prices. **Supply** refers to the quantities of a good or service that producers will provide on a particular date at various prices. In other words, *demand* refers to the behavior of buyers, while *supply* refers to the behavior of sellers. The two forces work together to impose a kind of dynamic order on the free-market system.

demand Buyers' willingness and ability to purchase products at various price points

supply A specific quantity of a product that the seller is able and willing to provide at various prices

UNDERSTANDING DEMAND

The airline industry offers a helpful demonstration of supply and demand. A **demand curve** is a graph that shows the relationship between the amount of product that buyers will purchase at various prices, all other factors being equal. Demand curves typically slope downward, implying that as price drops, more people are willing to buy. The black line labeled "Initial demand" in Exhibit 3 shows a possible demand curve for the monthly number of economy tickets on one airline's Chicago-to-Denver route. You can see that as price decreases, demand increases and vice versa. If demand is strong, airlines can keep their prices consistent or perhaps even raise them. If demand weakens, they can lower prices to stimulate more purchases. (Airlines use sophisticated *yield management* software to constantly adjust prices in order to keep average ticket prices as high as possible while also keeping their planes as full as possible.)

demand curve A graph of the quantities of a product that buyers will purchase at various prices

This movement up and down the demand curve is only part of the story, however. Demand at all price points can also increase or decrease in response to a variety of factors. If overall demand for air travel decreases, the entire demand curve moves to the left (the red line in Exhibit 3). If overall demand increases, the curve moves to the right (the

EXHIBIT 3	Demand Curve

The demand curve (black line) for economy seats on one airline's Chicago-to-Denver route shows that the higher the ticket price, the smaller the quantity of seats demanded and vice versa. Overall demand is rarely static, however; market conditions can shift the entire curve to the left (decreased demand at every price, red line) or to the right (increased demand at every price, green line).

green line). The bulleted lists in Exhibit 3 indicate the effects of some of the major factors that can cause overall demand to increase or decrease:

- Customer income
- Customer preferences toward the product (fears regarding airline safety, for example)
- The price of *substitute products* (products that can be purchased instead of air travel, including rail tickets, automobile travel, or web conferencing)
- The price of *complementary products* (such as hotel accommodations or restaurant dining for the airline industry)
- Marketing expenditures (for advertising and other promotional efforts)
- Customer expectations about future prices and their own financial well-being

For example, if the economy is down and businesses and consumers have less money to spend, overall demand for air travel is likely to shrink. Businesses will seek less expensive substitutes, such as videoconferencing and online meetings, and consumers may vacation closer to home so they can travel by car. Conversely, if customers have more money to spend, more of them are likely to travel, thereby increasing overall demand.

UNDERSTANDING SUPPLY

supply curve A graph of the quantities of a product that sellers will offer for sale, regardless of demand, at various prices

Demand alone is not enough to explain how a company operating in a free-market system sets its prices or production levels. In general, a firm's willingness to produce and sell a product increases as the price it can charge and its profit potential per item increase. In other words, as the price goes up, the quantity supplied generally goes up. The depiction of the relationship between prices and quantities that sellers will offer for sale, regardless of demand, is called a **supply curve**.

Movement along the supply curve typically slopes upward: As prices rise, the quantity that sellers are willing to supply also rises. Similarly, as prices decline, the quantity that sellers are willing to supply declines. Exhibit 4 shows a possible supply curve for the monthly number of economy tickets (seats) supplied on an airline's Chicago-to-Denver route at different prices. The graph shows that increasing prices for economy tickets on that route should increase the number of tickets (seats) an airline is willing to provide for that route and vice versa.

As with demand, supply is dynamic and is affected by a variety of internal and external factors. They include the cost of inputs (such as wages, fuel, and airport gate fees for the airlines), the number of competitors in the marketplace, and advancements in technology that allow companies to operate more efficiently. A change in any of these variables can shift the entire supply curve, either increasing or decreasing the amount offered at various prices, as Exhibit 4 suggests.

UNDERSTANDING HOW DEMAND AND SUPPLY INTERACT

equilibrium point The point at which quantity supplied equals quantity demanded

Buyers and sellers clearly have opposite goals: Buyers want to buy at the lowest possible price, and sellers want to sell at the highest possible price. Neither side can "win" this contest outright. Customers might want to pay $100 for a ticket from Chicago to Denver, but airlines aren't willing to sell many, if any, at that price. Conversely, the airlines might want to charge $1,000 for a ticket, but customers aren't willing to buy many, if any, at that price. So the market in effect arranges a compromise known as the **equilibrium point**, at which the demand and supply curves intersect (see Exhibit 5). At the equilibrium price point, customers are willing to buy as many tickets as the airline is willing to sell.

Because the supply and demand curves are dynamic, so is the equilibrium point. As variables affecting supply and demand change, so will the equilibrium price. For example, increased concerns about airline safety could encourage some travelers to choose alternatives

EXHIBIT 4   Supply Curve

This supply curve for economy seats on the Denver-to-Chicago route shows that the higher the price, the more tickets (seats) the airline would be willing to supply, all else being equal. As with demand, however, the entire supply curve can shift to the left (decreased supply) or the right (increased supply) as producers respond to internal and external forces.

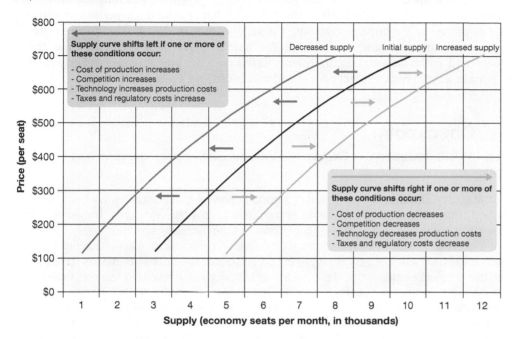

EXHIBIT 5   The Relationship Between Supply and Demand

The equilibrium price is established when the amount of a product that suppliers are willing to sell at a given price equals the amount that consumers are willing to buy at that price.

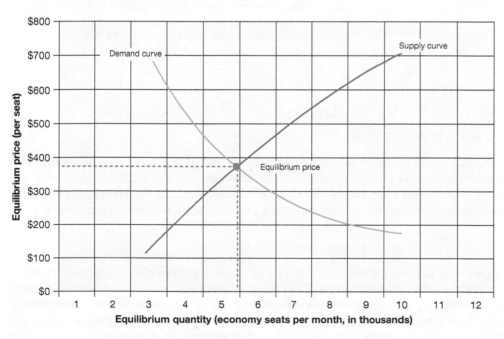

such as automobile travel or web conferencing, thus reducing the demand for air travel at every price and moving the equilibrium point as well. Suppliers might respond to such a reduction in demand by either cutting the number of flights offered or lowering ticket prices in order to restore the equilibrium level.

Questions of supply, demand, and equilibrium pricing are among the toughest issues you'll face as a manager. Imagine that you're a concert promoter planning for next year's summer season. You have to balance the potential demand for each performer across a range of prices, in the hope of matching the supply you can deliver (the seating capacity of each venue and the number of shows). You have to make these predictions months in advance and make financial commitments based on your predictions. Predict well, and you'll make a tidy profit. Predict poorly, and you could lose a pile of money.

✔ Checkpoint

LEARNING OBJECTIVE 3: Explain the interaction between demand and supply.

SUMMARY: *Demand* is the amount of a good or service that customers will buy at a given time at various prices; it can be shown visually as a *demand curve*. The entire demand curve can shift as market conditions change. Similarly, *supply* is the amount of a good or service that producers will provide on a particular date at various prices; it can be shown with a *supply curve*, which can also shift in response to market forces. In the simplest sense, demand and supply affect price in the following manner: When the price goes up, the quantity demanded goes down, but the supplier's incentive to produce more goes up. When the price goes down, the quantity demanded increases, but the quantity supplied may (or may not) decline. The point at which the demand and supply curves intersect—the point at which demand and supply are equal—is the *equilibrium point*.

CRITICAL THINKING: (1) How does the interaction of demand and supply keep a market in balance, at least approximately and temporarily? (2) If the prices of complementary products for a given product go up, what effect is this increase likely to have on demand for that product?

IT'S YOUR BUSINESS: (1) Are there any products or brands you are so loyal to that you will purchase them at almost any price? Will you accept less expensive substitutes? (2) Have you ever purchased something simply because it was on sale? Why?

KEY TERMS TO KNOW: demand, supply, demand curve, supply curve, equilibrium point

---

4 **LEARNING OBJECTIVE**

Identify four macroeconomic issues that are essential to understanding the behavior of the economy.

competition Rivalry among businesses for the same customers

pure competition A situation in which so many buyers and sellers exist that no single buyer or seller can individually influence market prices

The Macro View: Understanding How an Economy Operates

All the individual instances of supply and demand and all the thousands and millions of transactions that take place over time add up to the economy. This section explores four "big picture" issues in the economy that are essential to understanding the overall behavior of the economy: competition in a free-market system, business cycles, unemployment, and inflation.

COMPETITION IN A FREE-MARKET SYSTEM

Competition is the situation in which two or more suppliers of a product are rivals in the pursuit of the same customers. The nature of competition varies widely by industry, product category, and geography (see Exhibit 6). At one extreme is **pure competition**, in which no single firm becomes large enough to influence prices and thereby distort the workings of the free-market system. At the other extreme, in a **monopoly**, one supplier

EXHIBIT 6 Categories of Competition

Markets vary widely in the nature of competition they exhibit and the choices that buyers have. Here are five major categories of competition and the factors that distinguish them.

Pure Competition	Monopolistic Competition	Oligopoly	Pure Monopoly	Regulated Monopoly
Characteristics: • Many small suppliers • Virtually identical products • Low barriers to entry	**Characteristics:** • Can have few or many suppliers, of varying size • Products can be distinguished but are similar enough to be replacements • Variable barriers to entry but market open to all	**Characteristics:** • Small number of suppliers, even as few as just two (a *duopoly*) • Products can be distinguished in important ways, but replacements are still available • Barriers to entry tend to be high, making entering the market difficult	**Characteristics:** • Only one supplier in a given market • Monopoly achieved without government intervention, by innovation, specialization, exclusive contracts, or a simple lack of competitors • Products are unique, with no direct replacements available • Barriers to entry are extremely high, making entering the market difficult or impossible	**Characteristics:** • Only one supplier in a given market • Monopoly granted by government mandate, such as a license to provide cable TV and Internet service • No product competition is allowed • Barriers to entry are infinitely high; new competitors are not allowed
Price competition: • No single firm can grow large enough to influence prices across the market	**Price competition:** • Firms that excel in one or more aspects can gain some control over pricing	**Price competition:** • Individual firms can have considerable control over pricing	**Price competition:** • Suppliers can charge as much as they want, at least until people stop buying	**Price competition:** • Prices are set by government mandate
Buyers' choices: • Extensive	**Buyers' choices:** • Extensive	**Buyers' choices:** • Limited	**Buyers' choices:** • None	**Buyers' choices:** • None

so thoroughly dominates a market that it can control prices and essentially shut out other competitors. Monopolies can happen "naturally," as companies innovate or markets evolve (a *pure monopoly*) or by government mandate (a *regulated monopoly*). However, the lack of competition in a monopoly situation is considered so detrimental to a free-market economy that monopolies are often prohibited by law (see the section "Merger and Acquisition Approvals" later in this chapter).

Most of the competition in advanced free-market economies is **monopolistic competition**, in which a number of sellers offer products that can be distinguished from competing products in at least some small way. The risk/reward nature of capitalism promotes constant innovation in pursuit of competitive advantage, rewarding companies that do the best job of satisfying customers.

When the number of competitors in a market is quite small, a situation known as **oligopoly** is created. In an oligopoly, customers have some choice, unlike in a monopoly, but not as many choices as in monopolistic competition.

BUSINESS CYCLES

The economy is always in a state of change, expanding or contracting in response to the combined effects of factors such as technological breakthroughs, changes in investment patterns, shifts in consumer attitudes, world events, and basic economic forces. *Economic expansion* occurs when the economy is growing and consumers are spending more money,

monopoly A situation in which one company dominates a market to the degree that it can control prices

monopolistic competition A situation in which many sellers differentiate their products from those of competitors in at least some small way

oligopoly A market situation in which a very small number of suppliers, sometimes only two, provide a particular good or service

EXHIBIT 7   Fluctuations in the U.S. Economy

The U.S. economy has a long history of expansion and contraction. This chart shows the year-to-year change (as a percentage of the previous year) in *gross domestic product*, a key measure of the country's overall economic output. (Note that because this chart shows *percentage changes*, not absolute output, all the bars above zero represent years of economic expansion, even though a bar might be smaller than the one preceding. All the bars below zero represent years of contraction.)

U.S. Gross Domestic Product
Year-to-Year Change, 1930–2010

Source: U.S. Bureau of Economic Analysis, National Income and Product Accounts Tables, Table 1.1.1. Percent Change from Preceding Period in Real Gross Domestic Product, Revised 29 July 2011, www.bea.gov.

which stimulates higher employment and wages, which then stimulate more consumer purchases. *Economic contraction* occurs when such spending declines, employment drops, and the economy as a whole slows down.

If the period of downward swing is severe, the nation may enter into a **recession**, traditionally defined as two consecutive quarters of decline in the *gross domestic product*, a basic measure of a country's economic output. A deep and prolonged recession can be considered a *depression*, which doesn't have an official definition but is generally considered to involve a catastrophic collapse of financial markets.

When a downward swing or recession is over, the economy enters into a period of recovery. These up-and-down swings are commonly known as **business cycles**, although this term is somewhat misleading, because real economies do not expand and contract in regular and predictable "cycles." *Economic fluctuations* is a more accurate way to characterize the economy's real behavior (see Exhibit 7).[8]

recession A period during which national income, employment, and production all fall; defined as at least six months of decline in the GDP

business cycles Fluctuations in the rate of growth that an economy experiences over a period of several years

UNEMPLOYMENT

Unemployment is one of the most serious effects of economic contraction. It is traumatic at a personal level for idle workers and their families, and the decrease in the number of active workers affects the overall economy in terms of lost output.[9] Moreover, unemployed workers increase the financial burden on state governments when they collect unemployment benefit payments.

The **unemployment rate** indicates the percentage of the *labor force* currently without employment. The labor force consists of people aged 16 and older who are either working or looking for jobs.[10] Not all cases of unemployment are the same, however. As Exhibit 8 explains, each of the four types of unemployment—*frictional, structural, cyclical,* and *seasonal*—has unique implications for business and political leaders.

unemployment rate The portion of the labor force (everyone over 16 who has or is looking for a job) currently without a job

inflation An economic condition in which prices rise steadily throughout the economy

INFLATION

Like almost everything else in the economy, prices of goods and services rarely stay the same for very long. **Inflation** is a steady rise in the average prices of goods and services throughout the economy. **Deflation**, on the other hand, is a sustained fall in average prices.

deflation An economic condition in which prices fall steadily throughout the economy

EXHIBIT 8   Types of Unemployment

Economists identify four types of unemployment, each with unique causes and concerns.

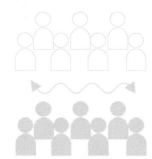

Frictional Unemployment	**Structural Unemployment**	**Cyclical Unemployment**	**Seasonal Unemployment**
• The "natural" flow of workers into and out of jobs, such as when a person leaves one job without first lining up a new job • Always some level of frictional unemployment in the economy	• A mismatch between workers' skills and current employer needs • Workers can't find jobs that match their qualifications, and employers can't find employees with the skills their job openings require • A never-ending concern as changes in the external environments of business make some skills obsolete and create demand for new skills	• Caused by economic fluctuations • When demand for goods and services drops, businesses reduce production, thereby requiring fewer workers • An increasing number of people who want to work can't find jobs • During catastrophic depressions, can run as high as 20 or 25 percent	• Predictable increases and decreases in the need for workers in industries with seasonal fluctuations in customer demand • Common in agriculture, leisure and entertainment, retailing, and accounting services

Source: Adapted from Roger LeRoy Miller, *Economics Today*, 15th ed. (Boston: Addison-Wesley, 2010), 164–165.

Inflation is a major concern for consumers, businesses, and government leaders because of its effect on *purchasing power,* or the amount of a good or service you can buy for a given amount of money. When prices go up, purchasing power goes down. If wages keep pace with prices, inflation is less worrisome, but if prices rise faster than wages, consumers definitely feel the pinch.

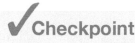 Checkpoint

LEARNING OBJECTIVE 4: Identify four macroeconomic issues that are essential to understanding the behavior of the economy.

SUMMARY: First, competition in a free-market system occurs on a spectrum from pure competition to monopolies; most competition in free-market economies is monopolistic competition, meaning that the number of sellers is large enough that none can dominate the market and products can be distinguished in at least some small way. Second, the economy expands and contracts, or fluctuates over time; this activity is commonly called the business cycle, although the fluctuations do not follow a regular cyclical pattern. Third, unemployment is a vitally important issue in economics, because of the serious effects it has on individuals, families, communities, and the economy as a whole. The types of unemployment include cyclical unemployment (when labor needs are reduced during an economic contraction), frictional unemployment (the normal inflow and outflow of workers as people change jobs), structural unemployment (when the skills workers possess do not align with the skills employers need), and seasonal unemployment (the ebb and flow of labor demand in certain industries over the course of a year). Fourth, inflation affects every aspect of economic activity because of the effects it has on prices of goods, services, and labor.

CRITICAL THINKING: (1) Are colleges and universities an example of pure competition or monopolistic competition? Why? (2) Are monopolies always harmful to consumers? Why or why not?

IT'S YOUR BUSINESS: (1) What state of the business cycle is the economy currently in? Is this influencing your career plans? (2) Have you ever been unemployed (at a time when you were actively looking for work)? Which of the four categories of unemployment would you have fallen under?

KEY TERMS TO KNOW: competition, pure competition, monopoly, monopolistic competition, oligopoly, recession, business cycles, unemployment rate, inflation, deflation

---

5 **LEARNING OBJECTIVE**

Outline the debate over deregulation and identify four key roles that governments play in the economy.

regulation Relying more on laws and policies than on market forces to govern economic activity

deregulation Removing regulations to allow the market to prevent excesses and correct itself over time

Government's Role in a Free-Market System

For as long as the United States has been in existence, people have been arguing over just how *free* the free market should be. In the broader view, this argument springs from profound philosophical differences over the role government should play in society as a whole. More narrowly, even professional economists don't always agree on what role the government should play in the economy.

Much of the debate about the government's role can be framed as a question of **regulation** versus **deregulation**—having more rules in place to govern economic activity or having fewer rules in place and relying more on the market to prevent excesses and correct itself over time. Generally speaking, proponents of more regulation assert that companies can't always be counted on to act in ways that protect stakeholder interests and that the market can't be relied on as a mechanism to prevent or punish abuses and failures. Proponents of deregulation contend that government interference can stifle innovations that ultimately help everyone by boosting the entire economy and that some regulations burden individual companies and industries with unfair costs.

Four major areas in which the government plays a role in the economy are protecting stakeholders, fostering competition, encouraging innovation and economic development, and stabilizing and stimulating the economy.

PROTECTING STAKEHOLDERS

Businesses have many stakeholders, including colleagues, employees, supervisors, investors, customers, suppliers, and society at large. In the course of serving one or more of these stakeholders, a business may sometimes neglect, or at least be accused of neglecting, the interests of other stakeholders in the process. For example, managers who are too narrowly focused on generating wealth for shareholders might not spend the funds necessary to create a safe work environment for employees or to minimize the business's impact on the community.

In an attempt to balance the interests of stakeholders and protect those who might be adversely affected by business, the U.S. federal government has established numerous regulatory agencies (see Exhibit 9), and state and local governments have additional agencies as well.

FOSTERING COMPETITION

Based on the belief that fair competition benefits the economy and society in general, governments intervene in markets to preserve competition and ensure that no single enterprise becomes too powerful. For instance, if a company has a monopoly, it can potentially harm

EXHIBIT 9	Major Government Agencies and What They Do

Government agencies protect stakeholders by developing and promoting standards, regulating and overseeing industries, and enforcing laws and regulations.

GOVERNMENT AGENCY OR COMMISSION	MAJOR AREAS OF RESPONSIBILITY
Consumer Product Safety Commission (CPSC)	Regulates and protects public from unreasonable risks of injury from consumer products
Environmental Protection Agency (EPA)	Develops and enforces standards to protect the environment
Equal Employment Opportunity Commission (EEOC)	Protects and resolves discriminatory employment practices
Federal Aviation Administration (FAA)	Sets rules for the commercial airline industry
Federal Communications Commission (FCC)	Oversees communication by telephone, telegraph, radio, and television
Federal Energy Regulatory Commission (FERC)	Regulates rates and sales of electric power and natural gas
Federal Highway Administration (FHA)	Regulates vehicle safety requirements
Federal Trade Commission (FTC)	Enforces laws and guidelines regarding unfair business practices and acts to stop false and deceptive advertising and labeling
Food and Drug Administration (FDA)	Enforces laws and regulations to prevent distribution of harmful foods, drugs, medical devices, and cosmetics
Interstate Commerce Commission (ICC)	Regulates and oversees carriers engaged in transportation between states: railroads, bus lines, trucking companies, oil pipelines, and waterways
Occupational Safety and Health Administration (OSHA)	Promotes worker safety and health
Securities and Exchange Commission (SEC)	Protects investors and maintains the integrity of the securities markets
Transportation Security Administration (TSA)	Protects the national transportation infrastructure

customers by raising prices or stifling innovation. Furthermore, because most monopolies have total control over certain products and prices and the market share for those products, it's extremely difficult for competitors to enter markets where monopolies exist. A number of laws and regulations have been established to help prevent individual companies or groups of companies from taking control of markets or acting in other ways that restrain competition or harm consumers.

Antitrust Legislation

Antitrust laws limit what businesses can and cannot do to ensure that all competitors have an equal chance of succeeding. Some of the earliest government moves in this arena produced such landmark pieces of legislation as the Sherman Antitrust Act, the Clayton Antitrust Act, and the Federal Trade Commission Act, which generally sought to rein in the power of a few huge companies that had financial and management control of a significant number of other companies in the same industry. Usually referred to as *trusts* (hence the label *antitrust legislation*), these huge companies controlled enough of the supply and distribution in their respective industries, such as Standard Oil in the petroleum industry, to muscle smaller competitors out of the way. More recently, government bodies in the United States and Europe have taken action against high-technology firms such as Microsoft and Intel to prevent unfair competitive practices.

Merger and Acquisition Approvals

To preserve competition and customer choice, governments occasionally prohibit companies from combining through mergers or acquisitions. In other cases, they may approve a combination but only with conditions, such as *divesting* (selling) some parts of the company or making other concessions. For example, as the Behind the Scenes explains, the U.S. Department of Justice allowed the merger of XM and Sirius, even though the combined firm now has a monopoly in the satellite radio market. Antitrust regulators concluded that satellite radio has so much competition from other technologies that consumer choice wasn't unduly limited; they also forced the company to make several major concessions, such as making more channels available for minority programming.

ENCOURAGING INNOVATION AND ECONOMIC DEVELOPMENT

Governments can use their regulatory and policymaking powers to encourage specific types of economic activity. A good example is encouraging the development and adoption of innovations that governments consider beneficial in some way, such as promoting the growth of solar power through economic incentives for customers. Governments can also encourage businesses to locate or expand in particular geographic areas by establishing *economic development zones*. These zones typically offer a variety of financial incentives such as tax credits, low-interest loans, and reduced utility rates to businesses that meet specific job creation and local investment criteria.

STABILIZING AND STIMULATING THE ECONOMY

monetary policy Government policy and actions taken by the Federal Reserve Board to regulate the nation's money supply

In addition to the specific areas of regulation and policy just discussed, governments have two sets of tools they can use to stabilize and stimulate the national economy: monetary policy and fiscal policy. **Monetary policy** involves adjusting the nation's *money supply,* the amount of "spendable" money in the economy at any given time, by increasing or decreasing interest rates. In the United States, monetary policy is controlled primarily by the Federal Reserve Board (often called "the Fed"), a group of government officials who oversee the country's central banking system.

fiscal policy Use of government revenue collection and spending to influence the business cycle

Fiscal policy involves changes in the government's revenues and expenditures to stimulate a slow economy or dampen a growing economy that is in danger of overheating and causing inflation. On the revenue side, governments can adjust the revenue they bring in by changing tax rates and various fees collected from individuals and businesses (see Exhibit 10). When the federal government lowers the income tax rate, for instance, it does so with the hope that consumers and businesses will spend and invest the money they save from lower tax bills.

EXHIBIT 10	Major Types of Taxes

Running a government is an expensive affair. Here are the major types of taxes that national governments, states, counties, and cities collect to fund government operations and projects.

TYPE OF TAX	LEVIED ON
Income taxes	Income earned by individuals and businesses. Income taxes are the government's largest single source of revenue.
Real property taxes	Assessed value of the land and structures owned by businesses and individuals.
Sales taxes	Retail purchases made by customers. Sales taxes are collected by retail businesses at the time of the sale and then forwarded to state governments. Disputes continue over taxes on e-commerce sales made across state lines
Excise taxes	Selected items such as gasoline, tobacco, and liquor. Often referred to as "sin" taxes, excise taxes are implemented in part to help control potentially harmful practices.
Payroll taxes	Earnings of individuals to help fund Social Security, Medicare, and unemployment compensation. Corporations match employee contributions.

On the expenditure side, local, state, and federal government bodies constitute a huge market for goods and services, with billions of dollars of collective buying power. Governments can stimulate the economy by increasing their purchases, sometimes even to the point of creating new programs or projects with the specific purpose of expanding employment opportunities and increasing demand for goods and services.

No instance of government spending in recent years has generated more heated controversy than the bailouts made during the financial crisis of 2008 and 2009. The federal government spent billions of dollars in investments and loans to troubled banks to encourage lending after the credit markets dried up and to prevent several large financial companies from collapsing. The government also stepped in to help save the automakers General Motors and Chrysler during this period.

Debate continues on whether it was wise to intervene by rescuing these ailing companies or whether the government should have let market forces play out. Would the money invested in saving one large company have been better spent in helping a dozen small, young companies get off the ground? In general, the rationale for stepping in to rescue any specific company is that its collapse would harm a significant portion of the economy as a whole. However, these decisions hit at the very heart of an economic system because they determine how a society chooses to deploy its scarce resources.

✔ Checkpoint

LEARNING OBJECTIVE 5: Outline the debate over deregulation, and identify four key roles that governments play in the economy.

SUMMARY: Proponents of increased regulation assert that companies can't always be counted on to act in ways that protect stakeholder interests and the market can't be relied on to prevent or punish abuses and failures. Proponents of deregulation contend that government interference can stifle innovations that ultimately help everyone by boosting the entire economy and that some regulations burden individual companies and industries with unfair costs. Four key roles the government plays in the economy are protecting stakeholders, fostering competition, encouraging innovation and economic development, and stabilizing and stimulating the economy.

CRITICAL THINKING: (1) Would it be wise for the government to put price controls on college tuition? Why or why not? (2) Under what conditions, if any, should the federal government step in to rescue failing companies?

IT'S YOUR BUSINESS: (1) How do you benefit from competition among the companies that supply you with the goods and services you need? (2) Does this competition have any negative impact on your life?

KEY TERMS TO KNOW: regulation, deregulation, monetary policy, fiscal policy

Economic Measures and Monitors

6 LEARNING OBJECTIVE

Identify the major ways of measuring economic activity.

economic indicators Statistics that measure the performance of the economy

Economic indicators are statistics such as interest rates, unemployment rates, housing data, and industrial productivity that let business and political leaders measure and monitor economic performance. *Leading indicators* suggest changes that may happen to the economy in the future and are therefore valuable for planning. In contrast, *lagging indicators* provide confirmation that something has occurred in the past.

Housing starts, for example, are a leading indicator that shows where several industries are headed. When housing starts drop, the construction industry contracts, and the effect soon ripples through other sectors of the economy, from the manufacture of plumbing fixtures, carpet, and appliances to a variety of services, including furniture retailing, real estate sales, and other areas that are dependent on housing-related transactions.

Another key leading indicator is durable-goods orders, or orders for goods that typically last more than three years (which can mean everything from desk chairs to airplanes).

A rise in durable-goods orders is a positive indicator that business spending is turning around. In addition to these indicators, economists closely monitor several *price indexes* and the nation's economic output to get a sense of how well the economy is working.

In contrast, unemployment is a key-lagging indicator. For example, companies tend to reduce their workforces after the economy has slowed down and sales revenues have dropped. Although they don't have the predictive power of leading indicators, lagging indicators give policy makers insights into how the economy is functioning and whether corrective steps might be needed.

PRICE INDEXES

Price changes, especially price increases, are a significant economic indicator. Price indexes offer a way to monitor the inflation or deflation in various sectors of the economy. An index is simply a convenient way to compare numbers over time and is computed by dividing the current value of some quantity by a baseline historical value and then multiplying by 100. Rather than saying something has increased by 28 percent, for example, economists would say the index is at 128.

Government statisticians compute a huge variety of price indexes, each designed to monitor a particular aspect of economic activity. The best known of these, the **consumer price index (CPI)**, measures the rate of inflation by comparing the change in prices of a representative "basket" of consumer goods and services, such as clothing, food, housing, and transportation (see Exhibit 11). The CPI has always been a hot topic because the government uses it to adjust Social Security payments, businesses use it to calculate cost-of-living increases for employees, and many use it as a gauge of how well the government is keeping inflation under control.

In contrast to the CPI, the **producer price index (PPI)** measures prices at the producer or wholesaler level, reflecting what businesses are paying for the products they need. (Like the CPI, the PPI is often referred to as a single index, but it is actually a family of more than 600 industry-specific indexes.) In addition to monitoring economic activity, PPIs have a number of managerial uses, from helping companies place an accurate value on inventories to protecting buyers and sellers with *price-escalation clauses* in long-term purchasing contracts.[11]

consumer price index (CPI) A monthly statistic that measures changes in the prices of a representative collective of consumer goods and services

producer price index (PPI) A statistical measure of price trends at the producer and wholesaler levels

EXHIBIT 11	Composition of the Consumer Price Index

The U.S. Bureau of Labor Statistics computes a variety of consumer price indexes by tracking prices for a representative collection of goods and services, and it periodically adjusts the mix to reflect consumer buying patterns. The particular CPI shown here, often referred to the "headline CPI" because it is the one usually mentioned in news reports, is officially called the "All Items CPI for All Urban Consumers." The "core CPI," in comparison, excludes the typically volatile categories of food and energy in an attempt to show long-term trends more accurately.

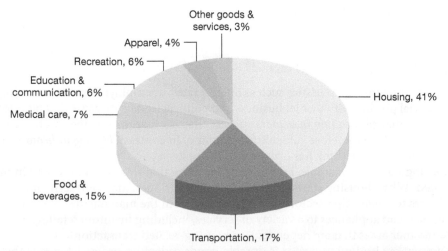

Other goods & services, 3%
Apparel, 4%
Recreation, 6%
Education & communication, 6%
Medical care, 7%
Housing, 41%
Food & beverages, 15%
Transportation, 17%

Source: U.S. Bureau of Labor Statistics, "Relative Importance of Items in the Consumer Price Index," December 2010, www.bls.gov.

NATIONAL ECONOMIC OUTPUT

The broadest measure of an economy's health is the **gross domestic product (GDP)**. The GDP measures a country's output—its production, distribution, and use of goods and services—by computing the sum of all goods and services produced for *final* use in a country during a specified period (usually a year). The products may be produced by either domestic or foreign companies as long as the production takes place within a nation's boundaries. Sales from a Honda assembly plant in California, for instance, would be included in the U.S. GDP, even though Honda is a Japanese company. Although far from perfect, the GDP enables a nation to evaluate its economic policies and to compare its current performance with prior periods or with the performance of other nations.

GDP has largely replaced an earlier measure called the *gross national product (GNP),* which excludes the value of production from foreign-owned businesses within a nation's boundaries and includes receipts from the overseas operations of domestic companies. GNP considers *who* is responsible for the production; GDP considers *where* the production occurs.

For the latest information on economic issues in business, visit http://real-timeupdates .com/bia6.

gross domestic product (GDP)
The value of all the final goods and services produced by businesses located within a nation's borders; excludes outputs from overseas operations of domestic companies

✓ Checkpoint

LEARNING OBJECTIVE 6: Identify the major ways of measuring economic activity.

SUMMARY: Economic activity is monitored and measured with statistics known as *economic indicators*; leading indicators help predict changes, and lagging indicators confirm changes that have already occurred. Two major indicators are *price indexes*, which track inflation or deflation over time for a fixed "basket" of goods and services, and *gross domestic product (GDP)*, the total value of the goods and services produced for final use in a country during a specified time period.

CRITICAL THINKING: (1) Why would anyone bother to monitor lagging indicators? (2) Why is GDP considered a more accurate measure of a country's economic health than GNP?

IT'S YOUR BUSINESS: (1) In your multiple economic roles as a consumer, employee, and investor, is inflation a good thing, a bad thing, or both? Explain your answer. (2) How is the federal budget deficit likely to affect you? How is it likely to affect your children as they grow up?

KEY TERMS TO KNOW: economic indicators, consumer price index (CPI), producer price index (PPI), gross domestic product (GDP)

BEHIND THE SCENES
THE PUSH FOR GRID PARITY AT SUNTECH POWER

MyBizLab

With energy costs trending upward and more people becoming attuned to the geopolitical complexities of petroleum-based energy and the environmental challenges of all major energy sources, interest in solar and other alternative energy sources continues to grow. Alternatives can't replace all the energy generated from conventional sources, but they can become increasingly important elements of the world's energy mix.

As the world's largest manufacturer of photovoltaic solar modules for generating electricity, China's Suntech

Power is ideally positioned to take advantage of the world-wide opportunities in solar power. Under the leadership of founder and CEO Zhengrong Shi, Suntech is lowering the cost and raising the energy-conversion efficiency of photovoltaic panels to achieve grid parity, meaning being cost-competitive with nonrenewable sources such as coal and natural gas.

Grid parity is a simple enough concept, but it is no small challenge to achieve—or even to calculate so you can tell when you've achieved it. Every form of energy has a unique mix of direct costs, from initial construction and installation costs to ongoing fuel, maintenance, and operations expenses. Every energy source also has a mix of indirect costs, including expenses that enable or mediate the effects of its use. Examples of such costs include health care expenses linked to air pollution caused by burning fossil fuels and the need to secure nuclear power plants from terrorist attacks. Also, every energy source, even "clean" energies such as solar and wind power, has an *ecological footprint*, the sum total of its impact on the environment throughout its entire life cycle.

Furthermore, even with a single type of energy source, specific implementations can have different cost profiles for different customers. For instance, when photovoltaic panels are installed on the roof of a house, the individual homeowner has to bear the full cost of installation (unless financial incentives are involved—more on this shortly), but there are no transmission costs because the electricity is used right where it is generated. Conversely, when a utility company builds a large-scale solar facility, the cost can be shared by all its customers—but large facilities require a lot of land and abundant sunshine, which means they are often built out in the desert and can require lengthy transmission lines and circuitry to connect to the electrical grid.

Location also plays a major role in cost comparisons, even for identical methods. For example, solar has an advantage over coal in Hawaii, given that state's abundant sunshine and the high cost of shipping coal across the ocean. And as if this all weren't complicated enough, costs rarely stand still, as supplies and demands fluctuate and technologies mature. Energy costs can be particularly volatile, making comparisons across energy formats even trickier.

Clearly, identifying all these costs accurately for each energy source is a complex task, and different assumptions in the calculations can lead to different conclusions. However, the numbers are starting to look appealing for solar. At least by some calculations and in some locations—such as Hawaii—photovoltaic energy has already reached parity with the grid. With prices for competing energies expected to keep rising, photovoltaic technology has another advantage in that it has become a big enough industry that it can start to put pressure on suppliers of silicon, a major component of solar modules, to lower their prices.

Now for those financial incentives mentioned a moment ago. In many locales, until the actual cost is driven down far enough by technical advances and production efficiencies, some governments are helping solar technology with tax credits and other incentives. One particularly interesting governmental boost is the *feed-in tariff*. Homeowners and businesses whose solar installations generate more electricity than they need can sell it back to utilities, and to spur the growth of solar energy, some governments pay these individual suppliers above-market rates for their power. Germany, for instance, one of the pioneers of feed-in tariffs, pays homeowners as much as four times the rate paid for electricity from a nuclear plant.

Shi and Suntech are counting on a combination of market forces like these and continuing improvements in photovoltaic performance to make solar power a viable competitor in the energy marketplace—and a viable business model. After revenues dropped by almost 90 percent during the global recession in 2009, Suntech has recovered and resumed its global expansion plans. Shi remains confident that solar power will reach grid parity in the near future and that photovoltaic energy will eventually be even cheaper than coal or gas. With its low-cost production, technical innovations, and worldwide presence, Suntech is well on its ways to meeting this ambitious goal.

Critical Thinking Questions

1. What effect are feed-in tariffs likely to have on electricity users who don't adopt solar power? Is this outcome fair? Why or why not?
2. If a particular government believes that solar is a more desirable energy source than nonrenewables such as coal and gas, why wouldn't it simply grant solar energy utilities monopoly rights?
3. Does it make sense for Suntech to acquire ailing competitors during a deep recession? Why or why not?

LEARN MORE ONLINE

Visit the Suntech website at **www.suntech-power.com** and explore the documents and videos aimed at homeowners. Does this information do a good job of helping website visitors understand the benefits of solar energy? Would it persuade you to consider solar energy for your home?

MyBizLab

Log on to www.mybizlab.com to access study and assessment aids associated with this chapter.

KEY TERMS

business cycles
capital
capitalism
competition
consumer price index (CPI)
deflation
demand

demand curve
deregulation
economic indicators
economic system
economics
economy
entrepreneurship

equilibrium point
fiscal policy
free-market system
gross domestic product (GDP)
human resources
inflation
knowledge
macroeconomics
microeconomics
monetary policy
monopolistic competition
monopoly
nationalizing

natural resources
oligopoly
opportunity cost
planned system
privatizing
producer price index (PPI)
pure competition
recession
regulation
socialism
supply
supply curve
unemployment rate

TEST YOUR KNOWLEDGE

Questions for Review

1. Why is the economic concept of scarcity a crucial concept for businesspeople to understand?
2. How does macroeconomics differ from microeconomics?
3. Does the United States have a purely free-market economy or a mixed economy?
4. Why is government spending an important factor in economic stability?
5. Why might a government agency seek to block a merger or an acquisition?

Questions for Analysis

6. Why is competition an important element of the free-market system?
7. Why do governments intervene in free-market systems?
8. How do countries know if their economic systems are working?

9. Are the fluctuations in the business cycle predictable?
10. Ethical Considerations. The risk of failure is an inherent part of free enterprise. Does society have an obligation to come to the aid of entrepreneurs who try but fail? Why or why not?

Questions for Application

11. How might government and education leaders work with businesses to minimize structural unemployment?
12. How would a decrease in Social Security benefits to retired persons affect the economy?
13. If you wanted to increase demand for your restaurant but are unable to lower prices or increase advertising, what steps might you take?
14. Concept Integration. What effect might the technological environment, have on the equilibrium point in a given market?

EXPAND YOUR KNOWLEDGE

Discovering Career Opportunities

Thinking about a career in economics? Find out what economists do by reviewing the *Occupational Outlook Handbook* in your library or online at www.bls.gov/oco. This is an authoritative resource for information about all kinds of occupations. Search for "economists" and then answer these questions:

1. Briefly describe what economists do and their typical working conditions.
2. What is the job outlook for economists? What is the average salary for starting economists?
3. What training and qualifications are required for a career as an economist? Are the qualifications different for jobs in the private sector than for those in the government?

Improving Your Tech Insights: Data Mining

To find a few ounces of precious gold, you dig through a mountain of earth. To find a few ounces of precious information, you dig through mountains of data, using *data mining,* a combination of technologies and techniques to extract important customer insights buried within thousands or millions of transaction records. (Data mining has many other uses as well, such as identifying which employees are most valuable to a firm. And a related technology, *text mining,* applies similar analysis tools to documents.)

Data mining is an essential part of *business intelligence* because it helps extract trends and insights from millions of pieces of individual data (including demographics, purchase histories, customer service records, and research results). Data mining helps marketers identify who their most profitable customers are, which goods and services are in highest demand in specific markets, how to structure promotional campaigns, where to target upcoming sales efforts, and which customers are likely to be high credit risks, among many other benefits. You may hear the terms *business analytics* and *predictive analytics* used in this context as well, to describe efforts to extract insights from databases.

Research one of the commercially available data mining or business analytics systems. (Leading companies in the field include FICO, IBM, KXEN, Oracle, SAS, and TIBCO.) In a brief email message to your instructor, describe how the system you've chosen can help companies market their goods and services more effectively.[12]

PRACTICE YOUR SKILLS

Sharpening Your Communication Skills

The subprime mortgage crisis that helped throw the economy into a recession in December 2007 bewildered a lot of people. In a brief paragraph (no more than 100 words), explain what a subprime mortgage is and why these loans helped trigger the recession.

Building Your Team Skills

Economic indicators help businesses and governments determine where the economy is headed. As part of a team assigned by your instructor, analyze these newspaper headlines for clues to the direction of the U.S. economy:

- "Housing Starts Lowest in Months"
- "Fed Lowers Discount Rate and Interest Rates Tumble"
- "Retail Sales Up 4 Percent Over Last Month"
- "Business Debt Down from Last Year"
- "Businesses Are Buying More Electronic Equipment"

- "Local Economy Sinks as Area Unemployment Rate Climbs to 9.2 Percent"
- "Telephone Company Reports 30-Day Backlog in Installing Business Systems"

Is each item good news or bad news for the economy? Why? What does each news item mean for large and small businesses? Report your team's findings to the class. Did all the teams come to the same conclusions about each headline? Why or why not? With your team, discuss how these different perspectives might influence the way you interpret economic news in the future.

Developing Your Research Skills

Some career paths have higher unemployment risks during the ups and downs of economic fluctuations. Research three business careers that should be relatively "recession proof" in the coming years, meaning employment doesn't drop dramatically during a recession (or may even increase during a recession). Summarize your findings in a one-page report.

REFERENCES

1. Suntech Power website, accessed 1 August 2011, www.suntech-power .com; "Levelized Cost of New Generation Resources in the Annual Energy Outlook 2011," U.S. Energy Information Administration, www.eia.gov; Bill Powell, "China's New King of Solar," *FSB: Fortune Small Business,* 11 February 2009, 68–71; Nick Hodge, "Grid Parity: Renewables vs. Coal," *Wealth Daily,* 28 November 2007, www.wealthdaily.com; Solar Energy Initiative, U.S. Department of Energy website, accessed 14 May 2009, www.eere.energy.gov; "Frost & Sullivan 2008 Global Solar Energy Development Company of the Year Award," Suntech Power website, accessed 15 May 2009, www .suntech-power.com; John Kell, "Earnings Preview: Solar Cos Focus on Financing, Margins," *Wall Street Journal,* 16 April 2009, http://online.wsj.com; Jennifer Kho, "Solar Prices Drop, Deeper Discounts Expected," Earth2tech, 23 February 2009, www .earth2tech.com; Kate Galbraith, "Europe's Way of Encouraging Solar Power Arrives in the U.S.," *New York Times,* 12 March 2006, www.nytimes.com; Jack Yetiv, "When Will Solar Achieve Grid Parity? We're Already There!" Seeking Alpha blog, 21 April 2008, www.seekingalpha.com; Kevin Kelleher, "Report: First Solar Reaches Grid Parity," Earth2tech, 21 December 2008, www.earth2tech.com; Josie Garthwaite, "Solar Shakeout Under Way, Serious Oversupply to Come, Report Says," Earth2tech, 18 February 2009, www.earth2tech.com.
2. Roger LeRoy Miller, *Economics Today,* 15th ed. (Boston: Addison-Wesley, 2010), 28.
3. Miller, *Economics Today,* 31.
4. Ronald M. Ayers and Robert A. Collinge, *Economics: Explore and Apply* (Upper Saddle River, N.J.: Pearson Prentice Hall, 2005), 97–103.
5. Landon Thomas, Jr., "Thriving Norway Provides an Economics Lesson," *New York Times,* 13 May 2009, www.nytimes.com.
6. Emily Thornton, "Roads to Riches," *BusinessWeek,* 7 May 2007, www.businessweek.com; Palash R. Ghosh, "Private Prisons Have a Lock on Growth," *BusinessWeek,* 6 July 2006, www .businessweek.com.
7. Peter Gumbel, "Saving Britain's Broken Bank," *Fortune,* 29 April 2009, http://money.cnn.com.
8. Miller, *Economics Today,* 174.
9. Miller, *Economics Today,* 160.
10. Miller, *Economics Today,* 160.
11. U.S. Bureau of Labor Statistics, Producer Price Indexes; Program Overview, accessed 29 July 2011, www.bls.gov.
12. Adapted from James Kobielus, "The Forrester Wave: Predictive Analytics and Data Mining Solutions, Q1 2010," SAS website, accessed 1 August 2011, www.sas.com; Stephen Baker, "How Much Is That Worker Worth?" *BusinessWeek,* 23 March 2009, 46–48; Doug Henschen, "IDC Reports on BI Sales: Which Vendors Are Hot?" *Intelligent Enterprise,* 1 July 2007, www .intelligententerprise.com; Angoss website, accessed 21 May 2009, www.angoss.com.

GLOSSARY

business cycles Fluctuations in the rate of growth that an economy experiences over a period of several years

capitalism Economic system based on economic freedom and competition

capital The funds that finance the operations of a business as well as the physical, human-made elements used to produce goods and services, such as factories and computers

competition Rivalry among businesses for the same customers

consumer price index (CPI) A monthly statistic that measures changes in the prices of a representative collective of consumer goods and services

deflation An economic condition in which prices fall steadily throughout the economy

demand Buyers' willingness and ability to purchase products at various price points

demand curve A graph of the quantities of a product that buyers will purchase at various prices

deregulation Removing regulations to allow the market to prevent excesses and correct itself over time

economic indicators Statistics that measure the performance of the economy

economics The study of how a society uses its scarce resources to produce and distribute goods and services

economic system The policies that define a society's particular economic structure; the rules by which a society allocates economic resources

economy The sum total of all the economic activity within a given region

entrepreneurship The combination of innovation, initiative, and willingness to take the risks required to create and operate new businesses

equilibrium point The point at which quantity supplied equals quantity demanded

fiscal policy Use of government revenue collection and spending to influence the business cycle

free-market system Economic system in which decisions about what to produce and in what quantities are decided by the market's buyers and sellers

gross domestic product (GDP) The value of all the final goods and services produced by businesses located within a nation's borders; excludes outputs from overseas operations of domestic companies

human resources All the people who work in an organization or on its behalf

inflation An economic condition in which prices rise steadily throughout the economy

knowledge Expertise gained through experience or association

macroeconomics The study of "big picture" issues in an economy, including competitive behavior among firms, the effect of government policies, and overall resource allocation issues

microeconomics The study of how consumers, businesses, and industries collectively determine the quantity of goods and services demanded and supplied at different prices

monetary policy Government policy and actions taken by the Federal Reserve Board to regulate the nation's money supply

monopolistic competition A situation in which many sellers differentiate their products from those of competitors in at least some small way

monopoly A situation in which one company dominates a market to the degree that it can control prices

nationalizing A government's takeover of selected companies or industries

natural resources Land, forests, minerals, water, and other tangible assets usable in their natural state

oligopoly A market situation in which a very small number of suppliers, sometimes only two, provide a particular good or service

opportunity cost The value of the most appealing alternative not chosen

planned system Economic system in which the government controls most of the factors of production and regulates their allocation

privatizing Turning over services once performed by the government and allowing private businesses to perform them instead

producer price index (PPI) A statistical measure of price trends at the producer and wholesaler levels

pure competition A situation in which so many buyers and sellers exist that no single buyer or seller can individually influence market prices

recession A period during which national income, employment, and production all fall; defined as at least six months of decline in the GDP

regulation Relying more on laws and policies than on market forces to govern economic activity

socialism Economic system characterized by public ownership and operation of key industries combined with private ownership and operation of less-vital industries

supply A specific quantity of a product that the seller is able and willing to provide at various prices

supply curve A graph of the quantities of a product that sellers will offer for sale, regardless of demand, at various prices

unemployment rate The portion of the labor force (everyone over 16 who has or is looking for a job) currently without a job

The Global Marketplace

LEARNING OBJECTIVES After studying this chapter, you will be able to

1 Explain why nations trade and describe how international trade is measured

2 Discuss the nature of conflicts in global business, including free trade and government interventions into international trade

3 Identify the major organizations that facilitate international trade and the major trading blocs around the world

4 Discuss the importance of understanding cultural and legal differences in the global business environment

5 Define the major forms of international business activity

6 Discuss the strategic choices that must be considered before entering international markets

MyBizLab

Where you see MyBizLab in this chapter, go to www.mybizlab.com for additional activities on the topic being discussed.

BEHIND THE SCENES MTV NETWORKS AFRICA: EXTENDING THE REACH OF ONE OF THE WORLD'S BIGGEST MEDIA BRANDS

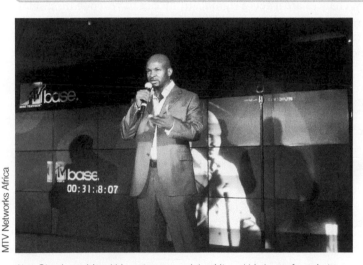

MTV Networks Africa

Alex Okosi combined his entrepreneurial spirit and his love of music to lead the successful launch of MTV Base Africa.

www.mtvbase.com

"Know your market" is one of the most fundamental principles of business, and Alex Okosi certainly knows his. A native of Nigeria, Okosi immigrated to the United States as a boy. After college in Vermont, he wound up out West, working for Viacom, the parent company of MTV Networks. However, a trip home convinced him that his future was back in Africa, not selling Viacom channels to cable operators in Idaho, Nevada, and Wyoming. And when he returned to Africa, he would bring MTV with him.

After years of colonialism, warfare, famine, widespread poverty, and rampant health problems ranging from malnutrition to the AIDS epidemic, Africa might not strike the average businessperson as a promising market. But Okosi saw reasons for hope, with economies showing signs of recovery in Angola, Uganda, Kenya, and elsewhere. He saw the incredibly rich music culture and the millions of people who were passionate about their music. The musical connection between Africa and America goes back centuries, actually, when the ancient singer-songwriter tradition from countries such as Mali found its way to the United States as a consequence of the slave trade. The music eventually evolved into American blues and jazz, which then inspired rock, soul, R&B, hip-hop, and other styles. Meanwhile, today's African popular music is a vibrant blend of traditional local styles and contemporary imports. For instance, the *hip-life* style popular in Ghana combines hip-hop with *highlife,* a jazzy, guitar-driven dance sound that dates from the 1920s.

From Chapter 3 of *Business in Action*, Sixth Edition. Courtland L. Bovée, John V. Thill. Copyright © 2013 by Pearson Education, Inc. Published by Pearson Business. All rights reserved.

When market research suggested that advertising, the lifeblood of any television business, was growing as local economies expanded, Okosi knew the time was right. "If you had any entrepreneurial spirit at all," he explained, "you'd say, 'Okay, I can do this.'" After several years of making contacts throughout the company, he transferred to MTV International's headquarters in London, ready to put his plans into action.

By this time, MTV had already launched nearly 100 country-specific channels around the world, so it was no stranger to doing business in the global marketplace. But none of those markets presented the challenges that Africa did. If you were in Alex Okosi's shoes, what steps would you take to bring MTV to Africa? How would you build a consumer market in a region where many people are still learning to adjust to the notion of a modern consumer economy?[1]

MyBizLab

For an interactive, real-world example of this topic, access this chapter's simulation entitled Going Global, located at **www.mybizlab.com**.

1 LEARNING OBJECTIVE

Explain why nations trade and describe how international trade is measured.

INTRODUCTION

The experience of MTV's Alex Okosi (profiled in the chapter-opening Behind the Scenes) in Africa is a great example of the opportunities and challenges of taking a business international. As you'll read in this chapter, international business has grown dramatically in recent years, and it's no stretch to say this growth affects virtually every company now, even those that never reach beyond their own borders. Studying international business is essential to your career, too. The future professionals and managers from Asia and Europe, people you'll be competing with for jobs in the global employment market, take international business very seriously.[2]

Fundamentals of International Trade

Wherever you're reading this, stop and look around for a minute. You might see cars that were made in Japan running on gasoline from Russia or Saudi Arabia, mobile phones made in South Korea, food grown in Canada or Mexico or Chile, a digital music player made in China, clothing from Vietnam or Italy, industrial equipment made in Germany—and dozens of other products from every corner of the globe. Conversely, if you or a family member works for a midsize or large company, chances are it gets a significant slice of its revenue from sales to other countries. In short, we live and work in a global marketplace. Moreover, while the United States remains one of the world's most competitive countries, dozens of other countries now compete for the same employees, customers, and investments (see Exhibit 1).

EXHIBIT 1	The World's Most Competitive Countries

According to the World Economic Forum, these are the 10 most competitive countries in the world, based on their ability to sustain economic growth.

2. Sweden
9. Denmark
7. Finland
5. Germany
8. Netherlands
1. Switzerland
10. Canada
4. United States
6. Japan
3. Singapore

1. Switzerland	6. Japan
2. Sweden	7. Finland
3. Singapore	8. Netherlands
4. United States	9. Denmark
5. Germany	10. Canada

Source: Klaus Schwab, *The Global Competitiveness Report 2010–2011*, World Economic Forum, www.weforum.org.

WHY NATIONS TRADE

Commerce across borders has been going on for thousands of years, but the volume of international business has roughly tripled in the past 30 years.[3] One significant result is **economic globalization**, the increasing integration and interdependence of national economies around the world. Six reasons help explain why countries and companies trade internationally:

- **Focusing on relative strengths.** The classic theory of *comparative advantage* suggests that each country should specialize in those areas where it can produce more efficiently than other countries, and it should trade for goods and services that it can't produce as economically. The basic argument is that such specialization and exchange will increase a country's total output and allow both trading partners to enjoy a higher standard of living.

- **Expanding markets.** Many companies have ambitions too large for their own back-yards. Well-known U.S. companies such as Microsoft and Boeing would be a fraction of their current size if they were limited to the U.S. marketplace. Similarly, companies based in other countries, from giants such as Toyota, Shell, and Nestlé to thousands of smaller but equally ambitious firms, view the U.S. consumer and business markets as a vast opportunity.

- **Pursuing economies of scale.** All this international activity involves more than just sales growth, of course. By expanding their markets, companies can benefit from **economies of scale**, which enable them to produce goods and services at lower costs by purchasing, manufacturing, and distributing higher quantities.[4]

- **Acquiring materials, goods, and services.** No country can produce everything its citizens want or need at prices they're willing to pay. For instance, the United States doesn't produce enough oil to meet its needs, so the nation buys oil from Canada, Russia, Saudi Arabia, and other countries that produce more than they can use. Similarly, most countries lack the ability to make commercial aircraft, so most of them buy planes from Boeing, a U.S. company, or Airbus, a consortium of companies based in Europe.

- **Keeping up with customers.** In some cases, companies have to expand in order to keep or attract multinational customers. For example, suppose a retailer with stores in 20 countries wants to hire a single advertising agency to manage all its ad campaigns. Any agency vying for the account might need to open offices in all 20 countries in order to be considered.

- **Keeping up with competitors.** Companies are sometimes forced to engage on a global scale simply because their competitors are doing so. Failing to respond can allow a competitor to increase its financial resources and become a greater threat everywhere the companies compete, even on home turf.[5]

These motivations have provided the energy behind the rapid growth in global business, but the level of growth would not have been possible without two key enablers. First, the world's borders are much more open to trade than they were just a few decades ago, thanks to the advent of international trade organizations and a growing awareness by most governments that healthy trade can help their economies. Second, advances in communication and transportation technologies have made global trade safer, easier, and more profitable.[6]

economic globalization The increasing integration and interdependence of national economies around the world

economies of scale Savings from buying parts and materials, manufacturing, or marketing in large quantities

HOW INTERNATIONAL TRADE IS MEASURED

Economists monitor certain key economic indicators to evaluate how well a country's economic system is performing, and several of these indicators measure international trade. As Exhibit 2 on the next page illustrates, the United States imports more goods than it exports, but it exports more services than it imports.

REAL-TIME UPDATES
Learn More by Exploring This Interactive Website

Get an interactive look at global economic data

This interactive Data Mapper tool from the International Monetary Fund makes it easy to explore and compare key economic data for countries around the world. Go to http://real-timeupdates.com/bia6 and click on Learn More. If you are using MyBizLab, you can access Real-Time Updates within the chapter or under Student Study Tools.

EXHIBIT 2   U.S. Exports and Imports Since 1990

The U.S. trade deficit has been growing dramatically in recent years. Although the United States maintains a trade surplus in services (middle graph), the international market for services isn't nearly as large as the market for goods. Consequently, the trade deficit in goods (top graph) far outweighs the trade surplus in services, resulting in an overall trade deficit (bottom graph).

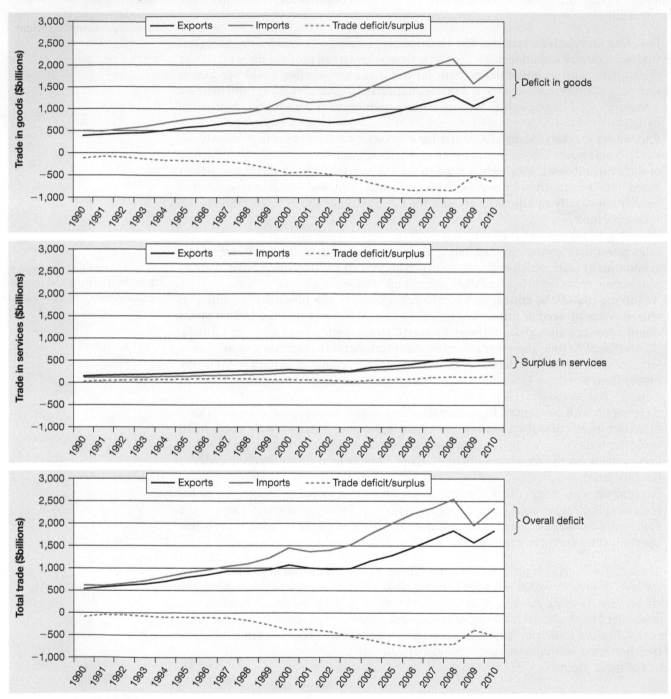

Source: "U.S. International Trade in Goods and Services," U.S. Bureau of Economic Analysis, accessed 30 July 2011, www.bea.gov.

balance of trade Total value of the products a nation exports minus the total value of the products it imports, over some period of time

trade surplus A favorable trade balance created when a country exports more than it imports

Two key measurements of a nation's level of international trade are the *balance of trade* and the *balance of payments*. The total value of a country's exports *minus* the total value of its imports, over some period of time, determines its **balance of trade**. In years when the value of goods and services exported by a country exceeds the value of goods and services it imports, the country has a positive balance of trade, or a **trade surplus**. The opposite is a **trade deficit**, when a country imports more than it exports.

The **balance of payments** is the broadest indicator of international trade. It is the total flow of money into the country *minus* the total flow of money out of the country over some period of time. The balance of payments includes the balance of trade plus the net dollars received and spent on foreign investment, military expenditures, tourism, foreign aid, and other international transactions. For example, when a U.S. company buys all or part of a company based in another country, that investment is counted in the balance of payments but not in the balance of trade. Similarly, when a foreign company buys a U.S. company or purchases U.S. stocks, bonds, or real estate, those transactions are part of the balance of payments.

trade deficit An unfavorable trade balance created when a country imports more than it exports

balance of payments The sum of all payments one nation receives from other nations minus the sum of all payments it makes to other nations, over some specified period of time

FOREIGN EXCHANGE RATES AND CURRENCY VALUATIONS

When companies buy and sell goods and services in the global marketplace, they complete the transaction by exchanging currencies. The process is called *foreign exchange,* the conversion of one currency into an equivalent amount of another currency. The number of units of one currency that must be exchanged for a unit of the second currency is known as the **exchange rate** between the currencies.

Most international currencies operate under a *floating exchange rate system*, meaning that a currency's value or price fluctuates in response to the forces of global supply and demand. The supply and demand of a country's currency are determined in part by what is happening in the country's own economy. Moreover, because supply and demand for a currency are always changing, the rate at which it is exchanged for other currencies may change a little each day.

A currency is called *strong* relative to another when its exchange rate is higher than what is considered normal and called *weak* when its rate is lower than normal ("normal" is a relative term here). Note that "strong" isn't necessarily good, and "weak" isn't necessarily bad when it comes to currencies, as Exhibit 3 illustrates. Exchange rates can dramatically affect a company's financial results by raising or lowering the cost of supplies it imports and raising or lowering the price of goods it exports.

exchange rate The rate at which the money of one country is traded for the money of another

EXHIBIT 3	Strong and Weak Currencies: Who Gains, Who Loses?

A strong dollar and a weak dollar aren't necessarily good or bad; each condition helps some people and hurts others.

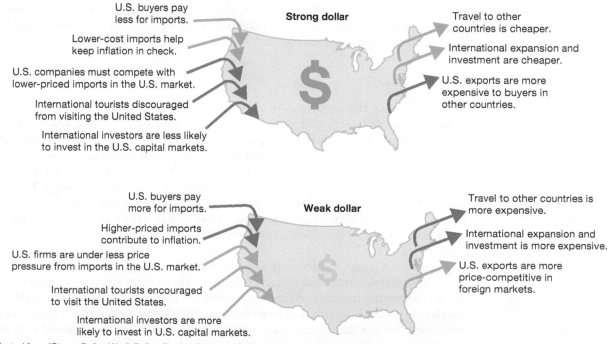

Strong dollar

U.S. buyers pay less for imports.

Lower-cost imports help keep inflation in check.

U.S. companies must compete with lower-priced imports in the U.S. market.

International tourists discouraged from visiting the United States.

International investors are less likely to invest in the U.S. capital markets.

Travel to other countries is cheaper.

International expansion and investment are cheaper.

U.S. exports are more expensive to buyers in other countries.

Weak dollar

U.S. buyers pay more for imports.

Higher-priced imports contribute to inflation.

U.S. firms are under less price pressure from imports in the U.S. market.

International tourists encouraged to visit the United States.

International investors are more likely to invest in U.S. capital markets.

Travel to other countries is more expensive.

International expansion and investment is more expensive.

U.S. exports are more price-competitive in foreign markets.

Source: Adapted from "Strong Dollar, Weak Dollar: Foreign Exchange Rates and the U.S. Economy," Federal Reserve Bank of Chicago website, www.chicagofed.org.

✔ Checkpoint

LEARNING OBJECTIVE 1: Explain why nations trade, and describe how international trade is measured.

SUMMARY: Nations and companies trade internationally for any of six reasons: focusing on their relative strengths (producing the goods and services in which they excel and trading for other products they need); expanding into new markets to increase sales revenues; pursuing economies of scale to achieve lower production costs; acquiring materials, goods, and services not available at home; tending to the needs of multinational customers; and keeping up with competitors that are expanding internationally. Two primary measures of a country's international trade are its *balance of trade*, which is exports minus imports, and its *balance of payments*, a broader measure that includes all incoming payments minus all outgoing payments.

CRITICAL THINKING: (1) Would it be wise for an advertising agency to open offices in Europe and Asia to service a single multinational client? Why or why not? (2) If IBM invests $40 million in a joint venture in China, would that amount be counted in the U.S. balance of trade or the balance of payments?

IT'S YOUR BUSINESS: (1) In the last major purchase you made, did you take into consideration whether the product was made in the United States or another country? (2) Does country of origin matter to you when you shop?

KEY TERMS TO KNOW: economic globalization, economies of scale, balance of trade, trade surplus, trade deficit, balance of payments, exchange rate

---

2 **LEARNING OBJECTIVE**

Discuss the nature of conflicts in global business, including free trade and government interventions into international trade.

Conflicts in International Trade

Just as employees compete with one another for jobs and companies compete for customers, countries compete with one another for both. The ability of firms such as Viacom, the company that owns MTV (profiled in the chapter-opening Behind the Scenes), to conduct business across national borders depends on the complex economic relationships the United States maintains with other countries. Naturally, the U.S. government promotes and protects the interests of U.S. companies, workers, and consumers. Other countries are trying to do the same thing for their stakeholders. As a consequence, international trade is a never-ending tug of war.

FREE TRADE

The benefits of the comparative advantage model are based on the assumption that nations don't take artificial steps to minimize their own weaknesses or to blunt the natural advantages of other countries. For example, if a country cannot produce a particular good at a cost that is competitive on the global market, its government might choose to *subsidize* exporters of this good with financial supports that allow them to charge lower prices than their business operations can naturally support. Trade that takes place without these interferences is known as **free trade**. (Like free-market capitalism, no trade is completely free in the sense that it takes place without regulations of any kind. Instead, international trade should be viewed along a continuum from "more free" to "less free.")

free trade International trade unencumbered by restrictive measures

Free trade is not a universally welcomed concept, despite the positive connotation of the word *free*. Supporters claim that it is the best way to ensure prosperity for everyone, and an overwhelming majority of U.S. economists say that the United States should eliminate barriers to trade.[7] Supporters of free trade generally acknowledge that it produces winners and losers but that the winners gain more than the losers lose, so the net effect is positive.[8]

Detractors call free trade unfair to too many people and a threat to the middle class.[9] In addition, some critics argue that free trade makes it too easy for companies to exploit workers around the world by pitting them against one another in a "race to the bottom," in which production moves to whichever country has the lowest wages and fewest restrictions regarding worker safety and environmental protection.[10] This complaint has been at the heart of recent protests over free trade and economic globalization in general. However, some researches rebut this criticism by saying that companies prefer to do business in countries with stable, democratic governments. Consequently, this camp says, less-developed nations are motivated to improve their economic and social policies, which not only helps business but can raise the standard of living.[11] As one example, from 1981 to 2005, a period during which China became much more actively involved in free-market capitalism and global trade, the country's poverty rate dropped by 68 percent.[12] Of course, such progress might be little comfort to workers in other countries who've lost jobs as the global labor market evolves in the direction of parity.

GOVERNMENT INTERVENTION IN INTERNATIONAL TRADE

When a government believes that free trade is not in the best interests of its national security, domestic industries, workforce, or consumers, it can intervene in a number of ways. Some of these methods are collectively known as **protectionism** because they seek to protect a specific industry or groups of workers. While they can help some parties in the short term, many protectionist measures actually end up hurting the groups they were intended to help. When an industry is isolated from real-life competition for too long, it can fail to develop and become strong enough to compete efficiently.[13]

The following are the most commonly used ways to intervene in international trade:

- **Tariffs.** Taxes, surcharges, or duties levied against imported goods are known as **tariffs**. Tariffs can be levied to generate revenue, to restrict trade, or to punish other countries for disobeying international trade laws.
- **Quotas. Import quotas** limit the amount of particular goods that countries allow to be imported during a given year.
- **Embargoes.** An **embargo** is a complete ban on the import or export of certain products or even all trade between certain countries.
- **Restrictive import standards.** Countries can assist their domestic producers by establishing restrictive import standards, such as requiring special licenses for doing certain kinds of business and then making it difficult or expensive for foreign companies to obtain such licenses.[14]
- **Export subsidies.** In addition to intervening on imported goods, countries can also intervene to help domestic industries export their products to other countries. **Export subsidies** are a form of financial assistance in which producers receive enough money from the government to allow them to lower their prices in order to compete more effectively in the world market.
- **Anti-dumping measures.** The practice of selling large quantities of a product at a price lower than the cost of production or below what the company would charge in its home market is called **dumping**. This tactic is most often used to try to win foreign customers or to reduce product surpluses. If a domestic producer can demonstrate that the low-cost imports are damaging its business, most governments will seek redress on their behalf through international trade organizations. Dumping is often a tricky situation to resolve, however; buyers of a product that is being dumped benefit from the lower prices, and proving what constitutes a fair price in the country of origin can be difficult.[15]
- **Sanctions.** Sanctions are politically motivated embargoes that revoke a country's normal trade relations status; they are often used as forceful alternatives short of war. Sanctions can include arms embargoes, foreign-assistance reductions and cutoffs, trade limitations, tariff increases, import-quota decreases, visa denials, air-link cancellations, and more.

protectionism Government policies aimed at shielding a country's industries from foreign competition

tariffs Taxes levied on imports

import quotas Limits placed on the quantity of imports a nation will allow for a specific product

embargo A total ban on trade with a particular nation (a sanction) or of a particular product

export subsidies A form of financial assistance in which producers receive enough money from the government to allow them to lower their prices in order to compete more effectively in the global market

dumping Charging less than the actual cost or less than the home-country price for goods sold in other countries

✓ Checkpoint

3 **LEARNING OBJECTIVE**

Identify the major organizations that facilitate international trade and the major trading blocs around the world.

International Trade Organizations

With international trade such a huge part of the world's economies, organizations that establish trading rules, resolve disputes, and promote trade play an important role in global business.

ORGANIZATIONS FACILITATING INTERNATIONAL TRADE

In an effort to ensure equitable trading practices and iron out the inevitable disagreements over what is fair and what isn't, governments around the world have established a number of important agreements and organizations that address trading issues, including the WTO, IMF, and World Bank.

The World Trade Organization (WTO)

The World Trade Organization (WTO), www.wto.org, is a permanent forum for negotiating, implementing, and monitoring international trade procedures and for mediating trade disputes among its more than 150 member countries. The organization's work is guided by five principles: preventing discriminatory policies that favor some trading partners over others or a country's own products over those of other countries, reducing trade barriers between countries, making trade policies more predictable and less arbitrary, discouraging unfair practices, and helping less-developed countries benefit from international trade.[16]

Critics of globalization often direct their ire at the WTO, but the organization says these criticisms are unjustified and based on misunderstandings of the WTO's missions and methods. For example, the WTO asserts that contrary to claims by some critics, it does not dictate policies to national governments, it does not ignore the special circumstances faced by the world's poorest countries, and it does not ignore health and environmental concerns when trying to mediate commercial disputes.[17] One point everyone seems to agree on is that the WTO's work is exceedingly complex and therefore excruciatingly slow. Reaching agreement to eventually eliminate agricultural export subsidies, in which government payments to farmers allow them to set artificially low prices on the world market, took several decades.[18]

The International Monetary Fund (IMF)

The International Monetary Fund (IMF), www.imf.org, was established in 1945 to foster international financial cooperation. Its primary functions are monitoring global financial developments, providing technical advice and training, providing short-term loans to countries that are unable to meet their financial obligations, and working to alleviate poverty in developing economies.[19] When they need money, the IMF's 187 member countries can borrow against the deposits they made to join the fund. However, to borrow more than 25 percent of its deposit amount, a country must agree to various conditions designed to ensure its ability to pay back the loan. These conditions can include significant changes to a country's economic policies, such as banking reforms and modifications to trade barriers.[20]

The World Bank

The World Bank (www.worldbank.org) is a United Nations agency owned by its 187 member nations. It was founded to finance reconstruction after World War II and is now involved in hundreds of projects around the world aimed at addressing poverty, health, education, and other concerns in developing countries.[21] While it is not as directly involved in international trade and finance as the WTO and IMF, the World Bank does indirectly contribute to trade by working to improve economic conditions throughout the developing world.

TRADING BLOCS

Trading blocs, or *common markets,* are regional organizations that promote trade among member nations (see Exhibit 4 on the next page). Although specific rules vary from group to group, their primary objective is to ensure the economic growth and benefit of members. As such, trading blocs generally promote trade inside the region while creating uniform barriers against goods and services entering the region from nonmember countries.

trading blocs Organizations of nations that remove barriers to trade among their members and that establish uniform barriers to trade with nonmember nations

North American Free Trade Agreement (NAFTA)

In 1994, the United States, Canada, and Mexico formed the North American Free Trade Agreement (NAFTA), paving the way for the free flow of goods, services, and capital within the bloc through the phased elimination of tariffs and quotas.[22] NAFTA primarily affects trade between the United States and Mexico and between the United States and Canada; trade between Mexico and Canada is small in comparison.[23]

NAFTA was controversial when first implemented, and it has remained controversial ever since. Mexican exports are up dramatically, and U.S. and other foreign companies have invested billions of dollars in Mexico. Some Mexican companies are thriving, thanks to those export opportunities, while others, particularly in agriculture, have been hurt severely by low-cost imports from the United States. Many of the manufacturing jobs Mexico hoped to attract wound up in China and other countries instead. And outside the business sphere, hoped-for improvements in education and health care in Mexico haven't materialized to the extent that NAFTA backers expected, although they place the blame on government inaction, not on the free-trade agreement. In the United States, critics of NAFTA claim that much of the promised benefits of lower consumer prices and steady export markets for small farmers didn't materialize, that benefits of NAFTA have gone mostly to huge agribusiness corporations, and that contrary to promises of job creation in the United States, NAFTA has cost U.S. jobs.[24]

The Office of the United States Trade Representative, the U.S. government agency responsible for negotiating international trade agreements, disputes many of the criticisms of NAFTA. For example, the agency offers statistics to show that NAFTA has more than tripled trade among the three countries and that unemployment rates in the United States were lower after NAFTA than before.[25] Arriving at clear answers in such disputes is often difficult, given the complexity of the economic relationships between countries, the shifting economic and political landscapes within countries, and the effects of developments in other countries.

The European Union (EU)

One of the largest trading blocs is the European Union (EU), http://europa.eu, whose membership now encompasses more than two dozen countries and a half billion people. Viewed as a whole, the EU now constitutes the world's largest economy. EU nations have eliminated hundreds of local regulations, variations in product standards, and protectionist measures that once limited trade among member countries. Trade now flows among member countries in much the same way it does among states in the United States. And the EU's reach extends far beyond the borders of Europe; to simplify design and manufacturing for world markets, many

EXHIBIT 4	Members of Major Trading Blocs

As the economies of the world become increasingly linked, many countries have formed powerful regional trading blocs that trade freely with one another but place restrictions on trade with other countries and blocs.

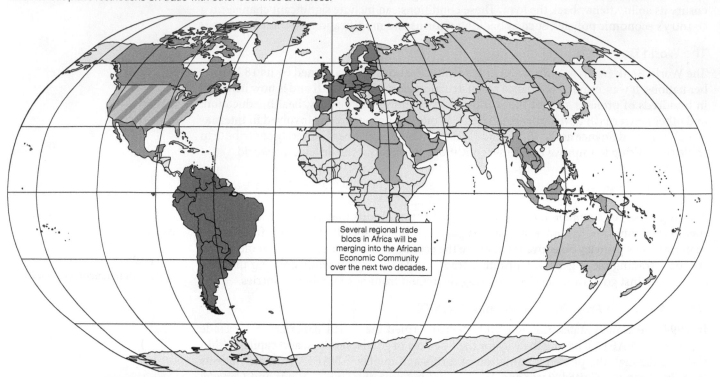

Several regional trade blocs in Africa will be merging into the African Economic Community over the next two decades.

European Union (EU)	North American Free Trade Agreement (NAFTA)	Association of Southeast Asian Nations (ASEAN)	Union of South American Nations	Asia-Pacific Economic Cooperation (APEC)	Greater Arab Free Trade Area (GAFTA)
Austria	Canada	Brunei Darussalam	Argentina	Australia	Bahrain
Belgium	Mexico	Cambodia	Bolivia	Brunei Darussalam	Egypt
Bulgaria	United States	Indonesia	Brazil	Canada	Iraq
Cyprus		Laos	Chile	Chile	Jordan
Czech Republic		Malaysia	Colombia	China	Kuwait
Denmark		Myanmar	Ecuador	Hong Kong	Lebanon
Estonia		Philippines	Guyana	Indonesia	Libya
Finland		Singapore	Paraguay	Japan	Morocco
France		Thailand	Peru	Republic of Korea	Oman
Germany		Vietnam	Suriname	Malaysia	Palestine
Greece			Uruguay	Mexico	Qatar
Hungary			Venezuela	New Zealand	Saudi Arabia
Ireland				Papua New Guinea	Syria
Italy				Peru	Sudan
Latvia				Philippines	Tunisia
Lithuania				Russia	United Arab Emirates
Luxembourg				Singapore	Yemen
Malta				Chinese Taipei	
Netherlands				Thailand	
Poland				United States	
Portugal				Vietnam	
Romania					
Slovakia					
Slovenia					
Spain					
Sweden					
United Kingdom					

Sources: Member country lists from Europa: Gateway to the European Union website, http://europa.eu; Association of Southeast Asian Nations website, www.asean.org; Union of South American Nations website, www.towardsunity.org; Union de Naciones Suramericanas website, www.pptunasur.com; Asia Pacific Economic Cooperation website, www.apec.org; Jordan Ministry of Industry & Trade website, www.mit.gov.jo. Membership information current as of 30 July 2011.

companies now create their products to meet EU specifications. If you've seen the "CE" marking on any products you may own, that stands for *Conformité Européene* and indicates that the product has met EU standards for safety, health, and environmental responsibility.[26]

The EU has taken a significant step beyond all other trading blocs in the area of money by creating its own currency, the *euro*, which has been adopted by more than half the member states of the EU. By switching to a common currency, these countries have made financial transactions simpler and less expensive. According to EU leadership, the euro has lowered inflation and interest rates, improved transparency in pricing, provided a more stable currency, and given the EU a stronger presence in global financial markets.[27] However, with widespread trade imbalances and ongoing financial crises in Greece, Italy, and several other nations weighing down the economies of all eurozone members, some observers now question whether the currency bloc can continue in its current configuration.

The Asia-Pacific Economic Cooperation (APEC)

The Asia-Pacific Economic Cooperation (APEC), www.apec.org, is an organization of 21 countries working to liberalize trade in the Pacific Rim (the land areas that surround the Pacific Ocean). Member nations represent 40 percent of the world's population and more than 50 percent of the world's gross domestic product. Like other trade blocs, APEC has a long-term goal of liberalizing and simplifying trade and investment among member countries and helping the region as a whole achieve sustainable economic growth. Since its establishment in 1989, APEC has reduced trade barriers between member nations by 70 percent.[28]

Checkpoint

LEARNING OBJECTIVE 3: Identify the major organizations that facilitate international trade and the major trading blocs around the world.

SUMMARY: Major organizations that facilitate trade include the World Trade Organization (WTO), the International Monetary Fund (IMF), and, at least indirectly, the World Bank. Major regional trading blocs include NAFTA (Canada, Mexico, and the United States), the European Union (more than two dozen countries across Europe), and APEC (21 countries around the Pacific Rim).

CRITICAL THINKING: (1) Why do trade disputes sometimes take years to resolve? (2) If a country currently benefits from high tariffs on imports, why might it consider joining a trading bloc that requires it to lower or eliminate those tariffs?

IT'S YOUR BUSINESS: (1) Can you identify any ways in which your life as an employee or a consumer has been affected by U.S. membership in trading blocs such as NAFTA and APEC? (2) How can you confirm that the effect was caused by trading bloc membership?

KEY TERM TO KNOW: trading blocs

The Global Business Environment

4 **LEARNING OBJECTIVE**

Discuss the importance of understanding cultural and legal differences in the global business environment.

Doing business internationally can be a boon for many companies, but it also presents many challenges. Every country has unique laws, customs, consumer preferences, ethical standards, labor skills, and political and economic forces. Understanding cultural and legal differences is an essential first step for any business contemplating international operations.

CULTURAL DIFFERENCES IN THE GLOBAL BUSINESS ENVIRONMENT

Culture is a shared system of symbols, beliefs, attitudes, values, expectations, and norms for behavior. Your cultural background influences the way you prioritize what is important in life, helps define your attitude toward what is appropriate in a situation, and establishes

culture A shared system of symbols, beliefs, attitudes, values, expectations, and norms for behavior

stereotyping Assigning a wide range of generalized attributes, which are often superficial or even false, to an individual based on his or her membership in a particular culture or social group

ethnocentrism Judging all other groups according to the standards, behaviors, and customs of one's own group

rules of behavior.[29] Successful global business leaders recognize and respect differences in language, social values, ideas of status, decision-making habits, attitudes toward time, use of space, body language, manners, religions, and ethical standards. Ignorance of or indifference to cultural differences is a common cause of communication breakdowns in international affairs. Above all else, businesspeople dealing with other cultures avoid the twin traps of **stereotyping**, assigning a wide range of generalized (and often superficial or even false) attributes to an individual on the basis of membership in a particular culture or social group, and **ethnocentrism**, the tendency to judge all other groups according to one's own group's standards, behaviors, and customs.

Education and an open mind are the best ways to prepare yourself for doing business with people from another culture. Numerous books and websites offer advice on traveling to and working in specific countries. Also try to sample newspapers, magazines, and even the music and movies of another country. For instance, a movie can demonstrate nonverbal customs even if you don't grasp the language. Learn everything you can about the culture's history, religion, politics, and customs—especially its business customs. Who makes decisions? How are negotiations usually conducted? Is gift giving expected? What is the proper attire for a business meeting? In addition to the suggestion that you learn about the culture, seasoned international businesspeople offer the following tips for improving communication with a person from another culture:

- **Be alert to the other person's customs.** Expect the other person to have values, beliefs, expectations, and mannerisms that may differ from yours.
- **Deal with the individual.** Don't stereotype the other person or react with preconceived ideas. Regard the person as an individual first, not as a representative of another culture.
- **Clarify your intent and meaning.** The other person's body language may not mean what you think, and the person may read unintentional meanings into your message. Clarify your true intent by repetition and examples. Ask questions and listen carefully.
- **Adapt your style to the other person's.** If the other person appears to be direct and straightforward, follow suit. If not, adjust your behavior to match.
- **Show respect.** Learn how respect is communicated in various cultures—through gestures, eye contact, social customs, and other actions.

These are just a few tips for doing business in the global marketplace. Successful international businesses learn as much as they can about political issues, cultural factors, and the economic environment before investing time and money in new markets. Exhibit 5 can guide you in your efforts to learn more about a country's culture before doing business in other countries.

LEGAL DIFFERENCES IN THE GLOBAL BUSINESS ENVIRONMENT

Differences in national legal systems may not be as immediately obvious as cultural differences, but they can have a profound effect on international business efforts. For instance, the legal systems in the United States and the United Kingdom are based on *common law*, in which tradition, custom, and judicial interpretation play important roles. In contrast, the system in countries such as France and Germany is based on *civil law*, in which legal parameters are specified in detailed legal codes. One everyday consequence of this difference is that business contracts tend to be shorter and simpler in civil law systems, since the existing legal code outlines more aspects of the transaction or relationship. A third type of legal system, *theocratic law*, or law based on religious principles, predominates in countries such as Iran and Pakistan. Beyond the differences in legal philosophies, the business of contracts, copyrights, and other legal matters can vary considerably from one country to another.

Perhaps no issue in international business law generates as much confusion and consternation as bribery. In some countries, payments to government and business officials are so common that some businesspeople consider them to be standard operating practice—and

EXHIBIT 5	Checklist for Doing Business Abroad

Use this checklist as a starting point when planning business activity in another country.

Action	Details to Consider
Understand social customs	• How do people react to strangers? Are they friendly? Hostile? Reserved? • How do people greet each other? Should you bow? Nod? Shake hands? • How do you express appreciation for an invitation to lunch, dinner, or someone's home? Should you bring a gift? Send flowers? Write a thank-you note? • Are any phrases, facial expressions, or hand gestures considered rude? • How do you attract the attention of a waiter? Do you tip the waiter? • When is it rude to refuse an invitation? How do you refuse politely? • What topics may or may not be discussed in a social setting? In a business setting? • How do social customs dictate interaction between men and women? Between younger people and older people?
Learn about clothing and food preferences	• What occasions require special attire? • What colors are associated with mourning? Love? Joy? • Are some types of clothing considered taboo for one gender or the other? • How many times a day do people eat? • How are hands or utensils used when eating? • Where is the seat of honor at a table?
Assess political patterns	• How stable is the political situation? • Does the political situation affect businesses in and out of the country? • Is it appropriate to talk politics in social or business situations?
Understand religious and social beliefs	• To which religious groups do people belong? • Which places, objects, actions, and events are sacred? • Do religious beliefs affect communication between men and women or between any other groups? • Is there a tolerance for minority religions? • How do religious holidays affect business and government activities? • Does religion require or prohibit eating specific foods? At specific times?
Learn about economic and business institutions	• Is the society homogeneous or heterogeneous? • What languages are spoken? • What are the primary resources and principal products? • Are businesses generally large? Family controlled? Government controlled? • What are the generally accepted working hours? • How do people view scheduled appointments? • Are people expected to socialize before conducting business?
Appraise the nature of ethics, values, and laws	• Is money or a gift expected in exchange for arranging business transactions? • Do people value competitiveness or cooperation? • What are the attitudes toward work? Toward money? • Is politeness more important than factual honesty?

Source: Courtland L. Bovée and John V. Thill, *Business Communication Today*, 11th ed. (Upper Saddle River, N.J.: Pearson Prentice Hall, 2012), 73.

companies sometimes fear they won't be able to compete if they don't play along. These payments are used to facilitate a variety of actions, from winning contracts for public works projects (such as roads or power plants) to securing routine government services (such as customs inspections) to getting preferential treatment (such as the approval to raise prices).[30]

These payment systems discourage much-needed investment in developing countries, undermine democratic processes and weaken trust in government, raise prices for consumers by inflating business costs, and can even present security risks by essentially putting officials' actions up for the highest bid. Some businesspeople have argued that critics of such payoffs are trying to impose U.S. values on other cultures, but Transparency International, a watchdog group that works to reduce business–government corruption around the world, discredits this argument by saying that all countries have laws against corruption, so it can hardly be considered a cultural issue.[31] (To learn more about Transparency International's work, visit www.transparency.org.)

All U.S. companies are bound by the Foreign Corrupt Practices Act (FCPA), which outlaws payments with the intent of getting government officials to break the laws of their own countries. The FCPA allows payments that expedite actions that are legal, such as clearing merchandise through customs, although critics such as Transparency International consider this behavior unethical as well because it permits private profits to be gained from public trust.[32] Other types of payments can also be considered forms of influence but aren't covered by the FCPA, such as foreign aid payments from one government to another, made with the intent of securing favorable decisions for business.

Significantly, the FCPA also gives the U.S. government authority to investigate and charge foreign companies that engage in bribery using subsidiaries, banks, or other resources based in the United States. The number of FCPA investigations has been increasing in recent years, with some companies even contacting the government on their own to make sure they haven't been in violation.[33] For example, when Johnson & Johnson discovered that its subsidiaries in Greece, Poland, and Romania had been bribing doctors to prescribe the company's products, executives alerted the U.S. Department of Justice. Johnson & Johnson was eventually hit with a $70 million fine for violating the FCPA.[34]

Following the FCPA, the Organisation for Economic Co-Operation and Development (OECD), an international body dedicated to fostering economic prosperity and combating poverty, had made bribery of foreign officials a criminal offence for its member nations as well.[35]

✔ Checkpoint

LEARNING OBJECTIVE 4: Discuss the importance of understanding cultural and legal differences in the global business environment.

SUMMARY: Elements of culture include language, social values, ideas of status, decision-making habits, attitudes toward time, use of space, body language, manners, religions, and ethical standards. Awareness of and respect for cultural differences is essential to avoiding communication breakdowns and fostering positive working relationships. Understanding differences in legal systems and specific laws and regulations in other countries is another vital aspect of successful international business. One of the most confusing and frustrating aspects of international trade law is the issue of bribery.

CRITICAL THINKING: (1) What steps could you take to help someone from another country adapt to U.S. business culture? (2) How can you convey respect for another person's culture even if you don't agree with it or even understand it?

IT'S YOUR BUSINESS: (1) Have you ever experienced a communication breakdown with someone from another country? (2) If so, how did you resolve it, and how could you apply this experience to your business career?

KEY TERMS TO KNOW: culture, stereotyping, ethnocentrism

5   **LEARNING OBJECTIVE**

Define the major forms of international business activity.

Forms of International Business Activity

Beyond cultural and legal concerns, companies that plan to go international also need to think carefully about the right organizational approach to support these activities. The five common forms of international business are importing and exporting, licensing, franchising, strategic alliances and joint ventures, and foreign direct investment; each has varying degrees of ownership, financial commitment, and risk (see Exhibit 6).

IMPORTING AND EXPORTING

importing Purchasing goods or services from another country and bringing them into one's own country

exporting Selling and shipping goods or services to another country

Importing, the buying of goods or services from a supplier in another country, and **exporting,** the selling of products outside the country in which they are produced, have existed for centuries. Exporting is one of the least risky forms of international business activity. It allows a firm to enter a foreign market gradually, assess local conditions, and then fine-tune its product offerings to meet the needs of local markets. In most cases, the firm's financial exposure is limited to the costs of researching the market, advertising, and either establishing a direct sales and distribution system or hiring intermediaries. Moreover, a

EXHIBIT 6 — Forms of International Business Activity

Depending on their goals and resources and the opportunities available, companies can choose from five different ways to conduct business internationally.

Importing and exporting: Buying and selling goods and services across national borders, without establishing a physical or legal business presence in other countries

International licensing: Licensing intellectual property such as a design patent to a company in another country, which then produces the product and sells it locally

International franchising: Selling the rights to use an entire business system, such as a fast-food restaurant, including the brand name and internal processes

International strategic alliances and joint ventures: Forming a long-term business partnership with an established company in a local market or creating a new, third company with a local business partner

Foreign direct investment: Buying an established company or launching a new company in another country

variety of intermediaries exist to help companies, even the smallest businesses, get started with exporting.

Many countries now have foreign trade offices to help importers and exporters interested in doing business within their borders. Other helpful resources include professional agents, local businesspeople, and the International Trade Administration of the U.S. Department of Commerce (http://export.gov), which offers a variety of services, including political and credit-risk analysis, advice on entering foreign markets, and financing tips.[36]

INTERNATIONAL LICENSING

Licensing is another popular approach to international business. License agreements entitle one company to use some or all of another firm's intellectual property (patents, trademarks, brand names, copyrights, or trade secrets) in return for a royalty payment.

Low up-front costs are an attractive aspect of international licensing. Pharmaceutical firms such as Germany's Boehringer Ingelheim routinely use licensing to enter foreign markets.[37] After a pharmaceutical company has developed and patented a new drug, it is often more efficient to grant existing local firms the right to manufacture and distribute the patented drug in return for royalty payments. (Licensing agreements are not restricted to international business, of course; a company can also license its products or technology to other companies in its domestic market.)

licensing Agreement to produce and market another company's product in exchange for a royalty or fee

INTERNATIONAL FRANCHISING

Some companies choose to expand into foreign markets by *franchising* their operations. Briefly, franchising involves selling the right to use a *business system*, including brand names, business processes, trade secrets, and other assets. For instance, there are more than 18,000 McDonald's restaurants in more than 100 countries outside the United States, and the vast majority of them are run by independent franchisees.[38] Franchising is an attractive option for many companies because it reduces the costs and risks of expanding internationally while leveraging their investments in branding and business processes.

REAL-TIME UPDATES
Learn More by Visiting This Website

Ready to take a business international?

Export.gov can help you at every step, including finding out if your company has what it takes to be a successful exporter. Go to http://real-timeupdates.com/bia6 and click on Learn More. If you are using MyBizLab, you can access Real-Time Updates within the chapter or under Student Study Tools.

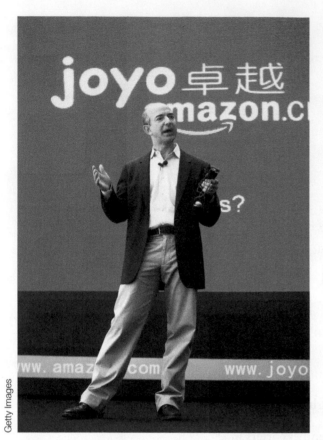

Amazon.com used foreign direct investment to enter the Chinese market, purchasing the established e-commerce company Joyo.

foreign direct investment (FDI) Investment of money by foreign companies in domestic business enterprises

multinational corporations (MNCs) Companies with operations in more than one country

INTERNATIONAL STRATEGIC ALLIANCES AND JOINT VENTURES

Strategic alliances, long-term partnerships between two or more companies to jointly develop, produce, or sell products, are another important way to reach the global marketplace. Alliance partners typically share ideas, expertise, resources, technologies, investment costs, risks, management, and profits. In some cases, a strategic alliance might be the only way to gain access to a market.

A *joint venture*, in which two or more firms join together to create a new business entity that is legally separate and distinct from its parents, is an alternative to a strategic alliance. In some countries, foreign companies are prohibited from owning facilities outright or from investing in local business, so establishing a joint venture with a local partner may be the only way to do business in that country.

FOREIGN DIRECT INVESTMENT

Many firms prefer to enter international markets through partial or whole ownership and control of assets in foreign countries, an approach known as **foreign direct investment (FDI).** To enter the Chinese market, for instance, Amazon.com purchased Joyo, an established e-commerce company. The copany is now known there as Joyo Amazon.cn (www.amazon.cn).[39] Some facilities are set up through FDI to exploit the availability of raw materials; others take advantage of low wage rates, while still others minimize transportation costs by choosing locations that give them direct access to markets in other countries. Companies that establish a physical presence in multiple countries through FDI are called **multinational corporations (MNCs).** MNCs can approach international markets in a variety of ways; see "Organizational Strategies for International Expansion" on the next page.

FDI typically gives companies greater control, but it carries much greater economic and political risk and is more complex than any other form of entry in the global marketplace. Consequently, most FDI takes place between the industrialized nations (a group that includes such large, stable economies as the United States, Canada, Japan, and most countries in Europe), which tend to offer greater protection for foreign investors.[40]

✓ Checkpoint

LEARNING OBJECTIVE 5: Define the major forms of international business activity.

SUMMARY: The major forms of international business activity are importing and exporting (buying and selling across national boundaries), licensing (conferring the rights to create a product), franchising (selling the rights to use an entire business system and brand identity), strategic alliances and joint ventures (forming partnerships with other companies), and foreign direct investment (buying companies or building facilities in another country).

CRITICAL THINKING: (1) Can a company successfully export to other countries without having staff and facilities in those countries? Why or why not? (2) Why does so much foreign direct investment take place between the industrialized nations?

IT'S YOUR BUSINESS: (1) What connotations does the word *imported* have for you? (2) On what do you base your reaction?

KEY TERMS TO KNOW: importing, exporting, licensing, foreign direct investment (FDI), multinational corporations (MNCs)

Strategic Approaches to International Markets

6 | LEARNING OBJECTIVE

Discuss the strategic choices that must be considered before entering international markets.

Expanding internationally is obviously not a decision any business can take lightly. The rewards can be considerable, but the costs and risks must be analyzed carefully during the planning stage. This section offers a brief look at overall organizational strategies for international expansion, followed by strategic questions in the various functional areas of the business.

ORGANIZATIONAL STRATEGIES FOR INTERNATIONAL EXPANSION

When a firm decides to establish a presence in another country, it needs to consider its long-term objectives, the nature of its products, the characteristics of the markets into which it plans to expand, and the management team's ability to oversee a geographically dispersed operation. These considerations can lead to one of several high-level strategies:[41]

- In the **multidomestic strategy**, a company creates highly independent operating units in each new country, giving local managers a great deal of freedom to run their operations almost as though they are independent companies. While this strategy can help a company respond more quickly and effectively to local market needs, it doesn't deliver the economy of scale advantages that other strategies can bring. In addition, the lack of centralized control can lead to situations in which local managers act in ways contrary to corporate strategy or guidelines. For example, when the French grocery retailer Carrefour learned that some of its local store managers in China were luring customers with low advertised prices but then charging more in their stores, the company clamped down on the practice, even though it is apparently widespread in Chinese retailing (despite being illegal).[42]

- In the **global strategy**, a company embraces the notion of economic globalization by viewing the world as a single integrated market. This is essentially the opposite of the multidomestic strategy. Managerial control with the global strategy is highly centralized, with headquarters in the home country making all major decisions.

- In the **transnational strategy**, a company uses a hybrid approach as it attempts to reap the benefits of international scale while being responsive to local market dynamics. This is the essence of the often-heard advice to "think globally, act locally." With this approach, major strategic decisions and business systems such as accounting and purchasing are often centralized, but local business units are given the freedom to make "on the ground" decisions that are most appropriate for local markets.

multidomestic strategy A decentralized approach to international expansion in which a company creates highly independent operating units in each new country

global strategy A highly centralized approach to international expansion, with headquarters in the home country making all major decisions

transnational strategy A hybrid approach that attempts to reap the benefits of international scale while being responsive to local market dynamics

FUNCTIONAL STRATEGIES FOR INTERNATIONAL EXPANSION

Choosing the right form of business to pursue is the first of many decisions that companies need to make when moving into other countries. Virtually everything you learn about in this course, from human resources to marketing to financial management, needs to be reconsidered carefully when going international. Some of the most important decisions involve products, customer support, pricing, promotion, and staffing:

- **Products.** You face two primary questions regarding products. First, which products should you try to sell in each market? Second, should you *standardize* your products, selling the same product everywhere in the world, or *customize* your products to accommodate the lifestyles and habits of local target markets? Customization seems like an obvious choice, but it can increase costs and operational complexity, so the decision to customize is not automatic. The degree of customization can also vary. A company may change only a product's name or packaging, or it can modify a product's components, size, and functions. Understanding a country's regulations, culture, and local competition plays into the decisions. For instance, LG Electronics, a South Korean appliance maker, markets refrigerators in India with extra-large vegetable compartments (catering to India's many vegetarians) and visually striking floral patterns, produces versions in Saudi Arabia that have a special cooler for dates (which are popular there), and sells versions in South Korea with a sealed compartment for *kimchi* (to keep the richly aromatic dish from interacting with other foods).[43]

- **Customer support.** Cars, computers, and other products that require some degree of customer support add another layer of complexity to international business. Many customers are reluctant to buy foreign products that don't offer some form of local support, whether it's a local dealer, a manufacturer's branch office, or a third-party organization that offers support under contract to the manufacturer.

- **Promotion.** Advertising, public relations, and other promotional efforts also present the dilemma of standardization versus customization. After years of trying to build global brands, many U.S. companies are putting new emphasis on crafting customized messages for each country. As one British advertising executive put it, "One size doesn't fit all. Consumers are more interesting for their differences rather than their similarities."[44]

- **Pricing.** Even a standardized strategy adds to the cost of doing business, from transportation to communication, and customized international strategies add even more. Before moving into other countries, businesses need to make sure they can cover all these costs and still be able to offer competitive prices.

- **Staffing.** Depending on the form of business a company decides to pursue in international markets, staffing questions can be major considerations. Many companies find that a combination of U.S. and local personnel works best, mixing company experience with local connections and lifelong knowledge of the working culture. Staffing strategies can evolve over time, too, as conditions change in various countries. In recent years, for example, U.S. and European countries with operations in China have begun filling more middle and upper management positions with local talent, rather than relocating managers from headquarters. The costs of hiring locally are often considerably lower, and there is less risk of a foreign manager failing to adapt to working and living in China.[45] When transferring managers to foreign posts, some U.S. companies have experienced failure rates as high as 50 percent.[46]

Given the number and complexity of the decisions to be made, you can see why successful companies plan international expansion with great care—and adapt quickly if their strategies and tactics aren't working. For the latest information on internal business, visit http://real-timeupdates.com/bia6.

✔ Checkpoint

LEARNING OBJECTIVE 6: Discuss the strategic choices that must be considered before entering international markets.

SUMMARY: The strategic choices a business must make include the basic organizational strategy that defines what kind of company the firm will be in each country and a variety of functional strategies involving such aspects as products, customer support, promotion, pricing, and staffing. Organizational strategies include *multidomestic* (a highly decentralized approach), *global* (a highly centralized approach), and *transnational* (a hybrid approach).

CRITICAL THINKING: (1) If a multidomestic approach gives local managers the most flexibility for responding to local market conditions, why wouldn't every international company use this strategy? (2) How might the choice of overall organizational strategy affect a company's staffing plans in each country?

IT'S YOUR BUSINESS: (1) Have you ever purchased an imported product that seemed poorly adapted to the U.S. market? (2) If so, what would you advise that the company do in order to satisfy U.S. customers more effectively?

KEY TERMS TO KNOW: multidomestic strategy, global strategy, transnational strategy

BEHIND THE SCENES

ADAPTING AN AMERICAN CULTURAL ICON TO THE AFRICAN MARKET

MyBizLab

By the time Alex Okosi was ready to launch MTV in Africa, the company had already set up 99 other versions of the music and entertainment channel around the world. International experience was not a problem. However, no market could have presented the challenges that Africa presented. From low consumer income to limited availability of television, the hurdles to success would require a unique approach. Plus, Okosi would have to compete with the South Africa–based Channel O, which had been broadcasting music videos across Africa for several years by the time MTV was primed to enter the market.

On the positive side, Okosi had the financial backing of a major corporation, the cachet of the MTV brand, and a ready supply of top-quality videos from MTV's global presence. What he didn't have was much in the way of locally produced content. To increase the supply, Okosi nurtured local talent, even visiting some aspiring directors in their homes to help them learn how to create broadcast-quality videos.

After several years of work, Okosi and his colleagues were ready to launch, and MTV Base Africa went live with "African Queen" by the popular Nigerian artist 2Face Idibia. Will Smith and Ludicris were among the American celebrities who helped launch the new channel at dance parties and other events around Africa.

In contrast to Channel O's almost exclusive focus on African artists, MTV Base Africa combines videos and shows produced in Africa with content imported from the United States. Locally produced videos account for about half of the channel's musical fare. Okosi describes the channel's goal as showcasing "the creativity and diversity of contemporary music in Africa, giving an international platform to African genres such as Kwaito, Hip-Life, Mbalax, and Zouk and putting African artists in the spotlight alongside their international peers." MTV Base Africa is also active in health and social causes, such as offering educational programming about HIV protection.

In spite of the many challenges present in the market, MTV Base Africa looks to be a success. The channel is profitable and attracts a variety of local and international advertisers. And it has already become a content exporter: Videos produced in Africa are now shown in a special program on MTV in the United Kingdom, and rising African stars such as D'Banj have appeared on MTV in the United States.

The audience continues to grow, with roughly a hundred million viewers across 48 countries. Okosi calls this a substantial number but adds, "it only scratches the surface of what is possible here on the African continent."[47]

Critical Thinking Questions

1. Why would MTV use the MTV brand name for its launch in Africa rather than coming up with a new name more closely identified with the target market, such as African Music Television?
2. What ethical responsibilities does MTV have relative to its expansion into Africa? Why?
3. Do global media such as MTV have the potential to improve international relations? Do they have the potential to harm international relations? Explain your answers.

LEARN MORE ONLINE

Visit the MTV Base Africa website, at www.mtvbase.com. Compare the site with MTV's U.S. homepage, at www.mtv.com. What differences and similarities do you see? How much American culture do you see reflected on the MTV Base Africa website, as either content on the site itself or content on the cable channel that is described on the website?

MyBizLab

Log on to www.mybizlab.com to access study and assessment aids associated with this chapter.

KEY TERMS

balance of payments
balance of trade
culture
dumping
economic globalization
economies of scale
embargo
ethnocentrism
exchange rate
export subsidies
exporting
foreign direct investment (FDI)
free trade

global strategy
import quotas
importing
licensing
multidomestic strategy
multinational corporations (MNCs)
protectionism
stereotyping
tariffs
trade deficit
trade surplus
trading blocs
transnational strategy

TEST YOUR KNOWLEDGE

Questions for Review

1. How can a company use a licensing agreement to enter world markets?
2. What two fundamental product strategies do companies choose between when selling their products in the global marketplace?
3. What is the balance of trade, and how is it related to the balance of payments?
4. What is protectionism?
5. What is a floating exchange rate?

Questions for Analysis

6. Why would a company choose to work through intermediaries when selling products in a foreign country?
7. How do companies benefit from forming international joint ventures and strategic alliances?
8. What types of situations might cause the U.S. government to implement protectionist measures?
9. How do tariffs and quotas protect a country's own industries?
10. **Ethical Considerations.** Is it unethical for a U.S. company to choose export markets specifically for their less-stringent consumer protection standards? Why or why not?

Questions for Application

11. Suppose you own a small company that manufactures baseball equipment. You are aware that Russia is a large market, and you are considering exporting your products there. However, you know you need to learn more about Russian culture before making contact with potential business partners. What steps could you take to improve your cultural awareness?
12. How has your current employer or any previous employer been affected by globalization? For instance, does your company compete with lower-cost imports? (If you don't have any work experience, ask a friend or family member.)
13. Would a major shopping mall developer with experience all across Europe be a good strategic alliance partner for your fast-food chain's first overseas expansion effort? Why or why not?
14. **Concept Integration.** You just received notice that a large shipment of manufacturing supplies you have been waiting for has been held up in customs for two weeks. A local business associate tells you that you are expected to give customs agents some "incentive money" to see that everything clears easily. How will you handle this situation? Evaluate the ethical merits of your decision by considering the approaches listed in Exhibit 4.

EXPAND YOUR KNOWLEDGE

Discovering Career Opportunities

If global business interests you, consider working for a U.S. government agency that supports or regulates international trade. For example, here are the duties of an international trade specialist working for the International Trade Administration of the U.S. Department of Commerce:[48]

> The International Trade Specialist, at the full performance level, will carry out a wide range of economic and trade analysis as a regional desk officer (Office covers Central and Southeast Europe). Will advise the Director of the Office of European Country Affairs and other departmental officials on matters pertaining to bilateral and multilateral trade policy development and implementation, market access and trade agreements compliance. Performance of these duties will require familiarity with and monitoring of U.S. and assigned countries' trade policies, programs and procedures. Will be responsive to companies' requests for assistance and perform outreach to the private sector. Will maintain close liaison and coordination with other departmental offices, other U.S. Government agencies, business organizations and foreign government entities. Will attend and report on meetings both in the Department and at other U.S. agencies, including but not limited to the Office of the U.S. Trade Representative and the Department of State. These meetings will involve development and advancement of trade policies, negotiating positions, and economic/commercial initiatives in the European region. He or she will prepare reports, talking points, speech materials, statistical data and correspondence for use by senior Commerce officials, utilizing word processing and computer software programs. Will review Foreign Service and intelligence reports on economic trends and issues in the region.

1. On the basis of this description, what education and skills (personal and professional) would you need to succeed as an international trade specialist?
2. How well does this job description fit your qualifications and interests?
3. How important would interpersonal skills be in this position? Why?

Improving Your Tech Insights: Telepresence

Telepresence systems start with the basic idea of videoconferencing but go far beyond, with imagery so real that colleagues thousands of miles apart virtually appear to be in the same room together. The interaction feels so lifelike that participants can forget that the person "sitting" on the other side of the table is actually in another city or even another country. The ability to convey nonverbal subtleties such as facial expressions and hand gestures makes these systems particularly good for negotiations, collaborative problem solving, and other complex discussions.[49]

Conduct research to identify a company that has installed a telepresence system. What kinds of meetings does the firm use the telepresence system for? What advantages does the system give the company?

PRACTICE YOUR SKILLS

Sharpening Your Communication Skills

Languages never translate on a word-for-word basis. When doing business in the global marketplace, choose words that communicate a single idea clearly. Avoid using slang or idioms (words that can have meanings far different from their individual components when translated literally). For example, if a U.S. executive tells an Egyptian executive that a change in plans "really threw us a curve ball," chances are that communication will fail.

Team up with two other students and list 10 examples of slang (in your own language) that would probably be misinterpreted or misunderstood during a business conversation with someone from another culture. Next to each example, suggest other words you might use to convey the same message. Make sure the alternatives mean exactly the same as the original slang or idiom. Compare your list with those of your classmates.

Building Your Team Skills

In April 2009, eight U.S. steel companies and the United Steelworkers union accused Chinese pipe manufacturers of dumping $2.7 billion worth of a particular type of stainless steel pipe on the American market the previous year. (Specifically, the type of pipe is called "oil country tubular goods" and is used in oil and gas wells.) In a petition to the U.S. International Trade Commission (ITC) and the U.S. Department of Justice (DOJ), the group said 2,000 U.S. employees had lost their jobs as a result of the unfairly priced Chinese imports. The petition asked for tariffs of up to 99 percent on the Chinese steel.[50]
With your team, research the outcome of the steel industry's petition. Did the ITC and DOJ enact tariffs on Chinese steel?

After you have discovered the outcome of the petition, analyze the potential effect of the government's position on the following stakeholders:

- U.S. businesses that buy this type of steel
- U.S. steel manufacturers
- Employees of U.S. steel manufacturers
- The United Steelworkers union
- Chinese steel manufacturers

Present your analysis to the class and compare your conclusions with those reached by other teams.

Developing Your Research Skills

Companies involved in international trade have to watch the foreign exchange rates of the countries in which they do business. Use your research skills to locate and analyze information about the value of the Japanese yen relative to the U.S. dollar. As you complete this exercise, make a note of the sources and search strategies you used.

1. How many Japanese yen does one U.S. dollar buy right now? (You can find the foreign exchange rate for the yen at www.x-rates.com and many similar sites.)
2. Investigate the foreign exchange rate for the yen against the dollar over the past month. Is the dollar growing stronger (buying more yen) or growing weaker (buying fewer yen)?
3. If you were a U.S. exporter selling to Japan, how would a stronger dollar be likely to affect demand for your products? How would a weaker dollar be likely to affect demand?

REFERENCES

1. MTV Base Africa website, accessed 2 August 2011, www.mtvbase .com; Christopher Vourlias, "MTV Africa Project Targets Aids, Teens," *Variety*, 15 February 2010, 17; Christopher Vourlias, "African Music's Battle of the Bands," *Variety*, 19 October 2009, 14–15; Ed Waller, "African Adventures for MTV Networks," C21 Media.net, 9 April 2009, www.c21media.net; MTV website, accessed 22 May 2009, www.mtv.com; Quentin Hardy, "Hope & Profit in Africa," *Forbes*, 18 June 2007, 92–117; Diane Coetzer, "Smith, Ludacris Help Launch African MTV Channel," Billboard.com, 21 April 2005, www.billboard.com; Damien Rafferty, "MTV Base (UK): Championing African Music," Fly Global Music Culture website, 31 May 2007, www.fly.co.uk; "MTV Base Africa on MTV Base UK," Africa on Your Street, BBC website, accessed 16 June 2007, www.bbc.co.uk; "The Road from Soldier Back to Child," *Africa Recovery*, October 2001, 10+; "Africa Gets Own MTV Channel Today," Afrol News, 22 February 2005, www.afrol.com; "MTV Music Channels Top Cool Survey Again," BizCommunity.com, 30 May 2007, www .bizcommunity.com.
2. Ricky W. Griffin and Michael W. Pustay, *International Business*, 6th ed. (Upper Saddle River, N.J.: Pearson Prentice Hall, 2010), 6.
3. Griffin and Pustay, *International Business*, 12.
4. Holley H. Ulbrich and Mellie L. Warner, *Managerial Economics* (New York: Barron's Educational Series, 1990), 190.
5. Griffin and Pustay, *International Business*, 13.
6. Griffin and Pustay, *International Business*, 14.
7. Robert Whaples, "The Policy Views of American Economic Association Members: The Results of a New Survey," *Econ Journal Watch*, September 2009, 337–348.
8. Uwe E. Reinhardt, "How Convincing Is the Case for Free Trade?" blog post, 18 February 2011, *New York Times*, www.nytimes.com.
9. "President Bush's Statement on Open Economies," FDCH Regulatory Intelligence Database, 10 May 2007, www.ebsco.com; Vladimir Masch, "A Radical Plan to Manage Globalization," *BusinessWeek*, 24 February 2007, 11; Philip Levy, "Trade Truths for Turbulent Times," *BusinessWeek*, 24 February 2007, 9.
10. "Twelve Myths About Hunger," Institute for Food and Development Policy website, accessed 27 January 2005, www.foodfirst.com.
11. Peter Davis, "Investment and the Development Theory Myth," *Ethical Corporation*, October 2006, 29–30.
12. Moisés Naim, "Globalization," *Foreign Policy*, March–April 2009, 28–34.
13. "Protectionism Fades, So EU Carmakers Must Fight," *Automotive News Europe*, 11 June 2007, 10.
14. "Common Trade Concerns and Problems Experienced by U.S. Textile/Apparel/Footwear/Travel Goods Exporters," U.S. Department of Commerce, International Trade Administration, Office of Textiles and Apparel website, accessed 1 August 2011, http://web.ita.doc.gov.
15. John D. Daniels, Lee H. Radebaugh, and Daniel P. Sullivan, *International Business*, 10th ed. (Upper Saddle River, N.J.: Pearson Prentice Hall, 2004), 182.

16. "Principles of the Trading System," World Trade Organization website, accessed 22 May 2009, www.wto.org.
17. "10 Common Misunderstandings About the WTO," World Trade Organization website, accessed 22 May 2009, www.wto.org.
18. Joe Chidley, "The WTO at the Brink," *Canadian Business*, 10 April 2009, 35–39.
19. International Monetary Fund website, accessed 1 August 2011, www.imf.org.
20. Griffin and Pustay, *International Business*, 189–190; "IMF Conditionality," International Monetary Fund website, accessed 1 August 2011, www.imf.org.
21. World Bank Group website, accessed 1 August 2011, www.worldbank.org.
22. "North American Free Trade Agreement (NAFTA)," USDA Foreign Agricultural Service website, accessed 29 June 2007, www.fas.usda.gov.
23. Griffin and Pustay, *International Business*, 288.
24. "Fool Me Twice? Chamber of Commerce Distorts NAFTA Record, Hides CAFTA Costs," Public Citizen, March 2005, www.citizen.org; "North American Free Trade Agreement (NAFTA)," Public Citizen website, accessed 28 January 2005, www.citizen.org; Debra Beachy, "A Decade of NAFTA," *Hispanic Business*, July/August 2004, 24–25; Geri Smith and Cristina Lindblad, "Mexico: Was NAFTA Worth It?" *BusinessWeek*, 22 December 2003, 66–72; Charles J. Walen, "NAFTA's Scorecard: So Far, So Good," *BusinessWeek*, 9 July 2001, 54–56.
25. "NAFTA Facts," Office of the United States Trade Representative website, March 2008, www.ustr.gov.
26. European Community website, accessed 1 August 2011, http://europa.eu.
27. "The Euro/Monetary Union," European Community website, accessed 1 August 2011, http://europa.eu.
28. "About APEC," APEC website, accessed 23 May 2009, www.apec.org.
29. Linda Beamer and Iris Varner, *Intercultural Communication in the Workplace*, 2nd ed. (New York: McGraw-Hill Irwin, 2001), 3.
30. Daniels, et al., *International Business*, 335.
31. "FAQs for Journalists; Facts and Figures on Corruption," Transparency International, accessed 23 May 2009, www.transparency.org.
32. "FAQs for Journalists; Facts and Figures on Corruption."
33. Dionne Searcey, "U.S. Cracks Down on Corporate Bribes," *Wall Street Journal*, 26 May 2009, http://online.wsj.com.
34. Daniel Wagner and Matthew Perrone, "Johnson & Johnson Settles Bribery Case for $70 Million," Seattle Times, 8 April 2011, www.seattletimes.com.
35. Organisation for Economic Co-Operation and Development website, accessed 1 August 2011, www.oecd.org.
36. Export.gov, accessed 1 August 2011, http://export.gov.
37. "Partnering for Success," Boehringer Ingelheim, accessed 23 May 2009, www.boehringer-ingelheim.com.
38. Hoovers, accessed 1 August 2011, www.hoovers.com.
39. Janet Ong, "Amazon to Boost Spending on China Unit," *Seattle Times*, 5 June 2007, http://seattletimes.nwsource.com.
40. U.S. Census Bureau, "U.S. Businesses Acquired or Established by Foreign Direct Investors—Investment Outlays by Industry of U.S. Business Enterprise and Country of Ultimate Beneficial Owner," accessed 1 August 2011, www.census.gov; Griffin and Pustay, *International Business*, 170.
41. Griffin and Pustay, *International Business*, 310–311.
42. "Carrefour in China: When the Price Isn't Right," Knowledge @ Wharton, 16 March 2011, www.knowledgeatwharton.com.
43. Naaptol website, accessed 1 August 2011, www.naaptol.com; Elizabeth Esfahni, "Thinking Locally, Succeeding Globally," *Business 2.0*, December 2005, 96–98.
44. Erin White and Jeffrey A. Trachtenberg, "'One Size Doesn't Fit All': At WPP, Sir Martin Sorrell Sees Limits to Globalization," *Wall Street Journal*, 1 October 2003, B1, B2.
45. Griffin and Pustay, *International Business*, 555.
46. Griffin and Pustay, *International Business*, 559.
47. See note 1.
48. Adapted from "USAJobs: International Trade Specialist," USA Jobs website, accessed 23 May 2009, http://jobsearch.usajobs.gov.
49. Adapted from Steve Lohr, "As Travel Costs Rise, More Meetings Go Virtual," *New York Times*, 22 July 2008, www.nytimes.com.
50. Adapted from Beth Murtagh, "U.S. Steel Files Trade Complaint Against China for Steel Dumping," *Pittsburgh Business Times*, 11 May 2009, www.bizjournals.com.

GLOSSARY

balance of payments The sum of all payments one nation receives from other nations minus the sum of all payments it makes to other nations, over some specified period of time

balance of trade Total value of the products a nation exports minus the total value of the products it imports, over some period of time

culture A shared system of symbols, beliefs, attitudes, values, expectations, and norms for behavior

dumping Charging less than the actual cost or less than the home-country price for goods sold in other countries

economic globalization The increasing integration and interdependence of national economies around the world

economies of scale Savings from buying parts and materials, manufacturing, or marketing in large quantities

embargo A total ban on trade with a particular nation (a sanction) or of a particular product

ethnocentrism Judging all other groups according to the standards, behaviors, and customs of one's own group

exchange rate The rate at which the money of one country is traded for the money of another

exporting Selling and shipping goods or services to another country

export subsidies A form of financial assistance in which producers receive enough money from the government to allow them to lower their prices in order to compete more effectively in the global market

foreign direct investment (FDI) Investment of money by foreign companies in domestic business enterprises

free trade International trade unencumbered by restrictive measures

global strategy A highly centralized approach to international expansion, with headquarters in the home country making all major decisions

importing Purchasing goods or services from another country and bringing them into one's own country

import quotas Limits placed on the quantity of imports a nation will allow for a specific product

licensing Agreement to produce and market another company's product in exchange for a royalty or fee

multidomestic strategy A decentralized approach to international expansion in which a company creates highly independent operating units in each new country

multinational corporations (MNCs) Companies with operations in more than one country

protectionism Government policies aimed at shielding a country's industries from foreign competition

stereotyping Assigning a wide range of generalized attributes, which are often superficial or even false, to an individual based on his or her membership in a particular culture or social group

tariffs Taxes levied on imports

trade deficit An unfavorable trade balance created when a country imports more than it exports

trade surplus A favorable trade balance created when a country exports more than it imports

trading blocs Organizations of nations that remove barriers to trade among their members and that establish uniform barriers to trade with nonmember nations

transnational strategy A hybrid approach that attempts to reap the benefits of international scale while being responsive to local market dynamics

Business Ethics and Corporate Social Responsibility

LEARNING OBJECTIVES   After studying this chapter, you will be able to

1 Discuss what it means to practice good business ethics and highlight three factors that influence ethical decision making

2 Define *corporate social responsibility (CSR)* and explain the difference between philanthropy and strategic CSR

3 Distinguish among the four perspectives on corporate social responsibility

4 Discuss the role of business in protecting the natural environment and define *sustainable development*

5 Identify four fundamental consumer rights and the responsibility of business to respect them

6 Explain the responsibilities businesses have toward their employees

MyBizLab

Where you see MyBizLab in this chapter, go to www.mybizlab.com for additional activities on the topic being discussed.

BEHIND THE SCENES   NIKE'S GLOBAL PRESENCE PUTS IT ON THE FRONT LINES OF CORPORATE SOCIAL RESPONSIBILITY

KRISTOPHER SKINNER/KRTC/Newscom

Nike has taken a leadership role in improving workplace conditions and environmental stewardship in factories around the globe.

www.nike.com

Imagine yourself in this dilemma. Much of the appeal of your products is based on their association with famous athletes, whose fame allows them to charge considerable sums for their endorsement of your products. Add this to your costs of doing business. You're in a ferociously competitive, trend-driven business, where you can drop off the public radar practically overnight if you don't invest heavily in constant promotion. Add this to your costs of doing business. Many of your products are technically innovative, which requires ongoing research and development. Add this to your costs of doing business. Finally, consumers want to be able to buy your products from thousands of retail outlets, at a moment's notice, wherever they like to shop, so you must keep a vast distribution network supplied with inventory. Add this to your costs of doing business.

Add up all these costs, and you still haven't paid for somebody to actually *make* your products. You could make them in the United States, with its comparatively high labor costs, which would force you to raise prices in order to sustain the profit margin your investors expect in return for the money they have entrusted to you. Of course, raise them too high, and consumers will decide that, as cool as your products are, they can get a better deal from your competitors.

Or you could move production to a country with significantly lower labor costs, taking the pressure off your prices and profit margins and allowing you to maintain high levels of investments in other areas. Looks great on paper, but you know that every decision in business involves trade-offs. Moving production overseas and into the hands of other companies entails a significant loss of control over the manufacturing process, materials sourcing, and working conditions.

You can measure financial costs and product quality, providing clear feedback on some important performance parameters. But what about the way your production partners conduct business? Do they conduct themselves in a manner that is consistent with your values and your public image? Do they treat workers humanely? Do they steward shared natural resources in a responsible manner? Do they minimize negative impacts on their communities?

You don't have direct control over how these companies perform, and you don't always know what they're up to, but you know one thing for certain: People are going to hold you accountable for the performance and behavior of these subcontractors, even if they are independent companies operating in other countries. Big companies make big targets, and you've been the focus of a number of campaigns by advocacy groups and other nongovernmental organizations.

Welcome to a day in the life of Mark Parker, president and CEO of Nike, the athletic footwear and apparel giant based in Beaverton, Oregon. If you were in Parker's Nikes, how would you balance the competing demands of investors, employees, retailers, advocacy groups, and business partners? How would you keep Nike on its path of strong growth while also being a responsible corporate citizen in the 160 countries where it does business?[1]

MyBizLab

Gain hands-on experience through an interactive, real-world scenario. This chapter's simulation entitled Navigating Murky Ethical Waters? is located at **www.mybizlab.com**.

INTRODUCTION

Like Nike's Mark Parker (profiled in the chapter-opening Behind the Scenes), managers in every industry today must balance the demands of running a profitable business with the expectations of running a socially responsible company. As a future business leader, you will face some of the challenges discussed in this chapter, and your choices won't always be easy. You may struggle to find ethical clarity in some situations, to even understand what your choices are and how each option might affect your company's various stakeholders. You may need to muster the courage to stand up to colleagues, bosses, or customers if you think ethical principles are being violated. Fortunately, by having a good understanding of what constitutes ethical behavior and what society expects from business today, you'll be better prepared to make these tough choices. This chapter explores the basic ideas of business ethics and corporate social responsibility and then takes a closer look at business's responsibility toward the natural environment, consumers, and employees.

---

1 | **LEARNING OBJECTIVE**

Discuss what it means to practice good business ethics, and highlight three factors that influence ethical decision making.

Ethics in Contemporary Business

Assessing the ethics of contemporary business is no simple matter, partly because of disagreement over what constitutes ethical behavior and partly because the behavior of individual companies runs the gamut from positive to neutral to negative. However, it is safe to say that there is significant concern about the ethics of current (and future) business leaders. Harvard Business School professor Rakesh Khurana probably speaks for many when he says, "One way of looking at the problem with American business today is that it has succeeded in assuming many of the appearances and privileges of professionalism, while evading the attendant constraints and responsibilities."[2] By and large, the general public seems to agree (see Exhibit 1).

The news is not all bad, of course. The vast majority of businesses are run by ethical managers and staffed by ethical employees whose positive contributions to their communities are unfortunately overshadowed at times by headline-grabbing scandals. Companies around the world help their communities in countless ways, from sponsoring youth sports teams to raising millions of dollars to build hospitals.

Moreover, even when companies are simply engaged in the normal course of business—and do so ethically—they contribute to society by making useful products, providing employment, and paying taxes. Business catches a lot of flak these days, some of it deserved, but overall, its contributions to the health, happiness, and well-being of society are beyond measure.

EXHIBIT 1   **Public Perceptions of Business Ethics**

One can argue whether public perceptions of business ethics accurately reflect the behavior of the entire community of business professionals or simply the behavior of businesses and individuals that make headlines. However, there is no argument on this point: The general public doesn't think too highly of business. This graph shows the percentage of Americans who rate the honesty and ethics of a particular profession as either "high" or "very high." Several business professions are shown, with several nonbusiness professions for comparison.

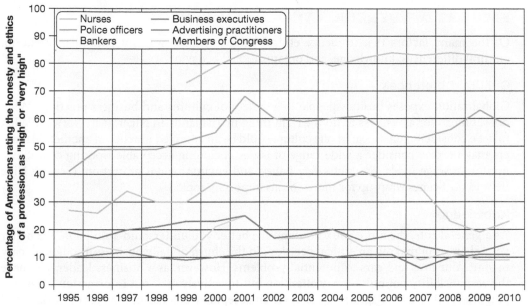

Notes: Based on data from USA Today/Gallup Poll. Nurses were not included in the survey prior to 1999. Several professions were asked about in two separate polls in 2002; for those professions, the 2002 figure shown in the graph is the average of the two scores for that year.

Source: Data from "USA Today/Gallup Poll, November Wave 1, Final Topline, 19–21 November 2010," www.gallup.com.

WHAT IS ETHICAL BEHAVIOR?

Ethics are the principles and standards of moral behavior that are accepted by society as right versus wrong. Practicing good business ethics involves, at a minimum, competing fairly and honestly, communicating truthfully, being transparent, and not causing harm to others:

ethics The rules or standards governing the conduct of a person or group

- **Competing fairly and honestly.** Businesses are expected to compete fairly and honestly and to not knowingly deceive, intimidate, or misrepresent themselves to customers, competitors, clients, employees, or the media.
- **Communicating truthfully.** Communicating truthfully is a simple enough concept: Tell the truth, the whole truth, and nothing but the truth. However, matters sometimes aren't so clear. For instance, if you plan to introduce an improved version of a product next year, do you have an obligation to tell customers who are buying the existing product this year? Suppose you do tell them, and so many decide to delay their purchases that you end up with a cash flow problem that forces you to lay off several employees. Would that be fair for customers but unfair for your employees?
- **Being transparent.** Business communication ethics often involve the question of **transparency**, which can be defined as "the degree to which information flows freely within an organization, among managers and employees, and outward to stakeholders."[3] For example, Facebook found itself the subject of criticism for a behind-the-scenes attempt to generate public outrage regarding alleged privacy violations by Google. After the company's use of a public relations agency to encourage bloggers and the news media to write critical stories about Google was exposed, Facebook admitted, "The issues are serious and we should have presented them in a serious and transparent way."[4]
- **Not causing harm to others.** All businesses have the capacity to cause harm to employees, customers, other companies, their communities, and investors. Problems can start when managers make decisions that put their personal interests above those of other stakeholders, underestimate the risks of failure, or neglect to consider potential

transparency The degree to which affected parties can observe relevant aspects of transactions or decisions

insider trading The use of unpublicized information that an individual gains from the course of his or her job to benefit from fluctuations in the stock market

effects on other people and organizations. For example, **insider trading**, in which company insiders use confidential information to gain an advantage in stock market trading, harms other investors. (Insider trading is illegal, in addition to being unethical.) Of course, harm can also result even when managers have acted ethically—but they are still responsible for these negative outcomes.

FACTORS INFLUENCING ETHICAL BEHAVIOR

Of the many factors that influence ethical behavior, three warrant particular attention: cultural differences, knowledge, and organizational behavior.

Cultural Differences

Globalization exposes businesspeople to a variety of cultures and business practices. What does it mean for a business to do the right thing in Thailand? In Nigeria? In Norway? What may be considered unethical in one culture could be an accepted practice in another. Managers may need to consider a wide range of issues, including acceptable working conditions, minimum wage levels, product safety issues, and environmental protection. (See the Nike Behind the Scenes wrap-up for more on this important topic.)

Knowledge

As a general rule, the more you know and the better you understand a situation, the better your chances of making an ethical decision. In the churn of daily business, though, it's easy to shut your eyes and ears to potential problems. However, as a business leader, you have the responsibility not only to pay attention but to actively seek out information regarding potential ethical issues. Ignorance is never an acceptable defense in the eyes of the law, and it shouldn't be in questions of ethics, either.

Organizational Behavior

Companies with strong ethical practices create cultures that reward good behavior—and don't intentionally or unintentionally reward bad behavior.[5] At United Technologies (www.utc.com), a diversified manufacturer based in Hartford, Connecticut, ethical behavior starts at the top; executives are responsible for meeting clearly defined ethical standards, and their annual compensation is tied to how well they perform.[6] To help avoid ethical breaches, many companies develop programs to improve ethical conduct, typically combine training, communication, and a **code of ethics** that defines the values and principles that should be used to guide decisions (see Exhibit 2 for an example).

code of ethics A written statement that sets forth the principles that guide an organization's decisions

Employees who observe unethical or illegal behavior within their companies and are unable to resolve the problems through normal channels may have no choice but to resort to **whistle-blowing**—expressing their concerns internally through formal reporting mechanisms or externally to the news media or government regulators. However, the decision to "blow the whistle" on one's own employer is rarely easy or without consequences. More than 80 percent of whistle-blowers in one survey said they were punished in some way for coming forward with their concerns.[7] In addition, the laws governing whistle-blowing are a complicated web of federal and state legislation that can be difficult for employees and employers to navigate through.[8]

whistle-blowing The disclosure of information by a company insider that exposes illegal or unethical behavior by others within the organization

Although whistle-blowing is sometimes characterized as "ratting on" colleagues or managers, it has an essential function. According to international business expert Alex MacBeath, "Often whistle-blowing can be the only way that information about issues such as rule breaking, criminal activity, cover-ups, and fraud can be brought to management's attention before serious damage is suffered."[9]

ETHICAL DECISION MAKING

When the question of what is right and what is wrong is clear, ethical decisions are easy to make: You simply choose to do the right thing. (At least making the decision is simple; *implementing* the decision may be another story.) If you choose the wrong course, such as cheating on your taxes or stealing from your employer, you commit what is known as an **ethical lapse**. The choices were clear, and you made the wrong one.

ethical lapse A situation in which an individual or a group makes a decision that is morally wrong, illegal, or unethical

EXHIBIT 2	AT&T's Code of Ethics (excerpts)

AT&T's Code of Ethics addresses nine areas of conduct and decision making. Selected guidelines for each of the nine principles are shown here; you can see the complete code at **www.att.com** (look in the "Investor Relations" section).

Principle	Selected Guidelines
I. Honest and Ethical Conduct	Each director, officer and employee owes a duty to the Company to act with integrity. Integrity requires, among other things, being honest and ethical.
II. Conflicts of Interest	A "conflict of interest" arises when an individual's personal interest interferes or appears to interfere with the interests of the Company. A conflict of interest can arise when a director, officer or employee takes actions or has personal interests that may make it difficult to perform his or her Company work objectively and effectively.
III. Disclosure	Each director, officer or employee . . . must not knowingly misrepresent, or cause others to misrepresent, facts about the Company to others, whether within or outside the Company, including to the Company's independent auditors, governmental regulators and self-regulatory organizations.
IV. Compliance	It is the Company's policy to comply with all applicable laws, rules and regulations. It is the personal responsibility of each employee, officer and director to adhere to the standards and restrictions imposed by those laws, rules and regulations in the performance of their duties for the Company, including those relating to accounting and auditing matters and insider trading.
V. Reporting and Accountability	Each director, officer or employee must: • Notify the appropriate Code of Ethics contact promptly of any existing or potential violation of this Code. • Not retaliate against any other director, officer or employee for reports of potential violations that are made in good faith.
VI. Corporate Opportunities	Employees, officers and directors are prohibited from taking (or directing to a third party) a business opportunity that is discovered through the use of corporate property, information or position, unless the Company has already been offered the opportunity and turned it down.
VII. Confidentiality	Employees, officers and directors must maintain the confidentiality of all information so entrusted to them, except when disclosure is authorized or legally mandated.
VIII. Fair Dealing	Each employee, officer and director should endeavor to deal fairly with the Company's customers, service providers, suppliers, competitors and employees.
IX. Protection and Proper Use of Company Assets	All employees, officers and directors should protect the Company's assets and ensure their efficient use. All Company assets should be used only for legitimate business purposes.

Source: Adapted from "AT&T Inc. Code of Ethics," AT&T website, accessed 2 August 2011, www.att.com.

However, you will encounter situations in which choices are not so clear. An **ethical dilemma** is a situation in which you must choose between conflicting but arguably valid options, or even situations in which all your options are unpleasant. As Exhibit 3 on the next page suggests, stakeholders' needs often conflict, requiring managers to make tough decisions about resource allocation.

ethical dilemma A situation in which more than one side of an issue can be supported with valid arguments

Consider the following points to help find the right answer whenever you face with an ethical dilemma:

- Make sure you frame the situation accurately, taking into account all relevant issues and questions.
- Identify all parties who might be affected by your decision, and consider the rights of everyone involved.
- Be as objective as possible. Make sure you're not making a decision just to protect your own emotions, and don't automatically assume you're viewing a situation fairly and objectively.
- Don't assume that other people think the way you do. The time-honored "Golden Rule" of treating others the way you want to be treated can cause problems when others don't *want* to be treated the same way you do.
- Watch out for **conflicts of interest**, situations in which competing loyalties can lead to ethical lapses. For instance, if you are in charge of selecting an advertising agency to handle your company's next campaign, you would have an obvious conflict of interest if your husband or wife worked for one of the agencies under consideration.

conflict of interest A situation in which competing loyalties can lead to ethical lapses, such as when a business decision may be influenced by the potential for personal gain

Exhibit 4 identifies six well-known approaches to resolving ethical dilemmas.

EXHIBIT 3	Stakeholders' Rights: A Difficult Balancing Act

Balancing the individual needs and interests of a company's stakeholders is one of management's most difficult tasks. Consider how these three examples could affect each of these five stakeholder groups in a different way. (Note that some people may fall into multiple groups. Employees, for example, are taxpayers and members of the local community, and they may also be shareholders. Also, these scenarios and outcomes offer a simplified view of what is likely to happen in each case, but they illustrate the mixed effects that can result from management decisions.)

Decision	Shareholders (entrust money to the company in anticipation of a positive return on their investment)	Employees (devote time, energy, and creativity to the company's success)	Customers (expect to receive quality products and maximum value for prices paid)	Local Community (can be affected both positively and negatively by the company's presence and actions)	Taxpayers (affected indirectly by the amount of tax revenue that local, state, and federal governments get from the company)
Company decides to *offshore* some of its production to another country with lower labor costs; lays off significant number of employees	⬆ Stand to benefit from lower production costs, which could increase sales, profits, or both, probably leading to increases in share price	⬇ Some employees lose their jobs; morale likely to suffer among those who keep theirs	⬆ Benefit from lower prices	⬇ Suffers from loss of spendable income in the local economy and taxes paid to local government; exodus of employees can drive down home values	⬇⬆ Might be hurt or helped by the move, depending on whether loss of income tax paid by U.S. employees is offset by increased income tax paid by the company, for example
Company institutes a generous pay and benefits increase to improve employee morale	⬇⬆ Might be hurt in the short term as the stock market punishes the company for increasing its cost structure and diverting funds away from development; could help over the long term if the moves boost employee productivity	⬆ Benefit from higher pay and more valuable benefits	⬇⬆ Could be hurt by higher prices if prices are raised to cover the added costs; could benefit from higher levels of employee satisfaction, leading to improved customer service	⬆ Benefits from more spendable income in the local economy and taxes paid to local government; better employee benefits could also mean less drain on community resources such as health clinics	⬆ Benefit from more money paid into government treasuries through higher income taxes
Company installs a multimillion-dollar waste water recirculation system that surpasses regulatory requirements; system will pay for itself in lower water bills, but not for 10 years	⬇⬆ Probably hurt as stock market punishes an investment with no immediate payback; increased goodwill and long-term cost savings help in years ahead	⬇⬆ Probably hurt in the short term as less money is available for raises and benefits; likely to benefit in the long term as the costs are recovered	⬇ Hurt as higher costs are passed along as higher prices	⬆ Helped by the company's efforts to conserve a shared natural resource	⬇ Hurt as the company writes off the cost of the system, thereby lowering the taxes it pays to the government

EXHIBIT 4	Approaches to Resolving Ethical Dilemmas

These approaches can help you resolve ethical dilemmas you may face on the job. Be aware that in some situations, different approaches can lead to different ethical conclusions.

Approach	Summary
Justice	Treat people equally or at least fairly in a way that makes rational and moral sense
Utilitarianism	Choose the option that delivers the most good for the most people (or protects the most people from a negative outcome)
Individual rights	To the greatest possible extent, respect the rights of all individuals, particularly their right to control their own destinies
Individual responsibilities	Focus on the ethical duties of the individuals involved in the situation
The common good	Emphasize qualities and conditions that benefit the community as a whole, such as peace and public safety
Virtue	Emphasize desirable character traits such as integrity and compassion

Sources: Adapted from Manuel Velasquez, Claire Andre, Thomas Shanks, and Michael J. Meyer, "Thinking Ethically: A Framework for Moral Decision Making," Markkula Center for Applied Ethics, Santa Clara University, accessed 3 June 2009, www.scu.edu; Ben Rogers, "John Rawls," *The Guardian*, 27 November 2002, www.guardian.co.uk; Irene Van Staveren, "Beyond Utilitarianism and Deontology: Ethics in Economics," *Review of Political Economy*, January 2007, 21–35.

 Checkpoint

LEARNING OBJECTIVE 1: Discuss what it means to practice good business ethics, and highlight three factors that influence ethical decision making.

SUMMARY: Three essential components of good business ethics are competing fairly and honestly, communicating truthfully, and not causing harm to others. Three major influences on ethical decision making are culture, knowledge, and organizational culture. When facing an ethical dilemma, you can often find clarity by starting with universal standards of justice, considering the rights of everyone involved, being as objective as possible, not assuming that other people think the way you do, and avoiding conflicts of interest.

CRITICAL THINKING: (1) If you go to work tomorrow morning and your boss asks you to do something you consider unethical, what factors will you take into consideration before responding? (2) How can you balance the business need to inspire employees to compete aggressively with the moral need to avoid competing unethically?

IT'S YOUR BUSINESS: (1) In your current job (or any previous job you've held), in what ways does your employer contribute to society? (2) Have you ever encountered an ethical dilemma in your work? If so, how did you resolve it?

KEY TERMS TO KNOW: ethics, transparency, insider trading, code of ethics, whistle-blowing, ethical lapse, ethical dilemma, conflicts of interest

Corporate Social Responsibility

Corporate social responsibility (CSR) is the notion that business has obligations to society beyond the pursuit of profits. There is a widespread assumption these days that CSR is both a moral imperative for business and a good thing for society, but the issues aren't quite as clear as they might seem at first glance.

THE RELATIONSHIP BETWEEN BUSINESS AND SOCIETY

What does business owe society, and what does society owe business? Any attempt to understand and shape this relationship needs to consider four essential truths:

- Consumers in contemporary societies enjoy and expect a wide range of benefits, from education and health care to credit and products that are safe to use. Most of these benefits share an important characteristic: They require money.

2 LEARNING OBJECTIVE

Define *corporate social responsibility (CSR),* and explain the difference between philanthropy and strategic CSR.

corporate social responsibility (CSR) The idea that business has obligations to society beyond the pursuit of profits

- Profit-seeking companies are the economic engine that powers modern society; they generate the vast majority of the money in a nation's economy, either directly (through their own taxes and purchases) or indirectly (through the taxes and purchases made by the employees they support).
- Much of what we consider when assessing a society's standard of living involves goods and services created by profit-seeking companies.
- Conversely, companies cannot hope to operate profitably without the many benefits provided by a stable, functioning society: talented and healthy employees, a legal framework in which to pursue commerce, a dependable transportation infrastructure, opportunities to raise money, and customers with the ability to pay for goods and services, to name just some of them.

Business and society clearly need each other—and each needs the other to be healthy and successful.

PHILANTHROPY VERSUS STRATEGIC CSR

philanthropy The donation of money, time, goods, or services to charitable, humanitarian, or educational institutions

Companies that engage in CSR activities can choose between two courses of action: general philanthropy or strategic CSR. **Philanthropy** involves donating money, employee time, or other resources to various causes without regard for any direct business benefits for the company. For instance, a company might support the arts in its hometown in the interest of enhancing the city's cultural richness. In addition to free products, employee time, use of company facilities, and other non-cash contributions, U.S. companies donate billions of dollars to charity every year.[10]

strategic CSR Social contributions that are directly aligned with a company's overall business strategy

In contrast to generic philanthropy, **strategic CSR** involves social contributions that are directly aligned with a company's overall business strategy. In other words, the company helps itself and society at the same time. This approach can be followed in a variety of ways. A company can help develop the workforce by supporting job training efforts, for example. A company can also help develop markets for its goods and services, as the British firm Thames Water did by assisting groups trying to improve water supplies in Africa.[11] And a company can make choices that address social concerns while giving it a competitive advantage. As you can read in the "Improving Your Tech Insights" activity at the end of the chapter, IBM and Microsoft are among the many companies that invest in *assistive technologies* that help people with disabilities while expanding market opportunities and access to employee talent.

Strategic CSR makes more sense than general philanthropy or an antagonistic business-versus-society mindset, for several reasons. First, because business and society are mutually dependent, choices that weaken one or the other will ultimately weaken both. Second, investments that benefit the company are more likely to be sustained over time. Third, making sizable investments in a few strategically focused areas will yield greater benefits to society than will spreading smaller amounts of money around through generic philanthropy.[12] Thames Water CEO Bill Alexander emphasizes, "Philanthropy won't be enough. To achieve real scale we need a new business model."[13]

Exactly how much can or should businesses contribute to social concerns? This is a difficult decision because all companies have limited resources that must be allocated to a number of goals, such as upgrading facilities and equipment, developing new products, marketing existing products, and rewarding employee efforts, in addition to contributing to social causes.

 Checkpoint

LEARNING OBJECTIVE 2: Define *corporate social responsibility (CSR)*, and explain the difference between philanthropy and strategic CSR.

SUMMARY: Corporate social responsibility (CSR) is the notion that business has obligations to society beyond the pursuit of profits. However, there is no general agreement over what those responsibilities are or which elements of society should determine those obligations or benefit from them. Philanthropy involves donating time, money, or other resources, without regard for any direct business benefits. In contrast, strategic CSR involves contributions that are aligned with the company's business needs and strategies.

CRITICAL THINKING: (1) Given that "society" is not an organized entity, how can society decide what the responsibilities of business are in a CSR context? (2) Is philanthropy morally superior to strategic CSR? Why or why not?

IT'S YOUR BUSINESS: (1) Have a company's philanthropic or CSR efforts ever influenced your purchasing behavior? (2) Have you ever benefited personally from a company's philanthropic or CSR efforts?

KEY TERMS TO KNOW: corporate social responsibility (CSR), philanthropy, strategic CSR

Perspectives on Corporate Social Responsibility

3 **LEARNING OBJECTIVE**

Distinguish among the four perspectives on corporate social responsibility.

To encourage ethical behavior and promote a mutually beneficial relationship between business and society, it is clearly necessary to establish expectations about how businesses should conduct themselves. However, both business and society are still grappling with exactly what those expectations should be. "Social responsibility" certainly sounds admirable, but it's not always clear which segments of society this involves or what those responsibilities are.[14] Approaches to CSR can be roughly categorized into four perspectives (see Exhibit 5), from minimalist through proactive.

EXHIBIT 5	Perspectives on Corporate Social Responsibility

The perspectives on CSR can be roughly divided into four categories, from minimalist to proactive. Companies that engage in CSR can pursue either *generic philanthropy* or *strategic CSR*.

Response: Philanthropy	Perspective (Motivation to Act)	Response: Strategic CSR
	Minimalist Companies do not have social responsibilities beyond earning money and obeying the law.	
Giving money to causes unrelated to the company's lines of business	**Cynical** Companies use CSR as a marketing ploy to distract attention from their self-centered behavior.	
Giving money to causes unrelated to the company's lines of business	**Defensive** Companies engage in CSR only after being shamed or forced into it.	
Giving money to causes unrelated to the company's lines of business	**Proactive** Companies have a responsibility to help society beyond simply paying taxes and obeying the law.	Investing in areas that are aligned with the company's business mission

MINIMALIST CSR

According to what might be termed the *minimalist* view, the only social responsibility of business is to pay taxes and obey the law. In a 1970 article that is still widely discussed today, Nobel Prize–winning economist Milton Friedman articulated this view by saying, "There is only one social responsibility of business: to use its resources and engage in activities designed to increase its profits so long as it stays within the rules of the game, which is to say, engages in open and free competition without deception or fraud."[15]

This view might seem selfish and even antisocial, but it raises a couple of important questions. First, any business that operates ethically and legally provides society with beneficial goods and services at fair prices. One can argue that doing so fulfills a company's primary obligation to society.

Second—and this is a vital point to consider even if you reject the minimalist view—should businesses be in the business of making social policy and spending the public's money? Proponents of the minimalist view claim that this is actually what happens when companies make tax-deductible contributions to social causes. For example, assume that in response to pressure from activists, a company makes a sizable contribution that nets it a $1 million tax break. That's $1 million taken out of the public treasury, where voters and their elected representatives can control how money is spent, and put it into whatever social cause the company chooses to support. In effect, the corporation and the activists are spending the public's money, and the public has no say in how it is spent. Would it be better for society if companies paid full taxes and let the people (through their elected representatives) decide how their tax dollars are put to work?

DEFENSIVE CSR

nongovernmental organizations (NGOs) Nonprofit groups that provide charitable services or promote social and environmental causes

Many companies today face pressure from a variety of activists and **nongovernmental organizations (NGOs)**, nonprofit groups that provide charitable services or promote causes, from workers' rights to environmental protection. One possible response to this pressure is to engage in CSR activities as a way to avoid further criticism. In other words, the company may take positive steps to address a particular issue only because it has been embarrassed into action by negative publicity.

Note that companies can engage in proactive CSR (see below) and still receive criticism from advocacy groups. A company and an NGO might disagree about responsibilities or outcomes, or in some cases an NGO might target a company for a problem that the company has already been working on. In other words, don't immediately conclude that a company is simply being defensive when it engages in CSR while in the glare of public criticism. (For an example, see the Nike Behind the Scenes wrap-up at the end of the chapter.)

CYNICAL CSR

One possible approach to CSR is purely cynical, in which a company accused of irresponsible behavior promotes itself as being socially responsible without making substantial improvements in its business practices. For example, environmental activists use the term *greenwash* (a combination of *green* and *whitewash*, a term that suggests covering something up) as a label for publicity efforts that present companies as being environmentally friendly when their actions speak otherwise. Ironically, some of the most ardent antibusiness activists and the staunchly probusiness advocates of the minimalist view tend to agree on one point: Many CSR efforts are disingenuous. Thirty-five years after his provocative article, Friedman said he believed that "most of the claims of social responsibility are pure public relations."[16]

REAL-TIME UPDATES
Learn More by Reading This Article

Taking the junk out of junk food

Learn how PepsiCo's nutritional scientists are working to create healthy—but still tasty—versions of soft drinks, potato chips, and other products that consumers can't seem to stop eating. Go to http://real-timeupdates.com/bia6 and click on Learn More. If you are using MyBizLab, you can access Real-Time Updates within the chapter or under Student Study Tools.

PROACTIVE CSR

In the fourth approach, proactive CSR, company leaders believe they have responsibilities beyond making a profit, and they back up their beliefs and proclamations with actions taken on their own initiative. Laurie Erickson is the founder and CEO of The Finest Accessories, a North Bend, Washington, company that markets handmade barrettes and other hair accessories to high-end department stores. After a customer asked Erickson if she sold any products for women who had lost their hair to chemotherapy, Erickson not only created a fashionable scarf that fit the bill but also launched a program of offering a free scarf to any cancer patient who asks for one. The company has now given away thousands of scarves, each accompanied with a get-well card signed by every employee in the company.[17]

RESOLVING THE CSR DILEMMA

So what's the right answer? Of the four perspectives on CSR, we can instantly eliminate the cynical approach simply because it is dishonest and therefore unethical. Beyond that, the debate is less clear, but the opinions are certainly strong. Some proponents of the minimalist view equate CSR with *collectivism*, a term that suggests socialism and even communism. Some consider CSR demands from activist groups and other outsiders to be little more than extortion.[18] Professor Alexei Marcoux of Loyola University in Chicago says that CSR is "fundamentally antagonistic to capitalist enterprise."[19] At the other extreme, some critics of contemporary business seem convinced that corporations can never be trusted and that every CSR initiative is a cynical publicity stunt.

A two-tiered approach to CSR can yield a practical, ethical answer to this complex dilemma. At the first tier, companies must take responsibility for the consequences of their actions and limit the negative impact of their operations. This approach can be summarized as "do no harm," and it is not a matter of choice. Just as a society has a right to expect certain behavior from all citizens, it has a right to expect a basic level of responsible behavior from all businesses, including minimizing pollution and waste, minimizing the depletion of shared natural resources, being honest with all stakeholders, offering real value in exchange for prices asked, and avoiding exploitation of employees, customers, suppliers, communities, and investors. Some of these issues are covered by laws, but others aren't, thereby creating the responsibility of ethical decision making by all employees and managers in a firm.

At the second tier, moving beyond "do no harm" becomes a matter of choice. Companies can choose to help in whatever way that investors, managers, and employees see fit, but the choices are up to the company and should not be the result of pressure from outside forces.

For the latest information on CSR, visit http://real-timeupdates.com/bia6.

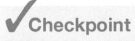

Checkpoint

LEARNING OBJECTIVE 3: Distinguish among the four perspectives on corporate social responsibility.

SUMMARY: The spectrum of viewpoints on CSR can be roughly divided into minimalist (business's only obligation is to compete to the best of its abilities without deception or fraud), defensive (in which businesses engage in CSR efforts only in response to social pressure), cynical (in which businesses engage in CSR as a public relations ploy), and proactive (in which businesses contribute to society out of a belief that they have an obligation to do so).

CRITICAL THINKING: (1) Do you agree that giving companies tax breaks for charitable contributions distorts public spending by indirectly giving companies and activists control over how tax revenues are spent? Why or why not? (2) If Company A takes a cynical approach to CSR while Company B takes a proactive approach but they make identical contributions to society, is one company "better" than the other? Why or why not?

IT'S YOUR BUSINESS: (1) Have you ever suspected a company of engaging in greenwashing or other disingenuous CSR activities? How would you prove or disprove such a suspicion? (2) If you were the head of a small company and wanted to give back to society in some way, how would you select which organizations or causes to support?

KEY TERM TO KNOW: nongovernmental organizations (NGOs)

---

4   **LEARNING OBJECTIVE**

Discuss the role of business in protecting the natural environment, and define *sustainable development*.

CSR: The Natural Environment

In the past few decades, few issues in the public dialog have become as politicized and polarized as pollution and resource depletion. Environmentalists and their political allies sometimes portray business leaders as heartless profiteers who would strip the Earth bare for a few bucks. Corporate leaders and their political allies, on the other hand, sometimes cast environmentalists as "tree huggers" who care more about bunnies and butterflies than about people. As is often the case, the shouting match between these extreme positions obscures real problems—and opportunities for real solutions.

To reach a clearer understanding of this situation, keep three important points in mind. First, the creation, delivery, use, and disposal of products that society values virtually always generate pollution and consume natural resources. For example, it's tempting to assume that web-based businesses are "clean" because there is no visible pollution. However, the Internet and all the computers attached to it have a voracious appetite for electricity; Google is one of the largest users of electricity in the world, for example.[20] (See more about Google's energy conservation efforts under "Efforts to Conserve Resources and Reduce Pollution.") Moreover, generation of electricity seriously affects the environment, as over 70 percent of the electricity used in the United States is generated by burning coal, oil, or natural gas (see Exhibit 6).[21]

Second, "environmental" causes are often as much about human health and safety as they are about forests, rivers, and wildlife. The availability of clean air, water, and soil affects everyone, not just people concerned with wild spaces.

Third, many of these issues are neither easy nor simple. They often require tough trade-offs, occasional sacrifice, disruptive change, and decision making in the face of uncertainty. Meeting these challenges will require people to be clear-headed, open-minded, adaptable, and courageous.

EFFORTS TO CONSERVE RESOURCES AND REDUCE POLLUTION

Concerns over pollution and resource depletion have been growing since the dawn of the Industrial Age in the 19th century. However, widespread concern for the environment really dates to the 1960s, when *ecology*, the study of the relationship between organisms and the natural environment, entered mainstream discussion. In 1963, federal, state, and

REAL-TIME UPDATES
Learn More by Exploring This Interactive Website

Create a more sustainable product with Nike's interactive tool

Nike's Environmental Design Tool measures the environmental impact of a manufactured product and helps design teams improve the sustainability of their products. You can plug in data from your own apparel to see how your clothing scores. Go to http://real-timeupdates.com/bia6 and click on Learn More. If you are using MyBizLab, you can access Real-Time Updates within chapter or under Student Study Tools.

EXHIBIT 6	Green and Clean? Where Our Electricity Comes From

Most of the electricity generated in the United States is produced by burning fossil fuels. Nuclear and hydroelectric power provide most of the rest. Renewable sources such as solar and wind have grown over the past decade, but they remain minor sources of electricity at this point.

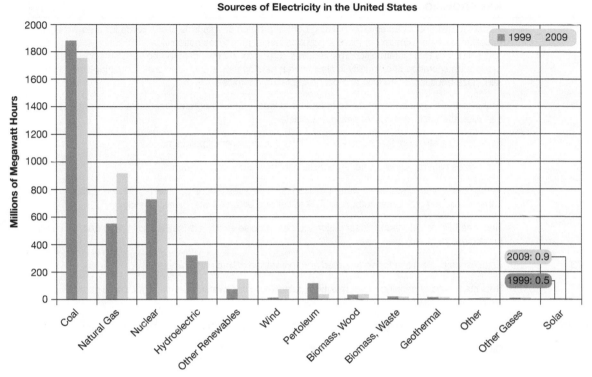

Sources of Electricity in the United States

Source: "Electric Power Annual, Summary Statistics for the United States," U.S. Energy Information Administration website, accessed 3 August 2011, www.eia.gov.

local governments began enacting laws and regulations to reduce pollution (see Exhibit 7 on the next page). Many states and cities have also passed their own tough clean-air laws.

You've no doubt heard the phrase "reduce, reuse, recycle" as advice for conserving resources and minimizing pollution. Google offers a great example of what businesses can do in this regard. As a major consumer of energy, the company is taking responsibility for that consumption in a number of significant ways, including reducing energy usage in its data centers (massive complexes that house the thousands of computers that make Google searches possible) by more than half, investing in renewable energy in ways that help this fledgling industry grow, using its position as a major corporation to help shape energy policy and public awareness, and sharing the results of its considerable research efforts with other companies to help them reduce resource usages as well.[22]

In addition to technological solutions to reduce pollution and resource consumption, businesses, governments, and NGOs are pursuing a variety of political and economic solutions. For example, **cap and trade** programs try to balance free-market economics with government intervention. Lawmakers first establish a maximum allowable amount of a particular pollutant that a designated group of companies or industries is allowed to emit (the "cap") and then distribute individual emission allowances to all the companies in that group. If a company lowers its emissions enough to stay under its prescribed limit, it can

REAL-TIME UPDATES
Learn More by Reading This Article

See how one of the world's biggest energy consumers is reducing, reusing, and recycling

Explore Google's efforts to reduce its energy usage and minimize its impact on the environment. Go to http://real-timeupdates.com/bia6 and click on Learn More. If you are using MyBizLab, you can access Real-Time Updates within the chapter or under Student Study Tools.

cap and trade A type of environmental policy that gives companies some freedom in addressing the environmental impact of specified pollutants, by either reducing emissions to meet a designated cap or buying allowances to offset excess emissions

EXHIBIT 7	Major Federal Environmental Legislation

Since the early 1960s, major federal legislation aimed at the environment has focused on providing cleaner air and water and reducing toxic waste. (Many of these laws have been amended since their original passage dates.)

LEGISLATION	KEY PROVISIONS
Clean Air Act (1963)	Assists states and localities in formulating control programs; sets federal standards for auto-exhaust emissions; sets maximum permissible pollution levels; authorizes nationwide air-pollution standards and limitations to pollutant discharge; requires scrubbers in new coal-fired power plants; directs EPA to prevent deterioration of air quality in clean areas; sets schedule and standards for cutting smog, acid rain, hazardous factory fumes, and ozone-depleting chemicals
Solid Waste Disposal Act (1965)	Authorizes research and assistance to state and local control programs; regulates treatment, storage, transportation, and disposal of hazardous waste
National Environmental Policy Act (1969)	Establishes a structure for coordinating all federal environmental programs
Resource Recovery Act (1970)	Subsidizes pilot recycling plants; authorizes nationwide control programs
Clean Water Act (1972)	Authorizes grants to states for water-pollution control; gives federal government limited authority to correct pollution problems; authorizes EPA to set and enforce water-quality standards
Noise Control Act (1972)	Requires EPA to set standards for major sources of noise and to advise Federal Aviation Administration on standards for airplane noise
Endangered Species Act (1973)	Establishes protections for endangered and threatened plants and animals
Safe Drinking Water Act (1974)	Sets standards of drinking-water quality; requires municipal water systems to report on contaminant levels; establishes funding to upgrade water systems
Toxic Substances Control Act (1976)	Requires chemicals testing; authorizes EPA to restrict the use of harmful substances
Resource Conservation and Recovery Act (1976)	Gives the EPA authority to control hazardous waste
Comprehensive Environmental Response, Compensation, and Liability Act (1980)	Establishes the "Superfund" program to oversee the identification and cleanup of uncontrolled or abandoned hazardous waste sites
Nuclear Waste Policy Act (1982)	Establishes procedures for creating geologic repositories of radioactive waste
Marine Protection, Research, and Sanctuaries Act (1988)	Prohibits ocean dumping that could threaten human health or the marine environment
Oil Pollution Act (1990)	Sets up liability trust fund; extends operations for preventing and containing oil pollution

Source: U.S. Environmental Protection Agency website, accessed 3 August 2011, www.epa.gov.

sell, trade, or save leftover allowances (the "trade"). If a company exceeds its emission allowances, it must buy or trade for enough allowances to cover the excess emissions. In this way, companies can choose the lowest-cost means of taking responsibility for their emissions.[23] During the 1990s, a cap and trade program to reduce sulfur dioxide emissions from coal-burning power plants, a leading cause of acid raid, reduced emissions by 50 percent.[24]

THE TREND TOWARD SUSTAINABILITY

sustainable development
Operating business in a manner that minimizes pollution and resource depletion, ensuring that future generations will have vital resources

Efforts to minimize resource depletion and pollution are part of a broader effort known as *sustainability,* or **sustainable development,** which the United Nations has defined as development that "meets the needs of the present without compromising the ability of future generations to meet their own needs."[25]

Sustainable development can certainly require changes to the way companies conduct business, but paying attention to a broader scope of stakeholders and managing for the longer term doesn't automatically mean that companies have to take a financial hit to go "green." Many businesses are discovering that taking steps now to reduce consumption and pollution can end up saving money down the road by reducing everything from cleanup and litigation expenses to ongoing production costs. As Xerox CEO Ursula Burns puts it, "The greener we get, the more we can reduce costs and boost efficiency."[26]

In other words, in addition to better stewardship of shared natural resources, sustainable development is also a smart business strategy. By taking a broad and long-term view of their companies' impact on the environment and stakeholders throughout the world, managers can ensure the continued availability of the resources their organizations need and be better prepared for changes in government regulations and shifting social expectations. In fact, some experts believe sustainability is a good measure of the quality of management in a corporation. According to investment researcher Matthew J. Kiernan, companies that take a sustainable approach "tend to be more strategic, nimble, and better equipped to compete in the complex, high-velocity global environment."[27]

© STOCKFOLIO/E / Alamy

When you upgraded your smartphone or laptop, where did the old one go?

✓ Checkpoint

LEARNING OBJECTIVE 4: Discuss the role of business in protecting the natural environment, and define *sustainable development*.

SUMMARY: As major users of natural resources and generators of waste products, businesses play a huge role in conservation and pollution-reduction efforts. Many businesses are making an effort to reduce, reuse, and recycle, and governments are trying market-based approaches such as *cap and trade* to encourage businesses to reduce emissions. All these efforts are part of a trend toward *sustainable development*, which can be defined as meeting the needs of the present without compromising the ability of future generations to meet their own needs.

CRITICAL THINKING: (1) Should all industries be required to meet the same levels of pollution control? Why or why not? (2) How would you respond to critics who say that cap and trade programs allow polluters to buy their way out of the responsibility of cleaning up their operations?

IT'S YOUR BUSINESS: (1) In what ways could your employer (or your college, if you're not currently working) take steps to reduce resource depletion? (2) How did you dispose of the last electronic product you stopped using?

KEY TERMS TO KNOW: cap and trade, sustainable development

CSR: Consumers

The 1960s activism that awakened business to its environmental responsibilities also gave rise to **consumerism**, a movement that put pressure on businesses to consider consumer needs and interests. (Note that some people use *consumerism* in a negative sense, as a synonym for *materialism*.) Consumerism prompted many businesses to create consumer affairs departments to handle customer complaints. It also prompted state and local agencies to set up bureaus to offer consumer information and assistance. At the federal level, President John F. Kennedy announced a "bill of rights" for consumers, laying the foundation for a wave of consumer-oriented legislation (see Exhibit 8 on the next page).

5 LEARNING OBJECTIVE

Identify four fundamental consumer rights and the responsibility of business to respect them.

consumerism A movement that pressures businesses to consider consumer needs and interests

EXHIBIT 8	Major Federal Consumer Legislation

Major federal legislation aimed at consumer protection has focused on food and drugs, false advertising, product safety, and credit protection.

LEGISLATION	MAJOR PROVISIONS
Food, Drug, and Cosmetic Act (1938)	Puts cosmetics, foods, drugs, and therapeutic products under Food and Drug Administration's jurisdiction; outlaws misleading labeling
Cigarette Labeling and Advertising Act (1965)	Mandates warnings on cigarette packages and in ads
Fair Packaging and Labeling Act (1966, 1972)	Requires honest, informative package labeling; labels must show origin of product, quantity of contents, uses or applications
Truth in Lending Act (Consumer Protection Credit Act) (1968)	Requires creditors to disclose finance charge and annual percentage rate; limits cardholder liability for unauthorized use
Fair Credit Reporting Act (1970)	Requires credit-reporting agencies to set process for assuring accuracy; requires creditors to explain credit denials
Consumer Product Safety Act (1972)	Creates Consumer Product Safety Commission
Magnuson-Moss Warranty Act (1975)	Requires complete written warranties in ordinary language; requires warranties to be available before purchase
Alcohol Beverage Labeling Act (1988)	Requires warning labels on alcohol products, saying that alcohol impairs abilities and that women shouldn't drink when pregnant
Children's Online Privacy Protection Act (1988)	Gives parents control over the collection or use of information that websites can collect about children
Nutrition Education and Labeling Act (1990)	Requires specific, uniform product labels detailing nutritional information on every food regulated by the FDA
American Automobile Labeling Act (1992)	Requires carmakers to identify where cars are assembled and where their individual components are manufactured
Deceptive Mail Prevention and Enforcement Act (1999)	Establishes standards for sweepstakes mailings, skill contests, and facsimile checks to prevent fraud and exploitation
Controlling the Assault of Non-Solicited Pornography and Marketing Act (2003)	Known as CAN-SPAM, attempts to protect online consumers from unwanted and fraudulent email
Consumer Product Safety Improvement Act (2008)	Strengthens standards for lead in children's products; mandates safety testing for imported children's products; creates a searchable database for reporting accidents, injuries, and illnesses related to consumer products
Dodd-Frank Wall Street Reform and Consumer Protection Act (2010)	Amends a number earlier acts and regulations in an attempt to improve stability of the banking and investment industries; establishes the Consumer Financial Projection Bureau

Sources: U.S. Food and Drug Administration website, accessed 3 August 2011, www.fda.gov; U.S. House of Representatives, Office of the Law Revision Counsel website, accessed 3 August 2011, http://uscode.house.gov; U.S. Federal Trade Commission website, accessed 3 August 2011, www.ftc.gov; U.S. Consumer Product Safety Commission website, accessed 3 August 2011, www.cpsc.com; Alcohol and Tobacco Tax and Trade Bureau website, accessed 3 August 2011, www.ttb.gov; U.S. Consumer Financial Projection Bureau website, accessed 3 August 2011, www.consumerfinance.gov.

THE RIGHT TO BUY SAFE PRODUCTS—AND TO BUY THEM SAFELY

As mentioned previously, doing no harm is one of the foundations of corporate social responsibility. The United States and many other countries go to considerable lengths to ensure the safety of the products sold within their borders. The U.S. government imposes many safety standards that are enforced by the Consumer Product Safety Commission (CPSC), as well as by other federal and state agencies. Companies that don't comply with these rules are forced to take corrective action, and the threat of product-liability suits and declining sales motivates companies to meet safety standards.

Product safety concerns range from safe toys, food, and automobiles to less-tangible worries such as online privacy and **identity theft**, in which criminals steal personal information and use it to take out loans, request government documents, get expensive medical procedures, and commit other types of fraud. According to Federal Trade Commission estimates, some 9 million Americans are victims of identity theft every year.[28] Companies—e-commerce websites in particular—play a vital role in fighting this crime because they frequently collect the information that identity thieves use to commit their fraud, including credit card and Social Security numbers. Any company that collects such information has a clear ethical obligation to keep it safe and secure.

REAL-TIME UPDATES

Learn More by Exploring This Interactive Website

Can you outsmart online crooks?

Play these games to find out how much you know about protecting your identity and your privacy online. Go to http://real-timeupdates.com/bia6 and click on Learn More. If you are using MyBizLab, you can access Real-Time Updates within the chapter or under Student Study Tools.

identity theft A crime in which thieves steal personal information and use it to take out loans and commit other types of fraud

THE RIGHT TO BE INFORMED

Consumers have a right to know what they're buying, how to use it, and whether it presents any risks to them. They also have a right to know the true price of goods or services and the details of purchase contracts. Accordingly, numerous government regulations have been put in place to make sure buyers get the information they need to make informed choices. Of course, buyers share the responsibility here, at least morally if not always legally. Not bothering to read labels or contracts or not asking for help if you don't understand them is no excuse for not being informed.

Fortunately, both consumers and businesses can turn to a wide range of information sources to learn more about the goods and services they purchase. The spread of social media and their use in *social commerce*, in which buyers help educate one another, has helped shift power from sellers to buyers. For just about every purchase you can envision these days, you can find more information about it before you choose.

THE RIGHT TO CHOOSE WHICH PRODUCTS TO BUY

Especially in the United States, the number of products available to consumers is staggering, even sometimes overwhelming. But how far should the right to choose extend? Are we entitled to choose products that are potentially harmful, such as cigarettes, alcoholic beverages, guns, sugary soft drinks, or fatty fried foods? Should the government take measures to make such products illegal, or should consumers always be allowed to decide for themselves what to buy?

Consider cigarettes. Scientists determined long ago that the tar and nicotine in tobacco are harmful and addictive. In 1965, the Federal Cigarette Labeling and Advertising Act was passed, requiring all cigarette packs to carry the Surgeon General's warnings. Over the years, tobacco companies have spent billions of dollars to defend themselves in lawsuits brought by smokers suffering from cancer and respiratory diseases. Lawsuits and legislative activity surrounding tobacco products continue to this day—and are likely to continue for years. Meanwhile, consumers can still purchase cigarettes in the marketplace. As one tobacco company executive put it, "Behind all the allegations . . . is the simple truth that we sell a legal product."[29]

THE RIGHT TO BE HEARD

The final component of consumer rights is the right to be heard. As with the challenge of gathering information, social media give consumers numerous ways to ask questions, voice concerns, provide feedback, and—if necessary—demand attention. Savvy companies monitor Twitter, blogs, and other online venues to catch messages from dissatisfied customers. Companies that fail to respond or that respond in defensive, inward-looking ways are likely to lose business to competitors that embrace this new media environment and the power it gives today's consumers.

Checkpoint

LEARNING OBJECTIVE 5: Identify four fundamental consumer rights and the responsibility of business to respect them.

SUMMARY: Four fundamental consumer rights that form the basis of much of the consumer-related legislation in the United States are the right to safe products, the right to be informed, the right to choose, and the right to be heard. Many specific aspects of these rights are now embodied in government regulations, but others rely on business professionals to practice ethical and responsive decision making.

CRITICAL THINKING: (1) Is there a point at which responsibility for product safety shifts from the seller to the buyer? Explain your answer. (2) If providing full information about products raises prices, should businesses still be required to do so? Why or why not?

IT'S YOUR BUSINESS: (1) Do you rely on social media when making purchases? (2) Have you ever lodged a complaint with a business? What was the outcome?

KEY TERMS TO KNOW: consumerism, identity theft

<table>
<tr><td>6</td><td>LEARNING OBJECTIVE</td></tr>
</table>

Explain the responsibilities businesses have toward their employees.

CSR: Employees

The past few decades have brought dramatic changes in the attitudes and composition of the global workforce. These changes have forced businesses to modify their recruiting, training, and promotion practices, as well as their overall corporate values and behaviors. This section discusses some key responsibilities that employers have regarding employees.

THE PUSH FOR EQUALITY IN EMPLOYMENT

discrimination In a social and economic sense, denial of opportunities to individuals on the basis of some characteristic that has no bearing on their ability to perform in a job

The United States has always stood for economic freedom and the individual's right to pursue opportunity. Unfortunately, in the past many people were targets of economic **discrimination**, being relegated to low-paying, menial jobs and prevented from taking advantage of many opportunities solely on the basis of their race, gender, disability, or religion.

The Civil Rights Act of 1964 established the Equal Employment Opportunity Commission (EEOC), the regulatory agency that addresses job discrimination. The EEOC is responsible for monitoring hiring practices and for investigating complaints of job-related discrimination. It has the power to file legal charges against companies that discriminate and to force them to compensate individuals or groups who have been victimized by unfair practices. The Civil Rights Act of 1991 amended the original act in response to a number of Supreme Court decisions that had taken place in the intervening quarter-century. Among its key provisions are limiting the amount of damage awards, making it easier to sue for discrimination, giving employees the right to have a trial by jury in discrimination cases, and extending protections to overseas employees of U.S. companies.[30]

Affirmative Action

affirmative action Activities undertaken by businesses to recruit and promote members of groups whose economic progress has been hindered through either legal barriers or established practices

In the 1960s, **affirmative action** programs were developed to encourage organizations to recruit and promote members of groups whose past economic progress has been hindered through legal barriers or established practices. Affirmative action programs address a variety of situations, from college admissions to hiring to conducting business with government agencies. Note that while affirmative action programs address a variety of population segments, from military veterans with disabilities to specific ethnic groups, in popular usage, "affirmative action" usually refers to programs based on race.

Affirmative action remains a controversial and politicized issue, with opponents claiming that it creates a double standard and can encourage reverse discrimination against white males; proponents say that it remains a crucial part of the effort to ensure equal opportunities for all. One of the key points of contention is whether affirmative action programs are still needed, given the various antidiscrimination laws now in place. Opponents assert that everyone has an equal shot at success now, so the programs are unnecessary and, if anything, should be based on income, not race; proponents argue that laws can't remove every institutionalized barrier and that discrimination going back decades has left many families and communities at a long-term disadvantage.[31]

Policy debates aside, well-managed companies across the country are finding that embracing diversity in the richest sense is simply good business.

People with Disabilities

In 1990, people with a wide range of physical and mental difficulties got a boost from the passage of the federal Americans with Disabilities Act (ADA), which guarantees equal opportunities in housing, transportation, education, employment, and other areas for the estimated 50 to 75 million people in the United States who have disabilities. As defined by the 1990 law, *disability* is a broad term that protects not only those with physical handicaps but also those with cancer, heart disease, diabetes, epilepsy, HIV/AIDS, drug addiction, alcoholism, emotional illness, and other conditions. In most situations, employers cannot legally require job applicants to pass a physical examination as a condition of employment. Employers are also required to make reasonable accommodations to meet the needs of employees with disabilities, such as modifying workstations or schedules.[32]

OCCUPATIONAL SAFETY AND HEALTH

Every year several thousand U.S. workers lose their lives on the job and many thousands more are injured (see Exhibit 9).[33] During the 1960s, mounting concern about workplace hazards resulted in the passage of the Occupational Safety and Health Act of 1970, which set mandatory standards for safety and health and also established the Occupational Safety and Health Administration (OSHA) to enforce them. These standards govern everything

---

EXHIBIT 9	Fatal Occupational Injuries

Transportation accidents are the leading cause of death on the job in the United States. Overall, U.S. workers suffer fatal on-the-job injuries at a rate of 3.5 deaths per 100,000 full-time employees per year.

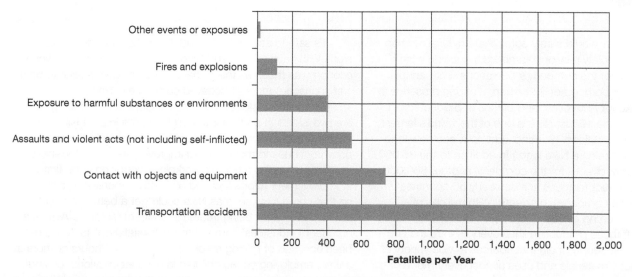

Source: "Census of Fatal Occupational Injuries," U.S. Bureau of Labor Statistics website, accessed 3 August 2011, www.bls.gov.

from hazardous materials to *ergonomics*, the study of how people interact with computers and other machines.

Concerns for employee safety can extend beyond a company's own workforce, and this concern is particularly acute for the many U.S. companies that contract out production to factories in Asia, Latin America, and parts of the United States to make products under their brand names. A number of these companies have been criticized for doing business with so-called *sweatshops*, a disparaging term applied to production facilities that treat workers poorly. As discussed in the Behind the Scenes wrap-up below, Nike is one of many companies taking positive steps to improve conditions in the factories that make their products. American colleges have been influential in this effort, too. More than 200 schools have joined the Fair Labor Association (www.fairlabor.org) to ensure that school-logo products are manufactured in an ethical manner.[34]

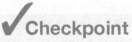 **Checkpoint**

LEARNING OBJECTIVE 6: Explain the responsibilities businesses have toward their employees.

SUMMARY: In addition to the impact a company has on its external stakeholders, corporate social responsibility applies within the company as well, to the way employees are treated. Major issues include the push for equal opportunity, which includes affirmative action programs and regulations to protect the rights of people with disabilities, and occupational safety and health.

CRITICAL THINKING: (1) Does affirmative action seem like a fair approach? Why or why not? (2) Should employees automatically get paid more to work in hazardous jobs? Why or why not?

IT'S YOUR BUSINESS: (1) Have you ever experienced or observed discrimination on the job? If so, how did you handle the situation? (2) Has this chapter changed your perspective about the relationship between business and society? Why or why not?

KEY TERMS TO KNOW: discrimination, affirmative action

BEHIND THE SCENES   MyBizLab

NIKE BUILDS A SUSTAINABLE BUSINESS THROUGH SUSTAINABLE DESIGN AND MANUFACTURING

Nike CEO Mark Parker would surely agree that any examination of Nike's business–society relationship needs to include a look at the massive scale of the company's operations. With annual revenues in the neighborhood of $20 billion, a strong presence in every continent except Antarctica, and billions of products sold since its founding in the 1960s, Nike is one of the world's largest and most visible corporations. (Starting right now, see how long you can go without seeing a Nike logo.) In addition to the 36,000 employees who work directly for the company, another 800,000 work in the 900 contract factories across nearly 50 countries that manufacture the company's products. With millions of shoes, garments, sporting goods, and other "Swoosh"-branded products rolling off those production lines every month, the company oversees a vast supply chain that sources a wide variety of natural and synthetic materials and uses almost every mode of transportation imaginable.

It's safe to say that Nike and the global community are stuck with each other—and Nike needs a vibrant, stable world economy as much as the global community needs Nike to be a well-managed and well-behaved corporate citizen.

Workplace conditions and sustainable manufacturing are two issues in particular that highlight the impact Nike has on stakeholders and the considerable investments the company continues to make toward improving its entire "business ecosystem." In the matter of workplace conditions, the first wave of improvement efforts focused on building monitoring systems so that companies such as Nike could get a better sense of how workers were being treated in contract factories. Across a number of industries, some of these "sweatshop" factories had been accused of forcing employees to work 24 hours or more at a time, employing young children in unsafe conditions, or virtually imprisoning workers in conditions that have at times been compared to slavery. Mattel, Reebok, Patagonia, Liz Claiborne, and Gap are among the other industry leaders that have been working at improving monitoring of contract factories.

However, Nike began to realize that setting standards and monitoring operations weren't improving conditions in its contract factories sufficiently, and the company is now working closely with vendors to improve their operations and practices. As the company explains, "What we've learned, after nearly a decade, is that monitoring alone hasn't solved the problems. And many of the problems are recurring in the industry. Our focus now is getting to the root of the problems."

A key part of that effort is an in-depth auditing process conducted by Nike inspectors, who look for evidence of compliance with Nike's own environmental safety, and health codes. Nike inspectors examine factory operations and interview supervisors as well as employees to make sure contract manufacturers are living up to the expectations outlined in Nike's *Code of Conduct*. Nike doesn't leave compliance to chance, either. The company's *Code Leadership Standards* is a comprehensive manual that describes exactly what a factory needs to do to meet Nike's standards. If a factory is out of compliance, Nike teams work with local management to help them figure where their processes are breaking down and how to improve.

In the area of sustainable manufacturing, Nike calls its efforts "considered design," which it describes as "reducing or eliminating toxics and waste, increasing the use of environmentally preferred materials and using Nike's innovation to create a future with more sustainable products." For example, the company's materials experts have worked for years to analyze and document the environmental impact of a wide variety of garment and shoe materials, and its designers now have a handy software tool to help them choose fabrics and other components that maximize product performance and resource sustainability. After spending several million dollars developing it, Nike released this tool for free public use to help other companies improve their design practices. (You can try this software yourself, actually—it's the Environmental Design Tool featured in the Real-Time Updates Learn More item.)

Recycling is another area of concentration for the company. Nike collects and grinds up millions of pairs of worn-out sneakers every year to produce shock-absorbing materials that are used in running tracks, tennis courts, playgrounds, and other playing surfaces. Nike designers are also ramping up their use of recycled polyester from discarded plastic bottles, keeping hundreds of millions of them out of landfills.

Fabric manufacturing uses enormous volumes of water, and Nike has had a water stewardship program in place since 2001 to help factories minimize water usage and to do a more responsible job of "borrowing" water, as the company phrases it. Given the number of factories it works with worldwide, Nike figures its efforts to improve water stewardship influence the usage of more than 500 billion gallons of water a year.

Even with the considerable investments it has made and the measurable progress that has come from those efforts, the scale of its operations and the visibility of its brand ensure that Nike will continue to attract the attention of stakeholders and advocacy groups. For example, Greenpeace recently launched a "detox challenge" publicity campaign in which the environmental advocacy group challenged Nike and arch-rival Adidas to reduce the discharge of toxic fabric-treatment chemicals from contract factories in China.

Nike's response included a comprehensive report on its progress toward eliminating toxic chemicals from the manufacturing process—efforts that had been underway for more than a decade. These included the process research and chemistry patents it has freely shared with other manufacturers through the GreenXchange intellectual property collaborative and an offer to work with Greenpeace and other NGOs on water usage issues.

Parker talks frankly of the lessons Nike has learned along the way. Reflecting on pressure the company received in the 1990s from worker rights groups, he says, "Our critics were smart (and right) to focus on the industry leader." After first defending conditions in the factories as just the way business was done in those countries, the company realized that change was needed, and it had to be fundamental change affecting every part of the company. Parker now welcomes collaboration with stakeholders and promotes the value of transparency, so that affected groups can see what the company is doing, and the company can learn from anybody who has great ideas to share. "For all the athletic and cultural and financial successes of the company," he says, "I believe our work in sustainable business and innovation has equal potential to shape our legacy."[35]

Critical Thinking Questions

1. This chapter covers three factors that influence ethical decisions: cultural differences, knowledge, and organizational behavior. How have these factors shaped Nike's CSR actions over the past two decades?
2. How does Mark Parker's phrase "sustainable business" relate to sustainable manufacturing?
3. Is it ethical for NGOs to put pressure on just one company in an industry when they are trying to effect change across the entire industry, given that responding to that pressure is likely to cost that one company more than its competitors?

LEARN MORE ONLINE

Visit Nike's consumer-oriented website, **www.nike.com**, and its corporate website, **www.nikebiz.com**. Study the messages presented on the two sites. How does Nike reach out to different stakeholder groups using these two separate sites? Read the "Letter to Shareholders" from Nike's latest annual report (available in the "Investors" section of its corporate website). How does Nike present itself to this vital stakeholder group? How does the company present its CSR efforts in a way that appeals to a reader whose primary interest is financial investment?

MyBizLab

Log on to www.mybizlab.com to access study and assessment aids associated with this chapter.

KEY TERMS

affirmative action	ethics
cap and trade	identity theft
code of ethics	insider trading
conflict of interest	nongovernmental organizations (NGOs)
consumerism	philanthropy
corporate social responsibility (CSR)	strategic CSR
discrimination	sustainable development
ethical dilemma	transparency
ethical lapse	whistle-blowing

TEST YOUR KNOWLEDGE

Questions for Review

1. How does ethics differ from corporate social responsibility?
2. What is a conflict of interest?
3. How do companies support ethical behavior?
4. How are businesses responding to the environmental issues facing society?
5. What is identity theft, and what responsibilities do businesses have to prevent it?

Questions for Analysis

6. Why can't legal considerations resolve every ethical question?
7. How do individuals employ philosophical principles in making ethical business decisions?
8. Why does a company need more than a code of ethics to be ethical?
9. Why is it important for a company to balance its social responsibility efforts with its need to generate profits?
10. **Ethical Considerations.** Is it ethical for companies to benefit from their efforts to practice corporate social responsibility?

Why or why not? How can anyone be sure that CSR efforts aren't just public relations ploys?

Questions for Application

11. What steps could a bookstore take to engage in strategic CSR?
12. Based on what you've learned about corporate social responsibility, what effect will CSR considerations have on your job search?
13. **Concept Integration.** If an employee leaves a company to work for a competitor, what types of knowledge would be ethical for the employee to share with the new employer, and what types would be unethical to share?
14. **Concept Integration.** Is it ethical for state and city governments to entice specific businesses to relocate their operations to that state or city by offering them special tax breaks that are not extended to other businesses operating in that area?

EXPAND YOUR KNOWLEDGE

Discovering Career Opportunities

Businesses, government agencies, and not-for-profit organizations offer numerous career opportunities related to ethics and social responsibility. How can you learn more about these careers?

1. Search the *Occupational Outlook Handbook* at www.bls.gov/oco for "occupational health and safety specialists and technicians," jobs concerned with a company's responsibility toward its employees. What are the duties and qualifications of the jobs you have identified? Are the salaries and future outlooks attractive for all of these jobs?
2. Select one job from the *Handbook* and search blogs, websites, and other sources to learn more about it. Try to find real-life information about the daily activities of people in this job. Can you find any information about ethical dilemmas or other conflicts in the duties of this position? What role do you think people in this position play within their respective organizations?
3. What skills, educational background, and work experience do you think employers are seeking in applicants for the specific job you are researching? What keywords do you think employers would search for when reviewing résumés submitted for this position?

Improve Your Tech Insights: Assistive Technologies

The term *assistive technologies* covers a broad range of devices and systems that help people with disabilities perform activities that might otherwise be difficult or impossible. These include technologies that help people communicate orally and visually, interact with computers and other equipment, and enjoy greater mobility, along with myriad other specific functions.

Assistive technologies create a vital link for thousands of employees with disabilities, giving them opportunities to pursue a greater range of career paths and giving employers access to a broader base of talent. Plus, the economy and society benefit when everyone who can make a contribution is able to, and assistive technologies will be an important part of the solution.

Research some of the technologies now on the market. AssistiveTech.net, www.assistivetech.net, is a great place to explore the thousands of assistive products now available; it also provides links to a variety of other sites. The Business Leadership Network (USBLN), www.usbln.org, helps companies develop policies and practices to encourage the full participation and advancement of employees with disabilities and to market goods and services to consumers with disabilities. Also visit the Rehabilitation Engineering and Assistive Technology Society of North America (RESNA), www.resna.org. (USBLN and RESNA sponsor annual conferences that bring together some of the best minds in the field of assistive technologies, too.) For a look at the federal government's efforts to promote these technologies, visit the National Institute on Disability and Rehabilitation Research, www.ed.gov/about/offices/list/osers/nidrr. Technology companies such as IBM, www.ibm.com/able, and Microsoft, www.microsoft.com/enable, also devote significant resources to developing assistive technologies and making information technology more accessible. Choose one assistive technology, and in a brief email to your instructor, explain how this technology can help companies support employees or customers with disabilities.[36]

PRACTICE YOUR SKILLS

Sharpening Your Communication Skills

Your employer makes a grand show of promoting strong ethics, with regular classes, posters in the hallways, a toll-free hotline, and more. However, as the economy has slowed down over the past few months, you've noticed that company managers aren't always practicing what they preach. They're cutting corners on product quality and squeezing suppliers by not paying bills on time. They even launched a frivolous lawsuit against an upstart competitor that will do little more than drain the new firm of funds and delay its entry into the market. This isn't the same company you were once so proud to work for. Write a brief email message to your immediate supervisor, requesting a meeting to discuss your concerns.

Building Your Team Skills

Every organization can benefit from having a code of ethics to guide decision making. But whom should a code of ethics protect, and what should it cover? In this exercise, you and the rest of your team are going to draft a code of ethics for your college or university.

Start by thinking about who will be protected by this code of ethics. What stakeholders should the school consider when making decisions? What negative effects might decisions have on these stakeholders? Then think about the kinds of situations you want your school's code of ethics to cover. One example might be employment decisions; another might be disclosure of confidential student information.

Next, using Exhibit 2 as a model, draft your school's code of ethics; identify general principles and then provide specific guidelines. Write a general introduction explaining the purpose of the code and who is being protected. Next, write a positive statement to guide ethical decisions in each situation you identified earlier in this exercise. Your statement about promotion decisions, for example, might read: "School officials will encourage equal access to job promotions for all qualified candidates, with every applicant receiving fair consideration."

Compare your code of ethics with the codes drafted by your classmates. Did all the codes seek to protect the same stakeholders? What differences and similarities do you see in the statements guiding ethical decisions?

Developing Your Research Skills

Articles on corporate ethics and social responsibility regularly appear in business journals and newspapers. Find one or more articles discussing one of the following ethics or social responsibility challenges faced by a business:

- Environmental issues, such as pollution, acid rain, and hazardous-waste disposal
- Employee or consumer safety measures
- Consumer information or education
- Employment discrimination or diversity initiatives
- Investment ethics
- Industrial spying and theft of trade secrets
- Fraud, bribery, and overcharging
- Company codes of ethics

1. What is the nature of the ethical challenge or social responsibility issue presented in the article? Does the article report any wrongdoing by a company or agency official? Was the action illegal, unethical, or questionable? What course of action would you recommend the company or agency take to correct or improve matters now?
2. What stakeholder group(s) is affected? What lasting effects will be felt by (a) the company and (b) this stakeholder group(s)?
3. Writing a letter to the editor is one way consumers can speak their mind. Review some of the letters to the editor in newspapers or journals. Why are letters to the editor an important feature for that publication?

REFERENCES

1. "Nike, Inc.'s Response to Greenpeace Report," 18 July 2011, Nike website, www.nikebiz.com; *Nike 2011 Annual Report*, accessed 4 August 2011, www.nikebiz.com; "Detox Campaign," Greenpeace, accessed 4 August 2011, www.greenpeace.org; *Nike Code Leadership Standard*, Nike website, accessed 7 August 2011, www.nikebiz.com; Nike corporate website, accessed 4 August 2011, www.nikebiz.com; GreenXchange, accessed 4 August 2011, www.greenxchange.cc; "Workers & Factories: Improving Conditions in Our Contract Factories," Nike website, accessed 4 August 2011, www.nike.com; Abigail Goldman, "Sweat, Fear, and Resignation Amid All the Toys," *Los Angeles Times*, 26 November 2004, A1, A30–A32; Edward Iwata, "How Barbie Is Making Business a Little Better," *USA Today*, 27 March 2006, B1–B2; "Nike Corporate Responsibility/Compliance ESH CLS Audit" worksheet, accessed 4 August 2011, www.nikebiz.com.

2. Rakesh Khurana, "The Future of Business School," *BusinessWeek*, 26 May 2009, www.businessweek.com.

3. James O'Toole and Warren Bennis, "What's Needed Next: A Culture of Candor," *Harvard Business Review*, June 2009, 54–61.

4. Barbara Ortutay, "Facebook Tries Dirty Tricks on Google But Is Found Out," *Seattle Times*, 12 May 2011, www.seattletimes.com.

5. O'Toole and Bennis, "What's Needed Next: A Culture of Candor," 59.

6. "Ethics and Business Practices," United Technologies website, accessed 3 August 2011, www.utc.com.

7. Ben Levisohn, "Getting More Workers to Whistle," *BusinessWeek*, 28 January 2008, 18.

8. Alan D. Berkowitz, Claude M. Tusk, J. Ian Downes, and David S. Caroline, "Whistleblowing," *Employee Relations Law Journal*, Vol. 36, No. 4, Spring 2011, 15–32.

9. "Less Than Half of Privately Held Businesses Support Whistleblowing," Grant Thornton website, accessed 13 October 2008, www.internationalbusinessreport.com.

10. Ian Wilhelm, "A Surge in Corporate Giving," *Chronicle of Philanthropy*, 17 August 2006, http://find.galegroup.com.

11. David Grayson and Adrian Hodges, "Forget Responsibility, Think Opportunities," *The Observer*, 4 June 2004, http://observer.guardian.co.uk.

12. Michael Porter and Mark Kramer, "Strategy & Society: The Link Between Competitive Advantage and Corporate Social Responsibility," *Harvard Business Review*, December 2006, 78–92.

13. "New Initiative Creates Partnerships on Water Projects Across Africa," Greenbiz.com, 7 June 2004, www.greenbiz.com.

14. Timothy M. Devinney, "Is the Socially Responsible Corporation a Myth? The Good, the Bad, and the Ugly of Corporate Social Responsibility," *Academy of Management Perspectives*, May 2009, 44–56.

15. Milton Friedman, "The Social Responsibility of Business Is to Increase Its Profits," *New York Times Magazine*, 13 September 1970, www.umich.edu/~thecore.

16. "Social Responsibility: 'Fundamentally Subversive'?" Interview with Milton Friedman, *BusinessWeek*, 15 August 2005, www.businessweek.com.

17. Krisi Heim, "In Person: Laurie Erickson Is a 'Wrap' Star to Cancer Patients," *Seattle Times*, 24 April 2011, www.seattletimes.com.

18. Henry G. Manne, "Milton Friedman Was Right," *WSJ Opinion Journal*, 24 November 2006, www.opinionjournal.com.

19. Alexei M. Marcoux, "Business Ethics Gone Wrong," *Cato Policy Report*, May/June 2000, www.cato.org.

20. Kas Thomas, "Google Uses More Electricity Than Most Countries on Earth," assertTrue() blog, 9 March 2009, http://asserttrue.blogspot.com; Rich Miller, "Google Data Center FAQ," Data Center Knowledge website, 26 August 2008, www.datacenterknowledge.com.

21. "Electric Power Annual," U.S. Department of Energy website, accessed 20 June 2007, www.energy.gov.

22. Urs Hölzle, "Energy and the Internet," The Official Google Blog, 11 May 2009, http://googleblog.blogspot.com; eSolar website, accessed 1 June 2009, www.esolar.com; "Google's Green PPAs: What, How, and Why," 29 April 2011, Google website, www.google.com; "Step 5: An Efficient and Clean Energy Future," Google website, accessed 1 June 2009, www.google.com; "Google Data Centers, Best Practices," Google website, accessed 3 August 2011, www.google.com.

23. Cap and Trade 101, U.S. Environmental Protection Agency website, accessed 1 June 2009, www.epa.gov.

24. John M. Broder, "From a Theory to a Consensus on Emissions," *New York Times*, 16 May 2009, www.nytimes.com.

25. "Report of the World Commission on Environment and Development," United Nations General Assembly, 96th Plenary Meeting, 11 December 1987, www.un.org.

26. Ursula M. Burns, "Is the Green Movement a Passing Fancy?" *BusinessWeek*, 27 January 2009, www.businessweek.com.

27. Pete Engardio, "Beyond the Green Corporation," *BusinessWeek*, 29 January 2007, www.businessweek.com.

28. "About Identity Theft," Federal Trade Commission website, accessed 30 May 2009, www.ftc.gov.

29. Action on Smoking and Health website, accessed 15 March 2005, www.ash.org; Chris Burritt, "Fallout from the Tobacco Settlement," *Atlanta Journal and Constitution*, 22 June 1997, A14; Jolie Solomon, "Smoke Signals," *Newsweek*, 28 April 1997, 50–51; Marilyn Elias, "Mortality Rate Rose Through '80s," *USA Today*, 17 April 1997, B3; Mike France, Monica Larner, and Dave Lindorff, "The World War on Tobacco," *BusinessWeek*, 11 November 1996; Richard Lacayo, "Put Out the Butt, Junior," *Time*, 2 September 1996, 51; Elizabeth Gleick, "Smoking Guns," *Time*, 1 April 1996, 50.

30. "The Civil Rights Act of 1991," U.S. Equal Employment Opportunity Commission website, accessed 7 August 2011, www.eeoc.gov.

31. Lorraine Woellert, "Anger on the Right, Opportunity for Bush," *BusinessWeek*, 7 July 2003, www.businessweek.com; Roger O. Crockett, "The Great Race Divide," *BusinessWeek*, 14 July 2003, www.businessweek.com; Earl Graves, "Celebrating the Best and the Brightest," *Black Enterprise*, February 2005, 16.

32. "Disability Discrimination," Equal Employment Opportunity Commission website, accessed 12 June 2007, www.eeoc.gov.

33. "Injuries, Illnesses, and Fatalities," Bureau of Labor Statistics, accessed 31 May 2009, www.bls.gov/iif.

34. Fair Labor Association website, accessed 4 August 2011, www.fairlabor.org.

35. See note 1.

36. Adapted from IBM Human Ability and Accessibility Center, accessed 4 August 2011, www.ibm.com/able; AssistiveTech.net, accessed 4 August 2011, www.assistivetech.net, Business Leadership Network website, accessed 4 August 2011, www.usbln.org; National Institute on Disability and Rehabilitation Research website, accessed 4 August 2011, www.ed.gov; Rehabilitation Engineering and Assistive Technology Society of North America website, accessed 4 August 2011, www.resna.org; Microsoft Accessibility, accessed 4 August 2011, www.microsoft.com/enable.

GLOSSARY

affirmative action Activities undertaken by businesses to recruit and promote members of groups whose economic progress has been hindered through either legal barriers or established practices

cap and trade A type of environmental policy that gives companies some freedom in addressing the environmental impact of specified pollutants, by either reducing emissions to meet a designated cap or buying allowances to offset excess emissions

code of ethics A written statement that sets forth the principles that guide an organization's decisions

conflict of interest A situation in which competing loyalties can lead to ethical lapses, such as when a business decision may be influenced by the potential for personal gain

consumerism A movement that pressures businesses to consider consumer needs and interests

corporate social responsibility (CSR) The idea that business has obligations to society beyond the pursuit of profits

discrimination In a social and economic sense, denial of opportunities to individuals on the basis of some characteristic that has no bearing on their ability to perform in a job

ethical dilemma A situation in which more than one side of an issue can be supported with valid arguments

ethical lapse A situation in which an individual or a group makes a decision that is morally wrong, illegal, or unethical

ethics The rules or standards governing the conduct of a person or group

identity theft A crime in which thieves steal personal information and use it to take out loans and commit other types of fraud

insider trading The use of unpublicized information that an individual gains from the course of his or her job to benefit from fluctuations in the stock market

nongovernmental organizations (NGOs) Nonprofit groups that provide charitable services or promote social and environmental causes

philanthropy The donation of money, time, goods, or services to charitable, humanitarian, or educational institutions

strategic CSR Social contributions that are directly aligned with a company's overall business strategy

sustainable development Operating business in a manner that minimizes pollution and resource depletion, ensuring that future generations will have vital resources

transparency The degree to which affected parties can observe relevant aspects of transactions or decisions

whistle-blowing The disclosure of information by a company insider that exposes illegal or unethical behavior by others within the organization

Management Roles, Functions, and Skills

Management Roles, Functions, and Skills

LEARNING OBJECTIVES After studying this chapter, you will be able to

1 Explain the importance of management and identify the three vital management roles

2 Describe the planning function and outline the strategic planning process

3 Describe the organizing function and differentiate among top, middle, and first-line management

4 Describe the leading function, leadership style, and organizational culture

5 Describe the controlling function and explain the four steps in the control cycle

6 Identify and explain four important types of managerial skills

MyBizLab

Where you see MyBizLab in this chapter, go to www.mybizlab.com for additional activities on the topic being discussed.

BEHIND THE SCENES WEGMANS SATISFIES CUSTOMERS BY PUTTING EMPLOYEES FIRST

Wegmans Food Markets, Inc.

Wegmans CEO Danny Wegman carries on the family tradition of satisfying customers by paying attention to employees and their needs.

www.wegmans.com

Thousands of companies use slogans such as "The customer is king," proclaiming in various ways that customers are their number-one priority. Not Wegmans, a regional grocery store chain based in Rochester, New York. Wegmans makes a clear statement of its priorities: employees first, customers second.

What do customers think about this, you ask? They love it. Customers routinely drive miles out of their way, past other grocery stores, to shop at Wegmans. The company receives thousands of letters of praise every year from current customers—and several thousand more letters from consumers in cities where it doesn't have stores, begging the chain to open a Wegmans nearby.

Such enthusiasm has helped the company post a solid record of success since its founding in 1915. As a private company, Wegmans isn't required to report its financial results to the public, but the numbers that are available are impressive. Its operating margin (a measure of profitability) is twice as high as that of national chains such as Safeway and Kroger. Sales per square foot, a key measure of selling efficiency, are estimated to be 50 percent higher than the industry average. The *Wall Street Journal* once called Wegmans the "best chain in the country, maybe in the world."

Such results would be impressive in any industry, but they're almost unfathomable in the grocery retailing business, one of the toughest industries on earth. Most grocery retailers struggle with constant price wars that guarantee paper-thin profit margins (making one or two cents on every dollar of revenue is typical), frequent labor troubles, high employee turnover, and a customer base that views most grocery stores as virtually indistinguishable from one another. As if those problems weren't enough, grocers face the steamrolling cost efficiencies of Walmart and other discount mass merchandisers, which have already captured one-third of the grocery business in the United States.

If you were Danny Wegman, the company's third-generation CEO, how would you sustain the Wegmans way of doing business in the face of relentless competitive pressures? How would you hold your own against the giant discounters that have rampaged through the grocery industry? How would you make sure that Wegmans attracts the best employees in the business and keeps them satisfied and productive?[1]

INTRODUCTION

Whether they are front-line supervisors or top executives such as Danny Wegman (profiled in the chapter-opening Behind the Scenes), managers have tremendous influence over the success or failure of the companies they lead. Leading seems to come naturally to Wegman, but he would probably be the first to tell you that **management**, the interrelated tasks of planning, organizing, leading, and controlling in pursuit of organizational goals,[2] is no easy job. In fact, according to one survey, more than one-third of the people who take on new managerial positions fail within the first 18 months.[3] Even those who eventually succeed can struggle with the transition from individual contributor to manager. If you aspire to become a manager, you can improve your chances of success by gaining a thorough understanding of what being a manager really entails. This chapter explores the *roles* that managers play, the *functions* they perform, and the essential *skills* they need.

> **management** The process of planning, organizing, leading, and controlling to meet organizational goals

The Roles of Management

Danny Wegman doesn't buy merchandise from wholesalers, stock shelves, or operate cash registers, but the decisions he makes, the organizational framework he establishes, the expectations he sets, the managers he hires to oversee employees, and the culture he establishes all have enormous impact on the company's success. Likewise, the managers who report to Wegman, including his daughter, company president Colleen Wegman, aren't directly engaged in the tasks of buying and selling groceries. However, within the scope of his or her own responsibilities, each of these managers also has significant influence on the company's fortunes. Although managers don't usually do the hands-on work in an organization, they create the environment and provide the resources that give employees opportunities to excel in their work.

In addition, given the effect that managerial decisions and behaviors have on employees, customers, investors, and other stakeholders, it's no exaggeration to say that management is one of the most vital professions in the contemporary economy. Managers who effectively and ethically guide their companies contribute greatly to our standard of living and our economic security. By the same measure, managers who fail, through poor planning, misguided decisions, or questionable ethics, can create havoc that extends far beyond the walls of their own companies. In other words, management is one of the most important functions in society, not just within the sphere of business.

All the **managerial roles** that leaders must play can be grouped into three main categories: interpersonal, informational, and decisional.

> **1** **LEARNING OBJECTIVE**
>
> Explain the importance of management, and identify the three vital management roles.

> **managerial roles** Behavioral patterns and activities involved in carrying out the functions of management; includes interpersonal, informational, and decisional roles

INTERPERSONAL ROLES

Management is largely a question of getting work accomplished through the efforts of other people, so a manager must play a number of interpersonal roles, including providing leadership to employees, building relationships, and acting as a liaison between groups and individuals both inside and outside the company (such as suppliers, government agencies, consumers, labor unions, and community leaders). Effective managers tend to excel at networking, fostering relationships with many people within their own companies and within the industries and communities where their companies do business. In fact, the number of connections a person has becomes an increasingly important asset the higher he or she rises in an organization.

INFORMATIONAL ROLES

MyBizLab

Gain hands-on experience through an interactive, real-world scenario. This chapter's simulation entitled Plan for Success is located at www.mybizlab.com.

Managers spend a fair amount of time gathering information from sources both inside and outside an organization. The higher up they are, the more they rely on subordinates to collect, analyze, and summarize information—and the greater the risk that they will fall out of touch with what is happening on "the front lines," where the essential day-to-day work of the organization is performed. Today's companies have devised powerful and clever ways to collect and process information for managers. A good example is the *executive dashboard*, which, just like the dashboard in a car, provides quick-read summaries of vital performance variables (see Exhibit 1).

The dashboard analogy is also a good way to think about the information challenges that managers face. As you're driving, making split-second decisions while keeping your eyes on the road, you don't need to know how full the water reservoir is or how fast the water pump is turning. Such details would overwhelm your decision making and serve no immediate purpose. However, if your engine is in danger of overheating because the water pump is failing, you need enough advance warning to take corrective action before it's too late, so your dashboard provides a quick summary through a temperature gauge or warning light. Similarly, managers must figure out what they need to know and when they need to know it. Generally speaking, as you progress higher up in an organization, you need to monitor more information sources but see fewer details from each one.

Managers also communicate information to employees, other managers, and other stakeholders. This communication involves virtually every form of information, from technical and administrative information to motivational pep talks to strategic planning sessions. And it involves every form of media, from private conversations to videoconferences that connect managers with employees across the country or around the world.

The increasing use of social media for both internal and external communication is changing the nature of the manager's informational role in many companies. In the past, communication was often concentrated in formal channels that tended to flow in only one direction at a time, such as from a manager down to his or her subordinates or from "the company" to customers. With social media, a more conversational model is emerging, in which more

EXHIBIT 1	Executive Dashboards

To help managers avoid information overload, many companies now use executive dashboards to present carefully filtered highlights of key performance parameters. The latest generation of software makes it easy to customize screens to show each manager the specific summaries he or she needs to see.

Source: Used with permission of StatCom.

people can participate and communication is more immediate and less formal. For example, on the Southwest Airlines Nuts About Southwest blog (www.blogsouthwest.com), a team of employee and manager bloggers from around the company conduct what amounts to multiple ongoing conversations with thousands of Southwest customers. The smart use of social media is helping managers learn more from employees and customers and communicate back to these and other stakeholder groups more effectively.

DECISIONAL ROLES

Managers up and down the organizational ladder face an endless stream of decisions. Many of these decisions are fairly routine, such as choosing which of several job candidates to hire or setting the prices of new products. Other decisions, however, might occur only once or twice in a manager's career, such as responding to a product-tampering crisis or the threat of a hostile takeover. Some decisions are made after extensive information gathering and analysis; others have to be made on the spot, with little but judgment and intuition to guide the manager's choice. One of the most significant changes occurring in business management in recent years is the effort to push decision making as far down the organizational pyramid as possible, giving whichever employees face a particular situation the authority to make decisions about it. This approach not only accelerates and improves work flow and customer service but also frees up higher-level managers to work on more strategic matters.

Being able to move among these roles comfortably while performing the basic management functions is just one of the many skills that managers must have. The following sections provide a closer look at those four functions—planning, organizing, leading, and controlling.

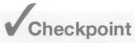

Checkpoint

LEARNING OBJECTIVE 1: Explain the importance of management, and identify the three vital management roles.

SUMMARY: While managers usually don't do the hands-on work in an organization, they create the environment and provide the resources that give employees the opportunities to excel in their work. Managerial responsibilities include creating the organizational framework, fostering a positive culture, setting expectations, and providing resources. The three vital managerial roles are interpersonal (interacting with others), informational (receiving and sharing information), and decisional (making decisions).

CRITICAL THINKING: (1) How are social media changing the nature of a manager's information role? (2) Would managers get more respect from employees if they "rolled up their sleeves" and pitched in with the daily work more often? Why or why not?

IT'S YOUR BUSINESS: (1) Review the process you went through to choose the college you are currently attending. What lessons from your experience could someone apply to managerial decision making? (2) Do you believe you have the right personality for management? If not, what areas would you work on?

KEY TERMS TO KNOW: management, managerial roles

The Planning Function

Managers engage in **planning** when they develop strategies, establish goals and objectives for the organization, and translate those strategies and goals into action plans. **Strategic plans** outline the firm's long-range (often two to five years) organizational goals and set a course of action the firm will pursue to reach its goals. The *strategic planning process* consists of six interrelated steps: defining the organization's mission, vision, and values; performing a SWOT analysis; developing forecasts; analyzing the competition; establishing goals and objectives; and developing action plans (see Exhibit 2 on the next page).

---

2 | **LEARNING OBJECTIVE**

Describe the planning function, and outline the strategic planning process.

planning Establishing objectives and goals for an organization and determining the best ways to accomplish them

strategic plans Plans that establish the actions and the resource allocation required to accomplish strategic goals; they're usually defined for periods of two to five years and developed by top managers

EXHIBIT 2	The Strategic Planning Process

Specific firms have their own variations of the strategic planning process, but these six steps offer a good general model. The circular arrangement is no coincidence, by the way. Strategic planning should be a never-ending process, as you establish strategies, measure outcomes, monitor changes in the business environment, and make adjustments as needed.

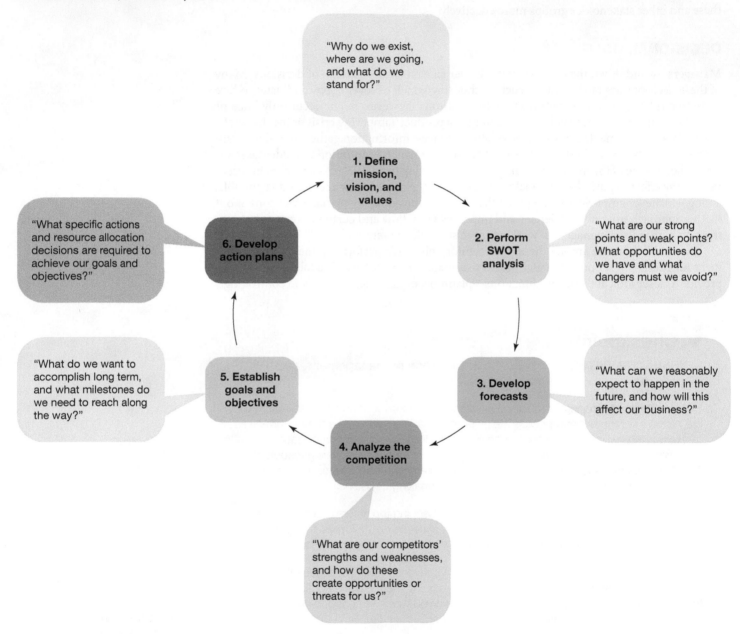

DEFINING THE MISSION, VISION, AND VALUES

To achieve any level of strategic clarity, planners first need to agree on the basic principles that define the organization, and such agreement can be articulated in three interrelated statements. First, a **mission statement** is a brief expression of *why* the company exists.[4] For example, the medical device manufacturer Welch Allyn defines its mission as "helping doctors, nurses, and other healthcare providers across the globe provide the best patient care by developing innovative products, breakthrough technologies, and cutting-edge solutions that help them see more patients, detect more conditions, and improve more lives."[5] This statement clearly defines the scope of the company's activities and its priorities in serving its target customers. Just as important, it eliminates activities the company could pursue, such as consumer products, but chooses not to.

mission statement A brief statement of why an organization exists; in other words, what the organization aims to accomplish for customers, investors, and other stakeholders

Second, a **vision statement** is a brief expression of *what* the company aspires to be. The defense contractor Northrop Grumman puts it this way: "Our vision is to be the most trusted provider of systems and technologies that ensure the security and freedom of our nation and its allies."[6] Notice how this statement differs in both content and tone from the mission statement above. It provides some focus (for example, saying the company wants to be the *most trusted* provider, not necessarily the largest or the most technologically advanced) without getting into the specifics of a mission statement. It also inspires employees with a clear sense of purpose. (Note that these definitions of *mission* and *vision* are not universally agreed upon, and some companies use these terms interchangeably.)

Third, a **values statement** identifies the principles that guide the company's decisions and behaviors and establish expectations for everyone in the organization. For instance, in addition to such attributes as honesty, service, fun, and inclusiveness, Enterprise Rent-a-Car identifies hard work as one of its values: "Learning how to run a successful business from the ground up and delivering our high standard of service is hard work. It's work that demands a deep personal commitment from each employee." In return, the company offers unusual opportunities to learn entrepreneurship and business management early in one's career.[7]

Mission, vision, and values statements are sometimes dismissed as vague "happy talk" that companies spend a lot of time creating but never look at again, and this criticism is sometimes deserved. However, if the statements are (1) crafted with the purpose of truly defining what the company stands for and (2) used in both strategic planning and the ongoing evaluation of the company's performance, they become essential parts of the company's "DNA."

vision statement A brief and inspirational expression of what a company aspires to be

values statement A brief articulation of the principles that guide a company's decisions and behaviors

ASSESSING STRENGTHS, WEAKNESSES, OPPORTUNITIES, AND THREATS

Before establishing long-term goals, a company needs to have a clear assessment of its strengths and weaknesses relative to the opportunities and threats it faces. This analysis is commonly referred to as *SWOT* (pronounced "swat"), which stands for strengths, weaknesses, opportunities, and threats (see Exhibit 3).

EXHIBIT 3	SWOT Analysis

Identifying a firm's strengths, weaknesses, opportunities, and threats is a common strategic planning technique. Here are some examples of the factors a company might identify during a SWOT analysis.

Internal

Strengths
Respected brand
Financial resources
Strong management
Design patents

Weaknesses
Aging facilities
Talent shortage
Narrow customer base

Positive, helpful — Negative, harmful

Opportunities
New products
Attractive merger candidates
New markets in Asia

Threats
Liability lawsuits
Pending regulations
Shrinking demand for existing products

External
(in some cases, threats can also come from internal sources)

Strengths are positive internal factors that contribute to a company's success, which can be anything from a team of expert employees to financial resources to unique technologies. For instance, Southern Cross Healthcare (www.schealthcare.co.uk) is the largest operator of elder-care homes in the United Kingdom. Two of its key strengths are its leading market position and its broad portfolio of services.[8] *Weaknesses* are negative internal factors that inhibit the company's success, such as obsolete facilities, inadequate financial resources to fund growth, or lack of managerial depth and talent. According to analysis by the research firm Datamonitor, one of Southern Cross's weaknesses was a failure to successfully integrate care homes that it acquired, which affected operating costs and service quality.[9] Identifying a firm's internal strengths and weaknesses helps management understand its current abilities so it can set proper goals.

After taking inventory of the company's internal strengths and weaknesses, the next step is to identify the external opportunities and threats that might significantly affect the firm's ability to attain desired goals. *Opportunities* are positive situations that represent the possibility of generating new revenue. As a provider of services to elderly consumers, for example, Southern Cross has significant opportunities to expand its sales based on the demographics of an aging population.[10] Shrewd managers and entrepreneurs recognize opportunities before others do and then promptly act on their ideas.

Threats are negative forces that could inhibit a firm's ability to achieve its objectives, including such external factors as new competitors, new government regulations, economic contraction, changes in interest rates, disruptions in supply, technological advances that render products obsolete, theft of intellectual property, product liability lawsuits, and even the weather. Depending on the company and the industry, it can also be helpful to consider internal threats if they have the potential to disrupt business. Datamonitor identifies increasing labor costs and intense competition as the two primary threats that Southern Cross faces.[11] The combination of rising costs (an internal threat) and increasing competition (an external threat) could put a serious squeeze on the company's profit margins.

DEVELOPING FORECASTS

By its very nature, planning requires managers to make predictions about the future. Forecasting is a notoriously difficult and error-prone part of strategic planning. Managers need to predict not only *what* will (or will not) occur, but *when* it will occur and *how* it will affect their business. Forecasting is crucial to every company's success because it influences the decisions managers make regarding virtually every business activity, and misreading the future can damage or even destroy a company.

Managerial forecasts fall under two broad categories: *quantitative forecasts*, which are typically based on historical data or tests and often involve complex statistical computations, and *qualitative forecasts*, which are based more on intuitive judgments. Neither method is foolproof, but both are valuable tools and are often used together to help managers fill in the unknown variables that inevitably crop up in the planning process. For example, managers can make statistical projections of next year's sales based on data from previous years while factoring in their judgment about the impact of new competitors, changing regulations, or other external forces.

As important as forecasting is, it represents a vexing paradox because, to a significant degree, the future is simply not predictable. Technology, fashion, and other influential forces often move forward in lurches and leaps that are difficult to predict. Extraordinary events—such as wars, economic meltdowns, or natural disasters can play havoc with the best forecasts. Moreover, a single surprising development can trigger a chain reaction of other developments that might have been impossible to envision before. One key element in the art of management, therefore, is crafting plans that are solid enough to move the company forward in a strategically coherent direction while staying alert to changing conditions and being flexible enough to adapt quickly when things do change.

ANALYZING THE COMPETITION

The competitive context in which a company operates needs to be thoroughly understood and factored into the strategic planning process. Performing a SWOT analysis on each of your major competitors is a good first step. Identifying *their* strengths and weaknesses helps pinpoint *your* opportunities and threats. For instance, if you discover that one of your competitors has been suffering customer satisfaction problems, that could be a sign of financial difficulties, product flaws, or other weaknesses that could be opportunities for you to capture additional market share. Similarly, identifying your competitors' opportunities and threats can give you insight into what they might do next, and you can then plan accordingly.

Competitive analysis should always keep the customer's perspective in mind. You may believe you have the best product, the best reputation, and the best customer service, but the only beliefs that matter are the target customer's. Conversely, you might believe that a competitor's less-expensive products are inferior, but those products might well be good enough to meet customers' needs—meaning that the higher cost of your higher-quality products puts you at a disadvantage.

ESTABLISHING GOALS AND OBJECTIVES

Although the terms are often used interchangeably, it helps to think of a **goal** as a broad, long-range accomplishment that the organization wants to attain and to think of an **objective** as a specific, short-range target designed to help reach that goal. For Wegmans, a *goal* might be to capture 15 percent of the grocery market in the mid-Atlantic region over the next five years, and an *objective* in support of that goal might be to open four new stores in Virginia in the next two years.

Business people are often advised to make their goals and objectives "SMART," as in *specific, measurable, attainable, relevant,* and *time limited.* For example, "substantially increase our sales" is a poorly worded statement because it doesn't define what *substantial* means or when it should be measured. This acronym can be a helpful reminder to set meaningful goals, but as with the paradox of forecasting, it's important to use good judgment and be flexible, too.[12] For example, you may not know whether a goal is really attainable until you try to reach it, or you might reach it easily and realize you set your sights too low.

goal A broad, long-range target or aim

objective A specific, short-range target or aim

DEVELOPING ACTION PLANS

With strategic goals and objectives in place, the next step is to develop a plan to reach them. Plans are often organized in a hierarchy, just as a company itself is. For instance, the overall strategic plan might be supported at the next level down by a research and development plan, a manufacturing plan, and a marketing plan, describing how each functional area will help the company reach its strategic goals and objectives.

The names and contents of these *tactical plans* or *operational plans* vary widely by industry, company, and business function. Some address all the actions required in a particular department or functional area over a recurring time frame, such as a quarter or a year, while others address all the tasks involved in a single project or event. For example, a *launch plan* for a new product might cover a period from several months or a year before the product is introduced to the public on through the launch date and several months afterward. Such a plan would identify all the actions needed to coordinate the launch of the product, including the production ramp-up, promotional activities, sales training, physical distribution, and every other task and resource allocation decision needed to get the new product off to a successful start.

By the way, crafting a solid plan and carrying it through to completion are great ways to make a name for yourself early in your career, even for relatively simple projects. Demonstrate that you can figure out what needs to be done, coordinate all the resources, and then bring it in on schedule and on budget. Upper managers will notice and keep you in mind when they need people to take on more challenging and important projects.

LEARNING OBJECTIVE 2: Describe the planning function, and outline the strategic planning process.

SUMMARY: Planning is the process of developing strategies, establishing goals and objectives for the organization, and translating those strategies and goals into action plans. Plans vary in their time frame and scope, from high-level, long-range strategic plans to lower-level, short-term tactical and operational plans. The strategic planning process consists of six interrelated steps: defining the organization's mission, vision, and values; performing a SWOT analysis; developing forecasts; analyzing the competition; establishing goals and objectives; and developing action plans.

CRITICAL THINKING: (1) Would Boeing and Old Navy develop strategic plans over the same time horizon? Why or why not? (2) How does the vision statement guide the planning process?

IT'S YOUR BUSINESS: (1) What is your personal vision statement for your career and your life? Have you ever thought about your future in this way? (2) Consider a career path that you might pursue upon graduation, and perform a quick SWOT analysis. What are some of your internal strengths and weaknesses and external opportunities and threats?

KEY TERMS TO KNOW: planning, strategic plans, mission statement, vision statement, values statement, goal, objective

3 **LEARNING OBJECTIVE**

Describe the organizing function, and differentiate among top, middle, and first-line management.

organizing The process of arranging resources to carry out the organization's plans

management pyramid An organizational structure divided into top, middle, and first-line management

The Organizing Function

Organizing, the process of arranging resources to carry out an organization's plans, is the second major function of managers. To organize effectively, managers must think through all the activities that employees perform, as well as all the facilities and equipment employees need in order to complete those activities. Managers also give people the ability to work toward company goals by determining who will have the authority to make decisions, to perform or supervise activities, and to distribute resources. The three levels of management in a typical corporate hierarchy—top, middle, bottom—is commonly known as the **management pyramid** (see Exhibit 4).

EXHIBIT 4	The Management Pyramid

Here are some of the typical jobs in the three basic levels of management.

Top managers → CEO, CTO, CFO, CIO, vice president

Middle managers → Controller, manager, director

First-line managers → Supervisor, department head

TOP MANAGERS

Top managers are the upper-level managers, such as Danny Wegman, who have the most power and who take overall responsibility for an organization. This tier includes corporate officers and usually the next layer or two of management beneath them, depending on the size and structure of the company. The term *executive* applies to top managers. Typical job titles include the "C" level positions, such as chief marketing officer (CMO) and chief financial officer (CFO) and vice presidents (the largest corporations may have dozens of vice presidents overseeing various divisions or functions).

Top managers establish the structure for the organization as a whole, and they select the people who fill the upper-level positions. Top managers also make long-range plans, establish major policies, and often represent the company to the media, the community, and other stakeholders. Two significant ways in which top management differs from lower management tiers are the long time frames with which executives must work and the magnitude of the decisions they need to make. Given the difficulty and importance of these strategic decisions, the ability to make tough judgment calls is highly valued in top executives.

top managers Those at the highest level of the organization's management hierarchy; they are responsible for setting strategic goals, and they have the most power and responsibility in the organization

MIDDLE MANAGERS

Middle managers have similar responsibilities but on a smaller scale, such as for an individual division or facility. The term *middle management* is somewhat vague, but in general, managers at this level report upward to top executives, while first-line managers report to them. In other words, they usually manage other managers, not workers. A smaller company might have a single layer of middle management (or none at all, in many cases), whereas a large corporation could have a half dozen or more layers of middle managers.

The term "middle management" is sometimes used disparagingly, giving the impression that middle managers are "bureaucrats" who clog up the works without adding much value. Some highly regarded opinion leaders have gone so far as to blame such managers for much that ails the modern corporation.[13] Many companies have also *flattened* their organizational structures by removing one or more layers of middle management.

However, middle managers play the essential role of translating strategic goals and objectives into the actions that allow the company to meet those targets. While they may not do the actual day-to-day work, middle managers are the ones who put the systems and resources in place so that front-line teams can work efficiently and with coordinated purpose. They also provide vital coaching and mentoring for first-line managers who are making the transition into management. As leadership consultant Steve Arneson emphasizes, "It's the leaders in the middle who must communicate and execute strategy, solve problems, create efficiencies, and manage performance."[14] In his analysis of the computer game industry, Wharton management professor Ethan Mollick concluded that middle managers who oversaw new game development had a greater impact on company performance than the top managers who set strategy or the developers who designed and created the games.[15]

middle managers Those in the middle of the management hierarchy; they develop plans to implement the goals of top managers and coordinate the work of first-line managers

FIRST-LINE MANAGERS

At the bottom of the management pyramid are **first-line managers** (or *supervisory managers*). They oversee the work of nonmanagerial employees, and they put into action the plans developed at higher levels. Titles at this level include supervisor, department head, and office manager.[16] The types of employees these managers supervise vary widely, from entry-level workers with limited experience and education to advanced experts in engineering, science, finance, and other professional specialties.

Like managers at the levels above them, first-line managers face challenges unique to their position in the hierarchy. As the direct interface between "management" and the employees, they have the most immediate responsibility for ensuring that necessary work is done according to agreed-upon performance standards. They must also deal with any friction that exists between employees and management. Supervisors are also usually quite involved in recruiting, hiring, and training of employees. In this role, they perform the vital task of making sure employees acquire the skills they need and adapt to the organization's culture.

first-line managers Those at the lowest level of the management hierarchy; they supervise the operating employees and implement the plans set at the higher management levels

✔ Checkpoint

LEARNING OBJECTIVE 3: Describe the organizing function, and differentiate among top, middle, and first-line management.

SUMMARY: The organizing function involves arranging an organization's resources in the best way possible to help reach its goals and objectives. Top managers grapple with long-range, strategic issues and often must make decisions about events and conditions several years into the future. They also have important communication roles, representing the company to external stakeholders. Middle managers usually have responsibility over individual divisions or facilities and are charged with translating strategic plans into the tactical plans that will allow the company to reach its goals and objectives. First-line managers supervise nonmanagement employees; they have the shortest time horizons and greatest tactical perspective.

CRITICAL THINKING: (1) Why might a manager need to deemphasize skills honed in previous positions as he or she rises through the organizational hierarchy? (2) Would top managers or first-line managers typically have more or less of the information they'd like to have for the decisions they need to make? Why?

IT'S YOUR BUSINESS: (1) Have you ever supervised others on the job or in volunteer work? If so, how would you rate your performance as a manager? (2) If you were suddenly promoted to manage the department you've been working in, would you change your "work" personality? Why or why not?

KEY TERMS TO KNOW: organizing, management pyramid, top managers, middle managers, first-line managers

---

4 LEARNING OBJECTIVE

Describe the leading function, leadership style, and organizational culture.

leading The process of guiding and motivating people to work toward organizational goals

The Leading Function

Leading is the process of influencing and motivating people to work willingly and effectively toward common goals. Managers with good leadership skills have greater success in influencing the attitudes and actions of others and motivating employees to put forth their best performance.

All managers have to be effective leaders to be successful, but management and leadership are not the same thing. One way to distinguish between the two is to view management as the rational, intellectual, and practical side of guiding an organization and to view leadership as the inspirational, visionary, and emotional side. Both management and leadership involve the use of power, but management involves *position power* (so called since it stems from the individual's position in the organization), whereas leadership involves *personal power* (which stems from a person's own unique attributes, such as expertise or charisma).[17]

Successful leaders tend to share many of the same traits, but no magical set of personal qualities automatically destines someone for leadership. Nevertheless, in general, good leaders possess a balance of several types of intelligence:

REAL-TIME UPDATES
Learn More by Reading This Article

Do you have what it takes to be a successful leader?

Rate yourself on 10 essential attributes of leadership. Go to http://real-timeupdates.com/bia6 and click on Learn More. If you are using MyBizLab, you can access Real-Time Updates within the chapter or under Student Study Tools.

- *Cognitive intelligence* involves reasoning, problem solving, memorization, and other rational skills. Obviously, leaders need a sufficient degree of cognitive intelligence to understand and process the information required for planning and decision making in their jobs.
- *Emotional intelligence* is a measure of a person's awareness of and ability to manage his or her own emotions. People with high emotional intelligence recognize their own emotional states and the effect those emotions have on others, they are able to regulate their emotional responses

in order to control or reduce disruptive impulses and moods, and they have a high degree of *empathy* (the ability to understand others' feelings).[18]

- *Social intelligence* involves looking outward to understand the dynamics of social situations and the emotions of other people, in addition to your own.[19] Socially adept managers have a knack for finding and building common ground with people of all kinds. Moreover, leaders, in a sense, "infect" their organizations with their own emotions, positive or negative.[20]

REAL-TIME UPDATES

Learn More by Listening to This Podcast

Find out why great leaders are made, not born

Explore the factors that produce great leaders and get advice on how to become one yourself. Go to http://real-timeupdates .com/bia6 and click on Learn More. If you are using MyBizLab, you can access Real-Time Updates within the chapter or under Student Study Tools.

All three types of intelligence are essential to building the competencies that lead to success. In fact, various studies suggest that in both leadership and life in general, emotional and social intelligence play a far greater role in success than purely cognitive intelligence.[21]

DEVELOPING AN EFFECTIVE LEADERSHIP STYLE

Leadership style can be viewed as finding the right balance between *what* the leader focuses on and *how* he or she makes things happen in the organization. Every manager has a definite style, although good leaders usually adapt their approach to match the requirements of the particular situation.[22] Across the range of leadership styles, you can find three basic types (see Exhibit 5). **Autocratic leaders** control the decision-making process in their organizations, often restricting the decision-making freedom of subordinates. Autocratic leadership generally has a bad reputation, and when it's overused or used inappropriately, it can certainly produce bad results or stunt an organization's growth. However, companies

autocratic leaders Leaders who do not involve others in decision making

EXHIBIT 5	Leadership Styles

Leadership styles fall on a continuum from *autocratic* (manager makes the decisions) to *democratic* (manager and subordinates make decisions together) to *laissez-faire* (subordinates make decisions on their own). Each style has strengths and weaknesses, and effective managers often adapt their style to suit specific situations.

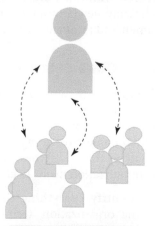

Autocratic leadership:

Manager makes the decisions and issues directives down the chain of command; subordinates have little or no freedom to make decisions, deviate from plans, or provide contrary input.

Democratic leadership:

Manager shares decision-making authority, seeking input and inviting subordinates to participate in a coordinated planning process; group can encourage a change of course if needed.

Laissez-faire leadership:

Manager acts as advisor and supporter, offering input when asked but generally letting subordinates chart and adjust their own course toward meeting agreed-upon goals and objectives.

can find themselves in situations where autocratic leadership is needed to guide the firm through challenging situations or to bring uncooperative units in line.

Democratic leaders, in contrast, delegate authority and involve employees in decision making. Also known as *collaborative* leaders, these managers invite and seek out input from anyone in the organization who can add insight to the decision-making process. For example, after Salesforce.com installed an internal social networking application that gave everyone in the company the chance to share information, CEO Mark Benioff began monitoring the flow of insights and realized that some of the most valuable information about customers was coming from employees whom upper management didn't normally communicate with. Inspired by that discovery, he opened the annual strategic planning meeting to the entire company via social networking.[23] This style is often called **participative management**.

The third leadership style takes its name from the French term *laissez-faire*, which can be translated roughly as "hands off." **Laissez-faire leaders** such as Danny Wegman take the role of supporters and consultants, encouraging employees' ideas and offering insights or opinions when asked. After the overall strategic direction and priorities are in place, they emphasize **employee empowerment**—giving employees the power to make decisions that apply to their specific aspects of work. As Wegman puts it, "Once you share a common set of values, you can go and be yourself."[24]

COACHING AND MENTORING

Leaders have an important responsibility for education and encouragement, which may take the form of coaching and mentoring. **Coaching** involves taking the time to meet with employees, discussing any problems that may hinder their ability to work effectively, and offering suggestions and encouragement to help them find their own solutions to work-related challenges. (Note that the term *executive coaching* usually refers to hiring an outside management expert to help senior managers.)

Mentoring is similar to coaching but is based on long-term relationships between senior and junior members of an organization. The mentor is usually an experienced manager or employee who can help guide other managers and employees through the corporate maze. Mentors have a deep knowledge of the business and can explain office politics, serve as role models for appropriate business behavior, and provide valuable advice about how to succeed within the organization. Mentoring programs are used in a variety of ways, such as helping newly promoted managers make the transition to leadership roles and helping women and minorities prepare for advancement.

MANAGING CHANGE

Change presents a major leadership challenge for one simple reason: Many people don't like it, or at least they don't like being told they need to change. They may fear the unknown, they may be unwilling to give up current habits or benefits, they may not trust the motives of the people advocating change, or they may simply have experienced too many change initiatives that didn't yield the promised results.[25] To improve the chances of success when the organization needs to change, managers can follow these steps:[26]

1. **Identify everything that needs to change.** Changes can involve the structure of the organization, technologies and systems, or people's attitudes, beliefs, skills, or behaviors.[27] One particular challenge for managers advocating change is understanding the ripple effect the change will have throughout the organization.[28]
2. **Identify the forces acting for and against a change.** By understanding these forces, managers can work to amplify the forces that will facilitate the change and remove or diminish the negative forces.
3. **Choose the approach best suited to the situation.** Managers can institute change through a variety of techniques, including communication, education, participation in decision making, negotiation, visible support from top managers or other opinion leaders, or coercive use of authority (usually recommended only for crisis situations). When managers engage people in the change, asking for their input and advice so they

---

*Sidebar definitions (left margin):*

democratic leaders Leaders who delegate authority and involve employees in decision making

participative management A philosophy of allowing employees to take part in planning and decision making

laissez-faire leaders Leaders who leave most decisions up to employees, particularly those concerning day-to-day matters

employee empowerment Granting decision-making and problem-solving authorities to employees so they can act without getting approval from management

coaching Helping employees reach their highest potential by meeting with them, discussing problems that hinder their ability to work effectively, and offering suggestions and encouragement to overcome these problems

mentoring A process in which experienced managers guide less-experienced colleagues in nuances of office politics, serving as a role model for appropriate business behavior, and helping to negotiate the corporate structure can help design the changes, they'll be much more likely to embrace the new way of doing things.[29]

4. **Reinforce changed behavior and monitor continued progress.** Once a change has been made, managers need to reinforce new behaviors and make sure old behaviors don't creep back in.

BUILDING A POSITIVE ORGANIZATIONAL CULTURE

Strong leadership is a key element in establishing a productive **organizational culture** (sometimes known as *corporate culture*)—the set of underlying values, norms, and practices shared by members of an organization (see Exhibit 6). Culture can be a negative or a

organizational culture A set of shared values and norms that support the management system and that guide management and employee behavior

EXHIBIT 6	Creating the Ideal Culture in Your Company

You can't create a culture directly, but you can establish the behaviors and values that in turn do create a culture. Use this list of questions to explore the many ways you can foster a positive culture—and avoid the growth of a negative culture.

Company Values

• Have you articulated a compelling vision for the company?

• Have you defined a mission statement, based on that vision, that employees understand and can implement?

• Do employees know how their work relates to this vision?

• Is there a common set of values that binds the organization together?

• Do you and other executives or owners demonstrate these values day in and day out?

People

• How are people treated?

• Do you foster an atmosphere of civility and respect?

• Do you value and encourage teamwork, with all ideas welcomed?

• Do you acknowledge, encourage, and act upon (when appropriate) ideas from employees?

• Do you give employees credit for their ideas?

• Have you shown a positive commitment to a balance between work and life?

Community

• Have you clarified how the company views its relationship with the communities it affects?

• Do your actions support that commitment to community?

Communication

• Do you practice and encourage open communication?

• Do you share operating information throughout the company so that people know how the company is doing?

• Do you regularly survey employees on workplace issues and ask for their input on solutions?

• Is there an open-door policy for access to management?

Employee Performance

• Do you handle personnel issues with fairness and respect?

• Do employees receive feedback regularly?

• Are employee evaluations based on agreed-upon objectives that have been clearly communicated?

Sources: Adapted from Andrew Bird, "Do You Know What Your Corporate Culture Is?" *CPA Insight*, February, March 1999, 25–26; Gail H. Vergara, "Finding a Compatible Corporate Culture," *Healthcare Executive*, January/February 1999, 46–47; Hal Lancaster, "To Avoid a Job Failure, Learn the Culture of a Company First," *Wall Street Journal*, 14 July 1998, B1.

positive force in an organization, and managers set the tone by establishing expectations, defining rules and policies that shape behavior, and acting as role models. When employees at Wegmans see Danny Wegman enthusiastically embrace the challenges of the day and treat customers and colleagues with respect, that positive energy radiates throughout the culture. As employee Elaine Danar puts it, "I have an incredible sense of pride to represent this company."[30]

Positive cultures create an environment that encourages employees to make smart decisions for the good of the company and its customers. At companies with legendary corporate cultures, such as Wegmans, Nordstrom, and Southwest Airlines, employees routinely go the extra mile to make sure customers are treated well. In contrast, negative, dysfunctional cultures can lead employees to make decisions that are bad for customers and bad for the company.

✓ Checkpoint

LEARNING OBJECTIVE 4: Describe the leading function, leadership style, and organizational culture.

SUMMARY: Leading is the art and science of influencing and motivating people to work toward common goals. Leaders can exhibit a range of styles in what they choose to focus on (strategic versus operational matters) and how they make things happen (forcing versus enabling). Three specific leadership styles are autocratic, democratic, and laissez-faire. Organizational culture is the set of underlying values, norms, and practices shared by members of an organization.

CRITICAL THINKING: (1) Are management and leadership the same thing? If not, why not? (2) Can a single individual be an autocratic, a democratic, *and* a laissez-faire leader? Why or why not?

IT'S YOUR BUSINESS: (1) What is your natural inclination in terms of the three basic leadership styles—autocratic, democratic, or laissez-faire? Think about times in school, at work, or in social situations in which you played a leadership role. How did you lead? (2) Does leadership experience in school activities such as student government and athletics help prepare you for business leadership? Why or why not?

KEY TERMS TO KNOW: leading, autocratic leaders, democratic leaders, participative management, laissez-faire leaders, employee empowerment, coaching, mentoring, organizational culture

---

5 | **LEARNING OBJECTIVE**

Describe the controlling function, and explain the four steps in the control cycle.

controlling The process of measuring progress against goals and objectives and correcting deviations if results are not as expected

The Controlling Function

Controlling is the management function of keeping a company's activities on track toward previously established goals. The nature of control varies widely, from directly intervening in a process to modifying policies or systems in a way that enables employees to reach their objectives.

THE CONTROL CYCLE

A good way to understand managerial control is to envision the *control cycle,* a four-step process of (1) establishing performance standards based on the strategic plan, (2) measuring performance, (3) comparing performance to standards, and (4) responding as needed (see Exhibit 7). Of course, the specific steps taken in any situation depend on the industry, the company, the functional area within the company, and the manager's leadership style. In

EXHIBIT 7	The Control Cycle

The control cycle starts with setting strategic goals and then establishing performance standards that will tell managers and employers whether the company is on track to meet those goals. As the company goes about its business, performance is measured along the way and then compared against the standards. If performance meets or exceeds the standards, no corrective action is required. However, if performance is below the standards, management can either take steps to improve performance (if the standards are still considered achievable) or lower the standards and possibly reset the goals (if they are deemed to be unachievable).

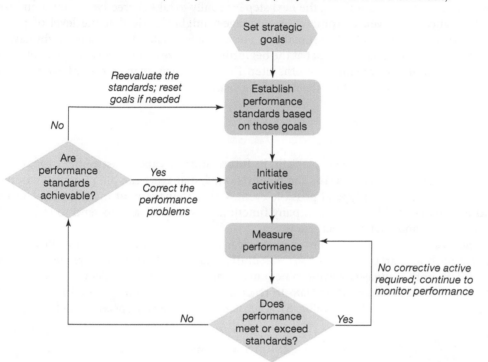

some cases, the control cycle is a formal process with explicit measurements, reports, and other tools. In others, control is subtle.

Establishing Performance Standards

In the first step of the control cycle, managers set **standards**, the criteria against which performance will be measured. Top managers set standards for the organization as a whole, such as revenue and profitability targets. Then for their individual areas of responsibility, middle and first-line managers set standards based on the overall organizational standards of performance.

Knowing which variables to use as standards and the values to set as performance targets can require a lot of experience and experimentation. Choosing variables that are truly meaningful rather than just easy to measure can also be a significant challenge. For example, *web analytics* software can deliver lots of data about online traffic, but it might not answer crucial questions such as why website visitors abandon their online shopping carts without buying anything.

A common approach to setting standards is **benchmarking**, comparing a company's key performance attributes with those of industry leaders.[31] For example, a company might discover that its average revenue per employee (total sales divided by the number of employees) is significantly lower than that of the best company in its industry. With this data point in hand, the company could look for ways to make its selling process more efficient, train sales people to go after bigger deals, or find other ways to improve the cost–revenue ratio.

One of the most important performance variables that fall under managerial control is **quality**—a measure of how closely activities or outcomes conform to predetermined standards and customer expectations. You'll learn more about quality in such areas as product and process quality in manufacturing and operations management and quality of hire in human resources.

standards Criteria against which performance is measured

benchmarking Collecting and comparing process and performance data from other companies

quality A measure of how closely a product conforms to predetermined standards and customer expectations

Measuring Performance and Responding as Needed

In the second step of the control cycle, managers assess performance, using both quantitative (specific, numerical) and qualitative (subjective) performance measures. For example, many companies now use a **balanced scorecard**, which monitors performance from multiple perspectives, including finances, operations, customer relationships, and the growth and development of employees and intellectual property.[32]

In the third step, managers compare performance with the established standards. If the level of performance falls short, the next step is usually to take corrective action to improve performance. However, in some cases, managers might decide that the level of performance originally hoped for is not realistic. For example, a sales department might have set aggressive goals for a new product at the beginning of the year, but then a tough competitor appeared out of nowhere three months later. The department manager may have no choice but to lower the sales target for the rest of the year.

CRISIS MANAGEMENT: MAINTAINING CONTROL IN EXTRAORDINARY CIRCUMSTANCES

No matter how well a company plans for its future, mistakes and catastrophes happen. And although not every specific crisis can be envisioned, managers can plan how the company should respond to each type of possible event. **Crisis management** involves the decisions and actions needed to keep a company functioning smoothly and to tend to stakeholder needs during and after an emergency.

Successful crisis management requires clear thinking and quick action while a crisis is unfolding, but smart companies don't wait until a crisis hits. A *crisis management* plan needs to contain both *contingency plans* to help managers make important decisions in a limited time frame and *communication plans* to reach affected parties quickly and forestall rumors and false information (see Exhibit 8). The plan should clearly specify which people are

balanced scorecard A method of monitoring the performance from four perspectives: finances, operations, customer relationships, and the growth and development of employees and intellectual property

crisis management Procedures and systems for minimizing the harm that might result from some unusually threatening situations

EXHIBIT 8	Communicating in a Crisis

Crisis situations test a manager's ability to make decisions and communicate clearly.

When a Crisis Hits:

Do	Don't
Prepare for trouble ahead of time by identifying potential problems, appointing and training a response team, and preparing and testing a crisis management plan.	Blame anyone for anything.
Get top management involved immediately.	Speculate in public.
	Refuse to answer questions.
Set up a news center for company representatives and the media that is equipped with phones, computers, and other electronic tools for preparing news releases and online updates. At the news center, take the following steps:	Release information that will violate anyone's right to privacy.
• Issue frequent news updates, and have trained personnel available to respond to questions around the clock.	Use the crisis to pitch products or services.
• Provide complete information packets to the news media as soon as possible.	Play favorites with media representatives.
• Prevent conflicting statements and provide continuity by appointing a single person trained in advance to speak for the company.	
• Tell receptionists and other employees to direct all phone calls to the designated spokesperson in the news center.	
• Provide updates when new information is available via blog postings, microblog updates, text messaging, Facebook, and other appropriate media.	
Tell the whole story—openly, completely, and honestly. If you are at fault, apologize.	
Demonstrate the company's concern by your statements and your actions.	

authorized to speak for the company, provide contact information for all key executives, and include a list of the news outlets and social media tools that will be used to disseminate information. In today's media-saturated environment, companies need to begin communicating literally within minutes after a crisis hits, to reach those who need information and to avoid the appearance of stonewalling or confusion.

REAL-TIME UPDATES
Learn More by Watching This Video

Crisis management in a social media landscape

Social media are changing every aspect of business communication, including crisis management. Learn how the rules are changing. Go to http://real-timeupdates.com/bia6 and click on Learn More. If you are using MyBizLab, you can access Real-Time Updates within the chapter or under Student Study Tools.

Checkpoint

LEARNING OBJECTIVE 5: Describe the controlling function, and explain the four steps in the control cycle.

SUMMARY: The controlling function consists of the activities and decisions involved in keeping a company's activities on track toward previously established goals. The four steps in the control cycle are establishing performance standards based on the strategic plan, measuring performance, comparing performance to standards, and responding as needed.

CRITICAL THINKING: (1) Why is it important to meet the needs of internal customers? (2) Is lowering performance standards in response to a failure to meet those standards necessarily a sign of "giving up"? Why or why not?

IT'S YOUR BUSINESS: (1) Do you benchmark your performance in any aspect of your personal or academic life? If yes, does it help you improve? If not, can you identify some aspects that could potentially benefit from benchmarking? (2) Think back over any crises you've faced in your life. How well did you respond? What would you do differently in a future crisis?

KEY TERMS TO KNOW: controlling, standards, benchmarking, quality, balanced scorecard, crisis management

Essential Management Skills

 6 LEARNING OBJECTIVE

Identify and explain four important types of managerial skills.

Managers rely on a number of skills to perform their functions and maintain a high level of quality in their organizations. These skills can be classified as *interpersonal*, *technical*, *conceptual*, and *decision making*. As managers rise through an organization's hierarchy, they may need to deemphasize skills that helped them in lower-level jobs and develop different skills. For instance, staying closely involved with project details is often a plus for first-line supervisors, but it can lead to serious performance issues for higher-level managers who should be spending time on more strategic issues.[33]

INTERPERSONAL SKILLS

The various skills required to communicate with other people, work effectively with them, motivate them, and lead them are **interpersonal skills**. Because managers mainly get things done through people at all levels of the organization, such skills are essential. Encouraging employees to work together toward common goals, interacting with employees and other managers, negotiating with partners and suppliers, developing employee trust and loyalty, and fostering innovation are all activities that require interpersonal skills.

Communication is the most important and pervasive interpersonal skill that managers use. Effective communication not only increases a manager's and an organization's

interpersonal skills Skills required to understand other people and to interact effectively with them productivity but also shapes the impressions made on colleagues, employees, supervisors, investors, and customers. In your role as a manager, communication allows you to perceive the needs of these stakeholders (your first step toward satisfying them), and it helps you respond to those needs.[34] Moreover, as the workforce becomes more diverse—and as more companies recognize the value of embracing diversity in their workforces—managers need to adjust their interactions with others, communicating in a way that considers the different needs, backgrounds, experiences, and expectations of their workforces.

TECHNICAL SKILLS

technical skills The ability and knowledge to perform the mechanics of a particular job

A person who knows how to operate a machine, prepare a financial statement, or use a web content management system has **technical skills**, the knowledge and ability to perform the tasks required in a particular job. Technical skills are most important at lower organizational levels because managers at those levels work directly with employees who are using the tools and techniques.

However, in today's increasingly technology-driven business environment, managers often need to have a solid understanding of the processes they oversee. One obvious reason is that they need to grasp the technical matters if they are to make smart decisions regarding planning, organizing, leading, and controlling. Another key reason for understanding technical matters is that demonstrating a level of technical aptitude gives managers credibility in the eyes of their employees. Maria Azua, a vice president at IBM, says her experience as a programmer earlier in her career helped her earn respect from the people she now leads. "They don't see me as a stodgy executive who doesn't understand, because I've done the same work they do."[35]

administrative skills Technical skills in information gathering, data analysis, planning, organizing, and other aspects of managerial work

Managers at all levels use **administrative skills**, which are the technical skills necessary to direct an organization, including scheduling, researching, analyzing data, and managing projects. Managers must know how to start a project or work assignment from scratch, map out each step in the process to its successful completion, develop project costs and timelines, and establish checkpoints at key project intervals.

CONCEPTUAL SKILLS

conceptual skills The ability to understand the relationship of parts to the whole

Managers need **conceptual skills** to visualize organizations, systems, markets, and solutions—both as complete entities on their own and as interrelated pieces of a whole. For example, the most visible part of a company's accounting system is probably its accounting software and the reports it produces, but the entire system also includes procedures, policies, and the people who process and use financial information. At the same time, the accounting system is also part of an overall business system and needs to integrate seamlessly with sales, purchasing, production, and other functions.

Conceptual skills are especially important to top managers because they are the strategists who develop the plans that guide the organization toward its goals. Managers use their conceptual skills to acquire and analyze information, identify both problems and opportunities, understand the competitive environment in which their companies operate, and develop strategies and plans. The ability to conceptualize solutions that don't yet exist, to see things as they could be rather than simply as how they are, is a vital skill for executives.

DECISION-MAKING SKILLS

decision-making skills The ability to identify a decision situation, analyze the problem, weigh the alternatives, choose an alternative, implement it, and evaluate the results

Decision-making skills involve the ability to define problems and opportunities and select the best course of action. To ensure thoughtful decision making, managers can follow a formal process such as the six steps highlighted in Exhibit 9:

1. **Recognize and define the problem or opportunity.** Most companies look for problems or opportunities by gathering customer feedback, conducting studies, or monitoring such warning signals as declining sales or profits, excess inventory buildup, or high customer turnover.

EXHIBIT 9	Steps in the Decision-Making Process

Following these six steps will help you make better decisions, particularly if you make a habit of applying what you learn from every decision outcome to the next decision you need to make.

2. **Identify and develop options.** The goal of this step is to develop a list of alternative courses of action. A problem that is easy to identify, such as a steady decline in sales revenue, might not have any easy answers. This step requires solid conceptual skills. Managers may need to break old thinking habits and throw away long-held assumptions in order to find promising solutions to tough problems.

3. **Analyze the options.** Once the ideas have been generated, they need to be studied and compared using criteria such as cost, feasibility, availability of resources, market acceptance, potential for revenue generation, and compatibility with the company's mission and vision. Some decisions present a simple yes/no choice, but others present multiple options that must be compared.

4. **Select the best option.** For some decisions, quantitative analysis can identify a clear choice from among the available options. For other decisions, however, managers might have to rely on intuition and experience to point the way.

5. **Implement the decision.** After an option has been selected, it's time to implement the decision.

6. **Monitor the results.** Finally, managers monitor the results of decisions over time to see whether the chosen alternative works, whether any new problems or opportunities arise because of the decision, and whether the decision should be modified to meet changing circumstances.

Although this list presents a logical and comprehensive method for decision making, it's important to realize that managers must frequently make decisions with incomplete or imperfect information. In other words, you may not have all the information you need, and you may not have as much time as you'd like to take. In fact, in today's fast-moving markets, the ability to make good decisions with incomplete information has become a highly valued management skill.[36]

For the latest information on managerial skills, visit http://real-timeupdates.com/bia6.

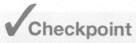

✔Checkpoint

LEARNING OBJECTIVE 6: Identify and explain four important types of managerial skills.

SUMMARY: Interpersonal skills are the abilities to communicate with, motivate, and lead others. Technical skills involve the "mechanics" of a particular job, including the administrative skills of project management. Conceptual skills are the abilities to visualize organizations, systems, markets, and solutions—even when they may not exist yet. Decision-making skills include defining problems and opportunities and selecting the best course of action to take in each case.

CRITICAL THINKING: (1) Why is trust a vital aspect of a manager's interpersonal skills? (2) What are the risks of defining problems or opportunities poorly prior to making decisions?

IT'S YOUR BUSINESS: (1) Would you succeed as a manager if you started a company right out of college, without having gained any experience as an employee in another company? Why or why not? (2) How would you rate your conceptual skills? Does "seeing the big picture" come easily to you? If not, how might you improve in this area?

KEY TERMS TO KNOW: interpersonal skills, technical skills, administrative skills, conceptual skills, decision-making skills

---

BEHIND THE SCENES   MyBizLab

CUSTOMERS BELIEVE IN WEGMANS BECAUSE WEGMANS BELIEVES IN ITS EMPLOYEES

The conventional response to all challenges in the retail grocery industry is to just keep squeezing everything—customer service, wages, employee benefits, training, and anything else—to keep prices low and still eke out a profit. However, CEO Danny Wegman and his colleagues are adamant that joining the discounters in a never-ending race to cut, cut, cut is not the Wegmans way. Instead, the company defines its mission as being "the very best at serving the needs of our customers." In pursuit of that mission, the company makes employees its number-one priority and counts on employees to then meet the needs of customers.

To compete successfully against both traditional grocers and Wal-Mart, Wegmans's strategy emphasizes a huge selection of products and employees who know food and love serving customers. The cheese department is a good example. Unlike the typical selection of two or three dozen varieties at other stores,

Wegmans offers four or five *hundred* varieties—and knowledgeable staff who can help customers select and serve the perfect cheese. In fact, chances are the department manager has been sent on a research tour of cheese-producing areas in Europe to gain first hand knowledge of the tastes and traditions of each region.

Such training is expensive, to be sure. Add in higher-than-average wages and employee benefits, and Wegmans's labor costs are higher than those of its competitors. Moreover, Wegmans managers exhibit a degree of personal concern for employees not often found in the hectic retail industry. As an example, when one manager whose job required frequent out-of-town travel learned that her mother had been diagnosed with cancer, Wegmans executives modified her responsibilities so that she could stay in town to care for her mother—before she even asked. Another indicator of the company's care for its employees is the investment it makes in their futures, even if those futures take them outside the company. More than 25,000 employees have received company scholarships, and roughly 4,000 employees attend college every year with financial assistance from Wegmans.

This investment in employees pays off in important ways. For starters, customers buy more when they understand how to use various products and are successful and satisfied with them. These positive experiences with Wegmans employees also help shoppers build emotional bonds with the store, further increasing customer loyalty. And employees who enjoy their work and feel they are treated with respect are more productive and less likely to leave for other jobs. Employee turnover (the percentage of the workforce that leaves and must be replaced every year) is a major expense for retailers, but turnover at Wegmans is a fraction of the industry average. As just one measure of the positive organizational culture at Wegmans, the company has made *Fortune* magazine's list of the 100 Best Companies to Work For every year since the survey began—and it is usually at or near the top of that list.

The mission to be the best at serving consumers extends to the company's decision-making style as well. For day-to-day decisions, laissez-faire management is widespread; executives want front-line employees to make whatever choices are needed to keep customers happy. As a Wegmans executive joked a few years ago, "We're a $3 billion company run by 16-year-old cashiers." The scheme must be working: The company is now approaching $6 billion in sales and shows no signs of slowing down.[37]

Critical Thinking Questions

1. Wegmans has always been managed by members of the Wegman family. Do you think the company could continue its winning ways if the next generation doesn't want to take over, forcing the company to hire someone from outside the family as CEO? Explain your answer.
2. Would the Wegmans approach work for a car dealer? A bookstore? A manufacturer of industrial goods? Explain you answers.
3. How does low employee turnover contribute to the distinct and positive corporate culture at Wegmans?

LEARN MORE ONLINE

Visit the Wegmans website, at **www.wegmans.com**, and click on "Careers." Read the information and watch the videos to learn more about working at Wegmans. Imagine yourself as someone who wants to join the company. Does the information on this website increase your interest in the company? Could you see yourself launching a career at Wegmans?

MyBizLab

Log on to www.mybizlab.com to access study and assessment aids associated with this chapter.

KEY TERMS

administrative skills
autocratic leaders
balanced scorecard
benchmarking
coaching
conceptual skills
controlling
crisis management
decision-making skills
democratic leaders
employee empowerment
first-line managers
goal
interpersonal skills
laissez-faire leaders
leading
management

management pyramid
managerial roles
mentoring
middle managers
mission statement
objective
organizational culture
organizing
participative management
planning
quality
standards
strategic plans
technical skills
top managers
values statement
vision statement

TEST YOUR KNOWLEDGE

Questions for Review

1. What is management? Why is it so important?
2. What is forecasting, and how is it related to the planning function?
3. What is the goal of crisis management?
4. How does leadership differ from management?
5. Why are interpersonal skills important to managers at all levels?

Questions for Analysis

6. Why is cognitive intelligence alone insufficient for effective leadership?
7. How do the three levels of management differ?
8. How do autocratic, democratic, and laissez-faire leadership styles differ?
9. Why are coaching and mentoring effective leadership techniques?

10. **Ethical Considerations.** When an organization learns about a threat that could place the safety of its workers or its customers at risk, is management obligated to immediately inform these parties of the threat? Explain your answer.

Questions for Application

11. Which would be more difficult to forecast 10 years from now: the number of 60-year-old residents or their average disposable income? Why?
12. What are your long-term goals? Develop a set of long-term career goals for yourself and several short-term objectives that will help you reach those goals. Make sure your goals are SMART.
13. This question was intentionally excluded from this edition.
14. **Concept Integration.** What is the principal difference between a business plan and a strategic plan?

EXPAND YOUR KNOWLEDGE

Discovering Career Opportunities

If you become a manager, how much of your day will be spent performing each of the four basic functions of management? This is your opportunity to find out. Arrange to shadow a manager (such as a department head, a store manager, or a shift supervisor) for a few hours. As you observe, categorize the manager's activities in terms of the four management functions and note how much time each activity takes. If observation is not possible, interview a manager in order to complete this exercise.

1. How much of the manager's time is spent on each of the four management functions? Is this the allocation you expected?
2. Ask whether this is a typical workday for this manager. If it isn't, what does the manager usually do differently? During a typical day, does this manager tend to spend most of the time on one particular function?
3. Of the four management functions, which does the manager believe is most important for good organizational performance? Do you agree?

Improving Your Tech Insights: Business Intelligence Systems

One of the maddening ironies of contemporary business is that many decision makers are awash in data but starved for true information and insights. *Business intelligence* (BI) systems, also called *business analytics*, aim to harness all that data and turn it into the information and insights that managers need.

Explore the business intelligence or business analytics products offered by several of the leading vendors, including Actuate (www.actuate.com), IBM (www.ibm.com), SAP Business Objects (www.sap.com), Information Builders (www.informationbuilders.com), Oracle (www.oracle.com), and SAS (www.sas.com). Research a system offered by one of these vendors, and in a brief email message to your instructor, summarize in your own words the system's benefits for managerial decision makers. (*Business intelligence* is a broad term that describes a variety of approaches, technologies, and specific products, so the field can be a bit confusing. Try several websites, if needed, to find a BI system that you can summarize briefly.)

PRACTICE YOUR SKILLS

Sharpening Your Communication Skills

Potential customers frequently visit your production facility before making purchase decisions. You and the people who report to you in the sales department have received extensive

training in etiquette issues because you deal with high-profile clients. However, the rest of the workforce has not received such training, and you worry that someone might inadvertently say or do something that would offend one of these potential customers. In a two-paragraph email, explain to the general manager why you think anyone who might come in contact with customers should receive basic etiquette training.

Building Your Team Skills

With a team of fellow students, perform a SWOT analysis for your college or university, from the perspective of recruiting new students. Identify as many significant strengths and weaknesses as you can think of, being as objective as possible. Next, identify any important opportunities and threats you can find, such as demographic shifts or changes in government funding. Summarize your findings in a chart modeled after Exhibit 3. Finally, evaluate your college's website and other promotional materials, if available, according to how well they present the school's strengths to prospective students.

Developing Your Research Skills

Find two articles in business journals or newspapers (print or online editions) that profile two senior managers who lead a business organization.

1. What experience, skills, and business background do the two leaders have? Do you see any striking similarities or differences in their backgrounds?

2. What kinds of business challenges have these two leaders faced? What actions did they take to deal with those challenges? Did they establish any long-term goals or objectives for their company? Did the articles mention a new change initiative?

3. Describe the leadership strengths of these two people as they are presented in the articles you selected. Is either leader known as a team builder? Long-term strategist? Shrewd negotiator? What are each leader's greatest areas of strength?

REFERENCES

1. Adapted from Wegmans website, accessed 13 August 2011, www .wegmans.com; "100 Best Companies to Work For," *Fortune*, accessed 13 August 2011, http://money.cnn.com/magazines/ fortune; Matthew Boyle, "The Wegmans Way," *Fortune*, 24 January 2005, www.fortune.com; William Conroy, "Rochester, N.Y.–Based Grocer Tops Magazine's Best Employer Rankings," *Asbury Park* (NJ) *Press*, 11 January 2005, www.ebsco.com; Matthew Boyle, "The Wegmans Way," *Fortune*, 24 January 2005, 62–68; "UCCNet Designated as U.S. Data Pool of Choice by Leading Retailers," UCCNet website, accessed 8 March 2005, www.uccnet .org; Joy Davis, "Caring for Employees Is Wegmans' Best Selling Point," (Rochester, NY) *Democrat and Chronicle*, 6 February 2005, www.democratandchronicle.com; Michael A. Prospero, "Employee Innovator: Wegmans," *Fast Company*, October 2004, 88; Matt Glynn, "Employees of Rochester, N.Y.–Based Grocer Celebrate Firm's Top Ranking," *Buffalo* (NY) *News*, 11 January 2005, www.ebsco.com.

2. Richard L. Daft, *Management*, 6th ed. (Mason, Ohio: Thompson South-Western, 2003), 5.

3. Anne Fisher, "Starting a New Job? Don't Blow It," *Fortune*, 24 February 2005, www.fortune.com.

4. Daniel S. Cochran, Fred R. David, and C. Kendrick Gibson, "A Framework for Developing an Effective Mission Statement," *Journal of Business Strategies*, Fall 2008, 27–39.

5. Welch Allyn website, accessed 13 August 2011, www.welchallyn .com.

6. Northrop Grumman website, accessed 13 August 2011, www .northropgrumman.com.

7. Enterprise Rent-A-Car Careers website, accessed 13 August 2011, www.erac.com.

8. Southern Cross Healthcare Group website, accessed 13 August 2011, www.schealthcare.co.uk; Datamonitor, "Southern Cross Healthcare Group SWOT Analysis," accessed 13 August 2011, www.ebsco.com.

9. "Southern Cross Healthcare Systems SWOT Analysis."

10. "Southern Cross Healthcare Systems SWOT Analysis."

11. "Southern Cross Healthcare Systems SWOT Analysis."

12. Alastair Dryburgh, "Don't You Believe It . . . It's Smart to Have SMART Objectives," *Management Today*, June 2011, 14.

13. Dean Foust, "Speaking up for the Organization Man," *BusinessWeek*, 9 March 2009, 78.

14. Steve Arneson, "Lead from the Middle," *Leadership Excellence*, March 2008, 19.

15. Why Middle Managers May Be the Most Important People in Your Company," Knowledge@Wharton, 25 May 2011, http:// knowledge.wharton.upenn.edu.

16. Daft, *Management*, 13.

17. Daft, *Management*, 514–515.

18. "Sometimes, EQ Is More Important Than IQ," CNN.com, 14 January 2005, www.cnn.com; Daniel Goleman, "What Makes a Leader?" *Harvard Business Review*, November–December 1998, 92–102; Shari Caudron, "The Hard Case for Soft Skills," *Workforce*, July 1999, 60–66.

19. James G. Clawson, *Level Three Leadership: Getting Below the Surface*, 2nd ed. (Upper Saddle River, N.J.: Prentice Hall, 2003), 116.

20. Cary Cherniss, "Emotional Intelligence: What It Is and Why It Matters," Consortium for Research on Emotional Intelligence in Organizations website, accessed 4 April 2009, www .eiconsortium.com.

21. Cherniss, "Emotional Intelligence: What It Is and Why It Matters."

22. Daniel Goleman, "Leadership That Gets Results," *Harvard Business Review*, March–April 2000, 78–90.

23. Herminia Ibarra and Morten T. Hansen, "Are You a Collaborative Leader?" *Harvard Business Review*, July/August 2011, 69–74.

24. Wegmans website, accessed 3 April 2009, www.wegmans.com.

25. Jeffrey D. Ford and Laurie W. Ford, "Decoding Resistance to Change," *Harvard Business Review*, April 2009, 99–103; Daft, *Management*, 382; Stephen Robbins and David DeCenzo, *Fundamentals of Management*, 4th ed. (Upper Saddle River, N.J.: Prentice Hall, 2003), 209.

26. Robbins and DeCenzo, *Fundamentals of Management*, 211; Daft, *Management*, 384, 396.

27. Robbins and DeCenzo, *Fundamentals of Management*, 210–211.

28. Ford and Ford, "Decoding Resistance to Change."
29. Paul Hebert, "People Don't Hate Change—They Hate You Trying to Change Them," Fistful of Talent blog, 6 April 2009, www.fistfuloftalent.com.
30. "High Standards," video, Wegmans website, accessed 3 April 2009, www.wegmans.com.
31. "Benchmarking," American Society for Quality, accessed 13 August 2011, http://asq.org.
32. Kevin J. Gregson, "Converting Strategy to Results," *American Venture*, September/October 2004, 16–18.
33. Robert E. Kaplan and Robert B. Kaiser, "Developing Versatile Leadership," *MIT Sloan Management Review*, Summer 2003, 19–26.
34. Courtland L. Bovée and John V. Thill, *Business Communication Today*, 9th ed. (Upper Saddle River, N.J.: Pearson Prentice Hall, 2008), 4.
35. Holly Ocasio Rizzo, "Patently Successful," *Hispanic Business*, April 2007, 34–36.
36. Geoff Gloeckler, "The Case Against Case Studies," *BusinessWeek*, 4 February 2008, 66–67.
37. See note 1.

GLOSSARY

administrative skills Technical skills in information gathering, data analysis, planning, organizing, and other aspects of managerial work

autocratic leaders Leaders who do not involve others in decision making

balanced scorecard A method of monitoring the performance from four perspectives: finances, operations, customer relationships, and the growth and development of employees and intellectual property

benchmarking Collecting and comparing process and performance data from other companies

coaching Helping employees reach their highest potential by meeting with them, discussing problems that hinder their ability to work effectively, and offering suggestions and encouragement to overcome these problems

conceptual skills The ability to understand the relationship of parts to the whole

controlling The process of measuring progress against goals and objectives and correcting deviations if results are not as expected

crisis management Procedures and systems for minimizing the harm that might result from some unusually threatening situations

decision-making skills The ability to identify a decision situation, analyze the problem, weigh the alternatives, choose an alternative, implement it, and evaluate the results

democratic leaders Leaders who delegate authority and involve employees in decision making

employee empowerment Granting decision-making and problem-solving authorities to employees so they can act without getting approval from management

first-line managers Those at the lowest level of the management hierarchy; they supervise the operating employees and implement the plans set at the higher management levels

goal A broad, long-range target or aim

interpersonal skills Skills required to understand other people and to interact effectively with them

laissez-faire leaders Leaders who leave most decisions up to employees, particularly those concerning day-to-day matters

leading The process of guiding and motivating people to work toward organizational goals

management pyramid An organizational structure divided into top, middle, and first-line management

management The process of planning, organizing, leading, and controlling to meet organizational goals

managerial roles Behavioral patterns and activities involved in carrying out the functions of management; includes interpersonal, informational, and decisional roles

mentoring A process in which experienced managers guide less-experienced colleagues in nuances of office politics, serving as a role model for appropriate business behavior, and helping to negotiate the corporate structure

middle managers Those in the middle of the management hierarchy; they develop plans to implement the goals of top managers and coordinate the work of first-line managers

mission statement A brief statement of why an organization exists; in other words, what the organization aims to accomplish for customers, investors, and other stakeholders

objective A specific, short-range target or aim

organizational culture A set of shared values and norms that support the management system and that guide management and employee behavior

organizing The process of arranging resources to carry out the organization's plans

participative management A philosophy of allowing employees to take part in planning and decision making

planning Establishing objectives and goals for an organization and determining the best ways to accomplish them

quality A measure of how closely a product conforms to predetermined standards and customer expectations

standards Criteria against which performance is measured

strategic plans Plans that establish the actions and the resource allocation required to accomplish strategic goals; they're usually defined for periods of two to five years and developed by top managers

technical skills The ability and knowledge to perform the mechanics of a particular job

top managers Those at the highest level of the organization's management hierarchy; they are responsible for setting strategic goals, and they have the most power and responsibility in the organization

values statement A brief articulation of the principles that guide a company's decisions and behaviors

vision statement A brief and inspirational expression of what a company aspires to be

Organization and Teamwork

BEHIND THE SCENES   REINVENTING THE RETAIL EXPERIENCE AT THE CONTAINER STORE

Effective team communication behind the scenes is key to creating positive customer experiences at The Container Score.

www.containerstore.com

Let's face it: Frontline jobs in retail don't have the greatest reputation. From an employee's perspective, these sales positions often combine low pay with high stress, leading to rapid burnout and frequent turnover. From a customer's perspective, frontline retail employees in some stores seem to fall into two categories: poorly trained, poorly motivated rookies or aggressive staffers who seem more intent on getting commissions than helping customers.

What if you wanted to put a new face on retailing? What if you wanted shopping to be a pleasant, welcome experience for both employees and customers? Too much to ask, perhaps?

This is the challenge Garrett Boone and Kip Tindell set for themselves when they opened the first The Container Store in Dallas, Texas. The chain, which has now expanded to several dozen locations across the country, carries a staggering array of products that help customers organize their lives. The Container Store has storage solutions for every room in the house, from the kitchen to the garage to the home office. Employees are expected to help customers solve every storage problem imaginable, from sweaters to DVDs to rubber stamps to tax records, with a variety of boxes, baskets, hangers, hooks, closet organizers, and more.

If you were in Boone's and Tindell's shoes, what steps would you take to break out of the retail rut and create a business that is satisfying for both customers and employees? How would you attract the best and the brightest employees and pull off a minor miracle in retailing—hanging on to them year after year? How would you organize the staffs in your stores? How much information would you share with them, and how would you communicate it?[1]

INTRODUCTION

Organization might not seem like the most exciting topic in the business world, but as Garrett Boone and Kip Tindell (profiled in the chapter-opening Behind the Scenes) would no doubt tell you, it is one of the most important. This chapter discusses the most important issues to consider in designing an organization structure, introduces you to the most common ways companies structure themselves, and explores the important matter of teamwork. It concludes with a look at the *unstructured organization*, which may be the structure of the future for many businesses. And if organization structures do strike you as a less-than-exhilarating topic, you might be surprised by some of the intriguing innovations going on with new technology-enabled work patterns.

Designing an Effective Organization Structure

A company's **organization structure** has a dramatic influence on the way employees and managers make decisions, communicate, and accomplish important tasks. This structure helps the company achieve its goals by providing a framework for managers to divide responsibilities, effectively distribute the authority to make decisions, coordinate and control the organization's work, and hold employees accountable for their work. In contrast, a poorly designed structure can create enormous waste, confusion, and frustration for employees, suppliers, and customers.

When managers design an organization's structure, they use an **organization chart** to provide a visual representation of how employees and tasks are grouped and how the lines of communication and authority flow (see Exhibit 1). An organization chart depicts the official design for accomplishing tasks that lead to achieving the organization's goals, a framework known as the *formal organization*. Every company also has an *informal organization*—the network of interactions that develop on a personal level among workers. Sometimes the interactions among people in the informal organization parallel their relationships in the formal organization, but often interactions transcend formal boundaries, such as when employees from various parts of the company participate in sports, social, or charitable activities together or use social media to reach across organizational barriers.

In the past, organizations were usually designed around management's desire to control workers, with everything set up in a hierarchy. Today, however, the goal of many companies is an **agile organization** that allows employees to respond quickly to customer needs and changes in the business environment and to bring the best mix of talents and resources to every challenge.

To identify the best structure for their organization, managers need to identify the organization's core competencies, clarify job responsibilities, define the chain of command, and organize the workforce in a way that maximizes effectiveness and efficiency.

IDENTIFYING CORE COMPETENCIES

Before they can decide how to organize, companies need to identify which business functions they should focus on themselves and which they should *outsource* to other companies. For instance, many companies outsource the payroll function because it doesn't make sense for them to invest the time needed to stay on top of frequent changes in income tax laws and related financial matters.[2] Many others outsource parts or all of the manufacturing process and concentrate on product design and marketing.

Core competencies are those activities in which a company excels and has the potential to create competitive advantages. For example, it's a virtual certainty that you've seen or used a product designed by Frog (www.frogdesign.com), a global design consultancy with talents in consumer research, design, and the commercialization phase of bringing new products to market. Frog has worked behind the scenes for many of the world's best-known companies, from Apple to Disney to Sony, but it stays focused on its core competencies in the research and development phase rather than becoming a manufacturer or consumers goods company itself.[3]

IDENTIFYING JOB RESPONSIBILITIES

Once a company knows what it wants to focus on, it can design each job needed to deliver those competencies. A key decision here is finding the optimal level of **work specialization**,

---

EXHIBIT 1	Simplified Organization Chart

An organization chart portrays the division of activities and responsibilities across a company.

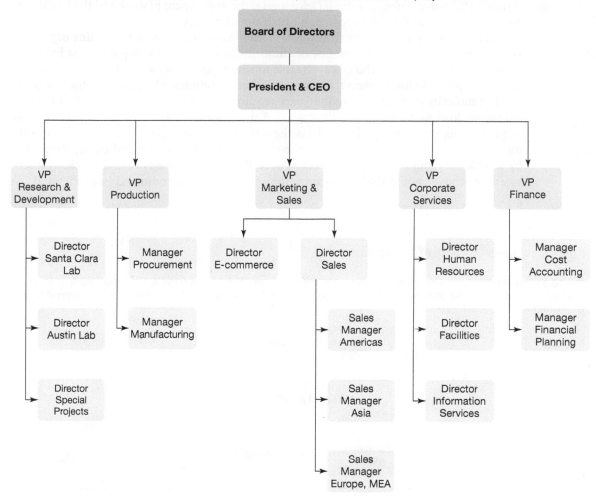

sometimes referred to as the *division of labor*—the degree to which organizational tasks are broken down into separate jobs.[4] Work specialization can improve organizational efficiency by enabling each worker to perform tasks that are well defined and that require specific skills. When employees concentrate on the same specialized tasks, they can perfect their skills and perform their tasks more quickly. In addition to aligning skills with job tasks, specialization prevents overlapping responsibilities and communication breakdowns.

However, organizations can overdo specialization. If a task is defined too narrowly, employees may become bored with performing the same limited, repetitive job over and over. They may also feel unchallenged and alienated. As you'll see later in the chapter, many companies are adopting a team-based approach to give employees a wider range of work experiences and responsibilities.

DEFINING THE CHAIN OF COMMAND

With the various jobs and their individual responsibilities identified, the next step is defining the **chain of command**, the lines of authority that connect the various groups and levels within the organization. The chain of command helps the organization function smoothly by making two things clear: who is responsible for each task and who has the authority to make decisions.

All employees have a certain amount of *responsibility*—the obligation to perform the duties and achieve the goals and objectives associated with their jobs. As they work toward the organization's goals, employees must also maintain their *accountability*, their obligation to report the results of their work to supervisors or team members and to justify any

chain of command A pathway for the flow of authority from one management level to the next outcomes that fall below expectations. Managers ensure that tasks are accomplished by exercising *authority*, the power to make decisions, issue orders, carry out actions, and allocate resources. Authority is vested in the positions that managers hold, and it flows down through the management pyramid. *Delegation* is the assignment of work and the transfer of authority, responsibility, and accountability to complete that work.[5]

line organization A chain-of-command system that establishes a clear line of authority flowing from the top down

line-and-staff organization An organization system that has a clear chain of command but that also includes functional groups of people who provide advice and specialized services

The simplest and most common chain-of-command system is known as **line organization** because it establishes a clear line of authority flowing from the top down, as Exhibit 1 depicts. Everyone knows who is accountable to whom, as well as which tasks and decisions each is responsible for. However, line organization sometimes falls short because the technical complexity of a firm's activities may require specialized knowledge that individual managers don't have and can't easily acquire. A more elaborate system, called **line-and-staff organization**, was developed to address the need to combine specialization with management control. In such an organization, managers in the chain of command are supplemented by functional groupings of people known as *staff*, who provide advice and specialized services but who are not in the line organization's overall chain of command (see Exhibit 2).

EXHIBIT 2	Simplified Line-and-Staff Structure

A line-and-staff organization divides employees into those who are in the direct line of command and those who provide staff (support) services to line managers at various levels. In this simplified example, the government affairs and legal departments report to the CEO but would provide support to any department in the company, as needed.

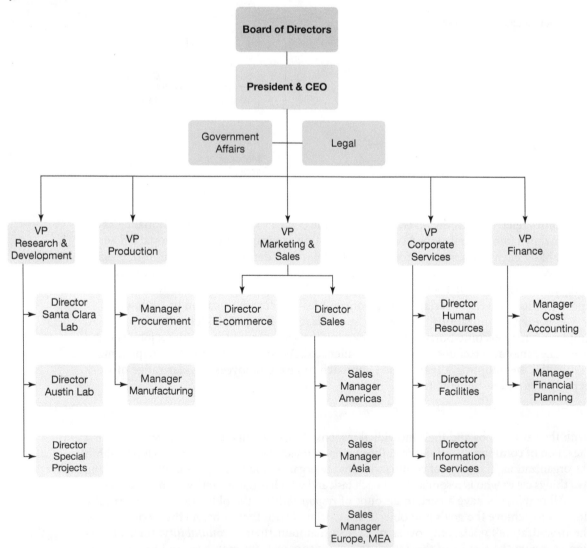

Span of Management

The number of people a manager directly supervises is called the **span of management**, or *span of control*. When a large number of people report directly to one person, that person has a wide span of management. This situation is common in *flat organizations* with relatively few levels in the management hierarchy. In contrast, *tall organizations* have many hierarchical levels, typically with fewer people reporting to each manager than is the case in a flat organization. In these organizations, the span of management is narrow.

To reduce the time it takes to make decisions, many companies are now flattening their organization structures by removing layers of management and pushing responsibilities and authority to lower levels (see Exhibit 3). Such moves have the additional benefit of putting senior executives in closer contact with customers and the daily action of the business.[6]

However, a flatter structure is not necessarily better in all respects. For example, it increases the demand on individual managers and gives them less time to spend with each employee. The Container Store, for instance, recently *added* a layer of management specifically to reduce the span of management in order to give each manager more time "to nurture and develop and train and counsel" his or her employees. "I think it's the best thing we ever did," Kip Tindell said, noting that even with the added costs, financial performance improved even more.[7]

Moreover, the deep experience base that midlevel managers have accrued, regarding both external market dynamics and internal working knowledge of the company itself, can be lost when these positions are eliminated. These managers can be particularly crucial in knowledge-driven industries, where insight and creative thinking are crucial to strategic decision making.[8]

Centralization Versus Decentralization

Organizations that focus decision-making authority near the top of the chain of command are said to be centralized. **Centralization** can benefit a company by utilizing top

span of management The number of people under one manager's control; also known as span of control

centralization Concentration of decision-making authority at the top of an organization

EXHIBIT 3	Flattening an Organization

In this simplified example, a layer of management (the business units) was removed to flatten the organization. In theory, this move reduces costs and speeds communication and decision making. Two obvious downsides are the increased span of management for the two group managers and the loss of knowledge and relationships that the business unit managers brought to the organization.

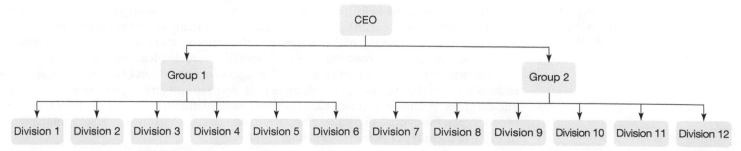

management's experience and broad view of organizational goals. In addition, it can help companies coordinate large undertakings more efficiently, accelerate decisions that might otherwise get bogged down in discussions and disagreements, and reduce the number of overlapping capabilities.

decentralization Delegation of decision-making authority to employees in lower-level positions

In contrast, **decentralization** pushes decision-making authority down to lower organizational levels—such as department heads—while control over essential companywide matters remains with top management. Implemented properly, decentralization can stimulate responsiveness because decisions don't have to be referred up the hierarchy.[9] However, decentralization does not work in every situation or in every company. At times, strong authority from the top of the chain of command may be needed to keep the organization focused on immediate goals. In other cases, a company may need strong central decision making to coordinate efforts on complex projects or to present a unified image to customers. Decentralization can also lead to inefficiencies, if multiple parts of a firm are doing the same basic task or replicating resources such as information systems. Managers should select the level of decision making that will most effectively serve the organization's needs, given the particular circumstances.[10]

✔ **Checkpoint**

LEARNING OBJECTIVE 1: Explain the major decisions needed to design an organization structure.

SUMMARY: The first major decision in designing an organization structure is identifying core competencies, those functions where the company excels and wants to focus. From there, managers can identify job responsibilities (who does what and how much work specialization is optimum), the chain of command, the span of management for each manager, and the degree of centralization or decentralization of decision-making authority.

CRITICAL THINKING: (1) What are the risks of a poorly designed organization structure? (2) How does a flat structure change the responsibilities of individual managers?

IT'S YOUR BUSINESS: (1) What would you say are your two or three core competencies at this point in your career? (2) Would you function better in a highly centralized or in a highly decentralized organization? Why?

KEY TERMS TO KNOW: organization structure, organization chart, agile organization, core competencies, work specialization, chain of command, line organization, line-and-staff organization, span of management, centralization, decentralization

---

2 | **LEARNING OBJECTIVE**

Define four major types of organization structure.

departmentalization Grouping people within an organization according to function, division, matrix, or network

Organizing the Workforce

The decisions regarding job responsibilities, span of management, and centralization versus decentralization provide the insights managers need in order to choose the best organization structure. The arrangement of activities into logical groups that are then clustered into larger departments and units to form the total organization is known as **departmentalization**.[11] The choice must involve both the *vertical structure*—how many layers the chain of command is divided into from the top of the company to the bottom—and the *horizontal structure*—how the various business functions and work specialties are divided across the company.

Variations in the vertical and horizontal designs of organizations can produce an almost endless array of structures—some flat, some wide; some simple and clear; others convoluted and complex. Within this endless variety of structure possibilities, most designs fall into one of four types: functional, divisional, matrix, and network. Companies can also combine two or more of these types in *hybrid structures*.

FUNCTIONAL STRUCTURES

The **functional structure** groups employees according to their skills, resource use, and job requirements. Common functional subgroups include research and development (R&D), production or manufacturing, marketing and sales, and human resources.

Splitting the organization into separate functional departments offers several advantages: (1) Grouping employees by specialization allows for the efficient use of resources and encourages the development of in-depth skills, (2) centralized decision making enables unified direction by top management, and (3) centralized operations enhance communication and the coordination of activities within departments. Despite these advantages, functional departmentalization can create problems with communication, coordination, and control, particularly as companies grow and become more complicated and geographically dispersed.[12] Moreover, employees may become too narrowly focused on departmental goals and may lose sight of larger company goals. Firms that use functional structures often try to counter these weaknesses by using *cross-functional teams* to coordinate efforts across functional boundaries, as you'll see later in the chapter.

functional structure Grouping workers according to their similar skills, resource use, and expertise

DIVISIONAL STRUCTURES

The **divisional structure** establishes self-contained suborganizations that encompass all the major functional resources required to achieve their goals—such as research and design, manufacturing, finance, and marketing.[13] In some companies, these divisions operate with great autonomy; such divisions are often called *business units*.

Many organizations use a structure based on *product divisions*—grouping around each of the company's products or family of products. In contrast, *process divisions* are based on the major steps of a production process. For example, Chevron has divisions (including separate companies in some cases) for such process steps as exploration, refining, pipeline distribution, shipping, and marketing.[14] The third approach, *customer divisions*, concentrates activities on satisfying specific groups of customers (see Exhibit 4). Finally, *geographic divisions* help companies respond more easily to local customs, styles, and product preferences.

Divisional structures offer both advantages and disadvantages. First, because divisions are self-contained, they can react quickly to change, making the organization more flexible. In addition, because each division focuses on a limited number of products, processes, customers, or locations, divisions can often provide better service to customers.

However, divisional departmentalization can also increase costs through duplication (if every product division has its own human resources department, for example). Furthermore, poor coordination between divisions may cause them to focus too narrowly on divisional goals and to neglect the organization's overall goals. Finally, divisions may compete with one another for resources and customers, causing rivalries that hurt the organization as a whole.[15]

divisional structure Grouping departments according to similarities in product, process, customer, or geography

EXHIBIT 4	Customer Division Structure

Focusing each division on a single type of customer can help a company market its products more efficiently and serve customers more responsively.

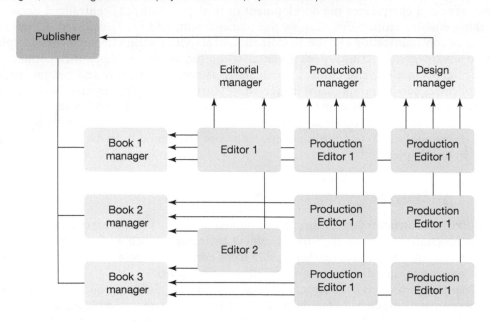

EXHIBIT 5 | **Matrix Structure**

In a matrix structure, each employee is assigned to both a functional group (with a defined set of basic functions, such as production management) and a project team (which consists of members of various functional groups working together on a project, such as bringing out a new consumer product). Even in this simplified model, you can sense how complex matrix management can be, when employees have multiple managers, and managers share employees with other projects and departments.

MATRIX STRUCTURES

matrix structure A structure in which employees are assigned to both a functional group and a project team (thus using functional and divisional patterns simultaneously)

A **matrix structure** is an organizational design in which employees from functional departments form teams to combine their specialized skills (see Exhibit 5). This structure allows the company to pool and share resources across divisions and functional groups. The matrix may be a permanent feature of the organization's design, or it may be established to complete a specific project.

The matrix structure can help big companies function like smaller ones by allowing teams to devote their attention to specific projects or customers without permanently reorganizing the company's structure. A matrix can also make it easier to deploy limited resources where they're needed the most and to bring a mix of skills to bear on important tasks. The pharmaceutical giant Bristol-Myers Squibb, for example, makes extensive uses of matrix structures to share expertise and to take advantage of resources spread throughout its global organization. According to executive Jane Luciano, "the matrix helps us to gain control of issues as they travel around the globe and to leverage economies of scale."[16]

On the downside, people in a matrix structure have to get used to reporting to two bosses, more communication and coordination is usually required, and struggles over resources can foster unhealthy competition between the two sides of the matrix.[17] Strong support from upper management, a culture that values collaboration, and hands-on attention from managers to make sure employees don't get lost in the matrix are essential to using this structural form successfully.[18]

REAL-TIME UPDATES
Learn More by Watching This Video

Surviving and thriving in the matrix

This brief overview identifies the portfolio of skills needed to make matrix management work for employees and manager alike. Go to http://real-timeupdates.com/bia6 and click on Learn More. If you are using MyBizLab, you can access Real-Time Updates within the chapter or under Student Study Tools.

NETWORK STRUCTURES

network structure A structure in which individual companies are connected electronically to perform selected tasks for a small headquarters organization

A **network structure** stretches beyond the boundaries of a company to connect a variety of partners and suppliers that perform selected tasks for a headquarters organization. Also called a *virtual organization*, a network organization can outsource engineering, marketing, research, accounting, production, distribution, or other functions. The design of a network structure stems from decisions about core competencies, with executives deciding which functions to focus on internally and which to outsource.

The network structure presents an intriguing blend of benefits and risks. A virtual structure can lower costs and increase flexibility, allowing a company to react more quickly to market demands. It can also boost competitiveness by taking advantage of specific skills and technologies available in other companies. On the other hand, relying too heavily on outsiders can render the company vulnerable to events beyond its control, such as key suppliers going out of business, offering the same goods and services to its competitors, or going into direct competition with the company. Moreover, outsourcing too many fundamental tasks, such as product design, can leave a company without any real competitive distinctions to speak of.[19] For more on contemporary uses of network structures, see "Managing an Unstructured Organization" later in this chapter.

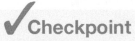
Checkpoint

LEARNING OBJECTIVE 2: Define four major types of organization structure.

SUMMARY: Companies can organize in four primary ways: by function, which groups employees according to their skills, resource use, and expertise; by division, which establishes self-contained departments formed according to similarities in product, process, customer, or geography; by matrix, which assigns employees from functional departments to interdisciplinary project teams and requires them to report to both a department head and a team leader; and by network, which connects separate companies that perform selected tasks for a headquarters organization.

CRITICAL THINKING: (1) Should The Container Store use the same organization structure in each of its stores around the country? Why or why not? (2) Why does a matrix structure create potential problems in the chain of command?

IT'S YOUR BUSINESS: (1) Do you think you would function well in a matrix structure, where you would need to report to two bosses simultaneously? Why or why not? (2) What about as a manger—could you share control with another manager?

KEY TERMS TO KNOW: departmentalization, functional structure, divisional structure, matrix structure, network structure

Organizing in Teams

3 LEARNING OBJECTIVE

Explain how a team differs from a group, and describe the six most common forms of teams.

While the vertical chain of command is a tried-and-true method of organizing for business, it is limited by the fact that decision-making authority is often located high up the management hierarchy, while real-world feedback from customers is usually located at or near the bottom of the hierarchy. Companies that organize vertically may become slow to react to change, and high-level managers may overlook many great ideas for improvement that originate in the lower levels of the organization. In addition, many business tasks and challenges demand the expertise of people who work in many parts of the company, isolated by the formal chain of command. To combat these issues, organizations such as The Container Store work to involve employees from all levels and functions of the organization in the decision-making process, using a variety of team formats in day-to-day operations.

This section looks at the most common types of teams, and the following two sections address the challenges of improving team productivity and fostering teamwork.

WHAT IS A TEAM?

A **team** is a unit of two or more people who work together to achieve a shared goal. Teams differ from work groups in that work groups interact primarily to share information and to make decisions to help one another perform within each member's area of responsibility.

team A unit of two or more people who share a mission and collective responsibility as they work together to achieve a goal

In other words, the performance of a work group is merely the summation of all group members' individual contributions.[20] In contrast, the members of a team have a shared mission and are collectively responsible for their work. By coordinating their individual efforts, the members of a successful team accomplish more together than they could individually, a result known as *synergy*.[21]

Although a team's goals may be set by either the team itself or someone in the formal chain of command, it is the job of the team leader to make sure the team stays on track to achieve those goals. Team leaders are often appointed by senior managers, but sometimes they emerge naturally as the team develops. Some teams complete their work and disband in a matter of weeks or months, while those working on complex projects can stay together for years.

TYPES OF TEAMS

The type, structure, and composition of individual teams within an organization depend on the organization's strategic goals and the objective for forming the team. Six common forms of teams are problem-solving teams, self-managed teams, functional teams, cross-functional teams, virtual teams, and social networks and virtual communities. Such classifications are not exclusive, of course. A problem-solving team may also be self-managed and cross-functional.

Problem-Solving Teams

A **problem-solving team** is assembled to find ways of improving quality, efficiency, or other performance measures. In some cases, a team attacks a single, specific problem and disbands after presenting or implementing the solution. In other cases, the team continues to meet over time, evaluating trends and fixing new problems as they crop up. At the Massachusetts Eye & Ear Infirmary, for example, a team charged with addressing insurance claim denials meets regularly to solve individual cases and to investigate systematic issues that might be causing problems with multiple patient cases.[22]

problem-solving team A team that meets to find ways of improving quality, efficiency, and the work environment

Self-Managed Teams

As the name implies, a **self-managed team** manages its own activities and requires minimal supervision. Typically, these teams control the pace of work and determination of work assignments. Fully self-managed teams select their own members. Self-managed teams represent a significant change for organizations and managers accustomed to rigid command-and-control structures. However, the potential advantages include lower costs, faster decision making, greater flexibility and innovation, and improved quality (stemming from the increased pride of ownership that an independent team feels in its work).[23]

self-managed team A team in which members are responsible for an entire process or operation

Functional Teams

A **functional team**, or *command team*, is organized along the lines of the organization's vertical structure and thus may be referred to as a *vertical team*. Such teams are composed of managers and employees within a single functional department, and the structure of a vertical team typically follows the formal chain of command. In some cases, the team may include several levels of the organizational hierarchy within the same functional department.[24]

functional team A team whose members come from a single functional department and that is based on the organization's vertical structure

Cross-Functional Teams

In contrast to functional teams, a **cross-functional team**, or *horizontal team*, draws together employees from various functional areas and expertise. Cross-functional teams can facilitate information exchange, help coordinate multiple organizational units, encourage new

cross-functional team A team that draws together employees from different functional areas solutions for organizational problems, and aid the development of new organizational policies and procedures.[25] However, collaborating across organizational boundaries can be challenging, particularly if participation on a cross-functional team conflicts with an individual's regular departmental workload or performance incentives.[26] Cross-functional teams often involve some form of matrix structure, even if temporarily, which brings with it the advantages and challenges of that form.

A cross-functional team can take on a number of formats. A **task force** is formed to work on a specific activity with a completion point. Several departments are usually involved so that all parties who have a stake in the outcome of the task are able to provide input. In contrast, a **committee** usually has a long life span and may become a permanent part of the organization structure. Committees typically deal with regularly recurring tasks, such as addressing employee grievances.

Virtual Teams

A **virtual team** is composed of members at two or more geographic locations. Research indicates that virtual teams can be as effective as face-to-face teams, as long as they take steps to overcome the disadvantages of not being able to communicate face to face.[27] For instance, some virtual teams meet in person at least once to allow the members to get to know one another before diving into their work.

To be successful, virtual teams should follow three basic rules. First, a virtual team should take full advantage of the diverse viewpoints, experiences, and skills of the various team members. One of the major benefits of virtual teams, in fact, is the opportunity to assemble teams of experts wherever they may be rather than rely on the people who happen to work in a given geographic location. Second, a virtual team should use technology to replicate resources that in-person teams rely on. *Shared online workspaces* are one of the most popular tools for virtual teams because they give everyone access to information and documents the team uses. Email and instant messaging (IM) can be effective for occasional communication, but many teams discover that either some people are left out of important message exchanges or everybody is deluged with every message. Blogs and wikis can cut down on the message overload and keep everyone in the loop. Third, a virtual team should take extra care to keep the team functioning effectively. The lack of the *nonverbal cues*, such as facial expressions and body language, which people rely on heavily when communicating in person, makes virtual communication especially challenging. Teleconferencing and videoconferencing can help in this regard.[28]

Social Networks and Virtual Communities

Social networking technologies are redefining teamwork and team communication by helping erase the constraints of geographic and organization boundaries. In addition to enabling and enhancing teamwork, social networks have numerous other business applications and benefits (see Exhibit 6 on the next page). While they are not always teams in the traditional sense, social networks and virtual communities often function as teams, helping people coordinate their efforts in pursuit of a shared goal. In addition, social networking has become an essential tool for many teams, matrix organizations, temporary organizations, and other structures.

Some companies use social networking technologies to form *virtual communities* or *communities of practice* that link employees with similar professional interests throughout the company and sometimes with customers and suppliers as well. The huge advantage that social networking brings is in identifying the best people to collaborate on each problem or project, no matter where they are around the world or what their official roles are in the organization. Such communities are similar to teams in many respects, but one major difference is in the responsibility for accumulating organizational knowledge over the long term. For example, the pharmaceutical company Pfizer has a number of permanent product safety communities that provide specialized advice on drug safety issues to researchers across the company.[29]

MyBizLab

Gain hands-on experience through an interactive, real-world scenario. This chapter's simulation entitled Team Management is located at **www.mybizlab.com.**

task force A team of people from several departments who are temporarily brought together to address a specific issue

committee A team that may become a permanent part of the organization and is designed to deal with regularly recurring tasks

virtual team A team that uses communication technology to bring together geographically distant employees to achieve goals

EXHIBIT 6	Business Uses of Social Networking Technology

Social networking has emerged as a powerful technology for enabling teamwork and enhancing collaboration in a variety of ways.

Business Challenge	Example of Social Networking in Action
Assembling teams	Identifying the best people, both inside the company and in other companies, to collaborate on projects
Fostering the growth of communities	Helping people with similar—or complementary—interests and skills find each other in order to provide mutual assistance and development
Accelerating the evolution of teams	Accelerating the sometimes slow process of getting to know one another and identifying individual areas of expertise
Maintaining business relationships	Giving people an easy way to stay in contact after meetings and conferences
Supporting customers	Allowing customers to develop close relationships with product experts within the company
Integrating new employees	Helping new employees navigate their way through the organization, finding experts, mentors, and other important contacts
Easing the transition after reorganizations and mergers	Helping employees connect and bond after internal staff reorganizations or mergers with other organizations
Overcoming structural barriers in communication channels	Bypassing the formal communication system in order to deliver information where it is needed in a timely fashion
Solving problems	Finding "pockets of knowledge" within the organization—the expertise and experience of individual employees
Preparing for major meetings and events	Giving participants a way to meet before an event takes place, helping to ensure that the meeting or event becomes more productive more quickly
Sharing and distributing information	Making it easy for employees to share information with people who may need it—and for people who need information to find employees who might have it
Finding potential customers, business partners, and employees	Identifying strong candidates by matching user profiles with current business needs and linking from existing member profiles

Sources: Adapted from Courtland L. Bovée and John V. Thill, *Business Communication Today*, 11th ed., (Upper Saddle River, N.J.: Pearson Prentice Hall, 2012), 181, 184; Christopher Carfi and Leif Chastaine, "Social Networking for Businesses & Organizations," white paper, Cerado website, accessed 13 August 2008, www.cerado.com; Anusorn Kansap, "Social Networking," PowerPoint presentation, Silpakorn University, accessed 14 August 2008, http://real-timeupdates.com; "Social Network Websites: Best Practices from Leading Services," white paper, 28 November 2007, FaberNovel Consulting www.fabernovel.com.

Social networking can also help a company maintain a sense of community even as it grows beyond the size that normally permits a lot of daily interaction. At the online retailer Zappos, fostering a supportive work environment is the company's top priority. To encourage the sense of community among its expanding workforce, Zappos uses social networking tools to track employee connections and encourage workers to reach out and build relationships.[30]

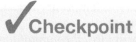 Checkpoint

LEARNING OBJECTIVE 3: Explain how a team differs from a group, and describe the six most common forms of teams.

SUMMARY: The primary difference between a team and a work group is that the members of a team work toward a shared goal, whereas members of a work group work toward individual goals. The six most common forms of teams are (1) problem-solving teams, which seek ways to improve a situation and then submit their recommendations; (2) self-managed teams, which manage their own activities and seldom require supervision; (3) functional teams, which are composed of employees within a single functional department; (4) cross-functional teams, which draw together employees from various departments and expertise in a number of formats such as task forces and committees; (5) virtual teams, which bring together employees from distant locations; and (6) social networks and virtual communities, which are typically less structured than teams but nonetheless share many aspects of teamwork and promote shared goals.

CRITICAL THINKING: (1) How might the work of a task force or committee disrupt the normal chain of command in an organization? (2) Should new hires with no business experience be assigned to virtual teams? Why or why not?

IT'S YOUR BUSINESS: (1) Would you function well in a virtual team setting that offered little or no chance for face-to-face contact with your colleagues? Why or why not? (2) If you had two similar job offers, one with a company that stresses teamwork and another with a company that stresses independent accomplishment, which would you choose? Why?

KEY TERMS TO KNOW: team, problem-solving team, self-managed team, functional team, cross-functional team, task force, committee, virtual team

Ensuring Team Productivity

Even though teams can play a vital role in helping an organization reach its goals, they are not appropriate for every situation, nor do they automatically ensure higher performance. Understanding the advantages and disadvantages of working in teams and recognizing the characteristics of effective teams are essential steps in ensuring productive teamwork.

4 | LEARNING OBJECTIVE

Highlight the advantages and disadvantages of working in teams, and list the characteristics of effective teams.

ADVANTAGES AND DISADVANTAGES OF WORKING IN TEAMS

Managers must weigh the pros and cons of teams when deciding whether and how to use them. A well-run team can provide a number of advantages:[31]

- **Higher-quality decisions.** Many business challenges require the input of people with diverse experiences and insights, and using teams can be an effective way to bring these multiple perspectives together. Working in teams can unleash new levels of creativity and energy in workers who share a sense of purpose and mutual accountability. Effective teams can be better than top-performing individuals at solving complex problems.[32]

- **Increased diversity of views.** Team members can bring a variety of perspectives to the decision-making process, which can result in more successful actions and decisions, as long as these diverse viewpoints are guided by a shared goal.[33]

- **Increased commitment to solutions and changes.** Employees who feel they've had an active role in making a decision are more likely to support the decision and encourage others to accept it.

- **Lower levels of stress and destructive internal competition.** When people work together toward a common goal rather than competing for individual recognition, their efforts and energies tend to focus on the common good. The sense of belonging to a group and being involved in a collective effort can also be a source of job satisfaction for most people.

- **Improved flexibility and responsiveness.** Because they don't have the same degree of permanence as formal departments and other structural elements, teams are easier to reformulate to respond to changing business needs.

REAL-TIME UPDATES
Learn More by Listening to This Podcast

Taking teams to the top

Listen to these hands-on techniques for developing, launching, leading, and evaluating world-class teams. Go to http://real-timeupdates.com/bia6 and click on Learn More. If you are using MyBizLab, you can access Real-Time Updates within the chapter or under Student Study Tools.

Furthermore, teams fill an individual worker's need to belong to a group, reduce employee boredom, increase feelings of dignity and self-worth, and reduce stress and tension among workers. While the advantages of teamwork help explain the wide spread popularity of teams in today's business environment, teams also present a number of potential disadvantages, particularly if they are poorly structured or poorly managed:[34]

- **Inefficiency.** Even successful teams need to be on constant watch for inefficiency—spending more time than necessary on their decisions and activities or simply losing sight of the team's ultimate goal. Potential sources of inefficiency include internal politics, too much emphasis on consensus, and excessive socializing among team members.
- **Groupthink.** Like all social structures, business teams can generate tremendous pressures to conform with accepted norms of behavior. **Groupthink** occurs when these peer pressures cause individual team members to withhold contrary or unpopular opinions. The result can be decisions that are worse than the team members might have made individually. Overcoming fear of conflict is essential to avoiding groupthink, which may require some coaching from experienced managers and continued attention to rules of engagement when conflict does arise.
- **Diminished individual motivation.** Balancing the need for group harmony with individual motivation is a constant issue with teams. Without the promise of individual recognition and reward, high-performance individuals may feel less incentive to keep working at high levels.
- **Structural disruption.** Teams can become so influential within an organization that they compete with the formal chain of command, in effect superimposing a matrix on the existing structure.
- **Excessive workloads.** The time and energy required to work on teams isn't free, and when team responsibilities are layered on top of individuals' regular job responsibilities, the result can be overload.

groupthink Uniformity of thought that occurs when peer pressures cause individual team members to withhold contrary or unpopular opinions

CHARACTERISTICS OF EFFECTIVE TEAMS

To be successful, teams need to be designed as carefully as any other part of an organization structure. Establishing the size of the team is one of the most important decisions; the optimal size for teams is generally thought to be between 5 and 12 members. Teams with fewer members may lack the necessary range of skills, while members of larger teams may have difficulty bonding properly and communicating efficiently. However, managers sometimes have no choice; complex challenges such as integrating two companies or designing complicated products can require teams of up to 100 people or more.[35]

The types of individuals on a team is also vital. People who assume the *task-specialist role* focus on helping the team reach its goals. In contrast, members who take on the *socioemotional role* focus on supporting the team's emotional needs and strengthening the team's social unity. Some team members are able to assume dual roles, contributing to the task and still meeting members' emotional needs. These members often make effective team leaders. At the other end of the spectrum are members who are *nonparticpators*, contributing little to reaching the team's goals or to meeting members' socioemotional needs. Obviously, a team staffed with too many inactive members isn't going to accomplish much of anything. Exhibit 7 outlines the behavior patterns associated with each of these roles.

Beyond the right number of the right sort of people, effective teams share a number of other characteristics:[36]

- **Clear sense of purpose.** Team members clearly understand the task at hand, what is expected of them, and their respective roles on the team.
- **Open and honest communication.** The team culture encourages discussion and debate. Team members speak openly and honestly, without the threat of anger, resentment, or retribution. They listen to and value feedback from others. As a result, all members participate. Conversely, members who either don't share valuable information because they don't understand that it's valuable or, worse, withhold information as a way to maintain personal power can undermine the team's efforts.[37]
- **Creative thinking.** Effective teams encourage original thinking, considering options beyond the usual.

EXHIBIT 7	Team Member Roles

Team members assume one of these four roles. Members who assume a dual role—emphasizing both task progress and people needs—often make the most effective team leaders.

Focus on task behaviors

Task-Specialist Role
- Focuses on task accomplishment over human needs
- Important role, but if adopted by everyone, team's social needs won't be met

Dual Role
- Focuses on both task accomplishment and people needs
- Often important but not essential if team is balanced with task and socioemotional roles

Nonparticpator
- Contributes little to either task or people needs of team
- A distraction at best and counterproductive "dead weight" at worst

Socioemotional Role
- Focuses on people needs rather than getting things done
- Important contribution, but if adopted by too many members, team won't get its work done

Focus on social behaviors

- **Accountability.** Team members commit to being accountable to each other.
- **Focus.** Team members get to the core issues of the problem and stay focused on key issues.
- **Decision by consensus.** On effective teams, all decisions are arrived at by consensus. But this point comes with a warning: Teams that worry too much about consensus can take a long time to make decisions. In many cases, members need to commit to the group's decision even though they may not support it 100 percent.

For a brief review of characteristics of effective teams, see Exhibit 8 on the next page.

✓ Checkpoint

LEARNING OBJECTIVE 4: Highlight the advantages and disadvantages of working in teams, and list the characteristics of effective teams.

SUMMARY: Teamwork has the potential to produce higher-quality decisions, increase commitment to solutions and changes, lower stress and destructive internal competition, and improve flexibility and responsiveness. The potential disadvantages include inefficiency, groupthink, diminished individual motivation, structural disruption, and excessive workloads. Effective teams have a clear sense of purpose, communicate openly and honestly, build a sense of fairness in decision making, think creatively, maintain accountability, stay focused on key issues, and emphasize consensus (while balancing the need for quick decision making).

CRITICAL THINKING: (1) Is groupthink similar to peer pressure? Why or why not? (2) Is supporting a group decision you don't completely agree with always a case of groupthink? Explain your answer.

IT'S YOUR BUSINESS: (1) How would you characterize the experience you've had working in teams throughout your high school and college years? (2) How can you apply experience gained on athletic teams and other collaborative activities to the business world?

KEY TERM TO KNOW: groupthink

EXHIBIT 8   **Characteristics of Effective Teams**

Effective teams practice these good habits.

Make Effective Teamwork a Top Management Priority

- Recognize and reward group performance where appropriate

- Provide ample training opportunities for employees to develop team skills

Select Team Members Wisely

- Involve key stakeholders and decision makers

- Limit team size to the minimum number of people needed to achieve team goals

- Select members with a diversity of views

- Select creative thinkers

Build a Sense of Fairness in Decision Making

- Encourage debate and disagreement without fear of reprisal

- Allow members to communicate openly and honestly

- Consider all proposals

- Build consensus by allowing team members to examine, compare, and reconcile differences—but don't let a desire for 100 percent consensus bog the team down

- Avoid quick votes

- Keep everyone informed

- Present all the facts

Manage Conflict Constructively

- Share leadership

- Encourage equal participation

- Discuss disagreements openly and calmly

- Focus on the issues, not the people

- Don't let minor disagreements boil over into major conflicts

Stay on Track

- Make sure everyone understands the team's purpose

- Communicate what is expected of team members

- Stay focused on the core assignment

- Develop and adhere to a schedule

- Develop rules and follow norms

---

5 LEARNING OBJECTIVE

Review the five stages of team development, and explain why conflict can arise in team settings.

Fostering Teamwork

Because teams are composed of unique individuals with different perspectives, the interpersonal relationships among team members require careful consideration. Two particularly important issues are team development and team conflict.

TEAM DEVELOPMENT

Teams often require some time and developmental change to reach full productive speed, and team leaders need to understand this process to help groups reach their potential as quickly as possible. Several models of team development have been proposed over the years. One well-known model defined by researcher Bruce Tuckman identifies five stages of development, nicknamed *forming, storming, norming, performing,* and *adjourning*:[38]

- **Forming.** The forming stage is a period of orientation and ice-breaking. Members get to know each other, determine what types of behaviors are appropriate within the group, identify what is expected of them, and become acquainted with each other's task orientation.
- **Storming.** In the storming stage, members show more of their personalities and become more assertive in establishing their roles. Conflict and disagreement often arise during the storming stage, as members jockey for position or form coalitions to promote their own perceptions of the team's mission. While it is necessary for this storming to occur, team members need to make sure the team doesn't lapse into counterproductive behaviors before it has a chance to resolve these emerging conflicts.
- **Norming.** During the norming stage, conflicts are resolved, and team harmony develops. Members come to understand and accept one another, reach consensus on who the leader is (if that hasn't already been established formally), and reach agreement on member roles.
- **Performing.** In the performing stage, members are really committed to the team's goals. Problems are solved, and disagreements are handled in the interest of task accomplishment.
- **Adjourning.** Finally, if the team has a specific task to perform, it goes through the adjourning stage after the task has been completed. In this stage, issues are wrapped up, and the team is dissolved.

As a team moves through these stages of development, two important developments occur. First, it develops a certain level of **cohesiveness**, a measure of how committed the members are to the team's goals. Cohesiveness is reflected in meeting attendance, team interaction, work quality, and goal achievement. Cohesiveness is influenced by many factors, particularly competition and evaluation. If a team is in competition with other teams, cohesiveness increases as the team strives to excel. In addition, if a team's efforts and accomplishments are recognized by the organization, members tend to be more committed to the team's goals. Strong team cohesiveness generally results in high morale. Moreover, when cohesiveness is coupled with strong management support for team objectives, teams tend to be more productive.

cohesiveness A measure of how committed team members are to their team's goals

The second development is the emergence of **norms**, informal but often powerful standards of conduct that members share and use to guide their behavior. Norms define acceptable behavior by setting limits, identifying values, and clarifying expectations. By encouraging consistent behavior, norms boost efficiency and help ensure the group's survival. Individuals who deviate from these norms can find themselves ridiculed, isolated, or even removed from the group entirely. (This fear is the leading cause of groupthink, by the way.) Norms can be established in various ways: from early behaviors that set precedents for future actions, from significant events in the team's history, from behaviors that come to the team through outside influences, and from a leader's or member's explicit statements that have an impact on other members.[39]

norms Informal standards of conduct that guide team behavior

TEAM CONFLICT

As teams mature and go about their work, conflicts can arise. Although the term *conflict* sounds negative, conflict isn't necessarily bad. It can be *constructive* if it brings important issues into the open, increases the involvement of team members, and generates creative ideas for solving a problem. Teamwork isn't necessarily about happiness and harmony; even teams that have some interpersonal friction can excel if they have effective leadership and team players committed to strong results. As teamwork experts Andy Boynton and Bill Fischer put it, "Virtuoso teams are not about getting polite results."[40]

REAL-TIME UPDATES
Learn More by Listening to This Podcast

Collaboration done right

Hear UC Berkeley's Morten Hansen explain the difference between good collaboration and bad collaboration. Go to http://real-timeupdates.com/bia6 and click on Learn More. If you are using MyBizLab, you can access Real-Time Updates within the chapter or under Student Study Tools.

In contrast, conflict is *destructive* if it diverts energy from more important issues, destroys the morale of teams or individual team members, or polarizes or divides the team.[41] Destructive conflict can lead to *win-lose* or *lose-lose* outcomes, in which one or both sides lose, to the detriment of the entire team. If you approach conflict with the idea that both sides can satisfy their goals to at least some extent (a *win-win strategy*), you can minimize losses for everyone. For a win-win strategy to work, everybody must believe that (1) it's possible to find a solution that both parties can accept, (2) cooperation is better for the organization than competition, (3) the other party can be trusted, and (4) greater power or status doesn't entitle one party to impose a solution.

Causes of Team Conflict

Team conflict can arise for a number of reasons. First, individuals may feel they are in competition for scarce or declining resources, such as money, information, and supplies. Second, team members may disagree over responsibilities. Third, poor communication can lead to misunderstandings and misperceptions. In addition, withholding information can undermine trust among members. Fourth, basic differences in values, attitudes, and personalities may lead to clashes. Fifth, power struggles may result when one party questions the authority of another or when people or teams with limited authority attempt to increase their power or exert more influence. Sixth, conflicts can arise because individual team members are pursuing different goals.[42]

Solutions to Team Conflict

As with any other human relationship, the way a team approaches conflict depends to a large degree on how well the team was functioning in the first place. A strong, healthy team is more likely to view a conflict as simply another challenge to overcome—and it can emerge from the conflict even stronger than before. In contrast, a generally dysfunctional team can disintegrate even further when faced with a new source of conflict.

The following seven measures can help team members successfully resolve conflict:

- **Proactive attention.** Deal with minor conflict before it becomes major conflict.
- **Communication.** Get those directly involved in a conflict to participate in resolving it.
- **Openness.** Get feelings out in the open before dealing with the main issues.
- **Research.** Seek factual reasons for a problem before seeking solutions.
- **Flexibility.** Don't let anyone lock into a position before considering other solutions.
- **Fair play.** Insist on fair outcomes and don't let anyone avoid a fair solution by hiding behind the rules.
- **Alliance.** Get opponents to fight together against an "outside force" instead of against each other.

Team members and team leaders can also take several steps to prevent conflicts. First, by establishing clear goals that require the efforts of every member, the team reduces the chance that members will battle over their objectives or roles. Second, by developing well-defined tasks for each member, the team leader ensures that all parties are aware of their responsibilities and the limits of their authority. Finally, by facilitating open communication, the team leader can ensure that all members understand their own tasks and objectives as well as those of their teammates. Communication builds respect and tolerance, and it provides a forum for bringing misunderstandings into the open before they turn into full-blown conflicts.

 Checkpoint

LEARNING OBJECTIVE 5: Review the five stages of team development, and explain why conflict can arise in team settings.

SUMMARY: Several models have been proposed to describe the stages of team development; the well-known model defined by researcher Bruce Tuckman identifies the stages as *forming*, *storming*, *norming*, *performing*, and *adjourning*. In the forming stage, team members become acquainted with each other and with the group's purpose. In the storming stage, conflict often arises as coalitions and power struggles develop. In the norming stage, conflicts are resolved and harmony develops. In the performing stage, members focus on achieving the team's goals. In the adjourning stage, the team dissolves upon completion of its task. Conflict can arise from competition for scarce resources; confusion over task responsibility; poor communication and misinformation; differences in values, attitudes, and personalities; power struggles; and incompatible goals.

CRITICAL THINKING: (1) How can a team leader know when to step in when conflict arises and when to step back and let the issue work itself out? (2) What are the risks of not giving new teams the time and opportunity to "storm" and "norm" before tackling the work they've been assigned?

IT'S YOUR BUSINESS: (1) Have you ever had to be teammates (in any activity) with someone you simply didn't like on a personal level? If so, how did this situation affect your performance as a team member? (2) Have you ever had to adapt your personality in order to succeed on a particular team? Was this a positive or negative experience?

KEY TERMS TO KNOW: cohesiveness, norms

Managing an Unstructured Organization

6   **LEARNING OBJECTIVE**

Explain the concept of an unstructured organization, and identify the major benefits and challenges of taking this approach.

Much of the thinking in past decades about organization strategies in business centered on the best way to structure a company to compete effectively and operate efficiently. However, a number of companies are concluding that the best way to organize might be with little or no structure at all, at least in terms of the traditional forms. Such **unstructured organizations** are using digital technologies—and global socioeconomic changes enabled by these technologies—to rapidly form and re-form work patterns that bear almost no resemblance to the classic structures.

unstructured organization An organization that doesn't have a conventional structure but instead assembles talent as needed from the open market; the virtual and networked organizational concepts taken to the extreme

These innovators are experimenting with various combinations of virtual organizations, networked organizations, crowdsourcing, outsourcing, and *hyperspecialization*, the division of work into narrowly focused tasks that can be assigned to specialists who become highly skilled at those discrete tasks.[43] The new "formless forms" are enabled by cloud computing, mobile communication, online collaboration platforms, and all manner of social networking tools. All of these elements have been in use for some time, but the mashup of new thinking and new technology promises to unleash them in revolutionary ways. In a sense, by binding together a temporary organization, these technologies take the place of the lines and boxes that define a traditional organization chart.

Just about any category and skill level of work seems a possible candidate for these new approaches—and particularly those that can be expressed digitally. Professions and functions already being affected include software development, product design, visual design, scientific research, legal research, business writing, clerical work, and customer support.[44]

For example, a solo entrepreneur can now quickly assemble a product development team to conceptualize and design a product, then immediately disassemble that team and build a manufacturing team to make the product, and then assemble a sales and customer support team to get the product on the market—all without hiring a single employee. Moreover, this entrepreneur could tap into some of the best technical talent in the world, with top scientists, engineers, and software developers competing to see who can do the best job on the new product. And rather than taking months to establish a company by recruiting employees, leasing office space, hiring supervisors, buying computers, setting up a payroll system, training staffers, and doing all the many other tasks involved in running a conventional company, this entrepreneur could sit at home in his or her pajamas and in a matter of days create an essentially formless company that successfully competes in the global marketplace.

The software development company TopCoder (www.topcoder.com) offers a great illustration of the potential of this new way of working. Billing itself as "The world's largest competitive community for software development and digital creation," TopCoder boasts a membership of more than 300,000 computer scientists and software engineers (including many who are still in college), representing virtually every country in the world. Clients such as our pajama-clad entrepreneur present TopCoder with one or more design challenges, and the members then compete to come up with the best solutions.[45] Instead of auditioning several regular vendors and hoping to make the right choice or hiring a small staff of generalists and hoping they'll be able to handle the many specialized tasks involved in developing the software for a new product, our entrepreneur could get the best of the best working on each part of the design. And when the design work is completed, the various TopCoder members move on to compete on other client projects, and the entrepreneur moves on to assembling teams of manufacturing and marketing specialists.

Just where these changes are taking the business enterprise is difficult to guess because the revolution is still underway. Some firms may adopt these structureless approaches extensively, while others may use them for specific projects. Even if you spend your career in a conventionally structured company, these changes are likely to affect you because they are accelerating the pace of business, influencing the worldwide talent market, and even changing the nature of work itself in some cases (such as introducing project-by-project talent competition).

The following sections take a look at some of the potential benefits and points of concern that are emerging in relation to these new approaches to organization (see Exhibit 9 for a summary).

POTENTIAL BENEFITS OF UNSTRUCTURED ORGANIZATIONS

Unstructured organization promises a number of benefits for firms of all sizes, from entrepreneurs who apply the concept to their entire operations to larger firms that use it for specific parts of the company or individual projects:[46]

- **Increased agility.** In many instances, virtual organizations can be assembled, reconfigured as needed, and disassembled much faster than a conventional employee-based organization can be created, changed, or dismantled. This agility makes it easier to jump on emerging market trends and then change course when the market changes again.
- **Lower fixed costs and more flexible capacity management.** Hiring employees to build organizational capacity increases a company's *fixed costs*, those costs that are incurred regardless of production or sales volumes. With the unstructured approach, companies have much more flexibility in adjusting their expense levels to match revenue levels.
- **Access to otherwise unreachable talent.** "Talent markets" such as TopCoder give many more companies access to these highly developed and often hyperspecialized talents. Companies that might never be able to attract or afford top experts in a field can essentially rent them project by project instead.
- **Benefits of competition.** While most employees are motivated to do good work most of the time, independent individuals working through TopCoder, Guru (www.guru.com), LiveOps (www.liveops.com), and other aggregators must do their best on every single project—and compete with other independents in what is essential a global marketplace—or risk not getting more assignments. Companies that engage contract talent clearly benefit from this competition. In addition, talent markets such as TopCoder and InnoCentive actually structure projects as competitions, in which potential solution providers compete to offer the best ideas and work products.

For workers, the unstructured model also offers several potential benefits:[47]

- **Performance-based evaluation.** Workers tend to be evaluated almost entirely on measurable performance, project by project—on what they can do for a client, not on who they know in the executive suite, where they went to college, or what they did last year.

EXHIBIT 9	Benefits and Challenges of Unstructured Organizations

The unstructured organization is an extreme version of the virtual and networked models, in which a company assembles freelance talent as needed from the open market rather than hiring and organizing employees in a conventional organizational structure.

Potential Benefits		Potential Challenges	
For Companies	**For Workers**	**For Companies**	**For Workers**
• **Increased agility:** Companies can respond to or create opportunities faster and then reorganize and move on when needed.	• **Performance-based evaluation:** The only thing that matters is getting the job done.	• **Complexity and control issues:** Workers often have competing demands on their time and attention, and managers lack many of the organizational control and incentive "levers" that a regular company has.	• **Uncertainty:** Workers can't be sure they'll have work from one project to the next.
• **Lower fixed costs:** Fewer employees means fewer bills to pay every month.	• **Freedom and flexibility:** Workers have more leeway in choosing which projects they want and how much they want to work.	• **Uncertainty:** Without staff at the ready, companies won't always know if they'll be able to get the talent they need.	• **Loss of meaning and connection:** Independent workers don't get the same sense of working together for a larger, shared purpose that employees get.
• **More flexible capacity management:** Firms can ramp capacity up and down more quickly and with less trauma.	• **Access to more interesting and more fulfilling work:** Workers can get access to opportunities that might be unreachable otherwise.	• **Diminished loyalty:** Managers have to deal with a workforce that doesn't have the same sense of loyalty to the organization that many full-time employees do.	• **Diminished loyalty:** Workers don't have the same sense employees often do that an organization is looking out for them and will reward sacrifices and effort above and beyond contractual obligations.
• **Access to star talent:** Managers can "rent" top talent that is too expensive to hire full time or unwilling to work full time.		• **Management succession:** Companies with fewer employees will find it harder to groom replacement managers and executives.	• **Career development:** Without full-time employers to guide, support, and train them, workers are left to fend for themselves and to keep their skills current at their own expense.
• **Benefitting from competition:** Firms can stage competitions in talent markets to see who can devise the best solutions to problems.		• **Accountability and liability:** Unstructured organizations lack the built-in accountability of conventional structures, and the distribution of work among multiple independent parties could create liability concerns.	

Sources: Adapted in part from Darren Dahl, "Want a Job? Let the Bidding Begin," *Inc.*, March 2011, 93–96; Thomas W. Malone, Robert J. Laubacher, and Tammy Johns, "The Age of Hyperspecialization," *Harvard Business Review*, July-August 2011, 56–65; Jennifer Wang, "The Solution to the Innovator's Dilemma," *Entrepreneur*, August 2011, 24–32; Marjorie Derven, "Managing the Matrix in the New Normal," *T+D*, July 2010, 42–47.

- **Freedom and flexibility.** The flip side of agility for companies is extreme flexibility for workers, particularly after they establish themselves in a field. Within the limits of financial need and project availability, of course, independent contractors can often pick and choose the clients and projects that interest them most and decide how much or how little they want to work.

- **Access to jobs that might be otherwise unattainable.** For people geographically removed from major employment centers, finding decent employment can be a serious challenge. The distributed, virtual approach gives people in rural areas and small towns greater access to job opportunities.

POTENTIAL CHALLENGES OF UNSTRUCTURED ORGANIZATIONS

For all its benefits, the unstructured approach presents some potential drawbacks, some of them considerable. These challenges will discourage many companies and workers from taking this route, and they'll make it more difficult for those who do:[48]

- **Complexity and control issues.** Unstructured organizations can be even more complex than matrix organizations because workers not only have multiple bosses but report to multiple bosses in multiple companies. In addition, even though companies can in effect hire and fire independent contractors more easily, they have less control over this talent than they have over permanent employees.

- **Uncertainty.** Without full-time staff at the ready, companies won't always know if they can get the talent they need for upcoming projects. Conversely, workers won't always know if they'll have a job from one project to the next.
- **Loss of meaning and connection.** Being a full-time employee of an organization means more than just employment to many people. Companies also provide a social structure that is as close as family for some employees. Moreover, the opportunity to help an organization succeed over the long haul, to work with others for a greater purpose, is an important motivator and provides a sense of pride for many employees. Independent contractors who move from project to project don't have the chance to form such bonds.
- **Diminished loyalty.** The bond that develops between employers and employees over time creates a sense of loyalty that can carry both parties through hard times. Employers often make accommodations for employees going through tough personal circumstances, for instance. And many employees are willing to make or at least accept short-term sacrifices that benefit their companies in the long term (such as helping colleagues in addition to doing their own work or accepting pay reductions during periods of slow sales). However, this sense of "all for one and one for all" is not likely to factor heavily in most unstructured scenarios, where workers are more like competing vendors than members of a family.
- **Career development.** Conventional organizations do much more than just put resources in place to tackle one project after another. They invest in employees over months or years, giving them time and opportunities to develop deep knowledge and skills, with the idea that the investment will pay off in the long term. However, independent contractors are responsible for developing themselves, while they're busy making a living, so keeping up with developments in their professions presents a greater burden than it does for typical employees.
- **Management succession.** As companies develop their employees, they also groom future managers and executives who understand both the company internally and its multiple external environments. Without these development channels in place, companies could be hard pressed to replace upper managers when the time comes.
- **Accountability and liability.** Conventional structures tend to have clear lines of accountability up and down the chain of command (meaning who is responsible if things go awry) and clear assignments of legal or financial liability in the event of major foul-ups. However, the situation might not be quite so clear in an unstructured organization that relies on a temporary assemblage of independent companies and contractors.

While these challenges should not be taken lightly by companies or workers, they are likely to be manageable in enough different scenarios that the unstructured approach will catch on in more and more industries. Exactly where unstructured organizations will take the world of business will be interesting to see.

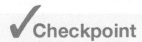

✓ Checkpoint

LEARNING OBJECTIVE 6: Explain the concept of an unstructured organization, and identify the major benefits and challenges of taking this approach.

SUMMARY: An unstructured organization doesn't rely on conventional organizational structures to assemble the resources needed to pursue business goals. Instead, it assembles independent contractors or companies, as needed, for specific tasks or functions, relying on electronic communications to replace much of the structural linkages in a conventional company. The potential benefits for companies are increased agility, lower fixed costs and more flexible capacity management, access to otherwise unreachable talent, and the benefits of competition among workers or service providers. For workers, the benefits include performance-based evaluation of their efforts, more freedom and flexibility to choose which projects to work on and how much to work, and access to jobs that might be otherwise unattainable. The potential disadvantages of the unstructured approach include complexity and control issues for managers, greater uncertainty for companies and workers, the loss of meaning and connection to a greater purpose for employees, diminished loyalty for both employers and employees, uncertainties in career development and management succession, and concerns over accountability and liability.

CRITICAL THINKING: (1) "Unstructured organization" is something of a contradiction in terms; are such companies still "organized" if they have no permanent structure? Why or why not? (2) How can workers develop marketable skills if they work as independent contractors?

IT'S YOUR BUSINESS: (1) Where do you think you would be most comfortable, as a regular employee in a conventionally structured firm or as an independent contractor, moving from project to project? Why? (2) Assume that you went to work for a conventional employer and then left to work as an independent contractor as soon as you developed enough of a skill set to make it on your own. (Assume as well that you were not violating any sort of employment contract and were free to leave.) Would you have any ethical concerns about leaving an employer who had invested in your professional development? Why or why not?

KEY TERM TO KNOW: unstructured organization

BEHIND THE SCENES

MyBizLab

TEAMING UP FOR SUCCESS AT THE CONTAINER STORE

The Container Store was not started with a modest goal. Founders Garrett Boone and Kip Tindell set out to become the "best retail store in the United States." Judging by feedback from customers and employees, they just might have succeeded.

As millions of frustrated consumers know all too well, though, delivering great customer service in retail environments isn't easy. The Container Store does it with strong company values, respect for employees, and a structure that promotes teamwork over individual competition. The company's values flow from the idea that people are its greatest asset because they are the key to exceptional service. The notion that "people are our greatest asset" is repeated often in the business world and often without substance to back it up, but The Container Store goes to extraordinary lengths to practice what it preaches. The company isn't bashful about saying employees are its number-one priority, either, saying that while business involves "an interdependent set of stakeholders—employees, customers, vendors, the community and shareholders. At The Container Store, we firmly believe our employee is the #1 stakeholder. In doing so, employees take better care of customers and ultimately the shareholders experience greater benefit from this approach to business."

To put employees first, however, the company makes sure it has the best employees it can find. Far from viewing employees as interchangeable parts, Tindell even says, "I choose employees and friends the same way." The Container Store uses a comprehensive interviewing and selection process to find the perfect person for each position, driven by the belief that "one great person equals three good people in terms of business productivity." Most employees are college educated, almost half come from employee referrals, and most have been customers of the store. They are also self-motivated, team oriented, and passionate about customer service.

Those traits are enhanced by extensive employee development: New full-time employees receive over 200 hours of training in their first year and nearly that much every year thereafter. In comparison, most retailers give new workers less than 10 hours of training per year. As a result, employees feel extremely confident in their ability to help customers, and positive feedback from customers continues to build that confidence.

The Container Store also pays three to four times the minimum wage, offering wages as much as 50 to 100 percent above those of other retailers. The financial security builds loyalty and helps keep annual turnover at a fraction of the typical turnover rates in the industry. What's more, salespeople are not paid commissions, unlike retail staffs in many other companies. Without the constant pressure to "make the numbers," it's easier for employees to take their time with customers, using their creative instincts and extensive training to design complete solutions to customers' storage problems. By not paying commissions, The Container Store also helps employees sense that they're all part of a team rather than being in competition with one another.

That emphasis on teamwork is reinforced twice a day, before opening and after closing, through a meeting called "the huddle." Similar to a huddle in football, it helps give everyone a common purpose: set goals, share information, boost morale, and bond as a team. Morning sessions feature spirited discussions of sales goals and product applications and may include a chorus of "Happy Birthday" for celebrating team members. Evening huddles include more team building and friendly competitions such as guessing the daily sales figures. Tindell believes that full, open communication with employees takes courage but says, "The only way that people feel really, really a part of something is if they know everything."

The Container Store differs dramatically from many other retail establishments in the way it embraces part-time employees. These workers are essential at the busiest times, such as evenings and holiday seasons, but they are treated as second-class citizens in some companies. Not at The Container Store. To begin with, the company refers to them as "prime-time" employees, not part-time, since these staffers are most valuable in those prime-time rush periods. And these people also receive extensive training and are treated as equal members of the team at each store. As one prime-timer in Houston puts it, "Everyone is treated as an important human being. I don't feel like a part-time employee at all—I feel like a professional. They make belonging easy and a source of pride."

By aligning its corporate values with its management practices and its organization structure, The Container Store paves the way for its employees to deliver great customer service. And by frequently astonishing its employees with enlightened leadership, the company sets a strong example for the people in blue aprons who are expected to astonish customers every day.

People outside the company notice, too. The Container Store has become a consistent winner in such nationwide forums as the annual Performance Through People Award, presented by Northwestern University, and *Fortune* magazine's annual list of "The 100 Best Companies to Work For."[49] And it all starts with teamwork. As Tindell says, "I think we do team as well as anybody I've ever seen."

Critical Thinking Questions

1. Based on what you've learned about the way employees at The Container Store interact with customers, do you think that the company emphasizes centralized or decentralized decision making? Explain your answer.
2. How might the company's emphasis on teamwork affect accountability and authority?
3. What effect might a change to commission-based compensation have on the team structure at The Container Store?

LEARN MORE ONLINE

Visit The Container Store's website, at **www.containerstore.com**, and read about the company's history, its culture, and the benefits it offers employees. What do you think of the company's belief that one great person equals three good people? What kinds of jobs are available in stores, the home office, and the distribution center?

MyBizLab

Log on to www.mybizlab.com to access study and assessment aids associated with this chapter.

KEY TERMS

agile organization	line-and-staff organization
centralization	matrix structure
chain of command	network structure
cohesiveness	norms
committee	organization chart
core competencies	organization structure
cross-functional team	problem-solving team
decentralization	self-managed team
departmentalization	span of management
divisional structure	task force
functional structure	team
functional team	unstructured organization
groupthink	virtual team
line organization	work specialization

TEST YOUR KNOWLEDGE

Questions for Review

1. What is an agile organization?
2. What are the characteristics of tall organizations and flat organizations?
3. What are the advantages and disadvantages of work specialization?
4. What are the advantages and disadvantages of functional departmentalization?
5. What are the potential benefits and potential disadvantages of the unstructured organizational model?

Questions for Analysis

6. Why is it important for companies to decide on their core competencies before choosing an organization structure?
7. How can a virtual organization reduce costs?
8. What can managers do to help teams work more effectively?
9. How can companies benefit from using virtual teams?
10. **Ethical Considerations.** You were honored to be selected to serve on the salary committee of the employee negotiations task force. As a member of that committee, you reviewed confidential company documents listing the salaries of all department managers. You discovered that other managers at your level are earning $25,000 more than you, even though you've been at the company the same amount of time. You feel that a raise is justified on the basis of this confidential information. How will you handle this situation?

Questions for Application

11. You are the leader of a cross-functional work team whose goal is to find ways of lowering production costs. Your team of eight employees has become mired in the storming stage. The team members disagree on how to approach the task, and they are starting to splinter into factions, each pursuing its own goal. What can you do to help the team move forward?

12. You've recently accepted a job as the U.S. sales manager for a German manufacturing company. One of your first assignments is serving on a virtual problem-solving team with colleagues from Germany, France, Japan, and South Korea. Budgets are tight, so you won't have the opportunity to meet with your teammates in person to get to know one another. What steps can you take to help the team develop into a cohesive and efficient unit?

13. **Concept Integration.** One of your competitors has approached you with an intriguing proposition. The company would like to merge with your company. The economies of scale are terrific. So are the growth possibilities. There's just one issue to be resolved. Your competitor is organized under a flat structure and uses lots of cross-functional teams. Your company is organized under a traditional tall structure that is departmentalized by function. Using your knowledge about culture clash, what are the likely issues you will encounter if these two organizations are merged?

14. This question was intentionally excluded from this edition.

EXPAND YOUR KNOWLEDGE

Discovering Career Opportunities

Whether you're a top manager, first-line manager (supervisor), or middle manager, your efforts will impact the success of your organization. To get a closer look at what the responsibilities of a manager are, log on to the Prentice Hall Student Success Super-Site, at www.prenhall.com/success. Click on Majors Exploration and select Business and then Management in the drop-down boxes. Then scroll down and read about careers in management.

1. What can you do with a degree in management?
2. What is the future outlook for careers in management?
3. Scroll down to "Advice from a Management Professor." After reading this information, does management appeal to you as a major? Why or why not?

Improving Your Tech Insights: Wireless Connectivity

Wireless connectivity—both local area Wi-Fi and wide area mobile phone networks—gives businesses three major benefits. The first is making information available where and when it can be most useful. The second is untethering workers from physical locations, allowing them to be productive wherever they want or need to be. The third major benefit is simplifying the connection between people and computers. This technology can help in a variety of ways, from making it easier to add networking to an older building that doesn't have wires running through the walls to enabling business teams to move around large corporate campuses (to attend team meetings, for example) without losing their connections to the company network. Research the ways businesses are using wireless connectivity to overcome organizational boundaries, enhance teamwork, improve customer service, or improve meetings. Identify three examples in a brief email to your instructor.

PRACTICE YOUR SKILLS

Sharpening Your Communication Skills

In group meetings, some of your colleagues have a habit of interrupting and arguing with the speaker, taking credit for ideas that aren't theirs, and shooting down ideas they don't agree with. You're the newest person in the group and not sure if this is accepted behavior in this company, but it concerns you both personally and professionally. Should you go with the flow and adopt their behavior or stick with your own communication style, even though you might get lost in the noise? In two paragraphs, explain the pros and cons of both approaches.

Building Your Team Skills

What's the most effective organization structure for your college or university? With your team, obtain a copy of your school's organization chart. If this chart is not readily available, gather information by talking with people in administration and then draw your own chart of the organization structure.

Analyze the chart in terms of span of management. Is your school a flat or a tall organization? Is this organization structure appropriate for your school? Does decision making tend to be centralized or decentralized in your school? Do you agree with this approach to decision making?

Finally, investigate the use of formal and informal teams in your school. Are there any problem-solving teams, task forces, or committees at work in your school? Are any teams self-directed or virtual? How much authority do these teams have to make decisions? What is the purpose of teamwork in your school? What kinds of goals do these teams have?

Share your team's findings during a brief classroom presentation and then compare the findings of all teams. Is there agreement on the appropriate organization structure for your school?

Developing Your Research Skills

Although teamwork can benefit many organizations, introducing and managing team structures can be a real challenge. Search past issues of business journals or newspapers (print or online editions) to locate articles about how an organization has overcome problems with teams.

1. Why did the organization originally introduce teams? What types of teams are being used?
2. What problems did each organization encounter in trying to implement teams? How did the organization deal with these problems?
3. Have the teams been successful from management's perspective? From the employees' perspective? What effect has teamwork had on the company, its customers, and its products?

REFERENCES

1. "Container Store's Hiring Secret," *Fortune* video, accessed 23 August 2011, http://money.cnn.com; The Container Store website, accessed 23 August 2011, www.containerstore.com; "100 Best Companies to Work For," *Fortune*, accessed 14 April 2009, www.fortune.com; Bob Nelson, "Can't Contain Excitement at The Container Store," BizJournals.com, accessed 11 March 2005, www.bizjournals.com; Mike Duff, "Top-Shelf Employees Keep Container Store on Track," *DSN Retailing Today*, 8 March 2004, 7, 49; Bob Nelson, "The Buzz at The Container Store," *Corporate Meetings & Incentives*, June 2003, 32; Jennifer Saba, "Balancing Act," *Potentials*, 1 October 2003, www.highbeam.com; Peter S. Cohan, "Corporate Heroes," *Financial Executive*, 1 March 2003, www.highbeam.com; Margaret Steen, "Container Store's Focus on Training a Strong Appeal to Employees," *Mercury News* (San Jose, Calif.), 6 November 2003, www.highbeam.com; Holly Hayes, "Container Store Brings Clutter Control to San Jose, Calif.," 17 October 2003, *Mercury News* (San Jose, Calif.), 1F; "Performance Through People Award," press release, 10 September 2003; David Lipke, "Container Store's CEO: People Are Most Valued Asset," *HFN*, 13 January 2003, www.highbeam.com; Lorrie Grant, "Container Store's Workers Huddle Up to Help You Out," 30 April 2002, *USA Today*, B1.
2. "Benefits of Outsourcing Payroll," *Practical Accountant*, November 2008, SR9.
3. "Capabilities" and "History," Frog Design website, accessed 16 August 2011, www.frogdesign.com.
4. Stephen P. Robbins and David A. DeCenzo, *Management*, 4th ed. (Upper Saddle River, N.J.: Pearson Prentice Hall, 2004), 142–143.
5. Charles R. Greer and W. Richard Plunkett, *Supervision: Diversity and Teams in the Workplace*, 10th ed. (Upper Saddle River, N.J.: Prentice Hall, 2003), 77.
6. Caroline Ellis, "The Flattening Corporation," *MIT Sloan Management Review*, Summer 2003, 5.
7. "Container Store's Hiring Secret."
8. "Why Middle Managers May Be the Most Important People in Your Company," Knowledge@Wharton, 25 May 2011, http://knowledge.wharton.upenn.edu.
9. Gareth R. Jones, *Organizational Theory, Design, and Change*, 4th ed. (Upper Saddle River, N.J.: Pearson Prentice Hall, 2004), 109.
10. Jones, *Organizational Theory, Design, and Change*, 109–111.
11. Richard L. Daft, *Management*, 6th ed. (Mason, Ohio: South-Western, 2003), 320.
12. Jones, *Organizational Theory, Design, and Change*, 163.
13. Jones, *Organizational Theory, Design, and Change*, 167.
14. "Our Businesses," Chevron website, accessed 16 August 2011, www.chevron.com.
15. Daft, *Management*, 324–327.
16. Marjorie Derven, "Managing the Matrix in the New Normal," *T+D*, July 2010, 42–47.
17. Jerald Greenberg and Robert A. Baron, *Behavior in Organizations*, 8th ed. (Upper Saddle River, N.J.: Prentice Hall, 2003), 558–560; Daft, *Management*, 329.
18. Derven, "Managing the Matrix in the New Normal."
19. Pete Engardio and Bruce Einhorn, "Outsourcing Innovation," *BusinessWeek*, 21 March 2005, 84–94.
20. Stephen P. Robbins, *Essentials of Organizational Behavior*, 6th ed. (Upper Saddle River, N.J.: Prentice Hall, 2000), 105.
21. Greer and Plunkett, *Supervision*, 293.
22. "Attacking Claim Denials," *Receivables Report for America's Health Care Financial Managers*, October 2007, 1–6.
23. Steven A. Frankforter and Sandra L. Christensen, "Finding Competitive Advantage in Self-Managed Work Teams," *Business Forum*, 2005, Vol. 27, Issue 1, 20–24.
24. Daft, *Management*, 594; Robbins and DeCenzo, *Fundamentals of Management*, 336.

25. Daft, *Management*, 618; Robbins and DeCenzo, *Fundamentals of Management*, 262.

26. Morten T. Hansen, "When Internal Collaboration Is Bad for Your Company," *Harvard Business Review*, April 2009, 82–88.

27. Jerry Fjermestad, "Virtual Leadership for a Virtual Workforce," *Chief Learning Officer*, March 2009, 36–39.

28. Jenny Goodbody, "Critical Success Factors for Global Virtual Teams," *Strategic Communication Management*, February/March 2005, 18–21; Ann Majchrzak, Arvind Malhotra, Jeffrey Stamps, and Jessica Lipnack, "Can Absence Make a Team Grow Stronger?" *Harvard Business Review*, May 2004, 131–137.

29. Richard McDermott and Douglas Archibald, "Harnessing Your Staff's Informal Networks," *Harvard Business Review*, March 2010, 82–89.

30. Tony Hsieh, "Why I Sold Zappos," *Inc.*, 1 June 2010, www.inc.com.

31. Robbins and DeCenzo, *Fundamentals of Management*, 257–258; Daft, *Management*, 634–636.

32. "Groups Best at Complex Problems," *Industrial Engineer*, June 2006, 14.

33. Max Landsberg and Madeline Pfau, "Developing Diversity: Lessons from Top Teams," *Strategy + Business*, Winter 2005, 10–12.

34. Derven, "Managing the Matrix in the New Normal"; Robert Kreitner, *Management*, 9th ed. (Boston: Houghton Mifflin, 2004), 475–481; Daft, *Management*, 635–636.

35. Lynda Gratton and Tamara J. Erickson, "8 Ways to Build Collaborative Teams," *Harvard Business Review*, November 2007, 100–109.

36. Jon R. Katzenbach and Douglas K. Smith, "The Discipline of Teams," *Harvard Business Review*, July/August 2005, 162–171; Laird Mealiea and Ramon Baltazar, "A Strategic Guide for Building Effective Teams," *Public Personnel Management*, Summer 2005, 141–160; Larry Cole and Michael Cole, "Why Is the Teamwork Buzz Word Not Working?" *Communication World*, February/March 1999, 29; Patricia Buhler, "Managing in the 90s: Creating Flexibility in Today's Workplace," *Supervision*, January 1997, 24+; Allison W. Amason, Allen C. Hochwarter, Wayne A. Thompson, and Kenneth R. Harrison, "Conflict: An Important Dimension in Successful Management Teams," *Organizational Dynamics*, Autumn 1995, 20+.

37. Jared Sandberg, "Some Ideas Are So Bad That Only a Team Effort Can Account for Them," *Wall Street Journal*, 29 September 2004, B1.

38. Mark K. Smith, "Bruce W. Tuckman—Forming, Storming, Norming, and Performing in Groups," Infed.org, accessed 5 July 2005, www.infed.org; Robbins and DeCenzo, *Fundamentals of Management*, 258–259; Daft, *Management*, 625–627.

39. Jones, *Organizational Theory, Design, and Change*, 112–113; Greenberg and Baron, *Behavior in Organizations*, 280–281; Daft, *Management*, 629–631.

40. Andy Boynton and Bill Fischer, *Virtuoso Teams: Lessons from Teams That Changed Their Worlds* (Harrow, UK: FT Prentice Hall, 2005), 10.

41. Thomas K. Capozzoli, "Conflict Resolution—A Key Ingredient in Successful Teams," *Supervision*, November 1999, 14–16.

42. Daft, *Management*, 631–632.

43. Darren Dahl, "Want a Job? Let the Bidding Begin," *Inc.*, March 2011, 93–96; Thomas W. Malone, Robert J. Laubacher, and Tammy Johns, "The Age of Hyperspecialization," *Harvard Business Review*, July–August 2011, 56–65.

44. Malone, et al., "The Age of Hyperspecialization."

45. "How Does It Work?" TopCoder website, accessed 18 August 2011, www.topcoder.com.

46. Adapted from Dahl, "Want a Job? Let the Bidding Begin," Malone, et al., "The Age of Hyperspecialization"; Jennifer Wang, "The Solution to the Innovator's Dilemma," *Entrepreneur*, August 2011, 24–32; Derven, "Managing the Matrix in the New Normal."

47. "LiveOps and Vision Perry Create New Work Opportunities for Rural Tennessee," LiveOps press release, 18 July 2011, www.liveops.com; Malone, et al., "The Age of Hyperspecialization."

48. Adapted from Dahl, "Want a Job? Let the Bidding Begin," Malone, et al., "The Age of Hyperspecialization"; Wang, "The Solution to the Innovator's Dilemma"; "Managing the Matrix in the New Normal."

49. See note 1.

GLOSSARY

agile organization A company whose structure, policies, and capabilities allow employees to respond quickly to customer needs and changes in the business environment

centralization Concentration of decision-making authority at the top of an organization

chain of command A pathway for the flow of authority from one management level to the next

cohesiveness A measure of how committed team members are to their team's goals

committee A team that may become a permanent part of the organization and is designed to deal with regularly recurring tasks

core competencies Activities that a company considers central and vital to its business

cross-functional team A team that draws together employees from different functional areas

decentralization Delegation of decision-making authority to employees in lower-level positions

departmentalization Grouping people within an organization according to function, division, matrix, or network

divisional structure Grouping departments according to similarities in product, process, customer, or geography

functional structure Grouping workers according to their similar skills, resource use, and expertise

functional team A team whose members come from a single functional department and that is based on the organization's vertical structure

groupthink Uniformity of thought that occurs when peer pressures cause individual team members to withhold contrary or unpopular opinions

line organization A chain-of-command system that establishes a clear line of authority flowing from the top down

line-and-staff organization An organization system that has a clear chain of command but that also includes functional groups of people who provide advice and specialized services8

matrix structure A structure in which employees are assigned to both a functional group and a project team (thus using functional and divisional patterns simultaneously)

network structure A structure in which individual companies are connected electronically to perform selected tasks for a small headquarters organization

norms Informal standards of conduct that guide team behavior

organization chart A diagram that shows how employees and tasks are grouped and where the lines of communication and authority flow

organization structure A framework that enables managers to divide responsibilities, ensure employee accountability, and distribute decision-making authority

problem-solving team A team that meets to find ways of improving quality, efficiency, and the work environment

self-managed team A team in which members are responsible for an entire process or operation

span of management The number of people under one manager's control; also known as span of control

task force A team of people from several departments who are temporarily brought together to address a specific issue

team A unit of two or more people who share a mission and collective responsibility as they work together to achieve a goal

unstructured organization An organization that doesn't have a conventional structure but instead assembles talent as needed from the open market; the virtual and networked organizational concepts taken to the extreme

virtual team A team that uses communication technology to bring together geographically distant employees to achieve goals

work specialization Specialization in or responsibility for some portion of an organization's overall work tasks; also called division of labor

Employee Motivation

Employee Motivation

LEARNING OBJECTIVES   After studying this chapter, you will be able to

1 Define *motivation* and identify the classical motivation theories

2 Explain why many consider *expectancy theory* to be the best current explanation of employee motivation

3 Identify the strengths and weaknesses of *goal-setting theory*

4 Describe the *job characteristics model* and explain how it helps predict motivation and performance

5 Define *reinforcement theory* and differentiate between positive and negative reinforcement

6 List five managerial strategies that are vital to maintaining a motivated workforce

MyBizLab

Where you see MyBizLab in this chapter, go to www.mybizlab.com for additional activities on the topic being discussed.

BEHIND THE SCENES TAKING A SECOND LOOK AT THE CAREER LADDER

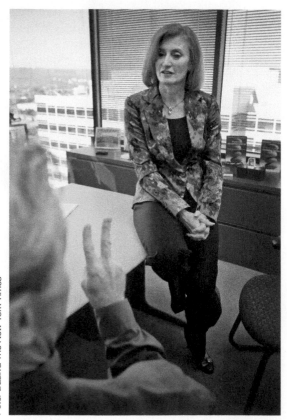

Peter Dasilva The New York Times

Having followed an unconventional career path herself, Cathy Benko helped redefine career options for Deloitte's employeés.

www.deloitte.com

The notion of a business career being a straight vertical ascent from the bottom to the top is so embedded in our thinking that it has its own well-used metaphor: *climbing the corporate ladder*. The basic idea is that you join the workforce after college, you work hard for 30, 40, or 50 years, and you are rewarded along the way with positions of increasing responsibility and reward.

There's just one small problem with this whole ladder idea: It has never been true for millions of business professionals, and it often doesn't work out even for those who believe in the promise of continuous career progress. Simple arithmetic will tell you that the continuous climb simply can't work for most people—there just aren't enough high-level jobs, and the number shrinks dramatically with each step up the ladder. Take the technology giant Intel, for example, which has roughly 130 vice presidents, 7 senior VPs, 4 executive VPs, and 1 CEO. That's about 140 slots up around the top of the ladder. This might sound like a lot of opportunities—until you consider that Intel has roughly 80,000 employees. Even if only 10 percent of these employees (8,000) aspire to reach the top level, 7,860 of them aren't going to make it.

The numbers don't tell the whole story, either. Many employees have other priorities and demands in life, from raising families and dealing with health issues to continuing their education and exploring different career specialties along the way. In other words, millions of employees are unwilling or unable to maintain a straight climb up the ladder, and reward systems built on a steady climb aren't going to do much to motivate these people. As consultant Bruce Tulgan puts it,

"Paying your dues, moving up slowly and getting the corner office—that's going away. In 10 years, it will be gone."

Cathy Benko is one of many executives who have been pondering this dilemma. As vice chairman and chief talent officer for Deloitte LLP, a diversified accounting, consulting, and financial advisory firm, Benko guides company strategy for attracting, developing, and motivating a highly skilled workforce. She realizes that the ladder metaphor has never quite fit many employees and that recent trends make it even less applicable to an ever-growing segment of the workforce. She knows the workplace needs to change to give employees a more satisfying, energizing, and motivating career path.

If you were Cathy Benko, what steps would you take to align the workplace with the changing workforce and make sure that every employee, on any career path, has a shot at success?[1]

INTRODUCTION

Deloitte's Cathy Benko (profiled in the chapter-opening Behind the Scenes) knows that a one-size-fits-all approach to managing and motivating employees has never been effective—and it is growing less effective every year as the workplace and the workforce continue to change. She could also tell you that although studying motivation is important, the task is challenging because no single theory or model can explain every motivational situation. The forces that affect motivation can vary widely from person to person and from situation to situation, and some managers and researchers continue to "rely on obsolete and discredited theories."[2] The various theories and models in this chapter each provide some insight into the complicated question of employee motivation. You'll notice a fair amount of overlap among some of the theories, but taken as a whole, they provide an overall picture of the challenges and rewards of motivating employees to higher performance.

MyBizLab

Gain hands-on experience through an interactive, real-world scenario. This chapter's simulation entitled Firing an Employee is located at **www.mybizlab.com**.

What Motivates Employees to Peak Performance?

Motivating employees is one of the most important challenges every manager faces. No matter how skillful employees may be and how supportive the work environment is, without the motivation to excel, they won't perform at a high level. This section digs into the meaning of motivation and then explores some of the early attempts to provide practical models for motivating employees.

1 LEARNING OBJECTIVE

Define *motivation,* and identify the classical motivation theories.

WHAT IS MOTIVATION?

Motivation is a complex subject that defies easy explanation, and some of the brightest minds in the field of management have been working for decades to understand this mysterious force. For one example, things that motivate you might have no effect on other people—or may even *demotivate* them. For another, some of the forces that motivate your behavior stem from deep within your subconscious mind, which means you might be driven by forces that you don't understand and can't even identify.

Starting with a basic definition, **motivation** is the combination of forces that drive individuals to take certain actions and avoid others in pursuit of individual objectives. Pay close attention to *drive* and *actions* in this definition; they are key to understanding motivation.

In a workplace setting, motivation can be assessed by measuring four indicators: *engagement, satisfaction, commitment,* and *rootedness*—the degree to which an employee intends to stay with his or her employer (see Exhibit 1 on the next page).[3] First, **engagement** reflects the degree of energy, enthusiasm, and effort each employee brings to his or her work. If you're "just not into it," chances are you won't perform at your best. Second, *satisfaction* indicates how happy employees are with the experience of work and the way they are treated. Third, *commitment* suggests the degree to which employees support the company and its mission. Fourth, *rootedness* (or its opposite, intention to quit) predicts

motivation The combination of forces that move individuals to take certain actions and avoid other actions

engagement An employee's rational and emotional commitment to his or her work

EXHIBIT 1	Four Indicators of Motivation

Employees can be said to be fully motivated when they are *engaged*, *satisfied*, *committed*, and *rooted*.

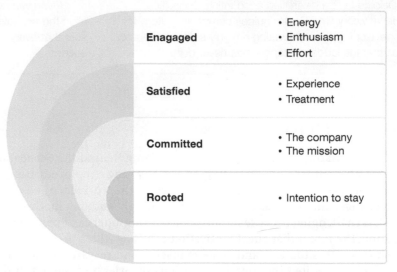

Enagaged	• Energy • Enthusiasm • Effort
Satisfied	• Experience • Treatment
Committed	• The company • The mission
Rooted	• Intention to stay

Source: Adapted from Nitin Nohria, Boris Groysberg, and Linda-Eling Lee, "Employee Motivation: A Powerful New Model," *Harvard Business Review*, July–August 2008, 78–84.

the likelihood that employees will stay or leave their jobs. A person who is engaged, satisfied, and committed and who has no intention of quitting can be safely said to be *motivated*.

These four indicators can identify who is motivated and who isn't, but they don't explain why. For that, it's necessary to dig deeper, looking into what drives people to choose certain actions and avoid others. Contemporary research suggests that motivation stems from four fundamental needs:[4]

- **The drive to acquire.** This includes the need for not only physical goods such as food and clothing but for enjoyable experiences and "psychological goods" such as prestige. Importantly, this drive is relative: Individuals want to know how well they're doing compared to others around them.
- **The drive to bond.** Humans are social creatures, and the need to feel a part of something larger is a vital aspect of employee motivation. This drive can be helpful, such as when it inspires employees to contribute to the common good, but it can also be harmful, such as when it pits groups of employees against one another in an "us versus them" mentality.
- **The drive to comprehend.** Learning, growing, meeting tough challenges, making sense of things—these are satisfying outcomes based on the drive to understand the world around us.
- **The drive to defend.** An instinct to protect and a sense of justice can lead human beings to vigorously defend the people, ideas, and organizations they hold dear. This drive is beneficial when it motivates people to fight for what is right, but it can be harmful as well, such as when it motivates people to resist change.

According to Harvard professor Nitin Nohria and his colleagues, who helped identify and explain these four drives, satisfying all four needs is essential to being motivated. When a need goes unsatisfied—or even worse, is betrayed, such as when employees believe an organization they've supported and defended no longer cares about them—poor motivation is the result.[5]

REAL-TIME UPDATES

Learn More by Watching This PowerPoint Presentation

Satisfying the four fundamental drives of employee behavior

Identify techniques that help satisfy the four fundamental drives in any workplace. Go to http://real-timeupdates.com/bia6 and click on Learn More. If you are using MyBizLab, you can access Real-Time Updates within the chapter or under Student Study Tools.

CLASSICAL THEORIES OF MOTIVATION

The quest to understand employee motivation has occupied researchers for more than a century. This section offers a brief overview of some of the important early theories that helped shape ideas about motivation. Although subsequent research has identified short-comings in all these theories, each contributed to our current understanding of motivation, and each continues to influence managerial practice.

Taylor's Scientific Management

One of the earliest motivational researchers, Frederick W. Taylor, a machinist and engineer from Philadelphia, studied employee efficiency and motivation in the late 19th and early 20th centuries. He is credited with developing **scientific management**, an approach that sought to improve employee efficiency through the scientific study of work. In addition to analyzing work and business processes in order to develop better methods, Taylor popularized financial incentives for good performance. His work truly revolutionized business and had a direct influence on the rise of the United States as a global industrial power in the first half of the 20th century.[6]

> **scientific management**
> A management approach designed to improve employees' efficiency by scientifically studying their work

Although money proved to be a significant motivator for workers, scientific management didn't consider other motivational elements, such as opportunities for personal satisfaction. For instance, scientific management can't explain why a successful executive will take a hefty pay cut to serve in government or a nonprofit organization. Therefore, other researchers have looked beyond money to discover what else motivates people.

The Hawthorne Studies and the "Hawthorne Effect"

Between 1924 and 1932, a series of pioneering studies in employee motivation and productivity were conducted at the Hawthorne Works of the Western Electric Company in Chicago. The Hawthorne studies are intriguing both for what they uncovered and as an example of how management ideas can get oversimplified and misunderstood over the course of time. The research began as an experiment in scientific management: testing the effect of various levels of electric lighting on worker productivity. The researchers varied the lighting level for one group of workers (the experimental group) and kept it the same for a second group (the control group). Both groups were engaged in the tedious and exacting task of wrapping wire to make telephone coils, so lighting presumably played a key role in eye strain and other factors influencing productivity.[7]

Whatever the researchers expected to find, they surely didn't expect to see productivity increase in *both* groups as the lighting level was increased for the experimental group—and it kept increasing in both groups even when the lighting level was then decreased for the experimental group. In other words, no correlation between the level of lighting and the level of productivity was observed, and productivity increased among the control group workers even though their environment hadn't changed at all. This perplexing outcome was followed by a range of tests on other variables in the work environment and in employee rewards. The research team eventually concluded that group norms affected individual performance more than any other factor and that to understand employee performance one needed to understand an employee's total emotional and cultural makeup, on and off the job.[8]

By themselves, these conclusions are important, and the Hawthorne studies helped launch the entire field of industrial psychology and began to enlighten the practice of management in general.[9] Then a couple of decades later, a researcher not connected with the studies suggested the phenomenon of the **Hawthorne effect**, in which the behavior of the Western Electric workers changed because they were being observed and given special treatment as research subjects. In the years that followed, the Hawthorne effect took on a life of its own and became widely assumed across many fields of research, from management to medicine, even though the original research never reached this conclusion. Moreover, the phenomenon has come to be defined in so many different ways that the use of the term could obscure more than it explains. The outcome of the Hawthorne studies has too often been reduced to this oversimplified and uncertain conclusion about the behavior of research subjects; their real and lasting contribution was opening a lot of eyes to the benefits of understanding human behavior in organizational settings.[10]

> **Hawthorne effect** A supposed effect of organizational research, in which employees change their behavior because they are being studied and given special treatment; the validity of the effect is uncertain, and the Hawthorne studies were richer and more influential than this simple outcome would suggest

Maslow's Hierarchy of Needs

Abraham Maslow suggested that needs on the lower levels of the hierarchy must be satisfied before higher-level needs can be addressed (examples are shown to the right). This model offers a convenient way to categorize needs, but it lacks empirical validation.

Source: Adapted from Andrew J. DuBrin, *Applying Psychology: Individual & Organizational Effectiveness*, 6th ed. (Upper Saddle River, N.J.: Pearson Prentice Hall, 2004), 122–124.

Maslow's Hierarchy of Needs

Maslow's hierarchy A model in which human needs are arranged in a hierarchy, with the most basic needs at the bottom and the more advanced needs toward the top

In 1943, psychologist Abraham Maslow hypothesized that behavior is determined by a variety of needs, which he organized into categories arranged in a hierarchy. As Exhibit 2 shows, the most basic needs are at the bottom of this hierarchy, while the more advanced needs are toward the top. In **Maslow's hierarchy** all of the requirements for basic survival—food, clothing, shelter, and the like—fall into the category of *physiological needs*. These basic needs must be satisfied before the person can consider higher-level needs such as *safety needs, social needs* (the need to give and receive love and to feel a sense of belonging), and *esteem needs* (the need for a sense of self-worth and integrity).[11]

At the top of Maslow's hierarchy is *self-actualization*—the need to become everything one can be. This need is also the most difficult to fulfill—and even to identify in many cases. Employees who reach this point work not just because they want to make money or impress others but because they feel their work is worthwhile and satisfying in itself.

Maslow's hierarchy is a convenient and logical tool for classifying human needs, and many people continue to use it to explain behavior. However, other researchers have not been able to experimentally verify that this is how motivation actually works.[12]

Theory X and Theory Y

Theory X A managerial assumption that employees are irresponsible, are unambitious, and dislike work and that managers must use force, control, or threats to motivate them

Theory Y A managerial assumption that employees enjoy meaningful work, are naturally committed to certain goals, are capable of creativity, and seek out responsibility under the right conditions

In the 1960s, psychologist Douglas McGregor proposed two radically different sets of assumptions that underlie most management thinking, which he classified as *Theory X* and *Theory Y*. According to McGregor, **Theory X**–oriented managers believe that employees dislike work and can be motivated only by the fear of losing their jobs or by *extrinsic rewards*—those given by other people, such as money and promotions. In contrast, **Theory Y**–oriented managers believe that employees like to work and can be motivated by working for goals that promote creativity or for causes they believe in. Consequently, Theory Y–oriented managers seek to motivate employees through *intrinsic rewards*—which employees essentially give to themselves.[13] As with Maslow's hierarchy, *Theory X* and *Theory Y* seem to have a permanent place in the management vocabulary, but they suffer from the same lack of empirical evidence.[14] (However, the distinction between intrinsic and extrinsic rewards remains a valid and essential aspect of many theories of motivation.)

EXHIBIT 3	Herzberg's Two-Factor Theory

According to Herzberg, *hygiene factors* such as working conditions and company policies can influence employee dissatisfaction. On the other hand, *motivators* such as opportunities for achievement and recognition can influence employee satisfaction.

Source: Adapted from *Management, Fourth Edition*, by Richard L. Daft copyright © 1997 by Harcourt Inc., reproduced by permission of the publisher.

Herzberg's Two Factors

Also in the 1960s, Frederick Herzberg and his associates explored the aspects of jobs that make employees feel satisfied or dissatisfied. The researchers found that two entirely different sets of factors were associated with dissatisfying and satisfying work experiences. In **Herzberg's two-factor theory** (see Exhibit 3), so-called *hygiene factors* are associated with dissatisfying experiences, and *motivators* are associated with satisfying experiences. Hygiene factors are mostly extrinsic and include working conditions, company policies, pay, and job security. Motivators tend to be intrinsic and include achievement, recognition, responsibility, and other personally rewarding factors.[15] According to Herzberg's model, managers need to remove dissatisfying elements *and* add satisfying elements—doing one or the other is not enough.[16]

Like Maslow's hierarchy and Theory X/Theory Y, the two-factor theory seems logical and helps explain part of the motivation puzzle. However, it has been criticized because of the methodology used in the original research and the inability of subsequent research to validate the model. Also, while there is a strong causal link between customer satisfaction and profitability, it is far less clear whether satisfied *employees* automatically lead to satisfied *customers*.[17]

Herzberg's two-factor theory
A model that divides motivational forces into satisfiers ("motivators") and dissatisfiers ("hygiene factors")

McClelland's Three Needs

The last of the classical theories to consider is the **three-needs theory** developed by David McClelland. McClelland's model highlights the *need for power* (having—and demonstrating—control over others), the *need for affiliation* (being accepted by others and having opportunities for social interaction), and the *need for achievement* (attaining personally meaningful goals).[18] Unlike with the other classical theories, there is a lot of research to validate McClelland's ideas and to explain particular outcomes in the workplace. For example, those with a high need for achievement tend to make successful entrepreneurs, but this focus on personal achievement can actually get in the way of managerial effectiveness, which relies on the ability to influence others toward shared goals.[19]

three-needs theory David McClelland's model of motivation that highlights the needs for power, affiliation, and achievement

Conversely, managers who are most successful in a conventional organizational structure tend to have a higher need for power and relatively little need for affiliation. They are less concerned with achieving personal goals or being well liked than they are with building up the influence needed to get things done through other people.[20]

While it helps explain motivation in various contexts, the biggest drawback to McClelland's approach is its limited practicality in terms of identifying needs and crafting motivational programs to harness them in beneficial directions. The three needs are subconscious, according to McClelland, and trained experts are required to help identify them in each individual.[21]

✔Checkpoint

LEARNING OBJECTIVE 1: Define *motivation,* **and identify the classical motivation theories.**

SUMMARY: Motivation is the combination of forces that prompt individuals to take certain actions and avoid others in pursuit of individual objectives. Research suggests that four drives underlie all motivation: the drive to acquire tangible and intangible rewards, the drive to bond with others, the drive to comprehend, and the drive to defend. The classical motivation theories and research that helped shape today's thinking include Taylor's scientific management, the Hawthorne studies, Maslow's hierarchy of needs, McGregor's Theory X and Theory Y, Herzberg's two factors, and McClelland's three needs.

CRITICAL THINKING: (1) How could a manager tap into the drive to defend as a way to help rally employees? (2) Could Herzberg's hygiene factors help explain the significant problem of employee theft and embezzlement? Why or why not?

IT'S YOUR BUSINESS: (1) If you are a typical college student who doesn't have much financial security at the moment but is also trying to fulfill higher-order needs such as social interaction and self-actualization through education, would it make more sense, according to Maslow, to drop out of college and work seven days a week so you could help ensure that your physiological and safety needs are met? (2) Do you think today's college students more closely match the descriptions of Theory X employees or Theory Y employees? What evidence can you provide to support your conclusion?

KEY TERMS TO KNOW: motivation, engagement, scientific management, Hawthorne effect, Maslow's hierarchy, Theory X, Theory Y, Herzberg's two-factor theory, three-needs theory

2 **LEARNING OBJECTIVE**

Explain why many consider *expectancy theory* to be the best current explanation of employee motivation.

expectancy theory The idea that the effort employees put into their work depends on expectations about their own ability to perform, expectations about likely rewards, and the attractiveness of those rewards

Explaining Employee Choices

The classical theories of motivation contributed in important ways to both managerial practices and the ongoing research into employee motivation, but each has been found wanting in some way or another. Starting with more contemporary theories, two models, known as expectancy theory and equity theory, help explain the choices that employees make.

EXPECTANCY THEORY

Expectancy theory, considered by some experts to offer the best available explanation of employee motivation, connects an employee's efforts to the outcome he or she expects from those efforts. Expectancy theory focuses less on the specific forces that motivate employees and more on the process they follow to seek satisfaction in their jobs. As shown in Exhibit 4, the effort employees will put forth depends on (1) their expectations regarding the level of performance they will be able to achieve, (2) their beliefs regarding the rewards that the organization will give in response to that performance, and (3) the attractiveness of those rewards relative to their individual goals.[22]

EXHIBIT 4	Expectancy Theory

Expectancy theory suggests that employees base their efforts on expectations of their own performance, expectations of rewards for that performance, and the value of those rewards.

Source: Adapted from Stephen P. Robbins and David A. DeCenzo, *Fundamentals of Management*, 4th ed. (Upper Saddle River, N.J.: Pearson Prentice Hall, 2004), 289.

Exploring these connections from both an employee's and a manager's perspective will give you an idea of how the expectancy model can explain employee behavior and prescribe managerial tactics to help motivate employees. First, as an employee, if you don't believe that the amount of effort you are willing or able to apply to a task will result in an acceptable level of performance, a natural response will be to say, "Well, why bother?" This uncertainty could come from many sources, such as doubts about your skills, confusion about the task, or a belief that "the system" is so broken that no matter how hard you try you can't succeed. Belief in your ability to complete a task is known as *self-efficacy*, and it can be increased by gaining experience, mimicking successful role models, getting encouragement from others, and sometimes even "psyching yourself up."[23] As a manager, your challenges would be to ensure that employees have the skills and confidence they need, that tasks are clearly defined, and that company policies and processes are functional.

Your second concern as an employee is whether the organization will recognize and reward your performance. Knowing you've done great work is its own reward, of course, but for many employees, this isn't enough. As a manager, your challenges include establishing reward systems and expectations to minimize employee uncertainty and taking time from the daily chaos to acknowledge the efforts your employees make.

Finally, if you're confident in your performance and the organization's response, your third concern is whether the promised reward is something you value. What if you are offered a raise but what you really want is for your boss to acknowledge how important your contributions have been to the company? As a manager, aligning rewards with employee priorities is an ongoing challenge; see "Reinforcing High-Performance Behavior" later in this chapter.

EQUITY THEORY

If you work side by side with someone, doing the same job and giving the same amount of effort, only to learn that your colleague earns more money, will you be satisfied in your work and motivated to continue working hard? Chances are, you will perceive a state of *inequity*, and you probably won't be happy with the situation. **Equity theory** suggests that employee satisfaction depends on the perceived ratio of inputs to outputs. To remedy a perception of inequity, you might ask for a raise, decide not to work as hard, try to change perceptions of your efforts or their outcomes, or simply quit and find a new job. Any one of these steps has the potential to bring your perceived input/output ratio back into balance.[24] Some of the choices employees can make to address perceived inequity are obviously not desirable from an employer's point of view, so it's important to understand why employees might feel they aren't getting a fair shake.

Equity issues can show up in a number of areas, such as in complaints about gender pay fairness and executive compensation and in many unionizing efforts,

equity theory The idea that employees base their level of satisfaction on the ratio of their inputs to the job and the outputs or rewards they receive from it whenever employees feel they aren't getting a fair share of corporate profits or are being asked to shoulder more than their fair share of hardships.

Research into equity theory has led to thinking about the broader concept of *organizational justice*, or perceptions of fairness in the workplace. These perceptions relate to outcomes, the processes used to generate those outcomes, and the way employees are treated during the process.[25] No reasonable employee expects to make as much as the CEO, for example, but as long as the process seems fair (both the employee's and the CEO's pay are related to performance, for example), most employees will be satisfied, and the disparity won't affect their motivation. In fact, perceptions of fairness can have as much impact on overall employee satisfaction as satisfaction with pay itself.[26]

✓ Checkpoint

LEARNING OBJECTIVE 2: Explain why many consider *expectancy theory* to be the best current explanation of employee motivation.

SUMMARY: Expectancy theory suggests that the effort employees put into their work depends on expectations about their own ability to perform, expectations about the rewards the organization will give in response to that performance, and the attractiveness of those rewards relative to their individual goals. This theory is thought to be a good model because it considers the linkages between effort and outcome. For instance, if employees think a linkage is "broken," such as having doubts that their efforts will yield acceptable performance or worries that they will perform well but no one will notice, they're likely to put less effort into their work.

CRITICAL THINKING: (1) What steps could managers take to alleviate the self-doubt employees often feel when they join a company or move into a new position? (2) If you were a human resources manager in a large corporation, how might you respond to employees who complain that the CEO makes two or three hundred times more than they make?

IT'S YOUR BUSINESS: (1) Have you ever given less than your best effort in a college course because you didn't believe you were capable of excelling in the course? (2) Was the outcome satisfying? Would you handle a similar situation the same way in the future?

KEY TERMS TO KNOW: expectancy theory, equity theory

Motivating with Challenging Goals

With the expectancy and equity theories offering some insight into why employees make the choices they do, the next step in understanding motivation is to explore specific leadership strategies that motivate employees. **Goal-setting theory**, the idea that carefully designed goals can motivate employees to higher performance, is one of the most important contemporary theories of motivation. It is both widely used and strongly supported by experimental research.[27] (However, as "Risks and Limitations of Goal-Setting Theory" explains, some researchers assert that the benefits of goal setting have been overstated and the risks have been understated, partly because some research studies fail to measure the full consequences of goal-driven behaviors.)

For goals to function as effective motivators, a number of criteria must be met. These criteria include[28]

- Goals that are specific enough to give employees clarity and focus
- Goals that are difficult enough to inspire energetic and committed effort
- Clear "ownership" of goals so that accountability can be established

- Timely feedback that lets people know if they're progressing toward their goals and, if not, how to change course
- Individuals' belief in their ability to meet their goals
- Cultural support for the individual achievement and independence needed to reach the goals

As today's companies face the twin challenges of increasing global competition and a slow economy, goal setting could play an even more important role than it already does.

MANAGEMENT BY OBJECTIVES

Goal-setting theory is frequently implemented through a technique known as **management by objectives (MBO)**, a companywide process that empowers employees and involves them in goal setting and decision making. This process consists of four steps: setting goals, planning actions, implementing plans, and reviewing performance (see Exhibit 5). Because employees at all levels are involved in all four steps, they learn more about company objectives and feel that they are an important part of the companywide team. Furthermore, they understand how their individual job functions contribute to the organization's long-term success.

One of the key elements of MBO is a collaborative goal-setting process. Together, a manager and an employee define the employee's goals, the responsibilities for achieving those goals, and the means of evaluating individual and group performance so that the employee's activities are directly linked to achieving the organization's long-term goals. Jointly setting clear and challenging but achievable goals can encourage employees to reach higher levels of performance, although participation alone is no guarantee of higher performance.[29]

REAL TIME UPDATES

Learn More by Exploring This Interactive Website

Plot your career path

See whether you've been on a straight path up the career ladder or have been moving around a career lattice. Go to http://real-timeupdates.com/bia6 and click on Learn More. If you are using MyBizLab, you can access Real-Time Updates within the chapter or under Student Study Tools.

management by objectives (MBO) A motivational approach in which managers and employees work together to structure personal goals and objectives for every individual, department, and project to mesh with the organization's goals

| EXHIBIT 5 | Management by Objectives |

The four steps of the MBO cycle are refined and repeated as managers and employees at all levels work toward establishing goals and objectives, thereby accomplishing the organization's strategic goals.

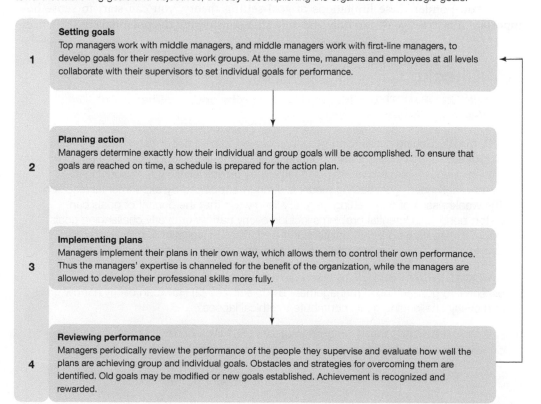

1 Setting goals
Top managers work with middle managers, and middle managers work with first-line managers, to develop goals for their respective work groups. At the same time, managers and employees at all levels collaborate with their supervisors to set individual goals for performance.

2 Planning action
Managers determine exactly how their individual and group goals will be accomplished. To ensure that goals are reached on time, a schedule is prepared for the action plan.

3 Implementing plans
Managers implement their plans in their own way, which allows them to control their own performance. Thus the managers' expertise is channeled for the benefit of the organization, while the managers are allowed to develop their professional skills more fully.

4 Reviewing performance
Managers periodically review the performance of the people they supervise and evaluate how well the plans are achieving group and individual goals. Obstacles and strategies for overcoming them are identified. Old goals may be modified or new goals established. Achievement is recognized and rewarded.

RISKS AND LIMITATIONS OF GOAL-SETTING THEORY

As powerful as goal setting can be, it can misfire in a variety of ways, with results ranging from employee frustration to systematic underperformance to serious ethical and legal problems:[30]

- **Overly narrow goals.** When goals are too narrow, people can miss or intentionally ignore vital aspects of the bigger picture. Salespeople trying to meet their quotas, for example, might be tempted to offer huge discounts or extend credit to customers who can't make the payments.

- **Overly challenging goals.** Lofty goals can inspire great performance, but they can also lead to risky behavior, belligerent negotiating tactics, and ethical lapses as employees cut corners to reach targets.

- **Inappropriate time horizons.** Too much emphasis on short-term performance can degrade long-term performance. A good example is the unhealthy focus that a publically traded company can place on quarterly performance in order to meet the stock market's expectations. This distorted focus can lead to decisions such as downsizing or cutting back on research that might help the bottom line in the short term but ultimately limit the company's ability to compete and grow.

- **Unintentional performance limitations.** Goals can limit performance potential when employees reach their targets and then stop trying, even though they could go beyond that level if reaching the goal didn't signal that it was acceptable to stop there.

- **Missed learning opportunities.** Employees can get so focused on meeting deadlines and other goals that they overlook opportunities to learn, whether to improve their own skills, fix process problems, or adapt to changes in the business environment—all of which could benefit the company more than meeting the original goal.[31]

- **Unhealthy internal competition.** Goals can pit groups within a company against each other, which can be beneficial if the competition is healthy but ultimately harmful if it is not. For example, healthy competitions among sales regions can be a great motivator, but what if several regions refuse to cooperate to help land a big national client?

- **Decreased intrinsic motivation.** Relying too heavily on public goals and their extrinsic rewards can eventually dull the intrinsic motivation to do well for the sake of the work itself—one of the most powerful and sustainable motivators.

As you ponder these limitations of goal-setting theory, you can start to sense how important it is to set goals carefully and only after considering the potential consequences.

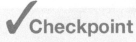 **Checkpoint**

LEARNING OBJECTIVE 3: Identify the strengths and weaknesses of *goal-setting theory*.

SUMMARY: Setting challenging goals has proven to be a dependable way to inspire employees to high levels of performance; goal setting is the foundation of a popular management system known as management by objectives (MBO). In addition to being widely used, goal-setting theory is strongly supported by experimental research. The weaknesses of goal setting generally lie in ways that the pursuit of goals can distort behavior. Potential problems include overly narrow or overly challenging goals, inappropriate time horizons, unintentional performance limitations, missed learning opportunities, unhealthy internal competition, and decreased intrinsic motivation.

CRITICAL THINKING: (1) Why is collaboration between employee and manager essential to goal setting in management by objectives? (2) How can overly narrow goals and overly challenging goals contribute to ethical lapses?

IT'S YOUR BUSINESS: (1) Do goals motivate you? Why or why not? (2) Does it depend on whether the goals are your own or imposed by someone else?

KEY TERMS TO KNOW: goal-setting theory, management by objectives (MBO)

Redesigning Jobs to Stimulate Performance

Along with setting challenging goals, many companies are exploring various ways to redesign the work itself to improve employee satisfaction and motivation.

4 **LEARNING OBJECTIVE**

Describe the *job characteristics model,* and explain how it helps predict motivation and performance.

THE JOB CHARACTERISTICS MODEL

Using the **job characteristics model** proposed by Richard Hackman and Greg Oldman has proven to be a reliable way to predict the effects of five *core job dimensions* on employee motivation and other positive outcomes:[32]

- **Skill variety**—the range of skills and talents needed to accomplish the responsibilities associated with the job. The broader the range of skills required, the more meaningful the work is likely to be to the employee.
- **Task identity**—the degree to which the employee has responsibility for completing an entire task. Greater task identity contributes to the sense of meaning in work.
- **Task significance**—the employee's perception of the impact the job has on the lives of other people.
- **Autonomy**—the degree of independence the employee has in carrying out the job.
- **Feedback**—timely information that tells employees how well they're doing in their jobs.

You can see that some of these dimensions relate to the nature of the work itself and others relate more to management decisions and leadership styles. All of them contribute in one way or another to three *critical psychological states:*

- **Experienced meaningfulness of the work**—a measure of how much employees care about the jobs they are doing.
- **Experienced responsibility for results**—the sense each employee has that his or her efforts contribute to the outcome.
- **Knowledge of actual results**—employees' awareness of the real-life results of their efforts.

As these psychological states increase in intensity, they lead to improvements in motivation, performance, job satisfaction, absenteeism (the amount of time employees miss work), and turnover (the rate at which employees leave their jobs). In other words, if employees believe their work is meaningful, believe their individual efforts are responsible at least in large part for the outcome of that work, and can see evidence of the results of their efforts, they are likely to be more motivated than they would otherwise. It's not hard to see that the reverse is true also. Employees who believe their work is meaningless, who don't feel much responsibility for the outcome, or who never get to see the results of their efforts aren't likely to be terribly motivated or satisfied.

One final aspect of job characteristics research explores how various types of employees respond to changes in the core job dimensions. Employees with strong *growth needs,* meaning they feel a strong need to increase self-esteem and self-actualization, respond more dramatically to improvements in job dimensions—and improvements in the critical psychological states will lead to greater increases in their motivation and the other positive outcomes.[33] Conversely, employees who feel little intrinsic need to grow can be among the most difficult to motivate, no matter what steps managers take.

The job characteristics model continues to offer helpful guidance as companies grapple with the challenges in today's work environment. For instance, as more companies increasingly rely on temporary workers to control costs or acquire skills that are needed only for specific projects, managers need to think carefully about the ways they supervise permanent versus temporary employees. As two examples, temporary workers may need to be assigned more discrete tasks that have enough task identity and autonomy to provide a sense of ownership and control, and managers need to make sure they don't take permanent employees for granted and fail to give them adequate feedback about their efforts.[34]

job characteristics model
A model suggesting that five core job dimensions influence three critical psychological states that determine motivation, performance, and other outcomes

APPROACHES TO MODIFYING CORE JOB DIMENSIONS

The job characteristics model identifies the generic aspects of a job that can be adjusted to improve motivation, but it's up to individual companies and departments to identify and make the specific changes that are relevant to each job in the organization. Three popular approaches are job enrichment, job enlargement, and cross-training:

job enrichment Making jobs more challenging and interesting by expanding the range of skills required

- **Job enrichment.** The strategy behind **job enrichment** is to make jobs more challenging and interesting by expanding the range of skills required—typically by expanding upward, giving employees some of the responsibilities previously held by their managers.[35] For example, an employee who had been preparing presentations for his or her boss to give to customers could be asked to give the presentations as well. Job enrichment needs to be approached carefully, however; some employees respond well, but for others, the increased responsibility is more a source of stress than of inspiration.[36]
- **Job enlargement.** Whereas job enrichment expands vertically, *job enlargement* is more of a horizontal expansion, adding tasks that aren't necessarily any more challenging. If it simply gives workers more to do, job enlargement won't do much to motivate and will more likely demotivate. However, if jobs are enlarged in ways that increase worker knowledge, expansion can improve job satisfaction.[37]

cross-training Training workers to perform multiple jobs and rotating them through these various jobs to combat boredom or burnout

- **Cross-training.** Job enrichment and job enlargement expand the scope of an individual job, whereas **cross-training**, or *job rotation*, involves training workers to perform multiple jobs and rotating them through these various jobs to combat boredom or burnout. Cross-training is also valuable in lean manufacturing because it lets companies keep staffs as small as possible and assign people wherever they are needed to handle fluctuations in workflow. And in a tight economy, cross-training helps companies address task needs without adding new staff.[38]

Not all the steps companies can take to improve motivation involve restructuring jobs, providing additional training, or making other explicit changes. Improvements can also come from making changes in management attitudes and practices, such as giving employees more control over their work and providing timely feedback. The best solution is usually a combination of changes that accommodate the nature of the work and the abilities and interests of individual employees and managers.

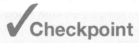

✓ Checkpoint

LEARNING OBJECTIVE 4: Describe the *job characteristics model,* and explain how it helps predict motivation and performance.

SUMMARY: The job characteristics model identifies five core job dimensions (skill variety, task identity, task significance, autonomy, and feedback) that create three critical psychological states (experienced meaningfulness of the work, experienced responsibility for results, and knowledge of actual results). Achieving these three states leads to improvements in motivation, job satisfaction, performance, absenteeism, and turnover.

CRITICAL THINKING: (1) Can the job characteristics model be used to motivate employees in such positions as janitors or security guards in a factory? How? (2) Is modifying the five core job dimensions likely to motivate employees who have low growth needs? Why or why not?

IT'S YOUR BUSINESS: (1) Has the requirement of working in teams ever lowered your motivation or satisfaction on a school project? If so, how does the job characteristics model explain this? (2) How does taking elective courses improve your experience of meaningfulness in your college "work"?

KEY TERMS TO KNOW: job characteristics model, job enrichment, cross-training

Reinforcing High-Performance Behavior

Challenging goals and creative job designs can motivate employees to higher levels of performance, but managers also need to make sure that performance can be sustained over time. Employees in the workplace, like people in all other aspects of life, tend to repeat behaviors that create positive outcomes for themselves and to avoid or abandon behaviors that bring negative outcomes. **Reinforcement theory** suggests that managers can motivate employees by shaping their actions through *behavior modification*. Using reinforcement theory, managers try to systematically encourage those actions considered beneficial to the company. Reinforcement is a valuable motivational tool, but it has broad application whenever managers want to shape employee behavior.

TYPES OF REINFORCEMENT

Reinforcement can be either *positive* or *negative*. In casual speech, the two terms are usually equated with praise for desirable behavior and criticism or punishment for undesirable behavior, respectively, but they have different and specific meanings in psychological terminology (see Exhibit 6). Both positive and negative reinforcement encourage behaviors to be repeated; the difference is in how they do it.

Positive reinforcement offers pleasant consequences for particular actions or behaviors, increasing the likelihood that the behaviors will be repeated. For example, even a simple but sincere "thank you" provides emotional reward and encourages employees to repeat whatever behavior elicited the praise.[39] Positive reinforcement can also have a multiplier effect, in which employees who receive positive reinforcement for one type of behavior are motivated to perform well in other areas, a process known as *chaining*.[40]

Many companies use some form of **incentives**, either monetary payments or other rewards of value, as positive reinforcement to motivate employees to achieve specific performance targets. Like praise and public recognition, incentive programs can become particularly important during economic slowdowns, when many employers can't afford to give big salary increases and companies aren't growing fast enough to create opportunities for career advancement.[41]

Again, don't be misled by the label "positive." Positive reinforcement can encourage bad behavior, so it isn't necessarily good. If an employee gets a compliment after taking credit for someone else's work, this positive feedback might encourage him or her to act unethically the next time the opportunity arises.

Negative reinforcement also encourages a particular behavior to be repeated, but it does so through the reduction, removal, or absence of an unpleasant outcome. Many people mistakenly use the term "negative reinforcement" when they are actually talking about *punishment*, which refers to actions used to diminish the repetition of unwanted behaviors by adding unpleasant outcomes.[42]

EXHIBIT 6   Reinforcement and Punishment

The terminology of reinforcement theory can be confusing because the terms are used differently in everyday speech than in psychology. Three points will help you keep the terms straight in your mind. First, both positive and negative reinforcement encourage a behavior to be repeated—they *reinforce* it, in order words. The difference is in how they work. Second, punishment (not negative reinforcement) is the opposite of positive reinforcement. Third, positive reinforcement can encourage undesirable behaviors, so it isn't necessarily a good thing, in spite of the "positive" label.

Recognition and reward programs can be powerful means for reinforcing desirable behaviors.

Masterfile Royalty Free Division

Of these three possibilities, you can see how positive reinforcement is the only one that injects positive energy into the situation. Fear can certainly be a powerful motivator, but it also adds stress and anxiety that can eventually lead to burnout and attrition as employees decide they don't want to deal with the constant pressure. And although punishment can be effective as a way to discourage particular behaviors, the effect isn't always permanent, and it can create serious morale problems.[43]

UNINTENDED CONSEQUENCES OF REINFORCEMENT

Reinforcement sounds like a simple enough concept, but the mechanisms of reinforcement can be subtle and the effects unexpected. Managers must be on constant alert for unintended consequences of incentives and other reinforcement efforts. For example, because they often focus on a single variable, incentive programs can distort performance by encouraging employees to focus on that variable to the detriment of other responsibilities.[44] If your salespeople get a bonus every time they land a new client but receive no penalties whenever an unhappy client leaves for a competitor, sales staffers will naturally tend to focus more on acquiring new clients than on making sure existing clients are satisfied.

Reinforcement doesn't have to involve explicit monetary incentives to distort behavior, either. For instance, imagine that a manager offers enthusiastic praise whenever employees suggest new ideas during meetings but never follows up to see whether those employees actually do any work to implement their great ideas. He or she can be encouraging empty "happy talk" through both positive reinforcement (there are pleasant consequences for spouting out ideas during meetings) *and* negative reinforcement (there are no unpleasant consequences for not doing any of the work, so employees will continue to not do it).

✓Checkpoint

LEARNING OBJECTIVE 5: Define *reinforcement theory,* and differentiate between positive and negative reinforcement.

SUMMARY: Reinforcement theory suggests that managers can motivate employees by systematically encouraging actions that are beneficial to the company. Positive and negative reinforcement both tend to increase the specific behavior in question, but positive reinforcement does so by providing pleasant consequences for engaging in the behavior, while negative reinforcement does so by removing unpleasant consequences. The term *negative reinforcement* is sometimes used in casual speech when people are really talking about *punishment,* which is discouraging a particular behavior by offering unpleasant consequences for it.

CRITICAL THINKING: (1) Is demoting an employee for failing to finish a project an attempt at negative reinforcement or punishment? Why? (2) In what ways is reinforcement theory similar to goal-setting theory?

IT'S YOUR BUSINESS: (1) How does your instructor in this course use positive reinforcement to motivate students to higher levels of performance? (2) If you study diligently to avoid being embarrassed when a professor calls on you in class, is this positive or negative reinforcement in action? Why?

KEY TERMS TO KNOW: reinforcement theory, positive reinforcement, incentives, negative reinforcement

Motivational Strategies

6 | LEARNING OBJECTIVE

List five managerial strategies that are vital to maintaining a motivated workforce.

Regardless of the specific motivational theories that a company chooses to implement in its management policies and reward systems, managers can improve their ability to motivate employees by providing timely and frequent feedback, personalizing motivational efforts, adapting to circumstances and special needs, tackling workplace problems before they have a chance to destroy morale, and being inspirational leaders.

PROVIDING TIMELY AND FREQUENT FEEDBACK

Imagine how you'd feel if you worked for weeks on a complex project for one of your classes, turned it in on time, and then heard . . . nothing. As days passed with no feedback, doubts would begin to creep in. Was your work so good that your professor is passing it around to other faculty members in sheer astonishment? Was it so bad that your professor is still searching for the words to describe it? Was your project simply lost in the shuffle, and no one cares enough to find it?

No matter which theory of motivation an organization or a manager subscribes to, providing timely and frequent feedback is essential. From the perspective of reinforcement theory, for example, feedback is the mechanism that shapes employee behavior. Without it, opportunities for reinforcement will be missed, and the effort put forth by employees will eventually wane because they'll see little reason to continue.

Feedback "closes the loop" in two important ways: It give employees the information they need in order to assess their own performance and make improvements if necessary, and it serves the emotional purpose of reassuring employees that someone is paying attention. Even if the feedback is constructive criticism, it lets employees know that what they do is important enough to be done correctly.

MAKING IT PERSONAL

A recurring theme in just about every attempt to explain motivation is that motivation is a deeply personal phenomenon. Rewards and feedback that stimulate one employee to higher achievement can have no effect on a second employee and may demotivate a third. As you'll see in Behind the Scenes at the end of the chapter, customizing career paths is an essential aspect of how Cathy Benko and her colleagues at Deloitte help to personalize motivation and rewards.

In an ideal world, managers would be able to personalize motivational efforts completely, giving each employee the rewards and feedback that spur him or her to peak achievement. However, the need for fairness and the demands on a manager's time place practical limits on the degree to which motivational efforts can be individualized. The situation calls for a three-pronged approach (see Exhibit 7 on the next page). First, establish systems and policies that are as equitable and as automatic as possible, and explain to employees why they are fair. Second, build in as much flexibility as you can, such as offering employees the cash equivalent of paid time off if they prefer money over time. Third, get to know employees as individuals in order to understand what is important to each person. For example, research suggests that younger employees are more likely to be demotivated by uninteresting work than their older counterparts.[45] (Another possible explanation is that older workers have learned to accept the fact that work can't always be exciting and are more willing to do whatever needs to be done.) If one person craves intellectual challenges, give him or her the tough problems to solve. If another thrives on recognition, give that employee the chance to give presentations to upper management.

Of course, managers need to give everyone an equal shot at opportunities, but as much as possible, they should let employees choose which opportunities and rewards they want to pursue. Employees understand that their managers can't always change "the system," but they do expect their managers to exercise some individual control over how policies are implemented and rewards are given.[46]

EXHIBIT 7	Personalizing Motivation

Making motivational efforts unique to the individual makes them more effective, but this must be done in a way that is fair for everyone. Achieving this balance is not always easy, because various employees are motivated by different things.

3. Get to know employees as individuals

2. Be as flexible as possible while still being fair

1. Establish systems and policies that are fair and automatic

ADAPTING TO CIRCUMSTANCES AND SPECIAL NEEDS

Just as the dynamics of motivation vary from person to person, they can vary from one situation to the next. For example, a slow economy and rising unemployment introduce a number of stresses into the workplace that need to be considered from a motivational perspective. Employers have less to spend on factors that can help avert employee dissatisfaction (salary, for example) or that can spur motivation (such as bonuses and other incentives). As a result, satisfaction and motivation are in danger of slipping, but employees have fewer options for finding new jobs if they aren't happy. The big exceptions are a company's top performers. When unemployment is rising and money is tight, high performers in any industry can often find new opportunities where average performers cannot. In other words, when companies are struggling, their best employees—the ones they need the most—are the ones most likely to leave. Consequently, managers need to work extra hard to keep these top performers happy and motivated.[47]

The threat of layoffs can motivate some employees but demoralize others. Some will work harder, in the hopes of minimizing their chances of being let go. Others, however, will wonder if there's any point in working hard if the economy is going to wipe out their jobs anyway. If layoffs are already starting to hit, survivors can be demoralized even further if they think the company is treating laid-off employees disrespectfully or unfairly.[48] Clearly, tough economic times put a huge motivational burden on managers, but those who treat employees with honesty and compassion stand the best chance of retaining the best people and keeping them motivated.

When the economy heats up again and unemployment drops, the balance of power shifts back toward workers. Employers who may have counted on job-loss fear as a motivator during the tough times will need to adjust strategies when employees have more options.[49]

ADDRESSING WORKPLACE NEGATIVITY

No workplace is immune to problems and conflicts, but negativity is an emotional "virus" that can infect an entire organization. Just as with physical health, managers must address workplace problems and conflicts quickly, before they multiply and erode employee morale. Left to fester long enough, these problems can destroy the sense of community in a company and leave employees feeling hopeless about the future.[50] Jumping on a problem quickly can have a double positive impact: It solves the problem, and it demonstrates to everyone that managers care about the emotional health of the workforce.

BEING AN INSPIRING LEADER

Theories and systems aside, inspired motivation in a business enterprise requires inspired leadership. To a large degree, good employees come to work already motivated—that's part of what makes them good employees. One of your jobs as a manager is to make sure you don't *demotivate* them. For example, in one survey of U.S. workers, more than one-third of respondents said their supervisors' habits of **micromanaging**—overseeing every small detail of employees' work and refusing to give them freedom or autonomy—were destroying their initiative.[51] Managers with low emotional intelligence can create toxic work environments that demotivate even the most driven employees, so it is essential for managers to understand the effect that their behaviors and attitudes have on employees.

micromanaging Overseeing every small detail of employees' work and refusing to give them freedom or autonomy

MOTIVATING YOURSELF

This chapter has focused on systems that organizations can put in place and various steps managers can take to motivate employees. However, this emphasis shouldn't obscure the role and responsibility of employees themselves. Every employee has an ethical obligation to find the motivation to accomplish the tasks for which he or she is getting paid. Managers can foster motivation (and they can certainly diminish it through clumsy leadership), but the motivation has to originate from within each employee.

For the latest information on motivation, visit http://real-timeupdates.com/bia6.

 Checkpoint

LEARNING OBJECTIVE 6: List five managerial strategies that are vital to maintaining a motivated workforce.

SUMMARY: No matter which motivational theories a company chooses to implement in its management policies and reward systems, managers can motivate employees more effectively by (1) providing timely and frequent feedback, (2) personalizing motivational efforts as much as possible while still being fair to all employees, (3) adapting motivational tactics to circumstances and special needs, (4) addressing workplace negativity before it has a chance to destroy morale, and (5) being inspirational leaders.

CRITICAL THINKING: (1) Referring to the job characteristics model, how does micromanaging destroy motivation? (2) Annual performance reviews are common in many companies; how might they fail to motivate employees?

IT'S YOUR BUSINESS: (1) If you are motivated more by the love of learning than the promised rewards of a grade, how can you motivate yourself when grades play a key role in your success as others perceive it? (2) Have you ever worked with someone (in a job or in school) whose negativity was contagious? How did you keep from letting that negativity drag down your own performance?

KEY TERM TO KNOW: micromanaging

BEHIND THE SCENES

MyBizLab

MOTIVATING INDIVIDUALS BY PERSONALIZING CAREERS AT DELOITTE

As the chief talent officer for a company brimming with talent, Deloitte's Cathy Benko knows how challenging it can be to create stimulating environments and opportunities to motivate a diverse workforce. And having traveled an unconventional path herself ("lots of zigs and zags" is how she describes it), she knows that a relentless 40-year climb up the corporate ladder is not for everyone.

The conventional ladder concept has never been right for many employees, and it is less appealing to a growing portion of the population. Benko explains that in the time span of just two generations, society and the workforce have been transformed to such an extent that the old ways of work don't work anymore. In studying this lack of fit between workplace and workforce, Benko and her colleagues identified five key issues:

- **A looming talent shortage.** Talk of not enough people to fill jobs might be difficult to fathom in the aftermath of a deep recession and continuing high unemployment, but the long-term trend is unmistakable. By 2025, the shortage of knowledge workers could be as high as 35 million people.
- **A vastly different society.** The corporate ladder—and with it the idea of devoting one's working life to a single company in order to climb one's way to the top—was conceived back in a time when two-thirds of U.S. households consisted of married couples in which one spouse (usually the husband) went to work and the other (usually the wife) stayed home. In a sense, this family structure helped support the corporate ladder by "freeing" the husband to devote himself to his company and career. Today, however, only about 15 percent of households fit that mold, and the old workplace ideals clearly don't fit them.
- **Expanded professional roles for women.** After years of gender imbalance in the workplace, women now hold more than half of all management jobs (although the ratio at the top of the ladder is still biased strongly toward men). Plus, women now earn nearly 60 percent of bachelor's and master's degrees, so the presence of women in professional positions is only going to expand.
- **Different desires and expectations from men.** A growing number of men are ready to explore a more balanced life with more flexibility and personal time than the constant ladder climb typically offers.
- **A dramatic shift in generational attitudes.** To a large degree, the Baby Boom generation (those born between 1946 and 1964) defined itself by work, and

the more of it the better, it seemed for many. However, the two generations that came after, Generation X and Generation Y, have different outlooks, with a much stronger desire to adapt their work to their lives rather than the other way around.

After pondering these tectonic shifts across the social landscape, Benko and Deloitte chose a new metaphor. Instead of a ladder, with its implication of a single path from bottom to top, they now speak in terms of a *lattice*, a crosshatch of horizontal and vertical lines. Just as a rosebush on a garden lattice can grow sideways and even downward for a while if upward isn't the best choice at the moment, a career lattice offers employees much the same flexibility.

Deloitte calls the model "mass career customization." Employees define where they've been, where they are, and where they'd like to go next, based on four variables: *pace* (from decelerated to accelerated), *workload* (reduced to full), *location/schedule* (restricted to not restricted), and *role* (individual contributor to leader). For example, to take time to have children or go back to college, a manager could step into a nonmanagerial individual contributor role with a reduced workload and less travel. "Our goal is to offer people options to keep their work and personal lives in sync," Benko explains, "and to give employers the loyalty of their best and brightest people. It ends up being a perfect fit."

Critical Thinking Questions

1. How might Deloitte's lattice approach help motivate employees and improve job satisfaction and performance?
2. How can managers determine whether a Deloitte employee is working at a decelerated pace in the career customization model or simply isn't working very hard?
3. What are the potential disadvantages, from the company's point of view, of giving employees this much flexibility?

LEARN MORE ONLINE

Visit the Mass Career Customization website, at www .masscareercustomization.com, which offers more information about the Deloitte lattice model. Read "About MCC" and then try the "Interactive Exercise," where you can chart your own career (real or imaginary). You can also download a brief version of the book Benko co-authored with another Deloitte executive, Anne Weisberg. Does the lattice model sound appealing to you?

MyBizLab

Log on to www.mybizlab.com to access study and assessment aids associated with this chapter.

KEY TERMS

cross-training
engagement
equity theory
expectancy theory
goal-setting theory
Hawthorne effect
Herzberg's two-factor theory
incentives
job characteristics model
job enrichment
management by objectives (MBO)

Maslow's hierarchy
micromanaging
motivation
negative reinforcement
positive reinforcement
reinforcement theory
scientific management
Theory X
Theory Y
three-needs theory

TEST YOUR KNOWLEDGE

Questions for Review

1. What is motivation?
2. What is expectancy theory?
3. What is management by objectives?
4. What are the core job dimensions in the job characteristics model?
5. What is negative reinforcement?

Questions for Analysis

6. How does expectancy theory explain the effect of self-doubt on employee motivation?
7. How might a deadline that is too easy to meet cause someone to work more slowly than he or she might otherwise work?
8. What effect will job enhancement likely have on someone with low growth needs? Why?
9. Why do managers often find it difficult to motivate employees who remain after downsizing?
10. Ethical Considerations. Motivational strategies that reward employees for meeting specific performance targets can encourage them to work hard—sometimes too hard. Overwork can contribute to mental and physical health problems as well as interfere with other aspects of employees' lives. As a manager, how do you determine how much work is too much for your employees?

Questions for Application

11. You manage the customer service department for an online clothing retailer. Customers tend to call or email with the same types of complaints and problems, day after day, and your employees are getting bored and listless. Some are starting to miss more days of work than usual, and several have quit recently. A few customers have called you directly to complain about poor treatment from your staff. Use the job characteristics model to identify several ways you could improve motivation, job satisfaction, and performance.
12. How do you motivate yourself when faced with school assignments or projects that are difficult or tedious? Do you ever try to relate these tasks to your overall career goals? Are you more motivated by doing your personal best or by outperforming other students?
13. Imagine yourself in one of the jobs you would like to land after graduation. Thinking about the importance of personalizing motivational tactics whenever possible, identify several steps your manager could take to make sure you stay motivated. Would these steps be fair to other employees as well?
14. This question was intentionally excluded from this edition.

EXPAND YOUR KNOWLEDGE

Discovering Career Opportunities

Whether you're a top manager, first-line manager (supervisor), or middle manager, your efforts will affect the success of your organization. To get a closer look at the responsibilities of a manager, log on to the Prentice Hall Student Success SuperSite, at www.prenhall.com/success. Click on "Majors Exploration" and then select "Business" and "Management" from the drop-down boxes. Then scroll down and read about careers in management. What can you do with a degree in management? What is the future outlook for careers in management?

Improving Your Tech Insights: Blogging and Microblogging.

Blogging and microblogging (of which Twitter is the best-known example) have revolutionized business communication in recent years. Far more than just another communication medium, blogging and microblogging help change the relationship between companies and their stakeholders by transforming communication from a formal "we talk, you listen" mindset to an informal and interactive conversational mindset.

Identify a company in which one or more managers are regular bloggers or Twitter users. In a brief email to your instructor, explain how the company uses blogging to build relationships with customers and potential customers, employees and potential employees, and other stakeholder groups.

PRACTICE YOUR SKILLS

Sharpening Your Communication Skills

Choose one of the major motivation theories discussed in this chapter: expectancy, goal-setting, job characteristics, or reinforcement theory. Create a brief electronic presentation (three to five slides) using PowerPoint, Keynote, Google Docs, or a similar tool explaining the theory and identifying its strengths and weaknesses as a practical management approach.

Building Your Team Skills

With your teammates, explore the careers sections of the websites of six companies in different industries. Look for descriptions of the work environment, incentive plans, career paths, and other information about how the company develops, motivates, and supports its employees. After you've compiled notes about each company, vote on the most appealing company to work for. Next, review the notes for this company and identify all the theories of motivation described in this chapter that the company appears to be using, based on the information on its website.

Developing Your Research Skills

Various periodicals and websites feature "best companies to work for" lists. Locate one of these lists and find a company that does a great job of attracting and motivating high performers. Learn as much as you can about the company's management philosophies. Which of the motivation theories does the company appear to be using? Summarize your findings in a brief email message to your instructor.

REFERENCES

1. "Learn About Our Leaders," Deloitte website, accessed 28 August 2011, www.deloitte.com; Cathy Benko, "Up the Ladder? How Dated, How Linear," *New York Times*, 9 November 2008, www.deloitteandtouche.org; Mass Career Customization website, accessed 28 August 2011, www.masscareercustomization.com; Anne Fisher, "When Gen X Runs the Show," *Time*, 25 May 2009, 48–49; Lisa Takeuchi Cullen, "Flex Work Is Not the Answer," Work in Progress blog, 10 October 2007, http://workinprogress.blogs.time.com; Laura Fitzpatrick, "We're Getting Off the Ladder," *Time*, 5 May 2009, 45; "Customizing Your Career," Deloitte website, accessed 17 June 2009, http://careers.deloitte.com; "Mass Career Customization," PBWC Connections website, accessed 17 June 2009, http://www.pbwcconnections.com; Intel Corporation website, accessed 28 August 2011, www.intel.com; "Intel Corporation," Hoovers, accessed 28 August 2011, www.hoovers.com.

2. Piers Steel and Cornelius J. König, "Integrating Theories of Motivation," *Academy of Management Review* 31, No. 4 (2006): 889–913.

3. Nitin Nohria, Boris Groysberg, and Linda-Eling Lee, "Employee Motivation: A Powerful New Model," *Harvard Business Review*, July–August 2008, 78–84.

4. Nohria, Groysberg, and Lee, "Employee Motivation: A Powerful New Model."

5. Nohria, Groysberg, and Lee, "Employee Motivation: A Powerful New Model."

6. Robbins and DeCenzo, *Fundamentals of Management*, 27–29.

7. Augustine Brannigan and William Zwerman, "The Real 'Hawthorne Effect'" *Society*, January/February 2001, 55–60; Stephen P. Robbins and Mary Coulter, *Management*, 10th ed. (Upper Saddle River, N.J.: Pearson Prentice Hall, 2009), 34.

8. Brannigan and Zwerman, "The Real 'Hawthorne Effect'"; Robbins and Coulter, *Management*, 34.

9. Frank Merrett, "Reflections on the Hawthorne Effect," *Educational Psychology*, February 2006, 143–146; Brannigan and Zwerman, "The Real 'Hawthorne Effect.'"

10. Mecca Chiesa and Sandy Hobbs, "Making Sense of Social Research: How Useful Is the Hawthorne Effect?" *European*

Journal of Social Psychology, 38, 67–74 (2008); Brannigan and Zwerman, "The Real 'Hawthorne Effect'"; Robbins and Coulter, *Management*, 34.

11. Andrew J. DuBrin, *Applying Psychology: Individual & Organizational Effectiveness*, 6th ed. (Upper Saddle River, N.J.: Pearson Prentice Hall, 2004), 122–124.
12. Robbins and Coulter, *Management*, 342.
13. Richard L. Daft, *Management*, 6th ed. (Mason, Ohio: Thomson South-Western, 2003), 547; Robbins and DeCenzo, *Fundamentals of Management*, 283–284; DuBrin, *Applying Psychology: Individual & Organizational Effectiveness*, 15–16.
14. Stephen P. Robbins and Timothy A. Judge, *Essentials of Organizational Behavior*, 10th ed. (Upper Saddle River, N.J.: Pearson Prentice Hall, 2010), 64.
15. Daft, *Management*, 552–553.
16. Robbins and Judge, *Essentials of Organizational Behavior*, 66.
17. Rosa Chun and Gary Davies, "Employee Happiness Isn't Enough to Satisfy Customers," *Harvard Business Review*, April 2009, 19; Robbins and Judge, *Essentials of Organizational Behavior*, 66.
18. Saundra K. Ciccarelli and Glenn E. Meyer, *Psychology* (Upper Saddle River, N.J.: Prentice Hall, 2006), 339–340.
19. "Seeking to Hire Strong Leaders? Buyer Beware!" *Compensation & Benefits for Law Offices*, September 2006, 1+.
20. David C. McClelland and David H. Burnham, "Power Is the Great Motivator," *Harvard Business Review*, January 2003, 117–126; Robbins and Judge, *Essentials of Organizational Behavior*, 66–67.
21. Robbins and Judge, *Essentials of Organizational Behavior*, 67.
22. Robbins and DeCenzo, *Fundamentals of Management*, 289.
23. Robbins and Judge, *Essentials of Organizational Behavior*, 72.
24. Daft, *Management*, 554–555.
25. Robbins and Judge, *Essentials of Organizational Behavior*, 75.
26. Deborah Archambeault, Christopher M. Burgess, and Stan Davis, "Is Something Missing from Your Company's Satisfaction Package?" *CMA Management*, May 2009, 20–23.
27. Robbins and Coulter, *Management*, 346.
28. Bill Lycette and John Herniman, "New Goal-Setting Theory," *Industrial Management*, September 2008, 25–30; Robbins and Coulter, *Management*, 346–347.
29. Robbins and Coulter, *Management*, 346.
30. Lisa Ordóñez, Maurice Schweitzer, Adam Galinsky, and Max Bazerman, "Goals Gone Wild: The Systematic Side Effects of Overprescribing Goal Setting," *Academy of Management Perspectives*, February 2009, 6–16.
31. Robert D. Ramsey, "Why Deadlines and Quotas Don't Always Work," *Supervision*, October 2008, 3–5.
32. Richard J. Hackman and Greg R. Oldman, "Motivation Through the Design of Work: Test of a Theory," *Organizational Behavior & Human Performance*, August 1976, 250–279; Robbins and Judge, *Essentials of Organizational Behavior*, 81–82; Jed DeVaro, Robert Li, and Dana Brookshire, "Analysing the Job Characteristics Model: New Support from a Cross-Section of Establishments," *International Journal of Human Resource Management*, June 2007, 986–1003.
33. Robbins and Judge, *Essentials of Organizational Behavior*, 82.
34. Stuart D. Galup, Gary Klein, and James J. Jiang, "The Impacts of Job Characteristics on IS Employee Satisfaction: A Comparison Between Permanent and Temporary Employees," *Journal of Computer Information Systems*, Summer 2008, 58–68.
35. Robbins and Coulter, *Management*, 348.
36. Scott Lazenby, "How to Motivate Employees: What Research Is Telling Us," *Public Management*, September 2008, 22–25.
37. Robbins and Coulter, *Management*, 348.
38. "Caution Urged in Expanding Cross-Training of CU Staff," *Credit Union Journal*, 5 January 2009, 18.
39. Debi O'Donovan, "Motivation Is Key in a Crisis and Words Can Be the Best Reward," *Employee Benefits*, April 2009, 5.
40. Timothy R. Hinkin and Chester A. Schriesheim, "Performance Incentives for Tough Times," *Harvard Business Review*, March 2009, 26.
41. Tom Washington, "Incentives Play Big Part in Motivation During Recession," *Employee Benefits*, April 2009, 14.
42. Ciccarelli and Meyer, *Psychology*, 179.
43. Robbins and Coulter, *Management*, 348.
44. Dan Heath and Chip Heath, "The Curse of Incentives," *Fast Company*, February 2009, 48–49.
45. "Tailor Motivation Techniques to the Worker," *Teller Vision*, March 2009, 5–6.
46. Nohria, Groysberg, and Lee, "Employee Motivation: A Powerful New Model."
47. Edward E. Lawler III, "Value-Based Motivation," *BusinessWeek*, 27 April 2009, 22.
48. Joan Lloyd, "Threat of Layoffs Demoralizes Employees," *Receivables Report for America's Health Care Financial Managers*, May 2009, 10–11.
49. Lawler, "Value-Based Motivation."
50. Betty MacLaughlin Frandsen, "Overcoming Workplace Negativity," *Long-Term Living: For the Continuing Care Professional*, March 2009, 26–27.
51. "Don't Be a Drag," *CA Magazine*, January–February 2009, 9.

GLOSSARY

cross-training Training workers to perform multiple jobs and rotating them through these various jobs to combat boredom or burnout

engagement An employee's rational and emotional commitment to his or her work

equity theory The idea that employees base their level of satisfaction on the ratio of their inputs to the job and the outputs or rewards they receive from it

expectancy theory The idea that the effort employees put into their work depends on expectations about their own ability to perform, expectations about likely rewards, and the attractiveness of those rewards

goal-setting theory A motivational theory suggesting that setting goals can be an effective way to motivate employees

Hawthorne effect A supposed effect of organizational research, in which employees change their behavior because they are being studied and given special treatment; the validity of the effect is uncertain, and

the Hawthorne studies were richer and more influential than this simple outcome would suggest

Herzberg's two-factor theory A model that divides motivational forces into satisfiers ("motivators") and dissatisfiers ("hygiene factors")

incentives Monetary payments and other rewards of value used for positive reinforcement

job characteristics model A model suggesting that five core job dimensions influence three critical psychological states that determine motivation, performance, and other outcomes

job enrichment Making jobs more challenging and interesting by expanding the range of skills required

management by objectives (MBO) A motivational approach in which managers and employees work together to structure personal goals and objectives for every individual, department, and project to mesh with the organization's goals

Maslow's hierarchy A model in which human needs are arranged in a hierarchy, with the most basic needs at the bottom and the more advanced needs toward the top

micromanaging Overseeing every small detail of employees' work and refusing to give them freedom or autonomy

motivation The combination of forces that move individuals to take certain actions and avoid other actions

negative reinforcement Encouraging the repetition of a particular behavior (desirable or not) by removing unpleasant consequences for the behavior

positive reinforcement Encouraging desired behaviors by offering pleasant consequences for completing or repeating those behaviors

reinforcement theory A motivational approach based on the idea that managers can motivate employees by influencing their behaviors with positive and negative reinforcement

scientific management A management approach designed to improve employees' efficiency by scientifically studying their work

Theory X A managerial assumption that employees are irresponsible, are unambitious, and dislike work and that managers must use force, control, or threats to motivate them

Theory Y A managerial assumption that employees enjoy meaningful work, are naturally committed to certain goals, are capable of creativity, and seek out responsibility under the right conditions

three-needs theory David McClelland's model of motivation that highlights the needs for power, affiliation, and achievement

Production Systems

Production Systems

1 Explain the systems perspective and identify seven principles of systems thinking that can improve your skills as a manager

2 Describe the *value chain* and *value web* concepts and discuss the controversy over offshoring

3 Define *supply chain management* and explain its strategic importance

4 Identify the major planning decisions in production and operations management

5 Explain the unique challenges of service delivery

6 Define *quality*, explain the challenge of quality and product complexity, and identify four major tools and strategies for ensuring product quality

MyBizLab

Where you see MyBizLab in this chapter, go to www.mybizlab.com for additional activities on the topic being discussed.

BEHIND THE SCENES CUSTOMIZING DREAMS AT CARVIN GUITARS

© Blend Images/Alamy

Carvin offers personalized guitars at affordable prices through a combination of sophisticated production systems and old-world handicraft.

www.carvinguitars.com

After beginning guitarists have mastered the nuances of "Mary Had a Little Lamb" and set their sights on making serious music, they often encounter a serious equipment dilemma. Low-cost, beginner guitars lack the materials and workmanship needed to produce top-quality sounds. Some are difficult to keep in tune, and some cannot produce true notes all the way up and down the neck. Plus, they just aren't very cool. Nobody wants to jump on stage in front of 50,000 adoring fans with a guitar purchased at the local discount store.

And so the shopping begins, as the aspiring guitarist looks to find a better "axe." As with just about every product category these days, the array of choices is dizzying. For a few hundred dollars, budding musicians can choose from several imports that offer improved quality. Jumping up toward $1,000 to $2,000, they can enter the world of such classic American brands as Fender, Gibson, and Martin—a world that goes up to $10,000 and beyond for limited-edition models. Musicians with that much to spend and several months to wait can also hire skilled instrument builders known as *luthiers* to create custom guitars that reflect their individual personalities and playing styles. Luthiers can custom-craft just about any attribute a guitarist might want, from the types of wood for the body to the radius of the fingerboard.

But what if our superstar-in-training wants it all: world-class quality, the personalized touch of a custom guitar, and a midrange price tag, without the long delays associated with handcrafted instruments?

That "sweet spot" in the guitar market is the territory staked out by Carvin, a San Diego company that has been in the instrument business for over 60 years. How can Carvin profitably do business in this seemingly impossible market segment? How could the company quickly customize guitars and sell them in the $750 to $1,500 range without compromising quality?[1]

INTRODUCTION

Carvin (profiled in the chapter-opening Behind the Scenes) faced a classic systems challenge: how to design and operate business processes that would enable the company to deliver its unique value to customers. This chapter starts with an overview of systems concepts that every manager can use in any functional area; it then explores systems-related issues in the production function, including value chains and value webs, supply chain management, production and operations management, services delivery, and product and process quality.

The Systems View of Business

One of the most important skills you can develop as a manager is the ability to view business from a systems perspective. A **system** is an interconnected and coordinated set of *elements* and *processes* that converts *inputs* into desired *outputs*. A company is made up of numerous individual systems in the various functional areas, not only in manufacturing or operations but also in engineering, marketing, accounting, and other areas that together constitute the overall system that is the company itself. Each of these individual systems can also be thought of as a *subsystem* of the overall business.

THINKING IN SYSTEMS

To grasp the power of systems thinking, consider a point, a line, and a circle (see Exhibit 1 on the next page). If you poked your head into a nearby office building, what would this snapshot tell you? You could see only one part of the entire operation—and only at this one point in time. You might see people in the advertising department working on plans for a new ad campaign or people in the accounting department juggling numbers in spreadsheets, but neither view would tell you much about what it takes to complete these tasks or how that department interacts with the rest of the company.

If you stood and observed for several days, though, you could start to get a sense of how people do their jobs in this department. In the advertising department, for instance, you could watch as the staff transforms ideas, information, and goals into a plan that leads to the creation of a new online advertising campaign. Your "point" view would thereby extend into a "line" view, with multiple points connected in sequence. However, you still wouldn't have a complete picture of the entire process in action. Was the campaign successful? What did the marketing department learn from the campaign that could help it do even better next time? To see the process operate over and over, you need to connect the end of the line (the completion of this ad campaign) back to the beginning of the line (the start of the next ad campaign) to create a circle. Now you're beginning to form a systems view of what this department does and how its performance can be improved.

This circular view helps you understand the advertising system better, but it still isn't complete, because it doesn't show you how the advertising system affects the rest of the company and vice versa. For instance, did the finance department provide enough money to run the ad campaign? Was the information technology group prepared to handle the surge in website traffic? Was the manufacturing department ready with enough materials

My BizLab

Gain hands-on experience through an interactive, real-world scenario. This chapter's simulation entitled Improving a Business is located at www.mybizlab.com.

1 | LEARNING OBJECTIVE

Explain the systems perspective, and identify seven principles of systems thinking that can improve your skills as a manager.

system An interconnected and coordinated set of *elements* and *processes* that converts *inputs* to desired *outputs*

EXHIBIT 1	From Point to Line to Circle: The Systems View

The systems view considers all the steps in a process and "closes the loop" by providing feedback from the output of one cycle back to the input of the next cycle.

Point view: single activity at single moment in time — Step 1

Line view: multiple activities in sequence — Step 1 → Step 2 → Step 3 → Step 4

Circle view: results of one cycle provide feedback to the next cycle

Step 1 → Step 2 → Step 3 → Step 4 → Measure and analyze results → Provide feedback to the next cycle → Step 1

to build the product after customers started placing orders? Were the sales and customer service departments ready to handle the increase in their workloads? All of these subsystems connect to form the overall business system. Only by looking at the interconnected business system can you judge whether the ad campaign was a success for the company as a whole.

MANAGING SYSTEMS FOR PEAK PERFORMANCE

Much of the art and science of management involves understanding systems or creating new systems and figuring out ways to make them work more efficiently (using fewer resources) and more effectively (meeting goals more successfully). In some instances, systems analysis can run computer simulations to experiment with changes before making any resource decisions (see Exhibit 2). However, even without these formal techniques and tools, you can benefit from systems thinking by keeping these principles in mind:[2]

- **Help everyone see the big picture.** It's human nature for individual employees and departments to focus on their own goals and lose sight of what the company as a whole is trying to accomplish. Showing people how they contribute to the overall goal—and rewarding them for doing so—helps ensure that the entire system works efficiently.
- **Understand how individual systems really work and how they interact.** Managers need to avoid the temptation to jump in and try to fix systems without understanding how each one works and how they interact with other systems. For instance, as a wholesaling distribution manager, you might notice that delivery drivers are spending more time at retail sites than deliveries really take, so you instruct drivers to reduce the amount of time they spend. However, it might be that drivers are spending that time gathering market intelligence that they turn over to the sales staff. If you're not careful, you might improve the distribution system but damage the sales system.

EXHIBIT 2   **Systems Diagram and Simulation**

This example of a formal systems diagram models the flow of people at a ski resort, from arriving at the chairlift to taking the lift up the hill to skiing back down, then returning to the lift line. The resort is anticipating a boom in business and needs to figure out how to handle the additional skiers. By mathematically modeling the number of skiers at each point in the system, the resort can simulate several options: doing nothing, getting a faster chairlift, switching to triple chairs, or switching to quadruple chairs. Doing nothing would result in a long line waiting to get on the lift, while getting a faster lift (shown in the graph) would solve that problem but result in overcrowding on the slope. The optimum solution turns out to be switching to quad chairs.

Ski Resort Dynamics
Core Model Structure

Ski Resort Dynamics
Simulate

Source: Used with permission from Isee Systems, Inc., www.iseesystems.com.

- **Understand problems before you try to fix them.** The most obvious answer is not always the right answer, and poorly conceived solutions often end up causing more harm than good. When you analyze system behavior and malfunctions, make sure you focus on things that are *meaningful*, not merely things that are *measurable*. For instance, it's easy to measure how many reports employees write every month, but that might not be the most meaningful gauge of how well a process is working.

- **Understand the potential impact of solutions before you implement them.** Let's say you manage the customer support department, and to encourage high productivity, you run a weekly contest to see who can handle the most calls. Trouble is, you're essentially rewarding people based on how quickly they can get the customer off the phone, not on how quickly they actually solve customer problems. Customers who aren't happy keep calling back—which adds to the department's workload and *decreases* overall productivity.

- **Don't just move problems around—solve them.** When one subsystem in a company is malfunctioning, its problems are sometimes just moved around from one subsystem to the next, without ever getting solved. For example, if the market research department does a poor job of understanding customers, this problem will get shifted to the engineering department, which is likely to design a product that doesn't meet customer needs. The problem will then get shifted to the advertising and sales departments, which will struggle to promote and sell the product. The engineering, advertising, and sales departments will all underperform, but the real problem is back in the market research department. Market research in this case is a *leverage point*, where a relatively small correction could make the entire company perform better.

- **Understand how feedback works in the system.** Systems respond to *feedback*, which is information from the output applied back to the input. In the case of an ad campaign, the response from target customers is a form of feedback that helps the department understand whether the campaign is working. Feedback can work in unanticipated ways, too. A good example is managers sending mixed signals to their employees, such as telling them that customer satisfaction is the top priority but then criticizing anyone who spends too much time helping customers. Employees will respond to this feedback by spending less time with customers, leading to a decline in customer satisfaction.

- **Use mistakes as opportunities to learn and improve.** When mistakes occur, resist the temptation to just criticize or complain and then move on. Pull the team together and find out why the mistake occurred, and then identify ways to fix the system to eliminate mistakes in the future.

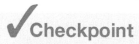 **Checkpoint**

LEARNING OBJECTIVE 1: Explain the systems perspective, and identify seven principles of systems thinking that can improve your skills as a manager.

SUMMARY: The systems perspective involves looking at business as a series of interconnected and interdependent systems rather than as a lot of individual activities and events. Seven principles of systems thinking that can help every manager are (1) helping everyone see the big picture, (2) understanding how individual systems really work and how they interact, (3) understanding problems before you try to fix them, (4) understanding the potential impact of solutions before you implement, (5) avoiding the temptation to just move problems from one subsystem to the next without fixing them, (6) understanding how feedback works in a system so that you can improve each process by learning from experience, and (7) using mistakes as opportunities to learn and improve a system.

Value Chains and Value Webs

The essential purpose of a business is adding value—transforming lower-value inputs into higher-value outputs. The details vary widely from industry to industry, but all businesses focus on some kind of transformation like this (see Exhibit 3). The **value chain** is a helpful way to consider all the elements and processes that add value as input materials are transformed into the final products made available to the ultimate customer.[3] Each industry has a value chain, and each company has its own value chain as well.

REDEFINING ORGANIZATIONS WITH VALUE WEBS

In the decades since Michael Porter introduced the value chain concept, many companies have come to realize that doing everything themselves is not always the most efficient or most successful way to run a business. Many now opt to focus on their core competencies and let other companies handle the remaining business functions—a strategy known as **outsourcing**. Hiring other firms to handle some tasks is not a new concept, to be sure;

EXHIBIT 3 | **Business Transformation Systems**

All businesses engage in a transformation process of some kind, converting one type of value (inputs) to another type (outputs).

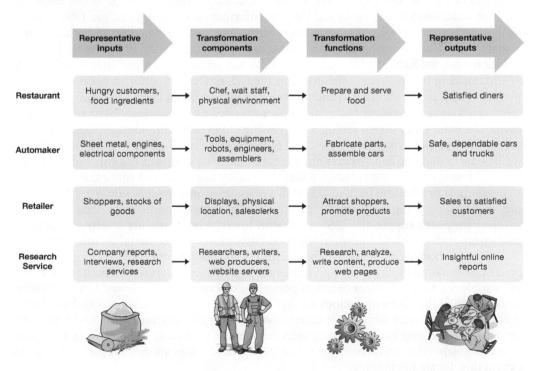

	Representative inputs	Transformation components	Transformation functions	Representative outputs
Restaurant	Hungry customers, food ingredients	Chef, wait staff, physical environment	Prepare and serve food	Satisfied diners
Automaker	Sheet metal, engines, electrical components	Tools, equipment, robots, engineers, assemblers	Fabricate parts, assemble cars	Safe, dependable cars and trucks
Retailer	Shoppers, stocks of goods	Displays, physical location, salesclerks	Attract shoppers, promote products	Sales to satisfied customers
Research Service	Company reports, interviews, research services	Researchers, writers, web producers, website servers	Research, analyze, write content, produce web pages	Insightful online reports

advertising, public relations, and transportation are among the services that have a long history of being handled by outside firms. The term *outsourcing* is usually applied when a firm decides to move a significant function that was previously done in house, such as information technology or manufacturing, to an outside vendor.

The combination of extensive globalization in many industries and the development of electronic networking has made it easy for companies to connect with partners around the world. Instead of the linear value chain, some businesses now think in terms of **value webs**, multidimensional networks of suppliers and outsourcing partners.[4] Value webs enable the virtual or network organization structures, and *unstructured organizations* can be viewed as dynamic value webs that grow, shrink, or change as the company's needs change.

value webs Multidimensional networks of suppliers and outsourcing partners

The outsourced, value web approach has several key advantages, including speed, flexibility, and the opportunity to access a wide range of talents and technologies that might be expensive or impossible to acquire otherwise. Established companies can narrow their focus to excel at their core competencies; entrepreneurs with product ideas can quickly assemble a team of designers, manufacturing plants, and distributors in far less time than it would take to build an entire company from scratch.

For all its potential advantages, outsourcing does carry some risks, particularly in terms of control. For example, to get its new 787 Dreamliner to market as quickly as possible, Boeing outsourced the manufacturing of many parts of the new plane to other manufacturers. Boeing managers initially decided not to impose the "Boeing way" on these suppliers, so it took a hands-off approach. However, the lack of control came to haunt the company. Many suppliers missed target dates and quality standards, throwing the Dreamliner off schedule by at least three years and costing Boeing billions of dollars in extra work, canceled sales, and delivery penalties.[5]

THE OFFSHORING CONTROVERSY

When companies outsource any function in the value chain, they usually eliminate many of the jobs associated with that function as well. In many cases, those jobs don't go across the street to another local company but rather around the world as companies pursue lower labor costs, a variation on outsourcing known as **offshoring**. (Offshoring can shift jobs to another company or to an overseas division of the same company.)

offshoring Transferring a part or all of a business function to a facility (a different part of the company or another company entirely) in another country

Offshoring has been going on for decades, but it began to be a major issue for U.S. manufacturing in the 1980s and then for information technology in the 1990s. Today, offshoring is affecting jobs in science, engineering, law, finance, banking, and other professional areas.[6] The offshoring debate is a great example of conflicting priorities in the stakeholder model; see Exhibit 4 for a summary of the key arguments for and against offshoring.

Measuring the impact of offshoring on the U.S. economy is difficult because isolating the effect of a single variable in such a complex system is not easy. For example, economists often struggle to identify the specific reasons one country gains jobs or another loses them. The emergence of new technology, phasing out of old technology, shifts in consumer tastes, changes in business strategies, and other factors can all create and destroy jobs.

As the offshoring debate rages on, the nature of offshoring is changing. The complexities and rising costs of long-distance manufacturing has prompted some U.S. companies to move their production back to U.S. soil, a phenomenon known as *reshoring*. For example, as manufacturing wages in China continue to increase and the demand for skilled workers outpaces supply, the U.S. states with lowest labor costs are starting to become cost-competitive with China when the total costs of offshoring are taken into account.[7]

While reshoring might reduce the amount of offshoring done by U.S. companies, globalized manufacturing is here to stay, so it's in everyone's best interest to make it work as well as possible for as many stakeholders as possible. For example, how should U.S. companies be taxed when they have operations all over the world? Also, should unions and regulatory agencies make it more difficult for companies to move jobs overseas, or would it be more beneficial in the long run to let companies compete as vigorously as possible and focus on retraining American workers for new jobs here? These issues are not simple, and you can expect this debate to continue.

EXHIBIT 4	The Offshoring Controversy

Offshoring, or shifting jobs performed by U.S. employees to countries with lower labor costs, is a complex controversy that pits some stakeholders against others. Here are the major arguments for and against the practice, along with some of the key stakeholder groups affected.

Arguments for Offshoring		Arguments Against or Concerns About Offshoring	
Stakeholders who benefit	**Argument**	**Stakeholders who suffer**	**Argument**
Shareholders	**Responsibility to shareholder interests:** Companies that engage in offshoring say they have a duty to manage shareholder investments for maximum gain, so it would be irresponsible not to explore cost-saving opportunities such as offshoring.	Workers	**Loss of well-paid U.S. jobs:** Opponents of offshoring say that companies are selling out the U.S. middle class in pursuit of profits and pushing a trend that can only harm the country.
Consumers	**Lower prices for U.S. consumers:** For goods in which labor represents a significant portion of production costs, dramatically lowering labor costs lets a company lower its prices to consumers.	Shareholders	**Hidden costs and risks:** Critics and some insiders say the real savings are not as great as proponents claim and that same companies fail to adequately analyze the costs and risks. Says J.Paul Dittman of the University of Tennessee, "Many firms are rethinking the mad rush to outsource . . . the long supply lines, incredibly volatile fuel costs, exchange rates, the geopolitical risks have all come home to roost."
Shareholders	**Lack of choice in competitive industries:** Given the pricing advantage that offshoring can give U.S. companies, as soon as one company in an industry does it, the others are put under pressure to lower their prices—and offshoring might be the only way for some to lower costs enough to do so.	Shareholders	**Business agility and responsiveness:** When companies rely on operations halfway around the world, marketplace trends and customer service matters.
Shareholders	**Support for local customers around the world:** Some companies say that as they expand into other countries, they have no choice but to hire overseas employees in order to support local customers.	Shareholders	**Knowledge transfer and theft risk:** By hiring other companies to perform technical and professional services, U.S. companies transfer important knowledge to these other countries—making them more competitive and potentially depleting the pools of expertise in the United States. Offshoring can also increase the risks of product piracy and theft of intellectual property.
U.S. economy	**U.S. competitiveness:** Proponents say that offshoring is crucial to the survival of many U.S. companies and that it saves other U.S. jobs by making U.S. companies more competitive in the global marketplace.	U.S. economy	
		Consumers	**Product safety issues:** Moving more production beyond U.S. borders increases concerns about the ability of regulators to oversee vital health and safety issues.
		United States	**National security and public health concerns:** The weapons and systems used for national defense require lots of steel, semiconductors, and other manufactured materials, and the health-care industry requires a vast supply of materials. What if the United States comes to rely too heavily on other countries for things it needs to protect its borders and its people?
		Consumers	

Sources: Adapted from J. Paul Dittmann, "WT100 and the University of Tennessee Supply Chain Survey," *World Trade 100*, July 2011, 42; Hayden Bush, "Reliance on Overseas Manufacturers Worries Supply Chain Experts," *Hospitals & Health Networks*, July 2011, 13; William T. Dickens and Stephen J. Rose, "Blinder Baloney," *The International Economy*, Fall 2007, 18+; "Supply Chain News: The Seven Timeless Challenges of Supply Chain Management," *SupplyChainDigest*, 2 June 2009, www.scdigest .com; Phil Fersht, Dana Stiffler, and Kevin O'Marah, "The Ins and Outs of Offshoring," *Supply Chain Management Review*, March 2009, 10–11; Ajay K. Goel, Nazgol Moussavi, and Vats N. Srivatsan, "Time to Rethink Offshoring?" *McKinsey Quarterly*, 2008 Issue 4, 108–111; Anita Hawser, "Offshoring Industry Faces New Opponent: Its Clients," *Global Finance*, November 2007, 6; Alan S. Brown, "A Shift in Engineering Offshore," *Mechanical Engineering*, March 2009, 24–29; John Ferreira and Len Prokopets, "Does Offshoring Still Make Sense?" *Supply Chain Management Review*, January/February 2009, 20–27; Dan Gilmore, "Can—and Should—Western Manufacturing Be Saved?" *SupplyChainDigest*, 28 May 2009, www.scdigest.com; Geri Smith and Justin Bachman, "The Offshoring of Airplane Care," *BusinessWeek*, 10 April 2008, www.businessweek .com; Susan Carey and Alex Frangos, "Airlines, Facing Cost Pressure, Outsource Crucial Safety Tasks," *Wall Street Journal*, 21 January 2005, A1, A5.

✔Checkpoint

LEARNING OBJECTIVE 2: Describe the *value chain* and *value web* concepts, and discuss the controversy over offshoring.

SUMMARY: The *value chain* includes all the elements and processes that add value as input materials are transformed into the final products made available to the ultimate customer. The *value web* concept expands this linear model to a multidimensional network of suppliers and outsourcing partners. In the complex argument over *offshoring*, the transfer of business functions to entities in other countries in pursuit of lower costs, proponents claim that (a) companies have a responsibility to shareholder interests to pursue the lowest cost of production, (b) offshoring benefits U.S. consumers through lower prices, (c) many companies don't have a choice once their competitors move offshore, (d) some companies need to offshore in order to support customers around the world, and (e) offshoring helps U.S. companies be more competitive. Those who question the value or wisdom of offshoring raise points about (a) the future of good jobs in the United States, (b) hidden costs and risks, (c) diminished responsiveness, (d) knowledge transfer and theft issues, (e) product safety issues, and (f) national security and public health concerns.

CRITICAL THINKING: (1) Do U.S. companies have an obligation to keep jobs in the United States? Why or why not? (2) Will global labor markets eventually balance out, with workers in comparable positions all over the world making roughly the same wages? Explain your answer.

IT'S YOUR BUSINESS: (1) In your own long-term career planning, have you taken the "offshorability" of your target profession into account? (2) Should such concerns affect your career planning?

KEY TERMS TO KNOW: value chain, outsourcing, value webs, offshoring

---

Define *supply chain management* and explain its strategic importance.

supply chain A set of connected systems that coordinates the flow of goods and materials from suppliers all the way through to final customers

supply chain management (SCM) The business procedures, policies, and computer systems that integrate the various elements of the supply chain into a cohesive system

Supply Chain Management

Regardless of how and where it is structured, the lifeblood of every production operation is the **supply chain**, a set of connected systems that coordinates the flow of goods and materials from suppliers all the way through to final customers. Companies with multiple customer bases can also develop a distinct supply chain to serve each segment.[8]

Supply chain management (SCM) combines business procedures and policies with information systems that integrate the various elements of the supply chain into a cohesive system. As companies rely more on outsourcing partners, SCM has grown far beyond the simple procurement of supplies to become a strategic management function that means the difference between success and failure. Successful implementation of SCM can have a profound strategic impact on companies and the broader economy, in several important ways:[9]

- **Managing risks.** SCM can help companies manage the complex risks involved in a supply chain, risks that include everything from cost and availability to health and safety issues.
- **Managing relationships.** SCM can coordinate the numerous relationships in the supply chain and help managers focus their attention on the most important company-to-company relationships.
- **Managing trade-offs.** SCM helps managers address the many trade-offs in the supply chain. These trade-offs can be a source of conflict within the company, and SCM helps balance the competing interests of the various functional areas. This holistic view helps managers balance both capacity and capability along the entire chain.

- **Promoting sustainability.** As the part of business that moves raw materials and finished goods around the world, supply chains have an enormous effect on resource usage, waste, and environmental impact. A major effort is underway in the field of SCM to develop greener supply chains. A key player in this effort is the giant retailer Walmart, which buys products from more than 100,000 suppliers and has tremendous influence on global supply chains. The company now works with its suppliers to help them meet sustainability targets in the areas of energy and climate, material efficiency, natural resources, and people and community.[10]

REAL-TIME UPDATES
Learn More by Watching This Video

Get a supplier's view of sustainability at Walmart

As the world's largest retailer, Walmart is using its considerable influence to increase sustainability in the global supply chain. This in-depth webinar shows how it is working with its suppliers to help them improve their operations. Go to http://real-timeupdates.com/bia6 and click on Learn More. If you are using MyBizLab, you can access Real-Time Updates within the chapter or under Student Study Tools.

SUPPLY CHAINS VERSUS VALUE CHAINS

The terms *supply chain* and *value chain* are sometimes used interchangeably, and the distinction between them isn't always clear in everyday usage. One helpful way to distinguish between the two is to view the supply chain as the part of the overall value chain that acquires and manages the goods and services needed to produce whatever it is the company produces and then deliver it to the final customer. Everyone in the company is part of the value chain, but not everyone is involved in the supply chain.[11]

Another way to distinguish the two is that the supply chain focuses on the "upstream" part of the process, collecting the necessary materials and supplies with an emphasis on reducing waste and inefficiency. The value chain focuses on the "downstream" part of the process and on adding value in the eyes of customers.[12]

Yet a third way that has recently emerged is talking about value chains as a strategic win-win business partnership rather than the more tactical, deal-driven arrangement of a supply chain. In this usage, "value" also encompasses *values*, including sustainability practices that make products more worthy and appealing in the eyes of customers.[13]

SUPPLY CHAIN SYSTEMS AND TECHNIQUES

The core focus of SCM is getting the right materials at the right price in the right place at the right time for successful production. Unfortunately, you can't just pile up huge quantities of everything you might eventually need, because **inventory**, the goods and materials kept in stock for production or sale, costs money to purchase and to store. On the other hand, not having an adequate supply of inventory can result in expensive delays. This balancing act is the job of **inventory control**, which tries to determine the right quantities of supplies and products to have on hand and then tracks where those items are. One of the most important technologies to emerge in inventory control in recent years is *radio frequency identification (RFID)*. RFID uses small antenna tags attached to products or shipping containers; special sensors detect the presence of the tags and can track the flow of goods through the supply chain.

Procurement, or *purchasing*, is the acquisition of the raw materials, parts, components, supplies, and finished products required to produce goods and services. The goal of purchasing is to make sure that the company has all the materials it needs, when it needs them, at the lowest possible cost. A company must always have enough supplies on hand to cover a product's *lead time*—the period that elapses between placing the supply order and receiving materials.

To accomplish these goals, operations specialists have developed a variety of systems and techniques over the years:

- **Material requirements planning (MRP).** MRP helps a manufacturer get the correct materials where they are needed, when they are needed, without unnecessary stockpiling. Managers use MRP software to calculate when certain materials will be required, when they should be ordered, and when they should be delivered so that storage costs

inventory Goods and materials kept in stock for production or sale

inventory control Determining the right quantities of supplies and products to have on hand and tracking where those items are

procurement The acquisition of the raw materials, parts, components, supplies, and finished products required to produce goods and services will be minimal. These systems are so effective at reducing inventory levels that they are used almost universally in both large and small manufacturing firms.

- **Manufacturing resource planning (MRP II).** MRP II expands MRP with links to a company's financial systems and other processes. For instance, in addition to managing inventory levels successfully, an MRP II system can help ensure that material costs adhere to target budgets.[14] Because it draws together all departments, an MRP II system produces a companywide game plan that allows everyone to work with the same numbers. Moreover, the system can track each step of production, allowing managers throughout the company to consult other managers' inventories, schedules, and plans.

- **Enterprise resource planning (ERP).** ERP extends the scope of resource planning and management even further to encompass the entire organization. ERP software programs are typically made up of modules that address the needs of the various functional areas, from manufacturing to sales to human resources. Some companies deploy ERP on a global scale, with a single centralized system connecting all their operations worldwide.[15]

Checkpoint

LEARNING OBJECTIVE 3: Define *supply chain management* **and explain its strategic importance.**

SUMMARY: Supply chain management (SCM) combines business procedures and policies with information systems that integrate the various elements of the supply chain into a cohesive system. SCM helps companies manage risks, relationships, and trade-offs throughout their supply chains, building partnerships that help everyone in the supply chain succeed.

CRITICAL THINKING: (1) Why can't companies just stockpile huge inventories of all the parts and materials they need rather than carefully manage supply from one day to the next? (2) Why would a company invest time and money in helping its suppliers improve their business practices? Why not just dump underperformers and get better suppliers?

IT'S YOUR BUSINESS: (1) In any current or previous job, what steps have supervisors taken to help you understand your role in the supply chain? (2) Is it dehumanizing to your colleagues and business partners to be participants in a supply chain? Why or why not?

KEY TERMS TO KNOW: supply chain, supply chain management (SCM), inventory, inventory control, procurement

4 LEARNING OBJECTIVE

Identify the major planning decisions in production and operations management.

production and operations management Overseeing all the activities involved in producing goods and services

Production and Operations Management

The term *production* suggests factories, machines, and assembly lines making automobiles, computers, furniture, motorcycles, or other tangible goods. With the growth in the number of service-based businesses and their increasing importance to the economy, however, the term *production* is now used to describe the transformation of resources into both goods and services. The broader term **production and operations management,** or simply *operations management,* refers to overseeing all the activities involved in producing goods and services. Operations managers are responsible for a wide range of strategies and decisions, from locating production facilities to managing the supply chain.

FACILITIES LOCATION AND DESIGN

Choosing the location of production facilities is a complex decision that must consider such factors as land, construction, availability of talent, taxes, energy, living standards, transportation, and proximity to customers and business partners. Support from local communities and governments often plays a key role in location decisions as well. To provide jobs and expand their income and sales tax bases, local, state, and national governments often compete to attract companies by offering generous financial incentives such as tax reductions.

After a site has been selected, managers turn their attention to *facility layout*, the arrangement of production work centers and other elements (such as materials, equipment, and support departments) needed to process goods and services. Layout planning includes such decisions as how many steps are needed in the process, the amount and type of equipment and workers needed for each step, how each step should be configured, and where the steps should be located relative to one another.[16]

Well-designed facilities help companies operate more productively by reducing wasted time and wasted materials, but that is far from the only benefit. Smart layouts support close communication and collaboration among employees and help ensure their safety, both of which are important for employee satisfaction and motivation. In the delivery of services, facility layout can be a major influence on customer satisfaction because it affects the overall service experience.[17]

FORECASTING AND CAPACITY PLANNING

Using customer feedback, sales orders, market research, past sales figures, industry analyses, and educated guesses about the future behavior of customers and competitors, operations managers prepare *production forecasts*—estimates of future demand for the company's products. After product demand has been estimated, management must balance that with the company's capacity to produce the goods or services. The term *capacity* refers to the volume of manufacturing or service capability that an organization can handle. **Capacity planning** is the collection of long-term strategic decisions that establish the overall level of resources needed to meet customer demand. When managers at Boeing plan for the production of an airliner, they have to consider not only the staffing of thousands of people but also massive factory spaces, material flows from hundreds of suppliers around the world, internal deliveries, cash flow, tools and equipment, and dozens of other factors. Because of the potential impact on finances, customers, and employees—and the difficulty of reversing major decisions—capacity choices are among the most important decisions that top-level managers make.[18]

capacity planning Establishing the overall level of resources needed to meet customer demand

SCHEDULING

In any production process, managers must do *scheduling*—determining how long each operation takes and deciding which tasks are done in which order. Manufacturing facilities often use a *master production schedule (MPS)* to coordinate production of all the goods the company makes. Service businesses use a variety of scheduling techniques as well, from simple appointment calendars for a small business to the comprehensive online systems that airlines and other large service providers use.

To plan and track projects of all kinds, managers throughout a company can use a *Gantt chart*, a special type of bar chart that shows the progress of all the tasks needed to complete a project (see Exhibit 5 on the next page). For more complex projects, the *program evaluation and review technique (PERT)* is helpful. PERT helps managers identify the optimal sequencing of activities, the expected time for project completion, and the best use of resources. To use PERT, managers map out all the activities in a network diagram (see Exhibit 6 on the next page). The longest path through the network is known as the **critical path** because it represents the minimum amount of time needed to complete the project. Tasks in the critical path usually receive special attention because they determine when the project can be completed.[19] (If anyone ever says that *you* are in the critical path, make sure you stay on schedule!)

critical path In a PERT network diagram, the sequence of operations that requires the longest time to complete

LEAN SYSTEMS

Throughout all the activities in the production process, operations managers pay close attention to **productivity**, or the efficiency with which they can convert inputs to outputs. (Put another way, productivity is equal to the value of the outputs divided by the value of the inputs.) Productivity is one of the most vital responsibilities in operations management because it is a key factor in determining the company's competitiveness and profitability.

productivity The efficiency with which an organization can convert inputs to outputs

EXHIBIT 5 — Gantt Charts for Project Management

A Gantt chart is a handy tool in project and production management because it shows the order in which tasks must be completed and which tasks are dependent on other tasks. For the new product launch shown here, for example, the analysis task is dependent on all three tasks before it, which means those tasks must be completed before analysis can begin. With periodic updates, it's also easy to show a team exactly where the project stands at any particular moment.

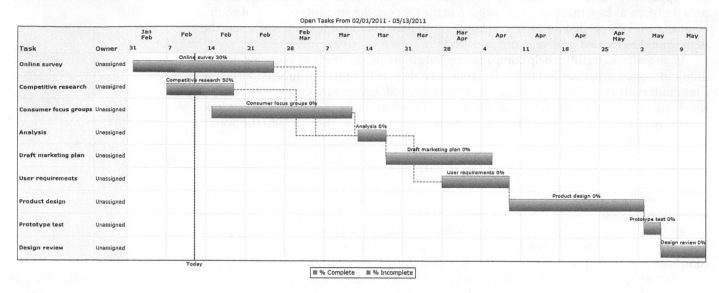

EXHIBIT 6 — Simplified PERT Diagram for a Store Opening

This PERT diagram shows a subset of the many tasks involved in opening a new retail store. The tasks involved in staffing are on the critical path because they take the longest time to complete (51 days), whereas the promotion tasks can be completed in 38 days, and the merchandise tasks can be completed in 39 days. In other words, some delay can be tolerated in the promotion or merchandise tasks, but any delay in any of the staffing tasks will delay the store's opening day.

lean systems Systems (in manufacturing and other functional areas) that maximize productivity by reducing waste and delays

just-in-time (JIT) Inventory management in which goods and materials are delivered throughout the production process right before they are needed

Companies that can produce similar goods or services with fewer resources have a distinct advantage over their competitors. Moreover, high productivity in the fullest sense also requires low waste, whether it's leftover materials, shoddy products that must be scrapped, or excess energy usage. Consequently, productivity improvements and sustainability improvements often complement each other.

Lean systems, which maximize productivity by reducing waste and delays, are at the heart of many productivity improvement efforts. Many lean systems borrow techniques from Toyota; the *Toyota Production System* is world renowned for its ability to continually improve both productivity and quality (see Exhibit 7).[20] Central to the notion of lean systems is **just-in-time (JIT)** inventory management, in which goods and materials are delivered

EXHIBIT 7 — Conceptual Diagram of the Toyota Production System

The Toyota Production System, one of the most influential production strategies in modern business history, has been studied, duplicated, and adapted by companies in a variety of industries around the world. Toyota refined the system over decades, but it has always been based on the two fundamental principles of just-in-time inventory management, so that expensive inventory doesn't pile up when it isn't being used, and *jidoka*, or "automation with a human touch," whereby the highly automated process can be stopped by any worker any time a problem appears, to avoid making more defective parts or cars. However, for all its abilities to reduce manufacturing defects, the system has not been able to prevent all failures—particularly now that cars are vast software systems as well as mechanical systems.

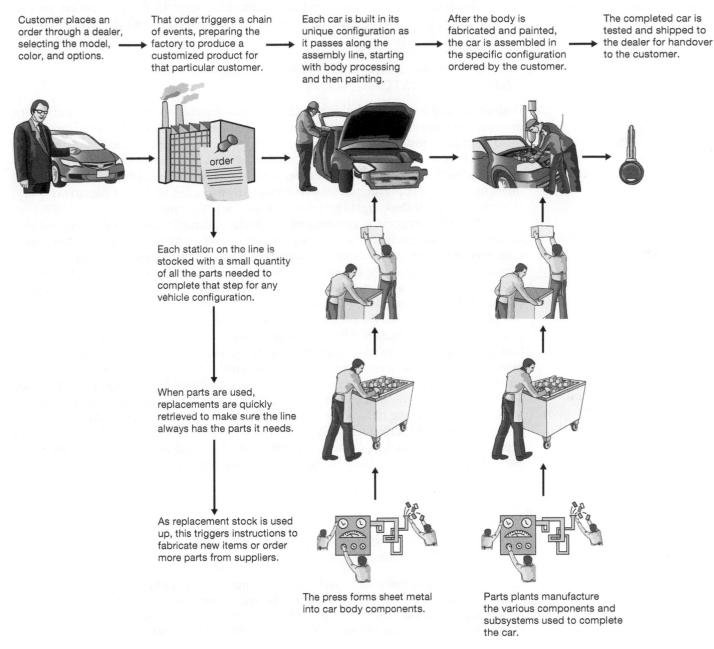

Customer places an order through a dealer, selecting the model, color, and options.

That order triggers a chain of events, preparing the factory to produce a customized product for that particular customer.

Each car is built in its unique configuration as it passes along the assembly line, starting with body processing and then painting.

After the body is fabricated and painted, the car is assembled in the specific configuration ordered by the customer.

The completed car is tested and shipped to the dealer for handover to the customer.

Each station on the line is stocked with a small quantity of all the parts needed to complete that step for any vehicle configuration.

When parts are used, replacements are quickly retrieved to make sure the line always has the parts it needs.

As replacement stock is used up, this triggers instructions to fabricate new items or order more parts from suppliers.

The press forms sheet metal into car body components.

Parts plants manufacture the various components and subsystems used to complete the car.

Source: Adapted from "Toyota Production System," Toyota Global website, accessed 25 August 2011, www.toyota-global.com.

throughout the production process right before they are needed rather than being stockpiled in inventories. Reducing stocks to immediate needs reduces waste and forces factories to keep production flowing smoothly. (For more on quality at Toyota, see "Quality and Complexity" later in this chapter.)

Achieving such benefits requires constant attention to quality and teamwork because with no spare inventory, there is no room for delays or errors.[21] Without stockpiles of extra parts and materials, each stage in the production process goes idle if the stages before it have not delivered on time.

MASS PRODUCTION, CUSTOMIZED PRODUCTION, AND MASS CUSTOMIZATION

mass production The creation of identical goods or services, usually in large quantities

customized production The creation of a unique good or service for each customer

mass customization A manufacturing approach in which part of the product is mass produced and the remaining features are customized for each buyer

Both goods and services can be created through *mass production, customized production,* or *mass customization,* depending on the nature of the product and the desires of target customers. In **mass production,** identical goods or services are created, usually in large quantities, such as when Apple churns out a million identical iPhones. Although not normally associated with services, mass production is also what American Airlines is doing when it offers hundreds of opportunities for passengers to fly from, say, Dallas to Chicago every day: Every customer on these flights gets the same service at the same time.

At the other extreme is **customized production,** sometimes called *batch-of-one production* in manufacturing, in which the producer creates a unique good or service for each customer. If you order a piece of furniture from a local craftsperson, for instance, you can specify everything from the size and shape to the types of wood and fabric used. Or you can hire a charter pilot to fly you wherever you want, whenever you want. Both products are customized to your unique requirements.

Mass production has the advantage of economies of scale, but it can't deliver many of the unique goods and services that today's customers demand. On the other hand, fully customized production can offer uniqueness but usually at a much higher price. An attractive compromise in many cases is **mass customization,** in which part of the product is mass produced and then the remaining features are customized for each buyer. With design and production technologies getting ever more flexible, the opportunities for customization continue to grow. For instance, the Italian motorcycle maker Ducati can now scan a customer's body shape and create the perfect seat to fit.[22] And as you'll read at the end of the chapter, this is the approach Carvin has taken: Customers get the same basic guitar bodies but with their own individual combinations of woods, fingerboard styles, finishes, and electronic components.

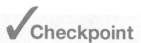 **Checkpoint**

LEARNING OBJECTIVE 4: Identify the major planning decisions in production and operations management.

SUMMARY: The major decisions in operations management include (1) facilities location and design; (2) forecasting and capacity planning to match resources with demand; (3) scheduling; (4) lean system design to reduce waste and delays; and (5) the choice of mass production, customized production, or mass customization.

CRITICAL THINKING: (1) Why is it essential to identify tasks in the critical path of a project? (2) How does mass customization help a company balance productivity and customer satisfaction?

IT'S YOUR BUSINESS: (1) The phrase "lean and mean" is sometimes used to describe lean systems. What are the risks of using such language? (2) Is this course an example of mass production, customization, or mass customization? Explain.

KEY TERMS TO KNOW: production and operations management, capacity planning, critical path, productivity, lean systems, just-in-time (JIT), mass production, customized production, mass customization

The Unique Challenges of Service Delivery

5 **LEARNING OBJECTIVE**

Explain the unique challenges of service delivery.

With the majority of workers in the United States now involved in the service sector, managers in thousands of companies need to pay close attention to the unique challenges of delivering services: perishability, location constraints, scalability challenges, performance variability and perceptions of quality, and customer involvement and service provider interaction.

PERISHABILITY

Most services are *perishable*, meaning that they are consumed at the same time they are produced and cannot exist before or after that time. For example, if a 200-seat airliner takes off half empty, those 100 sales opportunities are lost forever. The airline can't create these products ahead of time and store them in inventory until somebody is ready to buy. Similarly, restaurants can seat only so many people every night, so empty tables represent revenue lost forever. This perishability can have a profound impact on the way service businesses are managed, from staffing (making sure enough people are on hand to help with peak demands) to pricing (using discounts to encourage people to buy services when they are available).

LOCATION CONSTRAINTS

Perishability also means that for many services, customers and providers need to be in the same place at the same time. The equipment and food ingredients used in a restaurant can be produced just about anywhere, but the restaurant itself needs to be located close to customers. One of the most significant commercial advantages of the Internet is the way it has enabled many service businesses to get around this constraint. Online retailers, information providers, and other e-businesses can locate virtually anywhere on the planet.

SCALABILITY CHALLENGES AND OPPORTUNITIES

Any business that wants to grow must consider the issue of **scalability**, the potential to increase production by expanding or replicating its initial production capacity. Scaling up always creates some challenges, but service businesses that depend on the skills of specific professionals can be particularly difficult to scale. Examples range from chefs and interior designers to business consultants and graphic designers, particularly when the business is built around the reputation of a single person.

scalability The potential to increase production by expanding or replicating its initial production capacity

Of course, many goods businesses also rely on highly skilled production workers, but the potential to mechanize goods production can make it easier to scale up manufacturing in some cases. For example, by using computer-controlled routers to carve the bodies of its guitars, Carvin frees itself from the constraint of hiring enough skilled carvers to do it all by hand.

PERFORMANCE VARIABILITY AND PERCEPTIONS OF QUALITY

For many types of services, the quality of the service performance can vary from one instance to the next—and that quality is in the eye of the beholder and often can't be judged until after the service has been performed. If you manufacture scissors, you can specify a certain

One of the many challenges of providing services is that the evaluation of quality is often subjective.

© Radius Images/Alamy

grade of steel from your suppliers and use automated machinery to produce thousands of identical pairs of scissors of identical quality. Many key attributes such as the size and strength of the scissors are *objective* and measurable, and customers can experience the *subjective* variables such as the feel and action before they buy. In other words, there is little mystery and little room for surprise in the purchase.

However, if you create a haircut using a pair of those scissors, perceptions of quality become almost entirely subjective *and* impossible to judge until after the service is complete. Plus, hair styling is a good example of a service in which *quality of experience* is an important part of customer perceptions as well, which is why, for instance, most salons pay a lot of attention to architecture, interior design, lighting, music, and other amenities that have nothing to do with the actual haircut itself.

CUSTOMER INVOLVEMENT AND PROVIDER INTERACTION

Finally, one of the biggest differences between goods and services production is the fact that customers are often involved in—and thereby can affect the quality of—the service delivery. For instance, personal trainers can instruct clients in the proper way to exercise, but if the clients don't follow directions, the result will be unsatisfactory. Similarly, a business consultant relies on accurate information from managers in a client organization; lacking that, he or she will be unable to craft the most effective advice.

When customers and service providers interact, the quality of the interpersonal experience also affects customer perceptions of quality. In this sense, service delivery is something of a performance that needs to instill confidence in the client. Weak communication skills or poor etiquette can create dissatisfaction with a service that is satisfactory or even exceptional in all other respects.

✓ Checkpoint

LEARNING OBJECTIVE 5: Explain the unique challenges of service delivery.

SUMMARY: The delivery of services presents a number of unique challenges, including (1) perishability, which means that services are consumed at the same time they are produced; (2) location constraints, which often require that customers and service providers be in the same place at the same time; (3) scalability challenges, which can make some types of service businesses more difficult to expand; (4) performance variability and perceptions of quality, which heighten the challenge of delivering consistent quality and increase the subjectivity of the customer experience; and (5) customer involvement and service provider interaction, which can put some of the responsibility for service quality on the customer's shoulders and increase the importance of good interpersonal skills.

CRITICAL THINKING: (1) How can technology help some service businesses address the challenge of scalability? (2) If customers are paying for a service, why should they ever have to share in the responsibility of ensuring quality results?

IT'S YOUR BUSINESS: (1) Do you think you have a natural personality for working in a service business? Why or why not? (2) If you're not a "natural," what steps could you take to succeed in a service job anyway?

KEY TERM TO KNOW: scalability

Product and Process Quality

The term *quality* is often used in a vague sense of "goodness" or "excellence," but to be meaningful from a managerial standpoint, it needs to be defined in context. Hyundai and Aston Martin both make quality automobiles, but quality means dramatically different things to the makers and buyers of these two car brands. People who spend $15,000 or $20,000 on a Hyundai are likely to be satisfied with the quality they receive in return, but people who spend 10 times that much on an Aston Martin have very different expectations. Accordingly, **quality** is best defined as the degree to which a product or process meets reasonable or agreed-upon expectations. Within the framework of this general definition, a specific set of parameters can be identified that define quality in each situation.

Defining those expectations of quality and then organizing the resources and systems needed to achieve that level are vital responsibilities in today's competitive, resource-constrained environment. With numerous choices available in most product categories, consumers and business buyers alike tend to avoid or abandon products and companies that can't meet their expectations. Moreover, poor quality wastes time and money, squanders resources, frustrates customers and employees, erodes confidence in companies and their products, and can even put people in danger.

QUALITY AND COMPLEXITY

As many products become increasingly complex, defining and maintaining quality becomes an ever greater challenge. For example, even identical, mass-produced computers immediately become unique when their new owners start adding software, downloading files, and connecting to printers and other devices, each of which is a complex hardware/software system in its own right. All these changes and connections increase the chances that something will go wrong and thereby lower the functional quality of the product. In other words, even though the company verified the quality of the products before they left the factory, it could have thousands of quality issues on its hands over time.

Meeting expectations of quality in complicated, real-world operating conditions over time can present a sizable challenge but one that must be met to ensure buyer satisfaction. Dell, for example, has several dozen customer service specialists who monitor social media conversations for signs of discontent over its products. When they hear complaints, they jump in with advice and offers to help. This effort improves customer satisfaction and creates opportunities to sell additional goods and services—the company figures the program has generated more than $1 billion in additional sales—but it also gives Dell engineers valuable insights into how quality plays out in the messy real world outside the factory.[23]

The need to get feedback from the field and not just from the factory has been identified as one of the factors that contributed to quality issues that recently tarnished Toyota's reputation for safety and dependability—and prompted some observers to wonder whether the Toyota Production System was really all that effective at weeding out defects. The company made headlines in 2009 and 2010 by recalling millions of vehicles after complaints of unintended acceleration and other serious safety issues. A variety of causes were investigated, including floor mats being improperly installed by dealers or owners, software glitches, electromagnetic interference in the throttle control system (a problem that would affect virtually all new cars if it affected any), sticky pedals caused by humidity and material wear over time, driver error—the range of possibilities indicates how complex such problems can be. However, according to engineering professor Jeffrey Liker, who has researched and written extensively about Toyota, none of the recalls could be traced to production defects.[24]

One of the criticisms leveled at Toyota throughout these episodes is that the senior engineers in charge of design were isolated at company headquarters in Japan and too insulated from real-world feedback. In 2011, the company announced that North American engineering teams were being given more control over the development of vehicles designed for the North American market.[25]

STRATEGIES FOR ENSURING PRODUCT QUALITY

The traditional means of maintaining quality is called **quality control**—measuring quality against established standards after the good or service has been produced and weeding out

6 LEARNING OBJECTIVE

Define *quality*, explain the challenge of quality and product complexity, and identify four major tools and strategies for ensuring product quality.

quality The degree to which a product or process meets reasonable or agreed-upon expectations

quality control Measuring quality against established standards after the good or service has been produced and weeding out any defective products

quality assurance A more comprehensive approach of companywide policies, practices, and procedures to ensure that every product meets quality standards

any defects. A more comprehensive and proactive approach is **quality assurance**, a holistic system of integrated policies, practices, and procedures designed to ensure that every product meets preset quality standards. Quality assurance includes quality control as well as doing the job right the first time by designing tools and machinery properly, demanding quality parts from suppliers, encouraging customer feedback, training and empowering employees, and encouraging employees to take pride in their work.

Companies can use a variety of tools and strategies to help ensure quality; four of the most significant are continuous improvement, statistical process control, Six Sigma, and ISO 9000.

Continuous Improvement

Delivering quality goods and services is as much a mindset as it is a technical challenge. Companies that excel tend to empower their employees to continuously improve the quality of goods production or service delivery, a strategy often expressed through the Japanese word *kaizen*. By making quality everyone's responsibility, the kaizen approach encourages all workers to look for quality problems, halt production when necessary, generate ideas for improvement, and adjust work routines as needed.[26]

Statistical Process Control

statistical process control (SPC) The use of random sampling and tools such as control charts to monitor the production process

Any quality control or improvement effort depends on reliable feedback that tells workers and managers how well products and processes are performing. Quality assurance often includes the use of **statistical process control (SPC)**, which involves taking samples from the process periodically and analyzing these data points to look for trends and anomalies. One of the most important SPC tools is the *control chart*, which plots measured data over time and helps identify performance that is outside the normal range of operating conditions and therefore in need of investigation.[27]

Six Sigma

Six Sigma A rigorous quality management program that strives to eliminate deviations between the actual and desired performance of a business system

Whereas *kaizen* is more of a general mindset and SPC is a set of analytical tools, **Six Sigma** is a comprehensive approach that encompasses a philosophy of striving toward perfection, a rigorous methodology for measuring and improving quality, and specific tools such as SPC to track progress.[28] (The term *six sigma* is used in statistics to indicate 3.4 defects per 1 million opportunities—near perfection, in other words.) Six Sigma is a highly disciplined, systematic approach to reducing the deviation from desired goals in virtually any business process, whether it's eliminating defects in the creation of a product or improving a company's cash flow.[29] Six Sigma efforts typically follow a five-step approach, known as DMAIC for short (see Exhibit 8).[30]

| **EXHIBIT 8** | **The DMAIC Process in Six Sigma Quality Management** |

The five-step process of *define, measure, analyze, improve,* and *control* (DMAIC) is at the heart of Six Sigma quality management efforts.

Source: Adapted from Kelly D. Sloan, "The Path to a Sustainable Playbook," *Industrial Engineer*, April 2011, 41–46.

Many companies now marry the concepts of lean production and Six Sigma, seeking to reduce waste and defects simultaneously. And moving beyond operations, this hybrid approach of *Lean Six Sigma* is also being applied at a strategic level to help identify opportunities in the marketplace and align the resources needed to pursue them.[31]

ISO 9000

Buyers and business partners often want reassurance that the companies they do business with take quality seriously and have practices and policies in place to ensure quality outputs. **ISO 9000** is a globally recognized family of standards for quality management systems, administered by the International Organization for Standardization (ISO). ISO 9000 is based on eight quality management principles, including customer focus, a systematic approach to management, and fact-based decision making.[32]

Hundreds of thousands of organizations around the world have implemented ISO standards, making it a universally recognized indicator of compliance. Achieving ISO certification sends a reassuring signal to other companies that your internal processes meet these widely accepted standards, and many organizations now require that their supplies meet ISO standards. Even without the need to meet this requirement, ISO 9000 provides companies with a "tried and tested framework for taking a systematic approach to managing the organization's processes so that they consistently turn out products that satisfy customers' expectations."[33]

For the latest information on production systems, visit http://real-timeupdates.com/ bia6.

ISO 9000 A globally recognized family of standards for quality management systems

✓ Checkpoint

LEARNING OBJECTIVE 6: Define *quality*, explain the challenge of quality and product complexity, and identify four major tools and strategies for ensuring product quality.

SUMMARY: Quality is the degree to which a product or process meets reasonable or agreed-upon expectations. As products become more complex, the challenges of defining what quality means, ensuring quality production or service performance, and ensuring quality once the product is out in the field all increase. Four major tools and strategies for ensuring product quality are (1) continuous process improvement, enabling employees to search for and correct quality problems; (2) statistical process control (SPC), the use of random sampling and tools such as control charts to monitor the production process; (3) Six Sigma, a rigorous quality management program that strives to eliminate deviations between the actual and desired performance of a business system; and (4) ISO 9000, a globally recognized family of standards for quality management systems.

CRITICAL THINKING: (1) How significant is the role of software in product quality today? (2) How can process simplicity contribute to quality?

IT'S YOUR BUSINESS: (1) Are the grades you get in your various classes an example of quality control or of quality assurance? Explain your answer. (2) Have you ever tried anything like the Six Sigma DMAIC process in your own life, even partially or informally?

KEY TERMS TO KNOW: quality, quality control, quality assurance, statistical process control (SPC), Six Sigma, ISO 9000

BEHIND THE SCENES

MyBizLab

CARVIN'S PRODUCTION SYSTEM SATISFIES DEMANDING GUITARISTS

Carvin has made a name for itself among serious guitarists by filling the gap between mass-produced and fully custom guitars. The company's secret has been perfecting the art and science of *mass customization*, the ability to adapt standardized products to the tastes of individual customers. In five to seven weeks, and for roughly $700 to $1,500, Carvin can customize one of several dozen models of guitars and basses. All are available in a wide variety of woods, paints, stains, finishes, electronics, and even the slight curvature in the fingerboard; there are so many choices that the discussion boards on Carvin's website buzz with debates about which combinations are "best" for specific styles of music.

Carvin's factory combines old-world craftsmanship with new-world technologies. Because the custom guitars are built on a standard set of body shapes and styles, Carvin can use computer-controlled cutting and milling machines that cut and shape the bodies and necks quickly and precisely. A diamond-surface finishing machine mills fingerboards to tolerances of a thousandth of an inch. A dehumidification chamber removes internal stresses from the wood used in the guitar necks to minimize the chance of warping years down the road. Experienced craftspeople with sensitive eyes and ears take over from there, performing such tasks as matching veneer pieces on guitar tops (veneers are thin sheets of wood, usually exotic or expensive species), adjusting the action (the feel of the strings against the frets), and listening to the tone quality of finished instruments.

With this blend of automation and human touch, Carvin produces more than 5,000 instruments a year that win rave reviews from appreciative customers. "Nothing can touch it in terms of sound quality and workmanship" and "I haven't seen anything close to this price that can outperform it" are typical of the comments that Carvin customers post online. Upon hearing a salesperson in another music store speak disparagingly of the brand, one indignant Carvin owner retrieved his guitar from his car and put on an impromptu concert for the store's sales staff to demonstrate just how good the Carvin product sounded. With a proven manufacturing approach and customer loyalty like that, Carvin will be fulfilling the musical dreams of guitarists for years to come.[34]

Critical Thinking Questions

1. If Carvin experienced an increase in orders from its website over a period of two weeks, should it expand its production capacity to make sure it can handle increased demand in the future? Why or why not?
2. Watch the video of Carvin's production in action at **www.carvinchannel.com**. How does this information help convince potential buyers to consider Carvin?
3. Wooden musical instruments have been carved by hand for hundreds of years. Why wouldn't Carvin want to continue this tradition?

LEARN MORE ONLINE

Visit the Carvin website, at **www.carvinguitars.com**. How does the company promote its customized products? Step through the process of customizing a guitar or bass. Would you feel comfortable purchasing a musical instrument in this manner? Review comments on **www.carvinchannel.com** and **www.myspace.com/officialcarvin/comments**. What are Carvin employees and customers talking about these days?

MyBizLab

Log on to www.mybizlab.com to access study and assessment aids associated with this chapter.

KEY TERMS

capacity planning
critical path
customized production
inventory
inventory control
ISO 9000
just-in-time (JIT)
lean systems
mass customization
mass production

offshoring
outsourcing
procurement
production and operations
    management
productivity
quality
quality assurance
quality control
scalability

Six Sigma
statistical process control
(SPC)
supply chain

supply chain management (SCM)
system
value chain
value webs

TEST YOUR KNOWLEDGE

Questions for Review

1. What role does feedback play in a system?
2. Why is offshoring controversial?
3. What is mass customization?
4. What is a lean system?
5. What is scalability, in terms of managing a service business?

Questions for Analysis

6. Why is it important to monitor performance variables that are the most meaningful, not those that are the most easily measurable?
7. Why do some firms now think in terms of value webs instead of value chains?
8. How can supply chain management (SCM) help a company establish a competitive advantage?
9. How does perishability affect the delivery of services?
10. Ethical Considerations. How does society's concern for the environment affect a company's decisions about facility location and layout?

Questions for Application

11. Business is booming. Sales last month were 50 percent higher than the month before, and so far, this month is looking even better than last month. Should you hire more people to accommodate the increase? Explain your answer.
12. If 30 percent of the patrons eating at your restaurant say they won't eat there again, what steps would you take to define the problem(s) that needs to be solved, measure the relevant performance variables, and then analyze the root cause of the problems(s)?
13. You've developed a reputation as an outstanding math tutor, and you want to turn your talent into a full-time business after graduation. How will you address the challenge of scalability in your new venture?
14. Concept Integration. How might supply chain management issues influence your decision on how to expand your vitamin and nutritional supplements company internationally?

EXPAND YOUR KNOWLEDGE

Discovering Career Opportunities

Visit the *Occupational Outlook Handbook* at www.bls.gov/oco .com and locate "Industrial production managers" in the "Management" section.

1. What is the nature of the work for industrial production managers? Does the combination of people management and technical problem solving appeal to you?
2. What is the outlook for careers in this profession? If you were interested in this field, would you consider it, given the job outlook?
3. If you decide you want to work in a production-related job, what additional classes should you consider taking before you graduate?

Improving Your Tech Insights: Nanotechnology

Think small. Really small. Think about manufacturing products a molecule or even a single atom at a time. That's the scale of nanotechnology, a rather vague term that covers research and engineering done at nanoscale, or roughly 1/100,000 the width of a human hair.

The potential uses of nanotechnology range from the practical—smart materials that can change shape and heal themselves, more efficient energy generation and transmission, superstrong and superlight materials for airplanes, better cosmetics, smart medical implants, and ultrasmall computers—to the somewhat wilder—food-growing machines and microscopic robots that could travel through your body to cure diseases and fix injuries. (Like any new technology with lots of promise, nanotechnology also suffers from lots of hype.)

Well over 1,000 nanotechnology-enabled products have hit the market in a number of industries, from automotive materials to medicine to consumer products. Also, although they're slightly larger than the generally accepted scale of nanotechnology, *microelectromechanical systems (MEMS)* are having a major impact in some industries. These tiny machines (pumps, valves, and so on), some no bigger than a grain of pollen, are used in the nozzles of ink-jet printers, air bag sensors, and ultraprecise miniature laboratory devices.

Conduct research to identify a product currently on the market that uses nanotechnology in some fashion. In an email message to your instructor, describe the product, its target market, the role nanotechnology plays in the product's design, and any known safety concerns regarding the use of nanotechnology in this or similar products.[35]

PRACTICE YOUR SKILLS

Sharpening Your Communication Skills

As the newly hired manager of Campus Athletics, a shop featuring athletic wear bearing logos of colleges and universities, you are responsible for selecting the store's suppliers. Demand for merchandise with team logos and brands can be quite volatile. When a college team is hot, you've got to have merchandise. You know that selecting the right supplier is a task that requires careful consideration, so you have decided to host a series of selection interviews. Think about all the qualities you would want in a supplier, and develop a list of interview questions that will help you assess whether that supplier possesses those qualities.

Building Your Team Skills

Identify a company that has recently decided to offshore some part of its operations. (Search online news sources for "offshore outsourcing" or similar terms.) With the other members of your team, identify all the stakeholder groups that were or might be affected by this decision and speculate on the impact it had on each group. Weighing the effect on all the stakeholders, vote on whether this was a wise decision for the company. Be prepared to present your conclusions to the class.

Developing Your Research Skills

Seeking increased efficiency and productivity, a growing number of producers of goods and services are applying technology to improve the production process. Find an article in a business journal or newspaper that discusses how one company used computer-aided design (CAD), computer-aided engineering (CAE), computer-integrated manufacturing (CIM), robots, or other technological innovations to refit or reorganize its production operations.

1. What problems led the company to rethink its production process? What kind .of technology did it choose to address these problems? What goals did the company set for applying technology in this way?
2. Before adding the new technology, what did the company do to analyze its existing production process? What changes, if any, were made as a result of this analysis?
3. How did technology-enhanced production help the company achieve its goals for financial performance? For customer service? For growth or expansion?

REFERENCES

1. Carvin website, accessed 27 August 2011, www.carvinguitars .com; Carvin MySpace page, accessed 4 June 2009, www.myspace.com/officialcarvin; "Carvin AW175" (product reviews), Harmony Central website, accessed 18 March 2005, www.harmonycentral.com; "Carvin CT6M California Carved Top," *Guitar Player*, December 2004, www.guitarplayer.com; Rich Krechel, "Some Custom-Made Guitars Can Cost $4,000 to $8,000," *St. Louis Post Dispatch*, 27 September 2001, 16.
2. Adapted in part from Russell L. Ackoff, "Why Few Organizations Adopt Systems Thinking," Ackoff Center Weblog, 7 March 2007, http://ackoffcenter.blogs.com; Daniel Aronson, "Introduction to Systems Thinking," The Thinking Page website, accessed 21 June 2007, www.thinking.net; "What Is Systems Thinking?" The Systems Thinker website, accessed 21 June 2007, www .thesystemsthinker.com; Peter Senge, *The Fifth Discipline: The Art and Practice of the Learning Organization* (New York: Doubleday, 1994), 57–67.
3. Stephen P. Robbins and David A. DeCenzo, *Fundamentals of Management*, 4th ed. (Upper Saddle River, N.J.: Pearson Prentice Hall, 2004), 405.
4. Peter Fingar and Ronald Aronica, "Value Chain Optimization: The New Way of Competing," *Supply Chain Management Review*, September–October 2001, 82–85.
5. John Gillie, "Boeing Says Dreamliner Testing on Schedule for Third Quarter Delivery," *News Tribune* (Tacoma, Wash.), 25 February 2011, www.thenewstribune.com; Jeffrey Rothfeder, "Bumpy Ride," *Portfolio*, May 2009, www.portfolio.com.
6. Alan S. Brown, "A Shift in Engineering Offshore," *Mechanical Engineering*, March 2009, 24–29.
7. Lisa Harrington, "Is U.S. Manufacturing Coming Back?" *Inbound Logistics*, August 2011, www.inboundlogistics.com.
8. Bruce Constantine, Brian Ruwadi, and Josh Wine, "Management Practices That Drive Supply Chain Success," *McKinsey Quarterly*, no. 2 (2009): 24–26.
9. Tim Laseter and Keith Oliver, "When Will Supply Chain Management Grow Up?" *Strategy+Business*, Fall 2003, 32–36;

Robert J. Trent, "What Everyone Needs to Know About SCM," *Supply Chain Management Review*, 1 March 2004, www .manufacturing.net.
10. Ayse Bayat, Sekar Sundararajan, H. Robert Gustafson Jr., and Emory W. Zimmers Jr., "Sustainably Driven Supply Chains," *Industrial Engineer*, August 2011, 26–31; "Sustainability Index," Walmart, accessed 26 August 2011, http://walmartstores.com.
11. Trent, "What Everyone Needs to Know About SCM."
12. Andrew Feller, Dan Shunk, and Tom Callarman, "Value Chains Versus Supply Chains," *BPTrends*, March 2006, www .bptrends.com.
13. Patty Cantrell, "Sysco's Journey from Supply Chain to Value Chain," The Wallace Center, August 2009, www.ngfn.org.
14. Lee J. Krajewski and Larry P. Ritzman, *Operations Management: Processes and Value Chains*, 7th ed. (Upper Saddle River, N.J.: Pearson Prentice Hall, 2005), 744.
15. Malcolm Wheatley and Kevin Parker, "Rise in Global Enterprise Deployments Seen as Response to Far-Flung Supply Networks," *Manufacturing Business Technology*, May 2007, 26–27.
16. Krajewski and Ritzman, *Operations Management: Processes and Value Chains*, 299–300.
17. Russell and Taylor, *Operations Management: Focusing on Quality and Competitiveness*, 161.
18. Krajewski and Ritzman, *Operations Management: Processes and Value Chains*, 244–245.
19. Robert Kreitner, *Management*, 9th ed. (Boston: Houghton Mifflin, 2004), 202–203.
20. Krajewski and Ritzman, *Operations Management: Processes and Value Chains*, 482–483.
21. Russell and Taylor, *Operations Management: Focusing on Quality and Competitiveness*, 511.
22. Kenneth Korane, "Mass Production out, Mass Customization in," *Machine Design*, 21 August 2009, S2–S4.
23. Malcolm Wheatley, "Learning from Failure," *Engineering & Technology*, 11 September—24 September 2010, 56–58.

24. Jeffrey K. Liker, "The Way Back for Toyota," *Industrial Engineer*, May 2010, 28–33; Wheatley, "Learning from Failure."

25. Mark Rechtin, "Toyota Gives Development Clout to N.A.," *Automotive News*, 30 May 2011, 1, 23;

26. Russell and Taylor, *Operations Management*, 131.

27. Keith M. Bower, "Statistical Process Control," ASQ, accessed 27 August 2011, http://asq.org.

28. Donald W. Benbow and T. M. Kubiak, "Six Sigma," ASQ, accessed 27 August 2011, http://asq.org.

29. Steven Minter, "Six Sigma's Growing Pains," *IndustryWeek*, May 2009, 34–36; Tom McCarty, "Six Sigma at Motorola," *European CEO*, September–October 2004, www.motorola.com.

30. McCarty, "Six Sigma at Motorola"; General Electric, "What Is Six Sigma?" GE website, accessed 21 March 2005, www.ge.com.

31. George Byrne, Dave Lubowe, and Amy Blitz, "Driving Operational Innovation Using Lean Six Sigma," IBM, accessed 27 August 2011, www.ibm.com.

32. "Quality Management Principles," International Organization for Standardization website, accessed 27 August 2011, www.iso.org.

33. "ISO 9000 Essentials," International Organization for Standardization website, accessed 27 August 2011, www.iso.org.

34. See note 1.

35. Adapted from Project on Emerging Nanotechnologies website, accessed 27 August 2011, www.nanotechproject.org; National Nanotechnology Initiative website, accessed 28 June 2007, www.nano.gov; Barnaby J. Feder, "Technology: Bashful vs. Brash in the New Field of Nanotech," *New York Times*, 15 March 2004, www.nytimes.com; "Nanotechnology Basics," Nanotechnology Now website, accessed 16 April 2004, www.nanotech-now.com; Center for Responsible Nanotechnology website, accessed 16 April 2004, www.crnano.org; Gary Stix, "Little Big Science," *Scientific American*, 16 September 2001, www.sciam.com; Tim Harper, "Small Wonders," *Business 2.0*, July 2002, www.business2.com; Erick Schonfeld, "A Peek at IBM's Nanotech Research," *Business 2.0*, 5 December 2003, www.business2.com; David Pescovitz, "The Best New Technologies of 2003," *Business 2.0*, November 2003, 109–116.

GLOSSARY

capacity planning Establishing the overall level of resources needed to meet customer demand

critical path In a PERT network diagram, the sequence of operations that requires the longest time to complete

customized production The creation of a unique good or service for each customer

inventory Goods and materials kept in stock for production or sale

inventory control Determining the right quantities of supplies and products to have on hand and tracking where those items are

ISO 9000 A globally recognized family of standards for quality management systems

just-in-time (JIT) Inventory management in which goods and materials are delivered throughout the production process right before they are needed

lean systems Systems (in manufacturing and other functional areas) that maximize productivity by reducing waste and delays

mass production The creation of identical goods or services, usually in large quantities

mass customization A manufacturing approach in which part of the product is mass produced and the remaining features are customized for each buyer

offshoring Transferring a part or all of a business function to a facility (a different part of the company or another company entirely) in another country

outsourcing Contracting out certain business functions or operations to other companies

procurement The acquisition of the raw materials, parts, components, supplies, and finished products required to produce goods and services

productivity The efficiency with which an organization can convert inputs to outputs

production and operations management Overseeing all the activities involved in producing goods and services

quality The degree to which a product or process meets reasonable or agreed-upon expectations

quality assurance A more comprehensive approach of companywide policies, practices, and procedures to ensure that every product meets quality standards

quality control Measuring quality against established standards after the good or service has been produced and weeding out any defective products

scalability The potential to increase production by expanding or replicating its initial production capacity

Six Sigma A rigorous quality management program that strives to eliminate deviations between the actual and desired performance of a business system

statistical process control (SPC) The use of random sampling and tools such as control charts to monitor the production process

supply chain A set of connected systems that coordinates the flow of goods and materials from suppliers all the way through to final customers

supply chain management (SCM) The business procedures, policies, and computer systems that integrate the various elements of the supply chain into a cohesive system

system An interconnected and coordinated set of *elements* and *processes* that converts *inputs* to desired *outputs*

value chain All the elements and processes that add value as raw materials are transformed into the final products made available to the ultimate customer

value webs Multidimensional networks of suppliers and outsourcing partners

The Art and Science of Marketing

The Art and Science of Marketing

BEHIND THE SCENES   RED ANTS PANTS GIVE WORKING WOMEN A CHOICE THAT FITS

Sarah Calhoun of Red Ants Pants crafted a successful marketing mix to fulfill her mission of providing hardwearing pants for hardworking women.

Photo By Erik Peterson, Courtesy of Sarah Calhoun

www.redantspants.com

Something doesn't add up here:

1. Thousands and thousands of women work in heavy labor jobs, from farming and ranching to welding, construction, and pile driving. In fact, a quarter of the workforce in the building trades, agriculture, fishing, and forestry are women.
2. The kind of work these women perform quickly shreds regular clothing. They need heavy duty duds.
3. Carhartt and other work clothing suppliers sell heavy-duty pants that can stand up to the rigors of tough work, but when Sarah Calhoun surveyed the market, these suppliers focused on work pants made for men.
4. Women aren't shaped like men.

Calhoun wasn't a clothing designer, didn't work in the business, and wasn't chasing some lifelong entrepreneurial dream. But she was fed up—with men's work pants that didn't fit or women's regular pants that didn't hold up under the stress and strain of clearing trails, peeling logs, and doing the other sorts of work she took on in her adopted home state of Montana.

Tired of constantly putting down her tools so she could pull up her misfit britches, Calhoun decided to solve the problem herself. She launched Red Ants Pants with the single-minded goal of outfitting women who need rugged workwear.

Why "Red Ants Pants," by the way? In a conversation with a biologist about the social behaviors of ants, she learned that in red ant colonies, females do most of the work. In keeping with the cheeky style she adopted for all her company's communication, she uses the name as a salute to hardworking women everywhere.

Calhoun was convinced she had spotted a business opportunity, but what was the best way to pursue it? How could a total outsider—based in White Sulphur Springs, Montana, no less—break into the clothing industry? How could she design a product that would meet the needs of her target customers?

How many choices should she offer in terms of colors, styles, and sizes? What could she do to craft a compelling message and get that message in front of the buying public? How should she price the high-quality product she had in mind? What about distribution and the rest of the marketing mix? If you were in Calhoun's position, how would you go about marketing Red Ants Pants?[1]

INTRODUCTION

Sarah Calhoun's experience in introducing the Red Ants Pants brand (profiled in the chapter-opening Behind the Scenes) illustrates the complex challenge of fashioning an appealing blend of products, prices, distribution methods, and customer communication efforts—the essential elements of marketing. This chapter introduces the basic concepts of marketing.

MyBizLab

Gain hands-on experience through an interactive, real-world scenario. This chapter's simulation entitled Market Research Matters is located at **www.mybizlab.com**.

Marketing in a Changing World

Marketing requires a wide range of skills, from research and analysis to strategic planning to persuasive communication. On the job and in the media, you will encounter many uses of the term *marketing*, from the broad and strategic to the narrow and tactical. However, noted marketing professors Philip Kotler and Gary Armstrong offer a definition that does a great job of highlighting the contemporary flavor of customer-focused marketing: **Marketing** is "the process by which companies create value for customers and build strong customer relationships in order to capture value from customers in return."[2] The ideas of *value*, the *exchange* of value, and lasting *relationships* are essential elements of successful marketing.

In addition to goods and services, marketing applies to not-for-profit organizations, people, places, and causes. Politicians and celebrities constantly market themselves. So do places that want to attract residents, tourists, and business investments. **Place marketing** describes efforts to market geographic areas ranging from neighborhoods to entire countries. **Cause-related marketing** promotes a cause or a social issue—such as physical fitness, cancer awareness, environmental sustainability—while also promoting a company and its products.

1	LEARNING OBJECTIVE

Define *marketing*, and explain its role in society.

marketing The process of creating value for customers and building relationships with those customers in order to capture value back from them

place marketing Marketing efforts to attract people and organizations to a particular geographical area

cause-related marketing Identification and marketing of a social issue, cause, or idea to selected target markets

THE ROLE OF MARKETING IN SOCIETY

Marketing plays an important role in society by helping people satisfy their needs and wants and by helping organizations determine what to produce.

Needs and Wants

Individuals and organizations have a wide variety of needs, from food and water necessary for survival to transaction processing systems that make sure a retail store gets paid for all the credit card purchases it records. As a consumer, you experience **needs** any time there are differences or gaps between your actual state and your ideal state. You're hungry and you don't want to be hungry: You need to eat. Needs create the motivation to buy products and are, therefore, at the core of any discussion of marketing.

Your **wants** are based on your needs but are more specific. Producers do not create needs, but they do try to shape your wants by exposing you to attractive choices. For instance, when you *need* some food, you may *want* a Snickers bar, an orange, or a seven-course dinner at the swankiest restaurant in town. If you have the means, or *buying power*, to purchase the product you want, you create *demand* for that product.[3]

needs Differences between a person's actual state and his or her ideal state; they provide the basic motivation to make a purchase

wants Specific goods, services, experiences, or other entities that are desirable in light of a person's experiences, culture, and personality

Avon has made breast cancer awareness and research funding a focus of its cause-related marketing.

exchange process The act of obtaining a desired object or service from another party by offering something of value in return

transaction An exchange of value between parties

utility The power of a good or service to satisfy a human need

marketing concept An approach to business management that stresses customer needs and wants, seeks long-term profitability, and integrates marketing with other functional units within the organization

Exchanges and Transactions

When you participate in the **exchange process**, you trade something of value (usually money) for something else of value. When you make a purchase, you encourage the producer of that item to create or supply more of it. In this way, supply and demand tend toward balance, and society obtains the goods and services that are most satisfying. When the exchange actually occurs, it takes the form of a **transaction**. Party A gives Party B $1.29 and gets a medium Coke in return. A trade of values takes place.

Most transactions in today's society involve money, but money is not necessarily required. Bartering or trading, which predates the use of cash, is making a big comeback thanks to the Internet. Hundreds of online barter exchanges are now in operation in the United States alone. Intermediaries such as BizXchange (www.bizx.com) facilitate cashless trading among multiple members through a system of credits and debits. For instance, an advertising agency might trade services to a dairy farm, which then trades products to a catering company, which then trades services to the advertising agency. By eliminating the need for trading partners to have exactly complimentary needs at exactly the same time, these exchanges make it easy for companies to buy and sell without using cash.[4]

The Four Utilities

To encourage the exchange process, marketers enhance the appeal of their goods and services by adding **utility**, which is any attribute that increases the value that customers place on the product (see Exhibit 1). When organizations change raw materials into finished goods, they are creating *form utility* desired by consumers. When supermarkets provide fresh, ready-to-eat dishes as an alternative to food ingredients, they are creating form utility. In other cases, marketers try to make their products available when and where customers want to buy them, creating *time utility* and *place utility*. Overnight couriers such as FedEx create time utility, whereas coffee carts in office buildings and ATMs in shopping malls create place utility. Services such as Apple's iTunes create both time and place utility: You can purchase music almost instantly, without leaving your computer. The final form of utility is *possession utility*—the satisfaction that buyers get when they actually possess a product, both legally and physically. Mortgage companies, for example, create possession utility by offering loans that allow people to buy homes they could otherwise not afford.

THE MARKETING CONCEPT

Business's view of the marketing function has evolved rather dramatically over the decades. In years past, many companies pursued what was known as the *product concept*, which was essentially to focus on the production of goods and count on customers to figure out which products they needed and take the steps to find and purchase them. In other words, the product concept views the primary purpose of a business as making things, not satisfying customers. As markets evolved and competition heated up, the *sales concept* began to take over, which emphasizes building a business by generating as many sales transactions as possible. The customer features more prominently in the sales concept, but only as a target to be sold to, not as a partner in a mutually satisfying relationship.

In contrast, today's most successful companies tend to embrace the **marketing concept**, the idea that companies should respond to customers' needs and wants while seeking long-term profitability and coordinating their own marketing

EXHIBIT 1 — Examples of the Four Utilities

The utility of a good or service has four aspects, each of which enhances the product's value to the consumer.

Utility	Example
Form utility	Kettle Valley's Fruit Snack (www.kettlevalley.net) bars provide the nutritional value of real fruit in a form that offers greater convenience and longer storage life.
Time utility	LensCrafters (www.lenscrafters.com) has captured a big chunk of the market for eyeglasses by providing on-the-spot, one-hour service.
Place utility	By offering convenient home delivery of the latest fashion apparel and accessories, dELiA*s (www.delias.com) catalog and website have become favorites of teenage girls.
Possession utility	RealNetworks's Rhapsody music streaming service (www.rhapsody.com) gives customers the option of buying individual songs.

efforts to achieve the company's long-term goals (see Exhibit 2). These *customer-focused* companies build their marketing strategies around the goal of long-term relationships with satisfied customers.[5] The term **relationship marketing** is often applied to these efforts to distinguish them from efforts that emphasize production or sales transactions. One of the most significant goals of relationship marketing is **customer loyalty**, the degree to which customers continue to buy from a particular retailer or buy the products offered by a particular manufacturer. The payoff from becoming customer focused can be considerable, but the process of transforming a product-or sales-driven company into one that embraces the

relationship marketing A focus on developing and maintaining long-term relationships with customers, suppliers, and distribution partners for mutual benefit

customer loyalty The degree to which customers continue to buy from a particular retailer or buy the products of a particular manufacturer or service provider

EXHIBIT 2 — The Selling Concept Versus the Marketing Concept

Firms that practice the selling concept sell what they make rather than making what the market wants. In contrast, firms that practice the marketing concept determine the needs and wants of a market and deliver the desired product or service more effectively and efficiently than competitors do.

Source: Adapted in part from Philip Kotler and Gary Armstrong, *Principles of Marketing*, 13th ed. (Upper Saddle River, N.J.: Pearson Prentice Hall, 2010), 10.

marketing concept can take years and may involve changes to major systems and processes throughout the company, as well as the basic culture of the company.[6]

Why all the emphasis on customer service and customer satisfaction in the marketing concept? It's not just about being nice and helpful; satisfying customers is simply smart business. For one thing, keeping your existing customers is usually much cheaper and easier than finding new customers. For another, satisfied customers are the best promotion a company can hope for, particularly given the power of social media and social commerce.

✔ Checkpoint

LEARNING OBJECTIVE 1: Define *marketing*, **and explain its role in society.**

SUMMARY: Marketing can be defined as "the process by which companies create value for customers and build strong customer relationships in order to capture value from customers in return." The marketing function guides a company in selecting which products to offer, how much to charge for them, how to distribute them to customers, and how to promote them to potential buyers. Marketing plays an important role in society by helping people satisfy their needs and wants and by helping organizations determine what to produce.

CRITICAL THINKING: (1) Should every company see long-term relationships with customers to the same degree? Why or why not? (2) Would a company that already dominates its markets ever care about the marketing concept? Why or why not?

IT'S YOUR BUSINESS: (1) What is your reaction when you feel as though you're being "sold to" by a company that is clearly more interested in selling products than in meeting your needs as an individual consumer? (2) Do you want to have a "relationship" with any of the companies that you currently patronize as a customer? Why or why not?

KEY TERMS TO KNOW: marketing, place marketing, cause-related marketing, needs, wants, exchange process, transaction, utility, marketing concept, relationship marketing, customer loyalty

---

2 **LEARNING OBJECTIVE**

Identify three trends that help define contemporary marketing.

Challenges in Contemporary Marketing

As business has progressed from the product concept to the sales concept to the marketing concept—with the critical emergence of social commerce—the role of marketing has become increasingly complicated. You'll read about some specific challenges in this chapter, but here are three general issues that many marketing organizations are wrestling with today: involving the customer in the marketing process, making data-driven decisions, and conducting marketing activities with greater concern for ethics and etiquette.

INVOLVING THE CUSTOMER IN THE MARKETING PROCESS

REAL-TIME UPDATES
Learn More by Reading This Article

Read the inside story on being customer focused

Tony Hsieh, CEO of Zappos, explains how a culture deeply rooted in customer focus (and employee empowerment) is the foundation of the company's success. Go to http://real-timeupdates.com/bia6 and click on Learn More. If you are using MyBizLab, you can access Real-Time Updates within the chapter or under Student Study Tools.

A central element in the marketing concept is involving the customer as a partner in a mutually beneficial relationship rather than treating the customer as a passive recipient of products and promotional messages. Involving the customer has always been relatively easy for small, local companies and for large companies with their major customers. For instance, a neighborhood bistro or coffee shop can prepare foods and drinks just the way its regular customers want, and satisfied customers are happy to tell friends and relatives about their favorite places to eat and drink. At the other extreme, a maker of jet engines such as Pratt & Whitney or Rolls-Royce works closely with its airplane manufacturing customers to create exactly the products those customers want.

The challenge has been to replicate this level of intimacy on a broader scale, when a company has thousands of customers spread across the country or around the world. Two sets of technologies have helped foster communication and collaboration between companies and their customers. The first is **customer relationship management (CRM)** systems, which capture, organize, and capitalize on all the interactions that a company has with its customers, from marketing surveys and advertising through sales orders and customer support. A CRM system functions like an institutional memory for a company, allowing it to record and act on the information that is pertinent to each customer relationship.

CRM can be a powerful means to foster relationships, but to a certain degree, conventional CRM simply computerizes an existing way of doing business. A more dramatic step is enabling **social commerce**, using blogs, wikis, *user-generated content* such as online videos or customer-created advertising, and other social media technologies. These tools let customers communicate with companies, with each other, and with other influences in the marketplace such as prominent bloggers and journalists. For example, social networks such as Facebook have the potential to redefine advertising because consumers tend to view friends and peers as more reliable sources of product information than advertising.[7] Another valuable use of social media is listening to feedback from customers.[8] Innovative companies are beginning to integrate these two relationship technologies, combining the data capture and retrieval of CRM with the interactivity of social media.[9]

customer relationship management (CRM) A type of information system that captures, organizes, and capitalizes on all the interactions that a company has with its customers

social commerce The creation and sharing of product-related information among customers and potential customers

MAKING DATA-DRIVEN MARKETING DECISIONS

Learning more about customers is one aspect of the larger challenge of collecting, analyzing, and using data to make marketing decisions. Marketers in every industry would like to have better insights for making decisions and better ways of measuring the results of every marketing initiative. Pioneering retailer John Wannamaker said 100 years ago that "half the money I spend on advertising is wasted. The trouble is, I don't know which half."[10] Actually, Wannamaker was probably overly optimistic. In one extensive study, advertising was found to increase revenue for just over half of new products but for only one-third of existing products.[11] In other words, according to this research, the advertising campaigns for two-thirds of established products in the marketplace don't bring in more revenue.

Understandably, top executives are demanding that marketing departments do a better job of justifying their budgets and finding the most effective ways of meeting marketing objectives. However, this accountability challenge is not a simple one, and the problem may never be completely solvable for many companies. With so many sources of information in the marketplace, particularly with the continuing growth of online and mobile marketing channels, identifying which sources influence which aspects of buyer behavior can be difficult.

To get a better idea of how well their marketing budgets are being spent, companies can use a class of tools and techniques called *marketing analytics*. For example, Google Analytics helps online advertisers measure the effectiveness of specific search-term keywords and track the behavior of website visitors from their initial landing on an e-commerce site on through to a purchase.[12] By integrating such tools into an overall measurement system that evaluates both online and offline marketing activities, a company can improve its decision making and focus its time and money in the most productive marketing efforts.

The process of gathering and analyzing *market intelligence* about customers, competitors, and related marketing issues through any combination of methods is known as **marketing research**. As markets grow increasingly dynamic and open to competition from all parts of the globe, today's companies realize that information is the key to successful action. Without it, they're forced to use guesswork, analogies from other markets that may or may not apply, or experience from the past that may not correspond to the future.[13]

At the same time, however, marketing research can't provide the answer to every strategic or tactical question. As

marketing research The collection and analysis of information for making marketing decisions

REAL-TIME UPDATES
Learn More by Reading This Article

Marketing research tutorial

This three-part series offers a great overview of research strategies and techniques. Go to http://real-timeupdates.com/bia6 and click on Learn More. If you are using MyBizLab, you can access Real-Time Updates within the chapter or under Student Study Tools.

a manager or an entrepreneur, you'll find yourself in situations that require creative thinking and careful judgment to make the leap beyond what the data alone can tell you. Research techniques range from the basic to the exotic, from simple surveys to advanced statistical techniques to neurological scanning that tries to discover how and why customers' brains respond to visual and verbal cues about products. You can see a sample of techniques in Exhibit 3.

MARKETING WITH GREATER CONCERN FOR ETHICS AND ETIQUETTE

Under pressure to reach and persuade buyers in a business environment that gets more fragmented and noisy all the time, marketers occasionally step over the line and engage in practices that are rude, manipulative, or even downright deceptive. The result is an increasing degree of skepticism of and hostility toward advertising and other marketing activities.[14]

To avoid intensifying the vicious circle in which marketers keep doing the same old things, only louder and longer—leading customers to get more angry and more

| EXHIBIT 3 | Marketing Research Techniques |

Marketers can use a wide variety of techniques to learn more about customers, competitors, and threats and opportunities in the marketplace.

Technique	Examples
Observation	Any in-person, mechanical, or electronic technique that monitors and records behavior, including website usage tracking and monitoring of blogs and social networking websites.
Surveys	Data collection efforts that measure responses from a representative subset of a larger group of people; can be conducted in person (when people with clipboards stop you in a mall, that's called a *mall intercept*), over the phone, by mail or email, or online. Designing and conducting a meaningful survey requires thorough knowledge of statistical techniques such as *sampling* to ensure valid results that truly represent the larger group. For this reason, many of the simple surveys that you see online these days do not produce statistically valid results.
Interviews and focus groups	One-on-one or group discussions that try to probe deeper into issues than a survey typically does. *Focus groups* involve a small number of people guided by a facilitator while being observed or recorded by researchers. Unlike surveys, interviews and focus groups are not designed to collect statistics that represent a larger group; their real value is in uncovering issues that might require further study.
Process data collection	Any method of collecting data during the course of other business tasks, including warranty registration cards, sales transaction records, gift and loyalty program card usage, and customer service interactions.
Experiments	Controlled scenarios in which researchers adjust one or more variables to measure the effect these changes have on customer behavior. For instance, separate groups of consumers can be exposed to different ads to see which ad is most effective. *Test marketing*, the launch of a product under real-world conditions but on a limited scale (such as in a single city), is a form of experimental research.
Ethnographic research	A branch of anthropology that studies people in their daily lives to learn about their needs, wants, and behaviors in real-life settings.
Neuromarketing studies	Research that measures brain activity while customers are viewing or interacting with product, websites, or other elements.

Sources: Adapted from Ken Anderson, "Ethnographic Research: A Key to Strategy," *Harvard Business Review*, March 2009, 24; Emily R. Murphy, Judy Illes, and Peter B. Reiner, "Neuroethics of Neuromarketing," *Journal of Consumer Behaviour*, July–October 2008, 293–302; Dick Bucci, "Recording Systems Add More Depth When Capturing Answers," *Marketing News*, 1 March 2005, 50; Laurence Bernstein, "Enough Research Bashing!" *Marketing*, 24 January 2005, 10; Naresh K. Malhotra, *Basic Marketing Research* (Upper Saddle River, N.J.: Pearson Prentice Hall, 2002), 110–112, 208–212, 228–229.

defensive—some marketers are looking for a better way. Social commerce shows a lot of promise for redefining marketing communication from one-way promotion to two-way conversation. Another hopeful sign is **permission-based marketing**, in which marketers invite potential or current customers to receive information in areas that genuinely interest them. Many websites now take this approach, letting visitors sign up for specific content streams with the promise that they won't be bombarded with information they don't care about.

The widespread adoption of social media has also increased the attention given to transparency, which in this context refers to a sense of openness, of giving all participants in a conversation access to the information they need to accurately process the messages they are receiving. A key aspect of transparency is knowing who is behind the messages one receives. Consider the promotional event that Netflix staged in Toronto to announce the launch of its streaming video service in Canada. The outdoor news conference seemed to attract dozens of curious people who were excited about the availability of Netflix. However, many of these people who "spontaneously" showed up were actually paid actors with instructions to "look really excited, particularly if asked by media to do any interviews about the prospect of Netflix in Canada." The company apologized when the stunt was exposed.[15]

A major issue in business communication transparency is **stealth marketing**, which involves attempting to promote products and services to customers who don't know they're being marketed to. A common stealth marketing technique is rewarding someone for promoting products to his or her friends without telling them it's a form of advertising. Critics—including the U.S. Federal Trade Commission (FTC) and the Word of Mouth Marketing Association—assert that such techniques are deceptive because they don't give their targets the opportunity to raise their instinctive defenses against the persuasive powers of marketing messages.[16]

Aside from ethical concerns, trying to fool the public is simply bad for business. As LaSalle University professor Michael Smith puts it, "The public backlash can be long, deep, and damaging to a company's reputation."[17]

permission-based marketing
A marketing approach in which firms first ask permission to deliver messages to an audience and then promise to restrict their communication efforts to those subject areas in which audience members have expressed interest

stealth marketing The delivery of marketing messages to people who are not aware that they are being marketed to; these messages can be delivered by either acquaintances or strangers, depending on the technique

Checkpoint

LEARNING OBJECTIVE 2: Identify three trends that help define contemporary marketing.

SUMMARY: Three general issues that many marketing organizations are wrestling with today are involving the customer in the marketing process, making data-driven decisions, and conducting marketing with greater concern for ethics and etiquette. Allowing customers greater involvement is essential to relationship marketing and the marketing concept. Increasingly, this involvement is enabled by *social commerce*—customers using social media to converse with companies and each other. Data-driven decision making is a top priority as many companies struggle to justify and optimize marketing expenditures. Public opinion of business in general and marketing in particular is at a low point these days, prompting many professionals to take a closer look at their business practices and relationships with customers.

CRITICAL THINKING: (1) How can technology help companies replicate the community feel of a small neighborhood business on a global scale? (2) Why do some critics consider stealth marketing to be unethical?

IT'S YOUR BUSINESS: (1) Are you so loyal to any brands or companies that you refuse to accept substitutes—so much so that if you can't have your favorite product, you'll do without? What is it about these products that earns your continued loyalty? (2) Have you ever been a target of stealth marketing? If so, how did you feel about the company after you learned you had been marketed to without your knowledge?

KEY TERMS TO KNOW: customer relationship management (CRM), social commerce, marketing research, permission-based marketing, stealth marketing

Differentiate between consumer buying behavior and organizational buying behavior.

consumer market Individuals or households that buy goods and services for personal use

organizational market Companies, government agencies, and other organizations that buy goods and services either to resell or to use in the creation of their own goods and services

Understanding Today's Customers

To implement the marketing concept, companies must have good information about what customers want. Today's customers, both individual consumers and organizational buyers, are a diverse and demanding group, with little patience for marketers who do not understand them or will not adapt business practices to meet their needs. For instance, consumers faced with complex purchase decisions such as cars can now find extensive information online about products, prices, competitors, customer service rankings, safety issues, and other factors.

The first step toward understanding customers is recognizing the purchase and ownership habits of the **consumer market**, made up of individuals and families who buy for personal or household use, and the **organizational market**, composed of companies and a variety of noncommercial institutions, from local school districts to the federal government.

Exhibit 4 models two decision-making paths that buyers can take when they perceive the need to make a purchase, one for routine purchases and one for new, unusual, or highly significant purchases. Consumers and organizations can follow either path, depending on a specific purchase. Broadly speaking, however, organizational buyers tend to approach purchasing in a more rational, data-driven fashion, simply because organizational choices are nearly always about functional and financial value.

THE CONSUMER DECISION PROCESS

Think about several purchase decisions you've made recently. Classical economics suggests that your behavior would follow a rational process of first recognizing a need and then gathering information, identifying alternative solutions, and finally making your choice from those alternatives. But how often do you really make decisions in this way? Researchers now understand that consumer behavior tends to be far less logical and far more complicated—and more interesting—than this model suggests. In fact, some research suggests that as much as 95 percent of the decision-making process is subconscious and that sensory cues can play a much larger role than objective information.[18] The emerging field of *behavioral economics* is starting to offer better insights into consumer behavior by incorporating a broader (and somewhat less-flattering) view of the way people really make decisions.[19]

EXHIBIT 4	Buyer Decision Making

The steps buyers go through on the way to making a purchase vary widely, based on the magnitude of the purchase and the significance of the outcome. In general, businesses and other organizations use a more formal and more rational process than consumers, and nonroutine decisions in either sector require more time and energy than routine decisions. Defining *routine* is not a simple matter, however; a company might make huge resupply purchases automatically while a consumer spends days agonizing over a pair of jeans.

Even in situations in which consumers gather lots of information and appear to be making a well-thought-out, rational decision, they often are acting more on gut feelings and emotional responses. For instance, you might see some jaw-dropping sports car glide past you on the street, and in that split second—before you even start "thinking" about it—you've already decided to buy one just like it. Sure, you'll gather brochures, do research on the Internet, test-drive other models, and so on, but chances are you're not really evaluating alternatives. Instead, your rational, conscious brain is just looking for evidence to support the decision that your emotional, semiconscious brain has already made.

Moreover, consumers make all kinds of decisions that are hard to explain by any rational means. We might spend two weeks gathering data on $200 music players but choose a college with a $20,000 annual tuition simply because a best friend is going there. Sometimes we buy things for no apparent reason other than the fact that we have money in our pockets. As a result, at one time or another, all consumers suffer from **cognitive dissonance**, which occurs when one's beliefs and behaviors don't match. A common form of this situation is *buyer's remorse*, in which one makes a purchase and then regrets doing so—sometimes immediately after the purchase.

You can start to understand why so many decisions seem mysterious from a rational point of view if you consider all the influences that affect purchases:

- **Culture.** The cultures (and subgroups within cultures) that people belong to shape their values, attitudes, and beliefs and influence the way they respond to the world around them.
- **Socioeconomic level.** In addition to being members of a particular culture, people also perceive themselves as members of a certain social class—be it upper, middle, lower, or somewhere in between. In general, members of various classes pursue different activities, buy different goods, shop in different places, and react to different media—or at least like to believe they do.
- **Reference groups.** Individuals are influenced by *reference groups* that provide information about product choices and establish values that they perceive as important. Reference groups can be either *membership* or *aspirational*. As the name suggests, membership groups are those to which consumers actually belong, such as families, networks of friends, clubs, and work groups. In contrast, consumers are not members of aspirational reference groups but use them as role models for style, speech, opinions, and various other behaviors.[20] For instance, millions of consumers buy products that help them identify with popular musicians or professional athletes.
- **Situational factors.** These factors include events or circumstances in people's lives that are more circumstantial but that can influence buying patterns. Such factors can range from having a coupon to celebrating a holiday to being in a bad mood. If you've ever indulged in "retail therapy" to cheer yourself up, you know all about situational factors—and the buyer's remorse that often comes with it.
- **Self-image.** Many consumers tend to believe that "you are what you buy," so they make or avoid choices that support their desired self-images. Marketers capitalize on people's need to express their identity through their purchases by emphasizing the image value of goods and services.

THE ORGANIZATIONAL CUSTOMER DECISION PROCESS

The purchasing behavior of organizations is easier to understand than the purchasing behavior of consumers because it's more clearly driven by economics and influenced less by subconscious and emotional factors. Here are some of the significant ways in which organizational purchasing differs from consumer purchasing:[21]

- **An emphasis on economic payback and other rational factors.** Much more so than with consumer purchases, organizational purchases are carefully evaluated for financial impact, reliability, and other objective factors. Organizations don't always make the

REAL-TIME UPDATES
Learn More by Reading This Article

Take a closer look at consumer buying behavior

This tutorial dives into the "why" and "how" of consumer choices. Go to http://real-timeupdates.com/bia6 and click on Learn More. If you are using MyBizLab, you can access Real-Time Updates within the chapter or under Student Study Tools.

cognitive dissonance Tension that exists when a person's beliefs don't match his or her behaviors; a common example is *buyer's remorse*, when someone regrets a purchase immediately after making it

The Art and Science of Marketing

REAL-TIME UPDATES
Learn More by Reading This Article

Take a closer look at organizational buying behavior

Learn more about how businesses make purchasing decisions. Go to http://real-timeupdates.com/bia6 and click on Learn More. If you are using MyBizLab, you can access Real-Time Updates within the chapter or under Student Study Tools.

best choices, of course, but their choices are usually based on a more rational analysis of needs and alternatives. This isn't to say that emotions play little or no role in the purchase decision, however; organizations don't make decisions, people do. Fear of change, fear of failure, excitement about new technologies, and the pride of being associated with world-class suppliers are just a few of the emotions that can influence organizational purchases.

- **A formal buying process.** From office supplies to new factories, most organizational purchases follow a formal buying process, particularly in mid- to large-size companies.

- **Greater complexity in product usage.** The Apple iPhone is a great example of how consumer and organizational markets differ. It was instantly popular with vast numbers of consumers, but breaking into the corporate market was a much greater challenge for Apple because organizational buyers must address such issues as compatibility with corporate communication systems and legal requirements of data retention and security.[22] In addition, the *network effect*, in which the value of a product increases with the number of customers who use it, can be a key decision driver.[23] A major reason that other software providers have so much trouble putting a dent in Microsoft's dominance of the corporate market is that business users need compatibility, so it is simpler to select the tools that more people already use. Also, organizations sometimes continue to use products long after better substitutes become available if the costs and complexity of updating outweigh the advantages of the newer solutions.

- **The participation and influence of multiple people.** Except in the very smallest businesses, the purchase process usually involves a group of people. This team can include end users, technical experts, the manager with ultimate purchasing authority, and a professional purchasing agent whose job includes researching suppliers, negotiating prices, and evaluating supplier performance. Multiple family members play a part in many consumer purchases, of course, but not with the formality apparent in organizational markets.

- **Close relationships between buyers and sellers.** Close relationships between buyers and sellers are common in organizational purchasing. In some cases, employees of the seller even have offices inside the buyer's facility to promote close interaction.

 Checkpoint

LEARNING OBJECTIVE 3: Differentiate between consumer buying behavior and organizational buying behavior.

SUMMARY: Classical economic theory suggests that consumers follow a largely rational process of recognizing a need, searching for information, evaluating alternatives, making a purchase, and evaluating the product after use or consumption. However, recent research into behavioral economics and consumer psychology suggests that many consumer purchases are far less rational. Much of this decision making happens subconsciously and is driven to a large degree by emotion, culture, and situational factors. Organizational buying behavior comes much closer to the rational model of classical economics because purchases are usually judged by their economic value to the organization. The most significant ways in which organizational purchasing differs from consumer purchasing are an emphasis on economic payback, a formal buying process, greater complexity in product usage, purchasing groups, and close relationships between buyers and sellers.

CRITICAL THINKING: (1) Can business-to-business marketers take advantage of new insights into consumer buying behavior? Why or why not? (2) How could families and individual consumers benefit from adopting some elements of organizational buying behavior?

214

IT'S YOUR BUSINESS: (1) Do you read product reviews online before making important purchases? Why or why not? Have you ever contributed to social commerce by posting your own reviews or product advice? (2) Why did you buy the clothes you are wearing at this very moment?

KEY TERMS TO KNOW: consumer market, organizational market, cognitive dissonance

Identifying Market Opportunities

With insights into your customers' needs and behaviors, you're ready to begin planning your marketing strategies. **Strategic marketing planning** is a process that involves three steps: (1) examining the current marketing situation, (2) assessing opportunities and setting objectives, and (3) crafting a marketing strategy to reach those objectives (see Exhibit 5). Companies often record the results of their planning efforts in a formal *marketing plan*.

EXAMINING THE CURRENT MARKETING SITUATION

Examining your current marketing situation includes reviewing your past performance (how well each product is doing in each market where you sell it), evaluating your competition, examining your internal strengths and weaknesses, and analyzing the external environment.

Define *strategic marketing planning*, and identify the four basic options for pursuing new marketing opportunities.

strategic marketing planning
The process of examining an organization's current marketing situation, assessing opportunities and setting objectives, and then developing a marketing strategy to reach those objectives

EXHIBIT 5	**The Strategic Marketing Planning Process**

Strategic marketing planning can involve a range of major decisions that fall into three general steps: (1) examining the current marketing situation, (2) assessing opportunities and setting objectives, and (3) developing a marketing strategy. The nature of these steps can vary widely depending on the products and markets involved; for example, emerging markets and mature markets have very different sets of customer and competitor dynamics.

1. Examine current marketing situation

- Review past performance
- Evaluate competition
- Examine strengthes and weaknesses
- Analyze the business environment

2. Assess opportunities and set objectives

- Explore product and market opportunities
- Set sales targets that are invigorating while being realistic

3. Develop marketing strategy

- Divide market into strategically productive segments
- Choose best-fit segments
- Decide how to position in minds of target customers
- Develop marketing mix

Reviewing Performance

Unless you're starting a new business, your company has a history of marketing performance. Maybe sales have slowed in the past year, maybe you've had to cut prices so much that you're barely earning a profit, or maybe sales have been strong and you have money to invest in new marketing activities. Reviewing where you are and how you got there is critical because you want to learn from your mistakes and repeat your successes—without getting trapped in mindsets and practices that need to change for the future, even if they were successful in the past.

Evaluating Competition

In addition to reviewing past performance, you must evaluate your competition. If you own a Burger King franchise, for example, you need to watch what McDonald's and Wendy's are doing. You also have to keep an eye on Taco Bell, KFC, Pizza Hut, and other restaurants, as well as pay attention to any number of other ways your customers might satisfy their hunger—including fixing a sandwich at home. Furthermore, you need to watch the horizon for trends that could affect your business, such as consumer interest in organic foods or in locally produced ingredients.

Examining Internal Strengths and Weaknesses

Successful marketers try to identify sources of competitive advantage and areas that need improvement. They look at such factors as financial resources, production capabilities, distribution networks, brand awareness, business partnerships, managerial expertise, and promotional capabilities. On the basis of your internal analysis, you will be able to decide whether your business should (1) limit itself to those opportunities for which it possesses the required strengths or (2) challenge itself to reach higher goals by acquiring and developing new strengths.

Analyzing the External Environment

Marketers must also analyze trends and conditions in the business environment when planning their marketing strategies. For example, customer decisions are greatly affected by interest rates, inflation, unemployment, personal income, and savings rates. During recessions, consumers still aspire to enjoy the good life, but they are forced by circumstances to alter their spending patterns.[24] "Affordable luxuries" become particularly appealing during these times, for example. Recessions also create opportunities for agile and aggressive companies to take business away from companies weakened by poor sales and deteriorating finances.[25]

ASSESSING OPPORTUNITIES AND SETTING OBJECTIVES

After you've examined the current marketing situation, you're ready to assess your marketing opportunities and set your objectives. Successful companies are always on the lookout for new marketing opportunities, which can be classified into four options (see Exhibit 6).[26] **Market penetration** involves selling more of your existing products into the markets you already serve. **Product development** is creating new products for those current markets, while **market development** is selling your existing products to new markets. Finally, **diversification** involves creating new products for new markets.

Generally speaking, these four options are listed in order of increasing risk. Market penetration can be the least risky because your products already exist and the market has already demonstrated some level of demand for your products. At the other extreme, creating new products for new markets is usually the riskiest choice of all because you encounter uncertainties in both dimensions (you may fail to create the product you need, and the market might not be interested in it).

After you've framed the opportunity you want to pursue, you are ready to set your marketing objectives. A common marketing objective is to achieve a certain level of **market share**, which is a firm's portion of the total sales within a market (market share can be defined by either number of units sold or by sales revenue).

market penetration Selling more of a firm's existing products into the markets it already serves

product development Creating new products for a firm's current markets

market development Selling existing products to new markets

diversification Creating new products for new markets

market share A firm's portion of the total sales in a market

EXHIBIT 6 | **Pursuing Market Opportunities**

Every company has four basic options when it comes to pursuing market opportunities. The arrows show the increasing level of risk, from the lowest to the highest.

✓ **Checkpoint**

LEARNING OBJECTIVE 4: Define *strategic marketing planning*, **and identify the four basic options for pursuing new marketing opportunities.**

SUMMARY: Strategic marketing planning involves three steps: (1) examining the current marketing situation (including past performance, competition, internal strengths and weaknesses, and the external environment); (2) assessing market opportunities and setting marketing objectives; and (3) developing a marketing strategy to reach those objectives. The four basic options for pursuing market opportunities are *market penetration* (selling more existing products into the current markets), *product development* (creating new products for current markets), *market development* (selling existing products to new markets), and *diversification* (creating new products for new markets).

CRITICAL THINKING: (1) Why is it important to analyze past performance before assessing market opportunities and setting objectives? (2) Why is diversification considered riskier than market penetration, product development, and market development strategies?

IT'S YOUR BUSINESS: (1) Do you see yourself as a trendsetter in any aspect of your life? (2) How could the four options for pursuing market opportunities be applied to your career planning at various stages in your career? (Think of your skills as the products you have to offer.)

KEY TERMS TO KNOW: strategic marketing planning, market penetration, product development, market development, diversification, market share

Crafting a Marketing Strategy

Using the current marketing situation and your objectives as your guide, you're ready to develop a **marketing strategy**, which consists of dividing your market into *segments*, choosing your *target markets* and the *position* you'd like to establish in those markets, and then developing a *marketing mix* to help you get there.

5 | **LEARNING OBJECTIVE**

Identify the four steps in crafting a marketing strategy.

marketing strategy An overall plan for marketing a product; includes the identification of target market segments, a positioning strategy, and a marketing mix

DIVIDING MARKETS INTO SEGMENTS

market A group of customers who need or want a particular product and have the money to buy it

market segmentation The division of a diverse market into smaller, relatively homogeneous groups with similar needs, wants, and purchase behaviors

A **market** contains all the customers who might be interested in a product and can pay for it. However, most markets contain subgroups of potential customers with different interests, values, and behaviors. To maximize their effectiveness in reaching these subgroups, many companies subdivide the total market through **market segmentation**, grouping customers with similar characteristics, behaviors, and needs. Each of these market segments can then be approached by offering products that are priced, distributed, and promoted in a unique way that is most likely to appeal to that segment. The overall goal of market segmentation is to understand why and how certain customers buy what they buy so that you use your finite resources to create and market products in the most efficient manner possible.[27]

Four fundamental factors marketers use to identify market segments are demographics, psychographics, geography, and behavior:

demographics The study of statistical characteristics of a population

- **Demographics.** When you segment a market using **demographics**, the statistical analysis of a population, you subdivide your customers according to characteristics such as age, gender, income, race, occupation, and ethnic group.

psychographics Classification of customers on the basis of their psychological makeup, interests, and lifestyles

- **Psychographics.** Whereas demographic segmentation is the study of people from the outside, **psychographics** is the analysis of people from the inside, focusing on their psychological makeup, including attitudes, interests, opinions, and lifestyles. Psychographic analysis focuses on why people behave the way they do by examining such issues as brand preferences, media preferences, values, self-concept, and behavior.

geographic segmentation Categorization of customers according to their geographical location

- **Geography.** When differences in buying behavior are influenced by where people live, it makes sense to use **geographic segmentation**. Segmenting the market into geographic units such as regions, cities, counties, or neighborhoods allows companies to customize and sell products that meet the needs of specific markets and to organize their operations as needed.

behavioral segmentation Categorization of customers according to their relationship with products or response to product characteristics

- **Behavior. Behavioral segmentation** groups customers according to their relationship with products or response to product characteristics. To identify behavioral segments, marketers study such factors as the occasions that prompt people to buy certain products, the particular benefits they seek from a product, their habits and frequency of product usage, and the degree of loyalty they show toward a brand.[28]

Starting with these variables, researchers can also combine different types of data to identify target segments with even greater precision, such as merging geographic, demographic, and behavioral data to define specific types of consumer neighborhoods.

CHOOSING YOUR TARGET MARKETS

target markets Specific customer groups or segments to whom a company wants to sell a particular product

After you have segmented your market, the next step is to find appropriate target segments, or **target markets**, on which to focus your efforts. Marketers use a variety of criteria to narrow their focus to a few suitable market segments, including the magnitude of potential sales within each segment, the cost of reaching those customers, fit with a firm's core competencies, and any risks in the business environment.

Exhibit 7 diagrams four strategies for reaching target markets. Companies that practice *undifferentiated marketing* (also known as *mass marketing*) ignore differences among buyers and offer only one product or product line and present it with the same communication, pricing, and distribution strategies to all potential buyers. Undifferentiated marketing has the advantages of simplicity and economies of scale, but it can be less effective at reaching some portions of the market.

By contrast, companies that manufacture or sell a variety of products to several target customer groups practice *differentiated marketing*. This is Toyota's approach, for example, with the Scion brand aimed at young buyers, the Toyota brand designed for its core audience, and the Lexus brand targeted to those wanting luxury cars. Differentiated marketing is a popular strategy, but it requires substantial resources because the company has to tailor products, prices, promotional efforts, and distribution arrangements for each customer group. The differentiation should be based on meaningful differences that don't alienate any audiences.

EXHIBIT 7	Market-Coverage Strategies

Four alternative market-coverage strategies are undifferentiated marketing, differentiated marketing, concentrated marketing, and micromarketing.

Source: Adapted from Philip Kotler and Gary Armstrong, *Principles of Marketing*, 13th ed. (Upper Saddle River, N.J.: Pearson Prentice Hall, 2010), 201–207.

Concentrated marketing focuses on only a single market segment. With this approach, you acknowledge that various other market segments may exist but you choose to target just one. The biggest advantage of concentrated marketing is that it allows you to focus all your time and resources on a single type of customer (which is why this approach is usually the best option for start-up companies, by the way). The strategy can be risky, however, because you've staked your fortunes on just one segment.

Micromarketing, or *individualized marketing*, is the narrowest strategy of all, in which firms target a single location or even a single customer.[29] This approach can range from customizable products to *major accounts* sales teams that craft entire marketing programs for each of their largest customers.

Achieving success in any market segment can take time and significant investment, so embracing market segments for the long term is essential. For example, Procter & Gamble, the company behind the Pampers brand of disposable diapers, targets women before their babies are born and maintains a relationship with them for years afterward.[30] In fact, many companies now think in terms of *customer lifetime value*: the total potential revenue from each customer over a certain time span minus the cost of attracting and keeping that customer. This approach lets companies focus on their most valuable customers while deciding what to do with their less-profitable customers (such as abandoning those customers or changing marketing strategies to make pursuing them more profitable).[31]

STAKING OUT A POSITION IN YOUR TARGET MARKETS

After you have decided which segments of the market to enter, your next step is to decide what *position* you want to occupy in those segments. **Positioning** is the process of designing a company's offerings, messages, and operating policies so that both the company and its products occupy distinct and desirable competitive positions in your target customers' minds. For instance, for every product category that you care about as a consumer, you have some ranking of desirability in your mind—you believe that certain colleges are more prestigious than others, that certain brands of shoes are more fashionable than others, that one video game system is better than the others, and so on. Successful marketers are careful to choose the position they'd like to occupy in buyers' minds.

positioning Managing a business in a way designed to occupy a particular place in the minds of target customers

In their attempts to secure favorable positions, marketers can emphasize such variables as product attributes, customer service, brand image (such as reliability or sophistication), price (such as low cost or premium), or category leadership (such as the leading online bookseller). For example, BMW and Porsche work to associate their products with performance, Mercedes Benz with luxury, and Volvo with safety.

A vital and often overlooked aspect of positioning is that although marketers take all kinds of steps to position their products, it is *customers* who ultimately decide on the positioning: They're the ones who interpret the many messages they encounter in the marketplace and decide what they think and feel about each product. For example, you can advertise that you have a luxury product, but if consumers aren't convinced, it's not really positioned as a luxury product. The only result that matters is what the customer believes. One auto industry marketing executive put it this way: "Everyone works so hard to control and define what their brand stands for, when they ought to just let the consumer do it."[32]

✓ Checkpoint

LEARNING OBJECTIVE 5: Identify the four steps in crafting a marketing strategy.

SUMMARY: Crafting a marketing strategy involves dividing your market into *segments*, choosing your *target markets* and the *position* you'd like to establish in those markets, and developing a *marketing mix* to help you get there. Segmentation (using demographics, psychographics, geography, and behavior) allows a company to select parts of the market most likely to respond to specific marketing programs. Companies can use one of four approaches to selecting target markets: undifferentiated (mass) marketing, differentiated marketing (with a different marketing mix for each segment), concentrated marketing (focusing on a single market segment), and micromarketing or individualized marketing. A *position* refers to the position a company or brand occupies in the mind of the target market segments. In creating a *marketing mix*, companies define the products they will offer, the prices they will charge, distribution methods, and customer communication efforts.

CRITICAL THINKING: (1) Would two companies interested in the same group of customers automatically use the same target market approach (such as differentiated or concentrated)? Why or why not? (2) Why aren't marketers ultimately in control of the positions their products achieve in the marketplace?

IT'S YOUR BUSINESS: (1) Think of three car brands or specific models. How are these products positioned in your mind? What terms do you use to describe them? (2) Given your transportation needs in the near future (assuming you will need a car), which model is the most desirable? The least desirable?

KEY TERMS TO KNOW: marketing strategy, market, market segmentation, demographics, psychographics, geographic segmentation, behavioral segmentation, target markets, positioning

6 **LEARNING OBJECTIVE**

Describe the four main components of the marketing mix.

marketing mix The four key elements of marketing strategy: product, price, distribution, and customer communication

The Marketing Mix

After you've segmented your market, selected your target market, and taken steps to position your product, your next task is to develop a marketing mix. A firm's **marketing mix** consists of product, price, distribution, and customer communication (see Exhibit 8). (You might also hear references to "the four Ps" of the marketing mix, which is short for products, pricing, place or physical distribution, and promotion. However, with the advent of digital goods and services, distribution is no longer exclusively a physical concern. And many companies now view customer communication as a broader and more interactive activity than the functions implied by *promotion*.)

EXHIBIT 8 **The Marketing Mix**

The marketing mix consists of four key elements: the products a company offers to potential buyers, the price it asks in return, its methods of distributing those products to customers, and the various efforts it makes to communicate with customers before and after the sale.

PRODUCTS

In common usage, *product* usually refers to a tangible good, while *service* refers to an intangible performance. However, for the purposes of studying marketing, it is helpful to define **product** as the bundle of value offered for the purpose of satisfying a want or a need in a marketing exchange. In this expanded definition, both tangible goods and intangible services are considered products. The reason for taking this broader view of *product* is that it encourages a more holistic look at the entire offering, which can include the brand name, design, packaging, support services, warranty, the ownership experience, and other attributes.

> **product** A bundle of value that satisfies a customer need or want

For example, if you buy a pair of $200 Dolce & Gabbana sunglasses with the brand's prominent "DG" initials on the side, you are buying much more than a device that holds a couple of protective lenses in front of your eyes. You are buying a shopping and ownership experience that is distinctly different from that for buying a pair of $5 sunglasses from a discount drugstore. You are buying the opportunity to feel a particular way about yourself and to present a particular image to the world around you. You are buying the right to brand yourself with the Dolce & Gabbana brand and everything that brand means to you. All these elements constitute the Dolce & Gabbana product. You'll explore products in more detail in Chapter 14.

PRICING

Price, the amount of money customers pay for the product (including any discounts), is the second major component of a firm's marketing mix. Looking back at Kotler and Armstrong's definition of marketing, price is the *value captured* from customers in exchange for the value offered in the product. Setting and managing a product's price is one of the most critical decisions a company must make because price is the only element in a company's marketing mix that produces revenue; all other elements represent costs. Moreover, setting a product's price not only determines income but also can differentiate a product from the competition. Determining the right price is not an easy task, and marketers constantly worry whether they've turned away profitable customers by charging too much or "left money on the table" by charging too little.

> **price** The amount of money charged for a product or service

A number of factors influence pricing decisions, including marketing objectives, government regulations, production costs, customer perceptions, competition, and customer demand. A company's costs establish the minimum amount it can charge, and the various external forces establish the maximum. Somewhere in between those two extremes lies an optimum price point. Products also exhibit different levels of *price elasticity*, which is a measure of how sensitive customers are to changes in price. If you don't have a smart phone yet and the price of such phones drops by 25 percent, you might well be tempted to buy one. In contrast, if the price of broccoli drops by 25 percent, chances are you won't eat more veggies as a result.

DISTRIBUTION

distribution channels Systems for moving goods and services from producers to customers; also known as marketing channels

Distribution is the third marketing-mix element. It covers the organized network of firms and systems that move goods and services from the producer to the customer. This network is also known as *marketing channels*, *marketing intermediaries*, or **distribution channels**. As you can imagine, channel decisions are interdependent with virtually everything else in the marketing mix. Key factors in distribution planning include customer needs and expectations, market coverage, distribution costs, competition, positioning, customer support requirements, and sales support requirements. For example, when AstraZeneca introduced a cancer drug that required careful patient evaluation and education, it released the drug through a single specialty pharmacy so that it could manage pharmacist training more closely.[33]

Marketing intermediaries perform a variety of essential marketing functions, including providing information to customers, providing feedback to manufacturers, providing sales support, gathering assortments of goods from multiple producers to make shopping easier for customers, and transporting and storing goods. These intermediaries fall into two general categories: *wholesalers* and *retailers*. The basic distinction between them is that wholesalers sell to other companies whereas retailers sell to individual consumers. Across industries, you can find tremendous variety in the types of wholesalers and retailers, from independent representatives who sell products from several manufacturers to huge distribution companies with national or international scope to purely digital retailers such as Apple's iTunes service.

CUSTOMER COMMUNICATION

promotion A wide variety of persuasive techniques used by companies to communicate with their target markets and the general public

In traditional marketing thought, the fourth element of the marketing mix is **promotion**, all the activities a firm undertakes to promote its products to target customers. The goals of promotion include *informing*, *persuading*, and *reminding*. Among these activities are advertising in a variety of media, personal selling, public relations, and sales promotion. Promotion may take the form of direct, face-to-face communication or indirect communication through such media as television, radio, magazines, newspapers, direct mail, billboards, transit ads, social media, and other channels.

However, as "Involving the Customer in the Marketing Process" points out, forward-thinking companies have moved beyond the unidirectional approach of promotion to interactive customer communication. By talking *with* their customers instead of *at* their customers, marketers get immediate feedback on everything from customer service problems to new product ideas. As you'll read in the Behind the Scenes at the end of the chapter, Sarah Calhoun of Red Ants Pants literally sits in customers' living rooms, listening to their thoughts about work pants.

Promotion is still a vital part of customer communication, but by encouraging two-way conversations, whether it's two people talking across a desk or an online network spread across the globe, marketers can also learn while they are informing, persuading, and reminding. Moreover, by replacing "sales pitches" with conversations and giving customers some control over the dialog, marketers can also help break

REAL-TIME UPDATES
Learn More by Visiting This Website

See how airlines try to make connections through social media

The immediacy of social media tools makes them a natural fit for a time-sensitive business such as air travel. Go to http://real-timeupdates.com/bia6 and click on "Learn More."If you are using MyBizLab, you can access Real-Time Updates within the chapter or under Student Study Tools.

down some of the walls and filters that audiences have erected after years of conventional marketing promotion.[34] Chapter 16 offers a closer look at customer communication.

For the latest information on marketing principles, visit http://real-timeupdates.com/bia6.

Checkpoint

LEARNING OBJECTIVE 6: Describe the four main components of the marketing mix.

SUMMARY: The four elements of the marketing mix are product, price, distribution, and customer communication. Products are goods, services, persons, places, ideas, organizations, or anything else offered for the purpose of satisfying a want or need in a marketing exchange. Price is the amount of money customers pay for the product. Distribution is the organized network of firms that move the goods and services from the producer to the customer. Customer communication involves the activities used to communicate with and promote products to target markets.

CRITICAL THINKING: (1) Why is price sometimes referred to as *captured value*? (2) Why do companies that embrace relationship marketing focus on "customer communication" rather than "promotion"?

IT'S YOUR BUSINESS: (1) If you could buy a product from a website or a store right down the street and the prices were the same, where would you make your purchase? Why? (2) When buying products, do you tend to seek out products with visible logos (such as the Nike swoosh or the Dolce & Gabbana initials), or do you shun such products? Or do you not care one way or the other? Why?

KEY TERMS TO KNOW: marketing mix, product, price, distribution channels, promotion

---

BEHIND THE SCENES   MyBizLab

AGGRAVATION LEADS TO INSPIRATION FOR SARAH CALHOUN OF RED ANTS PANTS

Like many other entrepreneurs, frustration was the source of inspiration for Sarah Calhoun. When she couldn't find rugged work pants designed for women, she decided to meet this unmet market need herself. A chance encounter in a coffee shop with an experienced apparel industry insider (who noticed she was reading *Starting a Business for Dummies*) convinced her that a real opportunity was there and waiting for someone to pursue it.

Calhoun based all three key elements of her marketing strategy—segmentation, target markets, and positioning—on her mission of pursuing this opportunity. She founded Red Ants Pants with the singular focus on providing hardwearing pants for hardworking women, meeting the needs of customers whose work makes clothing a matter of practical utility and even on-the-job safety.

Red Ants Pants are made from tough, heavy cloth and in both "straight" and "curvy" styles to provide a better fit for more women. In addition, they come in two or three times as many waist/inseam combinations as typical pants, greatly increasing the chance that every woman will find exactly the size she needs.

In keeping with the capacity of a small business and the nature of her product offerings, simplicity is the key word in the product mix. Pants are available in exactly one color: chocolate brown. (It was only after buying $45,000 worth of the practical fabric that Calhoun learned "chocolate brown is the new black" in the fashion world.) A few years after introducing the pants, she expanded the product portfolio with a handful of complementary products, including shirts, hats, and belts.

Calhoun is adamant about keeping production in the United States, too, a rarity in the clothing business, which outsources most of its production to low-cost labor centers in other countries. Instead, she chose a mother/daughter-owned factory two states over, in Seattle, and she views supporting quality jobs in this country as "part of my responsibility as a business owner."

Referring to her production partners, she says, "They have 23 employees who are treated well, paid well and enjoy good working conditions."

At $129 a pair, the pants are not bargain-bin items, to be sure. However, like many purveyors of high-quality products, Calhoun emphasizes value, noting that customers would wear out several pairs of cheaper pants in the time they might wear out a single pair of Red Ants. Plus, the price reflects the structure she has chosen for her business: not offshoring in pursuit of the lowest possible production costs. At the rate her sales are growing, customers apparently agree that it's a fair price to pay for pants that keep them safe and comfortable on the job.

Distribution strategy was one of Calhoun's most important marketing and business decisions. Clothes in general and pants in particular are products for which individual fit and function can't be absolutely confirmed until the customer tries them on. Having her products available in hundreds of retail outlets would let more customers try them on—and give her tremendous visibility in the market. However, it would also put her at the mercy of retailers' demands regarding price and inventory. She opted to function as her own distribution channel, selling from her website, over the phone, and from her storefront operation in White Sulphur Springs, Montana. Having so many sizing options helps ensure that pants fit when customers receive them, but as with most online clothing retailers, she invites customers to exchange pants that don't fit.

Like millions of other small companies in recent years, Red Ants Pants has taken advantage of technology to overcome distribution hurdles. Calhoun explains, "The old quote of retail being location, location, location doesn't hold up as much. I have Internet and I have UPS and mail service, and that's all I need."

Customer communication is another aspect of the marketing mix in which Calhoun demonstrates both the greater flexibility that small companies often have compared to their larger, "more corporate" competitors—and the need to exercise creative brain power over brute-force budget power. Her communication style is more fun and more daring that the typical corporation would attempt, for example, and it seems to resonate with buyers. How many clothing companies would use photographs (discreetly staged, to be sure) to suggest that hardworking women would rather wear no pants than wear pants that don't fit?

Without a significant marketing budget, Calhoun looks for low-cost, high-visibility ways to reach customers. Her most unusual has been the Anthill, an ant-decorated Airstream travel trailer that she and her sales manager take on the road on trips they call the "Tour de Pants." They invite women to stage in-home gatherings, much like old-school Tupperware parties. Visiting customers in their homes and hearing stories about women working in what are often male-dominated professions, Calhoun also gets invaluable marketing research insights. And the Anthill is rolling advertising at its best. Some people even follow her down the highway to learn more about the company and its wares.

Calhoun's most ambitious communication effort so far has been sponsoring the Red Ants Pants Music Festival in 2011, which attracted such major Americana artists as Lyle Lovett and Guy Clark. All profits went to the Red Ants Pants Foundation, which she started to "support family farms and ranches, women in business, and rural initiatives."

The combination of meeting customer needs with quality products and a creative marketing effort is paying off. Red Ants Pants now has customers all across the country and around the world, from Europe to Australia, and even women working the research stations in Antarctica. Are customers satisfied with the product? "Putting on these pants was a religious experience," is how one phrased it.[35]

Critical Thinking Questions

1. How might Calhoun's decision to keep production in the United States help solidify her market position in the minds of her target customers?
2. If Red Ants Pants had investors looking for a quick return, how might that influence Calhoun's decision to continuing functioning as her own retail channel, rather than going through established retailers?
3. How could meeting small groups of women in their homes to talk about pants possibly be an efficient communication strategy?

LEARN MORE ONLINE

Visit the Red Ants Pants website, at **www.redantspants.com**, and its page on Facebook (search for "Red Ants Pants"). How are the various elements of the marketing mix represented? How does the style of communication help Red Ants Pants connect with customers? What sort of practical information is provided to help customers select and order products?

MyBizLab

Log on to www.mybizlab.com to access study and assessment aids associated with this chapter.

KEY TERMS

behavioral segmentation
cause-related marketing
cognitive dissonance
consumer market
customer loyalty

customer relationship management (CRM)
demographics
distribution channels
diversification
exchange process

geographic segmentation
market
market development
market penetration
market segmentation
market share
marketing
marketing concept
marketing mix
marketing research
marketing strategy
needs
organizational market
permission-based marketing
place marketing

positioning
price
product
product development
promotion
psychographics
relationship marketing
social commerce
stealth marketing
strategic marketing planning
target markets
transaction
utility
wants

TEST YOUR KNOWLEDGE

Questions for Review

1. Why are companies pushing for more accountability from the marketing function?
2. How does the organizational market differ from the consumer market?
3. What is strategic marketing planning, and what is its purpose?
4. What external environmental factors affect strategic marketing decisions?
5. What are the four basic components of the marketing mix?

Questions for Analysis

6. Why would consumers knowingly buy counterfeit luxury brands?
7. How can marketing research help companies improve their marketing efforts?
8. Why does a company need to consider its current marketing situation, including competitive trends, when setting objectives for market share?

9. Why do companies segment markets?
10. **Ethical Considerations.** Is it ethical to observe shoppers for the purposes of marketing research without their knowledge and permission? Why or why not?

Questions for Application

11. How might a retailer use relationship marketing to improve customer loyalty?
12. Think of a product you recently purchased and review your decision process. Why did you need or want that product? How did the product's marketing influence your purchase decision? How did you investigate the product before making your purchase decision? Did you experience cognitive dissonance after your decision?
13. If you were launching a new manufacturing company, would you draft your marketing plan or design your production processes first? Why?
14. **Concept Integration.** How might the key economic indicators, including consumer price index, inflation, and unemployment, affect a company's marketing decisions?

EXPAND YOUR KNOWLEDGE

Discovering Career Opportunities

Jobs in marketing cover a wide range of activities, including a variety of jobs such as personal selling, advertising, marketing research, product management, and public relations. You can get more information about various marketing positions by consulting the *Occupational Outlook Handbook* (www.bls.gov/oco), job-search websites such as Career Builder (www.careerbuilder.com) and Monster (www.monster.com), and other online resources.

1. Select a specific marketing job that interests you, and use the sites mentioned above to find out more about this career path. What specific duties and responsibilities do people in this position typically handle?
2. Search through help-wanted ads in newspapers, specialized magazines, or websites to find two openings in the field you are researching. What educational background and work experience are employers seeking in candidates for this position? What kind of work assignments are mentioned in these ads?
3. Now think about your talents, interests, and goals. How do your strengths fit with the requirements, duties, and responsibilities of this job? Do you think you would find this field enjoyable and rewarding? Why?

Improving Your Tech Insights: Search Engines

As most every web user knows, search engines identify individual webpages that contain specific words or phrases you've asked for. Search engines have the advantage of scanning millions of individual webpages, and they use powerful ranking algorithms to present the pages that are probably the most relevant to your search request. Because each engine uses a proprietary and secret algorithm to rank the displayed results, multiple engines can display different result sets for the same query.

To see how search engines can return markedly different results, search on the phrase "Apple computer market share" (use the quotation marks) using Google, Bing, and Yahoo!. In a brief email message to your instructor, describe the differences and similarities among the three search results. Which search engine gave you the best results? How many of the search results were more than a year out of date? How might the differences among the search engines affect the work of a businessperson preparing a report on Apple's share of the personal computer market?

PRACTICE YOUR SKILLS

Sharpening Your Communication Skills

In small groups, as assigned by your instructor, take turns interviewing each person in the group about a product that each person absolutely loves or detests. Try to probe for the real reasons behind the emotions, touching on all the issues you read about in this chapter, from self-image to reference groups. Do you see any trends in the group's collective answers? Do people learn anything about themselves when answering the group's questions? Does anyone get defensive about his or her reasons for loving or hating a product? Be prepared to share with the class at least two marketing insights you learned through this exercise.

Building Your Team Skills

In the course of planning a marketing strategy, marketers need to analyze the external environment to consider how forces outside the firm may create new opportunities and challenges. One important environmental factor for merchandise buyers at Sears is weather conditions. For example, when merchandise buyers for lawn and garden products think about the assortment and number of products to purchase for the chain's stores, they don't place any orders without first poring over long-range weather forecasts for each market. In particular, temperature and precipitation predictions for the coming 12 months are critical to the company's

marketing plan, because they offer clues to consumer demand for barbecues, lawn furniture, gardening tools, and other merchandise.

What other products would benefit from examining weather forecasts? With your team, brainstorm to identify at least three types of products (in addition to lawn and garden items) for which Sears should examine the weather as part of its analysis of the external environment. Share your recommendations with the entire class. How many teams identified the same products your team did?

Developing Your Research Skills

From recent issues of business journals and newspapers (print or online editions), select an article that describes in some detail a particular company's attempt to build relationships with its customers (either in general or for a particular product or product line).

1. Describe the company's market. What geographic, demographic, behavioral, or psychographic segments of the market is the company targeting?
2. How does the company communicate with and learn about its customers?
3. According to the article, how successful has the company been in understanding its customers?

REFERENCES

1. Adapted from Red Ants Pants website, accessed 8 September 2011, www.redantspants.com; Becky Warren, "Ants on the Pants," *Country Woman*, February–March 2011, www.countrywomanmagazine.com; Dan Testa, "Red Ants Pants: By Working Women, for Working Women," *Flathead Beacon*, 4 March 2010, www.flatheadbeacon.com; Sammi Johnson, "Outdoor Woman: Red Ants Pants," *406 Woman*, April/May 2010, 52–53; Beth Judy, "Fit for Her," *Montana Magazine*, March–April 2010, 14–16; *Montana Quarterly*, Summer 2010, www.redantspants.com; Devan Grote, "Red Ants Pants," *Gettysburg*, Spring 2009, www.redantspants.com.
2. Philip Kotler and Gary Armstrong, *Principles of Marketing*, 13th ed. (Upper Saddle River, N.J.: Pearson Prentice Hall, 2010), 5.
3. Kotler and Armstrong, *Principles of Marketing*, 6.
4. BizXchange website, accessed 13 July 2009, www.bizx.com.
5. June Lee Risser, "Customers Come First," *Marketing Management*, November/December 2003, 22–26.
6. Ranjay Gulati and James B. Oldroyd, "The Quest for Customer Focus," *Harvard Business Review*, April 2005, 92–101.
7. Jonathan L. Yarmis, "How Facebook Will Upend Advertising," *BusinessWeek*, 28 May 2008, www.businessweek.com
8. Paul Gunning, "Social Media Reality Check," *Adweek*, 8 June 2008, 18.
9. Jeremiah Owyang, "When Social Media Marries CRM Systems," Web Strategy blog, 3 June 2008, www.web-strategist.com.
10. "Sorry, John," *Adweek*, 22 June 2009, 9.
11. Dominique M. Hanssens, Daniel Thorpe, and Carl Finkbeiner, "Marketing When Customer Equity Matters," *Harvard Business Review*, May 2008, 117–123.

12. Google Analytics, accessed 24 October 2011, www.google.com/analytics.
13. Eric Almquist, Martin Kon, and Wolfgang Bock, "The Science of Demand," *Marketing Management*, March/April 2004, 20–26; David C. Swaddling and Charles Miller, "From Understanding to Action," *Marketing Management*, July/August 2004, 31–35.
14. "Marketing Under Fire," *Marketing Management*, July/August 2004, 5.
15. Michael Oliveira, "Netflix Apologizes for Using Actors to Meet Press at Canadian Launch," *Globe and Mail*, 22 September 2010, www.theglobeandmail.com.
16. Word of Mouth Marketing Association, "WOM 101," http://womma.org; Nate Anderson, "FTC Says Stealth Marketing Unethical," *Ars Technica*, 13 December 2006, http://arstechnica.com; "Undercover Marketing Uncovered," CBSnews.com, 25 July 2004, www.cbsnews.com; Stephanie Dunnewind, "Teen Recruits Create Word-of-Mouth 'Buzz' to Hook Peers on Products," *Seattle Times*, 20 November 2004, www.seattletimes.com.
17. Pophal, "Tweet Ethics: Trust and Transparency in a Web 2.0 World."
18. Dan Hill, "Why They Buy," *Across the Board*, November–December 2003, 27–32; Eric Roston, "The Why of Buy," *Time*, April 2004.
19. Dan Ariely, "The End of Rational Economics," *Harvard Business Review*, July/August 2009, 78–84.
20. Michael R. Solomon, *Consumer Behavior*, 6th ed. (Upper Saddle River, N.J.: Pearson Prentice Hall, 2004), 366–372.
21. Based in part on James C. Anderson and James A. Narus, *Business Market Management: Understanding, Creating, and Delivering Value*, 2nd ed. (Upper Saddle River, N.J.: Pearson Prentice Hall, 2004), 114–116.
22. Daniel Lyons, "Tough Customers," *Forbes Asia*, 7 April 2008, 69.
23. Gerard J. Tellis, Eden Yin, and Rakesh Niraj, "Does Quality Win? Network Effects Versus Quality in High-Tech Markets," *Journal of Marketing Research*, May 2009, 135–149.
24. Eric Beinhocker, Ian Davis, and Lenny Mendonca, "The 10 Trends You Have to Watch," *Harvard Business Review*, July/August 2009, 55–60.
25. Beinhocker, et al., "The 10 Trends You Have to Watch."
26. Kotler and Armstrong, *Principles of Marketing*, 43–46.
27. Gordon A. Wyner, "Pulling the Right Levers," *Marketing Management*, July/August 2004, 8–9.
28. Kotler and Armstrong, *Principles of Marketing*, 196–197.
29. Kotler and Armstrong, *Principles of Marketing*, 205–207.
30. Jeneanne Rae, "New Thinking About Consumer Marketing," *BusinessWeek*, 30 June 2009, 16.
31. Detlef Schoder, "The Flaw in Customer Lifetime Value," *Harvard Business Review*, December 2007, 26.
32. Mark Rechtin, "Scion's Dilemma," *AutoWeek*, 23 May 2006, www.autoweek.com.
33. Ben Comer, "AstraZeneca Signs Exclusive Distribution Deal for Vandetanib," PharmExec.com, 27 April 2011, http://blog.pharmexec.com.
34. Paul Gillin, *The New Influencers: A Marketer's Guide to the New Social Media* (Sanger, Calif.: Quill Driver Books, 2007), xi.
35. See note 1.

GLOSSARY

behavioral segmentation Categorization of customers according to their relationship with products or response to product characteristics

cause-related marketing Identification and marketing of a social issue, cause, or idea to selected target markets

cognitive dissonance Tension that exists when a person's beliefs don't match his or her behaviors; a common example is *buyer's remorse,* when someone regrets a purchase immediately after making it

consumer market Individuals or households that buy goods and services for personal use

customer loyalty The degree to which customers continue to buy from a particular retailer or buy the products of a particular manufacturer or service provider

customer relationship management (CRM) A type of information system that captures, organizes, and capitalizes on all the interactions that a company has with its customers

demographics The study of statistical characteristics of a population

distribution channels Systems for moving goods and services from producers to customers; also known as marketing channels

diversification Creating new products for new markets

exchange process The act of obtaining a desired object or service from another party by offering something of value in return

geographic segmentation Categorization of customers according to their geographical location

market A group of customers who need or want a particular product and have the money to buy it

market development Selling existing products to new markets

market penetration Selling more of a firm's existing products into the markets it already serves

market segmentation The division of a diverse market into smaller, relatively homogeneous groups with similar needs, wants, and purchase behaviors

market share A firm's portion of the total sales in a market

marketing concept An approach to business management that stresses customer needs and wants, seeks long-term profitability, and integrates marketing with other functional units within the organization

marketing mix The four key elements of marketing strategy: product, price, distribution, and customer communication

marketing research The collection and analysis of information for making marketing decisions

marketing strategy An overall plan for marketing a product; includes the identification of target market segments, a positioning strategy, and a marketing mix

marketing The process of creating value for customers and building relationships with those customers in order to capture value back from them

needs Differences between a person's actual state and his or her ideal state; they provide the basic motivation to make a purchase

organizational market Companies, government agencies, and other organizations that buy goods and services either to resell or to use in the creation of their own goods and services

permission-based marketing A marketing approach in which firms first ask permission to deliver messages to an audience and then promise to restrict their communication efforts to those subject areas in which audience members have expressed interest

place marketing Marketing efforts to attract people and organizations to a particular geographical area

positioning Managing a business in a way designed to occupy a particular place in the minds of target customers

price The amount of money charged for a product or service

product A bundle of value that satisfies a customer need or want

product development Creating new products for a firm's current markets

promotion A wide variety of persuasive techniques used by companies to communicate with their target markets and the general public

psychographics Classification of customers on the basis of their psychological makeup, interests, and lifestyles

relationship marketing A focus on developing and maintaining long-term relationships with customers, suppliers, and distribution partners for mutual benefit

social commerce The creation and sharing of product-related information among customers and potential customers

stealth marketing The delivery of marketing messages to people who are not aware that they are being marketed to; these messages can be delivered by either acquaintances or strangers, depending on the technique

strategic marketing planning The process of examining an organization's current marketing situation, assessing opportunities and setting objectives, and then developing a marketing strategy to reach those objectives

target markets Specific customer groups or segments to whom a company wants to sell a particular product

transaction An exchange of value between parties

utility The power of a good or service to satisfy a human need

wants Specific goods, services, experiences, or other entities that are desirable in light of a person's experiences, culture, and personality

Product and Pricing Strategies

From Chapter 14 of *Business in Action*, Sixth Edition. Courtland L. Bovée, John V. Thill. Copyright © 2013 by Pearson Education, Inc. Published by Pearson Business. All rights reserved.

Product and Pricing Strategies

BEHIND THE SCENES   TRANSFORMING A WORLD-CLASS ATHLETE INTO A WORLD-CLASS BRAND

Photo by Marc Serota/Getty Images

Professional golfer Annika Sorenstam is building a brand image to power her postgolf business career.

www.annikasorenstam.com

Start reading a list of Annika Sorenstam's accomplishments on the golf course, and you might have to stop halfway through and take a nap. Here's the short version: 89 tournament wins worldwide, including 10 major championships, and more than $20 million in prize winnings, with many millions more in product endorsements. Before she stepped away from competitive golf in late 2008, she dominated the woman's professional circuit as no one in recent memory had done before. And she rose high enough to achieve that ultimate badge of celebrity: one-name status. Millions of golf fans don't need to hear a last name; for them, she is simply Annika.

Her career on the course has clearly been a resounding success. But having achieved more before age 40 than most people could hope to achieve in several lifetimes, Sorenstam isn't ready to stop. In fact, she's starting all over again, this time in a multifaceted business career.

Sorenstam likes to measure herself against the best of the best. In fact, after dominating women's golf, she was the first woman to play in a professional men's tournament in more than 50 years. She did so not to make any kind of grand statement but simply to see how her skills compared to those of her male counterparts.

In her new career, Sorenstam is once again measuring herself against top performers, including such figures as basketball star Michael Jordan and golfers Arnold Palmer and Jack Nicklaus. Palmer and Nicklaus are particularly apt role models, both having built golf-centric business empires and having remained vibrant public figures years after hitting their last competitive shots.

Sorenstam believes it's high time a woman joined their ranks. "Ask a person on the street to name five male athletes who have made a name for themselves outside their sport— no problem," she says. "Ask the same question about women athletes? They can't name one." She plans to be the first. What advice would you give her to make the transition from golf star to business star, from Annika the athlete to Annika the brand?[1]

INTRODUCTION

This chapter explores two of the four elements in the marketing mix, product and price. Annika Sorenstam's challenge in defining the Annika brand (profiled in the chapter-opening Behind the Scenes) is an essential part of product strategy. She also faces another challenge that you'll read more about in this chapter: assembling the right mix of goods and services as part of a firm's overall product mix. Finally, as in every business, Sorenstam has to engage in careful financial analysis and make shrewd pricing decisions to stay both competitive and profitable.

MyBizLab

Gain hands-on experience through an interactive, real-world scenario. This chapter's simulation entitled Pricing Strategies and Objectives is located at **www.mybizlab.com**.

Characteristics of Products

1 LEARNING OBJECTIVE

Identify the main types of consumer and organizational products, and describe the four stages in the life cycle of a product.

As the central element in every company's exchanges with its customers, products naturally command a lot of attention from managers planning new offerings and coordinating the marketing mixes for existing offerings. To understand the nature of these decisions, it's important to recognize the various types of products and the stages that products go through during their "lifetime" in the marketplace.

TYPES OF PRODUCTS

Think about Doritos tortilla chips, Intel semiconductors, and your favorite musical artist. You wouldn't market all these products in the same way, because buyer behavior, product characteristics, market expectations, competition, and other elements of the equation are entirely different.

Classifying products on the basis of tangibility and application can provide useful insights into the best ways to market them. Some products are predominantly tangible; others are mostly intangible. Most products, however, fall somewhere between those two extremes. The *product continuum* indicates the relative amounts of tangible and intangible components in a product (see Exhibit 1).

EXHIBIT 1	The Product Continuum

Products contain both tangible and intangible components; predominantly tangible products are categorized as goods, whereas predominantly intangible products are categorized as services.

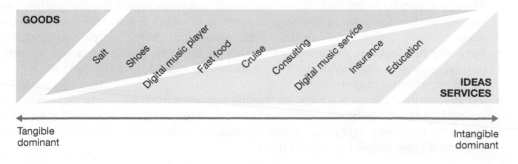

GOODS

Salt · Shoes · Digital music player · Fast food · Cruise · Consulting · Digital music service · Insurance · Education

IDEAS
SERVICES

Tangible dominant — Intangible dominant

EXHIBIT 2	Augmenting the Basic Product

Product decisions also involve how much or how little to augment the core product with additional goods and services.

Source: Adapted from Philip Kotler and Gary Armstrong, *Principles of Marketing*, 10th ed. (Upper Saddle River, N.J.: Pearson Prentice Hall, 2004), 279.

To provide a more complete solution to customer needs, many companies find success by *augmenting* a core product with accessories, services, and other elements (see Exhibit 2). For example, when GlaxoSmithKline introduced its Alli weight-loss pill, the company augmented Alli with a weight-loss program that included counseling, online networking, and other tools to help people use the product successfully.[2] In some cases, these enhancements are included in the price of the product, but product augmentation can also be a way to increase revenue, by offering new services and accessories or by charging for enhancements that were previously included at no charge.[3]

Consumer Products

Organizations and consumers use many of the same products, but they can use them for different reasons and in different ways. Products that are primarily sold to individuals for personal consumption are known as *consumer products*. Consumer products can be classified into four subgroups, depending on how people shop for them:

- Everyday goods and services that people buy frequently, usually without much conscious planning, are known as **convenience products**.
- **Shopping products** are fairly important goods and services that people buy less frequently, such as computers and college educations. Because the stakes are higher and the decisions more complex, such products require more thought and comparison shopping.
- **Specialty products** are particular brands that the buyer especially wants and will seek out, regardless of location or price, such as Suzuki violin lessons or Bang & Olufsen home entertainment gear.
- When it comes to some products, such as life insurance, cemetery plots, and items that are new to the marketplace, consumers aren't looking for them. The marketing challenges for these *unsought products* include making consumers aware of their existence and convincing people to consider them.

convenience products Everyday goods and services that people buy frequently, usually without much conscious planning

shopping products Fairly important goods and services that people buy less frequently with more planning and comparison

specialty products Particular brands that the buyer especially wants and will seek out, regardless of location or price

Industrial and Commercial Products

Organizational products, or *industrial and commercial products*, are generally purchased by organizations in large quantities and are used to create other products or to operate the organization. **Expense items** are relatively inexpensive goods that are generally used within a year of purchase, such as printer cartridges and paper. **Capital items** are more expensive products with a longer useful life. Examples include computers, vehicles, production machinery, and even entire factories. Businesses and other organizations also buy a wide variety of services, from facilities maintenance to temporary executives.

Aside from dividing products into expense and capital items, industrial buyers and sellers often classify products according to their intended use:

- *Raw materials* such as iron ore, crude petroleum, lumber, and chemicals are used in the production of final products.
- *Components* such as semiconductors and fasteners also become part of the manufacturers' final products.
- *Supplies* such as pencils, nails, and lightbulbs that are used in a firm's daily operations are considered expense items.
- *Installations* such as factories, power plants, and airports are major capital projects.
- *Equipment* includes items such as desks, computers, and factory robots.
- *Business services* range from landscaping and cleaning to complex services such as management consulting and auditing.

THE PRODUCT LIFE CYCLE

Most products undergo a **product life cycle**, passing through four distinct stages in sales and profits: introduction, growth, maturity, and decline (see Exhibit 3). The marketing challenge changes from stage to stage, sometimes dramatically.

The product life cycle can describe a product class (gasoline-powered automobiles), a product form (sport utility vehicles), or a brand or model (Ford Explorer). Product classes and forms tend to have the longest life cycles, specific brands somewhat shorter life cycles,

expense items Inexpensive products that organizations generally use within a year of purchase

capital items More expensive organizational products with a longer useful life, ranging from office and plant equipment to entire factories

product life cycle Four stages through which a product progresses: introduction, growth, maturity, and decline

EXHIBIT 3	The Product Life Cycle

Most products and product categories move through a life cycle similar to the one represented by the curve in this diagram, with new innovations pushing existing products along the time axis. However, the duration of each stage varies widely from product to product. Automobiles have been in the maturity stage for decades, but faxing services barely made it into the introduction stage before being knocked out of the market by low-cost fax machines that every business and home office could afford—which were themselves pushed along the curve by digital document formats.

Source: Adapted from Philip Kotler and Gary Armstrong, *Principles of Marketing*, 10th ed. (Upper Saddle River, N.J.: Pearson Prentice Hall, 2004), 330.

and individual products even shorter cycles. The amount of time that a product remains in any one stage depends on customer needs and preferences, economic conditions, the nature of the product, and the marketer's strategy. The proliferation of new products, changing technology, globalization, and the ability to quickly imitate competitors is hurtling many product forms and brands through their life cycles much faster today than in the past. In categories such as smartphones, individual models can go through the entire life cycle in as little as nine months.[4]

Introduction

The first stage in the product life cycle is the *introductory stage*, which extends from the research-and-development (R&D) phase through the product's first commercial availability. The introductory stage is a crucial phase that requires careful planning and often considerable investment. Marketing staffs often work long hours for weeks or months before a product launch, preparing promotional materials, training sales staff, completing packaging, finalizing the price, and wrapping up countless other tasks. Some markets offer the luxury of building demand over time if the introduction isn't a blockbuster, but in others, a weak introduction can doom a product. The opening weekend for a movie, for instance, often determines its success or failure—a tremendously stressful scenario for people who have invested months or years and many millions of dollars making the film.

Growth

After the introductory stage comes the *growth stage*, marked by a rapid jump in sales—if the product is successful—and, usually, an increase in the number of competitors and distribution outlets. As competition increases, so does the struggle for market share. This situation creates pressure to maintain large promotional budgets and competitive prices. With enough growth, however, a firm may be able to reach economies of scale that allow it to create and deliver its products less expensively than in the introduction phase. The growth stage can reap handsome profits for those who survive.

Maturity

During the *maturity stage*, usually the longest in the product life cycle, sales begin to level off. Markets tend to get saturated with all the supply that buyers demand, so the only way a firm can expand its sales in this phase is to win sales away from other suppliers. Because the costs of introduction and growth have diminished in this stage, most companies try to keep mature products alive so they can use the resulting profits to fund the development of new products (often referred to as "milking a cash cow").

Decline

Although maturity can be extended for many years, most products eventually enter the *decline stage*, when sales and profits slip and then fade away. Declines occur for several reasons: changing demographics, shifts in popular taste, overwhelming competition, and advances in technology. For instance, feature-rich smartphones are pushing a bunch of other product categories toward or into decline, including personal digital assistants (PDAs), handheld GPS navigation devices, music players, digital cameras, and portable gaming devices.[5]

When a product begins to decline, the company must decide whether to reduce the product's costs to compensate for declining sales or to discontinue it altogether and focus on developing newer products. Of course, companies can try to make their products more compelling and competitive at any stage. From subtle refinements to complete makeovers, product improvements can sometimes be a way to maintain competitiveness and maximize the returns on the money and effort invested in a product.

REAL-TIME UPDATES
Learn More by Reading This Article

Can these two major players keep up in the smartphone market?

Some experts think the relentless innovation cycles in smartphones could be leaving two of the biggest companies in the business scrambling to catch up. Go to http://real-timeupdates.com/bia6 and click on Learn More. If you are using MyBizLab, you can access Real-Time Updates within the chapter or under Student Study Tools.

✓ Checkpoint

LEARNING OBJECTIVE 1: Identify the main types of consumer and organizational products, and describe the four stages in the life cycle of a product.

SUMMARY: Consumer products can be identified as *convenience*, *shopping*, *specialty*, or *unsought*, distinguished primarily by the amount of thought and effort that goes into buying them. Organizational products are divided into *expense items*, less-expensive goods used in production or operations; *capital items*, more expensive goods and facilities with useful lives longer than a year; and *business services*. The product life cycle consists of (1) the introductory stage, during which marketers focus on stimulating demand for the new product; (2) the growth stage, when marketers focus on increasing the product's market share; (3) the maturity stage, during which marketers try to extend the life of the product by highlighting improvements or by repackaging the product in different sizes; and (4) the decline stage, when firms must decide whether to reduce the product's costs to compensate for declining sales or to discontinue it.

CRITICAL THINKING: (1) Do manufacturers have a responsibility to create safe products even if customers don't care and don't want to pay for safety features? Why or why not? (2) Do automobiles ever enter the decline stage of the product life cycle? Explain your answer.

IT'S YOUR BUSINESS: (1) Have you ever had the urge to be "the first one on the block" to buy a new product, try a new fashion, or discover a new musical artist? If so, were you pleased or displeased when "the masses" began to imitate your choice? What does your reaction say about you as a consumer? (2) Have you ever replaced a product (such as a computer or smartphone) that was still functional, just because a newer version had hit the market? What influenced your decision?

KEY TERMS TO KNOW: convenience products, shopping products, specialty products, expense items, capital items, product life cycle

The New-Product Development Process

 LEARNING OBJECTIVE

Describe six stages in the product development process.

product development process
A formal process of generating, selecting, developing, and commercializing product ideas

Mad scientists and basement inventors still create new products, but many of today's products appear on the market as a result of a rigorous, formal **product development process**—a method of generating, selecting, developing, and commercializing product ideas (see Exhibit 4 on the next page).

IDEA GENERATION

The first step in the new-product development process is to come up with some ideas that will satisfy unmet needs. Customers, competitors, and employees are often the best source of new-product ideas. Companies can also hire *trend watchers*, can monitor social media to spot shifts in consumer tastes, or can use *crowdsourcing* to invite the public to submit ideas or product designs. Some ideas are more or less sheer luck: The popular photo-sharing website Flickr (www.flickr.com) started as a feature in a massively multiplayer online game; developers soon realized the photo-sharing tool was a better business opportunity than the game they were creating.[6] Of course, many "new" product ideas are simply improvements to or variations on existing products, but even those slight alterations can generate big revenues.

IDEA SCREENING

From all the ideas under consideration, the company selects those that appear to be worthy of further development, applying broad criteria such as whether the product can use existing production facilities and how much technical and marketing risk is involved. Research suggests that sharply narrowing the possibilities at this stage is better than keeping a large

EXHIBIT 4   The Product Development Process

The product development process aims to identify the product ideas most likely to succeed in the marketplace. The process varies widely by company, of course; entrepreneurs and start-ups sometimes begin with a single product idea and take it all the way through to commercialization.

Idea generation	Idea screening	Business analysis	Prototyping	Test marketing	Commercialization

| Brainstorm product concepts that could satisfy unmet market needs or enhance the company's product portfolio | Subject those ideas to *feasibility* or *concept testing* to identify those with the best chance of turning into successful products | Subject those ideas to a *business-case analysis* based on estimates of production costs, sales volumes, and selling price | Develop functioning "pre-release" versions that can be used by target customers to check for design flaws, market appeal, and so on | Release a finished or nearly finished *(beta)* version to selected customers or market segments and measure customer reaction | Fine-tune the product design and the rest of the marketing mix and then officially launch the product and push sales in all target markets |

number of ideas alive, since each idea competes for attention or resources until it is abandoned or implemented as a real product.[7] This is often referred to as a *feasibility study*, in which the product's features are defined and its workability is tested. In the case of consumer products, marketing consultants and advertising agencies are often called in to help evaluate new ideas. In some cases, potential customers are asked what they think of a new product idea—a process known as *concept testing*. Some companies involve customers early in the design process to make sure new products truly meet customer needs instead of the design team's perception of customer needs. Xerox's Chief Technology Officer Sophie Vandebroek refers to her company's approach as "customer-led innovation" and says that "dreaming with the customer" is essential to creating the right products.[8]

BUSINESS ANALYSIS

A product idea that survives the screening stage is subjected to a business analysis. During this stage, the company reviews the sales, costs, and profit projections to determine whether they meet the company's objectives. In addition, it estimates the costs associated with various levels of production. Given these projections, analysts calculate the potential profit that will be achieved if the product is introduced. If the product meets the company's objectives, it can then move to the prototype development stage.

PROTOTYPE DEVELOPMENT

prototypes Preproduction samples of products used for testing and evaluation

At this stage, the firm may actually develop a product concept into a functioning "prerelease" product. For physical goods, the firm creates and tests a few samples, or **prototypes**, of the product, including its packaging. These units are rigorously analyzed for usability, durability, manufacturability, customer appeal, and other vital criteria, depending on the type of product. In addition, the company begins to plan for large-scale manufacturing (for tangible goods) or *scalability* (for digital services, for example), then identifies the resources required to bring the product to market.

TEST MARKETING

test marketing A product development stage in which a product is sold on a limited basis to gauge its market appeal

During **test marketing**, the firm introduces the product in selected markets and monitors consumer reactions. Test marketing gives the marketer experience with marketing the product before going to the expense of a full introduction. For instance, producers of television programs can test shows in local or regional markets to gauge viewer appeal before going nationwide. Companies can also release products early to get feedback from potential customers before finalizing features and functions. Software developers often do so through *beta* versions. Test marketing can be expensive and time-consuming, however, so not all companies choose to take this step with every new product.

COMMERCIALIZATION

It's go time. The final stage of development is **commercialization**, the large-scale production and distribution of products that have survived the testing process. This phase (also referred to as a *product launch*) requires the coordination of many activities—manufacturing, packaging, distribution, pricing, media relations, and customer communication.

commercialization Large-scale production and distribution of a product

 Checkpoint

LEARNING OBJECTIVE 2: Describe six stages in the product development process.

SUMMARY: The first two stages of product development involve generating and screening ideas to isolate those with the most potential. In the third stage, promising ideas are analyzed to determine their likely profitability. Those that appear worthwhile enter the fourth stage, the prototype development stage, in which a limited number of the products are created. In the fifth stage, the product is test marketed to determine buyer response. Products that survive the testing process are then commercialized, the final stage.

CRITICAL THINKING: (1) Apple claims to never do any marketing research for new product ideas but instead creates products that Apple employees themselves would be excited to have. What are the risks of this approach? Would it work for all consumer and organizational markets? (2) Consumers and government regulators sometimes complain about identical products being sold at different prices to different customers as part of test marketing efforts. Are such tests ethical? Why or why not?

IT'S YOUR BUSINESS: (1) What currently unavailable service can you think of that could be offered on mobile phones? (2) In addition to the mobile phone itself, what other product elements (such as a website or phone accessories) would be required to launch such a service?

KEY TERMS TO KNOW: product development process, prototypes, test marketing, commercialization

Product Identities

3 LEARNING OBJECTIVE

Define *brand*, and explain the concepts of brand equity and brand loyalty.

Creating an identity for products is one of the most important decisions marketers make. That identity is encompassed in the **brand**, which can have meaning at three levels: (1) a unique name, symbol, or design that sets the product apart from those offered by competitors; (2) the legal protections afforded by a trademark and any relevant intellectual property; and (3) the overall company or organizational brand.[9] For instance, the Nike "swoosh" symbol is a unique identifier on every Nike product, a legally protected piece of intellectual property, and a symbol that represents the entire company.

Branding helps a product in many ways. It gives customers a way of recognizing and specifying a particular product so that they can choose it again or recommend it to others. It provides consumers with information about the product. It facilitates the marketing of the product. And it creates value for the product. This notion of the value of a brand is also called **brand equity**. In fact, a brand name can be an organization's most valuable asset, and major brands are worth billions of dollars—and that's just the intangible value of the brand name.[10] Strong brands simplify marketing efforts because the target audience tends to associate

brand A name, term, sign, symbol, design, or combination of those used to identify the products of a firm and to differentiate them from competing products

brand equity The value that a company has built up in a brand

Brands help consumers make confident choices from the thousands of products available in today's supermarkets.

positive qualities with any product that carries a respected brand name—and vice versa.

Customers who buy the same brand again and again are evidence of the strength of **brand loyalty**, or commitment to a particular brand. Brand loyalty can be measured in degrees. The first level is *brand awareness*, which means that people are more likely to buy a product because they are familiar with it. The next level is *brand preference*, which means people will purchase the product if it is available, although they may still be willing to experiment with alternatives if they cannot find the preferred brand. The third and ultimate level of brand loyalty is *brand insistence*, the stage at which buyers will accept no substitute. Some brands, such as Harley-Davidson motorcycles and American Girl dolls, can acquire such a deep level of meaning to loyal consumers that the brands become intertwined with the narratives of the consumers' life stories.[11]

BRAND NAME SELECTION

Jeep, Levi's 501, and iPod are **brand names**, the portion of a brand that can be spoken, including letters, words, or numbers. Annika Sorenstam uses her first name in all capital letters as her brand name. In contrast, the McDonald's golden arches and the Nike "swoosh" symbol are **brand marks**, the portion of a brand that cannot be expressed verbally. The term **logo** (from *logotype*) once referred to typesetting treatment of a brand name but is now used more variably to refer to the nonverbal brand mark, the visual treatment of the brand name, or the combination of the two (see Exhibit 5).

The choice of a brand name and any associated brand marks can be a critical success factor. Imagine if Nike has chosen a cute fuzzy duckling or a static shape of some kind, rather than the dynamic and "athletic" swoosh shape—not to mention naming the brand after the Greek goddess of victory.

Brand names and brand symbols may be registered with the Patent and Trademark Office as **trademarks**, brands that have been given legal protection so that their owners have exclusive rights to their use. The Lanham Trademark Act prohibits the unauthorized use of a trademark on goods or services when the use would likely confuse consumers as to the origin of those goods and services.[12] Companies zealously protect their brand names because if a name becomes too widely used in a general sense, it no longer qualifies for protection under trademark laws. Cellophane, kerosene, linoleum, escalator, zipper, and shredded wheat are just a few of the many brand names that have since lost trademark protection and can now be used by anyone.[13]

BRAND OWNERSHIP

Brand names may be associated with a manufacturer, a retailer, a wholesaler, or a combination of business types. Brands offered and promoted by a national manufacturer, such as Procter & Gamble's Tide detergent and Pampers disposable diapers, are called **national brands**. **Private brands** are not linked to a manufacturer but instead carry a wholesaler's or a retailer's brand. DieHard batteries and Kenmore appliances are private brands sold by Sears. As an alternative to branded products, some retailers also offer *generic products*, which are packaged in plain containers that bear only the name of the product. Note that

brand loyalty The degree to which customers continue to purchase a specific brand

brand names The portion of brands that can be expressed orally, including letters, words, or numbers

brand marks The portion of brands that cannot be expressed verbally

logo A graphical and/or textual representation of a brand

trademarks Brands that have been given legal protection so that their owners have exclusive rights to their use

national brands Brands owned by manufacturers and distributed nationally

private brands Brands that carry the label of a retailer or a wholesaler rather than a manufacturer

EXHIBIT 5	Product Identities

Toyota's Facebook page shows its brand mark, brand name, and a *tagline*, often referred to as a *slogan*.

"generics" is also a term used in the pharmaceutical industry to describe products that are copies of an original drug (other companies are allowed to make these copies after the patent on the original drug expires).

Co-branding occurs when two or more companies team up to closely link their names in a single product, usually to leverage the brand associations and awareness of one product onto the other. Companies can also **license**, or offer to sell, the rights to well-known brand names and symbols. Mainstream movies, for example, often hit the market with an array of licensing deals with fast-food chains and other consumer products companies.

co-branding A partnership between two or more companies to closely link their brand names together for a single product

license An agreement to produce and market another company's product in exchange for a royalty or fee

PACKAGING

Most tangible products need some form of packaging to protect them from damage or tampering, but packaging can also play an important role in a product's marketing strategy. Packaging makes products easier to display, facilitates the sale of smaller products, serves as a means of product differentiation, and enhances the product's overall appeal and convenience. Packaging can significantly influence buyer perceptions, too, sometimes in surprising ways. For instance, packages with simple geometric lines (such as cylinders or rectangles) are perceived as being larger than geometrically complex packages of the same volume. Package designers can use these perceptual effects to create particular images for their products.[14]

Packaging can also involve decisions about which items to include as the product offering and in what quantities. For example,

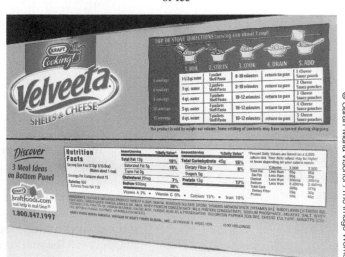

Product packaging usually has a number of functions, from promoting and protecting the product to displaying legally required health and safety information to providing instructions for use.

239

Costco and other warehouse-style retailers offer many of the same products available through regular grocery stores but in packages of larger quantities.

In the retailing environment, packaging plays a key role in reducing shoplifting; retailers have put a lot of pressure on manufacturers to adopt packages that are difficult to conceal or to open in the store. Those hard-to-open plastic packages known as "clamshells" that consumers love to hate—and that account for hundreds of injuries every year as people attempt to slice them open—are one such response to shoplifting.[15] Packaging is also a major environmental concern, in both the resources used and waste generated, so expect innovations and new regulations in this area in the coming years.

LABELING

Labeling is an integral part of packaging. Whether the label is a separate element attached to the package or a printed part of the container, it serves to identify a brand and communicate multiple types of information, from promotional messages to legally required safety or nutritional data. The labeling of foods, drugs, cosmetics, and many health products is regulated under various federal laws, which often require disclosures about potential dangers, benefits, and other issues consumers need to consider when making a buying decision.

✔ Checkpoint

LEARNING OBJECTIVE 3: Define *brand*, **and explain the concepts of brand equity and brand loyalty.**

SUMMARY: *Brand* encompasses the various elements of product identity and meaning. *Brand equity* reflects the value of a brand name based on its strength and appeal in the marketplace and its power as a communication vehicle. *Brand loyalty* can be defined at three levels: brand awareness, in which the buyer is familiar with the product; brand preference, in which the buyer will select the product if it is available; and brand insistence, in which the buyer will accept no substitute.

CRITICAL THINKING: (1) Can a brand with a bad reputation be rescued? Would a company be wiser to just drop a "bad brand" and start fresh with something new? (2) Is staying with the same product only a case of brand "loyalty"? Could other factors be in play that lead consumers or organizations not to switch brands? Explain your answer.

IT'S YOUR BUSINESS: (1) How many visible brand marks are you currently wearing? Are these common brands? (2) What do you think these brands say about you?

KEY TERMS TO KNOW: brand, brand equity, brand loyalty, brand names, brand marks, logo, trademarks, national brands, private brands, co-branding, license

---

4 LEARNING OBJECTIVE

Identify four ways of expanding a product line, and discuss two risks that product-line extensions pose.

brand managers Managers who develop and implement the marketing strategies and programs for specific products or brands

Product-Line and Product-Mix Strategies

In addition to developing product identities, a company must continually evaluate what kinds of products it will offer. To stay competitive, most companies continually add and drop products to ensure that declining items will be replaced by growth products. Companies that offer more than one product also need to pay close attention to how those products are positioned in the marketplace relative to one another. The responsibility for managing individual products, product lines, and product mixes is usually assigned to one or more managers in the marketing department. In a smaller company, the *marketing manager* tackles this effort; in larger companies with more products to manage, individual products or groups of products are usually assigned to **brand managers**, known in some companies as *product managers* or *product line managers*.

PRODUCT LINES

A **product line** is a group of products from a single manufacturer that are similar in terms of use or characteristics. The General Mills (www.generalmills.com) snack-food product line, for example, includes Bugles, Cascadian Farm organic snacks, and Nature Valley Granola Bars. Within each product line, a company confronts decisions about the number of goods and services to offer. On the one hand, offering additional products can help a manufacturer boost revenues and increase its visibility in retail stores. On the other hand, creating too many products and product variations can be expensive for everyone in the supply chain and can be confusing to buyers.

product line A series of related products offered by a firm

PRODUCT MIX

An organization with several product lines has a **product mix**—a collection of diverse goods or services offered for sale. The General Mills product mix includes cereals, baking products, desserts, snack foods, and entrees (see Exhibit 6). Three important dimensions of

product mix The complete portfolio of products that a company offers for sale

EXHIBIT 6	The Product Mix at General Mills (selected products)

These selected products from General Mills illustrate the various dimensions of its product mix. The mix is *wide* because it contains multiple product lines (cereals, fruit snacks, pasta, soup, yogurt, and more). The cereal product line is *long* because it contains many individual brands (only four of which are shown here). And these four cereal brands show different depths. The Trix brand is a shallow line, whereas the Cheerios brand is *deep*.

Source: Based on General Mills website, accessed 6 September 2011, www.generalmills.com.

a product mix are *width*, *length*, and *depth*, and each dimension presents its own set of challenges and opportunities. A product mix is *wide* if it has several product lines. A product mix is *long* if it carries several items in its product lines. For instance, General Mills produces multiple cereal brands within the ready-to-eat cereal line. A product mix is *deep* if it has a number of versions of *each* product in a product line. The Cheerios brand, for example, currently has about a dozen different varieties.[16]

When deciding on the dimensions of a product mix, a company must weigh the risks and rewards associated with various approaches. Some companies limit the number of product offerings and focus on selling a few items in higher quantities. Doing so can keep production and marketing costs lower through economies of scale. However, counting too heavily on a narrow set of products leaves a company vulnerable to competitive threats and market shifts. Other companies diversify their product offerings as a protection against shifts in consumer tastes, economic conditions, and technology, or as a way to build marketing synergy by offering complementary products.[17]

Retailers often have considerable influence in manufacturers' product line decisions, particularly in the store-based retail channel. In general, the more revenue a manufacturer represents, the better chance it has of getting all-important shelf space. Consequently, retail store aisles tend to be dominated by a few large brands, and manufacturers look for ways to build portfolios of best sellers that can command attention at the retail level.

Online retailing presents much better opportunities for large numbers of specialized and low-volume products. Without the physical limitations of a "bricks and mortar" facility, online retailers can offer a much greater variety of products. For example, the average physical bookstore might offer 40,000 volumes, whereas the major online book retailers offer several million.[18] While these products may individually sell at lower volumes, collectively they represent a substantial business opportunity that has been termed the *long tail* (referring to a sales volume graph in which a vast number of low-volume products stretches out toward infinity).[19]

PRODUCT EXPANSION STRATEGIES

As Exhibit 7 shows, you can expand your product line and mix in a number of ways. One approach is to introduce additional items in a given product category under the same brand name—such as new flavors, forms, colors, ingredients, or package sizes. Another approach

EXHIBIT 7	Expanding a Product Line

Companies use one or more of these product-line expansion methods to pursue new opportunities.

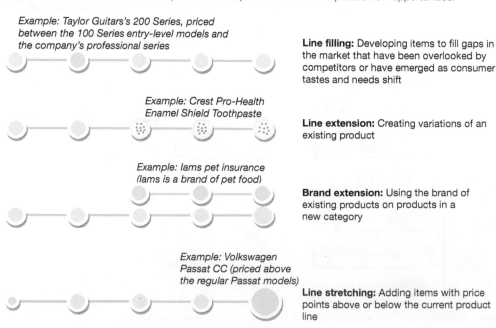

Example: Taylor Guitars's 200 Series, priced between the 100 Series entry-level models and the company's professional series

Line filling: Developing items to fill gaps in the market that have been overlooked by competitors or have emerged as consumer tastes and needs shift

Example: Crest Pro-Health Enamel Shield Toothpaste

Line extension: Creating variations of an existing product

Example: Iams pet insurance (Iams is a brand of pet food)

Brand extension: Using the brand of existing products on products in a new category

Example: Volkswagen Passat CC (priced above the regular Passat models)

Line stretching: Adding items with price points above or below the current product line is to expand a product line to add new and similar products with the same product name—a strategy known as **family branding**.

Conversely, in a **brand extension**, a company applies a successful brand name to a new product category in the hopes that the recognition and reputation of the brand will give it a head start in the new category. Building on the name recognition of an existing brand cuts the costs and risks of introducing new products. However, product-line extensions present two important risks that marketers need to consider carefully. First, stretching a brand to cover too many categories or types of products can dilute the brand's meaning in the minds of target customers. For instance, if the sports broadcaster ESPN were to branch out into business and financial news, its original sports audience might wonder whether the company is still committed to being a leader in sports journalism, and the business news audience might wonder what value a sports media company could bring to financial news. Second, additional products do not automatically guarantee increased sales revenue. Marketers need to make sure that new products don't simply *cannibalize*, or take sales away from, their existing products.

PRODUCT STRATEGIES FOR INTERNATIONAL MARKETS

Product adaptation is one of the key changes that companies need to consider when moving into other countries. First, managers must decide on which products and services to introduce in which countries. When selecting a country, they must take into consideration the type of government, market-entry requirements, tariffs and other trade barriers, cultural and language differences, consumer preferences, foreign-exchange rates, and differing business customs. Then, they must decide whether to standardize the product, selling it everywhere, or to customize the product to accommodate the lifestyles and habits of local target markets. A company may change only the product's name or packaging, or it can modify the product's components, size, and functions.

For example, the social network site hi5 (www.hi5.com) has become one of the world's most popular gaming and entertainment websites through extensive adaption, including localization in more than 50 languages around the world.[20] Similarly, French consumers have been eating at McDonald's (www.mcdonalds.fr) since the company first arrived in 1972, but the burger giant has a unique look in that country. To accommodate a culture known for its cuisine and dining experience, many McDonald's outlets in France have upgraded their decor to a level that would make them almost unrecognizable in the United States. And while the basic burger offerings remain roughly the same, menus include local cheeses, brioche (a soft bread), and *croques monsieurs* (a traditional grilled ham-and-cheese sandwich).[21]

For the latest information on product and branding strategies, visit http://real-timeupdates .com/bia6.

Checkpoint

LEARNING OBJECTIVE 4: Identify four ways of expanding a product line, and discuss two risks that product-line extensions pose.

SUMMARY: A product line can be expanded by filling gaps in the market, extending the line to include new varieties of existing products, extending the brand to new product categories, and stretching the line to include lower- or higher-priced items. Two of the biggest risks with product-line extensions are losing brand identity and coherence (weakening of the brand's meaning) and cannibalizing of sales of other products in the product line.

CRITICAL THINKING: (1) If McDonald's had been relatively unknown to French diners when the company entered that market in 1972, would it have made more sense to use a different and more "French-sounding" brand name? Why or why not? (2) Would a consumer-products manufacturer ever want to create more product extensions and variations than it could explain in terms of pure market appeal? Why or why not?

family branding Using a brand name on a variety of related products

brand extension Applying a successful brand name to a new product category

IT'S YOUR BUSINESS: (1) Citing specific examples, how has branding helped you as a consumer? Think about the assurance you have buying a known and trusted brand, for example. (2) Think about some of the consumer products you buy frequently, such as cereal, painkillers, or snack foods. Do you appreciate the range of choices available to you when you shop for these items, or do you wish that companies would narrow the options to a handful in each category? Why?

KEY TERMS TO KNOW: brand managers, product line, product mix, family branding, brand extension

5 LEARNING OBJECTIVE

List the factors that influence pricing decisions, and explain break-even analysis.

Pricing Strategies

The second key element in the marketing mix is pricing. Pricing involves *capturing value* back from the customer in exchange for the value provided in the product. Setting and managing prices is a combination of strategic considerations and careful financial analysis.

STRATEGIC CONSIDERATIONS IN PRICING

Managers must consider a variety of internal and external factors when establishing prices:

- **Marketing objectives**. The first step in setting a price is to match it to the objectives set in the strategic marketing plan. Is the goal to increase market share, increase sales, improve profits, project a particular image, or combat competition? Price is a flexible tool that can help a firm achieve a wide variety of marketing objectives.
- **Government regulations**. To protect consumers and encourage fair competition, governments around the world have enacted various price-related laws over the years. These regulations are particularly important in three areas of prohibited behavior: (1) *price discrimination*, unfairly offering attractive discounts to some customers but not to others; (2) *deceptive pricing*, pricing schemes that are considered misleading; and (3) *price fixing*, an agreement among two or more companies supplying the same type of products as to the prices they will charge. For example, the U.S. government recently fined 21 airlines more than $1.7 billion—and sent several airline executives to jail—for an extensive price-fixing scheme on flights to and from the United States. The scheme operated for more than five years, until two of the airlines, Lufthansa and Virgin Atlantic, took advantage of an amnesty program and turned themselves in.[22]
- **Customer perceptions**. Another consideration in setting price is the perception of quality and value that a price elicits from customers. An unexpectedly low price can trigger fears of low quality, but a high price can connote quality and even exclusivity. Specific numbers can have perceptual effect as well, such as the well-known "9 effect." You've probably noticed that many prices end in a 9, such as $9.99 or $5,999. Your conscious mind says, "Gimme a break; we all know that's really $10 or $6,000." However, research suggests that our minds equate that 9 with a bargain—even when it isn't. In one experiment, for example, a dress sold more when priced at $39 than when it was priced at $34.[23]
- **Market demand**. The discussion of supply and demand in Chapter 2 points out that market demand usually fluctuates as prices fluctuate. However, some goods and services are relatively *insensitive* to changes in price; others are highly *sensitive*. Buyers can also exhibit individual levels of price sensitivity. For instance, brand-loyal customers tend to be less sensitive to price, meaning they will stick with a brand even as the price increases, whereas other buyers will begin switching to cheaper alternatives.[24] Marketers refer to this sensitivity as **price elasticity**—how responsive demand will be to a change in price.
- **Competition**. Competitive prices are obviously a major consideration whenever a firm is establishing or changing its prices. Technology has profoundly shifted the balance of power in this respect from sellers to buyers in recent years, as social commerce websites

price elasticity A measure of the sensitivity of demand to changes in price

Prices that end in 9 (such as $9.99 or $5,499) try to convey a "bargain" message. However, marketers of higher-quality products often use even-numbered prices that end in 0 to emphasize a sense of luxury over low cost.

and mobile Internet access make it easy to find the lowest prices for a wide variety of goods and services. The easier it is for buyers to compare prices, for instance, the more important competitive prices become—particularly when buyers don't perceive much difference among the available products.

COST STRUCTURE AND BREAK-EVEN ANALYSIS

Every company has a particular *cost structure* that determines how much it must spend to create and market its products. Some costs remain the same regardless of production and sales volume. Such **fixed costs** include rent or mortgage payments, insurance premiums, real estate taxes, and salaries. These are costs incurred just to "keep the doors open," without creating or selling anything. In contrast, **variable costs**, including raw materials, supplies consumed during production, shipping, and sales commissions, vary with changes in production and sales volume. Obviously, the more a company can lower its cost structure, the more flexibility it has in setting prices and ensuring desirable levels of profit.

The cost to create and sell each product is a combination of fixed and variable costs. A critical calculation in setting prices is **break-even analysis**, determining the number of units a firm must sell at a given price to recoup both fixed and variable costs—to "break even," in other words. The **break-even point** is the minimum sales volume the company must achieve to avoid losing money. Sales volume beyond the break-even point will generate profits; sales volume below the break-even amount will result in losses.

You can determine the break-even point in number of units with this simple calculation:

$$\text{Break-even point} = \frac{\text{Fixed costs}}{\text{Selling price} - \text{Variable costs per unit}}$$

For example, if you wanted to price haircuts at $20 and you had fixed costs of $60,000 and variable costs per haircut of $5, you would need to sell 4,000 haircuts to break even:

$$\text{Break-even point} = \frac{\$60,000}{\$20 - \$5} = 4,000 \text{ units}$$

fixed costs Business costs that remain constant regardless of the number of units produced

variable costs Business costs that increase with the number of units produced

break-even analysis A method of calculating the minimum volume of sales needed at a given price to cover all costs

break-even point Sales volume at a given price that will cover all of a company's costs

Naturally, $20 isn't your only pricing option. Why not charge $30 instead? At that price, you need to sell only 2,400 haircuts to break even (see Exhibit 8). Of course, you would have to convince 2,400 people to pay the higher price, and depending on market dynamics and your cost structure, you might make more money selling at the lower price.

Note that break-even analysis doesn't dictate what price you *should* charge; rather, it provides some insight into the price you *can* charge and begin to generate profit. With the break-even point in hand, you can then factor in the various strategic considerations to determine price using one of the methods discussed in the next section.

EXHIBIT 8	Break-Even Analysis

The break-even point is the point at which revenues just cover costs. After fixed costs and variable costs have been met, any additional income represents profit. The graphs show that at $20 per haircut, the break-even point is 4,000 haircuts; charging $30 yields a break-even point at only 2,400 haircuts.

Checkpoint

LEARNING OBJECTIVE 5: List the factors that influence pricing decisions, and explain break-even analysis.

SUMMARY: Strategic considerations in pricing include marketing objectives, government regulations, customer perceptions, market demand, and competition. *Break-even analysis* is a way to determine how many units (the *break-even point*) a firm needs to produce in order to begin turning a profit by covering its fixed and variable costs. The break-even point is calculated by dividing fixed costs by the difference between the selling price and the variable costs per unit.

CRITICAL THINKING: (1) Why wouldn't a firm just drop any product that isn't selling in high enough volume to reach its break-even point? (2) Is "9" style pricing ethical? Why or why not?

IT'S YOUR BUSINESS: (1) Do you factor in the value of your time when you price-comparison shop? Why or why not? (2) As a consumer taking charge of your own financial future, what lessons could you take from the business concepts of fixed and variable costs?

KEY TERMS TO KNOW: price elasticity, fixed costs, variable costs, break-even analysis, break-even point

Pricing Methods

 LEARNING OBJECTIVE
Identify nine common pricing methods.

Break-even analysis and the various strategic considerations help managers establish an overall framework of pricing possibilities. You can think of costs as establishing the pricing "floor," whereas demand, competition, and other factors establish the "ceiling." Somewhere between those two limits lies the ideal price for each product. Managers can apply a variety of methods to pinpoint specific prices. Note that some of these methods aren't mutually exclusive; companies can use two or more methods, either in succession or at the same time.

COST-BASED PRICING

Some companies simplify the pricing task by using **cost-based pricing**, also known as *cost-plus pricing*, in which they start with the cost of producing a good or a service and then add a *markup* to arrive at the selling price. Cost-based pricing is simple, but it suffers from a major weakness: It doesn't consider any external factors such as customer demand or competitive prices. The price could be too high for market conditions, leaving the company uncompetitive, or it could be too low, generating less profit than it could otherwise.

cost-based pricing A method of setting prices based on production and marketing costs, rather than conditions in the marketplace

VALUE-BASED PRICING

In contrast to cost-based pricing, **value-based pricing** establishes a price on a product's potential or perceived value in the marketplace. In other words, rather than starting with cost and then figuring out a price, this method starts with a target price and works backward to identify a cost structure that will yield acceptable profit margins. The disadvantage of this method is that it requires more information and more analysis, because managers need to measure or at least estimate perceptions of customer value in order to establish the price. If a company lacks the information to establish a realistic price point based on value, one option is to introduce the product using cost-based pricing and then gradually shift to a value-based model as more is learned about how customers perceive the product.[25]

An additional challenge with value-based pricing is that perceptions of value change over time. For example, in a recession or depression, consumers take a much harder look at

value-based pricing A method of setting prices based on customer perceptions of value the value they are receiving for the money they spend. Many want more product value while paying the same price or the same product value at a lower price, while others are willing to give up some product value in exchange for lower prices. In all these cases, the perception of value changes, and companies that understand and can deliver on the new perceptions of value stand the best chance of surviving or even thriving during tough times.[26]

OPTIMAL PRICING

optimal pricing A computer-based pricing method that creates a demand curve for every product to help managers select a price that meets specific marketing objectives

Optimal pricing attempts to minimize the errors and guesswork of other methods by using computer software to generate the ideal price for every item, at each individual store, at any given time. A price-optimization program feeds reams of data from checkout scanners, seasonal sales figures, competitors, and other sources into probability algorithms to come up with an individual demand curve for each product in each store. From that, retailers can identify which products are the most price sensitive. Then they can adjust prices up or down according to each store's priorities—profit, revenue, or market share. Some systems also let store managers conduct "what if" analyses based on past sales data, helping them see the potential effect of proposed price changes.[27]

SKIM PRICING

skim pricing Charging a high price for a new product during the introductory stage and lowering the price later

During the introductory phase of the product life cycle, a company may opt to take advantage of strong demand before competitors can enter the market and exert downward pressure on prices. To achieve this goal, the company can charge a high initial price—a practice known as **skim pricing**—with the intention of dropping the price later. *Early adopters* are often willing to pay a premium to get their hands on new products as soon as possible. In consumer markets, some people simply want to have the latest and greatest before anyone else; in organizational markets, new types of equipment can give companies a short-term competitive advantage.

PENETRATION PRICING

penetration pricing Introducing a new product at a low price in hopes of building sales volume quickly

Skim prices are set high with the understanding that many customers won't be willing to pay them. In contrast, companies use **penetration pricing** to build sales volume by charging a low initial price. This approach has the added advantage of discouraging competition, because the low price—which competitors would be pressured to match—limits the profit potential for everyone. (If the intent of penetration is to drive competitors out of business, though, companies open themselves up to charges of illegal *predatory pricing*.)

However, penetration pricing doesn't work if the company can't sustain the low price levels profitably, if prices for a particular product are inelastic, or if customers weigh other factors more heavily than price. Moreover, as mentioned earlier, prices that are far below the market's expectations can raise concerns about quality, reliability, and safety. Everyone would like to pay less for medical care, but many people would be unwilling to go to cut-rate clinics if they thought their health might be jeopardized.

LOSS-LEADER PRICING

loss-leader pricing Selling one product at a loss as a way to entice customers to consider other products

As part of a larger marketing plan, some companies occasionally resort to **loss-leader pricing**, setting a price on one product so low that they lose money on every sale but recoup that loss by enticing customers to try a new product or buy other products. For instance, grocery stores can use milk and other staples as loss leaders to encourage shoppers to visit. (And there's a reason these products are often all the way at the back of the store—you have to walk past hundreds of higher-margin products that you might suddenly decide you can't live without.)

AUCTION PRICING

In an *auction*, the seller doesn't set a firm price but allows buyers to competitively bid on the products being sold. Auctions used to be confined to a few market sectors such as fine art, agricultural products, and government bonds, but that all changed when eBay turned selling and buying via auctions into a new national pastime. Many companies now use eBay and other auction sites to sell everything from modular buildings to tractors to industrial equipment. In *procurement auctions* or *reverse auctions*, potential buyers identify the goods or services they need and the prices they're willing to pay, then suppliers respond with offers at the prices they're willing to charge. The travel website Priceline.com, for example, lets buyers enter a price they're willing to pay and then see whether airlines, hotels, and other providers are willing to sell at that price (see Exhibit 9).[28]

EXHIBIT 9	Reverse Auction Pricing

Priceline was a pioneer in the concept of reverse auction pricing.

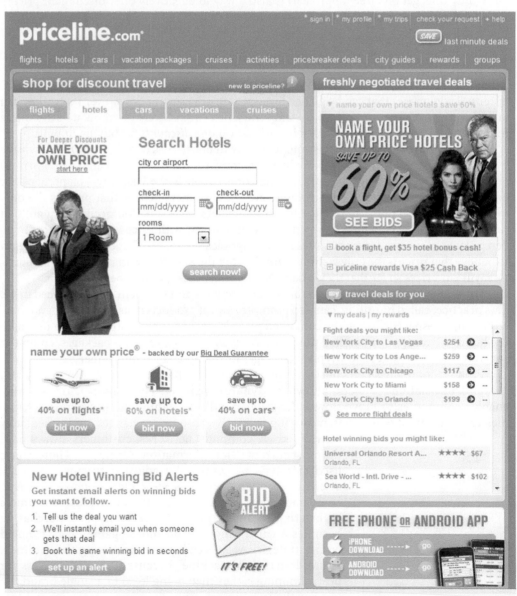

PARTICIPATIVE PRICING

participative pricing Allowing customers to pay the amount they think a product is worth

One of the most unusual pricing strategies is **participative pricing**, sometimes known as "pay what you want," in which customers literally get to pay as much as they think a product is worth. While it might sound like a strategy for financial disaster, with participative pricing, buyers sometimes pay *more* than the company would normally charge.[29] When the band Radiohead let buyers name their own price for one of its downloadable albums, the band made more money from that album than from downloads on all their other studio albums combined.[30]

FREE AND FREEMIUM PRICING

freemium pricing A hybrid pricing strategy of offering some products for free while charging for others, or offering a product for free to some customers while charging others for it

Even more radical than participative pricing is no price at all. However, giving away goods and services can make a lot of sense in the right situation, such as when a new company is trying to make a name for itself in the marketplace.[31] Another use of free pricing is when some customers are charged enough to provide free goods and services for other customers, a tactic known as **freemium pricing** (*free + premium*).[32] For example, a number of smartphone and tablet apps offer a free version with fewer capabilities and a paid version of the full product. Giving away some products while maintaining full prices for others (the common "buy one, get one free" approach) is also a way to effectively offer discounted pricing without the risk of creating expectations of lower prices.[33]

PRICE ADJUSTMENT TACTICS

discounts Temporary price reductions to stimulate sales or lower prices to encourage certain behaviors such as paying with cash

After they've established initial price points, companies need to stay on the lookout for potential advantages that can be gained by adjusting prices up or down over time. They can offer a variety of **discounts**, such as temporary price reductions to stimulate sales, price reductions for paying early or paying in cash, or *volume discounts* for buying in bulk.

Although offering discounts is a popular way to boost sales of a product, the downside is that discounts can set off *price wars* between competitors. Price wars can occur when (1) one supplier believes that underpricing the competition is the best way—or perhaps the only way—for it to increase sales volume and (2) customers believe that price is the only meaningful differentiator among the various suppliers. This situation occurs frequently in the air travel industry, which is why it has been wracked with price wars ever since it was deregulated years ago. Price wars present two significant dangers: that customers will begin to believe that price is the only factor to care about in the market and that desperate competitors will cut prices so far that they'll damage their finances—perhaps beyond repair.

bundling Offering several products for a single price that is presumably lower than the total of the products' individual prices

Sometimes sellers combine several of their products and sell them at one reduced price. This practice, called **bundling**, can also promote sales of products consumers might not otherwise buy—especially when the combined price is low enough to entice them to purchase the bundle. Examples of bundled products are season tickets, vacation packages, computer software with hardware, and wrapped packages of shampoo and conditioner.

dynamic pricing Continually adjusting prices to reflect changes in supply and demand

Finally, companies can constantly reprice their products in response to supply and demand fluctuations, a tactic known as **dynamic pricing**. Dynamic pricing not only enables companies to move slow-selling merchandise instantly but also allows companies to experiment with different pricing levels. Because price changes are immediately distributed via computer networks, customers always have the most current price information. Airlines and hotels have used this type of continually adjusted pricing for years, a technique often known as *yield management*. However, companies need to be careful not to alienate customers by creating so much pricing uncertainty that purchasing becomes a frustrating cat-and-mouse game. In fact, noted brand strategist Al Ries calls dynamic pricing the "ultimate brand destruction machine" because it rewards buyers for price shopping rather than being loyal to a single brand.[34]

For the latest information on pricing strategies and tactics, visit http://real-timeupdates.com/bia6.

REAL-TIME UPDATES
Learn More by Reading This Article

Can the business world survive Groupon?

Coupons have been a pricing dilemma for years, but Groupon and other social coupon schemes are turning couponing into a blessing for some companies and a nightmare for others. Go to http://real-timeupdates.com/bia6 and click on Learn More. If you are using MyBizLab, you can access Real-Time Updates within the chapter or under Student Study Tools.

✔ Checkpoint

LEARNING OBJECTIVE 6: Identify nine common pricing methods.

SUMMARY: (1) *Cost-based* or *cost-plus pricing* takes the cost of producing and marketing a product and adds a markup to arrive at the selling price. (2) *Value-based pricing* seeks to establish the perceived value of the product in the eyes of target customers and sets a price based on that. (3) *Optimal pricing* is a computer-based method that uses sales data to create a demand curve for every product, allowing managers to select prices based on specific marketing objectives. (4) *Skim pricing* involves setting an initial price that is relatively high in order to capitalize on pent-up demand or the lack of direct competition for a new product. (5) *Penetration pricing* is setting a price low enough to achieve targeted sales volumes. (6) *Loss-leader pricing* is setting the price artificially low on one product in order to attract buyers for other products. (7) *Auction pricing* lets buyers determine the selling price by bidding against one another; in a reverse auction, buyers state a price they are willing to pay and sellers choose whether to match it. (8) *Participative pricing* lets buyers pay whatever they think a product is worth. (9) *Freemium pricing* involves giving away products to some customers (as a means of attracting paying customers, for example) or giving away some products but charging for others.

CRITICAL THINKING: (1) What steps could a company take to determine the perceived value of its products in its target markets? (2) How can patterns of temporary price discounts "train" consumers to stop buying at full price?

IT'S YOUR BUSINESS: (1) Have you ever bid on anything on eBay, another online auction site, or an in-person auction? If so, how did you decide how much to bid? Did you set a maximum price you'd allow yourself to spend? Did you get caught up in the competitive emotions of bidding against someone else? (2) Have you ever purchased a hot new product as soon as it hit the market, only to see the price drop a few months later? If so, did you resolve never to buy so quickly again?

KEY TERMS TO KNOW: cost-based pricing, value-based pricing, optimal pricing, skim pricing, penetration pricing, loss-leader pricing, participative pricing, freemium pricing, discounts, bundling, dynamic pricing

---

BEHIND THE SCENES

BUILDING THE ANNIKA BRAND

MyBizLab

Annika Sorenstam is approaching her second career the same way she approached her first. In golf, she reached the top of her sport by learning from the best, surrounding herself with a supportive team, setting ambitious goals, and working as hard as it takes to reach those goals.

A central element in her business plan is the role she herself plays as the core of the "Annika" brand. As a young player in her native Sweden, she was so reluctant to step into the limelight that she would falter toward the end of tournaments to avoid winning and facing the media attention that came with it. She clearly fixed that problem, transforming herself into a quietly confident but ferocious competitor who often left other players in the dust as she went on to win nearly 90 times worldwide.

However, as she was nearing retirement from golf and ramping up her business activities, she realized that the persona she had become known for on the course didn't lend

itself to her ambitions for the Annika brand. Research by branding consultant Duane Knapp showed that people respected Sorenstam's competitive drive but really had no sense of who she was as a person. Even her own husband says she was viewed by the public as "the stoic Swede who will step on your throat" on the way to victory and not the "humble, pretty, and hilarious" woman he knew off the course.

Transforming Annika the feared competitor into Annika the warm and welcoming brand icon was a top priority. Good examples of this effort are her blog www.annikablog.com and her Twitter account http://twitter.com/#!/ANNIKA59, which give visitors the chance to know her as she lives off the course, including her love of gourmet cooking, her passion for skiing, and her role as a mother.

Along with crafting an inviting brand image that more accurately reflects her true personality, Sorenstam is busy expanding the Annika product line. She continues to endorse many of the same goods and services she promoted as an active player, including Callaway Golf, Lexus, and Rolex. Other business partnerships include an Annika-branded clothing line with Cutter & Buck, Annika wine, and Annika perfume.

A central element in her product portfolio is the Annika Academy, a golf instruction facility in Reunion, Florida, that offers lessons, corporate outings, golf vacations, and the opportunity to train with the same advisors and coaches who work with Sorenstam. For the ultimate golf experience, a few lucky visitors every year can buy the three-day, $12,000 "Soren-Slam" package, which includes nine holes of golf with Sorenstam herself.

Following another path blazed by her golf-business mentors, Sorenstam also launched a golf course design business, with courses stretching from Turkey to China to the United States. Having had the opportunity to play some of the finest and most historic golf courses in the world, she combines that experience with her insights as a professional to create challenging but playable courses. Her designs also aim to right an aesthetic wrong shared by too many golf courses: The best views of both the playing area and the surrounding landscape are found on the men's tee boxes. (Golf courses have different sets of tee boxes to reflect the different hitting lengths of average male and female players.) On her courses, women enjoy the same quality of experience as the men.

Sorenstam has had an interest in finance since any early age, and that passion is reflected in yet another part of the product mix, the Annika Financial Group. This small advisory firm helps other professional athletes manage their money and achieve financial security in their postathletic lives.

With a recrafted brand image and a growing product portfolio, Sorenstam is off to a hot start in her quest to be the first woman to join the exclusive club of former athletes who have truly made it big in business. Michael Jordan is "Air Jordan," Arnold Palmer is the "The King," Jack Nicklaus is "The Golden Bear," and Greg Norman, another golf empire builder, is "The Shark." Who knows—perhaps Annika is "The Avenger"?[35]

Critical Thinking Questions

1. Golfers who take lessons and purchase other services from the Annika Academy presumably share at least some of Sorenstam's passion for winning. Would toning down the competitive aspect of Sorenstam's public persona negatively affect the Annika brand in the eyes of Academy customers? Explain your answer.
2. Sorenstam's charitable efforts include the Annika Foundation, which you can read about on her website. How does her work with the Make-A-Wish Foundation and other activities contribute to her brand equity?
3. Explain how the brand extension efforts in wine, perfume, and financial advice can reasonably fit under the umbrella of the Annika brand.

LEARN MORE ONLINE
Visit Sorenstam's main website at www.annikasorenstam.com, her blog at www.annikablog.com, her Twitter account at http://twitter.com/#!/ANNIKA59, and the Annika Academy website at www.annikaacademy.com. What is your overall impression of Sorenstam as a businessperson and of the Annika brand as a product identifier? Do these communication efforts help in the effort to shift her public image away from that of the fierce competitor?

MyBizLab
Log on to www.mybizlab.com to access study and assessment aids associated with this chapter.

KEY TERMS

brand
brand equity
brand extension
brand loyalty
brand managers
brand mark
brand names
break-even analysis
break-even point
bundling
capital items
co-branding
commercialization
convenience products
cost-based pricing

discounts
dynamic pricing
expense items
family branding
fixed costs
freemium pricing
license
logo
loss-leader pricing
national brands
optimal pricing
participative pricing
penetration pricing
price elasticity
private brands

product development process

product life cycle

product line

product mix

prototypes

shopping products

skim pricing

specialty products

test marketing

trademarks

value-based pricing

variable costs

TEST YOUR KNOWLEDGE

Questions for Review

1. What are the four stages of the product life cycle?
2. What is test marketing?
3. What are the functions of packaging?
4. How many books will a publisher have to sell to break even if fixed costs are $100,000, the selling price per book is $60, and the variable costs per book are $40?
5. How does cost-based pricing differ from value-based pricing?

Questions for Analysis

6. How does branding help consumers?
7. Why are some well-established brands worth millions or even billions of dollars?
8. Why is cost-based pricing risky?
9. Why is it important to review the objectives of a strategic marketing plan before setting a product's price?
10. **Ethical Considerations.** If your college neighborhood is typical, many companies in the area adorn themselves in your school colors and otherwise seek to identify their names with your school name and thereby encourage business from students. Some of these firms probably have brand licensing agreements with your college or are involved in sponsoring various groups on campus. However, chances are some of them are using school colors and other branding elements without having any formal arrangement with the college. In other words, they may be getting commercial benefit from the association without paying for it.[36] Is this ethical? Why or why not?

Questions for Application

11. In what ways might Mattel modify its pricing strategies during the life cycle of a toy product?
12. Do you consider yourself an *early adopter* when it comes to trying out new products or new fashions, or do you tend to take a wait-and-see attitude? How does your attitude toward new products and new ideas influence your decision-making as a consumer?
13. This question was intentionally excluded from this edition.
14. This question was intentionally excluded from this edition.

EXPAND YOUR KNOWLEDGE

Discovering Career Opportunities

Being a marketing manager is a big responsibility, but it can be a lot of fun at the same time. Read what the U.S. Department of Labor has to say about the nature of the work, working conditions, qualifications, and job outlook for marketing managers by accessing the Bureau of Labor Statistics's *Occupational Outlook Handbook*, at www.bls.gov/oco.

1. What does a marketing manager do?

2. What are some key questions you might want to ask when interviewing for a job in marketing?

3. What training and qualifications should a marketing manager have?

Improving Your Tech Insights: Location and Tracking Technologies

Location and tracking technologies cover a wide range of capabilities. Radio frequency identification (RFID) technology uses small scannable tags attached to products or even people and pets. RFID is being implemented extensively in retail and wholesale distribution systems to enhance inventory management. Parents and caregivers can also use RFID to check on elderly relatives, pets, or children. The Great America amusement park in Santa Clara, California, offers RFID bracelets for $5 so parents and children can reconnect if they get separated in the crowds. The Food and Drug Administration (FDA) has approved an implantable device that stores medical information that emergency personnel could retrieve with a quick scan, even if the patient is unconscious.

The Global Positioning System (GPS) can pinpoint any location on Earth using a network of satellites and small transceivers. Trucking fleets use GPS to keep track of all their vehicles to optimize scheduling and make sure drivers stay on assigned routes. Some rental car companies use GPS to see whether drivers break the speed limit or venture outside of permitted rental territories. *Enhanced 911*, or *E911*, uses either GPS or cell phone towers to let emergency personnel pinpoint the location of people calling on cell phones. GPS-enabled smartphones are creating a dizzying array of new location-based services, from location-based social networking such as Loopt and Foursquare to shopping and dining guides to wireless payment systems.

Using online research tools, identify at least one emerging business opportunity that could take advantage of location and tracking technologies. In an email message to your instructor, describe the opportunity and briefly explain how the technology would be used.[37]

PRACTICE YOUR SKILLS

Sharpening Your Communication Skills

Now's your chance to play the role of a marketing specialist trying to convince a group of customers that your product concept is better than the competition's. You're going to wade into the industry battle over digital photo printing. Choose a side: either the photo printer manufacturers, who want consumers to buy printers to print their own digital photos (visit HP, at www.hp.com, for an overview of photo-quality printers), or the service providers, who claim their way is better (visit one of the many retailers that offer a service-based approach, such as www.cvs.com or www.walmart.com). Prepare a short presentation on why the approach you've chosen is better for consumers. Feel free to segment the consumer market and choose a particular target segment if that bolsters your argument.

Building Your Team Skills

Select a high-profile product with which you and your teammates are familiar. Do some online research to learn more about that brand. Then answer these questions and prepare a short group presentation to your classmates summarizing your findings:

- Is the product a consumer product, an organizational product, or both?
- At what stage in its life cycle is this product?
- Is the product a national brand or a private brand?
- How do the product's packaging and labeling help boost consumer appeal?

- How is this product promoted?
- Is the product mix to which this product belongs wide? Long? Deep?
- Is the product sold in international markets? If so, does the company use a standardized or a customized strategy?
- How is the product priced in relation to competing products?

Developing Your Research Skills

Scan recent business journals and newspapers (print or online editions) for an article related to one of the following:

- New product development
- The product life cycle
- Brand extensions
- Pricing strategies
- Packaging

1. Does this article report on a development in a particular company, several companies, or an entire industry? Which companies or industries are specifically mentioned?
2. If you were a marketing manager in this industry, what concerns would you have as a result of reading the article? What questions do you think companies in this industry (or related ones) should be asking? What would you want to know?
3. In what ways do you think this industry, other industries, or the public might be affected by this trend or development in the next five years? Why?

REFERENCES

1. Annika Sorenstam website, accessed 7 September 2011, www.annikasorenstam.com; Annika Academy website, accessed 7 September 2011, www.theannikaacademy.com; Jeff Chu, "A New Course for Sörenstam," *Time South Pacific* (Australia/New Zealand edition), 12 January 2009, 46–47; Brian McCallen, "Annika on Course," *Forbes*, 8 October 2007, 68–69; Eben Harrell, "Calling Time," *Time South Pacific* (Australia/New Zealand edition), 26 May 2008, 5; Edward Schmidt, Jr., "Fierce Competition," *Meeting News*, 8 October 2007, 60; Barry Janoff, "Sorenstam Scores with Sponsors; Foul Called on NBA's Offseason," *Brandweek*, 1 October 2007, 12; Jessica Shambora, "Stroke of Genius," *Fortune*, 10 November 2008, 62–64.

2. Jeneanne Rae, "New Thinking About Consumer Marketing," *BusinessWeek*, 30 June 2009, 16.
3. Werner Reinartz and Wolfgang Ulaga, "How to Sell Services More Profitably," *Harvard Business Review*, May 2008, 90–96.
4. Jung-Ah Lee and Evan Ramstad, "Samsung Pulls Galaxy Tab from Berlin Trade Show," *Wall Street Journal*, 6 September 2011, http://online.wsj.com.
5. Jenna Wortham, "Sending GPS Devices the Way of the Tape Deck?" *New York Times*, 7 July 2009, www.nytimes.com.
6. Michael V. Copeland and Om Malik, "How to Build a Bulletproof Startup," *Business 2.0*, June 2006, www.business2.com.

7. Nicolas Block, Kara Gruver, and David Cooper, "Slimming Innovation Pipelines to Fatten Their Returns," *Harvard Management Update*, August 2007, 3–5.

8. Nanette Byrnes, "Xerox' New Design Team: Customers," *BusinessWeek*, 7 May 2007, 72.

9. David Haigh and Jonathan Knowles, "How to Define Your Brand and Determine Its Value," *Marketing Management*, May/June 2004, 22–28.

10. David Kiley, "Best Global Brands," *BusinessWeek*, 6 August 2007, 56–64.

11. Nina Diamond, John F. Sherry, Albert M. Muñiz, Mary Ann McGrath, Robert V. Kozinets, and Stefania Borghini, "American Girl and the Brand Gestalt: Closing the Loop on Sociocultural Branding Research," *Journal of Marketing*, May 2009, 118–134.

12. Janell M. Kurtz and Cynthia Mehoves, "Whose Name Is It Anyway," *Marketing Management*, January/February 2002, 31–33.

13. Dictionary.com, accessed 24 October 2011, www.dictionary.com.

14. Lawrence L. Garber Jr., Eva M. Hyatt, and Ünal Ö. Boya, "The Effect of Package Shape on Apparent Volume: An Exploratory Study with Implications for Package Design," *Journal of Marketing Theory & Practice*, Summer 2009, 215–234.

15. Margaret Webb Pressler, "Do Not Pry Open Until Christmas: The Hard Truth About Hated 'Clamshell' Packaging," *Washington Post*, 30 November 2006, A1+; Jennifer Saranow, "The Puncture Wound I Got for Christmas," *Wall Street Journal*, 30 December 2004, D1+.

16. General Mills website, accessed 7 September 2011, www.generalmills.com.

17. Betsy Morris and Joan L. Levinstein, "What Makes Apple Golden," *Fortune*, 17 March 2008, 68–74; Bharat N. Anand, "The Value of a Broader Product Portfolio," *Harvard Business Review*, January 2008, 20–22.

18. Erik Brynjolfssson, Yu (Jeffrey) Hu, and Duncan Simester, "Goodbye Pareto Principle, Hello Long Tail: The Effects of Search Costs on the Concentration of Sales," research paper, February 2007, http://papers.ssrn.com.

19. Chris Anderson, "The Long Tail," *Wired*, October 2004, www.wired.com.

20. "About Us," hi5 Networks, accessed 7 September 2011, www.hi5networks.com; Jessi Hempel, "hi5 Guns for Facebook," *Fortune*, 27 October 2008, 14.

21. Andrew Shanahan, "Why Did France Fall in Love with McDonald's?" *The Guardian*, 24 July 2008, www.guardian.co.uk; Carol Matlack, "What's This? The French Love McDonald's?" *BusinessWeek*, 13 January 2003, 50; Shirley Leung, "Armchairs, TVs and Espresso–Is It McDonald's?" *Wall Street Journal*, 30 August 2002, A1, A6.

22. Alicia A. Caldwell, "21 Airlines Fined for Fixing Passenger, Cargo Fees," *Seattle Times*, 5 March 2011, www.seattletimes.com.

23. Eric Anderson and Duncan Simester, "Mind Your Pricing Cues," *Harvard Business Review*, September 96–103.

24. Edward Ramirez and Ronald E. Goldsmith, "Some Antecedents of Price Sensitivity," *Journal of Marketing Theory & Practice*, Summer 2009, 199–213.

25. Elisabeth A. Sullivan, "Value Pricing: Smart Marketers Know Cost-Plus Can Be Costly," *Marketing News*, 15 January 2008, 8.

26. Peter J. Williamson and Ming Zeng, "Value-for-Money Strategies for Recessionary Times," *Harvard Business Review*, March 2009, 66–74.

27. Revionics website, accessed 27 July 2009, www.revionics.com; Amy Cortese, "The Power of Optimal Pricing," *Business 2.0*, September 2002, 68–70.

28. Priceline website, accessed 7 September 2011, www.priceline.com.

29. Ju-Young Kim, Martin Natter, and Martin Spann, "Pay What You Want: A New Participative Pricing Mechanism," *Journal of Marketing*, January 2009, 44–58.

30. John Varcoe, "Lunatics in Charge," *NZ Marketing Magazine*, June 2009, 10.

31. Don Moyer, "That's Going to Cost You," *Harvard Business Review*, May 2009, 132.

32. Sunil Gupta and Carl F. Mela, "What Is a Free Customer Worth?" *Harvard Business Review*, November 2008, 102–109.

33. "How About Free? The Price Point That Is Turning Industries on Their Heads," Knowledge@Wharton, 4 March 2009, http://knowledge.wharton.upenn.edu.

34. Al Ries, "Variable Pricing Is Ultimate Brand-Destruction Machine," *Advertising Age*, 8 June 2009, 11.

35. See note 1.

36. Aubrey Kent and Richard M. Campbell, Jr., "An Introduction to Freeloading: Campus-Area Ambush Marketing," *Sport Marketing Quarterly* 16, no. 2 (2007), 118–122.

37. Adapted from Valerie Bennett and Andrew Capella, "Location-Based Services," IBM website, accessed 27 July 2009, www.ibm.com; David LaGress, "They Know Where You Are," *U.S. News & World Report*, 8 September 2003, 32–38; Christopher Elliott, "Some Rental Cars Are Keeping Tabs on Drivers," *New York Times*, 13 January 2004, C6; Kristi Heim, "Microchips in People, Packaging and Pets Raise Privacy Questions," *Seattle Times*, 18 October 2004, www.seattletimes.com; Andrew Heining and Christa Case, "Are Book Tags a Threat?" *Christian Science Monitor*, 5 October 2004, www.csmonitor.com; Corie Lok, "Wrist Radio Tags," *Technology Review*, November 2004, 25; Brian Albright, "RFID Dominates Frontline's Supply Chain Week," *Frontline Solutions*, November 2003, 10–13.

GLOSSARY

brand A name, term, sign, symbol, design, or combination of those used to identify the products of a firm and to differentiate them from competing products

brand equity The value that a company has built up in a brand

brand extension Applying a successful brand name to a new product category

brand loyalty The degree to which customers continue to purchase a specific brand

brand managers Managers who develop and implement the marketing strategies and programs for specific products or brands

brand marks The portion of brands that cannot be expressed verbally

brand names The portion of brands that can be expressed orally, including letters, words, or numbers

break-even analysis A method of calculating the minimum volume of sales needed at a given price to cover all costs

break-even point Sales volume at a given price that will cover all of a company's costs

bundling Offering several products for a single price that is presumably lower than the total of the products' individual prices

capital items More expensive organizational products with a longer useful life, ranging from office and plant equipment to entire factories

co-branding A partnership between two or more companies to closely link their brand names together for a single product

commercialization Large-scale production and distribution of a product

convenience products Everyday goods and services that people buy frequently, usually without much conscious planning

cost-based pricing A method of setting prices based on production and marketing costs, rather than conditions in the marketplace

discounts Temporary price reductions to stimulate sales or lower prices to encourage certain behaviors such as paying with cash

dynamic pricing Continually adjusting prices to reflect changes in supply and demand

expense items Inexpensive products that organizations generally use within a year of purchase

family branding Using a brand name on a variety of related products

fixed costs Business costs that remain constant regardless of the number of units produced

freemium pricing A hybrid pricing strategy of offering some products for free while charging for others, or offering a product for free to some customers while charging others for it

license An agreement to produce and market another company's product in exchange for a royalty or fee

logo A graphical and/or textual representation of a brand

loss-leader pricing Selling one product at a loss as a way to entice customers to consider other products

national brands Brands owned by manufacturers and distributed nationally

optimal pricing A computer-based pricing method that creates a demand curve for every product to help managers select a price that meets specific marketing objectives

participative pricing Allowing customers to pay the amount they think a product is worth

penetration pricing Introducing a new product at a low price in hopes of building sales volume quickly

price elasticity A measure of the sensitivity of demand to changes in price

private brands Brands that carry the label of a retailer or a wholesaler rather than a manufacturer

product development process A formal process of generating, selecting, developing, and commercializing product ideas

product life cycle Four stages through which a product progresses: introduction, growth, maturity, and decline

product line A series of related products offered by a firm

product mix The complete portfolio of products that a company offers for sale

prototypes Preproduction samples of products used for testing and evaluation

shopping products Fairly important goods and services that people buy less frequently with more planning and comparison

skim pricing Charging a high price for a new product during the introductory stage and lowering the price later

specialty products Particular brands that the buyer especially wants and will seek out, regardless of location or price

test marketing A product development stage in which a product is sold on a limited basis to gauge its market appeal

trademarks Brands that have been given legal protection so that their owners have exclusive rights to their use

value-based pricing A method of setting prices based on customer perceptions of value

variable costs Business costs that increase with the number of units produced

Distribution and Marketing Logistics

Distribution and Marketing Logistics

LEARNING OBJECTIVES   After studying this chapter, you will be able to

1 Explain the role of marketing intermediaries in contemporary business and list the eight primary functions that intermediaries can perform

2 Identify the major types of wholesalers and summarize four trends shaping the future of wholesaling

3 Identify the major retailing formats and summarize six trends shaping the future of retailing

4 Explain the strategic decisions that manufacturers must make when choosing distribution channels

5 Identify five key attributes of distribution channel design and management

6 Highlight the major components of physical distribution and logistics

MyBizLab

Where you see MyBizLab in this chapter, go to www.mybizlab.com for additional activities on the topic being discussed.

BEHIND THE SCENES COSTCO MAKES THE GOOD LIFE MORE AFFORDABLE

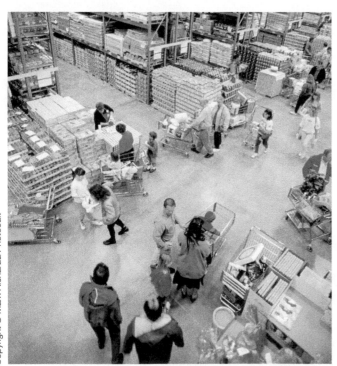

Copyright © Mark Richards/Photoedit

Costco shoppers have learned to look for great buys on both every-day items and an ever-changing mix of luxury and specialty goods.

www.costco.com

With an unusual mix of low prices and quality goods, Costco Wholesale has become the country's largest and most profitable warehouse club chain. The company knows that low prices on high-quality, high-end merchandise can transcend the common notion of "discount." And, in what amounts to a treasure hunt played out along Costco's cement-floor aisles, the high/low shopping experience is a powerful elixir for middle-class shoppers.

Once new members get the hang of the treasure hunt mentality, they get hooked on Costco, because even though they don't know what will be on display, they're sure it will be something at a price that will make the good life more affordable. Like other warehouse clubs, Costco Wholesale sells a mix of everything from giant boxes of cereal to patio furniture. In fact, Costco often asks vendors to change their factory runs to produce specially built packages that are bigger and less expensive. Unlike with other warehouse clubs, Costco shoppers can occasionally find $10,000 diamond rings and grand pianos along with mouthwash and laundry detergent. Costco also entices shoppers with in-store bakeries and ready-to-eat dishes, as well as optical departments, insurance, and other services that reflect the same high-quality, low-price model as the packaged merchandise.

If you were in charge of strategy at Costco, how would you keep Costco on the leading edge of retailing? How would you integrate your physical retail stores with your online e-commerce operation? What could you do to keep your bargain-conscious but demanding customers coming back for more?[1]

INTRODUCTION

Marketing intermediaries such as Costco (profiled in the chapter-opening Behind the Scenes) play an essential role in marketing products created by other companies. This chapter explores the many contributions these intermediaries make, both at the retailing stage that is visible to all consumers and at the less visible but no less important wholesaling stage. Manufacturers and other producers need to understand the distribution process in order to select the right intermediaries and work with them effectively. And, of course, wholesalers and retailers are business entities themselves, with their own strategic questions and operating challenges.

The Role of Marketing Intermediaries

A *distribution channel*, or *marketing channel*, is an organized network of firms that work together to get goods and services from producer to customer. Whether you're selling digital music files or scrap iron stripped out of old ships, your **distribution strategy**, or overall plan for moving products to buyers, will play a major role in your success.

Think of all the products you buy: food, cosmetics, clothing, sports equipment, train tickets, gasoline, stationery, appliances, music, books, and all the rest. How many of these products do you buy directly from the producer? For most people, the answer is not many. Most companies that create products do not sell these goods directly to the final users. Instead, producers in many industries work with **marketing intermediaries** to bring their products to market. Even some service companies rely on other firms to perform services on their behalf.

WHOLESALING VERSUS RETAILING

Intermediaries can be grouped into two general types: wholesalers and retailers. **Wholesalers** sell to organizational customers, including other wholesalers, companies, government agencies, and educational institutions. In turn, the customers of wholesalers either resell the products or use them to make products of their own.

Unlike wholesalers, **retailers** primarily sell products to consumers for personal use. Terminology in the distribution field can get a bit confusing, starting with the multiple uses of the term *wholesale*. For instance, even though Costco and other warehouse-type stores often use the "wholesale" label to describe themselves, they function as both wholesalers and retailers simultaneously. Small-business owners, for instance, are enthusiastic Costco shoppers because the store is a low-cost place to buy supplies and equipment. With these shoppers, Costco is functioning as a wholesaler. However, when selling to consumers, Costco is technically operating as a retailer, not a wholesaler. The distinction is important because business strategies for wholesaling and retailing are dramatically different in many ways. Even when they buy the same products, consumers and organizations usually make purchases for different reasons. Because their motivations and expectations are different, consumers (reached by retailers) and organizations (reached by wholesalers) don't respond to marketing programs the same way.

CONTRIBUTIONS OF MARKETING INTERMEDIARIES

Wholesalers and retailers are instrumental in creating three of the four forms of utility: They provide the items customers need in a convenient location (place utility), they save customers the time of having to contact each manufacturer to purchase a

1 | **LEARNING OBJECTIVE**

Explain the role of marketing intermediaries in contemporary business, and list the eight primary functions that intermediaries can perform.

distribution strategy A firm's overall plan for moving products through intermediaries and on to final customers

marketing intermediaries Businesspeople and organizations that assist in moving and marketing goods and services between producers and consumers

wholesalers Intermediaries that sell products to other intermediaries for resale or to organizations for internal use

retailers Intermediaries that sell goods and services to individuals for their own personal use good (time utility), and they provide an efficient process for transferring products from the producer to the customer (possession utility). In addition to creating utility, wholesalers and retailers perform the following distribution functions:

- **Matching buyers and sellers.** By making sellers' products available to multiple buyers, intermediaries such as Costco reduce the number of transactions between producers and customers. In the business-to-business market, the industrial distributor Grainger (www.grainger.com) is a good example of the enormous scale that can be achieved in bringing buyers and sellers together. Boasting a portfolio of more than 1 million products, Grainger connects some 3,000 suppliers with 2 million organizational customers.[2] These customers are saved the time and trouble of working with multiple suppliers, and the product suppliers get access to more customers than all but the very largest of them could ever hope to reach on their own. Although "cutting out the middleman" is sometimes used as a promotional slogan, intermediaries such as Grainger can actually make commerce more efficient by reducing the number of contact points between buyers and sellers (see Exhibit 1).

- **Providing market information.** Retail intermediaries, such as Amazon and Macy's, collect valuable data about customer purchases: who buys, how often, and how much.

| EXHIBIT 1 | How Intermediaries Simplify Commerce |

Intermediaries actually reduce the price customers pay for many goods and services because they reduce the number of contacts between producers and consumers that would otherwise be necessary. They also create place, time, and possession utility.

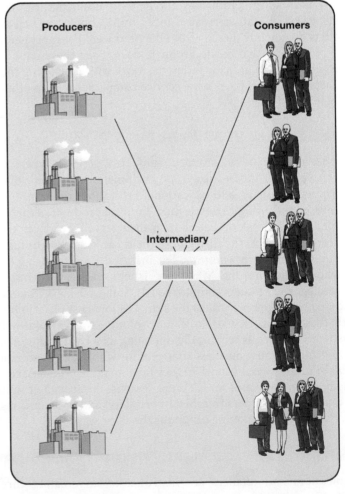

Number of transactions required when consumers buy directly from manufacturers

Number of transactions required when buying is conducted via intermediary

Source: Adapted from Philip Kotler, *Marketing Management*, 10th ed. (Upper Saddle River, N.J.: Pearson Prentice Hall, 2000), 491.

For example, e-commerce records and data from "frequent shopper" cards help retailers spot buying patterns, providing vital market information they can then share with producers to optimize product mixes and promotional efforts.

- **Providing promotional and sales support.** Many intermediaries assist with advertising, in-store displays, and other promotional efforts for some or all of the products they sell. Some also employ sales representatives who can perform a number of selling and customer relationship functions.
- **Gathering assortments of goods.** Many intermediaries receive bulk shipments from producers and break them into more convenient units (known as *breaking bulk*) by sorting, standardizing, and dividing bulk quantities into smaller packages.
- **Transporting and storing products.** Intermediaries often maintain inventories of merchandise that they acquire from producers so they can quickly fill customers' orders. In many cases, retailers purchase this merchandise from wholesalers who, in addition to breaking bulk, may also transport the goods from the producer to the retail outlets.
- **Assuming risks.** When intermediaries accept goods from manufacturers, they usually take on the risks associated with damage, theft, product perishability (in the sense of tangible goods that are vulnerable to rotting, for instance), and obsolescence.
- **Providing financing.** Large intermediaries sometimes provide loans to smaller producers.
- **Completing product solutions.** In some industries, producers rely on a class of intermediaries often called *value-added resellers (VARs)* or *system integrators* to complete or customize solutions for customers. For instance, Iris Professional Services (www.irisproservices.com) is a VAR for Apple, meaning it can combine Apple computers with other hardware and software elements to create information systems for its clients.[3] By partnering with companies such as Iris, Apple is able to reach a wider range of customers without the need to develop specialized expertise in multiple industries.
- **Facilitating transactions and supporting customers.** Intermediaries can perform a variety of functions that help with the selection, purchase, and use of products. Commercial real estate brokers, for example, can negotiate prices and contract terms on behalf of buyers and sellers. In a variety of industries, intermediaries help customers select the products that fit their needs and then provide customer support and technical assistance after the sale.

✔ Checkpoint

LEARNING OBJECTIVE 1: Explain the role of marketing intermediaries in contemporary business, and list the eight primary functions that intermediaries can perform.

SUMMARY: Intermediaries can be responsible for any and all aspects of distribution, one of the key elements in any firm's marketing mix. The two major categories are *wholesalers*, which buy from producers and sell to retailers, to other wholesalers, and to organizational customers such as businesses, government agencies, and institutions; and *retailers*, which buy from producers or wholesalers and sell the products to the final consumers. These marketing intermediaries bring products to market and help ensure that the goods and services are available in the right time, place, and amount. Depending on their position in the channel, intermediaries can perform the eight key functions of matching buyers and sellers; providing market information; providing promotional and sales support; sorting, standardizing, and dividing merchandise; transporting and storing products; assuming risks; providing financing; and completing production solutions.

CRITICAL THINKING: (1) Why wouldn't Apple develop the expertise to create professional video studios and other solutions that its channel partners now develop? (2) How can Costco be both a wholesaler and a retailer at the same time?

2 **LEARNING OBJECTIVE**

Identify the major types of wholesalers, and summarize four trends shaping the future of wholesaling.

Wholesaling and Industrial Distribution

Although largely unseen by consumers, wholesaling is a huge presence in the economy. More than 5 million people work in wholesaling in the United States, and the sector sees several trillion dollars in sales volume every year.[4] By connecting producers with retailers and organizational customers, wholesalers play a vital role in nearly every industry in the world.

MAJOR TYPES OF WHOLESALERS

merchant wholesalers
Independent wholesalers that take legal title to goods they distribute

Most wholesalers are independent companies that can be classified as *merchant wholesalers*, *agents*, or *brokers*. The majority of wholesalers are **merchant wholesalers**, independently owned businesses that buy from producers, take legal title to the goods, and then resell them to retailers or to organizational buyers. Most merchant wholesalers are small businesses, but the field includes a handful of multibillion-dollar firms such as Grainger in industrial supplies, Avnet (www.avnet.com) in electronic components, McKesson (www.mckesson.com) in health care, and Supervalu (www.supervalu.com) in groceries.

Full-service merchant wholesalers provide a wide variety of services, such as storage, selling, order processing, delivery, and promotional support. *Rack jobbers*, for example, are full-service merchant wholesalers that set up displays in retail outlets, stock inventory, and perform other services such as marking prices on merchandise. *Limited-service merchant wholesalers*, on the other hand, provide fewer services. Natural resources such as lumber, grain, and coal are usually marketed through a class of limited-service wholesalers called *drop shippers*, which take ownership but not physical possession of the goods they handle.

Merchant wholesalers can also be distinguished by their customers. Supervalu and others that sell primarily to other intermediaries are usually known in the trade simply as *wholesalers*. In contrast, Avnet and others that sell goods to companies for use in their own products and operations are usually called **distributors**.

distributors Merchant wholesalers that sell products to organizational customers for internal operations or the production of other goods, rather than to retailers for resale

Unlike merchant wholesalers, **agents and brokers** never actually own the products they handle, and they perform fewer services. Their primary role is to bring buyers and sellers together; they are generally paid a commission (a percentage of the money received) for arranging sales. Producers of industrial parts often sell to business customers through brokers. *Manufacturers' representatives*, another type of agent, sell various noncompeting products to customers in a specific region. By representing several manufacturers' products, these reps achieve enough volume to justify the cost of a direct sales call.

agents and brokers Independent wholesalers that do not take title to the goods they distribute but may or may not take possession of those goods

THE OUTLOOK FOR WHOLESALING

The business of wholesaling is changing in ways that are helping some wholesalers and threatening others. Four trends in particular are likely to reshape the wholesaling business in the coming years:

- **Integrated logistics management.** The outsourcing trend is definitely having an impact in the wholesaling sector as *third-party logistics (3PL)* firms continue to take over a wide range of tasks in supply chain management, including not only traditional wholesaling activities but also order fulfillment, product repair, customer service, and other functions. These 3PL firms have been growing rapidly in recent years, as more companies look to offload supply chain functions to focus on core business activities.[5]

The emergence of 3PL is coming from two directions, as transportation companies such as UPS and FedEx and wholesalers such as Supervalu and McKesson expand the scope of their services. In fact, you'd be hard pressed from McKesson's description of itself to recognize that the company is in fact a major wholesaler, referring to itself as a "health-care services company."[6]

- **Threat of disintermediation.** For many years, and particularly since the advent of the Internet and the growth of e-commerce, various observers have predicted the widespread **disintermediation** of wholesalers, meaning their role would be taken over by manufacturers on the upstream end or by customers (retailers and other organizational buyers) on the downstream end. While this has certainly happened in specific instances in various industries, and the share of wholesaling activity performed by independent wholesalers appears to be shrinking somewhat, wholesalers as a group have not disappeared to the extent that some predicted.[7] Even as the sector evolves, intermediaries will continue to play an integral role in the distribution process as long as they can add value and perform essential services more effectively and more efficiently than either manufacturers or customers.[8]

- **Unbundling of services.** The conventional way that merchant wholesalers generate revenue and earn profits is by purchasing products from manufacturers at a discount and reselling them to retailers or organizational buyers at a markup. Whatever services a wholesaler provides are covered by that markup. However, a growing number of wholesaling customers would like to see these services "unbundled" so they can pay for specific distribution services individually.[9] If this trend catches on, it could change the business model for many wholesalers.

- **Industry consolidation.** With all the forces at play in the marketplace, consolidation seems likely as large firms with economies of scale buy up or drive out smaller, less-competitive firms. In addition, a growing number of customers are pursuing *strategic sourcing*, in which they forge closer relationships with a smaller number of strategic distribution partners.[10]

disintermediation
The replacement of intermediaries by producers, customers, or other intermediaries when those other parties can perform channel functions more effectively or efficiently

✔ Checkpoint

LEARNING OBJECTIVE 2: Identify the major types of wholesalers, and summarize four trends shaping the future of wholesaling.

SUMMARY: Most wholesalers can be classified as *merchant wholesalers*, *agents*, or *brokers*. Merchant wholesalers are independently owned businesses that buy from producers, take legal title to the goods, and then resell them to retailers or to organizational buyers. Merchant wholesalers can be distinguished by level of service (*full-service* versus *limited-service*) and target customers (*wholesalers* that sell goods to retailers for the purpose of then reselling them to consumers and *distributors* that sell goods to organizations for internal operation use or to make other products). In contrast to merchant wholesalers, agents and brokers do not assume ownership but focus on bringing buyers and sellers together. Four trends shaping wholesaling are integrated logistics management, the threat of disintermediation, the unbundling of services, and industry consolidation.

CRITICAL THINKING: (1) Why does McKesson promote itself as a health care services company, rather than as a logistics company? (2) Why might a manufacturer choose to hire a third-party logistics firm rather than a conventional wholesaler or distributor?

IT'S YOUR BUSINESS: (1) Considering the forces shaping wholesaling, would you consider a career in this sector? Why or why not? (2) If your family ran a small industrial products wholesaler that was facing the threat of disintermediation, how would you respond?

KEY TERMS TO KNOW: merchant wholesalers, distributors, agents and brokers, disintermediation

Identify the major retailing formats, and summarize six trends shaping the future of retailing.

Retailing

In addition to providing convenient access to products and supporting consumers with a variety of presale and postsale services, retailers play a major role in the buying process because many consumer buying decisions are made in the retail setting. Consequently, retailing involves a blend of the distribution and customer communication elements of the marketing mix. The term *shopper marketing*, or *in-store marketing*, refers to communication efforts directed at consumers while they are in the retail setting. These efforts can range from printed signs to in-store video screens to smartphone apps that help shoppers find products or stores in a mall, for example.[11] To be sure, the degree to which decision making occurs in the store varies across product categories, consumers, and purchasing situations. For example, consumers engaged in home remodeling projects typically have a clear idea of what they want to buy before they get to the store, so the in-store decisions relate more to specific colors and textures than to broad product categories.[12] In other instances, in-store signs, product labels, and other factors can influence the types of products and specific brands that consumers choose.

Given the importance of the shopping environment, retailers spend considerable time and money crafting physical spaces and shopping experiences that are intended to shape consumer behavior, addressing everything from lighting and color palettes to music, aromas, and employee attire. No detail seems to be too small. For instance, the attractiveness of employees and even other shoppers can influence consumer choices. Although consumers are generally put off by the realization that other shoppers have touched the products on display in a store, if they see an *attractive* person touch a product, people tend to think more highly of that product.[13]

RETAILING FORMATS

With so much effort directed toward influencing buying decisions across so many categories of products and diverse segments in the consumer market, the retail sector has evolved into a dizzying array of store types and formats. Much of this evolution can be explained by a concept called the **wheel of retailing**. In this model, an innovative retailer with low operating costs attracts a following by offering low prices and limited service. As this store adds more services to broaden its appeal, its prices creep upward, opening the door for a new generation of lower-priced competitors. Eventually, these competitors also upgrade their operations and are replaced by still other lower-priced stores that later follow the same upward pattern.[14]

For instance, Walmart reshaped retailing with low prices enabled by the company's extraordinary abilities at cost control and efficiency but now finds itself facing new low-price competition from the likes of Family Dollar Stores and Dollar General. For instance, after having added more than 4,000 stores over the past decade, Family Dollar gained market share during the recent recession, as more shoppers turned to it for food and household essentials.[15]

Regardless of product offerings or target markets, all retailing efforts can be divided into *store* formats—based in physical store locations—and *nonstore* formats—which take place anywhere and everywhere outside of physical stores. Exhibit 2 summarizes the most important store formats. **Department stores** are the classic major retailers in the United States, with the likes of Bloomingdale's, Macy's, Nordstrom, Dillard's, and Kohl's generally offering a range of clothing, accessories, bedding, and other products for the home. **Specialty stores** such as jewelers and bicycle shops offer a limited number of product lines but an extensive selection of brands, styles, sizes, models, colors, materials, and prices within each line. Huge specialty stores such as The Home Depot and Bed Bath & Beyond that tend to dominate those sectors of retail are known as *category killers*.

Retailers can also be distinguished by their pricing strategies. Family Dollar Stores and Walmart, for example, are

wheel of retailing An evolutionary process by which stores that feature low prices gradually upgrade until they no longer appeal to price-sensitive shoppers and are replaced by a new generation of leaner, low-price competitors

department stores Large stores that carry a variety of products in multiple categories, such as clothing, house wares, gifts, bedding, and furniture

specialty stores Stores that carry only a particular type of goods, often with deep selection in those specific categories

EXHIBIT 2	Retail Store Formats

The term *retailer* covers many types of outlets. This table shows some of the most common types.

Retail Format	Key Features	Examples
Department store	Store that offers a wide variety of merchandise under one roof in departmentalized sections and many customer services	Dillard's, J.C. Penney, Nordstrom
Specialty store	Store that offers a complete selection in a narrow range of merchandise, often with extensive customer services	Payless Shoes, R.E.I.
Category killer	Type of specialty store that focuses on specific products on a massive scale and dominating retail sales in respective product categories	Office Depot, Bed Bath & Beyond, Lowe's
Discount store	Store that offers a wide variety of merchandise at low prices with relatively fewer services	Dollar General, Target, Walmart
Off-price store	Store that offers designer and brand-name merchandise at low prices and with relatively fewer services	T.J. Maxx, Marshalls
Convenience store	Store that offers limited range of convenience goods, long service hours, and quick checkouts	7-Eleven, AM-PM
Factory/retail outlet	Large outlet store that sells discontinued items, overruns, and factory seconds	Nordstrom Rack, Nike outlet store
Supermarket	Large, self-service store that offers a wide selection of food and nonfood merchandise	Kroger, Safeway
Hypermarket	Giant store that offers both food and general merchandise at discount prices	Walmart Super Centers, Carrefour
Warehouse club	Large, warehouse-style store that sells food and general merchandise at discount prices; some require club membership	Sam's Club, Costco
Online retailer	Web-based store that offers anything from a single product line to comprehensive selections in multiple product areas; can be web-only (e.g., Amazon.com) or integrated with physical stores (e.g., REI.com)	Amazon.com, REI.com

discount stores, which feature a wide variety of aggressively priced everyday merchandise. **Off-price retailers** such as Filene's Basement and T.J. Maxx take a slightly different approach, offering more limited selections of higher-end products such as designer label clothing at steeply discounted prices.[16]

In the nonstore arena, **online retailers** can be either Internet-only operations such as fashion retailer Bluefly (www.bluefly.com) or online extensions of store-based operations, such as the sites run by J.C. Penney (www.jcpenney.com) and other department stores. Online stores still account for less than 10 percent of U.S. retail sales overall, but they have become a major force in some product categories—such as books, for example, where online sales now outpace store sales.[17] Electronic commerce, or **e-commerce**, is not limited to retailing, to be sure. Companies ranging from small specialty wholesalers to the world's largest distribution firms rely on the Internet as well.

Meanwhile, the mail-order firms that inspired e-commerce are still going strong in many industries. Attractive catalogs are a powerful marketing tool, but printing and mailing them is expensive, so many mail-order firms are working to integrate their catalog efforts with e-commerce to maximize sales. Vending machines and interactive kiosks are an important format for many food and convenience goods as well. Redbox, for example, now has nearly 30,000 movie rental machines positioned around the United States.[18]

discount stores Retailers that sell a variety of everyday goods below the market price by keeping their overhead low

off-price retailers Stores that sell designer labels and other fashionable products at steep discounts

online retailers Companies that use e-commerce technologies to sell over the Internet; includes Internet-only retailers and the online arm of store-based retailers

e-commerce The application of Internet technologies to wholesaling and retailing

THE OUTLOOK FOR RETAILING

Retailing has always been a challenging field, and it's not getting any easier for many companies in the sector. Of course, disruption for some can mean opportunities for others. Retailers that survive and succeed over the long term tend to do the same things well: (1) maintaining a clear sense of purpose in the minds of target customers, (2) crafting an overall shopping experience that complements the purchases customers are making, (3) protecting the credibility of the retail brand, and (4) adapting to consumer trends without overreacting to short-term fads.[19]

Here are six major forces shaping the future of retailing:

- **Overcapacity.** In too many categories, there are simply too many stores to support current levels of business activity. Shopping malls in particular, those icons of contemporary consumer life, have become a symbol for much of what ails retailing. A furious spate of mall building in the past couple decades left the country with hundreds more malls than the economy could really support, at the same time as the rise of online retailing and the growth of stand-alone discounters were drawing shoppers away from malls. In fact, 100 or so malls across the country are now considered "dead" because they have such low revenues and high vacancy rates.[20] However, mall operators are learning to adapt to the loss of department store anchors, web-enabled shopping, and other challenges. Top-performing malls remain profitable retailing centers.[21]

- **Continued growth in online retailing.** The growth rate of online retailing has outpaced store-based retailing in recent years, and that trend is likely to continue. Not only are more consumers buying online, but many store-based retailers are trying to reduce their fixed costs by shifting more activity to the Internet.[22] The companies most likely to succeed online are store-based retailers with strong reputations and loyal customers, Internet-only retailers such as Amazon (www.amazon.com) and the jewelry store Blue Nile (www.bluenile.com) that have achieved the economies of scale necessary to be profitable, and niche players that can combine unusual products and great customer service—sometimes while operating as affiliates of major players such as Amazon.[23]

- **Growth of multichannel retailing.** The growth in online retailing reflects the fact that today's consumers increasingly combine online and offline shopping, such as researching products online and then making the purchase in a physical store or the other way around.[24] To stay in contact with consumers as they move from one retail channel to the next, more companies now emphasize **multichannel retailing**, a term for any coordinated effort to reach customers through more than one retail channel.[25]

- **Format innovations.** As companies endlessly search for the magic formula to attract customers and generate profitable sales, they continue to experiment with retailing formats. Two interesting innovations are *hybrid stores* that combine different types of retailers or different retail companies in the same facility and *pop-up stores* that exist for only a short time and are designed more as attention-getting events than as ongoing retail operations.[26]

- **Retail theater.** Increasingly, retail stores aren't just places to buy things; they're becoming places to research new technologies, learn about cooking, socialize, or simply be entertained for a few minutes while going through the drudgery of picking out the week's groceries—a tactic known as **retail theater.** Many of Apple's retail outlets look more like art galleries than stores, and they offer a multifaceted shopping and learning experience for both kids and adults.[27] CVS's Beauty 360 shops, which feel more like theater stages than traditional drug stores, give customers greater opportunities to learn about and experiment with various cosmetics.[28]

- **Threat of disintermediation.** Like wholesalers, retailers face the threat of disintermediation if suppliers or customers don't think they add sufficient value or if other types of retailers can do the job better.

multichannel retailing
Coordinated efforts to reach consumers through more than one retail channel

retail theater The addition of entertainment or education aspects to the retail experience

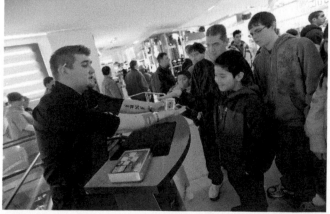

Product demonstrations, in-store classes, and other "retail theater" events help attract shoppers and build store loyalty.

✓ **Checkpoint**

LEARNING OBJECTIVE 3: Identify the major retailing formats, and summarize six trends shaping the future of retailing.

SUMMARY: Retailers come in many shapes and sizes, but the significant store formats include department stores, specialty stores, category killers, discount stores, and off-price retailers. The two most widely known nonstore retailers are online retailers and mail-order firms. The future of retailing is being shaped by such forces as overcapacity, continued growth in online retailing, the growth of multichannel retailing, format innovations such as hybrid stores, the use of retail theater, and the threat of intermediation.

CRITICAL THINKING: (1) Would it ever make sense for Amazon to open retail stores? Why or why not? (2) Moving into the future, what effect is online retailing likely to have on the oversupply of retail store space in the United States?

IT'S YOUR BUSINESS: (1) How have your shopping patterns changed in the past five years, in terms of how you research purchases and where you make those purchases? (2) Roughly what percentage of all your purchases do you make online? What could store-based retailers do to attract a greater portion of your business?

KEY TERMS TO KNOW: wheel of retailing, department stores, specialty stores, discount stores, off-price retailers, online retailers, e-commerce, multichannel retailing, retail theater

Distribution Strategies

 LEARNING OBJECTIVE

Explain the strategic decisions that manufacturers must make when choosing distribution channels.

Manufacturers and other producers face some critical decisions when selecting marketing channels for their product. Should they sell directly to end users or rely on intermediaries? Which intermediaries should they choose? Should they try to sell their products in every available outlet or limit distribution to a few exclusive outlets? Should they use more than one channel?

Building an effective channel system can take years and, as with all other marketing relationships, it requires commitment. Successful *trading partners*, a general term for any group of companies involved in a distribution network, work to establish relationships that are mutually beneficial and built on trust.

The ideal **distribution mix**—number and type of intermediaries—varies widely from industry to industry and even from company to company within the same industry. For example, Black & Decker (www.blackanddecker.com) distributes its power tools through hundreds of hardware stores and home centers such as Lowe's and The Home Depot along with a wide range of online retailers, including Amazon.com.[29] Black & Decker sells to both consumers and professionals; it wants to reach a broad audience, and its products don't require extensive support from retailers, so these mass market intermediaries make perfect sense. In contrast, Felder (www.feldergroupusa.com), an Austrian company that manufacturers top-of-the-line woodworking machines for professional use, makes its products available through only three company-owned stores in the entire United States.[30]

distribution mix A combination of intermediaries and channels a producer uses to reach target customers

CUSTOMER NEEDS AND EXPECTATIONS

The primary function of distribution channels is delivering value to customers, so channel strategy decisions should start with customer needs and expectations.[31] For instance, how do customers want and expect to purchase your product? If you have a food product, for example, are customers willing to drive to specialty stores to buy it, or does it need to be available in their regular grocery stores if you're to have any hope of selling it? Do customers expect to sample or try on products before they buy? Do they need help from trained product experts? What other goods and services do customers expect to be able to purchase at the same time or from the same supplier? By understanding these needs and expectations, producers can work backward, from their final customers back to their production facilities, to determine the right mix of channel features and functions.

PRODUCT SUPPORT REQUIREMENTS

Products vary widely in the amount of skilled support they may require before and after a sale. Laboratory instruments such as mass spectrometers require significant technical skills to sell and to support after the sale, which is why companies that make them, such as Agilent Technologies (www.agilent.com) generally sell them through their own salesforces.

SEGMENTATION, TARGETING, AND POSITIONING

Just as producers segment markets, choose target segments, and try to position their products within those segments, marketing intermediaries make strategic marketing decisions regarding their own businesses. For instance, Super Jock 'n Jill (www.superjocknjill.com) an athletic shoe retailer in Seattle, focuses on quality shoes and clothing for people who are serious about physical fitness. The store offers clinics on nutrition and injury prevention, sponsors races and running clubs, posts race results on its website, and takes other steps to support local walkers and runners.[32]

Super Jock 'n Jill doesn't sell shoes from its website because the company emphasizes individualized analysis and fitting by knowledgeable sales staff—and it offers the almost unheard-of option of letting shoppers lace on shoes and go for a run to test comfort and performance under real-life conditions. In other words, if you produce mass-market sneakers that are more about fashion than performance, this store won't help you reach your target audience.

COMPETITORS' DISTRIBUTION CHANNELS

Marketing managers must consider the distribution decisions that competitors have already made or are likely to make in the future. For instance, if you are a new producer trying to break into a particular market, you need to encourage buyers to consider your goods along with the products they already know about, so putting your products side-by-side with the competition in physical or online venues is probably the right choice. In other cases, you might want to distance yourself from competitors, either to make direct comparisons more difficult or to avoid being associated with competitive products.

Of course, marketing intermediaries have their own decisions to make about which products to carry and how to allocate their finite "bandwidth," whether it's the number of sales representatives or physical shelf space in a retail store. Because of these capacity limitations in the channel, producers often compete for the attention and resources of intermediaries. In some industries, channel capacity is at such a premium that retailers can demand payments from producers in exchange for carrying their products for an agreed-upon length of time. These *slotting allowances* are now common in the grocery business, for example, particularly for new products. Retailers are naturally reluctant to give up shelf space to unproven products, so slotting allowances help offset the financial risk of bringing in new products. Slotting allowances have grown common enough, in fact, that economic policymakers have begun to investigate their potential impact on competition and consumer prices.[33]

REAL-TIME UPDATES
Learn More by Visiting This Website

See how innovative retailers are embracing social media

Get an insider's view on how retailers use social media to find, connect with, and satisfy shoppers. Go to http://real-timeupdates .com/bia6 and click on "Learn More."If you are using MyBizLab, you can access Real-Time Updates within the chapter or under Student Study Tools.

ESTABLISHED INDUSTRY PATTERNS AND REQUIREMENTS

Over the years, all industries develop certain patterns of distribution. If you try to "buck the system," you might uncover a profitable new opportunity—or you might fail to reach your target customers entirely. Specific industries have other considerations as well, such as the need to get perishable food items to retail locations quickly or government regulations that dictate how and where certain products (hazardous chemicals and pharmaceuticals, for example) can be sold.

 Checkpoint

LEARNING OBJECTIVE 4: Explain the strategic decisions that manufacturers must make when choosing distribution channels.

SUMMARY: Defining a distribution strategy requires consideration of such issues as customer needs and expectations; product support requirements; segmentation, targeting, and positioning objectives; competitors' distribution channels; and established distribution patterns and requirements.

CRITICAL THINKING: (1) Would two manufacturers trying to reach the same customer segment with similar products use identical distribution mixes? Why or why not? (2) Is channel conflict necessarily always bad for everyone involved? Explain your answer.

IT'S YOUR BUSINESS: (1) You've probably seen television commercials advertising products that are "not available in stores." How does that lack of availability in stores affect your perception of those products? (2) Would knowing that a manufacturer had to pay a retailer to gain shelf space for a particular product change your perception of that product? Why or why not?

KEY TERM TO KNOW: distribution mix

Considerations in Channel Design and Management

5 **LEARNING OBJECTIVE**

Identify five key attributes of distribution channel design and management.

In addition to the strategic considerations discussed so far in this chapter, marketing managers need to consider five attributes that help define the function and effectiveness of any distribution channel: channel length, market coverage, distribution costs, channel conflict, and channel organization and control.

CHANNEL LENGTH

As you no doubt sense by now, distribution channels come in all shapes and sizes. Some channels are short and simple; others are long and complex. Many businesses purchase goods they use in their operations directly from producers, so those distribution channels are short. In contrast, the channels for consumer goods are usually longer and more complex (see Exhibit 3) on the next page.

The four primary channels for consumer goods are

- **Producer to consumer.** Producers that sell directly to consumers through catalogs, telemarketing, infomercials, and the Internet are using the shortest, simplest distribution channel. By selling directly to consumers, for example, Dell gains more control over pricing, promotion, service, and delivery. Although this approach eliminates payments to channel members, it also forces producers to handle distribution functions such as storing inventory and delivering products.

| EXHIBIT 3 | Common Distribution Channel Models |

Producers can choose from a variety of distribution channel configurations. Channels in consumer markets tend to be longer (with more participants) than channels in organizational markets.

Consumer goods and services

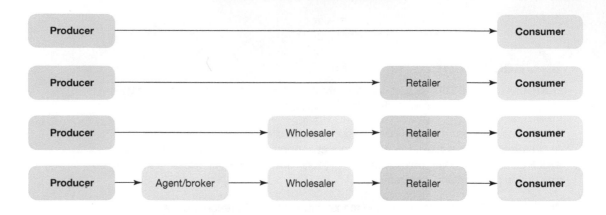

Organizational goods and services

AP Photo/Rene Macura

Marketers of luxury products often use exclusive distribution through carefully selected stores to ensure an optimum shopping experience for their customers.

- **Producer to retailer to consumer.** Producers that don't want to be involved in sales to consumers can sell their products to retailers, who then resell them to consumers.
- **Producer to wholesaler to retailer to consumer.** Manufacturers or suppliers of supermarket and pharmaceutical items often rely on two intermediary levels to reach consumers. They sell their products to wholesalers such as Supervalu, which in turn sell to the retailers. This approach works particularly well for small producers that lack the resources to sell or deliver merchandise to individual retail sites. It is also beneficial to retailers that lack the space to store container-size shipments of each product they sell.
- **Producer to agent/broker to wholesaler to retailer to consumer.** Additional channel levels are common in certain industries, such as agriculture, where specialists are required to negotiate transactions or to perform interim functions such as sorting, grading, or subdividing the goods.

MARKET COVERAGE

The appropriate market coverage—the number of wholesalers or retailers that will carry a product—depends on a number of factors in the marketing strategy. Inexpensive convenience goods or organizational supplies such as computer paper and pens sell best if they are available in as many outlets as possible. Such **intensive distribution** requires wholesalers and retailers of many types. In contrast, shopping goods such as home appliances and autos require different market coverage, because customers shop for such products by comparing features and prices. For these items, the best strategy is usually **selective distribution**, selling through a limited number of outlets that can give the product adequate sales and service support. If producers of expensive specialty or technical products do not sell directly to customers, they may choose **exclusive distribution**, offering products in only one outlet in each market area. With any of these approaches, producers need to choose the optimum number of outlets carefully to balance cost and market coverage and then continue to monitor market conditions to maintain a healthy balance.

intensive distribution A market coverage strategy that tries to place a product in as many outlets as possible

selective distribution A market coverage strategy that uses a limited number of carefully chosen outlets to distribute products

exclusive distribution A market coverage strategy that gives intermediaries exclusive rights to sell a product in a specific geographic area

DISTRIBUTION COSTS

Performing all the functions that are handled by intermediaries requires time and resources, so cost plays a major role in determining channel selection. Small or new companies often cannot afford to hire a salesforce large enough to sell directly to end users or to call on a host of retail outlets. Neither can they afford to build large warehouses and distribution centers to store large shipments of goods. These firms need the help of intermediaries, who can spread the cost of such activities across a number of products. To cover their costs and turn a profit, intermediaries generally buy products at a discount and then resell them at higher prices, although as noted earlier, some wholesaling customers are starting to push for per-item cost structures.

CHANNEL CONFLICT

Individual channel members naturally focus on running their own businesses as profitably as possible, which can lead to **channel conflict**, or disagreement over rights and responsibilities of the organizations in a distribution channel. Channel conflict may arise for a number of reasons, such as producers providing inadequate support to their channel partners; markets being oversaturated with intermediaries; producers trying to expand sales by adding additional channels, either on their own or through new intermediaries; or some intermediaries bearing the cost of developing new markets or promoting products only to see the sales revenue go to other intermediaries.

channel conflict Disagreement or tension between two or more members in a distribution channel, such as competition between channel partners trying to reach the same group of customers

For example, conflict between full-service and discount or online retailers continues to be an issue because shoppers can often take advantage of the opportunity to visit full-service retailers to examine products and get information from product experts—and they buy at lower prices from discounters or online stores. The full-service retailers not only lose the sale but end up helplessly helping their competitors make those sales—and websites and shopping apps on mobile phones are making this problem even worse for them.

CHANNEL ORGANIZATION AND CONTROL

To minimize costs and the potential for channel conflict, channel partners can take steps to work out issues of organization and control. Without some degree of coordination, the various companies involved will pursue their own economic interests, often to the detriment of the channel as a whole.

Producers and intermediaries can achieve this coordination through **marketing systems**, in which the channel participants agree to operate as a cohesive system under the leadership of one of the participants.[34] The agreement can be brought about through *ownership* (when the production and distribution firms are owned by a single company), *contracts* (when the participants have formal agreements that specify their rights and responsibilities, such as the franchising agreements, and *economic power* (when one player is so big that its

marketing systems Arrangements by which channel partners coordinate their activities under the leadership of one of the partners economic presence is enough to encourage or even force cooperation from the other participants in the channel).[35]

For example, one of the fundamentals of Costco's success is that it sells products in such high volume that many producers can't afford *not* to accommodate Costco's demands for specific price points and packaging configurations. If they don't play by Costco's rules, so to speak, they risk missing out on a major source of distribution for their products. Costco, Walmart, and other giant retailers offer enticing opportunities for manufacturers, but playing by their high-volume, low-cost rules can sometimes hurt a manufacturer more than help it.[36]

Exhibit 4 offers of a summary of the major factors to consider regarding distribution channels.

EXHIBIT 4	Factors That Influence Distribution Channel Choices

Designing a distribution mix is rarely a simple task; here are some of the most important factors to consider.

Factor	Issues to Consider
Customer needs and expectations	Where are customers likely to look for your products? How much customer service do they expect from the channel? Can you make your offering more attractive by choosing an unconventional channel?
Product support requirements	How much training do salespeople need to present your products successfully? How much after-sale support is required? Who will answer questions when things go wrong?
Segmentation, targeting, and positioning	Which intermediaries can present your products to target customers while maintaining your positioning strategy?
Competitors' distribution channels	Which channels do your competitors use? Do you need to use the same channels in order to reach your target customers, or can you use different channels to distinguish yourself?
Established industry patterns and requirements	Which intermediaries are already in place? Can you take advantage of them, or do you need to find or create alternatives? Will retailers demand that you use specific wholesalers or distributors?
Channel length	Do you want to deal directly with customers? *Can* you? Do you need to engage other intermediaries to perform vital functions?
Market coverage	Are you going for intensive, selective, or exclusive distribution? Are the right intermediaries available in your target markets? Can they handle the volumes at which you hope to sell?
Distribution costs	How much will intermediaries add to the price that final customers will eventually pay? Put another way, how much of a discount from the retail price will intermediaries expect from you?
Channel conflict	What are the potential sources of channel conflict, both now and in the future? If such conflict can't be avoided, how will you minimize its effect?
Channel organization and control	How much control do you need to maintain as products move through the channel—and how much can you expect to maintain with each potential intermediary? What happens if you lose control? Who leads the channel?

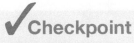

Checkpoint

LEARNING OBJECTIVE 5: Identify five key attributes of distribution channel design and management.

SUMMARY: Five key attributes of channel design and management are channel length (the number of layers between producers and target customers), market coverage needs (intense, selective, or exclusive distribution), distribution costs (all the costs involved in using a particular channel), channel conflict (disagreement and tension between channel partners), and channel organization and control (attempts to coordinate the activities of a channel into a cohesive marketing system).

CRITICAL THINKING: (1) Does exclusive distribution limit the potential size of a manufacturer's market? Why or why not? (2) Is it ethical for one participant in a channel to have power over the marketing system through sheer economic power alone? Why or why not?

IT'S YOUR BUSINESS: (1) Does knowing that a product is available only in selected retail outlets affect your assessment of its quality? (2) Have you ever been skeptical of "shipping and handling" charges added to products you've ordered? Did these charges affect your buying decisions?

KEY TERMS TO KNOW: intensive distribution, selective distribution, exclusive distribution, channel conflict, marketing systems

Physical Distribution and Logistics

6 LEARNING OBJECTIVE

Highlight the major components of physical distribution and logistics.

In addition to assembling and managing the organizations and systems that make up a distribution channel, any firm that deals in physical goods needs to figure out the best way to move those products so they are available to customers at the right place, at the right time, and in the right amount. **Physical distribution** encompasses all the activities required to move finished products from the producer to the consumer, including forecasting, order processing, inventory control, warehousing, and transportation (see Exhibit 5 on the next page).

physical distribution All the activities required to move finished products from the producer to the consumer

Physical distribution may not be the most glamorous aspect of business, but it is one of the most critical. Behind every luxury storefront or cutting-edge e-commerce website is a vast network of facilities, vehicles, and information systems that make sure products arrive at their destinations. The secret to making it all happen on time is **logistics**, the planning and movement of goods and information throughout the supply chain. As managers try to squeeze cost efficiencies and competitive advantages everywhere they can, logistics has taken on key strategic importance for many companies.

logistics The planning, movement, and flow of goods and related information throughout the supply chain

Success in physical distribution requires achieving a competitive level of customer service at the lowest total cost. Doing so requires trade-offs because as the level of service improves, the cost of distribution usually increases. For instance, if you reduce the level of inventory to cut your storage costs, you run the risk of being unable to fill orders in a timely fashion. Or, if you use slower forms of transportation, you can reduce your shipping costs, but you might aggravate customers. The trick is to optimize the total cost of achieving the desired level of service. This optimization requires a careful analysis of each step in the distribution process in relation to every other step in the physical distribution process. Of course, when companies reduce mistakes and eliminate inefficiencies, they can lower costs *and* improve service, which is the goal of every logistics manager.

FORECASTING

To control the flow of products through the distribution system, a firm must have an accurate estimate of demand. To some degree, historical data can be used to project future sales, but despite heavy investments in information technology, forecasting remains a major logistical challenge that is part hard numbers and part managerial judgment.

EXHIBIT 5	Steps in the Physical Distribution Process

Managing the physical distribution system is an attempt to balance a high level of customer service with the lowest overall cost.

Order Processing
The "paperwork" side of physical distribution, although it's computerized in most instances; requires speed and precision to keep customers happy and to avoid expensive mistakes.

Forecasting
One of the biggest challenges in all of physical distribution is trying to predict which quantities of which products need to be where and when.

Inventory Control
Inventory control requires constant balancing between forecasted and actual demand, making sure enough goods are available to ship without stockpiling so much that costs get out of hand.

Warehousing
Today's warehouses are often technological marvels, with robotics, RFID tracking, and advanced software.

Outboard Transportation
Depending on the product and market needs, companies can choose rail, trucks, ships and barges, air, pipelines, and digital networks.

ORDER PROCESSING

order processing Functions involved in receiving and filling customer orders

Order processing involves preparing orders for shipment and receiving orders when shipments arrive. It includes a number of activities, such as checking the customer's credit, recording the sale, making the appropriate accounting entries, arranging for the item to be shipped, adjusting the inventory records, and billing the customer. Because order processing involves direct interaction with the customer, it affects a company's reputation for customer service. To keep buyers happy, companies should establish ambitious standards for accuracy and timeliness in order fulfillment.

INVENTORY CONTROL

As a just-in-time systems points out, in an ideal world, a company would always have just the right amount of goods on hand to fill the orders it receives. In reality, however, inventory and sales are seldom in perfect balance. For instance, many firms like to keep a ready supply of finished goods on hand so that they can fill orders as soon as they arrive. But how much inventory is enough? If your inventory is too large, you incur extra expenses for storage space, handling, insurance, and taxes; you also run the risk of product obsolescence. On the other hand, if your inventory is too low, you may lose sales when the product is not in stock. The objective of inventory control is to resolve these issues. Inventory managers decide how much product to keep on hand and when to replenish the supply of goods in inventory. They also decide how to allocate products to customers if orders exceed supply.

WAREHOUSING

warehouses Facilities for storing inventory

Products held in inventory are physically stored in **warehouses**, which may be owned by the manufacturer, by an intermediary, or by a private company that leases space to others. Some warehouses are almost purely holding facilities, in which goods are stored for relatively long periods. Other warehouses, known as **distribution centers**, serve as command posts for moving products to customers. In a typical distribution center, goods produced at a variety of locations are collected, sorted, coded, and redistributed to fill customer orders. Leading-edge distribution centers use some of the most advanced technologies in business today, including satellite navigation and communication, voice-activated computers, wireless data services, machine vision, robots, radio frequency identification (RFID) tags and scanners, and planning software that relies on artificial intelligence.

distribution centers Advanced warehouse facilities that specialize in collecting and shipping merchandise

TRANSPORTATION

For any business, the cost of transportation is normally the largest single item in the overall cost of physical distribution. When choosing a mode of transportation, managers must also evaluate other marketing issues, including storage, financing, sales, inventory size, speed, product perishability, dependability, flexibility, and convenience. Each of the six major modes of transportation has distinct advantages and disadvantages:

- **Rail.** Railroads can carry heavier and more diverse cargo and a larger volume of goods than any other mode of transportation. The obvious disadvantage of trains is that they are constrained to tracks, so they can rarely deliver goods directly to customers.
- **Trucks.** Trucks offer the convenience of door-to-door delivery and the ease and efficiency of travel on public highways. However, large, heavy loads are often better handled by water or rail, and some perishable loads may need to travel by air for the shortest possible delivery time over long distances.
- **Ships and barges.** The cheapest method of transportation is via water, and this is the preferred method for such low-cost bulk items as oil, coal, ore, cotton, and lumber. Water transport is slow, however, and like rail, must be combined with another mode of delivery for most shipments.
- **Air.** Air transport offers the primary advantage of speed over long distances, but it imposes limitations on the size, shape, and weight of shipments. It also tends to be the most expensive form of transportation; however, when speed is a priority, air is usually the only way to go.
- **Pipelines.** For products such as gasoline, natural gas, and coal or wood chips (suspended in liquid), pipelines are an effective mode of transportation. The major downsides are slow speeds and inflexible routes.
- **Digital networks.** Any product that exists in or can be converted to digital format, from books and movies to software to product design files, can be transported over the Internet and other digital networks. The range of digital products is fairly limited, of course, but the Internet has certainly revolutionized industries such as entertainment and publishing.

Shippers can also combine the benefits of multiple modes by using **intermodal transportation**. With *containerized shipping*, for instance, standard-size freight containers can be moved from trucks to railroads to ships for maximum flexibility.

For the latest information on wholesaling, retailing, and marketing logistics, visit http://real-timeupdates.com/bia6.

intermodal transportation The coordinated use of multiple modes of transportation, particularly with containers that can be shipped by truck, rail, and sea

✔ **Checkpoint**

LEARNING OBJECTIVE 6: Highlight the major components of physical distribution and logistics.

SUMMARY: The major components of a firm's distribution process are order processing, inventory control, warehousing, materials handling, and outbound transportation. When choosing the best method of outbound transportation, such as truck, rail, ship, airplane, or pipeline, you should consider cost, storage, sales, inventory size, speed, product perishability, dependability, flexibility, and convenience.

CRITICAL THINKING: (1) Given the huge volume of small packages that Amazon ships every year, should it consider starting its own transportation company instead of giving all that business to FedEx and other shippers? Why or why not? (2) If another high-tech company approached Dell with a partnership proposal to build and operate several distribution centers that would ship both companies' products to customers, what would you advise Dell to do? Why?

IT'S YOUR BUSINESS: (1) Online retailers sometimes use free shipping as a promotional appeal. Do you think most consumers really believe the shipping is "free" and not just factored into the product's price? (2) Have you ever paid extra for expedited shipping for an order placed on a website? Was it worth the extra expense?

KEY TERMS TO KNOW: physical distribution, logistics, order processing, warehouses, distribution centers, materials handling, intermodal transportation

BEHIND THE SCENES

COSTCO PUSHES ITS SUPPLY CHAIN TO SATISFY CUSTOMERS

MyBizLab

The merchandise sold at Costco may be similar to that of its two main competitors—Sam's Club and BJ's—but Costco aims to be a cut above by offering many unique and unusual items. Its stores also look slightly more upscale than other club stores, the brands it carries have more cachet, and the products are often a bit more expensive, but they still offer extremely good value. And unlike some other discounters, Costco does not have everything under the sun. The stores carry only about 4,000 products each, which is a small fraction of the more than 100,000 items stocked by other warehouse clubs and conventional discounters such as Target and Walmart. About 3,000 of Costco's products are a consistent array of carefully chosen basics, from canned tuna to laundry detergent to printer cartridges. The other 1,000 items are a fast-moving assortment of goods such as designer-label clothing, watches, and premium wines. These items change from week to week, reinforcing the idea of buying something when you see it because it'll probably be gone next week.

Costco prefers to offer name-brand products and has successfully introduced some branded luxury items such as Kate Spade and Coach purses. However, high-end suppliers such as Cartier and Cannondale flinch at the idea of their goods being sold in a warehouse setting, so carrying those brands isn't always possible. Some suppliers, hoping to protect their higher-end retail customers, have been known to spurn Costco's offers "officially," only to call back later to quietly cut a deal. In other cases, Costco goes on its own treasure hunts, using third-party distributors to track down hot products, even though these "gray market" channels can be unpredictable. And if that doesn't work, Costco can commission another manufacturer to create a lookalike product—leather handbags are one example—with its own Kirkland Signature label.

To give its millions of members the best prices on everything, Costco negotiates directly—and fiercely—with suppliers. Aiming to be known as the toughest negotiators in the business, Costco's buyers won't let up until they get their target price on the merchandise. Often, the "right" price is determined by how much less expensively Costco can make a product itself. Using this approach, the company has managed to drive down price points in several categories, such as over-the-counter drugs. Costco then passes on the savings to customers, who never pay more than 15 percent above the company's cost. Cofounder and recently retired CEO Jim Sinegal was determined not to let the wheel of retailing take Costco for a spin, either. "When I started, Sears, Roebuck was the Costco of the country, but they allowed someone else to come in under them. We don't want to be one of the casualties. We don't want to turn around and say, 'We got so fancy we've raised our prices,' and all of a sudden a new competitor comes in and beats our prices."

Inventory turnover rate is also a key to Costco's financial success. By focusing on fast-selling items, the company moves its merchandise significantly faster than competitors—so quickly, in fact, that it often sells products to shoppers before it has to pay its suppliers.

Costco is rolling through its third decade with strong financial health, a dominant market position, and millions of consumers and business customers that rely on Costco bargains. Annual sales will break the $80 billion barrier soon, and $100 billion doesn't look too far out of reach. Online sales remain a fairly small fraction of total revenue, but the company expects those sales to pick up as the economy improves and consumers are more confident to spend on the more expensive items that are typically offered on the website. International expansion is another item on Costco's strategic menu, with sales recently growing at a faster clip outside the United States. Per-store sales are up in other countries, but the number of new store openings has tapered off over the past few years, thanks in part to the economy and in part to a cautious approach to finding the right locations. For instance, the company thinks Taiwan could support 20 Costco stores and Japan could support 50, but finding enough land for the giant footprint of a warehouse store—typically 15 acres—that is near population centers but not in areas with zoning regulations that prohibit big-box retailers is a particular challenge in some countries.[37]

Critical Thinking Questions

1. If customers repeatedly ask Costco to carry certain items that the company thinks are outside its price/quality "comfort zone" (because they're too expensive or not of high enough quality), should it give in and carry the items? Why or why not?
2. Most of the items on Costco's website are available only through Costco; should it expand its online product selection to include more commonly available products, since an online store doesn't have the physical constraints of a brick-and-mortar location? Why or why not?
3. If Costco can't find enough land in, say, Japan, to build its usual store format, should it leverage the Costco brand name anyway and build something such as conventional department stores or grocery stores in these areas? Why or why not?

LEARN MORE ONLINE

Explore the Costco website, at **www.costco.com**. What evidence do you see of "clicks-and-bricks" integration with the physical stores? Are sales promoted online? How much product information is available? Are nonmembers allowed to make purchases online? How does the online experience at Costco compare to that of another discounter, such as Walmart (**www.walmart.com**), or to a specialty retailer, such as Bluefly (**www.bluefly.com**)?

MyBizLab

Log on to www.mybizlab.com to access study and assessment aids associated with this chapter.

KEY TERMS

agents and brokers
channel conflict
department stores
discount stores
disintermediation
distribution centers
distribution mix
distribution strategy
distributors
e-commerce
exclusive distribution
intensive distribution
intermodal transportation
logistics
marketing intermediaries

marketing systems
merchant wholesalers
multichannel retailing
off-price retailers
online retailers
order processing
physical distribution
retail theater
retailers
selective distribution
specialty stores
warchouses
wheel of retailing
wholesalers

TEST YOUR KNOWLEDGE

Questions for Review

1. What is a distribution channel?
2. What are the two main types of intermediaries, and how do they differ from one another?
3. What forms of utility do intermediaries create?
4. What are some of the main causes of channel conflict?
5. How does a specialty store differ from a category killer and a discount store?

Questions for Analysis

6. How do marketing systems help avert channel conflict?
7. What are some of the challenges facing retailers and wholesalers today?
8. How might a once-valued intermediary find itself threatened with disintermediation?

9. How could strategic planning help a discount retailer avoid the pitfalls of the wheel of retailing?
10. **Ethical Considerations.** Manufacturers that have been selling to wholesalers and other intermediaries occasionally decide to start selling directly to end customers, which of course puts them in competition with the channel partners that have been selling for them. Even if this is legal, do you think such moves are ethical? Why or why not?

Questions for Application

11. Imagine that you own a small specialty store that sells hand-crafted clothing and jewelry. What are some of the nonstore retail options you might explore to increase sales? What are the advantages and disadvantages of each option?

12. Compare the prices of three products offered at a retail outlet with the prices charged if you purchase those products by mail order (catalog or phone) or over the Internet. Be sure to include extra costs such as handling and delivery charges. Which purchasing format offers the lowest price for each of your products?

13. This question was intentionally excluded from this edition.

14. This question was intentionally excluded from this edition.

EXPAND YOUR KNOWLEDGE

Discovering Career Opportunities

Retailing is a dynamic, fast-paced field with many career opportunities in both store and nonstore settings. In addition to hiring full-time employees when needed, retailers of all types often hire extra employees on a temporary basis for peak selling periods, such as the year-end holidays. You can find out about seasonal and year-round job openings by checking newspaper classified ads, looking for signs in store windows, browsing the websites of online retailers, and checking Craigslist (www.craigslist.org) and other sites.

1. Select a major retailer, such as a chain store in your area or a retailer on the Internet. Is this a specialty store, a discount store, a department store, or another type of retailer?

2. Visit the website of the retailer you selected. Does the site discuss the company's hiring procedures? If so, what are they? What qualifications are required for a position with the company?

3. Research your chosen retailer using library sources or online resources. Is this retailer expanding? Is it profitable? Has it recently acquired or been acquired by another firm? What are the implications of this acquisition for job opportunities?

Improving Your Tech Insights: Supply Chain Integration Standards

How do Amazon's computers know which book to reorder from its suppliers when you order one from Amazon's website? Who makes sure RFID readers know how to detect RFID tags accurately and ensures that databases know what to do with the data? How does every one of the billions of barcodes now in use get the right combination of black and white stripes? All these decisions are guided by industry groups that define the standards and technologies that make sure supply chains work together, from producers to wholesalers to retailers.

Supply chain standardization might not be the most pulse-pounding technology from a consumer's point of view, but global business simply wouldn't work without it—and consumers benefit from the lower prices and better service that standards enable. Moving forward, advances in supply-chain integration promise to remove billions of dollars of errors and inefficiencies from supply chains in many industries.

Visit the website of GS1 (www.gs1.org) a global, not-for-profit organization that develops and oversees a number of supply chain standards. The brochure "What Is GS1?" available on the "About Us" page, explains the importance of global business standards and describes bar codes, RFID tagging, the Global Data Synchronization Network, and other efforts. In a brief email message to your instructor, describe one of the GS1 standards and explain how it helps businesses operate more efficiently and serve customers more effectively.

PRACTICE YOUR SKILLS

Sharpening Your Communication Skills

Sales of your DJ equipment (turntables, amplifiers, speakers, mixers, and related accessories) have been falling for months, even as more and more music fans around the world try their hand at being DJs. Magazine reviews and professional DJs give your equipment high marks, your prices are competitive, and your advertising presence is strong. Suspecting that the trouble is in the distribution channel, you and a half dozen fellow executives go on an undercover shopping mission at retail stores that carry your products—and you're appalled by what you see. The salespeople in these stores clearly don't understand your products, so they either give potential customers bad information about your products or steer them to products from your competitors. No wonder sales are falling off a cliff.

The executive team is split over the best way to solve this dilemma; you convince them that retraining your existing channel partners would be less expensive and less disruptive than replacing them. Now you have to convince store managers to let you pull their staffs off the sales floor for a half day so you can train them. Each store will lose a half day's revenue, and each sales rep will lose commissions for that time as well. Draft a short email message for the store managers, explaining why the training would be well worth their time. Make up any details you need to complete the message.

Building Your Team Skills

Complicated or confusing shopping experiences are one of the biggest challenges for online retailing. Customers who can't find what they're looking for or who get lost filling out order forms, for instance, often just click away and leave their virtual shopping carts. Unfortunately, consumers don't always perceive the shopping experience the same way, so it's not always easy for website developers to craft the ideal e-retail experience.

Your team's task is to analyze the shopping experience on three competitive e-retail sites and from that analysis decide how a new competitor in the market could create a better customer experience. First, choose a product that everyone in the group finds interesting but that none of you have purchased online before. Then identify three websites that are likely to offer the product. Next, individually (so you can't guide each other), each person in the group should shop the three sites for your chosen product. (If you can't find the exact model, choose something similar.) Answer the following questions about each site:

1. How difficult was it to find the product you wanted?
2. How much information was available? Complete product details or just a few highlights? A static photo or a three-dimensional (3D) virtual experience that lets you explore the product from all angles?
3. How easy was it to compare this product to similar products?
4. Could you find the store's privacy and return policies? Were they acceptable to you?
5. How long did it take to get from the site's homepage to the point at which you could place an order for the specific product?
6. What forms of help were available in case you had questions or concerns?

7. Go ahead and place your item in the shopping cart to simulate placing an order. (Don't actually buy the product, of course!)
8. What social commerce and social elements did you encounter on the website? Were they helpful in your search?

Summarize your impression of each of the three sites and then compare notes with your teammates. Based on the strengths and weaknesses of each site, identify four pieces of advice for a company that wants to compete against these sites.

Developing Your Research Skills

Find an article in a business journal or newspaper (online or print editions) that discusses changes a company is making to its distribution strategy or channels. For example, is a manufacturer selling products directly to consumers? Is a physical retailer offering goods via a company website? Is a company eliminating an intermediary? Has a nonstore retailer decided to open a physical store? Is a category killer opening smaller stores? Has a major retail tenant closed its store in a mall?

1. What changes in the company's distribution structure or strategy have taken place? What additional changes, if any, are planned?
2. What were the reasons for the changes? What role, if any, did e-commerce play in the changes?
3. If you were a stockholder in this company, would you view these changes as positive or negative? What, if anything, might you do differently?

REFERENCES

1. "Costco Wholesale Corp," *Bloomberg Businessweek*, accessed 8 September 2011, http://investing.businessweek.com; Mark Brohan, "Web Sales Rebound for Costco in Fiscal 2010," Internet Retailer, 8 October 2010, www.internetretailer.com; *Costco 2010 Annual Report*; Datamonitor, "Costco Wholesale Corporation: Company Profile," 12 April 2010, www.ebscohost .com; Costco website, accessed 8 September 2011, www.costco .com; "Analyst Picks and Pans: MCD, COST, YUM, TSN," *BusinessWeek*, 21 May 2009, www.businessweek.com; Michelle V. Rafter, "Welcome to the Club," *Workforce Management*, April 2005, 41–46; David Meier, "It's the Employees, Stupid," MotleyFool.com, 17 September 2004, www.fool.com; Steven Greenhouse, "How Costco Became the Anti-Wal-Mart," *New York Times*, 17 July 2005, www.nytimes.com; Jeff Malester, "Costco Sales Rise 10%, Hit $12.4 Billion in Fis. Q2," *Twice*, 7 March 2005, 53; Ilana Polyak, "Warehouse Sale," *Kiplinger's Personal Finance*, May 2005, 67; Suzanne Wooley, "Costco? More Like Costgrow," *Money*, August 2002, 44–46; "Costco: A Cut Above," *Retail Merchandiser*, July 2002, 44; Pete Hisey, "Costco.com Means Business," *Retail Merchandiser*, October 2001, 36; Shelly Branch, "Inside the Cult of Costco," *Fortune*, 6 September 1999, 184–188.
2. "Grainger at a Glance," Grainger website, accessed 7 September 2011, www.grainger.com.
3. Iris Professional Services website, accessed 7 September 2011, www.irisproservices.com.
4. "Manufacturing & Trade Inventories & Sales," U.S. Census Bureau website, accessed 7 September 2011, www.census.gov; "Wholesale Trade," U.S. Bureau of Labor Statistics website, accessed 7 September 2011, www.bls.gov.

5. Joseph O'Reilly, "3PL Perspectives 2011: The Power of Three," *Inbound Logistics*, July 2011, www.inboundlogistics.com; Philip Kotler and Gary Armstrong, *Principles of Marketing*, 13th ed. (Upper Saddle River, N.J.: Pearson Prentice Hall, 2010), 362–363; Bert Rosenbloom, "The Wholesaler's Role in the Marketing Channel: Disintermediation Vs. Reintermediation," *International Review of Retail, Distribution & Consumer Research*, September 2007, 327–339.
6. McKesson website, accessed 7 September 2011, www.mckesson .com.
7. Rosenbloom, "The Wholesaler's Role in the Marketing Channel: Disintermediation vs. Reintermediation."
8. Rosenbloom, "The Wholesaler's Role in the Marketing Channel: Disintermediation vs. Reintermediation."
9. Rosenbloom, "The Wholesaler's Role in the Marketing Channel: Disintermediation vs. Reintermediation."
10. "Wholesale Trade"; Rosenbloom, "The Wholesaler's Role in the Marketing Channel: Disintermediation vs. Reintermediation."
11. Richard Brunelli, "Shopper Marketing? There's an App for That . . . ," *Adweek*, 14 March 2011, S1–S3.
12. Jeneanne Rae, "New Thinking About Consumer Marketing," *BusinessWeek*, 30 June 2009, 16.
13. Jennifer J. Argo, Darren W. Dahl, and Andrea C. Morales, "Positive Consumer Contagion: Responses to Attractive Others in a Retail Context," *Journal of Marketing Research*, December 2008, 690–701.
14. Don E. Schultz, "Another Turn of the Wheel," *Marketing Management*, March/April 2002, 8–9.
15. "Investor Overview," Family Dollar website, accessed 7 September 2011, www.familydollar.com; Kerry Grace Benn,

"Family Dollar Earnings Jump 36%, Boosts Fiscal-Year View," *Wall Street Journal*, 8 July 2009, http://online.wsj.com.

16. Teri Agins, "What Is 'Off-Price'?" *Wall Street Journal*, 17 July 2009, http://online.wsj.com.

17. "Web to Become Top Sales Channel by 2012," *Bookseller*, 24 April 2009, 10; "Quarterly Retail E-Commerce Sales: 2nd Quarter 2011," U.S. Census Bureau, 16 August 2011, www.census.gov.

18. "Facts About Redbox," Redbox website, accessed 7 September 2011, www.redbox.com.

19. "What the Leaders Do Right," *Chain Store Age*, February 2008, 7A.

20. Kris Hudson and Vanessa O'Connell, "Recession Turns Malls into Ghost Towns," *Wall Street Journal*, 22 May 2009, http://online.wsj.com; Glen A. Bere, "Big Boxes Pop Up in Regional Malls, Altering Landscape for Chain Stores," *National Jeweler*, 16 May 2005, 1+; Bruce Horovitz and Lorrie Grant, "Changes in Store for Department Stores?" *USA Today*, 21 January 2005, B1–B2; Dean Starkman, "As Malls Multiply, Developers Fight Fiercely for Turf," *Wall Street Journal*, 19 April 2002, A1, A6; Robert Berner and Gerry Khermouch, "Retail Reckoning," *BusinessWeek*, 10 December 2001, 72–77.

21. David Bodamer, "The Mall Is Not Dead," *Retail Traffic*, May/June 2011, 12.

22. Rick Braddock, "Lessons of Internet Marketing from FreshDirect," *Wall Street Journal*, 11 May 2009, http://online.wsj.com.

23. "Many-Stop Shopping? How Niche Retailers Are Thriving on Internet 2.0," Knowledge@Wharton, 11 May 2011, http://knowledge.wharton.upenn.edu; Cate T. Corcoran, "Delivering the Goods: E-Tailing Sales to Rise but Gains Seen Slowing," *Women's Wear Daily*, 5 May 2009, 1.

24. Jacques Bughin, Amy Guggenheim Shenkan, and Marc Singer, "How Poor Metrics Undermine Digital Marketing," *McKinsey Quarterly*, 2009 Issue 1, 106–107.

25. "Location-Free Shopping," *Chain Store Age*, February 2009, 13A.

26. Sharon Edelson, "Pop-ups Offer Retailers Multiple Benefits," *Women's Wear Daily*, 19 May 2009, 12.

27. Jim Dalrymple, "Inside the Apple Stores," *Macworld*, June 2007, 16–17; Andy Serwer, "The iPod People Have Invaded Apple's Stores," *Fortune*, 13 December 2004, 79.

28. Rob Eder, "CVS Unveils High-End Beauty 360 Store," *Drug Store News*, 17 November 2008, 1+.

29. Black & Decker website, accessed 7 September 2011, www.blackanddecker.com.

30. Felder website, accessed 7 September 2011, www.feldergroupusa.com.

31. Kotler and Armstrong, *Principles of Marketing*, 349.

32. Super Jock'n Jill website, accessed 26 October 2011, www.superjocknjill.com.

33. Øystein Foros and Hans Jarle Kind, "Do Slotting Allowances Harm Retail Competition?" *Scandinavian Journal of Economics* 110, no. 2 (2008), 367–384; U.S. Federal Trade Commission, "Slotting Allowances in the Retail Grocery Industry: Selected Case Studies in Five Product Categories," November 2003, www.ftc.gov.

34. Kotler and Armstrong, *Principles of Marketing*, 344.

35. Adapted from Kotler and Armstrong, *Principles of Marketing*, 344–345.

36. Andrew R. Thomas and Timothy J. Wilkinson, "The Devolution of Marketing," *Marketing Management*, Spring 2011, 19–25.

37. See note 1.

GLOSSARY

agents and brokers Independent wholesalers that do not take title to the goods they distribute but may or may not take possession of those goods

channel conflict Disagreement or tension between two or more members in a distribution channel, such as competition between channel partners trying to reach the same group of customers

department stores Large stores that carry a variety of products in multiple categories, such as clothing, house wares, gifts, bedding, and furniture

discount stores Retailers that sell a variety of everyday goods below the market price by keeping their overhead low

disintermediation The replacement of intermediaries by producers, customers, or other intermediaries when those other parties can perform channel functions more effectively or efficiently

distribution centers Advanced warehouse facilities that specialize in collecting and shipping merchandise

distribution mix A combination of intermediaries and channels a producer uses to reach target customers

distribution strategy A firm's overall plan for moving products through intermediaries and on to final customers

distributors Merchant wholesalers that sell products to organizational customers for internal operations or the production of other goods, rather than to retailers for resale

e-commerce The application of Internet technologies to wholesaling and retailing

exclusive distribution A market coverage strategy that gives intermediaries exclusive rights to sell a product in a specific geographic area

intensive distribution A market coverage strategy that tries to place a product in as many outlets as possible

intermodal transportation The coordinated use of multiple modes of transportation, particularly with containers that can be shipped by truck, rail, and sea

logistics The planning, movement, and flow of goods and related information throughout the supply chain

marketing intermediaries Businesspeople and organizations that assist in moving and marketing goods and services between producers and consumers

marketing systems Arrangements by which channel partners coordinate their activities under the leadership of one of the partners

merchant wholesalers Independent wholesalers that take legal title to goods they distribute

multichannel retailing Coordinated efforts to reach consumers through more than one retail channel

off-price retailers Stores that sell designer labels and other fashionable products at steep discounts

online retailers Companies that use e-commerce technologies to sell over the Internet; includes Internet-only retailers and the online arm of store-based retailers

order processing Functions involved in receiving and filling customer orders

physical distribution All the activities required to move finished products from the producer to the consumer

retail theater The addition of entertainment or education aspects to the retail experience

retailers Intermediaries that sell goods and services to individuals for their own personal use

selective distribution A market coverage strategy that uses a limited number of carefully chosen outlets to distribute products

specialty stores Stores that carry only a particular type of goods, often with deep selection in those specific categories

warehouses Facilities for storing inventory

wheel of retailing An evolutionary process by which stores that feature low prices gradually upgrade until they no longer appeal to price-sensitive shoppers and are replaced by a new generation of leaner, low-price competitors

wholesalers Intermediaries that sell products to other intermediaries for resale or to organizations for internal use

Customer Communication

LEARNING OBJECTIVES   After studying this chapter, you will be able to

1 Describe the three major tasks in crafting a communication strategy and identify four important legal aspects of marketing communication

2 Identify the major types of advertising, the most common advertising appeals, and the most important advertising media

3 Explain how direct marketing differs from advertising and identify the major forms of direct media

4 Describe consultative selling and explain the personal-selling process

5 Define *sales promotion* and identify the major categories of consumer and trade promotions

6 Explain the uses of social media in customer communication and the role of public relations

MyBizLab

Where you see MyBizLab in this chapter, go to www.mybizlab.com for additional activities on the topic being discussed.

BEHIND THE SCENES PULLING IN THE CROWDS AT SEAWORLD SAN ANTONIO

To quickly build interest in the new Journey to Atlantis water ride, SeaWorld San Antonio turned to a new generation of customer communication tools.

http://seaworldparks.com/seaworld-sanantonio

Theme parks offer plenty of ways for visitors to find a few hours of fun in the sun, enjoy some entertainment, and maybe give themselves a good scare on the roller coaster. From a marketing point of view, however, there is a never-ending challenge of creating new reasons to visit. Consumers who've "been there, done that" at a particular theme park are understandably tempted to take their entertainment dollars somewhere else unless the park can offer fresh attractions to lure them back.

One of three SeaWorld parks run by Busch Entertainment Corporation (the other two are in San Diego and Orlando), the 250-acre SeaWorld San Antonio is the world's largest marine life theme park. In addition to having numerous marine life exhibits, shows, and other attractions, the park offers several hair-raising rides, including the eight-story-high Great White roller coaster and the 65-mile-per-hour Steel Eel "hypercoaster." Both are exciting rides, but coaster enthusiasts who've already ridden them might not feel any immediate urge to revisit SeaWorld.

But visitors certainly would be interested in a new ride, and SeaWorld was ready to offer one with Journey to Atlantis, a combination roller coaster/water ride. Although not a thrill ride in the sense of pushing the limits of speed and performing gravity-defying stunts, Journey to Atlantis does offer great views of San

Antonio at the top and a grand splashdown into a lake at the bottom—a perfect way to cool off on a hot Texas afternoon.

With Journey to Atlantis nearing completion ahead of schedule, the customer communication team needed to get the word out quickly about this new attraction. If you were public relations specialist Kami Huyse, how would you identify the right audience and reach out to them with information about the new ride? How would you develop relationships with coaster enthusiasts—people who don't hesitate to travel just about anywhere to try a new ride—and encourage them to add Journey to Atlantis to their must-try lists? And how would you build excitement and energy around a product that really needs to be experienced to be fully appreciated?[1]

MyBizLab

Gain hands-on experience through an interactive, real-world scenario. This chapter's simulation entitled Promoting a Product is located at **www.mybizlab.com**.

1 LEARNING OBJECTIVE

Describe the three major tasks in crafting a communication strategy, and identify four important legal aspects of marketing communication.

social communication model An approach to communication based on interactive social media and conversational communication styles

INTRODUCTION

When SeaWorld San Antonio (profiled in the chapter-opening Behind the Scenes) needed to generate awareness for its new Journey to Atlantis ride, the company and its communication team had a dizzying array of options for reaching out to potential park visitors. This chapter, our final discussion of the marketing function, explains how marketers set communication goals, define messages, and choose from the ever-growing array of media options to reach target audiences.

Customer Communication: Challenges, Strategies, and Issues

Not long ago, marketing communication was largely about companies broadcasting carefully scripted messages to a mass audience that often had few, if any, ways to respond. Moreover, customers and other interested parties had few ways to connect with one another to ask questions about products, influence company decisions, or offer each other support.

However, a variety of technologies have enabled and inspired a new approach to customer communication. In contrast to the "we talk, you listen" mindset of the past, this new **social communication model** is *interactive* and *conversational*. Today's audiences are no longer passive recipients of messages; instead, they demand to be active participants in a meaningful conversation. On the surface, this approach might look like it has just added a few new electronic media tools to the traditional arsenal of television, radio, newspapers, and magazines. However, as Exhibit 1 shows, the changes are much deeper and more profound. "Social Media in the Marketing Process" on page 381 discusses this new model in more detail.

In this new world of interactive communication, it's more vital than ever to have a strategy that (1) establishes *clear communication goals*, (2) defines *compelling messages* to help achieve those goals, and (3) outlines a *cost-effective media mix* to engage target audiences.

ESTABLISHING COMMUNICATION GOALS

Communication activities can meet a wide range of marketing goals, but only if these activities are crafted with clear goals based on where the target audience is in the purchasing cycle.[2] Marketers take the following steps to move potential customers toward purchases:

- **Generating awareness.** People obviously can't buy things they don't know about, so creating awareness is essential for new companies and new products.
- **Providing information and creating positive emotional connections.** The next step is to build logical and emotional acceptance for the company and its products. Social media can work for or against companies in a significant way at this stage. If customers are pleased with a product, they'll help spread the message through the virtual word-of-mouth communication of social media. But they'll also spread the word if a product does not meet their expectations.

EXHIBIT 1	The Social Model of Customer Communication

The new social model of customer communication differs from the conventional promotion model in a number of significant ways.

Conventional Promotion Model Tendencies	Social Model Tendencies
Publication	Conversation
Lecture	Discussion
Intrusion	Permission
Unidirectional	Bidirectional, multidirectional
One to many	One to one, many to many
Control	Influence
Low message frequency	High message frequency
Few channels	Many channels
Information hoarding	Information sharing
Static	Dynamic
Hierarchical	Egalitarian
Structured	Amorphous
Isolation	Collaboration
Planned	Reactive
Rigid	Responsive

- **Building preference.** If buyers accept a product as a potential solution to their needs, the next step is to encourage them to prefer it over all other products they may be considering.
- **Stimulating action.** Now comes the most critical step: convincing a consumer or an organization to act on that product preference to make a purchase, using a compelling *call to action*.
- **Reminding past customers.** Past customers are often the best prospects for future sales, so *reminder advertising* tells these buyers that a product is still available or a company is ready to serve their needs.

DEFINING CUSTOMER MESSAGES

After establishing communication goals, the marketer's next step is to define the **core message**. This is the single most important idea the company hopes to convey to the target audience about a product. Ideally, the message can be expressed in a single sentence, such as "The Caterpillar 385C Ultra High Demolition Excavator can increase productivity at every stage of the most demanding demolition projects."[3] Notice how this statement highlights a key customer benefit (productivity) and identifies the target audience (companies that demolish buildings).

Of course, no one is going to shell out a million dollars for a 100-ton piece of equipment based on a single sentence. Think of the core message as the foundation on which the marketing team can build successive layers of detail and explanation, with each communication effort expanding on the core message. For instance, advertisements try to communicate a few key points quickly, without going into great detail. A sales presentation could go into more detail, and a technical brochure or a website can provide extensive information.

As Exhibit 1 notes, one of the most significant changes that the social communication model has brought to marketing is that companies now have far less control of their messages. After a message is released into the wild, so to speak, bloggers, reporters, industry analysts, and other parties will begin to repeat it, enhance it, change it, and even refute it. Starting with a clear and compelling core message increases the chances that the message will reach its target audience intact. If the core message is not clear or not credible, it will surely be altered or refuted as it passes from one outside commentator to the next.

core message The single most important idea an advertiser hopes to convey to the target audience about its products or the company

ASSEMBLING THE COMMUNICATION MIX

With clear goals and a compelling message, the next step is to share that message using a **communication mix**, also known as a *media mix* or *promotional mix*, through some combination of advertising, direct marketing, personal selling, sales promotion, social media, and public relations. Crafting the optimal mix is one of the toughest decisions marketing managers face and requires constant monitoring as markets and media choices evolve.

To assemble the best mix, companies have to consider a range of product, market, and distribution channel factors. Product factors include the type of product, its price range, and its stage in the product life cycle. For example, an innovative technical product may require intensive educational efforts in the introduction and growth stages to help customers understand and appreciate its value. Market factors include the type of intended customers (consumers versus organizations), the nature of the competition, and the size and geographic spread of the target market.

Channel factors include the need for intermediaries, the type of intermediaries available, and the ability of those companies to help with communication. A key decision is whether to focus communication efforts on the intermediaries or on final customers. With a **push strategy**, a producer focuses on intermediaries, trying to persuade wholesalers or retailers to carry its products and promote those products to *their* customers. Conversely, with a **pull strategy**, the producer appeals directly to end customers. Customers learn of the product through these communication efforts and request it from retailers (in the case of consumers) or wholesalers (in the case of business customers). For example, if a television commercial encourages you to "ask your pharmacist" about a specific product, the company is using a pull strategy. Many companies use both push and pull strategies to increase the impact of their promotional efforts.

With the number of communication vehicles continuing to expand, the need for companies to "speak with one voice" becomes even greater. **Integrated marketing communications (IMC)** is a strategy of coordinating and integrating all communication and promotional efforts to ensure clarity, consistency, and maximum communications impact.[4] However, companies obviously can't control all the messages their target audiences receive, particularly now that customers are empowered through social media. While the company is working to integrate its outgoing communication efforts, the customer is also integrating all the incoming messages he or she is receiving (see Exhibit 2).

communication mix A blend of communication vehicles—advertising, direct marketing, personal selling, sales promotion, social media, and public relations—that a company uses to reach current and potential customers

push strategy A promotional strategy that focuses on intermediaries, motivating them to promote, or *push*, products toward end users

pull strategy A promotional strategy that stimulates consumer demand via advertising and other communication efforts, thereby creating a *pull* effect through the channel

integrated marketing communications (IMC) A strategy of coordinating and integrating communication and promotion efforts with customers to ensure greater efficiency and effectiveness

| EXHIBIT 2 | Message Integration in Customer Communication |

To maximize efficiency and consistency, companies need to integrate their customer communication efforts. However, customers also integrate messages on the receiving end—including messages that might contradict messages from the company.

COMMUNICATION LAWS AND ETHICS

As marketing and selling grow increasingly complex, so do the legal ramifications of marketing communication. In the United States, the Federal Trade Commission (FTC) has the authority to impose penalties against advertisers that violate federal standards for truthful advertising. Other federal agencies have authority over advertising in specific industries, such as transportation and financial services. Individual states have additional laws that apply. The legal aspects of promotional communication can be quite complex, and they vary from state to state and from country to country. However, if you are involved in customer communication in any form, at a minimum you need to be aware of these legal issues:[5]

- **Marketing and sales messages must be truthful and nondeceptive.** The FTC considers messages to be deceptive if they include statements that are likely to mislead reasonable customers and the statements are an important part of the purchasing decision. Failing to include important information is also considered deceptive. The FTC also looks at *implied claims*—claims you don't explicitly make but that can be inferred from what you do or don't say.
- **You must back up your claims with evidence.** According to the FTC, offering a money-back guarantee or providing letters from satisfied customers is not enough; you must still be able to support claims for your product with objective evidence such as a survey or scientific study (see Exhibit 3). If you claim that your food product lowers cholesterol, you must have scientific evidence to support that claim.
- **"Bait and switch" advertising is illegal.** Trying to attract buyers by advertising a product that you don't intend to sell—and then trying to sell them another (and usually more expensive) product—is illegal.

EXHIBIT 3	Supporting Marketing Claims with Verifiable Evidence

Merck, the company that makes the hair-loss treatment Propecia, takes care to back up its product claims with solid evidence, out of respect for its audience and to ensure compliance with regulations regarding marketing and sales messages. The series of photos available through the "Evidence of Regrowth" link provides additional visual confirmation of the product's benefits.

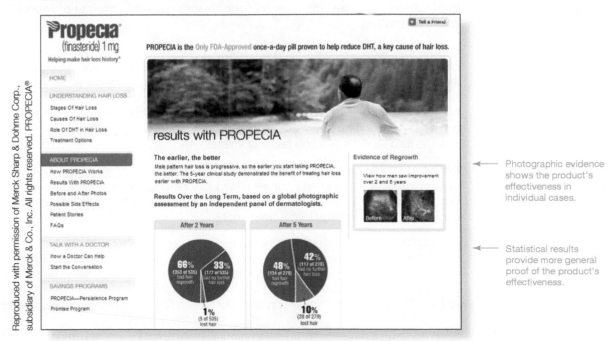

- **Marketing messages and websites aimed at children are subject to special rules.** For example, online marketers must obtain consent from parents before collecting personal information about children under age 13.
- **Marketing and sales messages are considered binding contracts in many states.** If you imply or make an offer and then can't fulfill your end of the bargain, you can be sued for breach of contract.
- **In most cases, you can't use a person's name, photograph, or other identity without permission.** Doing so is considered an invasion of privacy. You can use images of people considered to be public figures as long as you don't unfairly imply that they endorse your message.

Moreover, communicators must stay on top of changing regulations, such as the latest laws governing unsolicited bulk email ("spam"), customer privacy, data security, and disclosure requirements for bloggers who review products. Two of the latest ethical concerns that could produce new legislation are *behavioral targeting*, which tracks the online behavior of website visitors and serves up ads based on what they appear to be interested in, and *remarketing*, in which behaviorally targeted ads follow users even as they move on to other websites.[6]

Regarding privacy and other aspects of communication, responsible companies recognize the vital importance of ethical standards. Professional associations such as the American Association of Advertising Agencies (www.aaaa.org), the Direct Marketing Association (www.the-dma.org), and the American Marketing Association (www.marketingpower .com) devote considerable time and energy to ethical issues in marketing, including ongoing education for practitioners and self-regulation efforts aimed at avoiding or correcting ethical lapses. For instance, the National Advertising Review Council (www.narcpartners .org), whose members include advertisers, agencies, and the general public, works with the Better Business Bureau to investigate and resolve complaints of deceptive advertising in order to foster public trust.[7]

✓ Checkpoint

LEARNING OBJECTIVE 1: Describe the three major tasks in crafting a communication strategy, and identify four important legal aspects of marketing communication.

SUMMARY: The three major tasks in developing a communication strategy are establishing clear communication goals, defining compelling messages to help achieve those goals, and outlining a cost-effective media mix to engage target audiences. Four important issues in communications law are making sure advertising claims are truthful and nondeceptive, supporting claims with real evidence, recognizing that marketing and sales messages are contractual obligations in many cases, and avoiding the unauthorized use of a person's name or image.

CRITICAL THINKING: (1) Why do credit card companies target students even though most of them have little or no income? (2) Would it be wise for a manufacturer that is new to a particular industry (and unknown within it) to invest most of its promotional resources in a pull strategy? Why or why not?

IT'S YOUR BUSINESS: (1) What is your "core message" as a future business professional? How would you summarize, in one sentence, what you can offer a company? (2) Does knowing that advertisers are trying to track your online behavior in order to target you with personalized ads make you want to limit or change your web surfing? Do you think advertisers have the right to do this? Why or why not?

KEY TERMS TO KNOW: social communication model, core message, communication mix, push strategy, pull strategy, integrated marketing communications (IMC)

Advertising

2 | LEARNING OBJECTIVE

Identify the major types of advertising, the most common advertising appeals, and the most important advertising media.

Advertising can be defined as the "placement of announcements and persuasive messages in time or space purchased in any of the mass media."[8] In other words, advertisers buy time on radio or television and space in print and online media. Two key points here are that advertising is paid for, and it is carried by someone else's medium. (Companies sometimes own the media in which they advertise, but this is not the usual case.) This section offers a quick overview of the various types of advertising, the appeals most commonly used in advertising, and the advantages and disadvantages of major advertising media.

advertising The delivery of announcements and promotional messages via time or space purchased in various media

TYPES OF ADVERTISING

Companies can use advertising for a variety of purposes. The most common type, *product advertising*, promotes the features and benefits of specific products. The term *comparative advertising* is applied to ads that specifically highlight how one product is better than its competitors. Strong comparative messages can boost sales, but the approach is risky. Competitors are likely to sue if they believe their products have been portrayed unfairly, and sometimes *attack ads* can decrease sales for an entire product category (including the products of the advertiser) by emphasizing the negative aspects of the products in question.[9]

In some countries, comparative ads are tightly regulated and sometimes banned, but that is clearly not the case in the United States. Indeed, the FTC encourages advertisers to use direct product comparisons, with the intent of better informing customers. Comparative advertising is frequently used by competitors vying with the market leader, but it is useful whenever a company believes it has some specific product strengths that are important to customers. However, given the damage that unfair comparative advertising can cause, both federal regulations and industry guidelines established by the American Association of Advertising Agencies address the issues of fairness and accuracy in comparative advertising.[10]

Institutional advertising is designed to create goodwill and build a desired image for a company rather than to promote specific products. For example, a firm might promote its commitment to sustainable business practices or workforce diversity. Institutional ads that address public issues are called **advocacy advertising**. With recent efforts to overhaul health insurance in the United States, for instance, many companies with a financial stake in the outcome have been using advertising to present their points of view.[11]

institutional advertising Advertising that seeks to create goodwill and to build a desired image for a company, rather than to promote specific products

Advertising can also be classified according to the sponsor. *National advertising* is sponsored by companies that sell products on a nationwide basis. The biggest national advertisers spend a *lot* on advertising, with companies such as Verizon and AT&T spending over $1 billion a year.[12] In contrast, *local advertising* is sponsored by a local merchant; grocery store ads are a good example. *Cooperative advertising* involves a financial arrangement in which companies with products sold nationally share the costs of local advertising with local marketing intermediaries.

advocacy advertising Advertising that presents a company's opinions on public issues such as education or health care

ADVERTISING APPEALS

A key decision in planning a promotional campaign is choosing the **advertising appeal**, a creative tactic designed to capture the audience's attention and promote preference for the product or company being advertised. Marketers can choose from seven basic appeals (note that these appeals are not limited to advertising; they are used in other types of persuasive communication as well):[13]

advertising appeal A creative tactic designed to capture the audience's attention and promote preference for the product or company being advertised

- **Logic.** The basic approach with a logical appeal is to make a claim based on a rational argument supported by solid evidence. Not surprisingly, business-to-business advertising relies heavily on logical appeals because businesses have logical concerns—profitability, process improvements, quality, and other financial and technical concerns. However, marketers should not ignore the emotional aspects of business purchasing. Managers put their reputations and sometimes their careers on the line when they make major purchase decisions, so advertisers need to consider these emotional elements. Logical appeals are also used in consumer advertising whenever the purchase decision

289

has a rational component and logic might help persuade buyers to consider or prefer a particular product.

- **Emotion.** An emotional appeal calls on audience feelings and sympathies rather than facts, figures, and rational arguments (see Exhibit 4). Emotional appeals range from sentimental to terrifying. On the lighter side, flowers, greeting cards, and gifts are among the products usually sold with a positive emotional appeal. At the other end of the spectrum are appeals to a broad range of fears: personal and family safety, financial security, social acceptance, and business success or failure. To be effective, appeals to fear must be managed carefully. Laying it on too thick can anger the audience or even cause them to block out the message entirely.
- **Humor.** In a world cluttered with advertising, humor is frequently used to capture people's attention. However, humor can be tricky; sometimes it can offend audiences, tainting the brand, or the humor can be so memorable that audiences remember the joke but not the product being advertised.[14]
- **Celebrity.** The thinking behind celebrity involvement in advertising is that people will be more inclined to use products endorsed by a celebrity because they will identify with and want to be like this person (no matter how far-fetched such aspirations might be at a purely logical level). Celebrities can also bring new excitement, humor, energy, and even perceived value to a product. In addition to being expensive, however, celebrity endorsements can be risky because the brand's image becomes linked to the celebrity's image, including whatever image problems the celebrity experiences in his or her personal life.[15]
- **Sex.** Sex-oriented appeals are the most controversial type of advertising, in terms of both social reaction and promotional effectiveness. Although the phrase "sex sells" is often repeated, it isn't always true. Sexual appeals can definitely be effective, but the degree of effectiveness varies by product, audience, and the role of the sexual imagery or narrative in the advertising. For example, sexual appeals have been shown to be more effective with audiences that have a low level of emotional or intellectual engagement with the purchase than with audiences that are more involved.[16]
- **Music.** With its ability to create emotional bonds and "embed" itself in listeners' memories, music can be a powerful aspect of advertising. Marketers can take several approaches to integrating music into radio, television, or online advertising, including composing *jingles* specifically for commercials, licensing popular songs for use in commercials (although these fees can run into the millions of dollars for hit songs), or working with emerging artists to write songs specifically with advertising use in mind.[17]
- **Scarcity.** If a product is in limited supply or available only for a limited time, advertisers can use this scarcity to encourage consumer responses.

Note that these appeals are not mutually exclusive. For example, ads can use humor to catch an audience's attention and then use an emotional appeal to strengthen the bond with the brand or logic to show the superiority of a product.

ADVERTISING MEDIA

advertising media
Communications channels, such as newspapers, radio, television, and the World Wide Web

media mix A combination of print, broadcast, online, and other media used for an advertising campaign

Choosing **advertising media**, or channels of communication, can be as important as selecting the type of advertising and the advertising appeal. Major advertising media include newspapers, television, radio, magazines, product placement, fixed web (from computers), and mobile web (from mobile phones and other handheld devices). A *media plan* outlines the advertising budget, the schedule of when ads will appear, and a discussion of the **media mix**—the combination of print, broadcast, online, and other media to be used in the campaign. To create the media mix, advertising experts factor in the characteristics of the target audience, the types of media that will reach the largest audience in the most cost-effective way, and the strengths and weaknesses of the various media as they relate to the product and its marketing message (see Exhibit 5).

EXHIBIT 4	Emotional and Logical Appeals

All marketing messages strike a balance between logical and emotional appeals. Bigelow Tea uses textual and visual elements to convey the literal and figurative warmth offered by a cup of tea. In contrast, the stock brokerage TD Ameritrade provides a comprehensive, layered message that emphasizes logical supporting points. Investing one's hard-earned money obviously has a strong emotional angle, however, so TD Ameritrade also emphasizes points of safety and security.

Without using any images of people, the solitary teacup (left), the multiple glasses of iced tea (center), and the brunch setting suggested by the tea and food (right) convey both the pleasures of a quiet time alone as well as the pleasures of sharing tea with friends and family.

The red-orange color of the tea, enhanced with the glow of backlighting through the translucent liquid, speaks of warmth and comfort.

Complementary colors suggest freshness and elegance, adding to the emotional appeal.

The text uses the storytelling technique to explain the creation of Bigelow's signature Constant Comment tea flavor and does so in a way that highlights the emotional appeal of drinking tea.

Used with permission of R.C. Bigelow, Inc.

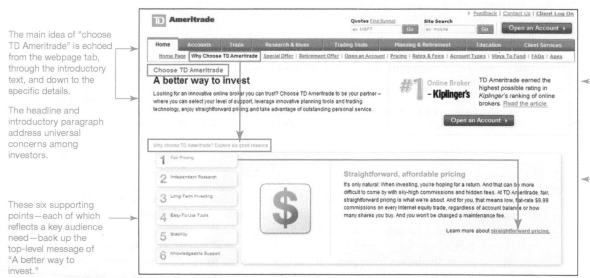

The main idea of "choose TD Ameritrade" is echoed from the webpage tab, through the introductory text, and down to the specific details.

The headline and introductory paragraph address universal concerns among investors.

These six supporting points—each of which reflects a key audience need—back up the top-level message of "A better way to invest."

An endorsement from a well-known source boosts the credibility of the company's promotional message.

Each of the six supporting points is presented at three levels of detail: (1) the short message of the button labels at the far left, (2) a short paragraph with a headline that echoes audience needs, and (3) additional pages (accessed via the link) with full details.

Image Courtesy of TD Ameritrade IP Company, Inc.

EXHIBIT 5	Advantages and Disadvantages of Major Advertising Media

Each medium has strengths and weaknesses; companies often combine two or more media in an advertising campaign to maximize their promotional effectiveness.

Medium	Advantages	Disadvantages
Newspapers	Extensive market coverage; low cost; short lead time for placing ads; good local market coverage; geographic selectivity; credibility	Poor graphic quality; short life span; cluttered pages; visual competition from other ads; printed papers have rapidly declining readership in many cities
Television	Great impact; broad reach; appealing to senses of sight, sound, and motion; creative opportunities for demonstration; high attention; entertainment carryover	High cost for production and air time; less audience selectivity; long preparation time; commercial clutter; short life for message; vulnerability to being skipped or muted; losing ground to new media options
Radio	Low cost; high frequency; immediacy; portability; high geographic and demographic selectivity	No visual possibilities; short life for message; commercial clutter; lower attention than television; declining audience share; low level of engagement
Magazines	Good production quality; long life; local and regional market selectivity; authority and credibility; multiple readers extend reach of each issue; close bond with readers	Limited demonstration possibilities; long lead time between placing and publishing ads; lots of ad clutter; high cost; declining readership for many titles
Product placement	Offers a way to get around viewers' advertising filters; chance for high visibility in the right program, movie, or game	Limited choice of vehicles; unpredictable; effectiveness is linked to the popularity of the programming; risk of overuse could reduce effectiveness over time
Fixed web (from stationary computers)	Rich media options and interactivity can make ads more compelling and more effective; changes and additions can be made quickly and easily in most cases; webpages can provide an almost unlimited amount of information; can be measured and personalized through tracking and targeting capabilities; instant links to online retailing and influence on store-based retail sales; growing audiences for Internet radio and video; social media connections can spread marketing messages through word of mouth	Extreme degree of audience fragmentation (millions of websites); increasing clutter (such as pop-up ads); technical glitches can interrupt ad display; not as portable as magazines, newspapers, or mobile web; ad-blocking software can prevent ads from being displayed
Mobile web (from mobile phones and other handheld devices)	In addition to almost every advantage of the fixed web other than display size: portability; constant, "always-on" presence (most people have their phones with them much of the time); opportunity for location-based advertising; possibilities for narrow targeting	Many users won't tolerate advertising intrusions via mobile phone; small screen size limits display possibilities

Sources: Adapted from Jeffrey M. O'Brien, "The Wizards of Apps," *Fortune*, 5 May 2009, 29–30; Christopher Meyer, "The Year of Marketing Dangerously," *Harvard Business Review*, October 2008, 26–27; Magid Abraham, "The Off-line Impact of Online Ads," *Harvard Business Review*, April 2008, 28; Michael A. Wiles and Anna Danielova, "The Worth of Product Placement in Successful Films: An Event Study Analysis," *Journal of Marketing*, July 2009, 44–63; Sarah Chung and Tina Hedges, "Is Your Digital Marketing a Turn-on?" *Global Cosmetic Industry*, July 2009, 22–24; Douglas MacMillan, "What Works in Online Video Advertising?" *BusinessWeek*, 28 January 2009, 26; Guy Yaniv, "Sold on Mobile Marketing: Effective Wireless Carrier Mobile Advertising and How to Make It Even More So," *International Journal of Mobile Marketing*, December 2008, 86–91; Kenneth E. Clow and Donald Baack, *Integrated Advertising, Promotion, and Marketing Communications*, 4th ed. (Upper Saddle River, N.J.: Pearson Prentice Hall, 2010), 219–229.

Three trends are likely to shape advertising media in the coming years. First, the media landscape will continue to fragment as new online and mobile formats emerge and conventional print and broadcast media fight to hang on to their share of advertisers' budgets. The days when advertisers could reach most consumers through a few television networks and major periodicals are long gone. Figuring out how to reach consumers who spread their attention across a variety of media and delivery platforms is one of the biggest challenges facing marketers today. With Facebook emerging as a multibillion-dollar advertising platform, for example, companies have yet another choice to consider when it comes to dividing up their advertising budgets.[18]

Second, the lines between advertising, entertainment, and *value-added content* (such as informative articles and how-to videos) will continue to blur. For example, more advertisers are borrowing storytelling techniques and other methods from the entertainment industry to make their TV commercials, online videos, and other ads more entertaining and thus more likely to be watched.[19] **Product placement**, in which companies pay to have their products displayed or used in television shows, movies, and video games, is already a multibillion-dollar business and is sure to grow as advertisers respond to the increasing number of ways consumers are able to ignore, skip, or block ads—and as content producers look for new cash flow opportunities. Product placement ranges from subtle brand displays in the background of a scene to active engagement with a product.[20]

Third, technical innovations will continue to create new advertising tools and techniques, including the behavioral targeting methods described on page 368 and more sophisticated tracking and pricing models that tie advertising costs to measurable results.[21] To counter the low response rates of conventional banner ads on websites, for instance, marketers are trying new ways of integrating advertising with site content.[22] The number of *hybrid media* will grow; one example is "webified" interactive purchasing systems that merge the television and Internet platforms so that consumers can use their TV remotes to buy products shown in a program.[23] As online video expands, so too will connections with advertising and retailing, including software that turns images of people and products in a video into clickable hyperlinks—so that a viewer can instantly order the same clothes an actor or a host is wearing, for example.[24]

REAL-TIME UPDATES
Learn More by Watching This Video

Inventing new ways to engage the audience

See how prominent television advertisers are responding to the changing world of media. Go to http://real-timeupdates.com/bia6 and click on Learn More. If you are using MyBizLab, you can access Real-Time Updates within each chapter or under Student Study Tools.

product placement The paid display or use of products in television shows, movies, and video games

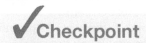

✔ Checkpoint

LEARNING OBJECTIVE 2: Identify the major types of advertising, the most common advertising appeals, and the most important advertising media.

SUMMARY: The major types of advertising based on the type of message are *product* advertising (which promotes the benefits of a product), *comparative* advertising (which compares a product to competitors' products), *institutional* advertising (which promotes a company or other organization), and *advocacy* advertising (which conveys information and opinions about public issues). Advertising can also be categorized by sponsor, including *national*, *local*, and *cooperative* advertising. The most common advertising appeals are logic, emotion, humor, celebrity, sex, music, and scarcity. Major advertising media include newspapers, television, radio, magazines, product placement, fixed web (from computers), and mobile web (from mobile phones and other handheld devices).

CRITICAL THINKING: (1) Do fragmented media make it easier or harder for marketers to engage in segmented or concentrated marketing? Explain your answer. (2) Why would a company such as McDonald's, which is already well known to virtually all consumers in the United States, continue to spend heavily on advertising?

IT'S YOUR BUSINESS: (1) Have you ever believed that you could create better advertising for a product than the company behind the product created? If so, explain the type of appeal you would've used and why. (2) Do you find that you tend to watch and listen to most television commercials, or do you mute or channel surf during commercials? If you pay attention to commercials, what captures your interest?

KEY TERMS TO KNOW: advertising, institutional advertising, advocacy advertising, advertising appeal, advertising media, media mix, product placement

3 **LEARNING OBJECTIVE**

Explain how direct marketing differs from advertising, and identify the major forms of direct media.

direct marketing Direct communication other than personal sales contacts designed to stimulate a measurable response

Direct Marketing

Although it is similar to advertising in many respects, **direct marketing**, defined as direct communication other than personal sales contacts, can differ from advertising in three important ways. (The lines continue to blur between types of media, so not all these distinctions hold true for every medium.) First, direct marketing often uses *personally addressable* media such as letters and email messages to deliver targeted messages to individual consumers or organizational purchasers. Second, except for infomercials, direct marketing doesn't involve the purchase of time or space in other media. The advertiser usually has control over the delivery mechanism and can decide when, where, and how the message is delivered. Third, direct marketing has a *direct response* aspect that often isn't present in advertising. While effective direct marketing works to build lasting relationships with customers, its primary emphasis is generating sales *now*.

According to the Direct Marketing Association (www.the-dma.org), a trade group of advertisers and marketing agencies, direct marketing efforts, on average, yield twice the return on investment of other marketing efforts.[25] Bear in mind, however, that direct marketing efforts often take place within a broader context of advertising and other activities. While they may get the credit for making the sale, they often don't work in isolation.

DIRECT MARKETING TECHNIQUES

Direct marketing has evolved dramatically from its early days, when pioneering promotional efforts such as the Sears catalog in the late 1800s helped establish *mail order* on a massive scale.[26] Direct marketing is now a computer-intensive multimedia effort that includes mail, telephone, and online media. The heart of any direct marketing effort is a customer database that contains contact histories, purchase records, and profiles of each buyer or potential buyer. (Direct marketing is sometimes referred to as *database marketing*.) The data can range from basic demographic information to records of all customer contacts to detailed purchasing records and other behavioral data. Such databases also play a vital role in relationship marketing because they enable a company to personalize its interaction with every customer.

The *measurability* of direct marketing is one of its greatest appeals. If you mail a promotional flyer to 1,000 people and 36 of them call to place an order, you know the campaign had a 3.6 percent response rate. Because direct responses are directly measurable (unlike many advertising efforts), direct marketing lends itself to constant experimentation and improvement. This is particularly true with online direct marketing efforts, where changes can be made cheaply and quickly.

Just as many retailers now reach out to customers in multiple ways through multichannel retailing (see page 348), many companies now integrate direct marketing with other communication efforts in *multichannel marketing campaigns*. For instance, customer databases are now expanding to include everything from widget usage on social networks to mobile web and phone usage.[27]

DIRECT MARKETING MEDIA

The catalogs that helped launch direct marketing over a hundred years ago are still a force today, as a peek inside any mailbox in the country will confirm. Here is a brief look at the major media used in direct marketing:

direct mail Printed materials addressed to individual consumers, households, or business contacts

- **Mail. Direct mail**, printed material addressed to an individual or a household, has the key advantage of being able to put promotional materials, ranging from simple letters and glossy catalogs to DVDs and product samples, directly into the hands of a target audience.
- **Email.** The ability to send millions of messages in a matter of minutes at almost no cost made email a hit with direct marketers—and practically destroyed email as a viable communication medium in the minds of some users tired of being deluged with unwanted "spam." The spam problem notwithstanding, email marketing remains the fastest-growing direct marketing medium.[28] To minimize the level of annoyance and to help potential customers get the information they really do want, many companies now emphasize *permission-based* email marketing, usually by asking customers or website visitors to *opt-in* to mailing lists.

- **Search engine marketing.** With millions of web users relying on search engines such as Google and Bing every day, **search engine marketing**, or *search advertising*, has become an important marketing medium (see Exhibit 6). Although it doesn't quite fit the traditional categories of either advertising or direct marketing, search engine marketing comes closer to being a direct medium because it is individualized to each web user. Search advertising works in two basic ways. First, advertisers can pay to have small ads presented whenever the keywords they select are used in a search. These are the "sponsored results" that can appear above and to the right of the actual search results. Second, these ads can also appear on the many websites that are in the search engine's *advertising exchange* or *advertising network*, a collection of websites that sell space on their pages for such ads.[29] These ads are triggered by content on a webpage and can appear anywhere on the page, even inserted between sections of an online article.

- **Direct response online.** The interactive, adaptable nature of websites allows them to go far beyond static advertising media to become direct, personalized communication channels. As Amazon.com founder Jeff Bezos explains, referring to the fact that every returning customer is greeted with a customized storefront based on his or her shopping patterns, "If we have 72 million customers, we should have 72 million stores."[30] *Targeted display advertising* involves ads with graphical (as opposed to just textual) content served up on web pages based on some knowledge of an individual's interests or behaviors. While Google is the most common conduit for search engine advertising, Facebook, with its massive user base, is the leader in the rapidly growing sector of online display advertising.[31]

- **Telephone.** The telephone is a major promotional tool in consumer and organizational markets and for both *inbound* (when buyers call in to place orders) and *outbound* (when sellers contact potential buyers with sales offers) marketing. After rising complaints from consumers about telemarketers interrupting them at home, Congress created the National Do Not Call Registry, which gives individuals the opportunity to have their numbers removed from telemarketers' lists. However, marketers can still call businesses as well as consumers who have purchased from them in the past.

- **Direct response television.** More commonly known as *infomercials*, **direct response television** programs have the major advantage of time, allowing companies to demonstrate products and engage viewers in a way that isn't possible with 30- or 60-second commercials.

search engine marketing Automated presentation of ads that are related to either the results of an online search or the content being displayed on other webpages

direct response television The use of television commercials and longer-format infomercials that are designed to stimulate an immediate purchase response from viewers

---

EXHIBIT 6   **Search Engine Marketing**

Sponsored search results display ads based on the terms entered into a search engine.

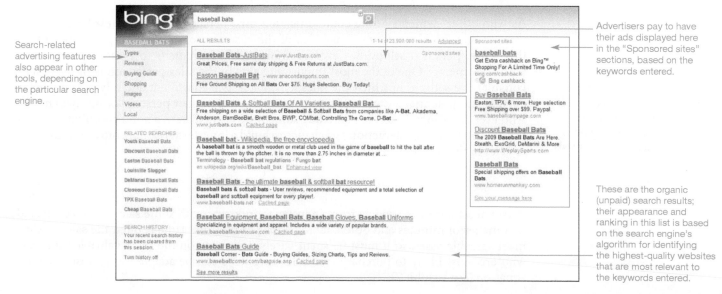

Search-related advertising features also appear in other tools, depending on the particular search engine.

Advertisers pay to have their ads displayed here in the "Sponsored sites" sections, based on the keywords entered.

These are the organic (unpaid) search results; their appearance and ranking in this list is based on the search engine's algorithm for identifying the highest-quality websites that are most relevant to the keywords entered.

LEARNING OBJECTIVE 3: Explain how direct marketing differs from advertising, and identify the major forms of direct media.

SUMMARY: Direct marketing differs from advertising in three important ways: (1) It uses *personally addressable* media such as letters and email messages to deliver targeted messages to individual consumers or organizational purchasers, (2) it doesn't involve the purchase of time or space in other media, and (3) it has a *direct response* aspect that often isn't present in advertising. The major categories of direct marketing media are mail (including catalogs), email, search engine marketing, telephone, and direct response television.

CRITICAL THINKING: (1) Would an iPhone app that streams QVC or another shopping channel to mobile phones be an effective direct marketing medium? Why or why not? (2) If direct marketing has a better return on investment than other forms of promotion, why do companies bother with anything but direct marketing?

IT'S YOUR BUSINESS: (1) As a rough guess, what percentage of the direct marketing messages you receive in a given week are effectively targeted to your needs as a consumer? Identify a recent example that was well targeted and one that was not. (2) Have you ever responded to the offer in a "spam" email message? If so, what enticed you to do so?

KEY TERMS TO KNOW: direct marketing, direct mail, search engine marketing, direct response television

---

Describe consultative selling, and explain the personal-selling process.

personal selling One-on-one interaction between a salesperson and a prospective buyer

consultative selling An approach in which a salesperson acts as a consultant and advisor to help customers find the best solutions to their personal or business needs

Personal Selling

Even with the rapid advance of e-commerce and other marketing technologies, **personal selling**, the one-on-one interaction between a salesperson and a prospective buyer, remains a fundamentally important part of the promotional mix in many consumer and organizational markets. Although a salesforce can't reach millions of customers at once like a website or a direct marketing program can, today's highly trained sales professionals are able to build relationships and solve problems in ways that impersonal media can't match.

CONTEMPORARY PERSONAL SELLING

As with other elements of the communication mix, personal selling has evolved over the years to support the contemporary idea of the customer-oriented marketing concept. In this sense, personal selling has evolved from *peddling products* to *creating partnerships* with customers.[32] One of the most important shifts in the sales profession is the advent of **consultative selling**, in which the salesperson acts as a consultant and advisor who helps current and potential customers find the best solutions to their personal or business needs. And even if a shopper isn't ready to buy something immediately, a good consultative salesperson will view the interaction as a chance to build a long-term relationship that could lead to sales in the future.[33]

THE PERSONAL-SELLING PROCESS

Personal selling varies widely from industry to industry, with some sales being completed in a matter of minutes and others taking weeks or months. Time is often the salesperson's most valuable asset, so it must be spent wisely—focusing on the most valuable prospects who are most likely to purchase. The following steps can be adapted to almost any sales situation (see Exhibit 7):

EXHIBIT 7	The Personal-Selling Process

The personal-selling process can involve up to seven steps, starting with prospecting for sales leads and ending with following up after the sale has been closed. This diagram gives you a general idea of how salespeople approach major sales opportunities.

1. Prospecting	2. Preparing	3. Approaching	4. Aligning with Customer Needs	5. Handling Objections	6. Closing	7. Following Up
Finding and qualifying potential customers; usually involves generating sales, identifying prospects, and qualifying prospects	Getting ready for the sales call; researching the customer in more depth, establishing objectives, and preparing a presentation	Taking steps to make a good first impression; crafting the right appearance, maintaining professional behavior, and preparing an engaging introduction	Listening to the prospect describe what is needed and proposing a solution to meet those needs	Addressing any concerns the prospect might raise; exploring the deeper reasons that might be behind the expressed objections	Asking the prospect to choose the solution being offered	Checking in with the customer after the sale to make sure the solution is working out as expected and to keep building a longterm relationship

- **Step 1: Prospecting.** The process of finding and qualifying potential customers is known as **prospecting**. This step usually involves three activities: (1) *generating sales leads*—names of individuals and organizations that might be likely prospects for the company's product; (2) *identifying prospects*—potential customers who indicate a need or a desire for the seller's product; and (3) *qualifying prospects*—the process of figuring out which prospects have both the authority and the available money to buy.

- **Step 2: Preparing.** With a list of strong prospects in hand, the next step is to prepare for the *sales call* (in person, over the phone, or online via videoconferencing or another method). In this research phase, the sales staff tries to learn more about the people and organizations they will be contacting regarding their buying needs, their motives for buying, and the names of current suppliers. The salesperson then establishes specific objectives to achieve during the sales call, which vary depending on where the buyer is in the decision cycle. Finally, the salesperson often prepares a presentation, which can be as basic as a list of points to discuss or as elaborate as a product demonstration or multimedia presentation.

- **Step 3: Approaching the prospect.** First impressions can make or break a sale, so knowledgeable salespeople take care to (1) craft the appropriate appearance for themselves and for everything that represents them; (2) maintain behaviors and attitudes that are professional, courteous, and confident without being arrogant; and (3) prepare opening lines that include a brief greeting and introduction, followed by a few carefully chosen words that establish a good rapport with the potential customer.

- **Step 4: Uncovering needs and presenting solutions.** After the conversation has been initiated, the next step is understanding the customer's specific needs. The biggest mistake a salesperson can make at this stage is talking instead of listening. The most extreme form of this error is the *canned sales pitch*, in which the salesperson recites or even reads a stock message, with no regard for the customer's unique circumstances. In contrast, today's enlightened sales professionals focus on questioning and listening before offering a solution that meets each prospect's unique needs.

- **Step 5: Handling objections.** Potential customers can express a variety of objections to the products they are considering, and salespeople need to be ready with answers and alternatives.

prospecting The process of finding and qualifying potential customers

Personal selling is an important promotional element for many business-to-business marketers.

© Peter Hvizdak / The Image Works

closing The point at which a sale is completed

- **Step 6: Closing.** Bringing the sales process to a successful conclusion by asking for and receiving an affirmative purchase decision is known as **closing**. Experienced professionals know to look for signs that the prospect is ready to make a decision, and they use a variety of techniques such as offering to write up an order to encourage a definitive answer.[34]
- **Step 7: Following up.** Most companies depend on repeat sales and referrals from satisfied customers, so it's important that salespeople follow up after the sale to make sure customers are satisfied with their purchases. Staying in touch gives a company the opportunity to answer questions, address areas of confusion or dissatisfaction with a purchase, and show customers it is a reliable partner for the long haul.

✓ Checkpoint

LEARNING OBJECTIVE 4: Describe consultative selling, and explain the personal-selling process.

SUMMARY: Consultative selling is a combination of persuasion and advice, in which the salesperson acts as a consultant and advisor who helps current and potential customers find the best solutions to their personal or business needs. The seven general steps in personal selling are (1) *prospecting*, finding prospects and qualifying them; (2) *preparing*, creating a prospect profile, setting objectives for the call, and preparing a presentation; (3) *approaching* the prospect, with the goal of making a positive first impression; (4) *uncovering* the customer's needs and *presenting* appropriate solutions; (5) *handling objections*, using audience comments as an opportunity to strengthen the presentation; (6) *closing*, focusing on completing the sale; and (7) *following up* after the sale to make sure the buyer is satisfied.

CRITICAL THINKING: (1) Why is the canned approach inadequate for many selling situations? (2) Why should a salesperson take the time to qualify sales leads?

IT'S YOUR BUSINESS: (1) Would you be comfortable in a personal-selling role? Why or why not? (2) What can you learn from professional selling methods to help you in a job interview?

KEY TERMS TO KNOW: personal selling, consultative selling, prospecting, closing

---

5 LEARNING OBJECTIVE

Define *sales promotion*, and identify the major categories of consumer and trade promotions.

sales promotion A wide range of events and activities designed to promote a brand or stimulate interest in a product

Sales Promotion

Sales promotion consists of short-term incentives to build the reputation of a brand, encourage the purchase of a product, or simply enhance relationships with current and potential customers. Sales promotion consists of two basic categories: consumer promotion and trade promotion.

CONSUMER PROMOTIONS

Companies use a variety of consumer promotional tools and incentives to stimulate repeat purchases and to entice new users:

- **Contests and other audience involvement tactics.** Giving consumers the opportunity to participate in contests, games, sweepstakes, surveys, and other activities, particularly if there is a chance for consumers to demonstrate cleverness or creativity, is a great way to build energy around a brand.
- **Coupons.** The biggest category of consumer promotion is **coupons**, printed or electronic certificates that spur sales by giving buyers a discount when they purchase specified products (see Exhibit 8). Paper couponing is an inefficient technique, however; consumers redeem only 1 percent of the 300 billion printed coupons distributed

coupons Printed or electronic certificates that offer discounts on particular items and are redeemed at the time of purchase

| EXHIBIT 8 | Consumer Promotions Using Social Media |

Blimpie is one of many companies that use Facebook as a channel for consumer promotions. "Liking" a company page such as this puts the company's Wall postings into your Facebook feed, making it a convenient way for the firm to reach out to customers.

Courtesy of Kahala Corp.

every year in the United States.[35] The rapid growth of mobile couponing via smartphones and new social systems such as Groupon (www.groupon.com) are revolutionizing couponing. While they are creating opportunities for businesses, the spread of these coupons is changing buyer behavior as more and more consumers now expect stores and restaurants to offer coupons.[36]

● **Rebates.** With **rebates**, companies offer partial reimbursement of the price as a purchase incentive. Rebates can be an effective tool for boosting sales, but they obviously cut into per-unit profits—and the effect can be more or less permanent when frequent rebates in an industry encourage buyers to delay purchases until a rebate program is available.

rebates Partial reimbursement of price, offered as a purchase incentive

point-of-purchase (POP) display
Advertising or other display materials set up at retail locations to promote products to potential customers as they are making their purchase decisions

- **Point-of-purchase.** A **point-of-purchase (POP) display** is an in-store presentation designed to stimulate immediate sales. POP displays are a vital element in the marketing effort for many products sold at retail stores. Not only do they represent the manufacturer's last chance to communicate with the consumer, but they help capture *impulse purchases*—unplanned purchases that can make up as much as 50 percent of sales in mass merchandise stores and supermarkets.[37]
- **Samples and trial-use versions.** Distributing samples is an effective way to introduce a new product, encourage nonusers to try an existing product, encourage current buyers to use the product in a new way, or expand distribution into new areas. Many software products are also offered as trial versions to let customers try before buying.
- **Special-event sponsorship.** Sponsoring special events has become one of the most popular sales promotion tactics, with thousands of companies spending billions of dollars to sponsor events ranging from golf to opera.
- **Other promotions.** Other popular consumer sales promotion techniques include in-store demonstrations, loyalty and frequency programs such as frequent-flyer programs, and **premiums**, which are free or bargain-priced items offered to encourage the consumer to buy a product. **Specialty advertising** (on pens, calendars, T-shirts, mouse pads, and other items) helps keep a company's name in front of customers for a long period of time.

premiums Free or bargain-priced items offered to encourage consumers to buy a product

specialty advertising Advertising that appears on various items such as coffee mugs, pens, and calendars, designed to help keep a company's name in front of customers

TRADE PROMOTIONS

trade promotions
Sales-promotion efforts aimed at inducing distributors or retailers to push a producer's products

Although shoppers are more aware of consumer promotions, **trade promotions** aimed at inducing wholesalers or retailers to sell a company's products actually account for the larger share of promotional spending and can be the single largest item in a manufacturer's marketing budget.[38] The most popular trade promotions are **trade allowances**, which involve discounts on product prices, free merchandise, or other payments, such as the retail slotting allowances. The intermediary can either pocket the savings to increase profits or pass the savings on to the consumer to generate additional sales. Trade allowances are commonly used when adopting a push marketing strategy because they encourage the intermediaries to carry new products or to sell higher volumes of current products.

trade allowances Discounts or other financial considerations offered by producers to wholesalers and retailers

The chief downside of trade allowances is that they can create the controversial practice of *forward buying*, in which customers load up on merchandise while the price is low. For example, if a producer offers retailers a 20 percent discount for a period of 6 weeks, a retailer might choose to buy enough inventory to last 8 or 10 weeks. Purchasing this excessive amount at the lower price increases the retailer's profit, but at the expense of the producer's profit.

Besides trade allowances, other popular trade promotions are dealer contests and bonus programs designed to motivate distributors or retailers to push particular merchandise. Product samples are also common in many business marketing efforts. For instance, semiconductor manufacturers often provide samples of electronic components to engineers who are designing new products, knowing that if the prototype is successful, it could lead to full-scale production—and orders for thousands or millions of components.

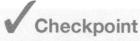 **Checkpoint**

LEARNING OBJECTIVE 5: Define *sales promotion*, **and identify the major categories of consumer and trade promotions.**

SUMMARY: The two main types of sales promotion are consumer promotion and trade promotion. Consumer promotions are intended to motivate the final consumer to try new products or to experiment with the company's brands. Examples include contests, coupons, rebates, point-of-purchase displays, samples, special-event sponsorship, premiums, and specialty advertising. Trade promotions are designed to induce wholesalers and retailers to promote a producer's products. Common trade promotions include trade allowances, dealer contests, bonus programs, and samples.

CRITICAL THINKING: (1) If 99 percent of coupons are never used, why do companies keep printing so many? (2) If wholesalers and retailers can make money selling a manufacturer's product, why would the manufacturer need to offer incentives such as sales contests?

IT'S YOUR BUSINESS: (1) How can sales promotions reduce the reluctance that buyers might feel about trying an unfamiliar product? (2) Have you ever participated in a sales promotion without realizing you were doing so? For example, have you ever "liked" a company on Facebook to enter a sweepstakes without realizing that in doing so you were also signing up for all its Wall postings in your Facebook feed?

KEY TERMS TO KNOW: sales promotion, coupons, rebates, point-of-purchase (POP) display, premiums, specialty advertising, trade promotions, trade allowances

Social Media and Public Relations

6 **LEARNING OBJECTIVE**

Explain the uses of social media in customer communication and the role of public relations.

All the communication methods discussed so far in this chapter involve activities by companies themselves to transmit carefully crafted and controlled messages to target audiences. The final two methods, social media and public relations, differ from the traditional methods in two key respects: They rely on others to forward or create promotional messages, and they don't provide anywhere near the level of control over those messages that conventional marketing methods offer.

SOCIAL MEDIA IN THE MARKETING PROCESS

Social media are any electronic media that transform passive audiences into active participants in the communication process by allowing them to share, revise, or respond to existing content, or to contribute new content. These media include social networks, blogs, microblogs such as Twitter, wikis, *user-generated content (UGC) sites* such as Flickr and YouTube, *community Q&A sites* such as LinkedIn Answers and Get Satisfaction's customer support sites, and *community participation websites* such as Yelp. To varying degrees, all of these media play a role in contemporary marketing.

social media Any electronic media that transform passive audiences into active participants in the communication process by allowing them to share content, revise content, respond to content, or contribute new content

Social media activities combine the newest communication technologies with the oldest form of marketing communication in the world, **word of mouth**—customers and other parties transmitting information about companies and products through personal conversations. Word-of mouth marketing is often called *viral marketing*, in reference to the transmission of messages in much the same way that biological viruses are transmitted from person to person. However, viral marketing is not really an accurate metaphor. As author Brian Solis puts it, "There is no such thing as viral marketing."[39] Real viruses spread from host to host on their own, whereas word-of-mouth marketing spreads *voluntarily* from person to person. The distinction is critical because marketers need to give people a good reason—good content, in other words—to pass along their messages.

word of mouth Communication among customers and other parties, transmitting information about companies and products through online or offline personal conversations

The social communication model is by no means limited to the consumer sector. Technical professionals were using the Internet for communication years before the World Wide Web was invented, and now businesspeople in just about every industry use social media to share ideas, conduct research, and evaluate products. In fact, many businesspeople are far more active in social media than the average consumer.[40]

Communication Strategies for Social Media

Audiences in the social media environment are not willing to be passive recipients in a structured, one-way information delivery process—or to rely solely on promotional

REAL-TIME UPDATES
Learn More by Watching This Video

Spending less on media and more on the good stuff

New York City's 4food burger restaurant relies on low-cost social media efforts to spread the word specifically so that it can spend its money on high-quality ingredients. Go to http://real-timeupdates .com/bia6 and click on Learn More. If you are using MyBizLab, you can access Real-Time Updates within each chapter or under Student Study Tools.

messages from marketers. This notion of interactive participation is the driving force behind **conversation marketing**, in which companies *initiate* and *facilitate* conversations in a networked community of customers, journalists, bloggers, Twitter users, and other interested parties. Social media can be a powerful communication channel, but companies should follow these guidelines in order to meet audience expectations:[41]

- **Remember that it's a conversation, not a lecture or a sales pitch.** One of the great appeals of social media is the feeling of conversation, of people talking *with* one another instead of one person talking *at* everyone else.
- **Facilitate community building.** Make sure customers and other audiences can connect with the company and with each other.
- **Initiate and respond to conversations within the community.** Marketers can start or join conversations by providing useful information to current and potential customers. As you can see in the Behind the Scenes wrap-up at the end of the chapter, this effort was key to SeaWorld's success in launching its new water coaster ride.
- **Identify and support champions.** In marketing, *champions* are enthusiastic fans of a company and its products—so enthusiastic that they help spread the company's message, defend it against detractors, and help other customers use its products.
- **Restrict conventional promotional efforts to the right time and right place.** Persuasive communication efforts are still valid for specific communication tasks, such as regular advertising and the product information pages on a website, but efforts to inject "salespeak" into social media conversations will be rejected by the audience.

Brand Communities

Another major impact of social media has been the rapid spread of **brand communities**, people united by their interest in and ownership of particular products (see Exhibit 9). These communities can be formal membership organizations, such as the longstanding Harley Owners Group (HOG), or informal networks of people with similar interests. They can be fairly independent from the company behind the brand or can have the active support and involvement of company management, as is the case of Harley-Davidson's support of the motorcycle enthusiasts who are members of HOG (*hog* is an affectionate nickname for a Harley).[42]

Social media are natural communication vehicles for brand communities because these tools let people bond and share information on their own terms. And because a strong majority of consumers now trust their peers more than any other source of product information—including conventional advertising techniques—formal and informal brand communities are becoming an essential information source in consumer buying behavior.[43]

PUBLIC RELATIONS

Public relations encompasses a wide variety of nonsales communications that businesses have with their many stakeholders, including communities, investors, industry analysts, government agencies, and activists. Companies rely on public relations to build a favorable corporate image and foster positive relations with all these groups.

Public relations efforts often involve the news media, with companies offering information to print, broadcast, and online journalists in the hope that these intermediaries will pass the message along to their audiences. If the information is likely to interest their audiences, journalists will help "spread the word," in the best cases generating high levels of public awareness at a much lower cost than a company could achieve on its own through paid advertising.[44]

Two standard tools for communicating with the media are the press release and the press conference. A traditional **press release** is a short message sent to the media covering topics that are of potential news interest; a *video news release* is a brief video clip sent to television stations. Companies use news releases in the hopes of getting favorable news coverage about themselves and their products. When a business has significant news to announce, it will often arrange a **press conference**, at which reporters can listen to company representatives and ask questions.

---

conversation marketing
An approach to customer communication in which companies initiate and facilitate conversations in a networked community of potential buyers and other interested parties

brand communities Formal or informal groups of people united by their interest in and ownership of particular products

public relations Nonsales communication that businesses have with their various audiences (including both communication with the general public and press relations)

press release A brief statement or video program released to the press announcing new products, management changes, sales performance, and other potential news items; also called a *news release*

press conference An in-person or online gathering of media representatives at which companies announce new information; also called a *news conference*

EXHIBIT 9 | Using Social Media to Promote Brand Communities

The Segway Social online network connects owners of these unique personal vehicles, including helping teams organize Segway polo matches and other events.

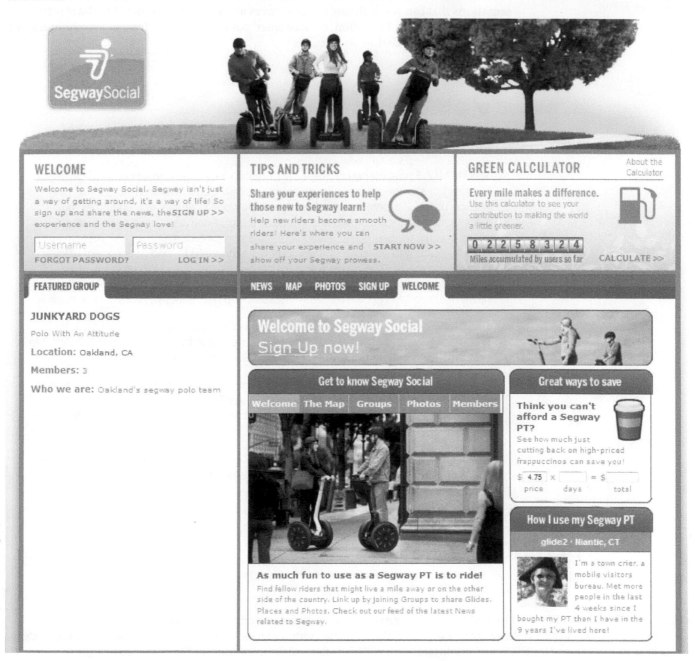

Until recently, press releases were intended only for members of the news media and were crafted in a way to provide information to reporters who would then write their own articles. However, the nature of the press release is changing. Many companies now view it as a general-purpose tool for communicating directly with customers and other audiences, writing *direct-to-consumer press releases*. As news media expert David Meerman Scott puts it, "Millions of people read press releases directly, unfiltered by the media. You need to be speaking directly to them."[45]

The newest twist on news releases is the *social media release*, which has several advantages over the traditional release. First, the social media release emphasizes bullet-point content over narrative paragraphs so that bloggers, editors, and others can assemble their own stories rather than being forced to rewrite the material in a traditional release. Second,

303

as an electronic-only document (a specialized webpage, essentially), the social media release offers the ability to include videos and other multimedia elements. Third, social bookmarking buttons make it easy for people to help publicize the content.[46] Similarly, the traditional press conference is being replaced or augmented in many cases with *webcasts*, online presentations that can reach thousands of viewers at once and be archived for later retrieval.

For the latest information on customer communication strategies, techniques, and tools, visit http://real-timeupdates.com/bia6.

✓ Checkpoint

LEARNING OBJECTIVE 6: Explain the uses of social media in customer communication and the role of public relations.

SUMMARY: Social media have several potential uses in customer communication, including customer service, rumor control, research, and relationship building. They can also be used for promotion, but that should be done in an indirect, customer-focused manner. Because consumers and investors support companies with good reputations, smart companies use public relations to build and protect their images. They communicate with consumers, investors, industry analysts, and government officials through the media. They pursue and maintain press relations with representatives of newspapers, television, and other broadcast media so that they can provide effective news releases (also known as press releases) and hold effective news conferences.

CRITICAL THINKING: (1) If marketers are advised against blatantly promoting their products in social media, why should they bother using these media at all? (2) Why are press relations critical to the launch of many new products?

IT'S YOUR BUSINESS: (1) Have you ever used social media to ask questions about a product or to criticize or compliment a company? Did anyone from the company respond? (2) Do you consider yourself a member of any brand communities (formal or informal)? If so, what effect do these groups have on your purchasing behavior?

KEY TERMS TO KNOW: social media, word of mouth, conversation marketing, brand communities, public relations, press release, press conference

---

BEHIND THE SCENES   MyBizLab

SEAWORLD SAN ANTONIO GETS SOCIAL TO BUILD INTEREST IN NEW RIDE

When SeaWorld San Antonio needed to get the word out quickly about its new Journey to Atlantis water coaster ride, public relations specialist Kami Huyse of My PR Pro (http://myprpro.com) worked with SeaWorld's Director of Communications Fran Stephenson to survey the options. The team had three objectives: (1) build relationships with the community of coaster enthusiasts, (2) create awareness of the new ride, and (3) increase visitor traffic. You can see that these goals stretch across three time frames: long-term relationship building, midterm awareness, and short-term sales. It's a lot to ask of any communication campaign—and particularly a campaign with the time and budget limits that Huyse and Stephenson faced.

Hard-core roller coaster enthusiasts are *really* enthusiastic about their coasters. They like to learn about new rides, compare their impressions of rides they've been on, organize trips to visit

rides around the country, and even work to preserve some of the classic old roller coasters that dot the American landscape. Dozens of websites, forums, blogs, and coaster groups share information, including the 7,000-member American Coaster Enthusiasts (www.aceonline.org). With Huyse's expertise in social media, she recognized an opportunity when she saw one: They would connect with the "thrill ride" community online.

Their research identified 22 blogs and forums that were particularly active and influential in the enthusiast community. "The primary strategy was to treat coaster bloggers as a VIP audience and to create content to suit their needs," Huyse explains. These bloggers were also invited to attend a special prelaunch media day to test-drive Journey to Atlantis.

As part of this effort to provide opinion influencers and the general public with enticing content about the new ride,

SeaWorld's in-house communication staff created 11 videos and a 45-image photo collection that were made available for public use through YouTube, Flickr, and Veoh. The staff also created a content-rich website with social media functionality to add to SeaWorld's existing web presence to serve as the "hub" of the launch campaign.

The results? One of the knocks against social media as a business communication platform is that its effects can be difficult or impossible to measure. While that is true in many cases, Huyse and her colleagues were able to make three specific measurements that highlight the success of SeaWorld's social media effort. First, of the 22 targeted VIP enthusiast groups, more than half covered the opening in their blogs or forums, including the influential Theme Park Insider website (www.themeparkinsider.com). Second, more than 50 other websites created links to the Journey to Atlantis campaign website, and 30 of those were from coaster enthusiast websites. These numbers might sound small, but remember that social media is a game of multiplication: Small numbers of people spreading a message can quickly turn into large numbers.

The third and ultimately most important measurement is the impact on SeaWorld's business. Fortunately for Huyse's team, a measuring device was already in place: the exit surveys that SeaWorld routinely conducts, asking park visitors about their experiences and decisions to visit. Using data from this survey, the team could identify which media efforts drove visitors to the park most effectively and then calculate the cost-effectiveness of each method to see how the social media campaign compared to SeaWorld's other, ongoing promotional efforts. While television was almost as effective as online efforts at driving traffic through the front gate, the net cost to get one visitor through the front gate was nearly five times higher for television. And in terms of actual sales, based on SeaWorld's average per capita revenue figure, the social media campaign generated more than $2.6 million in revenue—for only $44,000 in total costs. From a marketing point of view, that's even more thrilling than a ride on the latest roller coaster.[47]

Critical Thinking Questions

1. With social media proving to be a cost-effective way to attract park visitors, should SeaWorld abandon its other promotional efforts and focus everything on social media? Why or why not?
2. What steps can SeaWorld take to maintain a relationship with coaster enthusiasts, now that the excitement surrounding the new ride has faded?
3. Do coaster fans such as members of American Coaster Enthusiasts constitute a brand community as described in the chapter? Why or why not?

LEARN MORE ONLINE

Search online for commentary and media materials relating to the Journey to Atlantis ride at SeaWorld San Antonio. (Be aware that different rides with the same name exist at the other SeaWorld parks.) Imagine that you're a coaster enthusiast. Based on what you see online, would you consider visiting San Antonio to ride Journey to Atlantis? Why or why not?

MyBizLab

Log on to www.mybizlab.com to access study and assessment aids associated with this chapter.

KEY TERMS

advertising
advertising appeal
advertising media
advocacy advertising
brand communities
closing
communication mix
consultative selling
conversation marketing
core message
coupons
direct mail
direct marketing
direct response television
institutional advertising
integrated marketing communications (IMC)
media mix
personal selling

point-of-purchase (POP) display
premiums
press conference
press release
product placement
prospecting
public relations
pull strategy
push strategy
rebates
sales promotion
search engine marketing
social communication model
social media
specialty advertising
trade allowances
trade promotions
word of mouth

TEST YOUR KNOWLEDGE

Questions for Review

1. What are two key ways in which the social communication model differs from conventional promotional communication?
2. What is the difference between using a push strategy and using a pull strategy to promote products?
3. What are the advantages of personal selling over other forms of customer communication?
4. What is an advertising appeal?
5. What are some common types of consumer promotion?

Questions for Analysis

6. Why is it important for sales professionals to qualify prospects?
7. What are the potential disadvantages of using celebrity appeals in advertising?
8. Why do some companies avoid email marketing, particularly to noncustomers?
9. Do marketers have any control over social media? Why or why not?
10. **Ethical Considerations.** Is your privacy being violated when a website you visit displays ads that are personalized in any way, even if it's just geographically targeted to the local area (based on your computer's Internet address)? Why or why not?

Questions for Application

11. If you were a real estate agent, how would you determine whether it's worth investing a significant amount of time in a particular prospect?
12. Think about an advertisement (in any medium) that had either a strongly positive or strongly negative effect on your attitude toward the product being advertised or the advertiser itself. Why did the ad have this effect? If you responded positively to the ad, do you think you were being manipulated in any way? If you responded negatively—and you are a potential buyer of the product that was advertised—what changes would you make to the ad to make it more successful?
13. Would it be a good idea to "repurpose" conventional press releases as posts on your company blog? Why or why not?
14. **Concept Integration.** Should companies involve their marketing channels in the design of their customer communication programs? What are the advantages and disadvantages of doing so?

EXPAND YOUR KNOWLEDGE

Discovering Career Opportunities

Jobs in customer communication—advertising, direct marketing, personal selling, sales promotion, social media, and public relations—are among the most exciting and challenging in all of marketing. Choose a particular job in one of these areas. Using personal contacts, local directories of businesses or business professionals, or online resources such as company websites or search engines (including Twitter and blog search tools), arrange a brief phone, email, or personal interview with a professional working in your chosen marketing field.

1. What are the daily activities of this professional? What tools and resources does this person use most often on the job? What does this professional like most and least about the job?
2. What talents and educational background does this professional bring to the job? How are the person's skills and knowledge applied to handle the job's daily activities?
3. What advice does the person you are interviewing have for newcomers entering this field? What can you do now to get yourself started on a career path toward this position?

Improving Your Tech Insights: Individualized Advertising

Don't be surprised if you look out the window one morning to see clouds in the sky arranged in letters that spell out your name and invite you to try a refreshing bottle of Coke or remind you to get your oil changed at Jiffy Lube.

Maybe it won't get quite that far, but advertisers are perfecting a variety of technologies that allow them to pinpoint individual audience members with customized messages. One interesting effect of this is that some advertising media or retailing formats are starting to look more like direct marketing media. As the chapter notes, Amazon.com already personalizes a store front for every one of its customers. Here are a few other examples: personalized magazine covers (including one that showed an aerial photograph of each subscriber's neighborhood with his or her home or office circled in red); commercials on digital cable systems that can be targeted to viewers in an individual neighborhood or even an individual household (with messages shaped by the demographics of the residents of the house); narrowly focused audio messages that can be aimed at a single shopper in a retail store; Google's Gmail email service, which serves up ads based on specific words in your email messages; and Google's behavioral targeting technology (its "interest-based advertising"), which displays ads based on your web-surfing patterns.

Identify one form of individualized advertising now in use (you can search for "individualized advertising," "personalized advertising," "behavioral targeting," or "interest-based advertising"). In a brief email message to your instructor, describe the technology, explain how it helps businesses reach customers more effectively, and identify any privacy concerns involved with the medium.[48]

PRACTICE YOUR SKILLS

Sharpening Your Communication Skills

The good news: The current events blog you started as a hobby has become quite popular. The bad news: The blog now takes up so much of your time that you've had to quit a part-time job you were using to supplement your regular income. After some discussions with other bloggers, you decide to join Google's AdSense program (www.google.com/adsense) to help pay for the costs of operating your blog. With this program, small ads triggered by keywords in the content you publish will appear on your site. However, you're worried that your audience will think you've "sold out" because you're now generating revenue from your blog. Write a short message that could be posted on your blog, explaining why you consider it necessary to run ads and assuring your readers of your continued objectivity, even if that means criticizing organizations whose ads might appear on your blog.

Building Your Team Skills

In small groups, discuss three or four recent ads or consumer promotions (in any media) that you think were particularly effective. Using the knowledge you've gained from this chapter, try to come to agreement on which attributes contributed to the success of each ad or promotion. For instance: Was it persuasive? Informative? Competitive? Creative? Did it have logical or emotional appeal? Did it stimulate you to buy the product? Why? Compare your results with those of other teams. Did you mention the same ads? Did you list the same attributes?

Developing Your Research Skills

Choose an article from recent issues of business journals or newspapers (print or online editions) that describes the advertising or promotion efforts of a particular company or trade association.

1. Who is the company or trade association targeting?
2. What specific marketing objectives is the organization trying to accomplish?
3. What role does advertising play in the promotion strategy? What other promotion techniques does the article mention? Are any of them unusual or noteworthy? Why?

REFERENCES

1. SeaWorld San Antonio website, accessed 10 September 2011, http://seaworldparks.com/seaworld-sanantonio; Kami Huyse, "Case Study: ROI of Social Media Campaign for SeaWorld San Antonio—A Year Later," Communication Overtones blog, 18 April 2008, http://overtonecomm.blogspot.com; Shel Israel, "GNTV: Making a Splash with Social Media Measurement," Global Neighbourhoods blog, 28 March 2008, http://redcouch.typepad.com/weblog; American Coaster Enthusiasts website, accessed 18 August 2009, www.aceonline.org.
2. Philip Kotler and Gary Armstrong, *Principles of Marketing*, 13th ed. (Upper Saddle River, N.J.: Pearson Prentice Hall, 2010), 409–140.
3. Adapted from Caterpillar website, accessed 2 August 2009, www.cat.com.
4. Kotler and Armstrong, *Principles of Marketing*, 405.
5. "How to Comply with the Children's Online Privacy Protection Rule," U.S. Federal Trade Commission website, accessed 17 July 2010, www.ftc.gov; "Frequently Asked Advertising Questions: A Guide for Small Business," U.S. Federal Trade Commission website, accessed 17 July 2010, www.ftc.gov.
6. Miguel Helft and Tanzina Vega, "Retargeting Ads Follow Surfers to Other Sites," *New York Times*, 29 August 2010, www.nytimes.com.
7. National Advertising Review Council website, accessed 3 August 2009, www.narcpartners.org.
8. American Marketing Association website, accessed 3 August 2009, www.marketingpower.com.
9. Emily Bryson York, "The Gloves Are Off: More Marketers Opt for Attack Ads," *Advertising Age*, 25 May 2009, 4.
10. William Wells, John Burnett, and Sandra Moriarty, *Advertising: Principles & Practice*, 6th ed. (Upper Saddle River, N.J.: Pearson Prentice Hall, 2003), 47–48.
11. Peter Overby, "Millions Spent on Ad War over Health Care Overhaul," National Public Radio website, 21 July 2009, www.npr.org.
12. Maureen Morrison, "Verizon Tops AT&T as Most-Advertised Brand," *Advertising Age*, 22 June 2009, http://adage.com.
13. Adapted from Kenneth E. Clow and Donald Baack, *Integrated Advertising, Promotion, and Marketing Communications*, 4th ed. (Upper Saddle River, N.J.: Pearson Prentice Hall, 2010), 153–167.
14. Clow and Baack, *Integrated Advertising, Promotion, and Marketing Communications*, 155–156.
15. Steve McKee, "The Trouble with Celebrity Endorsements," *BusinessWeek*, 17 November 2008, 10.
16. Sanjay Putrevu, "Consumer Responses Toward Sexual and Nonsexual Appeals," *Journal of Advertising*, Summer 2008, 57–69.
17. Clow and Baack, *Integrated Advertising, Promotion, and Marketing Communications*, 162–164.
18. Todd Wasserman, "Facebook to Take Number 1 Spot in Display Ad Market This Year," Mashable, 20 June 2011, http://mashable.com.
19. Kotler and Armstrong, *Principles of Marketing*, 436–437.
20. Janet Stilson, "The Clutter Busters," *Adweek*, 2 March 2009, 7.
21. Ben Kunz, "A Pricing Revolution Looms in Online Advertising," *BusinessWeek*, 7 April 2009, 20.
22. Brian Morrissey, "Thinking Beyond the Banner," *Adweek*, 8 June 2009, 9.
23. "The $56 billion Ad Question," *Fortune*, 3 January 2011, http://tech.fortune.cnn.com; Meyer, "The Year of Marketing Dangerously."
24. Douglas MacMillan, "What Works in Online Video Advertising?" *BusinessWeek*, 28 January 2009, 26.
25. "What Is the Direct Marketing Association?" Direct Marketing Association website, accessed 15 August 2009, www.the-dma.org.
26. "History of the Sears Catalog," Sears Archives, accessed 15 August 2009, www.searsarchives.com.
27. "Direct Marketing Association 2008 Annual Report," Direct Marketing Association website, www.the-dma.org.
28. Carol Krol, "E-Mail, Fastest Growing Direct Marketing Segment, Expands Double Digits," *DMNews*, 4 August 2009, www.dmnews.com.
29. "Google Adwords," Google website, accessed 18 August 2007, www.google.com; Danny Sullivan, "Major Search Engines and Directories," *Search Engine Watch*, 28 March 2007, http://search-enginewatch.com; Thomas Claburn, "Google, Yahoo Gain Search

Market Share; Microsoft, Time Warner Lose," *InformationWeek*, 21 November 2006, www.informationweek.com.

30. Kotler and Armstrong, *Principles of Marketing*, 489.
31. Wasserman, "Facebook to Take Number 1 Spot in Display Ad Market This Year."
32. Gerald L. Manning and Barry L. Reece, *Selling Today*, 9th ed. (Upper Saddle River, N.J.: Pearson Prentice Hall, 2004), 7–8.
33. Howard Feiertag, "Build Your Group Sales by Consultative Selling," *Hotel & Motel Management*, 15 June 2009, 10.
34. Kotler and Armstrong, *Principles of Marketing*, 474–475.
35. Dan Balaban, "Will Tough Times Spell Greater Opportunity for Mobile Coupons?" *Cards & Payments*, March 2009, 14–17.
36. Jay Goltz, "Is Groupon Ruining Retailing?" *New York Times*, 16 March 2011, www.nytimes.com.
37. Clow and Baack, *Integrated Advertising, Promotion, and Marketing Communications*, 284.
38. Clow and Baack, *Integrated Advertising, Promotion, and Marketing Communications*, 340.
39. Brian Solis, *Engage!* (Hoboken, N.J.: Wiley, 2010), 86.
40. Josh Bernoff, "Why B-to-B Ought to Love Social Media," *Marketing News*, 15 April 2009, 20.
41. Josh Bernoff, "Social Strategy for Exciting (and Not So Exciting) Brands," *Marketing News*, 15 May 2009, 18; Larry Weber, *Marketing to the Social Web* (Hoboken, N.J.: Wiley, 2007), 12–14; David Meerman Scott, *The New Rules of Marketing and PR* (Hoboken, N.J.: Wiley, 2007), 62; Paul Gillin, *The New Influencers* (Sanger, Calif.: Quill Driver Books, 2007), 34–35; Jeremy Wright, *Blog Marketing: The Revolutionary Way to Increase Sales, Build*

Your Brand, and Get Exceptional Results (New York: McGraw-Hill, 2006), 263–365.
42. Susan Fournier and Lara Lee, "Getting Brand Communities Right," *Harvard Business Review*, April 2009, 105–111.
43. Patrick Hanlon and Josh Hawkins, "Expand Your Brand Community Online," *Advertising Age*, 7 January 2008, 14–15.
44. Steve McKee, "Why PR Is the Prescription," *BusinessWeek*, 13 April 2009, 8.
45. David Meerman Scott, *The New Rules of Marketing and PR* (Hoboken, N.J.: Wiley, 2007), 62.
46. Shel Holz, "Next-Generation Press Releases," CW Bulletin, September 2009, www.iabc.com; Steph Gray, "Baby Steps in Social Media News Releases," Helpful Technology blog, 15 May 2009, http://blog.helpfultechnology.com.
47. See note 1.
48. Adapted from Miguel Helft, "Google to Offer Ads Based on Interests," *New York Times*, 11 March 2009, www.nytimes.com; "Nick Gillespie Discusses the Personalized Cover of *Reason* Magazine and the Possibilities of Database Technology" (interview), Talk of the Nation, National Public Radio, 4 May 2003, www.highbeam.com; Kevin J. Delaney, "Will Users Care if Gmail Invades Privacy?" *Wall Street Journal*, 6 April 2004, B1, B3; Allison Fass, "Spot On," *Forbes*, 23 June 2003, 140; "Hey You! How About Lunch?" *Wall Street Journal*, 1 April 2004, B1, B5.

GLOSSARY

advertising appeal A creative tactic designed to capture the audience's attention and promote preference for the product or company being advertised

advertising media Communications channels, such as newspapers, radio, television, and the World Wide Web

advertising The delivery of announcements and promotional messages via time or space purchased in various media

advocacy advertising Advertising that presents a company's opinions on public issues such as education or health care

brand communities Formal or informal groups of people united by their interest in and ownership of particular products

closing The point at which a sale is completed

communication mix A blend of communication vehicles—advertising, direct marketing, personal selling, sales promotion, social media, and public relations—that a company uses to reach current and potential customers

consultative selling An approach in which a salesperson acts as a consultant and advisor to help customers find the best solutions to their personal or business needs

conversation marketing An approach to customer communication in which companies initiate and facilitate conversations in a networked community of potential buyers and other interested parties

core message The single most important idea an advertiser hopes to convey to the target audience about its products or the company

coupons Printed or electronic certificates that offer discounts on particular items and are redeemed at the time of purchase

direct mail Printed materials addressed to individual consumers, households, or business contacts

direct marketing Direct communication other than personal sales contacts designed to stimulate a measurable response

direct response television The use of television commercials and longer-format infomercials that are designed to stimulate an immediate purchase response from viewers

institutional advertising Advertising that seeks to create goodwill and to build a desired image for a company, rather than to promote specific products

integrated marketing communications (IMC) A strategy of coordinating and integrating communication and promotion efforts with customers to ensure greater efficiency and effectiveness

media mix A combination of print, broadcast, online, and other media used for an advertising campaign

personal selling One-on-one interaction between a salesperson and a prospective buyer

point-of-purchase (POP) display Advertising or other display materials set up at retail locations to promote products to potential customers as they are making their purchase decisions

premiums Free or bargain-priced items offered to encourage consumers to buy a product

press conference An in-person or online gathering of media representatives at which companies announce new information; also called a *news conference*

press release A brief statement or video program released to the press announcing new products, management changes, sales performance, and other potential news items; also called a *news release*

product placement The paid display or use of products in television shows, movies, and video games

prospecting The process of finding and qualifying potential customers

public relations Nonsales communication that businesses have with their various audiences (including both communication with the general public and press relations)

pull strategy A promotional strategy that stimulates consumer demand via advertising and other communication efforts, thereby creating a *pull* effect through the channel

push strategy A promotional strategy that focuses on intermediaries, motivating them to promote, or *push*, products toward end users

rebates Partial reimbursement of price, offered as a purchase incentive

sales promotion A wide range of events and activities designed to promote a brand or stimulate interest in a product

search engine marketing Automated presentation of ads that are related to either the results of an online search or the content being displayed on other webpages

social communication model An approach to communication based on interactive social media and conversational communication styles

social media Any electronic media that transform passive audiences into active participants in the communication process by allowing them to share content, revise content, respond to content, or contribute new content

specialty advertising Advertising that appears on various items such as coffee mugs, pens, and calendars, designed to help keep a company's name in front of customers

trade allowances Discounts or other financial considerations offered by producers to wholesalers and retailers

trade promotions Sales-promotion efforts aimed at inducing distributors or retailers to push a producer's products

word of mouth Communication among customers and other parties, transmitting information about companies and products through online or offline personal conversations

Financial Information and Accounting Concepts

Financial Information and Accounting Concepts

LEARNING OBJECTIVES After studying this chapter, you will be able to

1 Define *accounting* and describe the roles of private and public accountants

2 Explain the impact of accounting standards such as GAAP and the Sarbanes-Oxley Act on corporate accounting

3 Describe the *accounting equation* and explain the purpose of *double-entry bookkeeping* and the *matching principle*

4 Identify the major financial statements and explain how to read a balance sheet

5 Explain the purpose of the income statement and the statement of cash flows

6 Explain the purpose of ratio analysis and list the four main categories of financial ratios

MyBizLab

Where you see MyBizLab in this chapter, go to www.mybizlab.com for additional activities on the topic being discussed.

BEHIND THE SCENES REALITY COMES KNOCKING AT THE GOOGLEPLEX

When expenses began to grow faster than revenues, Google CFO Patrick Pichette began a systematic evaluation of how the company was spending its cash.

David Eulitt/MCT/Newscom

www.google.com

You may have received some nice employee benefits somewhere along the line, but did an armored truck ever back up to your company's front door to hand out $1,000 to every employee at Christmas time?

As Google's dominance in the profitable search engine market grew in recent years and its stock price soared, the company looked like it just might end up with all the cash in the world. To create one of the world's best places to work, the Mountain View, California, Internet giant sometimes spent money as if it had unlimited cash, too. Employee perks ranged from a companywide ski trip and an annual cash bonus—which really was delivered by armored truck—to free meals cooked by gourmet chefs and on-site massages, doctors, and car service.

Beyond these mere amenities, Google created one of the most interesting and stimulating workplaces imaginable. Engineers were allowed to spend up to 20 percent of their time exploring whatever fascinated them, even if those adventures weren't directly related to the company's current business efforts. Those explorations often did lead to new products and features, though, as Google's product line expanded far beyond its original search engine.

As it launched new projects and business initiatives right and left, Google kept hiring the best and the brightest; by 2008, the company had 20,000 employees and another 10,000 contractors. It had also acquired more than 50 other companies, paying from a few million dollars to get small niche companies on up to $1.65 billion to buy YouTube and $3.1 billion to buy the online advertising company DoubleClick.

Cash was flowing in, cash was flowing out, and all was good in the Googleplex, as the company's headquarters complex is known. But reality has a way of catching up to even the highest-flying companies, and Google would prove no exception. Internally, after a decade of rampant growth, expenses were eating up an ever-larger share of revenue. Externally, the global economy was cooling off quickly, and one company after another began trimming advertising budgets. Despite its many product innovations and explorations, Google still depended on search engine advertising for nearly all its revenue. Online advertising wasn't getting chopped quite as severely as ads for television and other traditional media, but the spending reductions were serious enough to slow Google's sales growth. With expenses growing faster than revenue, something had to give.

If you were Patrick Pichette, Google's chief financial officer, how would you bring spending under control without alienating a workforce that has come to expect a certain level of pampering—and without stifling innovation, the engine behind the company's spectacular growth?[1]

INTRODUCTION

With years of experience managing complex business operations, Google's Patrick Pichette (profiled in the chapter-opening Behind the Scenes) could tell you how vital it is to have accurate, up-to-date accounting information. After providing an introduction to what accountants do and the rules they are expected to follow, this chapter explains the fundamental concepts of the accounting equation and double-entry bookkeeping. It then explores the primary "report cards" used in accounting: the balance sheet, income statement, and statement of cash flows. The chapter wraps up with a look at trend analysis and ratio analysis, the tools that managers, lenders, and investors use to predict a company's ongoing health.

Understanding Accounting

1 LEARNING OBJECTIVE

Define *accounting*, and describe the roles of private and public accountants.

Accounting is the system a business uses to identify, measure, and communicate financial information to others, inside and outside the organization. Accurate and timely financial information is important to businesses such as Google for two reasons: First, it helps managers and owners plan and control a company's operations and make informed business decisions. Second, it helps outsiders evaluate a business. Suppliers, banks, and other lenders want to know whether a business is creditworthy; investors and shareholders are concerned with its profit potential; government agencies are interested in its tax accounting.

accounting Measuring, interpreting, and communicating financial information to support internal and external decision making

Because outsiders and insiders use accounting information for different purposes, accounting has two distinct facets. **Financial accounting** is concerned with preparing financial statements and other information for outsiders such as stockholders and *creditors* (people or organizations that have lent a company money or have extended its credit); **management accounting** is concerned with preparing cost analyses, profitability reports, budgets, and other information for insiders such as management and other company decision makers. To be useful, all accounting information must be accurate, objective, consistent over time, and comparable to information supplied by other companies.

financial accounting The area of accounting concerned with preparing financial information for users outside the organization

management accounting The area of accounting concerned with preparing data for use by managers within the organization

WHAT ACCOUNTANTS DO

Some people confuse the work accountants do with **bookkeeping**, which is the clerical function of recording the economic activities of a business. Although some accountants do perform bookkeeping functions, their work generally goes well beyond the scope of this activity. Accountants prepare financial statements, analyze and interpret financial information, prepare financial forecasts and budgets, and prepare tax returns. Some accountants specialize in certain areas of accounting, such as *cost accounting* (computing and analyzing production and operating costs), *tax accounting* (preparing tax returns and interpreting tax law), *financial analysis* (evaluating a company's performance and the financial implications of strategic decisions such as product pricing, employee benefits,

bookkeeping Recordkeeping; the clerical aspect of accounting and business acquisitions), or *forensic accounting* (combining accounting and investigating skills to assist in legal and criminal matters).

In addition to traditional accounting work, accountants may also help clients improve business processes, plan for the future, evaluate product performance, analyze profitability by customer and product groups, design and install new computer systems, assist companies with decision making, and provide a variety of other management consulting services. Performing these functions requires a strong business background and a variety of business skills beyond accounting.

PRIVATE ACCOUNTANTS

private accountants In-house accountants employed by organizations and businesses other than a public accounting firm; also called *corporate accountants*

controller The highest-ranking accountant in a company, responsible for overseeing all accounting functions

certified public accountants (CPAs) Professionally licensed accountants who meet certain requirements for education and experience and who pass a comprehensive examination

public accountants Professionals who provide accounting services to other businesses and individuals for a fee

Private accountants work for corporations, government agencies, and not-for-profit organizations. Their titles vary by function and include *corporate accountant*, *managerial accountant*, and *cost accountant*.[2] Private accountants generally work together as a team under the supervision of the organization's **controller**, who reports to the vice president of finance or the chief financial officer (CFO). Exhibit 1 shows the typical finance department of a large company. In smaller organizations, the controller may be in charge of the company's entire finance operation and report directly to the president.

Although certification is not required of private accountants, many are licensed **certified public accountants (CPAs)**. Specific requirements vary by state, but to receive a CPA license, an individual must complete a certain number of hours of college-level coursework, have a minimum number of years of work experience in the accounting field, and pass the Uniform CPA Exam.[3] A growing number of private accountants are becoming *certified management accountants (CMAs)*; to do so, they must pass an intensive exam sponsored by the Institute of Management Accountants.[4]

PUBLIC ACCOUNTANTS

In contrast to private accountants, **public accountants** are independent of the businesses, organizations, and individuals they serve. Most public accountants are employed by public

EXHIBIT 1	Typical Finance Department

Here is a typical finance department of a large company. In smaller companies, the controller may be the highest-ranking accountant and report directly to the president. The top executive in charge of finance is often called the chief financial officer (CFO).

accounting firms that provide a variety of accounting and consulting services to their clients. The largest of these, four international networks known as the "Big Four," are Deloitte Touche Tohmatsu (www.deloitte.com), Ernst & Young (www.ey.com), KPMG (www.kpmg.com), and Price-waterhouseCoopers, or PwC (www.pwc.com). Whether they belong to one of these giant networks (each of which employs over 100,000 people) or to a smaller independent firm, public accountants generally are CPAs and must obtain CPA and state licensing certifications before they are eligible to conduct an **audit**—a formal evaluation of a company's accounting records and processes to ensure the integrity and reliability of a company's financial statements.

By the way, if you've shied away from accounting as a career choice because of popular stereotypes about it being a dull job fit only for "bean counters," it's time to take another look. Partly as a consequence of financial scandals in recent years and the growing complexity of accounting regulations, accounting specialists are now in demand in many industries. Employment is growing faster than average for all accounting occupations, while salaries and benefits are increasing as everybody from the Big Four to the FBI to corporations both large and small actively recruits accountants to help navigate the challenging landscape of contemporary business finance.[5]

REAL-TIME UPDATES

Learn More by Reading This Article

Considering a career in accounting?

This comprehensive directory can help you explore the profession and find potential employers. Go to http://real-timeupdates.com/bia6 and click on Learn More. If you are using MyBizLab, you can access Real-Time Updates within the chapter or under Student Study Tools.

audit Formal evaluation of the fairness and reliability of a client's financial statements

✓ Checkpoint

LEARNING OBJECTIVE 1: Define *accounting*, **and describe the roles of private and public accountants.**

SUMMARY: Accounting is the system a business uses to identify, measure, and communicate financial information to others, inside and outside the organization. Accountants perform a wide variety of tasks, including preparing financial statements, analyzing and interpreting financial information, preparing financial forecasts and budgets, preparing tax returns, interpreting tax law, computing and analyzing production costs, evaluating a company's performance, and analyzing the financial implications of business decisions. Private accountants work for corporations, government agencies, and not-for-profit organizations, performing various accounting functions for their employers. Public accountants, in contrast, sell their services to individuals and organizations. One of the most important functions of public accountants is performing audits, a formal evaluation of a company's accounting records and processes.

CRITICAL THINKING: (1) Why would a private accountant bother with becoming a CPA? (2) What effect can unreliable or uncertain accounting have on the economy?

IT'S YOUR BUSINESS: (1) How rigorous are your personal bookkeeping and accounting efforts? Do you keep accurate records, analyze spending, and set budgets? (2) If you don't really account for your personal finances, how might doing so help you, now and in the future?

KEY TERMS TO KNOW: accounting, financial accounting, management accounting, bookkeeping, private accountants, controller, certified public accountants (CPAs), public accountants, audit

The Rules of Accounting

In order to make informed decisions, investors, bankers, suppliers, and other parties need some means to verify the quality of the financial information that companies release to the public. They also need some way to compare information from one company to the next. To accommodate these needs, financial accountants are expected to follow a number of rules, some of which are voluntary and some of which are required by law.

2 **LEARNING OBJECTIVE**

Explain the impact of accounting standards such as GAAP and the Sarbanes-Oxley Act on corporate accounting.

ACCOUNTING STANDARDS: GAAP AND IFRS

Accounting is based on numbers, so it might seem like a fairly straightforward task to tally up a company's revenues and costs to determine its net profits. However, accounting is often anything but simple. For instance, *revenue recognition*, how and when a company records incoming revenue, is a particularly complex topic.[6] As just one example, should a company record revenue (a) when it ships products to customers, (b) when it bills customers, (c) when customers actually pay, or (d) after everyone has paid and any products that are going to be returned for refunds have been returned (since refunds reduce revenue)? If customers are in financial trouble and taking a long time to pay or are not paying at all, or if a poorly designed product is generating a lot of returns, the differences can be substantial.

Standardizing Through GAAP

From booking revenues and expenses to placing a value on assets and liabilities, the decisions just discussed affect just about every aspect of a company's stated financial picture. That picture in turn affects how much tax the company has to pay, how attractive it is as an investment opportunity, how creditworthy it is from a lender's point of view, and other significant outcomes.

> **GAAP (generally accepted accounting practices)** Standards and practices used by publicly held corporations in the United States and a few other countries in the preparation of financial statements; on course to converge with IFRS

To help ensure consistent financial reporting so that all stakeholders understand what they're looking at, over the years regulators, auditors, and company representatives have agreed on a series of accounting standards and procedures. **GAAP (generally accepted accounting principles)**, overseen in the United States by the Financial Accounting Standards Board (FASB), aims to give a fair and true picture of a company's financial position and enable outsiders to make confident analyses and comparisons. GAAP can't prevent every reporting abuse, but it does make distorting financial results in order to fool outsiders more difficult.[7] Companies can still provide "non-GAAP" financial results to investors in addition to their GAAP figures—as Google does, for example—but they must label these figures as non-GAAP data.

> **external auditors** Independent accounting firms that provide auditing services for public companies

Companies whose stock is publicly traded in the United States are required to file audited financial statements with the Securities and Exchange Commission (SEC). During an audit, CPAs who work for an independent accounting firm, also known as **external auditors**, review a client's financial records to determine whether the statements that summarize these records have been prepared in accordance with GAAP. The auditors then summarize their findings in a report attached to the client's published financial statements. Sometimes these reports disclose information that might materially affect the client's financial position, such as the bankruptcy of a major supplier, a large obsolete inventory, costly environmental problems, or questionable accounting practices. When a company receives a clean audit report, this means that to the best of the auditors' knowledge the company's financial statements are accurate.

To assist with the auditing process, many large organizations use *internal auditors*—employees who investigate and evaluate the organization's internal operations and data to determine whether they are accurate and whether they comply with GAAP, federal laws, and industry regulations. Although this self-checking process is vital to an organization's financial health, an internal audit is not a substitute for having an independent auditor look things over and render an unbiased opinion.

The Evolution Toward Global Accounting Standards

GAAP has helped standardize accounting and financial reporting for companies in the United States, but the situation is more complex at the international level because GAAP standards are not used in most other countries. The lack of global standardization creates extra work for U.S. multinationals, essentially forcing them to keep two sets of books.[8] In addition, it complicates cross-border transactions, mergers, and investments because companies don't have a single set of benchmarks to compute assets, liabilities, and other vital quantities.

> **international financial reporting standards (IFRS)** Accounting standards and practices used in many countries outside the United States

For the past decade, the FASB has been working with the London-based International Accounting Standards Board to harmonize GAAP with the **international financial reporting standards (IFRS)** now used in most countries. At present, the earliest the SEC plans to require or at least allow U.S. corporations to begin using IFRS-compatible standards is 2015, and many details remain to be worked out. However, it is clear that the eventual standards will bring pervasive changes to the accounting profession, financial management, information systems, stock-based compensation and bonuses, and other aspects of managing a public corporation.[9]

Just how complex and expensive it will be for U.S. companies to shift from GAAP to IFRS (or an IFRS-friendly version of GAAP) isn't clear yet. In general, the shift could take several years of work and will require a comprehensive reevaluation of a company's finances. The implications could be significant. For example, corporate income tends to come out higher under IFRS than it does under GAAP, which could conceivably increase companies' tax obligations.[10]

Changing to IFRS should help investors who want to purchase stocks of companies based in other countries, help U.S. stock exchanges by making them more competitive in world capital markets, help foreign companies that want to sell stock in the United States, and help multinational companies by letting them settle on a single set of accounting standards. Another key potential benefit is that companies will find it easier to staff financial positions around the world because everyone will be trained in the same financial language.[11]

SARBANES-OXLEY

The need for and complexity of financial reporting standards is highlighted in the controversial story of **Sarbanes-Oxley**, the informal name of the Public Company Accounting Reform and Investor Protection Act. (You'll hear it referred to as "Sox" or "Sarbox" as well.) Passed in 2002 in the wake of several cases of massive accounting fraud, most notably involving the energy company Enron and the telecom company WorldCom, Sarbanes-Oxley changed public company accounting in the United States in a number of important ways. Its major provisions include[12]

- Outlawing most loans by corporations to their own directors and executives
- Creating the Public Company Accounting Oversight Board (PCAOB) to oversee external auditors
- Requiring corporate lawyers to report evidence of financial wrongdoing
- Prohibiting external auditors from providing certain nonaudit services
- Requiring that audit committees on the board of directors have at least one financial expert and that the majority of board members be independent (not employed by the company in an executive position)
- Prohibiting investment bankers from influencing stock analysts
- Requiring CEOs and CFOs to sign statements attesting to the accuracy of their financial statements
- Requiring companies to document and test their internal financial controls and processes

The last item in particular, the result of the brief "Section 404" of the legislation, generated considerable controversy. Representative Michael Oxley, co-sponsor of the legislation, says that "99.9 percent of the complaints you hear are about 404." Oxley adds that it's not the two paragraphs in this section of the legislation that caused so much grief but rather the several hundred pages of regulations the PCAOB generated to enforce it.[13] As one financial writer put it, the requirements were so sweeping that they left financial executives "awash in a vast sea of details, with little ability to set priorities about what to focus on in their compliance efforts."[14]

After a lot of initial criticism about the costs of compliance and a shift in the PCAOB's stance to let companies focus on monitoring the riskiest financial decisions instead of every mundane transaction, complaints about Sarbox have leveled off in recent years.[15]

Sarbanes-Oxley
The informal name of comprehensive legislation designed to improve integrity and accountability of financial information

✓ **Checkpoint**

LEARNING OBJECTIVE 2: Explain the impact of accounting standards such as GAAP and the Sarbanes-Oxley Act on corporate accounting.

SUMMARY: Accounting standards such as GAAP help ensure consistent financial reporting, which is essential for regulators and investors to make informed decisions. To ensure consistency on a global scale, GAAP is likely to be merged with the international financial reports standards (IFRS) in the coming years. Sarbanes-Oxley introduced a number of rules covering the way publicly traded companies manage and report their finances, including restricting loans to directors and executives, creating a new board to oversee public auditors, requiring corporate lawyers to report financial wrongdoing, requiring CEOs and CFOs to sign financial statements under oath, and requiring companies to document their financial systems.

CRITICAL THINKING: (1) Should U.S. public companies with no significant overseas business activity be forced to follow international accounting standards? Why or why not? (2) How does requiring CEOs to personally attest to the accuracy of financial statements eliminate errors and misrepresentations?

IT'S YOUR BUSINESS: (1) How might the convergence of GAAP and IFRS in the coming years affect you as an investor? (2) If you were considering buying stock in a company, would you support rigorous and detailed financial accountability such as that called for by Section 404 of Sarbanes-Oxley? Why or why not?

KEY TERMS TO KNOW: GAAP (generally accepted accounting principles), external auditors, international financial reporting standards (IFRS), Sarbanes-Oxley

---

3 LEARNING OBJECTIVE

Describe the *accounting equation*, and explain the purpose of *double-entry bookkeeping* and the *matching principle.*

assets Any things of value owned or leased by a business

liabilities Claims against a firm's assets by creditors

owners' equity The portion of a company's assets that belongs to the owners after obligations to all creditors have been met

accounting equation The basic accounting equation, stating that assets equal liabilities plus owners' equity

Fundamental Accounting Concepts

In their work with financial data, accountants are guided by three basic concepts: the *fundamental accounting equation*, *double-entry bookkeeping*, and the *matching principle*. Here is a closer look at each of these essential ideas.

THE ACCOUNTING EQUATION

For thousands of years, businesses and governments have kept records of their **assets**—valuable items they own or lease, such as equipment, cash, land, buildings, inventory, and investments. Claims against those assets are **liabilities**, or what the business owes to its creditors—such as lenders and suppliers. For example, when a company borrows money to purchase a building, the lender has a claim against the company's assets. What remains after liabilities have been deducted from assets is **owners' equity**:

$$\text{Assets} - \text{Liabilities} = \text{Owners' equity}$$

As a simple example, if your company has $1,000,000 in assets and $800,000 in liabilities, your equity would be $200,000:

$$\$1,000,000 - \$800,000 = \$200,000$$

Using the principles of algebra, this equation can be restated in a variety of formats. The most common is the simple **accounting equation**, which serves as the framework for the entire accounting process:

$$\text{Assets} = \text{Liabilities} + \text{Owners' equity}$$
$$\$1,000,000 = \$800,000 + \$200,000$$

This equation suggests that either creditors or owners provide all the assets in a corporation. Think of it this way: If you were starting a new business, you could contribute cash to the company to buy the assets you needed to run your business or you could borrow money from a bank (the creditor) or you could do both. The company's liabilities are placed before owners' equity in the accounting equation because creditors get paid first. After liabilities have been paid, anything left over belongs to the owners. As a business engages in economic activity, the dollar amounts and composition of its assets, liabilities, and owners' equity change. However, the equation must always be in balance; in other words, one side of the equation must always equal the other side.

REAL-TIME UPDATES

Learn More by Reading This Article

Introduction to the accounting equation

Get a better feel for the accounting equation with these practical examples. Go to http://real-timeupdates.com/bia6 and click on Learn More. If you are using MyBizLab, you can access Real-Time Updates within the chapter or under Student Study Tools.

DOUBLE-ENTRY BOOKKEEPING AND THE MATCHING PRINCIPLE

To keep the accounting equation in balance, most companies use a **double-entry bookkeeping** system that records every transaction affecting assets, liabilities, or owners' equity. Each transaction is entered twice, once as a *debit* and once as a *credit*, and they must offset each other to keep the accounting equation in balance. The double-entry method predates computers by hundreds of years and was originally created to minimize errors caused by entering and adding figures by hand; accounting software typically handles all this behind the scenes now.

The **matching principle** requires that expenses incurred in producing revenues be deducted from the revenue they generated during the same accounting period. This matching of expenses and revenue is necessary for the company's financial statements to present an accurate picture of the profitability of a business. Accountants match revenue to expenses by adopting the **accrual basis** of accounting, which states that revenue is recognized when you make a sale or provide a service, not when you get paid. Similarly, your expenses are recorded when you receive the benefit of a service or when you use an asset to produce revenue—not when you pay for it.

Accrual accounting focuses on the economic substance of an event rather than on the movement of cash. It's a way of recognizing that revenue can be earned either before or after cash is received and that expenses can be incurred when a company receives a benefit (such as a shipment of supplies) either before or after the benefit is paid for.

If a business runs on a **cash basis**, the company records revenue only when money from the sale is actually received. Your checking account is a simple cash-based accounting system: You record checks, debit card charges, and ATM withdrawals at the time of purchase and record deposits at the time of receipt. Cash-based accounting is simple, but it can be misleading. It's easy to inflate income, for example, by delaying the payment of bills. For that reason, public companies are required to keep their books on an accrual basis.

Depreciation, or the allocation of the cost of a tangible long-term asset over a period of time, is another way that companies match expenses with revenue. (For intangible assets, this allocation over time is known as *amortization*.) When Google buys a piece of real estate, for example, instead of deducting the entire cost of the item at the time of purchase, the company *depreciates* it, or spreads the cost over a certain number of years as specified by tax regulations because the asset will likely generate income for many years. If the company were to expense long-term assets at the time of purchase, its apparent financial performance would be distorted negatively in the year of purchase and positively in all future years when these assets generate revenue.

double-entry bookkeeping A method of recording financial transactions that requires a debit entry and credit entry for each transaction to ensure that the accounting equation is always kept in balance

matching principle The fundamental principle requiring that expenses incurred in producing revenue be deducted from the revenues they generate during an accounting period

accrual basis An accounting method in which revenue is recorded when a sale is made and an expense is recorded when it is incurred

cash basis An accounting method in which revenue is recorded when payment is received and an expense is recorded when cash is paid

depreciation An accounting procedure for systematically spreading the cost of a tangible asset over its estimated useful life

✔Checkpoint

LEARNING OBJECTIVE 3: Describe the *accounting equation*, and explain the purpose of *double-entry bookkeeping* and the *matching principle*.

SUMMARY: The basic accounting equation is Assets = Liabilities + Owners' equity. Double-entry bookkeeping is a system of recording every financial transaction as two counterbalancing entries in order to keep the accounting equation in balance. The matching principle makes sure that expenses incurred in producing revenues are deducted from the revenue they generated during the same accounting period.

CRITICAL THINKING: (1) How does double-entry bookkeeping help eliminate errors? (2) Why is accrual-based accounting considered more fraud-proof than cash-based accounting?

IT'S YOUR BUSINESS: (1) Does looking at the accounting equation make you reconsider your personal spending habits? (Think about taking on liabilities that don't create any long-term assets, for example.) (2) How would accrual basis accounting give you better insights into your personal finances?

KEY TERMS TO KNOW: assets, liabilities, owners' equity, accounting equation, double-entry bookkeeping, matching principle, accrual basis, cash basis, depreciation

---

4 LEARNING OBJECTIVE

Identify the major financial statements, and explain how to read a balance sheet.

closing the books
Transferring net revenue and expense account balances to retained earnings for the period

Using Financial Statements: The Balance Sheet

As a company conducts business day after day, sales, purchases, and other transactions are recorded and classified into individual accounts. After these individual transactions are recorded and then summarized, accountants must review the resulting transaction summaries and adjust or correct all errors or discrepancies before **closing the books**, or transferring net revenue and expense items to *retained earnings*. Exhibit 2 illustrates the *accounting cycle* that companies go through during a given accounting period, such as a month.

In a way, this is what you do every month when you get your bank statement. You might think you have $50 left in your account but then see your statement and realize with delight that you forgot to record depositing the $100 check your grandmother sent you, and your true balance is $150. Or you might realize with dismay that you forgot to record the $300 ATM withdrawal you made on spring break, and your true balance is −$250. Before you know how much money you'll have to spend next month—your retained earnings—you have to accurately close the books on this month.

UNDERSTANDING FINANCIAL STATEMENTS

Financial statements consist of three separate but interrelated reports: the *balance sheet*, the *income statement*, and the *statement of cash flows*. These statements are required by law for all publicly traded companies, but they are vital management tools for every company, no matter how large or small. Together, these statements provide information about an organization's financial strength and ability to meet current obligations, the effectiveness of its sales and collection efforts, and its effectiveness in managing its assets. Organizations and individuals use financial statements to spot opportunities and problems, to make business decisions, and to evaluate a company's past performance, present condition, and future prospects.

The following sections examine the financial statements of Computer Central Services, a hypothetical company engaged in direct sales and distribution of personal computers and accessories. In the past year, the company shipped more than 2.3 million orders, amounting to more than $1.7 billion in sales—a 35 percent increase in sales over the prior year. The company's daily sales volume has grown considerably over the last decade—from $232,000 to $6.8 million. Because of this tremendous growth and the increasing demand for new computer products, the company recently purchased a 276,000-square-foot building.

BALANCE SHEET

balance sheet
A statement of a firm's financial position on a particular date; also known as a *statement of financial position*

The **balance sheet**, also known as the *statement of financial position*, is a snapshot of a company's financial position on a particular date (see Exhibit 3). In effect, it freezes all business actions and provides a baseline from which a company can measure change from that point forward. This statement is called a balance sheet because it includes

EXHIBIT 2	The Accounting Cycle

Here are the general steps in the accounting process, or *accounting cycle*, from recording transactions to making sure the books are in balance to closing the books for a particular accounting period (usually a month). Steps 1 through 3 are done as transactions occur; steps 4 through 8 are usually performed at the end of the accounting period.

1. Perform *transactions*
A transaction is any relevant accounting event, including making a sale, making a purchase, or making a debt payment.

2. Analyze and record transactions in a *journal*
Journalizing means analyzing the *source document* (e.g., a sales receipt or a customer invoice) for each transaction, then separating the transaction into its debit and credit components and recording these chronologically in a journal.

3. *Post* journal entries to the *ledger*
Entries from the chronological journals are moved to the account-based ledger. Over the course of the month or other accounting period, each account (e.g., sales revenue or expenses) in the ledger fills up with the various transaction records posted from the journals. These accounts are considered temporary because they are closed out at the end of the accounting period (see step 8).

4. Prepare a *trial balance*
At the end of the accounting period, the debits and credits in the ledger are totaled, and then the two amounts are compared. If they don't equal, one or more errors have crept in somewhere in the previous three steps and need to be found and corrected.

5. Make *adjusting entries*, as needed
Not all relevant changes are generated by transaction records during the accounting period, so accountants enter items such as asset depreciation or transactions whose revenues or expenses occur before or after the accounting period.

6. Prepare an adjusted trial balance
This is the same procedure as in step 4 but includes the adjusting entries made in step 5. Again, if the debits total and the credits total don't match, the error needs to be investigated and corrected.

7. Prepare *financial statements*
With the accounts adjusted and in balance for the accounting period, various managerial and government compliance reports can now be generated.

8. *Close the books* for the accounting period
Transfer the balances from temporary ledger accounts to the permanent balance sheet and income statement. Record *reversing entries* as needed to start fresh temporary accounts at the beginning of the next period.

Sources: Adapted from Jeffery Slater, *College Accounting: A Practical Approach*, 11th ed. (Upper Saddle River, N.J.: Pearson Prentice Hall, 2010), 78, 104, 148; "The Accounting Process," NetMBA, www.netmba.com; Bob Schneider, "Accounting Basics: The Accounting Process," Investopedia.com, www.investopedia.com.

all elements in the accounting equation and shows the balance between assets on one side of the equation and liabilities and owners' equity on the other side.

Every company prepares a balance sheet at least once a year, most often at the end of the **calendar year**, covering January 1 to December 31. However, many business and government bodies use a **fiscal year**, which may be any 12 consecutive months. Some companies prepare a balance sheet more often than once a year, such as at the end of each month or quarter. Every balance sheet is dated to show the exact date when the financial snapshot was taken.

calendar year
A 12-month accounting period that begins on January 1 and ends on December 31

fiscal year
Any 12 consecutive months used as an accounting period

321

EXHIBIT 3   **Balance Sheet for Computer Central Services**

The categories used on the year-end balance sheet for Computer Central Services are typical.

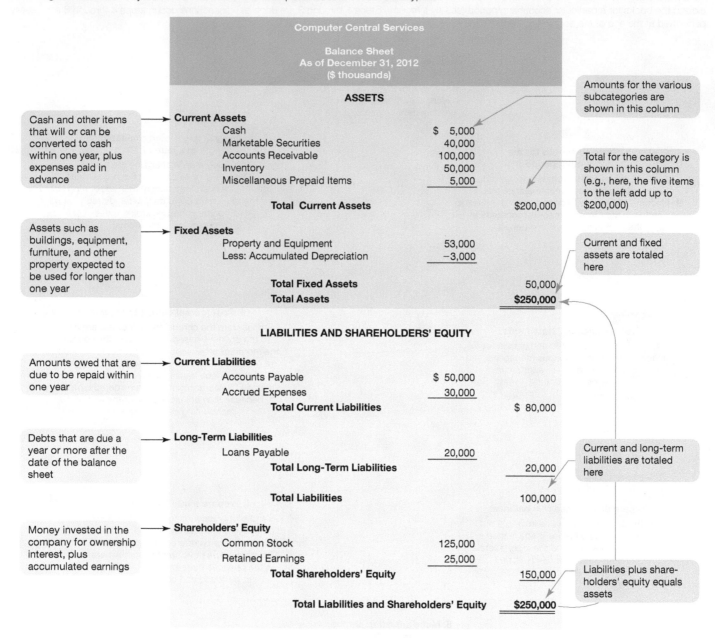

By reading a company's balance sheet, you should be able to determine the size of the company, the major assets owned, any asset changes that occurred in recent periods, how the company's assets are financed, and any major changes that have occurred in the company's debt and equity in recent periods.

Assets

As discussed earlier in the chapter, an asset is something owned by a company with the intent to generate income. Assets can be *tangible* or *intangible*. Tangible assets include land, buildings, and equipment. Intangible assets include intellectual property (such as patents and business methods), *goodwill* (which includes company reputation), brand awareness and recognition, workforce skills, management talent, and even customer relationships.[16]

As you might expect, assigning value to intangible assets is not an easy task (and is one of the major points of difference between GAAP and IFRS, incidentally), but these assets make up an increasingly important part of the value of many contemporary companies.[17] For instance, much of the real value of a company such as Google is not in its tangible assets but in its search engine algorithms, software designs, brand awareness, and the brainpower of its workforce. For example, a recent balance sheet for the company listed over $8 billion in goodwill and other intangibles.[18]

The asset section of the balance sheet is often divided into *current assets* and *fixed assets*. **Current assets** include cash and other items that will or can become cash within the following year. **Fixed assets** (sometimes referred to as *property, plant, and equipment*) are long-term investments in buildings, equipment, furniture and fixtures, transportation equipment, land, and other tangible property used in running the business. Fixed assets have a useful life of more than one year.

Assets are listed in descending order by *liquidity*, or the ease with which they can be converted into cash. Thus, current assets are listed before fixed assets. The balance sheet gives a subtotal for each type of asset and then a grand total for all assets. The current assets of Computer Central Services consist primarily of cash, investments in short-term marketable securities such as money-market funds, *accounts receivable* (amounts due from customers), and inventory (such as computers, software, and other items the company sells to customers).

current assets Cash and items that can be turned into cash within one year

fixed assets Assets retained for long-term use, such as land, buildings, machinery, and equipment; also referred to as *property, plant, and equipment*

Liabilities

Liabilities may be current or long term, and they are listed in the order in which they will come due. The balance sheet gives subtotals for **current liabilities** (obligations that will have to be met within one year of the date of the balance sheet) and **long-term liabilities** (obligations that are due one year or more after the date of the balance sheet), and then it gives a grand total for all liabilities.

Current liabilities include accounts payable, short-term financing, and accrued expenses. *Accounts payable* includes the money the company owes its suppliers as well as money it owes vendors for miscellaneous services (such as electricity and telephone charges). *Accrued expenses* are expenses that have been incurred but for which bills have not yet been received. For example, because salespeople at Computer Central Services earn commissions, the company has a liability to those employees after the sale is made—regardless of when a check is issued to the employee. If such expenses and their associated liabilities were not recorded, the company's financial statements would be misleading and would violate the matching principle because the commission expenses earned at the time of sale would not be matched to the revenue generated from the sale.

Long-term liabilities include loans, leases, and bonds. A borrower makes principal and interest payments to the lender over the term of the loan, and its obligation is limited to these payments. Rather than borrow money to make purchases, a firm may enter into a *lease*, under which the owner of an item allows another party to use it in exchange for regular payments. Bonds are certificates that obligate the company to repay a certain sum, plus interest, to the bondholder on a specific date. Bonds are traded on organized securities exchanges.

current liabilities Obligations that must be met within a year

long-term liabilities Obligations that fall due more than a year from the date of the balance sheet

Owners' Equity

The owners' investment in a business is listed on the balance sheet under owners' equity (or *shareholders' equity* or *stockholders' equity* for corporations). Sole proprietorships list owner's equity under the owner's name with the amount (assets minus liabilities). Small partnerships list each partner's share of the business separately, and large partnerships list the total of all partners' shares. In a corporation, the shareholders' total investment value is

retained earnings
The portion of shareholders' equity earned by the company but not distributed to its owners in the form of dividends

the sum of two amounts: the total value of the all the shares currently held, plus **retained earnings**—cash that is kept by the company rather than distributed to shareholders in the form of dividends. As Exhibit 3 shows, Computer Central Services has retained earnings of $25 million. The company doesn't pay dividends—many small and growing corporations don't—but rather builds its cash reserves to fund expansion in the future. (Shareholders' equity can be slightly more complicated than this, depending on how the company's shares were first created, but this summary gives you the basic idea of how the assets portion of the balance sheet works.)

✓Checkpoint

LEARNING OBJECTIVE 4: Identify the major financial statements, and explain how to read a balance sheet.

SUMMARY: The three major financial statements are the balance sheet, the income statement, and the statement of cash flows. The balance sheet provides a snapshot of the business at a particular point in time. It shows the size of the company, the major assets owned, the ways the assets are financed, and the amount of owners' investment in the business. Its three main sections are assets, liabilities, and owners' equity.

CRITICAL THINKING: (1) Why do analysts need to consider different factors when evaluating a company's ability to repay short-term versus long-term debt? (2) Would the current amount of the owners' equity be a reasonable price to pay for a company? Why or why not?

IT'S YOUR BUSINESS: (1) What are your current and long-term financial liabilities? Are these liabilities restricting your flexibility as a student or consumer? (2) As a potential employee, what intangible assets can you offer a company?

KEY TERMS TO KNOW: closing the books, balance sheet, calendar year, fiscal year, current assets, fixed assets, current liabilities, long-term liabilities, retained earnings

---

| 5 | LEARNING OBJECTIVE |

Explain the purpose of the income statement and the statement of cash flows

Using Financial Statements: Income and Cash Flow Statements

In addition to the balance sheet, the two other fundamentally important financial statements are the income statement and the statement of cash flows.

INCOME STATEMENT

income statement A financial record of a company's revenues, expenses, and profits over a given period of time; also known as a *profit and loss statement*

expenses Costs created in the process of generating revenues

net income Profit earned or loss incurred by a firm, determined by subtracting expenses from revenues; casually referred to as the *bottom line*

If the balance sheet is a snapshot, the income statement is a movie. The **income statement**, or *profit-and-lose statement* or simply "P&L," shows an organization's profit performance over a period of time, typically one year. It summarizes revenue from all sources as well as all **expenses**, the costs that have arisen in generating revenues. Expenses and income taxes are then subtracted from revenues to show the actual profit or loss of a company, a figure known as **net income**—also called profit or, informally, the *bottom line*. By briefly reviewing a company's income statements, you should have a general sense of the company's size, its trend in sales, its major expenses, and the resulting net income or loss. Owners, creditors, and investors can evaluate the company's past performance and future prospects by comparing net income for one year with net income for previous years. Exhibit 4 shows the income statement for Computer Central Services.

Expenses include both the direct costs associated with creating or purchasing products for sale and the indirect costs associated with operating the business. If a company manufactures or purchases inventory, the cost of storing the product for sale (such as heating the warehouse, paying the rent, and buying insurance on the storage facility) is added to the difference between the cost of the beginning inventory and the cost of the ending inventory

EXHIBIT 4   Income Statement for Computer Central Services

An income statement summarizes the company's financial operations over a particular accounting period, usually a year.

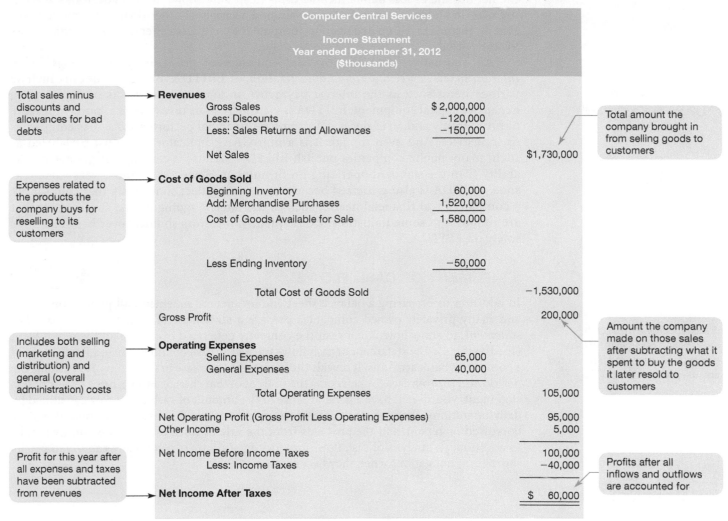

Computer Central Services		
Income Statement		
Year ended December 31, 2012		
($thousands)		

Total sales minus discounts and allowances for bad debts →

Revenues
Gross Sales	$ 2,000,000	
Less: Discounts	−120,000	
Less: Sales Returns and Allowances	−150,000	
Net Sales		$1,730,000

Total amount the company brought in from selling goods to customers

Expenses related to the products the company buys for reselling to its customers →

Cost of Goods Sold
Beginning Inventory	60,000	
Add: Merchandise Purchases	1,520,000	
Cost of Goods Available for Sale	1,580,000	
Less Ending Inventory	−50,000	
Total Cost of Goods Sold		−1,530,000
Gross Profit		200,000

Amount the company made on those sales after subtracting what it spent to buy the goods it later resold to customers

Includes both selling (marketing and distribution) and general (overall administration) costs →

Operating Expenses
Selling Expenses	65,000	
General Expenses	40,000	
Total Operating Expenses		105,000
Net Operating Profit (Gross Profit Less Operating Expenses)		95,000
Other Income		5,000
Net Income Before Income Taxes		100,000
Less: Income Taxes		−40,000

Profit for this year after all expenses and taxes have been subtracted from revenues →

Net Income After Taxes $ 60,000

Profits after all inflows and outflows are accounted for

---

in order to compute the actual cost of items that were sold during a period—or the **cost of goods sold**. The computation can be summarized as follows:

Cost of goods sold = Beginning inventory + Net purchases − Ending inventory

As shown in Exhibit 4, cost of goods sold is deducted from sales to obtain a company's **gross profit**—a key figure used in financial statement analysis. In addition to the costs directly associated with producing goods, companies deduct **operating expenses**, which include both *selling expenses* and *general expenses*, to compute a firm's *net operating income*. Net operating income is often a better indicator of financial health because it gives an idea of how much cash the company is able to generate. For instance, a company with a sizable gross profit level can actually be losing money if its operating expenses are out of control—and if it doesn't have enough cash on hand to cover the shortfall, it could soon find itself bankrupt.[19]

Selling expenses are operating expenses incurred through marketing and distributing the product (such as wages or salaries of salespeople, advertising, supplies, insurance for the sales operation, depreciation for the store and sales equipment, and other sales department expenses such as telephone charges). *General expenses* are operating expenses incurred in the overall administration of a business. They include such items as professional services (such as accounting and legal fees), office salaries, depreciation of office equipment, insurance for office operations, and supplies.

cost of goods sold The cost of producing or acquiring a company's products for sale during a given period

gross profit The amount remaining when the cost of goods sold is deducted from net sales; also known as *gross margin*

operating expenses All costs of operation that are not included under cost of goods sold

A firm's net operating income is then adjusted by the amount of any nonoperating income or expense items such as the gain or loss on the sale of a building. The result is the net income or loss before income taxes (losses are shown in parentheses), a key figure used in budgeting, cash-flow analysis, and a variety of other financial computations. Finally, income taxes are deducted to compute the company's after-tax net income or loss for the period.

An alternative—and controversial—measure of profitability is *earnings before interest, taxes, depreciation, and amortization*, or **EBITDA**. Because it doesn't include various items such as the interest payments on loans or the effects of depreciating expensive capital equipment, EBITDA is viewed by some investors as a "purer" measure of profitability and an easier way to compare financial performance across companies or industries. And even though it is a non-GAAP indicator and must be labeled as such, many public companies publish EBITDA because it can suggest greater profitability than the standard operating profit number. However, for those very same reasons, EBITDA is also criticized because it doesn't reflect some costs that could mask a company's real financial health, such as the large, ongoing capital investments that are required in some industries. Consequently, investors should never base decisions solely on EBITDA.[20]

EBITDA
Earnings before interest, taxes, depreciation, and amortization

STATEMENT OF CASH FLOWS

statement of cash flows
A statement of a firm's cash receipts and cash payments that presents information on its sources and uses of cash

In addition to preparing a balance sheet and an income statement, all public companies and many privately owned companies prepare a **statement of cash flows**, or *cash flow statement*, to show how much cash the company generated over time and where it went (see Exhibit 5). The statement of cash flows tracks the cash coming into and flowing out of a company's bank accounts. It reveals the increase or decrease in the company's cash for the period and summarizes (by category) the sources of that change. From a brief review of this statement, you should have a general sense of the amount of cash created or consumed by daily operations, the amount of cash invested in fixed or other assets, the amount of debt borrowed or repaid, and the proceeds from the sale of stock or payments for dividends. In addition, an analysis of cash flows provides a good idea of a company's ability to pay its short-term obligations when they become due.

✔ Checkpoint

LEARNING OBJECTIVE 5: Explain the purpose of the income statement and the statement of cash flows.

SUMMARY: The income statement, also known as the profit and loss statement, reflects the results of operations over a period of time. It gives a general sense of a company's size and performance. The statement of cash flows shows how a company's cash was received and spent in three areas: operations, investments, and financing. It gives a general sense of the amount of cash created or consumed by daily operations, fixed assets, investments, and debt over a period of time.

CRITICAL THINKING: (1) How could two companies with similar gross profit figures end up with dramatically different net operating income? (2) How might a statement of cash flows help a turnaround expert decide how to rescue a struggling company?

IT'S YOUR BUSINESS: (1) What would your personal income statement look like today? Are you operating "at a profit" or "at a loss"? (2) What steps could you take to reduce your "operating expenses"?

KEY TERMS TO KNOW: income statement, expenses, net income, cost of goods sold, gross profit, operating expenses, EBITDA, statement of cash flows

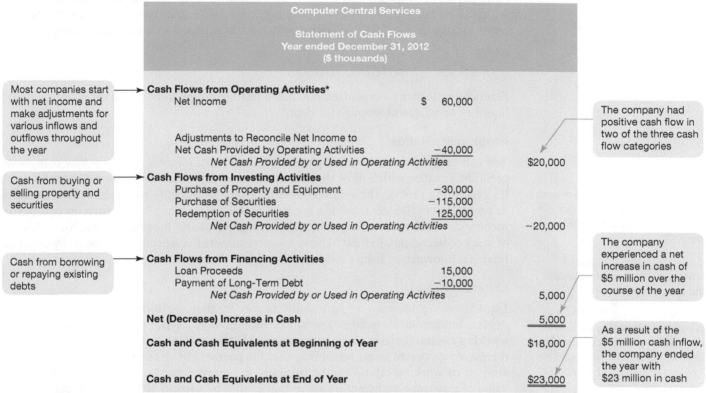

EXHIBIT 5	Statement of Cash Flows for Computer Central Services

A statement of cash flows shows a firm's cash receipts and cash payments as a result of three main activities—operating, investing, and financing—for an identified period of time (such as the year indicated here).

Computer Central Services

Statement of Cash Flows
Year ended December 31, 2012
($ thousands)

Most companies start with net income and make adjustments for various inflows and outflows throughout the year

Cash Flows from Operating Activities*

Net Income	$ 60,000	
Adjustments to Reconcile Net Income to		
Net Cash Provided by Operating Activities	−40,000	
Net Cash Provided by or Used in Operating Activities		$20,000

The company had positive cash flow in two of the three cash flow categories

Cash from buying or selling property and securities

Cash Flows from Investing Activities

Purchase of Property and Equipment	−30,000	
Purchase of Securities	−115,000	
Redemption of Securities	125,000	
Net Cash Provided by or Used in Operating Activities		−20,000

Cash from borrowing or repaying existing debts

Cash Flows from Financing Activities

Loan Proceeds	15,000	
Payment of Long-Term Debt	−10,000	
Net Cash Provided by or Used in Operating Activites		5,000

The company experienced a net increase in cash of $5 million over the course of the year

Net (Decrease) Increase in Cash	5,000
Cash and Cash Equivalents at Beginning of Year	$18,000
Cash and Cash Equivalents at End of Year	$23,000

As a result of the $5 million cash inflow, the company ended the year with $23 million in cash

*Numbers preceded by minus sign indicate cash outflows.

Analyzing Financial Statements

6 LEARNING OBJECTIVE

Explain the purpose of ratio analysis, and list the four main categories of financial ratios.

After financial statements have been prepared, managers, investors, and lenders use these statements to evaluate the financial health of the organization, make business decisions, and spot opportunities for improvements by looking at the company's performance in relation to its past performance, the economy as a whole, and the performance of its competitors.

TREND ANALYSIS

The process of comparing financial data from year to year is known as *trend analysis*. You can use trend analysis to uncover shifts in the nature of a business over time. Of course, when you are comparing one period with another, it's important to take into account the effects of extraordinary or unusual items such as the sale of major assets, the purchase of a new line of products from another company, weather, or economic conditions that may have affected the company in one period but not the next. These extraordinary items are usually disclosed in the text portion of a company's annual report or in the notes to the financial statements.

RATIO ANALYSIS

Unlike trend analysis, which tracks *absolute* numbers from one year to the next, ratio analysis creates *relative* numbers by comparing sets of figures from a single year's performance. By using ratios rather than absolute amounts, analysts can more easily assess a company's performance from one year to the next or compare it with other companies. A variety of commonly used ratios help companies understand their current operations and answer some key questions: Is inventory too large? Are credit customers paying too slowly? Can the company pay its bills? Ratios also allow comparison with other companies within an industry, which helps gauge how well a company is doing relative to its competitors. Every industry tends to have its own "normal" ratios, which act as yardsticks for individual companies.

TYPES OF FINANCIAL RATIOS

Financial ratios can be organized into the following groups, as Exhibit 6 shows: profitability, liquidity, activity, and leverage (or debt).

Profitability Ratios

You can analyze how well a company is conducting its ongoing operations by computing *profitability ratios*, which show the state of the company's financial performance or how well it's generating profits. Three of the most common profitability ratios are **return on sales**, or *profit margin* (the net income a business makes per unit of sales); **return on equity** (net income divided by owners' equity); and **earnings per share** (the profit earned for each share of stock outstanding). Exhibit 6 shows how to compute these profitability ratios by using the financial information from Computer Central Services.

Liquidity Ratios

Liquidity ratios measure a firm's ability to pay its short-term obligations. As you might expect, lenders and creditors are keenly interested in liquidity measures. A company's **working capital** (current assets minus current liabilities) is an indicator of liquidity because it represents current assets remaining after the payment of all current liabilities. The dollar amount of working capital can be misleading, however. For example, it may include the value of slow-moving inventory items that cannot be used to help pay a company's short-term debts.

A different picture of the company's liquidity is provided by the **current ratio**—current assets divided by current liabilities. This figure compares the current debt owed with the current assets available to pay that debt. The **quick ratio**, also called the *acid-test ratio*, is computed by subtracting inventory from current assets and then dividing the result by current liabilities. This ratio is often a better indicator of a firm's ability to pay creditors than the current ratio because the quick ratio leaves out inventories—which at times might be difficult to sell. Analysts generally consider a quick ratio of 1.0 to be reasonable, whereas a current ratio of 2.0 is considered a safe risk for short-term credit. Exhibit 6 shows that both the current and quick ratios of Computer Central Services are well above these benchmarks and industry averages.

Activity Ratios

Activity ratios analyze how well a company is managing and making use of its assets. For companies that maintain inventories, the most common activity ratio is the **inventory turnover ratio**, which measures how fast a company's inventory is turned into sales. Inventory is a constant balancing act—hold too little, and you risk being out of stock when orders arrive; hold too much, and you raise your costs. When inventory sits on the shelf, money is tied up without earning interest; furthermore, the company incurs expenses for its storage, handling, insurance, and taxes. In addition, there is often a risk that the inventory will become obsolete or go out of style before it can be converted into finished goods and sold. Car dealers, for example, face the never-ending challenge of selling this year's models before next year's arrive. Newer models usually make the older models a lot less attractive in buyers' eyes, often requiring dealers to resort to steep discounts just to get rid of aging inventory.[21]

A recent study of U.S. manufacturers found wide disparities in inventory turnover, with the best performers moving their inventory four or five times faster than lower performers.[22] As with all ratios, however, it's important to dig below the surface after making an initial

---

return on sales The ratio between net income after taxes and net sales; also known as the *profit margin*

return on equity The ratio between net income after taxes and total owners' equity

earnings per share A measure of a firm's profitability for each share of outstanding stock, calculated by dividing net income after taxes by the average number of shares of common stock outstanding

working capital Current assets minus current liabilities

current ratio A measure of a firm's short-term liquidity, calculated by dividing current assets by current liabilities

quick ratio A measure of a firm's short-term liquidity, calculated by adding cash, marketable securities, and receivables, then dividing that sum by current liabilities; also known as the *acid-test ratio*

inventory turnover ratio A measure of the time a company takes to turn its inventory into sales, calculated by dividing cost of goods sold by the average value of inventory for a period

EXHIBIT 6	How Well Does This Company Stack Up?

Financial ratios offer a quick and convenient way to evaluate how well a company is performing in relation to prior performance, the economy as a whole, and the company's competitors.

	Ratio		Significance	How It Is Calculated			Company	Industry
Profitability	Return on Sales	1	How well company generates profits out of sales	Net income* / Net sales	60,000 / 1,730,000	=	3.47%	4.10%
	Return on Equity	2	Income earned on owners' investment	Net income* / Total owners' equity	60,000 / 150,000	=	40.00%	35.20%
	Earnings per Share	3	Profit earned per share outstanding	Net income* / Average number of shares	60,000 / 21,000	=	$2.86	$1.47
Liquidity	Current Ratio	4	Whether company can pay its bills	Current assets / Current liabilities	200,000 / 80,000	=	2.50	1.90
	Quick Ratio	5	Whether company can pay its bills without selling inventory	Current assets less inventory / Current liabilities	150,000 / 80,000	=	1.88	1.60
Activity	Inventory Turnover	6	How well company manages inventory	Cost of goods sold / Average inventory	1,530,000 / 55,000	=	27.82	15.50
	Accounts Receivable Turnover	7	How well credit and collection policies are working	Net sales / Average accounts receivable	1,730,000 / 124,000	=	13.95	9.20
Leverage	Debt to Equity	8	How much the company is financed by debt and equity	Total liabilities / Total equity	100,000 / 150,000	=	0.67	2.50
	Debt to Total Assets	9	What percentage of total funds is provided by creditors	Total liabilities / Total assets	100,000 / 250,000	=	0.40	2.15

* Net income after taxes

comparison. For instance, a decline in a manufacturer's inventory turnover ratio could indicate that sales are slowing down, or it could mean sales are steady but the company made some forecasting errors and as a result produced more goods than it needed. Conversely, a company with a high ratio could be discounting heavily and not making as much money as it could by raising prices and lowering its sales volume.

Another useful activity ratio is the **accounts receivable turnover ratio**, which measures how well a company's credit and collection policies are working by indicating how frequently accounts receivable are converted to cash. The volume of receivables outstanding depends on the financial manager's decisions regarding several issues, such as who qualifies for credit and who does not, how long customers are given to pay their bills, and how aggressive the firm is in collecting its late payments. Be careful here as well. If the ratio is going up, you need to determine whether the company is doing a better job of collecting or if sales are rising. If the ratio is going down, it may be because sales are decreasing or because collection efforts are lagging.

Leverage, or Debt, Ratios

A company's ability to pay its long-term debts is reflected in its *leverage ratios*, also known as *debt ratios*. Both lenders and investors use these ratios to judge a company's risk and growth potential. The **debt-to-equity ratio** (total liabilities divided by total equity) indicates the extent to which a business is financed by debt as opposed to invested capital (equity). From a lender's standpoint, the higher this ratio is, the riskier the loan, because the company must devote more of its cash to debt payments. From an investor's standpoint, a higher ratio indicates that the company is spending more of its cash on interest payments than on investing in activities that will help raise the stock price.[23]

The **debt-to-assets ratio** (total liabilities divided by total assets) indicates how much of the company's assets are financed by creditors. As with the debt-to-equity ratio, the higher this ratio gets, the riskier the company looks to a lender. From an investor's perspective, though, a high level of debt relative to assets could indicate that a company is making aggressive moves to grow without diluting the value of existing shares by offering more shares for sale.[24] However, having a high level of debt to assets, or being *highly leveraged*, puts a company at risk. Those assets may not be able to generate enough cash to pay back the debt, or lenders and suppliers might cut off the company's credit.

Again, you can use every ratio as a helpful initial indicator but be sure to dig below the surface to see what the number really means.

For the latest information on accounting practices and financial reporting, visit http://real-timeupdates.com/bia6.

---

accounts receivable turnover ratio A measure of the time a company takes to turn its accounts receivable into cash, calculated by dividing sales by the average value of accounts receivable for a period

debt-to-equity ratio A measure of the extent to which a business is financed by debt as opposed to invested capital, calculated by dividing the company's total liabilities by owners' equity

debt-to-assets ratio A measure of a firm's ability to carry long-term debt, calculated by dividing total liabilities by total assets

---

✓ **Checkpoint**

LEARNING OBJECTIVE 6: Explain the purpose of ratio analysis, and list the four main categories of financial ratios.

SUMMARY: Financial ratios provide information for analyzing the health and future prospects of a business. Ratios facilitate financial comparisons among different-size companies and between a company and industry averages. Most of the important ratios fall into one of four categories: profitability ratios, which show how well the company generates profits; liquidity ratios, which measure the company's ability to pay its short-term obligations; activity ratios, which analyze how well a company is managing its assets; and debt ratios, which measure a company's ability to pay its long-term debt.

CRITICAL THINKING: (1) Why is it so important to be aware of extraordinary items when analyzing a company's finances? (2) Why is the quick ratio frequently a better indicator than the current ratio of a firm's ability to pay its bills?

IT'S YOUR BUSINESS: (1) Assume that you are about to make a significant consumer purchase, and the product is available at two local stores, one with high inventory turnover and one with low. Which store would you choose based on this information? Why? (2) If you were applying for a home mortgage loan today, would a lender view your debt-to-assets ratio favorably? Why or why not?

KEY TERMS TO KNOW: return on sales, return on equity, earnings per share, working capital, current ratio, quick ratio, inventory turnover ratio, accounts receivable turnover ratio, debt-to-equity ratio, debt-to-assets ratio

BEHIND THE SCENES

MyBizLab

GOOGLE THIS: "COST CONTROL"

By just about any measure you can think of, Google is one of the most spectacular success stories in the history of business. However, even a company as wealthy as Google has to control its spending.

Google's case is unusual in the sense of its sheer scale, but the story is not unique. When a young company is growing quickly and money is pouring in from sales or from investors, the natural tendency is to focus on building the business and capturing market opportunities. The less exciting—but ultimately no less important—task of creating a sustainable cost structure with rigorous expense management often doesn't get as much attention in the early years.

In some companies, rapid growth in a hot economy can mask serious underlying problems that threaten the long-term viability of the enterprise. In the dot-com boom of the late 1990s, for instance, more than a few high-flying companies fell to earth when investors who had enjoyed a rocket ride in the stock market realized the companies didn't have workable business models.

During the mid-2000s, Google's revenue had been increasing at a spectacular pace, from $10.6 billion in 2006, to $16.6 billion in 2007, to $21.8 billion in 2008. However, expenses were growing at an even faster rate. As a result, the company's profit margin dropped from 29 percent in 2006 to around 20 percent in 2008 (still 5 percentage points better than the industry average); 2008 ended with the first-ever drop in quarterly profits in the company's history.

The cooling economy and slowing profits didn't expose any fatal flaws in the Google business model, but the drop certainly was a wake-up call that emphasized the need to transition to the next stage of organizational development. It was time for the accounting and financial management functions to play a more prominent role and to transform a wild and wooly entrepreneurial success story into a major corporation with stable finances.

Back in 2001, Google cofounders Larry Page and Sergey Brin brought in Eric Schmidt, a seasoned technology industry executive, to guide the company's growth beyond its initial start-up stage. Under Schmidt's leadership, Google expanded from 200 employees to more than 20,000 and secured its place as one of the world's most influential companies. In 2008, facing the need for a more methodical approach to accounting and financial management, Schmidt brought in another executive with a proven track record in corporate leadership. Patrick Pichette made his name helping Bell Canada reduce operating expenses by $2 billion, and his proven ability to bring expenses in line with revenue was just what Google needed.

Pichette and other executives tackled expenses at three levels: employee perks, staffing, and project investment. It's safe to say the employee perks at Google are still better than you'll find just about anywhere, but they have been trimmed back to save money. The company no longer pays for the annual trip, and the $1,000 annual cash bonus was replaced with a $400 smartphone. The 50 percent discount on Google-branded clothes and other products was reduced to 20 percent, and the subsidy on hybrid vehicles was trimmed as well. On the plus side, employees still get free gourmet meals and subsidized concierge services to take some of the hassle out of handling life's little chores.

At the staffing level, Google is taking a much harder look at hiring practices to better align staffing with project needs. Tellingly, the first layoffs in the company's history, in January 2009, involved 100 recruiters whose services were no longer needed because Google's hiring rate had slowed so dramatically. Thousands of contract workers were let go as well. The vaunted "20 percent time" was reevaluated, too, with the company deciding to focus engineers' time more directly on core projects.

At the project and program levels, Google is scrutinizing its investments more carefully and pulling the plug on less-promising activities. Some of the higher-profile shutdowns in the past few years include Lively, a virtual world that would have competed with SecondLife; dMarc Broadcasting, a radio advertising company; Google Wave, a collaboration platform; and Google Labs, which did a lot of the company's speculative tinkering and experimentation. "More wood behind fewer arrows" is how Google describes its new emphasis on putting its resources into the projects most likely to have sizable long-term success.

Pichette leads by example when it comes to cost control, too—flying economy class in North America and riding to work on a bicycle that is so beat up he says he doesn't even bother to lock it up.

While continuing to manage costs more carefully, the company is also stepping up its efforts to generate more revenue. Key areas of focus include expanding the company's activities in mobile phone advertising and display advertising (graphical ads as opposed to the text-only ads that now appear next to Google searches), expanding Google+ to take on the mighty Facebook in social networking, growing its software and e-book revenue, and continuing to push YouTube toward profitability.

To say the effort has been a success would be a bit of an understatement. Expenses are down, and free cash flow is up dramatically. Even after that rough patch when the economy slowed ad sales, Google still ended 2008 with over $20 billion in current assets—and it raised that to almost $30 billion in 2009, over $40 billion in 2010 and headed for $50 billion and beyond.

Asked why the company was sitting on so much cash, Pichette explains that in the fast-changing world of search and other digital services, Google might need to jump on an acquisition almost overnight, with potentially billions of dollars of cash in hand. It might not have an infinite supply of money, but with a new focus

on careful accounting, Google will have plenty of cash to keep its innovation engine churning out new ideas for years to come.[25]

Critical Thinking Questions

1. Given the eventual need for rigorous financial management, should every company have extensive cost controls in place from the first moment of operation? Explain your answer.
2. Google recently had a debt-to-equity ratio of 0.04. Microsoft, one of its key competitors, had a debt-to-equity ratio of 0.15. From a bank's point of view, which of the two companies is a more attractive loan candidate, based on this ratio? Why?
3. At the end of 2008, Google's current ratio was 8.77. Midway through 2009, the current ratio was up to 11.91. Does this make Google more or less of a credit risk in the eyes of potential lenders? Why?

LEARN MORE ONLINE

Visit Google's "Investor Relations" section, at http://investor.google.com. Peruse the latest financial news. How does the company's financial health look at present? What do the trends for revenue, expenses, and income look like? Does the company report both GAAP and non-GAAP financial results? Why does it report non-GAAP figures?

MyBizLab

Log on to www.mybizlab.com to access study and assessment aids associated with this chapter.

KEY TERMS

accounting
accounting equation
accounts receivable turnover ratio
accrual basis
assets
audit
balance sheet
bookkeeping
calendar year
cash basis
certified public accountants (CPAs)
closing the books
controller
cost of goods sold
current assets
current liabilities
current ratio
debt-to-assets ratio
debt-to-equity ratio
depreciation
double-entry bookkeeping
earnings per share
EBITDA
expenses
external auditors

financial accounting
fiscal year
fixed assets
GAAP (generally accepted accounting principles)
gross profit
income statement
international financial reporting standards (IFRS)
inventory turnover ratio
liabilities
long-term liabilities
management accounting
matching principle
net income
operating expenses
owners' equity
private accountants
public accountants
quick ratio
retained earnings
return on equity
return on sales
Sarbanes-Oxley
statement of cash flows
working capital

TEST YOUR KNOWLEDGE

Questions for Review

1. What is GAAP?
2. What is an audit, and why are audits performed?
3. What is the matching principle?
4. What are the three main profitability ratios, and how is each calculated?
5. What is the value of an income statement?

Questions for Analysis

6. Why are the GAAP and IFRS standards being converged?
7. Why would a company bother with double-entry bookkeeping?
8. Why are the costs of fixed assets depreciated?
9. Why would a bank lending officer be interested in the cash flow statement of a company that is applying for a loan?
10. **Ethical Considerations.** In the process of closing the company books, you encounter a problematic transaction. One of the company's customers was invoiced twice for the same project materials, resulting in a $1,000 overcharge. You immediately notify the controller, whose response is, "Let it go, it happens often. It'll probably balance out on some future transaction." What should you do now?

Questions for Application

11. The senior partner of an accounting firm is looking for ways to increase the firm's business. What other services besides traditional accounting can the firm offer to its clients? What new challenges might this additional work create?
12. Visit the websites of Google and Microsoft and retrieve their annual reports. Using these financial reports, compute the working capital, current ratio, and quick ratio for each company. Does one company appear to be more liquid than the other? Why?
13. If you were asked to lend money to your cousin's clothing store to help her through a slow sales period, would you be more interested in looking at the current ratio or the quick ratio as a measure of liquidity? Why?
14. **Concept Integration.** Your appliance manufacturing company recently implemented a just-in-time inventory system for all parts used in the manufacturing process. How might you expect this move to affect the company's inventory turnover rate, current ratio, and quick ratio?

EXPAND YOUR KNOWLEDGE

Discovering Career Opportunities

People interested in entering the field of accounting can choose among a wide variety of careers with diverse responsibilities and challenges. Visit the Accountants and Auditors page at www.bls.gov/oco/ocos001.htm to read more about career opportunities in accounting.

1. What are the day-to-day duties of this occupation? How would these duties contribute to the financial success of a company?
2. What skills and educational qualifications would you need to enter this occupation? How do these qualifications fit with your current plans, skills, and interests?
3. What kinds of employers hire people for this position? According to your research, does the number of employers seem to be increasing or decreasing? How do you think this trend will affect your employment possibilities if you choose this career?

Improving Your Tech Insights: GRC Software

The Sarbanes-Oxley Act's requirement that publicly traded companies regularly verify their internal accounting controls spurred the development of software tools to help companies flag and fix problems in their financial systems. In the past few years, a number of software vendors have gone beyond Sarbox compliance to integrate the monitoring of a wide range of legal and financial issues that require management attention. This new category of software is generally known as *governance, risk, and compliance (GRC) software*. GRC capabilities can either be built into other software packages (such as accounting and finance software, process management software, or business intelligence software) or offered as standalone compliance programs. Vendors that offer GRC capabilities include Oracle (www.oracle.com), SAP (www.sap.com), and OpenPages (www.openpages.com), among many others.

Explore one GRC software solution. In a brief email message to your instructor, describe the benefits of using this particular software package.[26]

PRACTICE YOUR SKILLS

Sharpening Your Communication Skills

Obtain a copy of the annual report of a business and examine what the report shows about finances and current operations.

- Consider the statements made by the CEO regarding the past year: Did the company do well, or are changes in operations necessary to its future well-being? What are the projections for future growth in sales and profits?
- Examine the financial summaries for information about the fiscal condition of the company: Did the company show a profit?

- If possible, obtain a copy of the company's annual report from the previous year and compare it with the current report to determine whether past projections were accurate.
- Prepare a brief written summary of your conclusions.

Building Your Team Skills

Divide into small groups and compute the following financial ratios for Alpine Manufacturing, using the company's balance sheet and income statement. Compare your answers to those of your classmates:

- Profitability ratios: return on sales; return on equity; earnings per share
- Liquidity ratios: current ratio; quick ratio
- Activity ratios: inventory turnover; accounts receivable turnover
- Leverage ratios: debt to equity; debt to total assets

ALPINE MANUFACTURING INCOME STATEMENT YEAR ENDED DECEMBER 31, 2012	
Sales	$1,800
Less: Cost of Goods Sold	1,000
Gross Profit	$ 800
Less: Total Operating Expenses	450
Net Operating Income Before Income Taxes	350
Less: Income Taxes	50
Net Income after Income Taxes	$ 300

ALPINE MANUFACTURING BALANCE SHEET DECEMBER 31, 2012		
ASSETS		
Cash	$ 100	
Accounts Receivable (beginning balance $350)	300	
Inventory (beginning balance $250)	300	
Current Assets	700	
Fixed Assets	2,300	
Total Assets		$3,000
LIABILITIES AND SHAREHOLDERS' EQUITY		
Current Liabilities (beginning balance $300)	$ 400	
Long-Term Debts	1,600	
Shareholders' Equity (100 common shares outstanding valued at $12 each)	1,000	
Total Liabilities and Shareholders' Equity		$3,000

Developing Your Research Skills

Select an article from a business journal or newspaper (print or online editions) that discusses the quarterly or year-end performance of a company that industry analysts consider notable for either positive or negative reasons.

1. Did the company report a profit or a loss for this accounting period? What other performance indicators were reported? Is the company's performance improving or declining?
2. Did the company's performance match industry analysts' expectations, or was it a surprise? How did analysts or other experts respond to the firm's actual quarterly or year-end results?
3. What reasons were given for the company's improvement or decline in performance?

REFERENCES

1. James Manyika, "Google's CFO on Growth, Capital Structure, and Leadership," McKinsey Quarterly, August 2011, www.mckinseyquarterly.com; Google financial profile on Trefis, accessed 10 September 2011, www.trefis.com; Bill Coughran, "More Wood Behind Fewer Arrows," Google blog, 20 July 2011, http://googleblog.blogspot.com; Julianne Pepitone, "Google Beats Profit Estimates," CNNMoney.com, 16 April 2009, http://money.cnn.com; "Frugal Google," Fortune, 22 January 2009, http://money.cnn.com/magazines/fortune; Miguel Helft, "Google's Profit Surges in Quarter," New York Times, 16 July 2009, www.nytimes.com; Catherine Clifford, "Layoffs Hit Google: 200 Jobs Cut," CNNMoney.com, 26 March 2009, http://money.cnn.com; Adam Lashinsky, "Belt-Tightening at Google," Fortune, 22 January 2009, http://money.cnn.com/magazines/fortune;

Adam Lashinsky, "The Axman Comes to Google," Fortune, 23 March 2009, http://money.cnn.com/magazines/fortune; Google website, accessed 23 August 2009, www.google.com; Jessica E. Vascellaro and Scott Morrison, "Google Gears Down for Tougher Times," Wall Street Journal, 3 December 2008, http://online.wsj.com; Abbey Klaassen, "A Maturing Google Buckles Down and Searches for Cost Savings," Advertising Age, 1 December 2008, 3, 29.

2. "Accountants and Auditors," Occupational Outlook Handbook, 2010–11 Edition, U.S. Bureau of Labor Statistics website, www.bls.gov.

3. "Frequently Asked Questions," American Institute of Certified Public Accountants website, accessed 19 August 2009, www.aicpa.org.

4. "CMA: The Essential Credential," Institute of Management Accountants, accessed 10 September 2011, www.imanet.org.

5. "Accountants and Auditors," *Occupational Outlook Handbook, 2010-11 Edition*; Nanette Byrnes, "Green Eyeshades Never Looked So Sexy," *BusinessWeek*, 10 January 2005, 44; "Rules Make Accountants Newly Hot Commodity," *Oregonian*, 13 April 2005, www.ebsco.com.

6. Sarah Johnson, "Goodbye GAAP," *CFO*, 1 April 2008, www.cfo.com.

7. "Detecting Two Tricks of the Trade," Investopedia.com, accessed 19 August 2009, www.investopedia.com.

8. Johnson, "Goodbye GAAP."

9. American Institute of CPAs, "International Financial Reporting Standards (IFRS): An AICPA Backgrounder," 2011; PricewaterhouseCoopers, "IFRS and US GAAP: Similarities and Differences," September 2010; KPMG, "IFRS Compared to US GAAP: An Overview," September 2010.

10. American Institute of CPAs, "International Financial Reporting Standards (IFRS): An AICPA Backgrounder"; Johnson, "Goodbye GAAP."

11. Johnson, "Goodbye GAAP."

12. "Summary of SEC Actions and SEC Related Provisions Pursuant to the Sarbanes-Oxley Act of 2002," SEC website, accessed 9 May 2004, www.sec.gov; "Sarbanes-Oxley Act's Progress," *USA Today*, 26 December 2002, www.highbeam.com.

13. Scott Leibs, "Five Years and Counting," *CFO*, 1 July 2007, www.cfo.com.

14. David M. Katz, "CFOs Seek Sarbox Triage," *CFO*, 9 February 2006, www.cfo.com.

15. Sarah Johnson, "PCAOB Chairman Mark Olson to Retire," *CFO*, 9 June 2009, www.cfo.com.

16. Thayne Forbes, "Valuing Customers," *Journal of Database Marketing & Customer Strategy Management*, October 2007, 4–10.

17. Baruch Lev, "Sharpening the Intangibles Edge," *Harvard Business Review*, June 2004, 109–116.

18. "Google Inc. Financial," Google Finance, accessed 10 September 2011, www.google.com/finance.

19. "How to Spot Trouble in Your Financials," *Inc.*, October 2004, 96.

20. Ben McClure, "A Clear Look at EBITDA," Investopedia.com, 17 April 2010, www.investopedia.com; "Bobbie Gossage," Cranking Up the Earnings," *Inc.*, October 2004, 54; Lisa Smith, "EBITDA: Challenging the Calculation," Investopedia.com, 20 November 2009, www.investopedia.com.

21. Amy Wilson, "Old Vehicles Clog Dealer Lots," *Automotive News*, 11 May 2009, 4.

22. "Inventory Turnover," *Controller's Report*, October 2008, 13–14.

23. Jeffery Slater, *College Accounting: A Practical Approach*, 11th ed. (Upper Saddle River N.J.: Pearson Prentice Hall, 2010), 741.

24. Slater, *College Accounting: A Practical Approach*, 735.

25. See note 1.

26. Adapted from Mary Hayes Weier, "Companies Look to Contain Risk with GRC Software," *InformationWeek*, 5 April 2008, www.informationweek.com; OpenPages website, accessed 24 August 2009, www.openpages.com; Oracle website, accessed 24 August 2009, www.oracle.com; GRC Software Seems to be Rising," *FierceComplianceIT*, 12 March 2007, www.fiercecomplianceit.com; James Kobielus, "Compliance-Enabling Technologies via SOA on the Rise," *ITWorldCanada*, 8 March 2007, www.itworldcanada.com.

GLOSSARY

accounting equation The basic accounting equation, stating that assets equal liabilities plus owners' equity

accounting Measuring, interpreting, and communicating financial information to support internal and external decision making

accounts receivable turnover ratio A measure of the time a company takes to turn its accounts receivable into cash, calculated by dividing sales by the average value of accounts receivable for a period

accrual basis An accounting method in which revenue is recorded when a sale is made and an expense is recorded when it is incurred

assets Any things of value owned or leased by a business

audit Formal evaluation of the fairness and reliability of a client's financial statements

balance sheet A statement of a firm's financial position on a particular date; also known as a *statement of financial position*

bookkeeping Recordkeeping; the clerical aspect of accounting

calendar year A 12-month accounting period that begins on January 1 and ends on December 31

cash basis An accounting method in which revenue is recorded when payment is received and an expense is recorded when cash is paid

certified public accountants (CPAs) Professionally licensed accountants who meet certain requirements for education and experience and who pass a comprehensive examination

closing the books Transferring net revenue and expense account balances to retained earnings for the period

controller The highest-ranking accountant in a company, responsible for overseeing all accounting functions

cost of goods sold The cost of producing or acquiring a company's products for sale during a given period

current assets Cash and items that can be turned into cash within one year

current liabilities Obligations that must be met within a year

current ratio A measure of a firm's short-term liquidity, calculated by dividing current assets by current liabilities

debt-to-assets ratio A measure of a firm's ability to carry long-term debt, calculated by dividing total liabilities by total assets

debt-to-equity ratio A measure of the extent to which a business is financed by debt as opposed to invested capital, calculated by dividing the company's total liabilities by owners' equity

depreciation An accounting procedure for systematically spreading the cost of a tangible asset over its estimated useful life

double-entry bookkeeping A method of recording financial transactions that requires a debit entry and credit entry for each transaction to ensure that the accounting equation is always kept in balance

earnings per share A measure of a firm's profitability for each share of outstanding stock, calculated by dividing net income after taxes by the average number of shares of common stock outstanding

EBITDA Earnings before interest, taxes, depreciation, and amortization

expenses Costs created in the process of generating revenues

external auditors Independent accounting firms that provide auditing services for public companies

financial accounting The area of accounting concerned with preparing financial information for users outside the organization

fiscal year Any 12 consecutive months used as an accounting period

fixed assets Assets retained for long-term use, such as land, buildings, machinery, and equipment; also referred to as *property, plant, and equipment*

GAAP (generally accepted accounting practices) Standards and practices used by publicly held corporations in the United States and a few other countries in the preparation of financial statements; on course to converge with IFRS

gross profit The amount remaining when the cost of goods sold is deducted from net sales; also known as *gross margin*

income statement A financial record of a company's revenues, expenses, and profits over a given period of time; also known as a *profit and loss statement*

international financial reporting standards (IFRS) Accounting standards and practices used in many countries outside the United States

inventory turnover ratio A measure of the time a company takes to turn its inventory into sales, calculated by dividing cost of goods sold by the average value of inventory for a period

liabilities Claims against a firm's assets by creditors

long-term liabilities Obligations that fall due more than a year from the date of the balance sheet

management accounting The area of accounting concerned with preparing data for use by managers within the organization

matching principle The fundamental principle requiring that expenses incurred in producing revenue be deducted from the revenues they generate during an accounting period

net income Profit earned or loss incurred by a firm, determined by subtracting expenses from revenues; casually referred to as the *bottom line*

operating expenses All costs of operation that are not included under cost of goods sold

owners' equity The portion of a company's assets that belongs to the owners after obligations to all creditors have been met

private accountants In-house accountants employed by organizations and businesses other than a public accounting firm; also called *corporate accountants*

public accountants Professionals who provide accounting services to other businesses and individuals for a fee

quick ratio A measure of a firm's short-term liquidity, calculated by adding cash, marketable securities, and receivables, then dividing that sum by current liabilities; also known as the *acid-test ratio*

retained earnings The portion of shareholders' equity earned by the company but not distributed to its owners in the form of dividends

return on equity The ratio between net income after taxes and total owners' equity

return on sales The ratio between net income after taxes and net sales; also known as the *profit margin*

Sarbanes-Oxley The informal name of comprehensive legislation designed to improve integrity and accountability of financial information

statement of cash flows A statement of a firm's cash receipts and cash payments that presents information on its sources and uses of cash

working capital Current assets minus current liabilities

Financial Management

Financial Management

1 Identify three fundamental concepts that affect financial decisions and identify the primary responsibilities of a financial manager

2 Describe the budgeting process, three major budgeting challenges, and the four major types of budgets

3 Compare the advantages and disadvantages of debt and equity financing and explain the two major considerations in choosing from financing alternatives

4 Identify the major categories of short-term debt financing

5 Identify the major categories of long-term debt financing

6 Describe the two options for equity financing and explain how companies prepare an initial public offering

MyBizLab

Where you see MyBizLab in this chapter, go to www.mybizlab.com for additional activities on the topic being discussed.

BEHIND THE SCENES CHARGING AHEAD: VISA SEARCHES FOR FUNDS

Photo by Chris Hondros/Getty Images

Visa faced the challenge of going public during the worst economic conditions in recent memory. The executive team is shown here at the New York Stock Exchange on the day the company went public.

www.visa.com

The story of Visa, Inc., is a story of big numbers. As the world's largest processor of credit and debit card transactions, Visa provides essential services to more than 16,000 financial institutions, which have issued 1.7 billion Visa-branded cards. The 28 million merchants that accept Visa ring up nearly 60 billion transactions a year.

Visa's history began in 1958, when Bank of America premiered the BankAmericard in Fresno, California, just as the concept of general-purpose credit cards was taking hold across the Unites States. (*Charge cards* issued and accepted by a single company, such as a gas station or department store, had been around for several decades by then.) These new *revolving* credit accounts, which let consumers charge purchases and pay them off over time, revolutionized consumer and business purchasing and changed the way consumers and companies manage their finances.

Over the next 50 years, the business venture that began as BankAmericard grew and transformed into the Visa International Service Association, a global payment-processing system jointly owned by thousands of member banks and other financial institutions. The BankAmericard became the Visa card, and Visa became one of the world's best-known and most valuable brands.

With growth and change came challenges, and by 2007 Visa had more than a few challenges on its hands. While Visa remained a privately held joint venture, archrival MasterCard had become a public company in 2006, raising $2.4 billion with its initial stock offering. MasterCard's stock price continued to climb, giving an already strong competitor more financial power and flexibility, including the ability to attract and motivate top employees with stock options. As competition—and opportunities—grew, Visa needed cash to keep investing in payment-processing technologies, including smart cards with embedded computer chips and phone-based mobile commerce payments. At the same time, Visa was also facing several billion dollars in liabilities from lawsuits filed by merchants and rival card companies American Express and Discover. To top it off, the six major banks that were Visa's primary owners were facing a massive liquidity crisis after the subprime mortgage crisis and the global credit freeze that followed. They needed cash by the bucketful.

Selling stock for the first time through an initial public offering (IPO) of its own seemed like the obvious answer to Visa's funding challenges. However, did an IPO make sense when the global economy was in the process of falling off a cliff? Did Visa choose the right financing option and the right time to execute it? Would the IPO be another big number in a company history of big numbers, or would it be a big-time failure?[1]

INTRODUCTION

From the coffee shop down the street to the world's largest corporations, every business enterprise needs cash, although not always the billions of dollars that Visa needed. In this chapter, you'll learn about the major financial decisions companies make, starting with the process of developing a financial plan, then creating and maintaining budgets, and finally comparing ways to finance both ongoing operations and growth opportunities.

The Role of Financial Management

Planning for a firm's money needs and managing the allocation and spending of funds are the foundations of **financial management**, or *finance*. In most smaller companies, the owner is responsible for the firm's financial decisions, whereas in larger operations, financial management is the responsibility of the finance department. This department, which includes the accounting function, reports to a vice president of finance or a chief financial officer (CFO).

No matter what size the company, decisions regarding company finances must consider three fundamental concepts (see Exhibit 1 on the next page). First, if the firm spends too much money meeting short-term demands, it won't have enough money to make strategic investments for the future, such as building new facilities, developing the next generation of products, or being able to jump on a strategic acquisition. Conversely, if the firm spends too little in the short term, it can lose key employees to better-paying competitors, compromise product quality or customer service, or create other problems with long-term consequences.

Second, most financial decisions involve balancing potential risks against potential rewards, known as a **risk/return trade-off**. Generally speaking, the higher the perceived risk, the higher the potential reward, and vice versa. However, this situation doesn't always hold true. For example, a company with free cash could (a) invest it in the stock market, which offers potentially high returns but at moderate to high risk; (b) put the money in a bank account, which has little to no risk but very low return; or (c) invest in a new facility or a new product, which could yield high returns, moderate returns, or no returns at all. Moreover, the *safest* choice isn't always the *best* choice. For instance, if you're hording cash in a safe place while competitors are investing in new products or new stores, you could be setting yourself up for a big decline in revenue.

Third, financial choices can have a tremendous impact on a company's flexibility and resilience. For example, companies that are *highly leveraged* (that is, carrying a lot of debt) are forced to devote more of their cash flow to debt service and therefore can't spend that money on advertising, staffing, or product development. Heavy debt loads and low cash flow make a company especially vulnerable to economic downturns, too. In contrast, companies with lots of cash on hand can weather tough times and make strategic moves that their debt-constrained competitors can't make. In fact, well-funded companies often view recessions as opportunities to take market share from weaker competitors or simply to buy

1 LEARNING OBJECTIVE

Identify three fundamental concepts that affect financial decisions, and identify the primary responsibilities of a financial manager.

financial management Planning for a firm's money needs and managing the allocation and spending of funds

risk/return trade-off The balance of potential risks against potential rewards

EXHIBIT 1 | **Financial Management: Three Fundamental Concepts**

Whether it's the owner of a small company or the chief financial officer (CFO) of a major corporation, a financial manager must grapple with these three fundamental concepts.

1. **Balancing short-term and long-term demands**
   - Must have ready cash to pay salaries, bills, and taxes
   - Need a financial cushion to ride out rough times
   - May need money for acquisitions or other extraordinary expenses
   - Must make strategic long-term investments

2. **Balancing potential risks and potential rewards**
   - Every decision involves a risk/reward trade-off
   - Higher risks may yield higher rewards
   - The safest choices aren't always the best choices

3. **Balancing leverage and flexibility**
   - Can use debt strategically and sometimes out of necessity
   - Debt can be a tool, but it can also be a trap
   - Highly leveraged companies have far less ability to maneuver and are more vulnerable to setbacks

them outright.[2] The semiconductor giant Intel uses downturns to invest in major facility upgrades, enabling it to respond more aggressively when the economy turns around and demand picks up.[3]

DEVELOPING A FINANCIAL PLAN

financial plan A document that outlines the funds needed for a certain period of time, along with the sources and intended uses of those funds

Successful financial management starts with a **financial plan**, a document that outlines the funds a firm will need for a certain period of time, along with the sources and intended uses of those funds. The financial plan takes its input from three information sources:

- The strategic plan, which establishes the company's overall direction and identifies the need for major investments, expanded staffing, and other activities that will require funds
- The company's financial statements, including the income statement and the statement of cash flows, which tell the finance manager how much cash the company has now and how much it is likely to generate in the near future
- The external financial environment, including interest rates and the overall health of the economy

By considering information from these three sources, managers can identify how much money the company will need and how much it will have to rely on external resources to complement its internal resources over the span of time covered by the financial plan (see Exhibit 2).

MONITORING CASH FLOW

Overall income, as identified in the income statement, is important, but knowing precisely how much cash is flowing into and out of the company—and when—is critical because cash is necessary to purchase the assets and supplies a company needs to operate, to meet payroll, and to pay dividends to shareholders (for those corporations that pay dividends). Cash flow is generally related to net income; that is, companies with relatively high accounting profits generally have relatively high cash flow, but the relationship is not precise.

EXHIBIT 2 **Finding and Allocating Funds**

Financial management involves finding suitable sources of funds and deciding on the most appropriate uses for those funds.

Companies that don't keep a close eye on cash flow can find themselves facing a *liquidity crisis*, having insufficient cash to meet their short-term needs. In the worst-case scenario, a firm in a liquidity crisis finds itself in a credit crisis, too, meaning it doesn't have the cash it needs and can't borrow any more. During the recent recession, many companies caught with no money and no way to borrow had no choice but to reduce their workforces. Whenever economic storm clouds are gathering, financial managers need to jump into action to strengthen balance sheets and do whatever they can to ensure positive cash flow as conditions deteriorate.[4]

A vital step in maintaining positive cash flow is monitoring *working capital accounts*: accounts receivable, accounts payable, inventory, and cash (see Exhibit 3 on the next page).

Managing Accounts Receivable and Accounts Payable

Keeping an eye on **accounts receivable**—the money owed to a firm by its customers—is one way to manage cash flow effectively. The volume of receivables depends on a financial manager's decisions regarding several issues: who qualifies for credit and who does not, how long customers are given to pay their bills, and how aggressive the firm is in collecting its debts. In addition to setting guidelines and policies for handling these issues, a financial manager analyzes the firm's outstanding receivables to identify patterns that might indicate problems and establishes procedures for collecting overdue accounts.

The flip side of managing receivables is managing **accounts payable**—the bills that the company owes to its suppliers, lenders, and other parties. Here the objective is generally to postpone paying bills until the last moment, because doing so allows the firm to hold on to its cash as long as possible. However, a financial manager also needs to weigh the advantages of paying promptly if doing so entitles the firm to cash discounts. In

accounts receivable Amounts that are currently owed to a firm

accounts payable Amounts that a firm currently owes to other parties

EXHIBIT 3 — Monitoring the Working Capital Accounts

The working capital accounts represent a firm's cash on hand as well as economic value that can be converted to cash (inventory) or is expected from customers (accounts receivable), minus what it is scheduled to pay out (accounts payable).

Accounts Receivable (A/R, or receivables)

- Amounts owed to the company but not yet received

- Need to be monitored closely and managed carefully so that the firm gets the revenues it is expecting on time

Cash Reserves

- Cash or cash equivalents (financial instruments that can be converted to cash quickly)

- Readily available and under the company's control

Inventory

- Has the potential to be converted to cash but must be sold first

- Represents a cost while it's sitting there waiting to be sold

Accounts Payable (A/P, or payables)

- Amounts the company owes but hasn't paid yet

- Firms generally wait as long as possible to pay unless given incentives to pay early

addition, paying on time is essential to maintaining a good credit rating, which lowers the cost of borrowing.

Managing Inventory

Inventory is another area in which financial managers can fine-tune the firm's cash flow. Inventory sitting on the shelf represents capital that is tied up without earning interest. Furthermore, the firm incurs expenses for storage and handling, insurance, and taxes. In addition, there is always a risk that inventory will become obsolete before it can be converted into finished goods and sold. Thus, the firm's goal is to maintain enough inventory to fill orders in a timely fashion at the lowest cost. To achieve this goal, financial managers work with operations managers and marketing managers to determine the *economic order quantity (EOQ)*, or quantity of materials that, when ordered regularly, results in the lowest ordering and storage costs.

MANAGING CASH RESERVES

Financial managers also serve as guardians of a company's cash reserves, whether that cash is from investors that have funded a start-up venture or from profitable product sales in an established company. The nature of this challenge varies widely, depending on the business, the firm's overall financial health, and management's predictions for the economy. For instance, start-ups usually have a finite pool of cash from their investors and need to manage that cash wisely so they don't run out of funds before the new business can start to generate cash on its own. At the other extreme, an established company with many successful and profitable products can generate more cash than it needs for both ongoing operations and "rainy day" emergency funds.

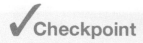

Checkpoint

LEARNING OBJECTIVE 1: Identify three fundamental concepts that affect financial decisions, and identify the primary responsibilities of a financial manager.

SUMMARY: Decisions regarding company finances must take into account three fundamental concepts. First, every company has to balance short-term and long-term financial demands. Failure to do so can lead to serious cash flow problems and even bankruptcy. Second, most financial decisions involve a *risk/return trade-off* in which, generally speaking, the higher the perceived risk, the higher the potential reward, and vice versa. Third, financial choices can have a tremendous impact on a company's flexibility and resilience. Overburdening a company with debt limits its strategic options and makes it vulnerable to economic slowdowns. Financial managers are responsible for developing and implementing a firm's financial plan, monitoring cash flow and managing excess funds, and budgeting for expenditures and improvements. In addition, these managers raise capital as needed and oversee the firm's relationships with banks and other financial institutions.

CRITICAL THINKING: (1) What role does a company's strategic plan play in the process of financial management? (2) Does it ever make sense for a profitable company with positive cash flow to seek external financing? Why or why not?

IT'S YOUR BUSINESS: (1) What is your financial plan for getting through college? (2) How well do you budget your personal finances? If you don't budget, how do you monitor cash flow to make sure you don't run out of money each month?

KEY TERMS TO KNOW: financial management, risk/return trade-off, financial plan, accounts receivable, accounts payable

The Budgeting Process

In addition to developing a financial plan and monitoring cash flow, financial managers are responsible for developing a **budget**, a financial guide for a given period, usually the company's fiscal year, or for the duration of a particular project. Like a good personal or household budget, a company budget identifies where and when money will be spent throughout the year. Particularly in larger organizations, budgeting is often a combination of *top-down mandate*, in which top executives specify the amount of money each functional area can have based on the company's total available budget for the year, and *bottom-up requests*, in which individual supervisors and managers add up the amounts they need based on number of employees, project expenses, supplies, and other costs.

Finalizing a budget is usually a matter of negotiation and compromise in which financial managers try to reconcile the top-down and bottom-up numbers. After a budget has been developed, the finance manager compares actual results with projections to discover variances and recommends corrective action, a process known as **financial control**.

BUDGETING CHALLENGES

The budgeting process might sound fairly straightforward, but in practice, it can be an exhausting, time-consuming chore that everyone dreads and few managers find satisfactory. Budgeting is a challenge for several reasons (see Exhibit 4 on the next page). First, a company always has a finite amount of money available to spend each year, and every group in the company is fighting for a share of it. Consequently, individual department managers can spend a considerable amount of time making a case for their budgetary needs, and top executives frequently need to make tough choices that won't please everybody.

2 LEARNING OBJECTIVE

Describe the budgeting process, three major budgeting challenges, and the four major types of budgets.

budget A planning and control tool that reflects expected revenues, operating expenses, and cash receipts and outlays

financial control The process of analyzing and adjusting the basic financial plan to correct for deviations from forecasted events

EXHIBIT 4	Budgeting Challenges

Budgeting can be a tough challenge that requires tough choices; here are three big issues managers usually face.

1. Every company has a limited amount of money to spend.
- Projects and departments are often in competition for resources.
- Managers need to make tough choices, occasionally taking money from one group and giving it to another.

2. Revenues and costs are often difficult to predict.
- Sales forecasts are never certain, particularly for new products or in sales into new markets.
- Fixed costs are easy to predict, but variable costs can be hard to predict, particularly more than a few months out.

3. It's not always clear how much should be spent.
- With some expenses, such as advertising, managers aren't always sure how much is enough.
- Uncertainty leads to budgeting based on past expenditures, which might be out of line with current strategic needs.

hedging Protecting against cost increases with contracts that allow a company to buy supplies in the future at designated prices

Second, managers often can't predict with complete accuracy how much revenue will come in or how much the various items covered by the budget will cost during the time frame covered by the budget. For instance, some expenses are routine and predictable, but others are variable and some can be almost impossible to predict. Fixed salaries are easy to predict month to month, but energy costs fluctuate—sometimes wildly so. In some cases, companies can protect themselves against future price increases by **hedging**, arranging contracts that allow them to buy supplies in the future at designated prices. The obvious risk of hedging against rising prices is that prices could instead drop over the duration of the contract, leaving a company paying more than it would have otherwise.

Another alternative is *rolling forecasts*, in which the company starts the year with a budget based on revenue and cost assumptions made at that point but then reviews economic performance every month or every quarter to see whether the budget needs to be modified as the year progresses.[5] For example, Google CFO Patrick Pichette and his colleagues review projects every quarter, analyzing what has been accomplished in the past three months and what can be accomplished in the next three. Projects that appear to be losing momentum might get their funding reduced, whereas projects making strong headway might get a budget increase.[6]

Another effective tool in volatile situations is *scenario planning*, in which managers identify two or more possible ways that events could unfold—different scenarios, that is—and have a budgetary response ready for each one. Scenario planning is particularly valuable for long-range planning because the longer the time frame, the harder it is to pin down revenues and costs with any degree of accuracy.

Third, even if they can predict how much revenue will come in or how much various things will cost, managers can't always be sure how much they *should* spend in each part of the budget. A common practice is to take the amounts spent the previous year and raise or lower them by some amount to arrive at this year's budget. However, this practice is a bit like cost-plus pricing in that it is simple to do but can produce seriously flawed numbers by ignoring real-world inputs. This practice also encourages a "use it or lose it" mentality: At the end of the year managers hurriedly spend any remaining money in their budgets, even if doing so doesn't make financial sense, because they know if they don't spend it all, their budgets will be reduced for the next year.

A more responsive approach is **zero-based budgeting**, in which each department starts from zero every year and must justify every item in the budget.[7] This approach forces each department to show how the money it wants to spend will support the overall strategic plan. The downside to zero-based budgeting is the amount of time it takes. One practical alternative is a hybrid approach in which zero-basing is reserved for those areas of the budget with the greatest flexibility, such as advertising and various development projects.[8]

REAL-TIME UPDATES
Learn More by Reading This Article

Small business budgeting: how to make it work

Follow these six steps to create a better budget for your small business. Go to http://real-timeupdates.com/bia6 and click on Learn More. If you are using MyBizLab, you can access Real-Time Updates within the chapter or under Student Study Tools.

TYPES OF BUDGETS

A company can have up to four types of budgets, depending on the nature and age of its business:

- Before a new company starts business, the entrepreneurial team assembles a **start-up budget**, or *launch budget*, that identifies all the money it will need to spend to "get off the ground." A major concern at this stage is the *burn rate*, the rate at which the company is using up the funds from its initial investors. If the burn rate is too high, the firm risks running out of money before it can start generating sustainable sales revenues and become self-funding. Start-up budgets can be the most difficult of all because the company doesn't have any operating history to use as a baseline. Feedback from other entrepreneurs, experienced early-stage investors, and advisors such as SCORE executives or business incubators can be invaluable.

- After a company gets through the start-up phase, the financial manager's attention turns to the **operating budget**, sometimes known as the *master budget*, which identifies all sources of revenue and coordinates the spending of those funds throughout the coming year. Operating budgets help financial managers estimate the flow of money into and out of the business by structuring financial plans within a framework of estimated revenues, expenses, and cash flows. The operating budget incorporates any special budgets, such as *capital* and *project budgets*.

- A **capital budget** outlines expenditures for real estate, new facilities, major equipment, and other **capital investments**. For smaller capital purchases, a company might designate a certain percentage of its annual operating budget for capital items every year. Significant capital investments might require planning over the course of multiple years as the company assembles the necessary funds and makes payments on the purchases while maintaining its ongoing operating budget.

- Another special type of budget that has to be coordinated with the operating budget is the **project budget**, which identifies the costs needed to accomplish a particular project, such as conducting the research and development of a new product or moving a company to a new office building. Project managers typically request funding based on their estimates of the cost to complete the project and its value to the company. They then have the responsibility of making sure the project is completed on budget.

zero-based budgeting A budgeting approach in which each department starts from zero every year and must justify every item in the budget, rather than simply adjusting the previous year's budget amounts

start-up budget A budget that identifies the money a new company will need to spend to launch operations

operating budget Also known as the *master budget*, a budget that identifies all sources of revenue and coordinates the spending of those funds throughout the coming year

capital budget A budget that outlines expenditures for real estate, new facilities, major equipment, and other capital investments

capital investments Money paid to acquire something of permanent value in a business

project budget A budget that identifies the costs needed to accomplish a particular project

Checkpoint

LEARNING OBJECTIVE 2: Describe the budgeting process, three major budgeting challenges, and the four major types of budgets.

SUMMARY: A budget is a financial guide for a given time period or project that indentifies how much money will be needed and where and when it will be spent. Budgeting often combines top-down mandates, whereby company executives identify how much money each functional area will have to spend, and bottom-up requests, whereby individual division or department managers add up the funding they'll need to meet their respective goals. Three major budgeting challenges are (1) reconciling the competing demands on the finite amount of money the company has to spend, (2) trying to predict future costs, (3) and deciding how much to spend in each area of the budget. Four major types of budgets are the *start-up budget*, which guides companies during the launch phase of a new company; the *operating* or *master budget*, which outlines all spending during a given time period (typically a year) and incorporates various special budgets; the *capital budget*, which plans expenditures on major capital purchases; and the *project budget*, which guides spending on projects such as new product launches.

CRITICAL THINKING: (1) What are some of the risks of failing to create and manage budgets? (2) How does zero-based budgeting help a company spend its cash in the most effective ways possible?

IT'S YOUR BUSINESS: (1) What steps would you take to identify the costs of a two-week trip to Scotland next summer? (2) Assume that you need to raise $3,000 between now and graduation for a down payment on a car. How would budgeting and financial control help you meet this objective?

KEY TERMS TO KNOW: budget, financial control, hedging, zero-based budgeting, start-up budget, operating budget, capital budget, capital investments, project budget

---

Compare the advantages and disadvantages of debt and equity financing, and explain the two major considerations in choosing from financing alternatives.

Financing Alternatives: Factors to Consider

Every firm's need for cash and its ability to get money from various external sources is unique, and it's up to financial executives to find the right source or combination of sources. This section explores the factors that finance managers consider when they are looking for outside funds, and the next three sections cover the three major categories of financing: short-term debt, long-term debt, and equity.

DEBT FINANCING VERSUS EQUITY FINANCING

debt financing Arranging funding by borrowing money

equity financing Arranging funding by selling ownership shares in the company, publicly or privately

The most fundamental decision a company faces regarding financing is whether it will obtain funds by **debt financing**, which is borrowing money, or by **equity financing**, which is selling ownership shares in the company. To meet their changing needs over time, many firms use a combination of debt and equity financing, and many use several kinds of debt financing at the same time for different purposes.

Note that business debt usually doesn't have the same negative connotations as consumer debt. Whereas consumers are advised to avoid most kinds of debt if at all possible, and being in debt is often a sign of financial trouble or financial mismanagement, robust and well-run businesses of all shapes and sizes use debt as a routine element of financial management. The key difference is that—unlike with nearly all consumer debt other than loans for education—businesses can make money by borrowing money. Of course, companies can get into debt trouble through bad choices and bad luck, just as consumers can, and it's up to financial managers to make smart borrowing choices.

When choosing between debt and equity financing, companies consider a variety of issues, including the prevailing interest rates, maturity, the claim on income, the claim on assets, and the desire for ownership control. Exhibit 5 summarizes these considerations.

EXHIBIT 5	Debt Financing Versus Equity Financing

When choosing between debt and equity financing, companies evaluate the characteristics of both types of funding.

Characteristic	Debt Financing	Equity Financing
Maturity	**Specific:** In most cases, specifies a date by which debt must be repaid.	**N/A:** Equity funding does not need to be repaid.
Claim on income	**Nondiscretionary, usually a recurring cost and usually fixed:** Debt obligations must be repaid, regardless of whether the company is profitable; payments can be regular (e.g., monthly), balloon (repaid all at once), or a combination.	**Discretionary cost:** At management's discretion and if company is profitable, shareholders may receive dividends after creditors have been paid; however, company is not required to pay dividends.
Claim on assets	**Priority:** Lenders have prior claims on assets.	**Residual:** Shareholders have claims only after the firm satisfies claims of lenders.
Influence over management	**Usually little:** Lenders usually have no influence over management unless debit vehicles come with conditions or management fails to make payments on time.	**Varies:** As owners of the company, shareholders can vote on some aspects of corporate operations, although in practice only large shareholders have much influence. Private equity holders (such as venture capitalists) can have considerable influence.
Tax consequences	**Deductible:** Debt payments reduce taxable income, lowering tax obligations.	**Not deductible:** Dividend payments are not tax deductible.
Employee benefit potential	**N/A:** Debt financing does not create any opportunities for compensation alternatives such as stock options.	**Stock options:** Issuing company shares creates the opportunity to use stock options as a motivation or retention tool.

Of course, not every firm has access to every financing option, and sometimes companies have to take whatever they can get. For instance, only companies that are already public or are prepared to go public (see "Public Stock Offerings" later in this chapter) can raise funds by selling shares on the open market. Similarly, as you'll read in the sections on debt financing, some debt options are not available to small companies.

LENGTH OF TERM

Financing can be either short term or long term. **Short-term financing** is financing that will be repaid within one year, whereas **long-term financing** is financing that will be repaid in a period longer than one year. The primary purpose of short-term financing is to ensure that a company maintains its liquidity, or its ability to meet financial obligations (such as inventory payments) as they become due. By contrast, long-term financing is used to acquire long-term assets such as buildings and equipment or to fund expansion via any number of growth options.

short-term financing Financing used to cover current expenses (generally repaid within a year)

long-term financing Financing used to cover long-term expenses such as assets (generally repaid over a period of more than one year)

COST OF CAPITAL

In general, a company wants to obtain money at the lowest cost and with the least amount of risk. However, lenders and investors want to receive the highest possible return on their investment, also at the lowest risk. A company's **cost of capital** is the average rate of interest it must pay on its debt and equity financing. For any form of financing to make economic sense, the expected returns must exceed the cost of capital. Consequently, financial managers study capital costs carefully in relation to the intended uses of those funds. At the same time, the potential sources of external funds, from banks to stock market investors to

cost of capital The average rate of interest a firm pays on its combination of debt and equity suppliers who sell on credit, also analyze a company's plans and prospects to determine whether helping the company is a safe and sensible use of their capital.

During the recent credit crisis, when sources of available credit shrunk dramatically and the limited credit that was available became quite expensive, most companies were forced to rethink their approaches to financing.

Cost of capital depends on three main factors: the risk associated with the company, the prevailing level of interest rates, and management's selection of funding vehicles.

Risk

Lenders that provide money to businesses expect their returns to be in proportion to the two types of risk they face: the quality and length of time of the venture. Obviously, the more financially solid a company is, the less risk investors face and the less money they will demand in compensation. Just as with consumer credit, in which protecting your *credit score* is vital to securing credit at reasonable rates, companies must also guard their reputations as being good credit and investment risks.

In addition to perceived risk, time also plays a vital role. Because a dollar will be worth less tomorrow than it is today, lenders need to be compensated for waiting to be repaid. As a result, for a given type of debt, long-term financing generally costs a company more than short-term financing.

Interest Rates

prime interest rate The lowest rate of interest that banks charge for short-term loans to their most creditworthy customers

Regardless of how financially solid a company is, the cost of money will vary over time because interest rates fluctuate. The **prime interest rate** (often called simply the *prime*) is the lowest interest rate offered on short-term bank loans to preferred borrowers. The prime changes irregularly and, at times, quite frequently. Sometimes it changes because of supply and demand; at other times it changes because the prime rate is closely tied to the *discount rate*, the interest rate that the Federal Reserve charges on loans to commercial banks and other depository institutions (see page 464).

Companies must take such interest rate fluctuations into account when making financing decisions. For instance, a company planning to finance a short-term project when the prime rate is 3 percent would want to reevaluate the project if the prime rose to 6 percent a few months later. Even though companies try to time their borrowing to take advantage of drops in interest rates, this option is not always possible. A firm's need for money doesn't always coincide with a period of favorable rates. At times, a company may be forced to borrow when rates are high and then renegotiate the loan when rates drop. Sometimes projects must be put on hold until interest rates become more affordable.

Opportunity Cost

leverage The technique of increasing the rate of return on an investment by financing it with borrowed funds

Using a company's own cash to finance its growth has one chief attraction: No interest payments are required. Nevertheless, such internal financing is not free; using money for any particular purpose has an *opportunity cost*, defined in Chapter 2 as the value of the most appealing alternative from among those that weren't chosen. For instance, a company might be better off investing its excess cash in external opportunities, such as stocks of other companies, and borrowing money to finance its own growth. Doing so makes sense as long as the company can earn a greater *rate of return* (the percentage increase in the value of an investment) on those investments than the rate of interest paid on borrowed money. This concept is called **leverage** because the loan acts like a lever: It magnifies the power of the borrower to generate profits (see Exhibit 6).

capital structure A firm's mix of debt and equity financing

However, leverage works both ways: Borrowing may magnify your losses as well as your gains. Because most companies require some degree of external financing from time to time, the issue is not so much whether to use outside money; rather, it's a question of how much should be raised, by what means, and when. The answers to such questions determine the firm's **capital structure**, the total mix of debt and equity it uses to meet its short- and long-term needs.

EXHIBIT 6	Financial Leverage

Leverage can be your best friend if investments work out well—or it can be your worst enemy if they don't. Assume that you have $10,000 of your own funds to invest in the stock market or some business venture. You also have the opportunity to borrow an additional $50,000 at 6 percent interest. Should you invest just your own $10,000 or leverage your investment by borrowing the $50,000 so you can invest $60,000 instead? If the investment returns 12 percent after a year, you'll earn a healthy $1,200 if you invest just your own money. But with leverage, you would earn more than three and a half times that amount, even after you pay the cost of borrowing the $50,000. However, look at what happens if the investment turns sour. If it loses 12 percent that first year instead, the leveraging will wipe out your entire $10,000.

No leverage; 12% return			5x leverage; 12% return	
Funds	$10,000		Funds	$10,000
Debt	$0		Debt	$50,000
Total to invest	$10,000		Total to invest	$60,000
Annual return (12%)	$1,200		Annual return (12%)	$7,200
Cost of debt	$0		Cost of debt (6%)	($3,000)
Profit (loss)	$1,200		Profit (loss)	$4,200
No leverage; –12% return			5x leverage; –12% return	
Funds	$10,000		Funds	$10,000
Debt	$0		Debt	$50,000
Total to invest	$10,000		Total to invest	$60,000
Annual return (–12%)	($1,200)		Annual return (–12%)	($7,200)
Cost of debt	$0		Cost of debt (6%)	($3,000)
Profit (loss)	($1,200)		Profit (loss)	($10,200)

✓ Checkpoint

LEARNING OBJECTIVE 3: Compare the advantages and disadvantages of debt and equity financing, and explain the two major considerations in choosing from financing alternatives.

SUMMARY: Debt financing offers a variety of funding alternatives and is available to a wider range of companies than equity financing. It also doesn't subject management to outside influence the way equity financing does, and debt payments reduce a company's tax obligations. On the downside, except for trade credit, debt financing always puts a demand on cash flow, so finance managers need to consider whether a company can handle debt payments. The major advantages of equity financing are the fact that the money doesn't have to be paid back and the resulting discretionary drain on cash flow (publicly held companies don't have to pay regular dividends if they choose not to). The major disadvantages are the dilution of management control and the fact that equity financing—public equity financing in particular—is not available to many firms. The two major considerations in choosing financing alternatives are *length of term* (the duration of the financing) and *cost of capital* (the average cost to a company of all its debt and equity financing).

CRITICAL THINKING: (1) What factors might lead a company to gain additional funds through debt financing rather than through equity financing? (2) Why does consumer debt have a more negative connotation than business debt?

IT'S YOUR BUSINESS: (1) Do you know your credit score, or have you ever looked at your credit report? To learn more about free credit reports, visit www.ftc.gov/freereports. (2) How should the cost of capital figure into your decisions about attending college, buying cars, and buying housing?

KEY TERMS TO KNOW: debt financing, equity financing, short-term financing, long-term financing, cost of capital, prime interest rate, leverage, capital structure

Identify the major categories of short-term debt financing.

Financing Alternatives: Short-Term Debt

Financial managers have a number of options when it comes to short-term debt financing, including *credit cards, trade credit, secured loans, unsecured loans, commercial paper*, and an alternative to borrowing known as *factoring* (see Exhibit 7).

CREDIT CARDS

Half of all small companies and start-ups use credit cards to help fund their operations. Credit cards are one of the most expensive forms of financing, but they are sometimes the only form available to business owners. In the years leading up to the 2008 credit crunch, anyone with a pulse and mailbox could get multiple credit card offers, making cards a tempting way to get cash to start or expand a business, or simply to stay afloat during rough patches. However, card issuers recently began cutting credit limits for millions of card holders, even those with strong credit histories, and these cutbacks are affecting many small businesses whose owners use their personal credit cards to provide funds for their companies.[9]

EXHIBIT 7	Sources of Short-Term Debt Financing

Businesses have a variety of short-term debt financing options, each with advantages and disadvantages.

Source	Funding Mechanism	Length of Term	Advantages	Disadvantages and Limitations
Credit cards	Essentially creates a short-term loan every time cardholder makes purchases or gets a cash advance	Revolving (no fixed repayment date)	Widely available; convenient; no external scrutiny of individual purchases	High interest rates; availability decreasing since the credit crunch; ease of use and lack of external scrutiny can lead to overuse
Trade credit	Allows buyer to make purchases without immediately paying for them	Typically 30 to 90 days	Usually free (no interest) as long as payment is made by due date; enables purchaser to manage cash flow more easily; consolidates multiple purchases into a single payment	Buyer often needs to establish a payment history with seller before credit will be extended; availability and terms vary from seller to seller; some sellers may require promissory note and charge interest
Secured loans	Lender provides cash using borrower's assets (such as inventory or equipment) as collateral; also known as *asset-based loans*	Up to 1 year (for short-term loans)	Can provide financing for companies that don't qualify for unsecured loans or other alternatives	More expensive than some other options
Unsecured loans	Lender provides lump sum of cash via a promissory note or on-demand access to cash via a credit line	Up to 1 year (for short-term loans)	Provides cash or access to cash without requiring borrower to pledge assets as collateral	Cost varies according to borrower's credit rating; often not available to customers with unproven or poor credit history
Commercial paper	Participating in the global *money market*, large institutional investors provide unsecured, short-term loans to corporations	Up to 270 days (longer in special cases)	Less expensive and less trouble to get than conventional loans; can generate very large amounts of cash fairly quickly, from $100,000 to many millions	Available only to large corporations with strong credit ratings; proceeds can only be used to purchase current assets, not fixed assets
Factoring	Company sells its accounts receivable to an intermediary that collects from the customer	N/A	Frees up working capital; makes cash flow more predictable; can provide some protection from bad debts and customer bankruptcies; often can be arranged more quickly than a loan	Expensive (annualized costs can be 30–40 percent)

TRADE CREDIT

Trade credit, often called *open-account purchasing*, occurs when suppliers provide goods and services to their customers without requiring immediate payment. Such transactions create the accounts receivable. From the buyer's perspective, trade credit allows a company to get the goods and services it needs without immediately disrupting its cash flow. Trade credit can also lower transaction costs for buyers (as well as sellers) by consolidating multiple purchases into a single payment. In many cases, credit is extended at no interest for a short period (typically 30 days).

From the seller's perspective, offering credit terms is often a competitive necessity, and doing so can allow a supplier to sell more to each customer because purchase levels aren't constrained to buyers' immediate cash balances. However, like all other forms of credit, trade credit involves costs and risks. Allowing customers to delay payments affects the seller's cash flow and exposes it to the risk that some customers won't be able to pay when their bills come due. Extending trade credit can also reduce the company's own credit worthiness because lenders will look at how quickly it is closing its accounts receivable. Companies that offer trade credit should be sure to check the credit worthiness of all buyers, keep credit limits low for new customers until they establish a reliable payment history, and keep a close eye on every customer's payment status.[10]

trade credit Credit obtained by a purchaser directly from a supplier

SECURED LOANS

Secured loans are those backed by something of value, known as **collateral**, that may be seized by the lender in the event that the borrower fails to repay the loan. Common types of collateral include property, equipment, accounts receivable, inventories, and securities.

secured loans Loans backed up with assets that the lender can claim in case of default, such as a piece of property

collateral A tangible asset a lender can claim if a borrower defaults on a loan

UNSECURED LOANS

Unsecured loans are ones that require no collateral. Instead, the lender relies on the general credit record and the earning power of the borrower. To increase the returns on such loans and to obtain some protection in case of default, most lenders insist that the borrower maintain some minimum amount of money on deposit at the bank—a **compensating balance**—while the loan is outstanding.

A common example of an unsecured loan is a **line of credit**, which is an agreed-on maximum amount of money a bank is willing to lend a business. Once a line of credit has been established, the business may obtain unsecured loans for any amount up to that limit. The key advantage of a line of credit over a regular loan is that interest (or at least full interest) is usually not charged on the untapped amount.

unsecured loans Loans that require a good credit rating but no collateral

compensating balance The portion of an unsecured loan that is kept on deposit at a lending institution to protect the lender and increase the lender's return

line of credit An arrangement in which a financial institution makes money available for use at any time after the loan has been approved

COMMERCIAL PAPER

When businesses need a sizable amount of money for a short period of time, they can issue **commercial paper**—short-term *promissory notes*, or contractual agreements, to repay a borrowed amount by a specified time with a specified interest rate. Commercial paper is usually sold only by major corporations with strong credit ratings, in denominations of $100,000 or more and with maturities of up to 270 days (the maximum allowed by the Securities and Exchange Commission (SEC) without a formal registration process). Commercial paper is normally issued to secure funds for short-term needs such as buying supplies and paying rent rather than for financing major expansion projects. Because the amounts are generally large, these notes are usually purchased by various investment funds and not by individual investors.

commercial paper Short-term promissory notes, or contractual agreements, to repay a borrowed amount by a specified time with a specified interest rate

FACTORING AND RECEIVABLES AUCTIONS

Businesses with slow-paying trade credit customers—some organizational customers can take months to pay their bills—and tight cash flow have the option of selling their accounts receivable, a method known as **factoring**. Although it's not really a form of borrowing in the conventional sense, factoring is an alternative to short-term debt financing.

factoring Obtaining funding by selling accounts receivable

351

Factoring involves several steps. First, a *factor* or *factoring agent* purchases a company's receivables, paying the company a percentage of the total outstanding amount, typically 70 to 90 percent. Second, the factoring agent collects the amounts owed, freeing the company from the administrative tasks of collection. Third, after a customer pays the factor, the factor makes a second payment to the company, keeping a percentage as a fee for its services. Some factors assume the risk that customers won't ever pay (and their fees are naturally higher), while others don't, in which case the company has to refund the initial payment it received from the factor.[11]

The use of factoring has increased in recent years, particularly as banks and other lenders have reduced the level of credit that many businesses rely on to manage cash flow. Because it is a comparatively expensive method, factoring is generally best suited for profitable, growing companies with pressing cash flow needs and large, creditworthy customers (businesses or government agencies, not consumers) that are likely to pay their bills but are just slow in doing so.[12] Particularly for companies that sell to retailers, factoring is sometimes a necessity because they have contracts that require them to keep retailers supplied with inventory on a regular schedule and need the cash flow to do so.[13]

An innovative twist on factoring is the *receivables auction*, pioneered by The Receivables Exchange (www.receivablesxchange.com). Using an online format somewhat like eBay and other auction sites, companies post their receivables for investors to bid on. Those who offer the best combination of funding amount and fees win the business, and the sellers get their money the next day. The average auction duration is one day; the fastest deal was done in just three seconds.[14]

Checkpoint

LEARNING OBJECTIVE 4: Identify the major categories of short-term debt financing.

SUMMARY: The major categories of short-term debt financing are *credit cards*, *trade credit* (the option to delay paying for purchases for 30 to 60 days or more), *secured loans* (loans backed by sellable assets such as land, equipment, or inventory), *unsecured loans* (loans and lines of credit extended solely on the borrower's creditworthiness), *commercial paper* (short-term promissory notes issued by major corporations), and *factoring* (selling a firm's accounts payable to a third-party financer; strictly speaking, not a form of debt financing).

CRITICAL THINKING: (1) How does getting a secured loan using accounts receivable as collateral differ from factoring? (2) Why would any seller offer trade financing, since it ties up working capital without generating any income through interest payments?

IT'S YOUR BUSINESS: (1) Would you launch a new company if the only way to finance it was through the use of your personal credit cards? Why or why not? (2) Which of the short-term debt alternatives identified in this section are available to you as a consumer?

KEY TERMS TO KNOW: trade credit, secured loans, collateral, unsecured loans, compensating balance, line of credit, commercial paper, factoring

5 LEARNING OBJECTIVE

Identify the major categories of long-term debt financing.

Financing Alternatives: Long-Term Debt

In addition to the various short-term debt alternatives, a number of long-term debt financing options are available as well. Although some of them are similar in concept to short-term debt, the longer time spans create a different set of decisions for both borrowers and lenders. The most common long-term debt alternatives are *long-term loans*, *leases*, and *corporate bonds* (see Exhibit 8).

EXHIBIT 8	Sources of Long-Term Debt Financing

Long-term debt financing can provide funds for major asset purchases and other investments needed to help companies grow.

Source	Funding Mechanism	Length of Term	Advantages	Disadvantages and Limitations
Long-term loans	Bank or other lender provides cash; borrower agrees to repay according to specific terms	From 1 to 25 years	Can provide substantial sums of money without diluting ownership through sale of equity; allows company to make major purchases of inventory, equipment, and other vital assets	Not all companies can qualify for loans and acceptable terms; payments tie up part of cash flow for the duration of the loan; purchases made via loans require substantial down payments
Leases	Company earns the right to use an asset in exchange for regular payments; arrangement can be directly between lessor and lessee or can involve a third party such as a bank	Typically several years for equipment and vehicles; longer for real estate	Usually require lower down payments than loans; can provide access to essential assets for companies that don't qualify for loans; let company avoid buying assets that are likely to decline in value or become obsolete; often free company from maintenance and other recurring costs	Can restrict how assets can be used; company doesn't gain any equity in return for lease payments, except in the case of lease-to-own arrangements; can be more expensive than borrowing to buy
Corporate bond	Company sells bonds to investors, with the promise to pay interest and repay the principle according to a set schedule	Typically from 10 to 30 years	Can generate more cash with longer repayment terms than are possible with loans	Available only to large companies with strong credit ratings

LONG-TERM LOANS

Long-term loans, sometimes called *term loans*, can have maturities between 1 and 25 years or so, depending on the lender and the purpose of the loan. (Some lenders designate loans with maturities between one and three years as *intermediate-term loans*.[15]) Common reasons for taking out long-term loans are to buy real estate, to build or expand facilities, to acquire other companies, to purchase equipment or inventory, to refinance existing debt at lower interest rates, or to provide working capital.[16] Long-term loans on real estate are called *mortgages*.

Long-term loans can be an attractive option for borrowers because such loans can provide substantial capital without the need to sell equity in the company. However, because they tie up a lender's capital for a long period of time and usually involve large sums of money, lending standards tend to be fairly stringent and not all companies can qualify. Lenders usually look at "the five Cs" when considering applications for these loans:[17]

- **Character.** This aspect includes not only the personal and professional character of the company owners but also their experience and qualifications to run the type of business for which they plan to use the loan proceeds.
- **Capacity.** To judge the company's capacity or ability to repay the loan, lenders scrutinize debt ratios, liquidity ratios, and other measures of financial health. For small businesses, the owners' personal finances are also evaluated.
- **Capital.** Lenders want to know how well *capitalized* the company is—that is, whether it has enough capital to succeed. For small-business loans in particular, lenders want to know how much money the owners themselves have already invested in the business.
- **Conditions.** Lenders look at the overall condition of the economy as well as conditions within the applicant's specific industry to determine whether they are comfortable with the business's plans and capabilities.

- **Collateral.** Long-term loans are usually secured with collateral of some kind. Lenders expect to be repaid from the borrower's cash flow, but in case that is inadequate, they look for assets that could be used to repay the loan, such as real estate or equipment.

An old joke about applying for bank loans suggests that the only way to qualify for a loan is to prove you don't need the money. This is an exaggeration, of course, but it is grounded in fact. Before they will part with their capital, particularly in tough economic conditions, responsible lenders want a high degree of assurance that they'll get their money back.

LEASES

lease An agreement to use an asset in exchange for regular payment; similar to renting

Rather than borrow money to purchase an asset, a firm may enter into a **lease**, under which the owner of an asset (the *lessor*) allows another party (the *lessee*) to use it in exchange for regular payments. (Leasing is similar to renting; a key difference is that leases fix the terms of the agreement for a specific amount of time.) Leases are commonly used for real estate, major equipment, and vehicles. In some cases, the lease arrangement is made directly between the asset owner and the lessee. In other cases, a bank or other financial firm provides leasing services to its clients and takes care of payments to the lessor.

Leasing may be a good alternative for a company that has difficulty obtaining a loan because of a poor credit rating or that is unwilling or unable to use its working capital for a down payment on a loan. A creditor is more willing to provide a lease than a loan because, should the company fail, the lessor need not worry about a default on loan payments; it can simply repossess the asset it legally owns. Some firms use leases to finance significant portions of their assets, particularly in industries such as airlines, where assets are mostly large, expensive pieces of equipment. Leasing can also provide more flexibility than purchasing through a loan. For instance, a growing company with expanding office space requirements can lease additional space when needed without the cost and delay of buying and selling real estate.

CORPORATE BONDS

bonds A method of funding in which the issuer borrows from an investor and provides a written promise to make regular interest payments and repay the borrowed amount in the future

secured bonds Bonds backed by specific assets that will be given to bondholders if the borrowed amount is not repaid

debentures Corporate bonds backed only by the reputation of the issuer

convertible bonds Corporate bonds that can be exchanged at the owner's discretion into common stock of the issuing company

When a company needs to borrow a large sum of money, it may not be able to get the entire amount from a single source. Under such circumstances, it may try to borrow from many individual investors by issuing **bonds**—certificates that obligate the company to repay a certain sum, plus interest, to the bondholder on a specific date. (Note that although bondholders buy bonds, they are acting as lenders.)

Companies issue a variety of corporate bonds. **Secured bonds**, like secured loans, are backed by company-owned property (such as airplanes or plant equipment) that passes to the bondholders if the issuer does not repay the amount borrowed. *Mortgage bonds*, one type of secured bond, are backed by real property owned by the issuing corporation. **Debentures** are unsecured bonds, backed only by the corporation's promise to pay. Because debentures are riskier than other types of bonds, the companies that issue them must pay higher interest rates to attract buyers. **Convertible bonds** can be exchanged at the investor's option for a certain number of shares of the corporation's common stock. Because of this feature, convertible bonds generally pay lower interest rates.

Of course, organizations that issue bonds must eventually repay the borrowed amount to the bondholders. Normally, this repayment is done when the bonds mature, but the cost of retiring the debt can be staggering because bonds are generally issued in quantity—perhaps thousands of individual bonds in a single issue. To ease the cash flow burden of redeeming its bonds all at once, a company can issue *serial bonds*, which mature at various times, as opposed to *term bonds*, which mature all at the same time.

Another way of relieving the financial strain of retiring many bonds all at once is to set up a *sinking fund*. When a corporation issues a bond payable by a sinking fund, it must set aside a certain sum of money each year to pay the debt. This money may be used to retire a few bonds each year, or it may be set aside to accumulate until the issue matures.

With most bond issues, a corporation retains the right to pay off the bonds before maturity. Bonds containing this provision are known as *callable bonds*, or *redeemable bonds*. If a company issues bonds when interest rates are high and then rates fall later on, it may want to pay off its high-interest bonds and sell a new issue at a lower rate. However, this feature carries a price tag: Investors must be offered a higher interest rate to encourage them to buy callable bonds.

Checkpoint

LEARNING OBJECTIVE 5: Identify the major categories of long-term debt financing.

SUMMARY: The three major categories of long-term debt financing are *long-term loans* (substantial amounts of capital for major purchases or other needs, on terms up to 25 years, usually secured by assets), *leases* (similar to renting, conferring the rights to use an asset in exchange for regular payments), and *bonds* (certificates that obligate the company to repay a specified sum, plus interest, to the bondholder on a specific date).

CRITICAL THINKING: (1) How could rates of technological change affect a company's decision about whether to buy or lease equipment, vehicles, and other assets? (2) Why would lenders want to see that a business already has some level of capitalization before giving it access to more capital by means of a loan?

IT'S YOUR BUSINESS: (1) If you have just moved to a new city to start a new job, would you prefer to lease or rent an apartment? Why? (2) Assume you are in the market for a new car. Will you lease or buy? Why?

KEY TERMS TO KNOW: lease, bonds, secured bonds, debentures, convertible bonds

6 LEARNING OBJECTIVE

Describe the two options for equity financing, and explain how companies prepare an initial public offering.

Financing Alternatives: Equity

The most far-reaching alternative for securing funds is to sell shares of ownership in a company. Even the most thorough loan application reviews and strict repayment terms can't match the degree to which selling equity changes the way a company is managed. In the most extreme cases, selling equity can lead to the founders of a firm being ousted from the company. Even when owners retain control, equity financing can complicate operations by adding new layers of public scrutiny and accountability. Finally, the process of obtaining equity financing is expensive and time-consuming, so even companies that could obtain it don't always choose to do so—and some that sell equity to the public choose to reverse the decision by buying it back.

With all these caveats, why would any company bother with equity financing? The answer is the tremendous upside potential for the company as a whole and for any individual or organization that owns shares. Equity financing has fueled the growth of most of the major corporations in the world, and it has contributed to the financial security of millions of employees (and made millionaires out of thousands of employees, too). Plus, unlike debt financing, selling stock can continue to generate money for years if share prices continue to increase.

Although this option is available to only a small fraction of companies, it is one of the most powerful forms of financing. Moreover, it directly and indirectly plays a huge role in the economy by giving both individual and institutional investors the opportunity to increase their own capital by investing in company shares. This section takes a quick look at the private and public varieties of equity financing.

VENTURE CAPITAL AND OTHER PRIVATE EQUITY

Venture capitalists (VCs), as well as angel investors for companies that aren't yet ready for VC funding, are a key source of equity financing for a certain class of start-up companies. In exchange for a share of ownership, VCs can invest millions of dollars in companies long before those firms can qualify for most other forms of financing, so they represent an essential form of funding for high-growth ventures. VCs also provide managerial expertise and industry connections that can be crucial to new companies.

However, VCs are one of the most specialized and least widely available forms of funding, and most firms have no chance of getting venture capital. VCs typically look for privately held firms that are already well established enough to be able to use a significant amount of money and are positioned to grow aggressively enough to give the VCs a good shot at eventually selling their interests at an acceptable profit. Not all VC-backed firms grow enough to pay back their investors, so VCs count on getting very high returns from a handful of winners.

private equity Ownership assets that aren't publicly traded; includes venture capital

Venture capital is a specialized form of funding known as **private equity** (ownership assets that aren't publicly traded), and other forms of private equity can provide funding for companies that are beyond the start-up stage. Leveraged buyouts are usually done with private equity funds. Other uses of private equity are taking companies private by buying up all publicly held shares and rescuing companies that are on the verge of bankruptcy.

PUBLIC STOCK OFFERINGS

Going public, offering shares of stock to the public through a stock market such as the New York Stock Exchange, can generate millions or even billions of dollars in funding. As you can read in the Behind the Scenes wrap-up, this is the financing path Visa chose, and its initial public offering (IPO) raised a record $19.6 billion.[18]

However, going public is not for the faint of heart. The process takes months of management time and attention, it can cost several million dollars, and it exposes the company to rigorous scrutiny (which isn't necessarily a bad thing, of course). Complaining that the process had become too difficult in the wake of some high-profile accounting scandals that tightened oversight of public companies, former PayPal CEO Peter Thiel once remarked, "Going public today is a process I wouldn't wish upon my worst enemy."[19] Moreover, companies have no assurance that efforts to go public will pay off. Some offerings fail to sell at the hoped-for share price, and some offerings are withdrawn before going public because their backers don't think the market conditions are strong enough. Like the economy as a whole, the market for IPOs runs in cycles, and timing an IPO is one of the key factors for success (see Exhibit 9).

Despite the costs and risks, the potential rewards are so high that every year thousands of companies around the world attempt to go public. The legal, financial, and promotional steps in the process can be grouped into three phases:[20]

underwriter A specialized type of bank that buys the shares from the company preparing an IPO and sells them to investors

- **Preparing the IPO.** Preparing an offering involves assembling a team of advisors that includes legal experts, a public accounting firm to serve as auditor, and an **underwriter**, a specialized type of bank known as an *investment bank* that buys the shares from the company and sells them to investors. (To spread the risk, a lead underwriter usually assembles a syndicate of other underwriters.) Working with company management, this team prepares required financial statements, organizes a board of directors, hires a public relations firm to begin promoting the upcoming offering, and engages in *due diligence* to make sure the company's financial policies and systems meet the expectations and legal requirements of public ownership.

prospectus An SEC-required document that discloses required information about the company, its finances, and its plans for using the money it hopes to raise

- **Registering the IPO.** Before a company can sell shares to the public in the United States, it must first register with the SEC. This process includes submitting a **prospectus**, which discloses required information about the company, its finances, and its plans for using the money it hopes to raise. The SEC reviews the information and typically requests modifications and additional information to make the filing conform with all applicable regulations.

- **Selling the IPO.** Before the stock is officially offered for sale, the company and its team promote the offering privately to institutional investors through a series of meetings called the *road show*. Although the IPO is the first "public" offering, shares are usually offered only to institutional investors or selected individual investors before the IPO date. Based on the demand they perceive during the road show, the company and the underwriter decide how to price the IPO shares. After the SEC approves the registration, the stock begins trading on a designated stock exchange, and the company is now officially public.

REAL-TIME UPDATES
Learn More by Visiting This Website

Get the inside scoop on IPO activity

Renaissance Capital is the go-to source for information on IPOs. Go to http://real-timeupdates.com/bia6 and click on Learn More. If you are using MyBizLab, you can access Real-Time Updates within the chapter or under Student Study Tools.

As with corporate bonds, this chapter's coverage of stocks is from the stock issuer's perspective.

For the latest information on financial management and funding alternatives, visit http://real-timeupdates.com/bia6.

EXHIBIT 9	Global IPO Activity

The number of initial public offerings (IPOs) tends to track the stock market's ups and downs. This graph compares global IPO activity with the year-end level of the S&P 500 Index, a common composite measure of stock market values.

**Global IPO Activity
1998–2010**

	1998	1999	2000	2001	2002	2003	2004	2005	2006	2007	2008	2009	2010
Number of IPOs	1042	1372	1883	832	839	864	1517	1537	1729	1979	769	577	1393
S&P 500 Index	1229.23	1469.25	1320.28	1148.08	879.82	1111.92	1211.92	1248.29	1418.3	1468.36	903.25	1115.10	1257.64

Sources: IPO activity from *Global IPO Trends Report 2011*, Ernst & Young, 2011, 6; S&P 500 data from "S&P 500 Index," Google Finance, accessed 11 September 2011, www.google.com/finance.

✔ Checkpoint

LEARNING OBJECTIVE 6: Describe the two options for equity financing, and explain how companies prepare an initial public offering.

SUMMARY: Equity financing can be accomplished through *private equity* (ownership assets that aren't publicly traded the way shares of company stock are) or the issuance of public stock. Private equity investments such as venture capital are often used at specific points in a company's growth history, such as to get the company off the ground or to perform a leveraged buyout. Preparing for an initial public offering (IPO) involves a number of financial, legal, and promotional activities that fall into three stages: (1) preparing the IPO by assembling a team that includes a public auditor and an underwriter, preparing required financial statements, and making sure the company's financial statements and systems are up to public company standards; (2) registering the IPO with the SEC and responding to any demands for additional information from the SEC; and (3) selling the IPO, primarily through a *road show*, a series of presentations to institutional investors aimed at getting them interested in buying blocks of the soon-to-be-released stock.

CRITICAL THINKING: (1) High-technology firms tend to dominate IPO filings year after year; why do you suppose this is so? (2) Why does the volume of IPOs tend to track the ups and downs of the stock market?

IT'S YOUR BUSINESS: (1) If you had the choice between working at a company still in the pre-IPO stage, which is offering a lower salary but a share of ownership that will become shares of company stock after the IPO, or a higher paying job with no stock, what additional information would you need before you would be comfortable making a choice? (2) Choose any business that you might like to start as an entrepreneur. How would you make a compelling pitch to private equity investors to encourage them to invest in your company?

KEY TERMS TO KNOW: private equity, underwriter, prospectus

BEHIND THE SCENES

MyBizLab

VISA FUNDS ITS FUTURE WITH RECORD-SETTING IPO

If ever a company needed a few billion dollars, it was Visa in late 2007. Still operating as a privately held joint venture owned by its member banks, Visa didn't have access to the stock market as a fundraising mechanism. Archrival MasterCard was reaping the benefits of its recent IPO, generating several billion dollars in fresh capital and creating the opportunity to use stock options to recruit and reward employees. Moreover, after settling lawsuits brought against it by merchants and two other credit card companies, Visa had rung up more than $4 billion in legal liabilities. Plus, the six large banks that made up the primary ownership group within the Visa association were desperately in need of cash to help ride out the recession and the credit crunch. On top of these challenges, Visa had to keep investing in new payment-processing systems and technologies as consumers around the world continued to increase their use of conventional credit and debit cards and as promising new opportunities such as mobile commerce were coming up to speed.

An IPO could help solve all these funding dilemmas, but it would prove to be much more complicated than a normal IPO.

One of the essential steps was creating a company that could actually go public. In late 2007, Visa Inc., was spun off from the Visa association as a wholly owned subsidiary. This new firm is the company that actually filed the IPO—with the U.S. economy in the depths of the worst downturn since the Great Depression of the 1930s and the financial services industry in turmoil. One could hardly have picked a worse time to go public, as evidenced by the fact that the normal annual flow of IPOs had slowed to a trickle.

However, Visa had several factors working in its favor. First, with one of the world's best-known brand names and a half century of growth behind it, Visa didn't need to introduce itself to investors the way most companies do when pitching an IPO. Second, in investor-speak, Visa had a wide "economic moat," meaning its revenue-generating capacity was safeguarded by barriers to entry—including a powerful brand, established relationships with millions of companies worldwide, and a global transaction-processing network—that new market entrants would find hard to overcome. Third, and most important from the timing perspective, Visa isn't really a financial services company in the sense of lending money or issuing credit cards, so it wasn't exposed to the credit meltdown the way banks and credit card companies were. Although it is intertwined with the financial sector, Visa is actually more of a data processing company than a finance company.

In its prospectus, Visa indicated that it expected to net $16 or $17 billion from the IPO and intended to distribute $10 billion of that to its member institutions, use another $3 billion toward its legal liabilities, and reserve the remaining few billion for general corporate purposes. This was a staggering amount of money to generate in an IPO during the best of times and an almost unimaginable amount to generate during the worst of times.

But that is exactly what Visa did. It went public on March 19, 2008, and broke the record for the largest IPO ever by a U.S. company—over $19 billion after some optional shares were redeemed by the two lead underwriters on the giant deal, Goldman Sachs and JPMorgan Chase. As both an underwriter earning fees on the IPO and one of the cash-hungry member banks of the Visa association benefiting from the stock sale, JPMorgan Chase made over $1 billion on the deal.

In a turbulent stock market and an even rougher economy over the past several years, Visa's new stock has fared well, all things considered. By late 2011, it was up around 30 percent from its IPO price. Archrival MasterCard's stock did slightly better, and both companies were outpacing the overall stock market by a healthy margin.

Visa's growth in the coming years could be hampered by any protracted slowdown in consumer spending, because fewer purchases means fewer transactions for Visa to process. However, more transactions are shifting from cash to cards, mobile commerce is on the rise, and credit card use is only just beginning to ramp up in many areas around the world—and between its core processing business and recent acquisitions, Visa is positioned to benefit from all three trends.[21]

Critical Thinking Questions

1. How might Visa executives use scenario planning in the budgeting process?
2. Could Visa have accomplished its funding goals through short-term or long-term debt financing instead? Why or why not?
3. As Visa continues to explore growth opportunities, should it consider becoming a lender by issuing cards itself or lending money to banks that issue cards? Why or why not?

LEARN MORE ONLINE

Visit Visa's website, at **www.visa.com**, and locate the investors section. Has the company reported any significant financial news in the past year? Has it resolved its outstanding legal issues? What were its net income and earnings per share for the more recent fiscal year? Has company management expressed any concerns about ongoing cash flow issues?

MyBizLab

Log on to www.mybizlab.com to access study and assessment aids associated with this chapter.

KEY TERMS

accounts payable
accounts receivable
bonds
budget
capital budget
capital investments
capital structure
collateral
commercial paper
compensating balance
convertible bonds
cost of capital
debentures
debt financing
equity financing
factoring
financial control
financial management
financial plan

hedging
lease
leverage
line of credit
long-term financing
operating budget
prime interest rate
private equity
project budget
prospectus
risk/return trade-off
secured bonds
secured loans
short-term financing
start-up budget
trade credit
underwriter
unsecured loans
zero-based budgeting

TEST YOUR KNOWLEDGE

Questions for Review

1. What is the primary goal of financial management?
2. What types of investments and expenditures are typically considered in the capital budgeting process?
3. What is the difference between a secured loan and an unsecured loan?
4. What does it mean when someone refers to a company's *capital structure*?
5. How can factoring help a company manage its cash flow?

Questions for Analysis

6. Would it be wise for a young company that is growing quickly but still hasn't achieved profitability to attempt to issue bonds as a way to expand its working capital? Why or why not?
7. Why is careful management of accounts receivable and accounts payable so essential to ensuring positive cash flow?
8. How does factoring differ from short-term debt?
9. Why do lenders often refuse to finance 100 percent of the cost of a purchase, requiring borrowers to make a down payment that covers a portion (typically from 10 to 25 percent) of the purchase price? After all, a lender could potentially earn more by financing the entire purchase amount.
10. **Ethical Considerations.** Budget projections always involve a degree of judgment because managers can never predict the future with total accuracy. For instance, one manager with an optimistic view and another manager with a pessimistic view could look at the same set of facts and arrive at distinctly different conclusions about the company's financial prospects. When budgets will influence decisions made by investors or lenders, how should the people who prepare the budgets deal with the variance between optimistic and pessimistic viewpoints? On the one hand, being too pessimistic could result in lower levels of funding, which could be detrimental to employees, existing investors, existing creditors, and other financial stakeholders. On the other hand, being too optimistic could be detrimental to prospective investors or creditors. How do you find the right balance?

Questions for Application

11. The company you cofounded last year is growing rapidly and has strong prospects for an IPO in the next year or two. The additional capital that an IPO could raise would let you hire the brightest people in the industry and continue to innovate with new product research. There is one potential glitch: You and the rest of the executive team have been so focused on launching the business that you haven't paid much attention to financial control. You've had plenty of funds from venture capitalists and early sales, so working capital hasn't been a problem, but an experienced CEO in your industry recently told you that you'll never have a successful IPO unless you clean up the financial side of the house. Your cofounders say they are too busy chasing great opportunities right now, and they want to wait until right before the IPO to hire a seasoned financial executive to put things in order. What should you do and why?
12. Why might a company's board of directors decide to lease office space even though it would be more economical to purchase the property and finance it with a long-term loan?
13. You're getting ready to expand your woodworking hobby into a full-time business of building custom kitchen cabinets. To create top-quality cabinets, you know you'll need to upgrade from the consumer-grade machinery you have now to industrial-grade equipment. The new equipment will be much more expensive, but, if properly cared for, should last for decades, and you hope to be in business for at least 20 years. If the overall costs of leasing this equipment or borrowing money to buy it are roughly the same, which financing method would you choose? Why?
14. This question was intentionally excluded from this edition.

EXPAND YOUR KNOWLEDGE

Discovering Career Opportunities

People interested in entering the field of financial management can choose among a wide variety of careers with diverse responsibilities and challenges. Visit the "Financial Managers" page at www.bls.gov/oco/ocos010.htm to read more about career opportunities in financial management.

1. What are the day-to-day duties of this occupation? How would these duties contribute to the financial success of a company?
2. What skills and educational qualifications would you need to enter this occupation? How do these qualifications fit with your current plans, skills, and interests?
3. What kinds of employers hire people for this position? According to your research, does the number of employers seem to be increasing or decreasing? How do you think this trend will affect your employment possibilities if you choose this career?

Developing Your Tech Insights: Credit Scoring Software

Credit scoring software is a type of business intelligence software that measures the credit worthiness of applications for credit cards, mortgages, business loans, and other forms of credit. It has the dual objective of filtering out applications that don't meet a lender's criteria and speeding up the process for applications that do meet the criteria.

Using sophisticated mathematical models based on historical records, credit scoring software helps lenders decide which applicants to accept and how much credit to extend to each one. In addition, software with *predictive modeling* or *predictive analytics* helps predict which applicants will make the best customers (lowest risk and highest profit potential) for a given lender. Explore the credit scoring and risk assessment products offered by Fair Isaac (www.fico.com), Equifax (www.equifax.com), or another company in this industry. Choose one product. In a brief email message to your instructor, explain how this tool can help lenders make better decisions.

PRACTICE YOUR SKILLS

Sharpening Your Communication Skills

You've just been hired as the CFO of a start-up company that is a few months away from launching its first products. Unfortunately, the company is running short of cash and doesn't have enough to pay for initial manufacturing costs. Your boss, Connie Washington, is getting frantic. She has worked for several years to get to this point, and she doesn't want the company to collapse before it even starts selling products. She comes to you, asking for ideas to generate some funds—immediately. Several investors have expressed interest in helping with financing, but Washington doesn't want to surrender any control by using equity financing. She wants to start applying for loans, or even stacks of credit cards, if that's what it takes.

However, you don't think piling on debt is a wise idea at this point. The company doesn't have any revenue yet, and there's no guarantee that the new products will be successful. You'd rather share the risk with some equity investors, even if doing so means that Washington will have to give up some of her managerial authority. Draft a short memo to her, explaining why you think equity financing is a better option at this stage (make up any details you need).

Building Your Team Skills

You and your team are going to build an operating expense budget worksheet for a neighborhood Domino's Pizza franchise. Begin by brainstorming a list of expenses that are typical of a franchise delivery restaurant. One way to do so is to think about the company's process—from making the pizza to delivering it. List the types of expenses and then group your list into categories such as delivery, marketing, manufacturing, financing, and so on. Leave the budget dollar amounts blank. Finally, develop a list of capital investments your company will make over the next three to five years. Compare your budget worksheets to those of the other teams in your class. Which operating and capital expenses did other teams have that your team didn't? Which expenses did your team have that other teams didn't? Did all the teams categorize the expenses in a similar manner?

Developing Your Research Skills

Choose a recent article from a business journal or newspaper (print or online editions) that discusses the financing arrangements or strategies of a particular company.

1. What form of financing did the company choose? Does the article indicate why the company selected this form of financing?
2. Who provided the financing for the company? Was this arrangement considered unusual, or was it routine?
3. What does the company intend to do with the arranged financing—purchase equipment or other assets, finance a construction project, finance growth and expansion, or do something else?

REFERENCES

1. Michael Kon, "Visa Is Set to Benefit from the Growth in Electronic Payments," Morningstar, 17 August 2011, www.morningstar.com; "Visa Inc.," Google Finance, accessed 11 September 2011, www.google.com/finance; "Visa Inc. Posts Strong Fiscal Third Quarter 2011 Earnings Results and Authorizes New $1 Billion Share Repurchase Program," press release, 27 July 2011, http://investor.visa.com; *Visa Inc. Annual Report 2010*, Visa website, accessed 11 September 2011, http://investor.visa.com; *Visa Inc. Annual Report 2008*, Visa website, accessed 2 September 2009, www.visa.com; "Visa Inc, Corporate Overview," Visa website, accessed 2 September 2009, www.visa.com; Katie Benner, "Visa's Record IPO Rings up 28% Gain," *Fortune*, 19 March 2008, http://money.cnn.com; Tami Luhby, "JPMorgan Chase makes $1B-plus on Visa IPO," CNNMoney.com, 21 March 2008, http://money.cnn.com; M.J. Stephey, "A Brief History of: Credit Cards," *Time*, 23 April 2009, www.time.com. "Form S-1 Registration Statement, Visa Inc." U.S. Securities and Exchange Commission website, accessed 2 September 2009, www.sec.gov; *Visa Inc.*, Datamonitor, 9 March 2009.
2. Emily Thornton and Frederick Jespersen, "Corporate Cash: Big Stockpiles for Tough Times," *BusinessWeek*, 5 March 2009, 11.
3. David McCann, "For Intel, the Future Is Now," *CFO*, 25 August 2009, www.cfo.com.
4. Janice DiPietro, "Protecting Liquidity in Tough Times," *Financial Executive*, June 2009, 61.
5. Mahmut Akten, Massimo Giordano, and Mari A. Scheiffele, "Just-in-Time Budgeting for a Volatile Economy," *McKinsey Quarterly*, 2009, Issue 3, 115–121.
6. James Manyika, "Google's CFO on Growth, Capital Structure, and Leadership," *McKinsey Quarterly*, August 2011, www.mckinseyquarterly.com;
7. Martin Labbe, "Budgeting the Proper Way," *Fleet Owner*, December 2008, 39.
8. Akten, et al., "Just-in-Time Budgeting for a Volatile Economy."

9. "Banks Cut Credit for 58M Card Holders in 1 Year," *New York Times*, 20 August 2009, www.nytimes.com.
10. "How to Create a Smart Credit Policy," *Inc.*, March 2009, 37–40.
11. "Turn Your Receivables into Quick Cash," CNNMoney.com, 21 November 2008, http://money.cnn.com/smallbusiness; David Worrell, "Taking the Sting out of Receivables," Investopedia.com, accessed 28 August 2009, www.investopedia.com.
12. Maureen Farrell, "The Check Is in the Mail," *Forbes*, 11 May 2009, 56–57; "Invoice Factoring Basics," Invoice Factoring Group, accessed 28 August 2009, http://factoring.qlfs.com; "Turn Your Receivables into Quick Cash"; Worrell, "Taking the Sting out of Receivables."
13. "Demand for Factoring High," *The Secured Lender*, April 2009, 26–29.
14. "How It Works," The Receivables Exchange, accessed 11 September 2011, www.receivablesxchange.com.
15. "Bank-Term Loans," *Entrepreneur*, accessed 29 August 2009, www.entrepreneur.com.
16. "Small Business Administration (SBA) Loans," U.S. Bank website, accessed 29 August 2009, www.usbank.com.
17. "Bank-Term Loans"; "Financing for Your Future—The Five C's of Credit," PNC website, accessed 29 August 2009, www.pnc.com.
18. Ben Steverman, "IPOs: Back from the Dead?" *BusinessWeek*, 9 March 2008, 12.
19. Marguerite Rigoglioso, "The Risky Business of Going Public," *Stanford GSB News*, March 2003, www.gsb.stanford.edu.
20. "The Corporate Handbook Series: Going Public," U.S. Securities and Exchange Commission website, accessed 29 August 2009, www.sec.gov; Matt H. Evans, "Excellence in Financial Management: Course 13: Going Public," Excellence in Financial Management website, accessed 29 August 2009, www.exinfm.com.
21. See note 1.

GLOSSARY

accounts payable Amounts that a firm currently owes to other parties

accounts receivable Amounts that are currently owed to a firm

bonds A method of funding in which the issuer borrows from an investor and provides a written promise to make regular interest payments and repay the borrowed amount in the future

budget A planning and control tool that reflects expected revenues, operating expenses, and cash receipts and outlays

capital budget A budget that outlines expenditures for real estate, new facilities, major equipment, and other capital investments

capital investments Money paid to acquire something of permanent value in a business

capital structure A firm's mix of debt and equity financing

collateral A tangible asset a lender can claim if a borrower defaults on a loan

commercial paper Short-term *promissory notes*, or contractual agreements, to repay a borrowed amount by a specified time with a specified interest rate

compensating balance The portion of an unsecured loan that is kept on deposit at a lending institution to protect the lender and increase the lender's return

convertible bonds Corporate bonds that can be exchanged at the owner's discretion into common stock of the issuing company

cost of capital The average rate of interest a firm pays on its combination of debt and equity

debentures Corporate bonds backed only by the reputation of the issuer

debt financing Arranging funding by borrowing money

equity financing Arranging funding by selling ownership shares in the company, publicly or privately

factoring Obtaining funding by selling accounts receivable

financial control The process of analyzing and adjusting the basic financial plan to correct for deviations from forecasted events

financial management Planning for a firm's money needs and managing the allocation and spending of funds

financial plan A document that outlines the funds needed for a certain period of time, along with the sources and intended uses of those funds

hedging Protecting against cost increases with contracts that allow a company to buy supplies in the future at designated prices

lease An agreement to use an asset in exchange for regular payment; similar to renting

leverage The technique of increasing the rate of return on an investment by financing it with borrowed funds

line of credit An arrangement in which a financial institution makes money available for use at any time after the loan has been approved

long-term financing Financing used to cover long-term expenses such as assets (generally repaid over a period of more than one year)

operating budget Also known as the *master budget*, a budget that identifies all sources of revenue and coordinates the spending of those funds throughout the coming year

prime interest rate The lowest rate of interest that banks charge for short-term loans to their most creditworthy customers

private equity Ownership assets that aren't publicly traded; includes venture capital

project budget A budget that identifies the costs needed to accomplish a particular project

prospectus An SEC-required document that discloses required information about the company, its finances, and its plans for using the money it hopes to raise

risk/return trade-off The balance of potential risks against potential rewards

secured bonds Bonds backed by specific assets that will be given to bondholders if the borrowed amount is not repaid

secured loans Loans backed up with assets that the lender can claim in case of default, such as a piece of property

short-term financing Financing used to cover current expenses (generally repaid within a year)

start-up budget A budget that identifies the money a new company will need to spend to launch operations

trade credit Credit obtained by a purchaser directly from a supplier

underwriter A specialized type of bank that buys the shares from the company preparing an IPO and sells them to investors

unsecured loans Loans that require a good credit rating but no collateral

zero-based budgeting A budgeting approach in which each department starts from zero every year and must justify every item in the budget, rather than simply adjusting the previous year's budget amounts

Information Systems

Information represents one of the most intriguing challenges you'll face as both an employee and a manager. Many companies now find themselves drowning in an ocean of data—but struggling to find real insights that can mean the difference between success and failure.

The first step in turning information into a competitive advantage is understanding the difference between **data** (recorded facts and statistics), **information** (useful knowledge, often extracted from data), and **insight** (a deep level of understanding about a particular situation). The transformation of data into insight requires a combination of technology, information-management strategies, creative thinking, and business experience—and companies that excel at this transformation have a huge advantage over their competitors. In fact, entire industries can be created when a single person looks at the same data and information everyone else is looking at but sees things in a new way, yielding insights that no one has ever had before (see Exhibit 1).

Businesses collect data from a wide array of sources, from checkout scanners and website clicks to research projects and electronic sensors. A single customer order can generate hundreds of data points, from a credit card number to production statistics to accounting totals that end up on a tax form. Even a small business can quickly amass thousands or millions of individual data points; large companies generate billions and even trillions of data points.[1]

To keep all these data points under control and to extract useful information from them, companies rely on **databases**, computerized files that collect, sort, and cross-reference data. In addition to helping with the daily chores of sending out bills, ordering new parts, and doing everything else that keeps the company running, databases can also be used for *data mining*, a powerful computerized analysis technique that identifies previously unknown relations among individual data points.[2]

Most large organizations employ a top-level manager, often called a **chief information officer (CIO)**, whose job is to understand the company's information needs and to create systems and procedures to deliver that information to the right people at the right time. This manager is expected to deliver quality information, which can be defined as *relevant* (directly pertinent to the recipient's needs), *accurate* (both current and free from errors), *timely* (delivered in time to make a difference), and *cost-effective* (costs a reasonable amount of money compared to the value it offers).

How Businesses Use Information

Companies invest heavily in information for the simple reason that they can't live without it. Here's a small sample of the ways managers rely on information:

- **Research and development.** In a sense, the cycle of information use starts with understanding customer needs

EXHIBIT 1	From Data to Information to Insight

Businesses generate massive amounts of data, but a key challenge is transforming all those individual data points into useful information and then applying creative thinking (sometimes with the additional help of computers) to extract deeper insights from the information.

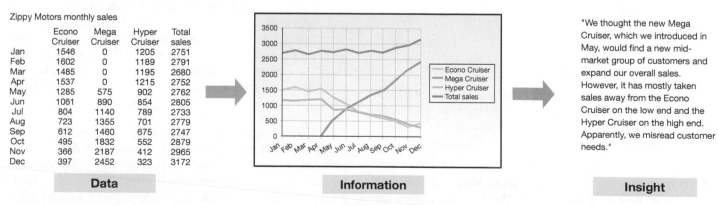

Zippy Motors monthly sales

	Econo Cruiser	Mega Cruiser	Hyper Cruiser	Total sales
Jan	1546	0	1205	2751
Feb	1602	0	1189	2791
Mar	1485	0	1195	2680
Apr	1537	0	1215	2752
May	1285	575	902	2762
Jun	1061	890	854	2805
Jul	804	1140	789	2733
Aug	723	1355	701	2779
Sep	612	1460	675	2747
Oct	495	1832	552	2879
Nov	366	2187	412	2965
Dec	397	2452	323	3172

Data **Information** **Insight**

"We thought the new Mega Cruiser, which we introduced in May, would find a new mid-market group of customers and expand our overall sales. However, it has mostly taken sales away from the Econo Cruiser on the low end and the Hyper Cruiser on the high end. Apparently, we misread customer needs."

and then moves to developing new goods and services to meet those needs. Information is vital at every step, from researching markets to analyzing competitors to testing new products.

- **Planning and control.** Two of the most important functions of management are planning and control—deciding what to do and making sure it gets done. Accounting managers need accurate financial information, sales managers need to know if their teams are meeting their sales goals, human resource managers need to make sure the company has enough of the right kind of employees, and so on.
- **Marketing and sales.** Thanks to technology, marketing and sales have evolved from "gut feel" activities to more scientific, information-driven functions.
- **Communication and collaboration.** Throughout an organization, employees, managers, and teams of every size and shape rely on information to communicate and collaborate. In fact, information technology is changing the very definition of what an organization means, thanks to the Internet's ability to connect people from every corner of the globe.

Types of Business Information Systems

Over the years, the collective label for the technologies used to manage information has changed; what used to be called *data processing* is now called either **information systems (IS)** or **information technology (IT)**, depending on the context. The types of information systems used by a company generally fall into two major categories: (1) operational systems and (2) professional and managerial systems. (The specific systems you'll encounter in your career are likely to have their own names, often arcane acronyms that make no sense to outsiders.) Most systems meet the information needs of people at specific levels in the organization. In contrast, *enterprise systems* are designed to connect everyone in the organization, giving each person the information he or she needs to meet specific job responsibilities.

OPERATIONAL SYSTEMS

Operational systems are the "frontline" workhorses of IT, collecting and processing the data and information that represent the day-to-day work of the business enterprise. These systems typically support daily operations and decision making for lower-level managers and supervisors:

- **Transaction processing systems.** Much of the daily flow of data into and out of the typical business organization, particularly regarding sales, is handled by a *transaction processing system (TPS)*, which captures and

organizes raw data and converts these data into information. Common transaction processing systems take care of customer orders, billing, employee payroll, inventory changes, and other essential transactions. Such systems are a vital part of supply chain management.

- **Process and production control systems.** Operational systems are also used to make routine decisions that control operational processes. *Process control systems* monitor conditions such as temperature or pressure change in physical processes. *Production control systems* are used to manage the production of goods and services by controlling production lines, robots, and other machinery and equipment.
- **Office automation systems.** *Office automation systems* address a wide variety of typical office tasks. Office automation systems range from a single personal computer with word-processing software to *content management systems* that help companies organize the content on their websites.
- **Customer relationship management systems.** *Customer relationship management (CRM) systems* capture, organize, and capitalize on all the interactions that a company has with its customers, from marketing surveys and advertising through sales orders and customer support. Companies continue to find ways to integrate social media into customer communication, too, from using Twitter to answer customer support questions to offering coupons and other special deals on Facebook pages.

PROFESSIONAL AND MANAGERIAL SYSTEMS

In contrast to operational systems, *professional and managerial systems* help with such higher-level tasks as designing new products, analyzing financial data, identifying industry trends, and planning long-term business needs. These systems are used by professionals such as engineers and marketing specialists and by managers up to the top executive and board of directors. An important advance for many professionals is the idea of a *knowledge management (KM) system*, which collects the expertise of employees across an organization.

A **management information system (MIS)** provides managers with information and support for making routine decisions. (Note that *MIS* is sometimes used synonymously with both *IS* and *IT* to describe an overall IT effort.) An MIS takes data from a database and summarizes or restates it into useful information such as monthly sales summaries, daily inventory levels, product manufacturing schedules, employee earnings, and so on.

Whereas an MIS typically provides structured, routine information for managerial decision making, a *decision support system (DSS)* assists managers in solving highly unstructured and nonroutine problems through the use of decision models and specialized databases. Compared with an MIS, a DSS is more interactive (allowing the user to interact with the system instead of simply receiving information), and it usually relies on both internal and external information. Similar in concept to a DSS is an *executive support system (ESS)*, which helps top executives make strategic decisions.

Employee performance management systems help managers set employee performance goals, develop improvement plans, and reward employees based on measurable performance. By making performance evaluation more transparent and objective, such systems can help companies improve employee retention and job satisfaction.[3]

One of the most intriguing applications for computers in decision making and problem solving is the development of **artificial intelligence**—the ability of computers to solve problems through reasoning and learning and to simulate human sensory perceptions. For instance, an *expert system* mimics the thought processes of a human expert to help less-experienced individuals make decisions.

Information Systems Management Issues

As you already know from your experiences as a student and a consumer, technology can deliver some amazing benefits and every year seems to bring new technological miracles. As a business manager or entrepreneur, you can capitalize on all these benefits as well, but you'll also be responsible for a variety of legal, ethical, and administrative issues, starting with the challenge of ensuring privacy and security.

ENSURING SECURITY AND PRIVACY

Linking computers via networking technology creates enormous benefits for businesses and consumers, but there's a dark side to connecting everyone everywhere. Managers need to be constantly vigilant these days to make sure their computer systems remain secure and that data on them remain private. In recent years, millions of employee and customer records have been stolen or exposed, and billions of dollars have been lost to damage from computer viruses. The financial damage from computer-based crime is estimated to be as much as $100 billion annually and is getting worse every year.[4] Moreover, the collection, storage, and use of private information raises a host of legal and ethical issues that managers must consider.

The sources of potential trouble seem to multiply with every passing year and each new technological breakthrough:

- **Malicious software. Malware**, short for *malicious software*, is the term often applied to the diverse and growing collection of computer programs designed to disrupt websites, destroy information, or enable criminal activity. **Viruses** are invasive programs that reproduce by infecting legitimate programs; *worms* are a type of virus that can reproduce by themselves. *Trojan horses* allow outsiders to hijack infected computers and use them for purposes such as retransmitting spam email. *Spyware* sneaks onto computers with the intent of capturing passwords, credit card numbers, and other valuable

information. Chances are you've also met spyware's less-malicious cousin, *adware*, which creates pop-up ads on your computer screen.

- **Security breaches.** Any time a computer is connected to any network, it becomes vulnerable to security breaches. Given the enormous value of information stored on business information systems, particularly credit card numbers and other personal data that can be used for identity theft, there is financial motivation for outsiders to break in and insiders to sell out. For example, a security breach at United Health Services gave identity thieves access to the personal data of students enrolled in a health insurance program at the University of California, Irvine. The thieves used the information to collect bogus tax refunds by filing false tax returns.[5]

- **Unauthorized software and services.** IT departments in many companies face a constant battle with employee use of unauthorized software and online services. Employees not only expose their companies to security risks but also legal risks if they download or transmit inappropriate content on company networks.

- **Social media.** Social media technologies such as wikis, social networking sites, and video-sharing sites help companies create a more open communication environment for employees, customers, and other communities. Unfortunately, these technologies also create new system vulnerabilities, such as virus-infected Facebook pages and employee blogs that divulge company secrets.[6]

- **Misuse of information systems.** Companies must monitor for intentional or unintentional misuse of information systems, such as sending inappropriate files through email or using company resources for personal communication. Many employers now monitor both internal and external email. This monitoring can involve both automated scans using software programmed to look for sensitive content and manual scans in which selected email messages are actually read by security staff.[7]

- **Poor security planning and management.** Many viruses and worms are able to wreak their havoc and gain intruders access because computer owners haven't bothered to install available security patches in their software or haven't installed *firewalls*, hardware or software devices that block access to intruders. As larger companies with more resources and expertise work to improve their security, many criminals are now going after small businesses.[8] As the networking options multiply, so do the areas of risk; new areas of concern include viruses sent through VoIP Internet phone service, viruses on smartphones (including viruses downloaded from ringtone websites, viruses transmitted from phone to phone over Bluetooth wireless, and viruses hiding inside software apps), nasty things lurking on public wireless networks, and hacked accounts on Twitter, Facebook, and other social networking sites.[9]

- **Lack of physical control.** Software and network security isn't enough. Some of the most egregious security lapses involve the loss or theft of laptops that contain sensitive data such as employee or customer records.

Whether it's human issues such as background checks on new hires and ongoing security training or technical issues such as firewalls, encryption, or disaster recovery plans, all managers need to devote time and energy to potentially harmful side effects of IT. Sadly, as long as criminals can profit from digital theft and malware writers can amuse themselves by destroying the hard work of others, the problems are likely to get worse.

PROTECTING PROPERTY RIGHTS

Digital technology has increased concerns over the protection of digital products (including software and entertainment products available in digital format) and intellectual property (which includes a wide range of creative outputs with commercial value, such as design ideas, manufacturing processes, brands, and chemical formulas). One of the most controversial issues in this area is *digital rights management (DRM)*, the protection of owners' rights in products that are in digital format. DRM limits the ways consumers can use music files, movies, and other digital purchases, and critics worry that major corporations are using DRM to stifle creativity and control popular culture. Intellectual property protection remains a contentious and complex issue, as copyright owners, privacy advocates, and consumer groups battle over how digital products can or can't be used.

GUARDING AGAINST INFORMATION OVERLOAD

From simple RSS newreaders to enterprise-wide sales reporting systems, it's not uncommon for businesspeople to be stunned by how quickly their computerized systems start piling up data and information. The overuse or misuse of communication technology can lead to *information overload*, in which people receive more information than they can effectively process. Information overload makes it difficult to discriminate between useful and useless information, lowers productivity, and amplifies employee stress both on the job and at home—even to the point of causing health and relationship problems.[10]

Anyone who has sampled today's electronic media offerings has probably experienced this situation: You find a few fascinating blogs, a few interesting people to follow on Twitter, a couple of podcast channels with helpful business tips, and then *wham*—within a few hours of signing up, your computer is overflowing with updates. Even if every new item is useful (which is unlikely), you receive so many that you can't stay ahead of the incoming flood. Between Twitter updates, newsfeeds, email, instant messaging, and social networks—not to mention a desk phone and a mobile phone—today's business professionals could easily spend their entire days just trying to keep up with incoming messages and never get any work done.

To keep social media from turning into a source of stress and information anxiety, consider these tips:

- **Understand what information you really need in order to excel in your current projects and along your intended career path.** Unfortunately, taking this advice is even trickier than it sounds because you can't always

know what you need to know, so you can't always predict which sources will be helpful. However, don't gather information simply because it is interesting or entertaining; collect information that is useful or at least potentially useful.

- **Face the fact that you cannot possibly handle every update from every potentially interesting and helpful source.** You have to set priorities and make tough choices to protect yourself from information overload.
- **Add new information sources slowly.** Give yourself a chance to adjust to the flow and judge the usefulness of each new source.
- **Prune your sources vigorously and frequently.** Bloggers run out of things to say; your needs and interests change; higher-priority sources appear.
- **Remember that information is an enabler, a means to an end.** Collecting vast amounts of information won't get you a sweet promotion with a big raise. *Using* information creatively and intelligently will.

MONITORING PRODUCTIVITY

Facebook, Twitter, and other technologies are key parts of what has been called the "information technology paradox," in which tools designed to save time can waste as much time as they save. For instance, many employers are so concerned about productivity losses from personal use of the Internet at work that they place restrictions on how employees can use it, such as installing software that limits Internet access to business-related sites during working hours.[11]

Managers also need to guide their employees in productive use of information tools. The speed and simplicity of these tools is also one of their greatest weaknesses: It's simply too easy to send too many messages and to subscribe to too many blog feeds, Twitter follows, and other information sources. The flood of messages from an expanding array of electronic sources can significantly affect employees' ability to focus on their work. In one study, in fact, workers exposed to a constant barrage of emails, IMs, and phone calls experienced an average 10-point drop in their functioning intelligence quotient (IQ).[12]

MANAGING TOTAL COST OF OWNERSHIP

The true costs of IT are a concern for every company. The *total cost of ownership (TCO)* of IT systems, which includes the purchase costs of hardware, software, and networking plus expenses for installation, customization, training, upgrades, and maintenance, can be three to five times higher than the purchase price.[13] And that's for IT that companies really need and actively use. Managers also need to guard against the all-too-common problems of buying technology they don't need and building poorly planned systems that are redesigned or even scrapped before being completed.

DEVELOPING EMPLOYEE SKILLS

With the pervasiveness of IT, virtually everyone from the mailroom to the executive suite is expected to have some level of technology skills. Not only will you need to keep your own skills up to date so that you can manage yourself and others efficiently, but you'll also need to make sure your employees have the skills they need. With so much business communication taking place through electronic channels these days, managers and employees need more skills than ever to stay connected.

MAINTAINING THE HUMAN TOUCH

Technology can do wonderful things for business, but it can also get in the way of communication and collaboration. Even in the best circumstances, technology can't match the rich experience of person-to-person contact. Let's say you IM a colleague, asking how she did with her sales presentation to an important client, and her answer comes back simply as "Fine." What does *fine* mean? Is an order expected soon? Did she lose the sale and doesn't want to talk about it? Was the client rude, and she doesn't want to talk about it? If you communicate in person, she might provide additional information, or you might be able to offer advice or support during a difficult time. As technological options increase, people seem to need the human touch even more. In fact, some firms have taken such steps as banning email one day a week to force people to communicate in person or at least over the phone.

Moreover, in-person communication is important to your career. You can create amazing documents and presentations without ever leaving your desk or meeting anyone in person. But if you stay hidden behind technology, people won't get to know the real you. Jill Smart, an executive with the consulting firm Accenture, often takes advantage of the company's advanced telepresence facilities but still travels frequently to meet with clients—particularly clients in other countries and cultures. "You get things from being there, over breakfast and dinner, building relationships face to face."[14]

TEST YOUR KNOWLEDGE

Questions for Review

1. What is the difference between data and information?
2. What is the key difference between a management information system and a decision support system?
3. What is information overload?
4. What is the purpose of data mining?
5. How do operational information systems differ from managerial systems?

Questions for Analysis

6. Why do social media technologies present a potential information security threat?

7. What steps can you take to balance the need for relevant, timely information with the need to protect your productivity?
8. Why would a firm invest in an expert system if it already employs the experts whose knowledge and experience would be used to develop the system's decision support capabilities?
9. Why is new information technology sometimes considered both a benefit and a curse?
10. Ethical Considerations. Should employees be allowed to use company-owned information technologies for personal use during work hours? Why or why not?

APPENDIX GLOSSARY

data Facts, numbers, statistics, and other individual bits and pieces of data that by themselves don't necessarily constitute useful information

information Useful knowledge, often extracted from data

insight A deep level of understanding about a particular subject or situation

databases Computerized files that collect, sort, and cross-reference data

chief information officer (CIO) A high-level executive responsible for understanding a company's information needs and creating systems and procedures to deliver that information to the right people at the right time

information systems (IS) A collective label for all technologies and processes used to manage business information

information technology (IT) A generally accepted synonym for information systems; many companies use *IT* to refer to the department that manages information systems

management information system (MIS) A computer system that provides managers with information and support for making routine decisions

artificial intelligence The ability of computers to solve problems through reasoning and learning and to simulate human sensory perceptions

malware Short for *malicious software*; computer programs that are designed to disrupt websites, destroy information, or enable criminal activity

viruses Invasive programs that reproduce by infecting legitimate programs

MyBizLab

For an interactive, real-world example of this topic, access this chapter's simulation entitled Technolgy Direction, located at **www.mybizlab.com.**

REFERENCES

1. Daniel Lyons, "Too Much Information," *Forbes*, 13 December 2004, 110–115.
2. Irma Becerra-Fernandez, Avelino Gonzalez, and Rajiv Sabherwal, *Knowledge Management* (Upper Saddle River, N.J.: Pearson Prentice Hall, 2004), 200.
3. Victoria Murphy Barret, "Fight the Jerks," *Forbes*, 2 July 2007, 52–54.
4. "Cyber-Gloom on the Horizon," *Accountancy*, January 2009, 59; Spencer E. Ante and Brian Grow, "Meet the Hackers," *BusinessWeek*, 29 May 2006, www.businessweek.com.
5. Robert McMillan, "Data Scam Hits Grad Students," *Computerworld*, 9 June 2008, 6.
6. Jenny Williams, "Top Three Internet Scams to Avoid in 2011," ComputerWeekly.com, 12 January 2011, www.computerweekly.com; "Boom Time for Cybercrime," *Consumer Reports*, June 2009, 18–21; Sharon Gaudin, "The Move to Web 2.0 Increases Security Challenges," *InformationWeek*, 24 May 2007, www.informationweek.com.
7. Greg Burns, "For Some, Benefits of Email Not Worth Risk," *San Diego Union-Tribune*, 16 August 2005, A1, A8; Pui-Wing Tam, Erin White, Nick Wingfield, and Kris Maher, "Snooping Email by Software Is Now a Workplace Norm," *Wall Street Journal*, 9 March 2005, B1+.
8. Jeffrey Gangemi, "Cybercriminals Target Small Biz," *BusinessWeek*, 11 December 2006, www.businessweek.com.
9. Williams, "Top Three Internet Scams to Avoid in 2011"; Todd Wasserman, "Facebook Says 600,000 Accounts Compromised per Day," Mashable, 28 October 2011, http://mashable.com; Al Senia, "High-Tech Handsets Are Hacker Bait," *BusinessWeek*, 10 January 2007, www.businessweek.com; Ken Belson, "Hackers Are Discovering a New Frontier: Internet Telephone Service," *New York Times*, 2 August 2004, C4; Yuki Noguchi, "Hold the Phone: Hackers Starting to Infect Our Cells," *Seattle Times*, 26 November 2004, www.seattletimes.com; Steven Ranger, "Mobile Virus Epidemic Heading This Way," *Test Bed Blog*, 10 February 2005, www.vnunet.com; Stephanie N. Mehta, "Wireless Scrambles to Batten Down the Hatches," *Fortune*, 18 October 2004, 275–280.
10. Tara Craig, "How to Avoid Information Overload," *Personnel Today*, 10 June 2008, 31; Jeff Davidson, "Fighting Information Overload," *Canadian Manager*, Spring 2005, 16+.
11. Sushil K. Sharma and Jatinder N. D. Gupta, "Improving Workers' Productivity and Reducing Internet Abuse," *Journal of Computer Information Systems*, Winter 2003–2004, 74–78.
12. Jack Trout, "Beware of 'Infomania,'" *Forbes*, 11 August 2006, www.forbes.com.
13. Laudon and Laudon, *Management Information Systems*, 208.
14. Steve Lohr, "As Travel Costs Rise, More Meetings Go Virtual," *New York Times*, 22 July 2008, www.nytimes.com.

Introduction to Business Analytics

Learning Objectives

After studying this chapter, you will be able to:

- Define business analytics.
- Explain why analytics is important in today's business environment.
- State some typical examples of business applications in which analytics would be beneficial.
- Summarize the evolution of business analytics and explain the concepts of business intelligence, operations research and management science, and decision support systems.
- Explain and provide examples of descriptive, predictive, and prescriptive analytics.
- State examples of how data are used in business.
- Explain the difference between a data set and a database.
- Define a metric and explain the concepts of measurement and measures.
- Explain the difference between a discrete metric and continuous metric, and provide examples of each.

- Describe the four groups of data classification, categorical, ordinal, interval, and ratio, and provide examples of each.
- Explain the concept of a model and various ways a model can be characterized.
- Define and list the elements of a decision model.
- Define and provide an example of an influence diagram.
- Use influence diagrams to build simple mathematical models.
- Use predictive models to compute model outputs.
- Explain the difference between uncertainty and risk.
- Define the terms optimization, objective function, and optimal solution.
- Explain the difference between a deterministic and stochastic decision model.
- List and explain the steps in the problem-solving process.

You may likely be one of the millions of subscribers to Netflix; even if you're not, you are probably familiar with it. Netflix changed the DVD-rental industry by offering a vast array of titles through the mail, with no due dates or late fees. A new customer is prompted to enter his or her genre preferences into the Netflix computer system and rate a selection of movies with one to five stars. Films in the Netflix inventory are tagged with attributes such as "gritty," "superhero," "strong female lead," and so on. Customer ratings are compared with these attributes, along with people who have similar viewing and preference histories. These data are used to predict movies that a customer is likely to enjoy and create personalized recommendations. The more movies a customer rates, the more accurate are the recommendations generated by the system. This information also helps Netflix manage its film inventory. For example, the system often recommends older movies to balance demand for newer releases.[1]

How does Netflix do all this? By using business analytics! Analytics is used everywhere, from marketing to operations to customer service. Netflix collects extensive data using surveys, Web site user testing, brand-awareness studies, and segmentation research, just to name a few approaches. It even uses analytics to help decide what price to pay for the rights to distribute new DVDs.[2] Despite recent controversy, analytics has been fundamental to the company's success.

In recent years, analytics has become increasingly important in the world of business, particularly as organizations have access to more and more data. Managers today no longer make decisions based on pure judgment and experience; they rely on factual data and the ability to manipulate and analyze data to support their decisions. As a result, many companies have recently established analytics departments; for instance, IBM reorganized its consulting business and established a new 4,000-person organization focusing on analytics.[3] Companies are increasingly

[1] Sources: Michael V. Copeland, "Reed Hastings: Leader of the Pack," *Fortune* (December 6, 2010): 121–130; Netflix Consumer Press Kit; Netflix Investor Press Kit.
[2] Thomas H. Davenport and Jeanne G. Harris, *Competing on Analytics: The New Science of Winning* (Boston: Harvard Business School Press, 2007).
[3] Matthew J. Liberatore and Wenhong Luo, "The Analytics Movement: Implications for Operations Research," *Interfaces*, 40, 4 (July–August 2010): 313–324.

seeking business graduates with the ability to understand and use analytics. In fact, in 2011, the U.S. Bureau of Labor Statistics predicted a 24% increase in demand for professionals with analytics expertise.

No matter what your academic business concentration is, you will most likely be a future user of analytics to some extent and work with analytics professionals. In this chapter we introduce you to the field of business analytics, and set the foundation for many of the concepts and techniques that you will learn.

What Is Business Analytics?

Everyone makes decisions. Individuals face personal decisions such as choosing a college or graduate program, making product purchases, selecting a mortgage instrument, and investing for retirement. Managers in business organizations make numerous decisions every day. Some of these decisions include what products to make and how to price them, where to locate facilities, how many people to hire, where to allocate advertising budgets, whether or not to outsource a business function or make a capital investment, and how to schedule production. Many of these decisions have significant economic consequences; moreover, they are difficult to make because of uncertain data and imperfect information about the future. Thus, managers need good information and assistance to make such critical decisions that will impact not only their companies but also their careers. What makes business decisions complicated today is the overwhelming amount of available data and information. Data to support business decisions—including those specifically collected by firms as well as through the Internet and social media such as Facebook—are growing exponentially and becoming increasingly difficult to understand and use. This is one of the reasons why analytics is important in today's business environment.

Business analytics, or simply **analytics**, is the use of data, information technology, statistical analysis, quantitative methods, and mathematical or computer-based models to help managers gain improved insight about their business operations and make better, fact-based decisions. Business analytics is "a process of transforming data into actions through analysis and insights in the context of organizational decision making and problem solving."[4] Business analytics is supported by various tools such as Microsoft Excel and various Excel add-ins, commercial statistical software packages such as SAS or Minitab, and more-complex business intelligence suites that integrate data with analytical software.

---

[4]Liberatore and Luo, "The Analytics Movement."

Tools and techniques of business analytics are used across many areas in a wide variety of organizations to improve the management of customer relationships, financial and marketing activities, human capital, supply chains, and many other areas. Leading banks use analytics to predict and prevent credit fraud, saving millions. Manufacturers use analytics for production planning, purchasing, and inventory management. Retailers use analytics to predict the best location for stores and how to stock them. Pharmaceutical firms use it to get life-saving drugs to market more quickly. Even sports teams are using business analytics to determine both game strategy and optimal ticket prices.[5] Among the many organizations that use analytics to make strategic decisions and manage day-to-day operations are Harrah's Entertainment, the Oakland Athletics baseball and New England Patriots football teams, Amazon.com, Procter and Gamble, United Parcel Service, and Capital One bank.

Some common types of decisions that can be enhanced by using analytics include

- pricing decisions (for example, consumer and industrial goods, government contracts, and maintenance contracts),
- decisions to target consumer segments (for example, retailers, insurers, and credit card firms),
- merchandising decisions (for example, brands to buy, quantities, and allocations),
- location decisions (for example, bank branches or where to service industrial equipment), and many others in operations and supply chains, finance, marketing, and human resources—in fact, in every discipline of business.[6]

Various research studies have discovered strong relationships between a company's performance in terms of profitability, revenue, and shareholder return and its use of analytics. Top-performing organizations (those that outperform their competitors) are three times more likely to be sophisticated in their use of analytics than lower performers and are more likely to state that their use of analytics differentiates them from competitors.[7] However, research has also suggested that organizations are overwhelmed by data and struggle to understand how to use data to achieve business results and that most organizations simply don't understand how to use analytics to improve their businesses. Thus, understanding the capabilities and techniques of analytics is vital to managing in today's business environment.

One of the emerging applications of analytics is helping businesses learn from social media and exploit social media data for strategic advantage.[8] Using analytics, firms can integrate social media data with traditional data sources such as customer surveys, focus groups, and sales data; understand trends and customer perceptions of their products; and create informative reports to assist marketing managers and product designers.

---

[5]Jim Davis, "8 Essentials of Business Analytics," in "Brain Trust—Enabling the Confident Enterprise with Business Analytics" (Cary, NC: SAS Institute, Inc., 2010): 27–29. www.sas.com/bareport

[6]Thomas H. Davenport, "How Organizations Make Better Decisions," edited excerpt of an article distributed by the International Institute for Analytics published in "Brain Trust—Enabling the Confident Enterprise with Business Analytics" (Cary, NC: SAS Institute, Inc., 2010): 8–11. www.sas.com/bareport

[7]Thomas H. Davenport and Jeanne G. Harris, *Competing on Analytics* (Boston: Harvard Business School Press 2007): 46; Michael S. Hopkins, Steve LaValle, Fred Balboni, Nina Kruschwitz and Rebecca Shockley, "10 Data Points: Information and Analytics at Work," *MIT Sloan Management Review*, 52, 1 (Fall 2010): 27–31.

[8]Jim Davis, "Convergence—Taking Social Media from Talk to Action," *SASCOM* (First Quarter 2011): 17.

Evolution of Business Analytics

Analytical methods, in one form or another, have been used in business for more than a century. However, the modern evolution of analytics began with the introduction of computers in the late 1940s and their development through the 1960s and beyond. Early computers provided the ability to store and analyze data in ways that were either very difficult or impossible to do manually. This facilitated the collection, management, analysis, and reporting of data, which is often called **business intelligence**, a term that was coined in 1958 by an IBM researcher, Hans Peter Luhn.[9] Business intelligence software can answer basic questions such as: How many units did we sell last month? What did customers buy and how much did they spend? How many credit card transactions were completed yesterday? It can also create simple rules to flag exceptions for automatic reporting, for example, reporting on transactions greater than $10,000 to the Internal Revenue Service.[10]

Much of modern business analytics stems from the analysis and solution of complex decision problems using mathematical or computer-based models—a discipline known as *operations research,* or *management science.* **Operations research (OR)** was born from efforts to improve military operations prior to and during World War II. After the war, scientists recognized that the mathematical tools and techniques developed for military applications could be applied successfully to problems in business and industry. A significant amount of research was carried on in public and private think tanks during the late 1940s and through the 1950s. As the focus on business applications expanded, the term **management science (MS)** became more prevalent. Many people use the terms *operations research* and *management science* interchangeably, and in recent years, the term *analytics* is being used more to refer to OR and MS techniques. INFORMS, the Institute for Operations Research and the Management Sciences, is the leading professional society devoted to analytics and publishes a bimonthly magazine called *Analytics* (http://analytics-magazine.com/). Digital subscriptions may be obtained free of charge at the Web site.

Decision support systems (DSS) began to evolve in the 1960s by combining business intelligence concepts with MS models to create analytical-based computer systems to support decision making. DSSs include three components:

1. *Data management.* The data management component includes databases for storing data and allows the user to input, retrieve, update, and manipulate data.
2. *Model management.* The model management component consists of various statistical tools and management science models and allows the user to easily build, manipulate, analyze, and solve models.
3. *Communication system.* The communication system component provides the interface necessary for the user to interact with the data and model management components.[11]

Decision support systems have been used for many applications, including pension fund management, portfolio management, work-shift scheduling, global manufacturing and facility location, advertising-budget allocation, media planning, distribution planning,

---

[9]H. P. Luhn, "A Business Intelligence System." *IBM Journal* (October 1958).

[10]Jim Davis, "Business Analytics: Helping You Put an Informed Foot Forward," in "Brain Trust—Enabling the Confident Enterprise with Business Analytics," (Cary, NC: SAS Institute, Inc., 2010): 4–7. www.sas.com/bareport

[11]William E. Leigh and Michael E. Doherty, *Decision Support and Expert Systems* (Cincinnati, OH: South-Western Publishing Co., 1986).

airline operations planning, inventory control, library management, classroom assignment, nurse scheduling, blood distribution, water pollution control, ski-area design, police-beat design, and energy planning.[12]

Perhaps the most influential developments that propelled the use of business analytics have been the personal computer and spreadsheet technology. Personal computers and spreadsheets provide a convenient way to manage data, calculations, and visual graphics simultaneously, using intuitive representations instead of abstract mathematical notation. Although the early applications of spreadsheets were primarily in accounting and finance, spreadsheets have developed into powerful general-purpose managerial tools for applying techniques of business analytics. The power of analytics in a personal computing environment was noted some 20 years ago by business consultants Michael Hammer and James Champy, who said, "When accessible data is combined with easy-to-use analysis and modeling tools, frontline workers—when properly trained—suddenly have sophisticated decision-making capabilities."[13]

Scope of Business Analytics

Business analytics begins with the collection, organization, and manipulation of data and is supported by three major components:[14]

1. *Descriptive analytics.* Most businesses start with **descriptive analytics**—the use of data to understand past and current business performance and make informed decisions. Descriptive analytics is the most commonly used and most well understood type of analytics. These techniques categorize, characterize, consolidate and classify data to convert it into useful information for the purposes of understanding and analyzing business performance. Descriptive analytics summarizes data into meaningful charts and reports, for example, about budgets, sales, revenues, or cost. This process allows managers to obtain standard and customized reports and then drill down into the data and make queries to understand the impact of an advertising campaign, for example, review business performance to find problems or areas of opportunity, and identify patterns and trends in data. Typical questions that descriptive analytics helps answer are: How much did we sell in each region? What was our revenue and profit last quarter? How many and what types of complaints did we resolve? Which factory has the lowest productivity? Descriptive analytics also helps companies to classify customers into different segments, which enables them to develop specific marketing campaigns and advertising strategies.

2. *Predictive analytics.* **Predictive analytics** analyzes past performance in an effort to predict the future by examining historical data, detecting patterns or relationships in these data, and then extrapolating these relationships forward in time. For example, a marketer might wish to predict the response of

---

[12]H. B. Eom and S. M. Lee, "A Survey of Decision Support System Applications (1971–April 1988)," *Interfaces*, 20, 3 (May–June 1990): 65–79.

[13]Michael Hammer and James Champy, *Reengineering the Corporation* (New York: HarperBusiness, 1993): 96.

[14]Parts of this section are adapted from Irv Lustig, Brenda Dietric, Christer Johnson, and Christopher Dziekan, "The Analytics Journey," *Analytics* (November/December 2010). Analyticsmagazine.com

different customer segments to an advertising campaign, a commodities trader might wish to predict short-term movements in commodities prices, or a skiwear manufacturer might want to predict next season's demand for skiwear of a specific color and size. Predictive analytics can predict risk and find relationships in data not readily apparent with traditional analyses. Using advanced techniques, predictive analytics can help to detect hidden patterns in large quantities of data to segment and group data into coherent sets in order to predict behavior and detect trends. For instance, a bank manager might want to identify the most profitable customers or predict the chances that a loan applicant will default, or alert a credit-card customer to a potential fraudulent charge. Predictive analytics helps to answer questions such as: What will happen if demand falls by 10% or if supplier prices go up 5%? What do we expect to pay for fuel over the next several months? What is the risk of losing money in a new business venture?

3. *Prescriptive analytics.* Many problems, such as aircraft or employee scheduling and supply chain design, for example, simply involve too many choices or alternatives for a human decision maker to effectively consider. **Prescriptive analytics** uses optimization to identify the best alternatives to minimize or maximize some objective. Prescriptive analytics is used in many areas of business, including operations, marketing, and finance. For example, we may determine the best pricing and advertising strategy to maximize revenue, the optimal amount of cash to store in ATMs, or the best mix of investments in a retirement portfolio to manage risk. The mathematical and statistical techniques of predictive analytics can also be combined with optimization to make decisions that take into account the uncertainty in the data. Prescriptive analytics addresses questions such as: How much should we produce to maximize profit? What is the best way of shipping goods from our factories to minimize costs? Should we change our plans if a natural disaster closes a supplier's factory: if so, by how much?

Although the tools used in descriptive, predictive, and prescriptive analytics are different, many applications involve all three. Here is a typical example in retail operations.

EXAMPLE 1 Retail Markdown Decisions[15]

As you probably know from your shopping experiences, most department stores and fashion retailers clear their seasonal inventory by reducing prices. The key question they face is what prices should they set—and when should they set them—to meet inventory goals and maximize revenue? For example, suppose that a store has 100 bathing suits of a certain style that go on sale April 1 and wants to sell all of them by the end of June. Over each week of the 12-week selling season, they can make a decision to discount the price. They face 2 decisions: when to reduce the price and by how much? This results in 24 decisions to make. For a major national chain that may carry thousands of products, this can easily result in millions of decisions that store managers have to make. Descriptive analytics can be used to examine historical data for similar products, such as the number of units sold, price at each point of sale, starting and ending inventories, and special promotions, newspaper ads, direct marketing ads, and so on, to understand what the results of past decisions achieved. Predictive analytics can be used to predict sales based on pricing decisions. Finally, prescriptive analytics can be applied to find the best set of pricing decisions to maximize the total revenue.

---

[15]Inspired by a presentation by Radhika Kulkarni, SAS Institute, "Data-Driven Decisions: Role of Operations Research in Business Analytics," INFORMS Conference on Business Analytics and Operations Research, April 10–12, 2011.

Analytics in Practice: Harrah's Entertainment[16]

One of the most cited examples of the use of analytics in business is Harrah's Entertainment. Harrah's owns numerous hotels and casinos and uses analytics to support revenue management activities, which involve selling the right resources to the right customer at the right price to maximize revenue and profit. The gaming industry views hotel rooms as incentives or rewards to support casino gaming activities and revenues, not as revenue-maximizing assets. Therefore, Harrah's objective is to set room rates and accept reservations to maximize the expected gaming profits from customers. They begin with collecting and tracking of customers' gaming activities (playing slot machines and casino games) using Harrah's "Total Rewards" card program, a customer loyalty program that provides rewards such as meals, discounted rooms, and other perks to customers based on the amount of money and time they spend at Harrah's. The data collected are used to segment customers into more than 20 groups based on their expected gaming activities. For each customer segment, analytics forecasts demand for hotel rooms by arrival date and length of stay. Then Harrah's uses a prescriptive model to set prices and allocate rooms to these customer segments. For example, the system might offer complimentary rooms to customers who are expected to generate a gaming profit of at least $400 but charge $325 for a room if the profit is expected to be only $100. Marketing can use the information to send promotional offers to targeted customer segments if it identifies low-occupancy rates for specific dates.

The impact of applying business analytics can be significant. For example, 1-800-FLOWERS.COM uses analytic software to target print and online promotions with greater accuracy; change prices and offerings on its Web site (sometimes hourly); and optimize its marketing, shipping, distribution, and manufacturing operations, resulting in a $50 million cost savings in one year.[17]

Business analytics is changing how managers make decisions.[18] To thrive in today's business world, organizations must continually innovate to differentiate themselves from competitors, seek ways to grow revenue and market share, reduce costs, retain existing customers and acquire new ones, and become faster and leaner. IBM suggests that traditional management approaches are evolving in today's analytics-driven environment to include more fact-based decisions as opposed to judgment and intuition, more prediction rather than reactive decisions, and the use of analytics by everyone at the point where decisions are made rather than relying on skilled experts in a consulting group.[19] Nevertheless, organizations face many challenges in developing analytics capabilities, including lack of understanding of how to use analytics, competing business priorities, insufficient analytical skills, difficulty in getting good data and sharing information, and not understanding the benefits versus perceived costs of analytics studies.

Data for Business Analytics

Since the dawn of the electronic age and the Internet, both individuals and organizations have had access to an enormous wealth of data and information. *Data* are numerical facts and figures that are collected through some type of measurement process. *Information*

---

[16]Based on Liberatore and Luo, "The Analytics Movement"; and Richard Metters et al., "The 'Killer Application' of Revenue Management: Harrah's Cherokee Casino & Hotel," *Interfaces*, 38, 3 (May–June 2008): 161–175.

[17]Jim Goodnight, "The Impact of Business Analytics on Performance and Profitability," in "Brain Trust—Enabling the Confident Enterprise with Business Analytics" (Cary, NC: SAS Institute, Inc., 2010): 4–7. www.sas.com/bareport

[18]*Analytics: The New Path to Value*, a joint MIT Sloan Management Review and IBM Institute for Business Value study.

[19]"Business Analytics and Optimization for the Intelligent Enterprise" (April 2009). www.ibm.com/qbs/intelligent-enterprise

comes from analyzing data—that is, extracting meaning from data to support evaluation and decision making.

Data are used in virtually every major function in a business. Modern organizations—which include not only for-profit businesses but also nonprofit organizations—need good data to support a variety of company purposes, such as planning, reviewing company performance, improving operations, and comparing company performance with competitors' or best-practice benchmarks. Some examples of how data are used in business include the following:

- Annual reports summarize data about companies' profitability and market share both in numerical form and in charts and graphs to communicate with shareholders.
- Accountants conduct audits to determine whether figures reported on a firm's balance sheet fairly represent the actual data by examining samples (that is, subsets) of accounting data, such as accounts receivable.
- Financial analysts collect and analyze a variety of data to understand the contribution that a business provides to its shareholders. These typically include profitability, revenue growth, return on investment, asset utilization, operating margins, earnings per share, economic value added (EVA), shareholder value, and other relevant measures.
- Economists use data to help companies understand and predict population trends, interest rates, industry performance, consumer spending, and international trade. Such data are often obtained from external sources such as Standard & Poor's Compustat data sets, industry trade associations, or government databases.
- Marketing researchers collect and analyze extensive customer data. These data often consist of demographics, preferences and opinions, transaction and payment history, shopping behavior, and a lot more. Such data may be collected by surveys, personal interviews, focus groups, or from shopper loyalty cards.
- Operations managers use data on production performance, manufacturing quality, delivery times, order accuracy, supplier performance, productivity, costs, and environmental compliance to manage their operations.
- Human resource managers measure employee satisfaction, training costs, turnover, market innovation, training effectiveness, and skills development.

Such data may be gathered from primary sources such as internal company records and business transactions, automated data-capturing equipment, or customer market surveys and from secondary sources such as government and commercial data sources, custom research providers, and online research.

Perhaps the most important source of data today is data obtained electronically from the Web. With today's technology, marketers collect extensive information about Web behaviors, such as the number of page views, visitor's country, time of view, length of time, origin and destination paths, products they searched for and viewed, products purchased, what reviews they read, and many others. Not only can marketers understand what customers have done, but they can better predict what they intend to do in the future. For example, if a bank knows that a customer has browsed for mortgage rates and home owner's insurance, they can target the customer with homeowner loans rather than credit cards or automobile loans. Traditional Web data are now being enhanced with social media data from Facebook, cell phones, and even Internet-connected gaming devices.

As one example, a home furnishings retailer wanted to increase the rate of sales for customers who browsed their Web site. They developed a large data set that covered more than 7,000 demographic, Web, catalog, and retail behavioral attributes for each customer.

They used predictive analytics to determine how well a customer would respond to different e-mail marketing offers and customized promotions to individual customers. This not only helped them to determine where to most effectively spend marketing resources but doubled the response rate compared to previous marketing campaigns, with a projected multimillion dollar increase in sales.[20]

Data Sets and Databases

A **data set** is simply a collection of data. Marketing survey responses, a table of historical stock prices, and a collection of measurements of dimensions of a manufactured item are examples of data sets. A **database** is a collection of related files containing records on people, places, or things. The people, places, or things for which we store and maintain information are called **entities**.[21] A database for an online retailer that sells instructional fitness books and DVDs, for instance, might consist of a file for three entities: publishers from which goods are purchased, customer sales transactions, and product inventory. A database file is usually organized in a two-dimensional table, where the columns correspond to each individual element of data (called **fields**, or **attributes**), and the rows represent records of related data elements. A key feature of computerized databases is the ability to quickly relate one set of files to another.

Databases are important in business analytics for accessing data, making queries, and other data and information management activities. Software such as Microsoft Access provides powerful analytical database capabilities. However, we won't be delving deeply into databases or database management systems but will work with individual database files or simple data sets. Because spreadsheets are convenient tools for storing and manipulating data sets and database files, we will use them for all examples and problems.

EXAMPLE 2   A Sales Transaction Database File[22]

Figure 1 shows a portion of sales transactions on an Excel worksheet for a particular day for an online seller of instructional fitness books and DVDs. The fields are shown in row 3 of the spreadsheet and consist of the customer ID, region, payment type, transaction code, source of the sale, amount, product purchased, and time of day. Each record (starting in row 4) has a value for each of these fields.

Metrics and Data Classification

A **metric** is a unit of measurement that provides a way to objectively quantify performance. For example, senior managers might assess overall business performance using such metrics as net profit, return on investment, market share, and customer satisfaction. A plant manager might monitor such metrics as the proportion of defective parts produced or the number of inventory turns each month. For a Web-based retailer, some useful metrics are the percentage of orders filled accurately and the time taken to fill a customer's

---

[20]Based on a presentation by Bill Franks of Teradata, "Optimizing Customer Analytics: How Customer Level Web Data Can Help," INFORMS Conference on Business Analytics and Operations Research, April 10–12, 2011.

[21]Kenneth C. Laudon and Jane P. Laudon, *Essentials of Management Information Systems*, 9th ed. (Upper Saddle River, NJ: Prentice Hall, 2011): 159.

[22]Adapted and modified from Kenneth C. Laudon and Jane P. Laudon, *Essentials of Management Information Systems*.

	A	B	C	D	E	F	G	H
1	Sales Transactions: July 14							
2								
3	Cust ID	Region	Payment	Transaction Code	Source	Amount	Product	Time Of Day
4	10001	East	Paypal	93816545	Web	$20.19	DVD	22:19
5	10002	West	Credit	74083490	Web	$17.85	DVD	13:27
6	10003	North	Credit	64942368	Web	$23.98	DVD	14:27
7	10004	West	Paypal	70560957	Email	$23.51	Book	15:38
8	10005	South	Credit	35208817	Web	$15.33	Book	15:21
9	10006	West	Paypal	20978903	Email	$17.30	DVD	13:11
10	10007	East	Credit	80103311	Web	$177.72	Book	21:59
11	10008	West	Credit	14132683	Web	$21.76	Book	4:04
12	10009	West	Paypal	40128225	Web	$15.92	DVD	19:35
13	10010	South	Paypal	49073721	Web	$23.39	DVD	13:26

Figure 1

A Portion of Excel File *Sales Transaction* Database

order. **Measurement** is the act of obtaining data associated with a metric. **Measures** are numerical values associated with a metric.

Metrics can be either discrete or continuous. A **discrete metric** is one that is derived from counting something. For example, a delivery is either on time or not; an order is complete or incomplete; or an invoice can have one, two, three, or any number of errors. Some discrete metrics associated with these examples would be the proportion of on-time deliveries; the number of incomplete orders each day, and the number of errors per invoice. **Continuous metrics** are based on a continuous scale of measurement. Any metrics involving dollars, length, time, volume, or weight, for example, are continuous.

Another classification of data is by the type of measurement scale. Data may be classified into four groups:

1. **Categorical (nominal) data**, which are sorted into categories according to specified characteristics. For example, a firm's customers might be classified by their geographical region (North America, South America, Europe, and Pacific); employees might be classified as managers, supervisors, and associates. The categories bear no quantitative relationship to one another, but we usually assign an arbitrary number to each category to ease the process of managing the data and computing statistics. Categorical data are usually counted or expressed as proportions or percentages.

2. **Ordinal data**, which are ordered or ranked according to some relationship to one another. College football or basketball rankings are ordinal; a higher ranking signifies a stronger team but does not specify any numerical measure of strength. Ordinal data are more meaningful than categorical data because data can be compared to one another. A common example in business is data from survey scales—for example, rating a service as poor, average, good, very good, or excellent. Such data are categorical but also have a natural order (excellent is better than very good) and, consequently, are ordinal. However, ordinal data have no fixed units of measurement, so we cannot make meaningful numerical statements about differences between categories. Thus, we cannot say that the difference between excellent and very good is the same as between good and average, for example. Similarly, a team ranked number 1 may be far superior to the number 2 team, whereas there may be little difference between teams ranked 9th and 10th.

3. **Interval data**, which are ordinal but have constant differences between observations and have no natural zero. Common examples are time and temperature. Time is relative to global location, and calendars have arbitrary starting dates. Both the Fahrenheit and Celsius scales represent a specified measure of distance—degrees—but have no natural zero. Thus we cannot take meaningful ratios; for example, we cannot say that 50 degrees is twice as hot as 25 degrees. Another example is SAT or GMAT scores. The scores can be used to rank students, but only differences between scores provide information on how much better one student performed over another; ratios make little sense. In contrast to ordinal data, interval data allow meaningful comparison of ranges, averages, and other statistics.

   In business, data from survey scales, while technically ordinal, are often treated as interval data when numerical scales are associated with the categories (for instance, 1 = poor, 2 = average, 3 = good, 4 = very good, 5 = excellent). Strictly speaking, this is not correct because the "distance" between categories may not be perceived as the same (respondents might perceive a larger gap between poor and average than between good and very good, for example). Nevertheless, many users of survey data treat them as interval when analyzing the data, particularly when only a numerical scale is used without descriptive labels.

4. **Ratio data**, which are continuous and have a natural zero. Most business and economic data, such as dollars and time, fall into this category. For example, the measure dollars has an absolute zero. Ratios of dollar figures are meaningful. For example, knowing that the Seattle region sold $12 million in March whereas the Tampa region sold $6 million means that Seattle sold twice as much as Tampa.

This classification is hierarchical in that each level includes all the information content of the one preceding it. For example, ratio information can be converted to any of the other types of data. Interval information can be converted to ordinal or categorical data but cannot be converted to ratio data without the knowledge of the absolute zero point. Thus, a ratio scale is the strongest form of measurement.

EXAMPLE 3   Classifying Data Elements in a Purchasing Database[23]

Figure 2 shows a portion of a data set containing all items that an aircraft component manufacturing company has purchased over the past 3 months. The data provide the supplier; order number; item number, description, and cost; quantity ordered; cost per order, the suppliers' accounts payable (A/P) terms; and the order and arrival dates. We may classify each of these types of data as follows:

- Supplier—categorical
- Order Number—categorical
- Item Number—categorical
- Item Description—categorical

- Item Cost—ratio
- Quantity—ratio
- Cost per Order—ratio
- A/P Terms—ratio
- Order Date—interval
- Arrival Date—interval

We might use these data to evaluate the average speed of delivery and rank the suppliers (thus creating ordinal data) by this metric.

---

[23]Based on Laudon and Laudon, *Essentials of Management Information Systems.*

⊿	A	B	C	D	E	F	G	H	I	J
1	Purchase Orders									
2										
3	Supplier	Order No	Item No.	Item Description	Item Cost	Quantity	Cost per order	A/P Terms (Months	Order Date	Arrival Date
4	Spacetime Technologies	A0111	6489	O-Ring	$ 3.00	900	$ 2,700.00	25	10/10/11	10/18/11
5	Steelpin Inc.	A0115	5319	Shielded Cable/ft.	$ 1.10	17,500	$ 19,250.00	30	08/20/11	08/31/11
6	Steelpin Inc.	A0123	4312	Bolt-nut package	$ 3.75	4,250	$ 15,937.50	30	08/25/11	09/01/11
7	Steelpin Inc.	A0204	5319	Shielded Cable/ft.	$ 1.10	16,500	$ 18,150.00	30	09/15/11	10/05/11
8	Steelpin Inc.	A0205	5677	Side Panel	$195.00	120	$ 23,400.00	30	11/02/11	11/13/11
9	Steelpin Inc.	A0207	4312	Bolt-nut package	$ 3.75	4,200	$ 15,750.00	30	09/01/11	09/10/11
10	Alum Sheeting	A0223	4224	Bolt-nut package	$ 3.95	4,500	$ 17,775.00	30	10/15/11	10/20/11
11	Alum Sheeting	A0433	5417	Control Panel	$255.00	500	$ 127,500.00	30	10/20/11	10/27/11
12	Alum Sheeting	A0443	1243	Airframe fasteners	$ 4.25	10,000	$ 42,500.00	30	08/08/11	08/14/11
13	Alum Sheeting	A0446	5417	Control Panel	$255.00	406	$ 103,530.00	30	09/01/11	09/10/11
14	Spacetime Technologies	A0533	9752	Gasket	$ 4.05	1,500	$ 6,075.00	25	09/20/11	09/25/11
15	Spacetime Technologies	A0555	6489	O-Ring	$ 3.00	1,100	$ 3,300.00	25	10/05/11	10/10/11

Figure 2

Portion of Excel File
Purchase Orders Data

Data Reliability and Validity

Data used in business analytics need to be reliable and valid. Care must be taken when working with data, and every effort should be made to ensure that data are sufficiently accurate. Sample data do not always reflect reality. People do not always behave the same when observed, nor do they always act as they say they act. Poor data can result in poor decisions. In one situation, a distribution system design model relied on data obtained from the corporate finance department. Transportation costs were determined using a formula based on the latitude and longitude of the locations of plants and customers. But when the solution was represented on a geographic information system (GIS) mapping program, one of the customers was in the Atlantic Ocean.

Decision Models

To make a decision, we must be able to specify the decision alternatives that represent the choices that can be made and criteria for evaluating the alternatives. Specifying decision alternatives might be very simple; for example, you might need to choose one of three corporate health plan options. Other situations can be more complex; for example, in locating a new distribution center, it might not be possible to list just a small number of alternatives. The set of potential locations might be anywhere in the United States or even within entire continents. Decision criteria might be to maximize discounted net profits, customer satisfaction, or social benefits or to minimize costs, environmental impact, or some measure of loss.

Decision problems can be formalized using a model. A **model** is an abstraction or representation of a real system, idea, or object. Models capture the most important features of a problem and present them in a form that is easy to interpret. A model can be as simple as a written or verbal description of some phenomenon, a visual representation such as a graph or a flow chart, or a mathematical or spreadsheet representation. In business, we typically use models in the form of logical flowcharts, spreadsheets, mathematical functions, and relationships.

A **decision model** is a logical or mathematical representation of a problem or business situation that can be used to understand, analyze, or facilitate making a decision. Decision models are usually developed from theory or observation and establish

EXAMPLE 4   Three Forms of a Model

The sales of a new product, such as a first-generation iPad, Android phone, or 3D television, often follow a common pattern. We might represent this in one of three ways:

1. A simple verbal description of sales might be: The rate of sales starts small as early adopters begin to evaluate a new product and then begins to grow at an increasing rate over time as positive customer feedback spreads. Eventually, the market begins to become saturated and the rate of sales begins to decrease.

2. A sketch of sales as an S-shaped curve over time, as shown in Figure 3, is a visual model that conveys this phenomenon.

3. Finally, analysts might identify a mathematical model that characterizes this curve. Several different mathematical functions do this; one is called a *Gompertz curve* and has the formula: $S = ae^{be^{ct}}$, where S = sales, t = time, e is the base of natural logarithms, and a, b, and c are constants. Of course, you would not be expected to know this; that's what analytics professionals do.

relationships between actions that decision makers might take and results that they might expect, thereby allowing the decision makers to predict what might happen based on the model.

Most decision models have three types of input:

1. *Data*, which are assumed to be constant for purposes of the model. Some examples would be costs, machine capacities, and intercity distances.
2. *Uncontrollable variables*, which are quantities that can change but cannot be directly controlled by the decision maker. Some examples would be customer demand, inflation rates, and investment returns. Often, these variables are uncertain.
3. *Decision variables*, which are controllable and can be selected at the discretion of the decision maker. Some examples would be production quantities, staffing levels, and investment allocations.

Figure 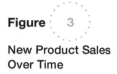 3

New Product Sales
Over Time

Figure 4

Nature of Decision Models

Decision models characterize the relationships among the data, uncontrollable variables, and decision variables, and the outputs of interest to the decision maker (see Figure 4). Decision models can be represented in various ways, most typically with mathematical functions and spreadsheets. Spreadsheets are ideal vehicles for implementing decision models because of their versatility in managing data, evaluating different scenarios, and presenting results in a meaningful fashion.

Models complement decision makers' intuition and often provide insights that intuition cannot. For example, one early application of analytics in marketing involved a study of sales operations. Sales representatives had to divide their time between large and small customers and between acquiring new customers and keeping old ones. The problem was to determine how the representatives should best allocate their time. Intuition suggested that they should concentrate on large customers and that it was much harder to acquire a new customer than to keep an old one. However, intuition could not tell whether they should concentrate on the 500 largest or the 5,000 largest customers or how much effort to spend on acquiring customers. Models of sales force effectiveness and customer response patterns provided the insight to make these decisions. However, it is important to understand that all models are only representations of the real world and, as such, cannot capture every nuance that decision makers face in reality. Decision makers must often modify the policies that models suggest to account for intangible factors that they might not have been able to incorporate into the model.

Decision models are used in each of the three major areas of business analytics—descriptive, predictive, and prescriptive analytics.

Descriptive Decision Models

Descriptive models simply tell "what is" and describe relationships; they do not tell a manager what to do. However, managers can use descriptive models to evaluate different decisions. A simple descriptive model is a visual representation called an

---

EXAMPLE 5   A Sales-Promotion Model

In the grocery industry, managers typically need to know how best to use pricing, coupons, and advertising strategies to influence sales. Grocers often study the relationship of sales volume to these strategies by conducting controlled experiments to identify the relationship between them and sales volumes.[24] That is, they implement different combinations of pricing, coupons, and advertising, observe the sales that result, and use analytics to

develop a predictive model of sales as a function of these decision strategies.

For example, suppose that a grocer who operates three stores in a small city varied the price, coupons (yes = 1, no = 0), and advertising expenditures in a local newspaper over a 16-week period and observed the following sales:

(continued)

---

[24]"Flanking in a Price War," *Interfaces*, 19, 2 (1989): 1–12.

Week	Price ($)	Coupon (0,1)	Advertising ($)	Store 1 Sales (Units)	Store 2 Sales (Units)	Store 3 Sales (Units)
1	$6.99	0	$0	501	510	481
2	$6.99	0	$150	772	748	775
3	$6,99	1	$0	554	528	506
4	$6.99	1	$150	838	785	834
5	$6.49	0	$0	521	519	500
6	$6.49	0	$150	723	790	723
7	$6.49	1	$0	510	556	520
8	$6.49	1	$150	818	773	800
9	$7.59	0	$0	479	491	486
10	$7.59	0	$150	825	822	757
11	$7.59	1	$0	533	513	540
12	$7.59	1	$150	839	791	832
13	$5.49	0	$0	484	480	508
14	$5.49	0	$150	686	683	708
15	$5.49	1	$0	543	531	530
16	$5.49	1	$150	767	743	779

Using business analytics, the grocer might have developed the following model:

$$\text{sales} = 500 - 0.05 \times \text{price} + 30 \times \text{coupons} + 0.08 \times \text{advertising} + 0.25 \times \text{price} \times \text{advertising}$$

In this model, the decision variables are price, coupons, and advertising. The values 500, –0.05, 30, 0.08, and 0.25 are effects of the input data to the model that are estimated from the data obtained from the experiment. They reflect the impact on sales of changing the decision variables. For example, an increase in price of $1 results in a 0.05-unit decrease in weekly sales; using coupons results in a 30-unit increase in weekly sales. In this example, there are no uncontrollable input variables. The output of the model is the sales units of the product. For example, if the price is $6.99, no coupons are offered and no advertising is done (the experiment corresponding to week 1), the model estimates sales as

$$\text{sales} = 500 - 0.05 \times \$6.99 + 30 \times 0 + 0.08 \times 0 + 0.25 \times \$6.99 \times 0 = 500 \text{ units}$$

We see that the actual sales in week 1 varied between 481 and 510 in the three stores. Thus, the model predicts a good estimate for sales but does not tell us anything about the potential variability. However, the manager can use this model to evaluate different pricing, promotion, and advertising strategies, and help choose the best strategy to maximize sales or profitability.

influence diagram because it describes how various elements of the model influence, or relate to, others. An influence diagram is a useful approach for conceptualizing the structure of a model and can assist in building a mathematical or spreadsheet model. The elements of the model are represented by circular symbols called *nodes*. Arrows called *branches* connect the nodes and show which elements influence others. Example 6 shows how to construct simple influence diagrams.

Descriptive models may also be mathematical. Example 7 shows how to build a mathematical model for profit, drawing upon the influence diagram. How can we use the model in Example 7 to help make a decision? Suppose that a manufacturer has the option of producing a part in-house or outsourcing it from a supplier. Should the firm produce the part or outsource it? The decision depends on the anticipated

EXAMPLE 6   An Influence Diagram for Total Cost

The general equation that describes the total cost of producing a fixed volume of a product is

$$\text{total cost} = \text{fixed cost} + \text{variable cost} \tag{1}$$

Thus, a simple influence diagram that shows these relationships is given in Figure 5.

We can develop a more detailed model by noting that the variable cost depends on the unit variable cost as well as the quantity produced. The enhanced model is shown in Figure 6. In this figure, all the nodes that have no branches pointing into them are inputs to the model. We can see that the unit variable cost and fixed costs are data inputs in the model. The quantity produced, however, is a decision variable because it can be controlled by the manager of the operation. The total cost is the output (note that it has no branches pointing out of it) that we would be interested in calculating. The variable cost node links some of the inputs with the output and can be considered as a "building block" of the model for total cost.

volume of demand; for high volumes, the cost to manufacture in-house will be lower than outsourcing, because the fixed costs can be spread over a large number of units. For small volumes, it would be more economical to outsource. Knowing the cost of both alternatives and the break-even point would facilitate the decision; this is shown in Example 8.

Figure   5

An Influence Diagram
Relating Total Cost to Its
Key Components

Figure   6

An Expanded Influence
Diagram for Total Cost

EXAMPLE 7   A Mathematical Model for Total Cost

To develop a mathematical model from the influence diagram in Figure 6, we need to first specify the precise nature of the relationships among the various quantities. For example, we have already stated that total cost = fixed cost + variable cost. Logic also suggests that the variable cost is the unit variable cost times the quantity produced. Thus,

$$\text{total cost} = \text{fixed cost} + \text{variable cost} \qquad (2)$$

and

$$\text{variable cost} = (\text{unit cost})(\text{quantity produced}) \qquad (3)$$

By substituting this into equation (2), we have

$$\begin{aligned}\text{total cost} &= \text{fixed cost} + \text{variable cost}\\ &= \text{fixed cost} + (\text{unit cost})(\text{quantity produced}) \qquad (4)\end{aligned}$$

We may develop a mathematical representation by defining symbols for each of these quantities:

TC = total cost
V = unit variable cost
F = fixed cost
Q = quantity produced

This results in the model

$$TC = F + VQ \qquad (5)$$

EXAMPLE 8   A Break-Even Decision Model

Suppose that a manufacturer can produce a part for $125/unit with a fixed cost of $50,000. The alternative is to outsource production to a supplier at a unit cost of $175. The total manufacturing cost is expressed by using equation (5):

$$TC \text{ (manufacturing)} = \$50,000 + \$125 \times Q$$

and the total outsourcing cost can be written as

$$TC \text{ (outsourcing)} = \$175 \times Q$$

Mathematical models are easy to manipulate; for example, it is easy to find the break-even volume by setting TC (manufacturing) = TC (outsourcing) and solving for Q:

$$\$50,000 + \$125 \times Q = \$175 \times Q$$
$$\$50,000 = 50 \times Q$$
$$Q = 1,000$$

Thus, if the anticipated production volume is greater than 1,000, it is more economical to manufacture the part; if it is less than 1,000, then it should be outsourced. This is shown graphically in Figure 7.

We may develop a general formula for the break-even point by letting C be the unit cost of outsourcing the part and setting TC (manufacturing) = TC (outsourcing) using the general formulas:

$$F + VQ = CQ$$
$$Q = F/(C - V) \qquad (6)$$

Figure 7

Graphical Illustration of Break-Even Analysis

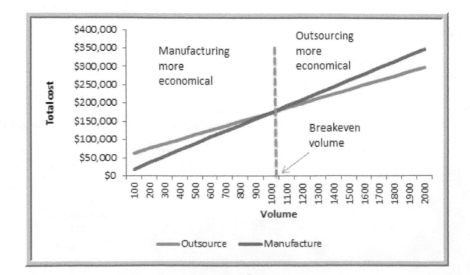

Predictive Decision Models

Predictive models aim to predict what will happen in the future. For instance, we might wish to predict the pattern of sales of a new product over time in order to plan production or inventory levels or sales efforts. Another example is trying to predict how demand (an uncontrollable variable) is influenced by price (a controllable variable). Economic theory tells us that demand for a product is negatively related to its price. Thus, as prices increase, demand falls, and vice versa. Many different mathematical models can describe this phenomenon. In the following examples, we illustrate two of them.

EXAMPLE 9   A Linear Demand Prediction Model

In microeconomic theory, we often assume that a relationship exists between price and demand. Typically, as price increases, demand falls. A simple model to predict demand as a function of price is the linear model

$$D = a - bP \qquad (7)$$

where D is the demand rate, P is the unit price, a is a constant that estimates the demand when the price is zero, and b is the slope of the demand function. This model is most applicable when we want to predict the effect of small changes around the current price. For example, suppose that $a = 20{,}000$ and $b = 10$. If the price is \$100, the model predicts demand as

$$D = 20{,}000 - 10(100) = 19{,}000 \text{ units}$$

If the price is decreased to \$80, the predicted demand is

$$D = 20{,}000 - 10(80) = 19{,}200 \text{ units}$$

A graph of demand as a function of price is shown in Figure 8.

Both models in Examples 9 and 10 make predictions of demand. The task of the modeler is to select or build an appropriate model that best represents the behavior of the real situation. This involves critical examination of assumptions and often requires testing and evaluation with real data.

As we all know, the future is always uncertain. Thus, many predictive models incorporate uncertainty and help decision makers analyze the risks associated with their decisions. **Uncertainty** is imperfect knowledge of what will happen; **risk** is associated with

Figure 8

Graph of Linear
Demand Model
$D = a - bP$

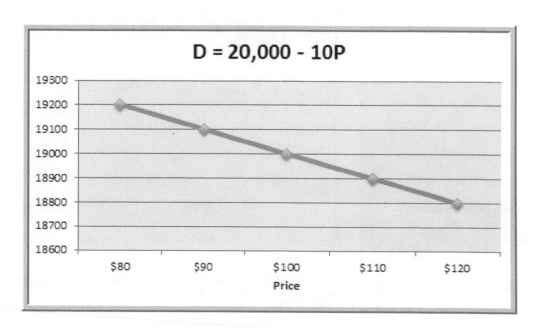

EXAMPLE 10   A Nonlinear Demand Prediction Model

An alternative model assumes that price elasticity—the ratio of the percentage change in demand to the percentage change in price—is constant. In this case, the appropriate model is

$$D = cP^{-d} \tag{8}$$

where, again, c and d (where $d > 0$ is the price elasticity) are constants. For example, suppose that $c = 20,000$ and $d = 0.03$. If the price is $100, then demand is predicted to be

$$D = 20,000(100)^{-0.03} = 17,419$$

If the price increases to $120, then the predicted demand is

$$D = 20,000(120)^{-0.03} = 17,324$$

A graph of demand as a function of price is shown in Figure 9. The predicted demand falls in a slight nonlinear fashion as price increases.

the consequences of what actually happens. Even though uncertainty may exist, there may be no risk. For example, the change in the stock price of Apple on the next day of trading is uncertain. This uncertainty has no impact if you don't own Apple stock. However, if you do, then you bear the risk associated with the possibility of losing money. Thus, risk is an outcome of uncertainty.

The importance of risk in business has long been recognized. The renowned management writer, Peter Drucker, observed in 1974:

> To try to eliminate risk in business enterprise is futile. Risk is inherent in the commitment of present resources to future expectations. Indeed, economic progress can be defined as the ability to take greater risks. The attempt to eliminate risks, even the attempt to minimize them, can only make them irrational and unbearable. It can only result in the greatest risk of all: rigidity.[25]

Figure 9

Graph of Nonlinear Demand Model $D = cP^{-d}$

[25]P. F. Drucker, *The Manager and the Management Sciences in Management: Tasks, Responsibilities, Practices* (London: Harper and Row, 1974).

Consideration of risk is a vital element of decision making. For instance, you would probably not choose an investment simply on the basis of the return you might expect because, typically, higher returns are associated with higher risk. Therefore, you have to make a trade-off between the benefits of greater rewards and the risks of potential losses. Analytic models can help assess this.

Prescriptive Decision Models

A prescriptive decision model helps decision makers to identify the best solution to a decision problem. **Optimization** is the process of finding a set of values for decision variables that minimize or maximize some quantity of interest—profit, revenue, cost, time, and so on—called the **objective function**. Any set of decision variables that optimizes the objective function is called an **optimal solution**. In a highly competitive world where one percentage point can mean a difference of hundreds of thousands of dollars or more, knowing the best solution can mean the difference between success and failure.

EXAMPLE 11   A Prescriptive Pricing Model

To illustrate an example of a prescriptive model, suppose that a firm wishes to determine the best pricing for one of its products to maximize revenue over the next year. A market research study has collected data that estimate the expected annual sales for different levels of pricing. Analysts determined that sales can be expressed by the following model:

$$sales = -2.9485 \times price + 3{,}240.9$$

Because revenue equals price × sales, a model for total revenue is

$$
\begin{aligned}
total\ revenue &= price \times sales \\
&= price \times (-2.9485 \times price + 3240.9) \\
&= -2.9485 \times price^2 + 3240.9 \times price
\end{aligned}
$$

The firm would like to identify the price that maximizes the total revenue.

Although the pricing model did not, most optimization models have **constraints**—limitations, requirements, or other restrictions that are imposed on any solution, such as "do not exceed the allowable budget" or "ensure that all demand is met." For instance, a consumer products company manager would probably want to ensure that a specified level of customer service is achieved with the redesign of the distribution system. The presence of constraints makes modeling and solving optimization problems more challenging.

For some prescriptive models, analytical solutions—closed-form mathematical expressions or simple formulas—can be obtained using such techniques as calculus or other types of mathematical analyses. In most cases, however, some type of computer-based procedure is needed to find an optimal solution. An **algorithm** is a systematic procedure that finds a solution to a problem. Researchers have developed algorithms to solve many types of optimization problems. For example, Microsoft Excel has a built-in add-in called *Solver* that allows you to find optimal solutions to optimization problems formulated as spreadsheet models. However, we will not be concerned with the detailed mechanics of these algorithms; our focus will be on the use of the algorithms to solve the models we develop.

If possible, we would like to ensure that an algorithm such as the one *Solver* uses finds the best solution. However, some models are so complex that it is impossible to solve them optimally in a reasonable amount of computer time because of the extremely large number of computations that may be required or because they are so complex that finding the best solution cannot be guaranteed. In these cases, analysts use **search algorithms**—solution procedures that generally find good solutions without guarantees of finding the best one. Researchers have developed powerful search algorithms to obtain good solutions to extremely difficult optimization problems.

Prescriptive decision models can be either *deterministic* or *stochastic*. A **deterministic model** is one in which all model input information is either known or assumed to be known with certainty. A **stochastic model** is one in which some of the model input information is uncertain. For instance, suppose that customer demand is an important element of some model. We can make the assumption that the demand is known with certainty; say, 5,000 units per month. In this case we would be dealing with a deterministic model. On the other hand, suppose we have evidence to indicate that demand is uncertain, with an average value of 5,000 units per month, but which typically varies between 3,200 and 6,800 units. If we make this assumption, we would be dealing with a stochastic model.

Problem Solving and Decision Making

The fundamental purpose of analytics is to help managers solve problems and make decisions. The techniques of analytics represent only a portion of the overall problem-solving and decision-making process. **Problem solving** is the activity associated with defining, analyzing, and solving a problem and selecting an appropriate solution that solves a problem. Problem solving consists of several phases:

1. recognizing a problem
2. defining the problem
3. structuring the problem
4. analyzing the problem
5. interpreting results and making a decision
6. implementing the solution

Recognizing a Problem

Managers at different organizational levels face different types of problems. In a manufacturing firm, for instance, top managers face decisions of allocating financial resources, building or expanding facilities, determining product mix, and strategically sourcing production. Middle managers in operations develop distribution plans, production and inventory schedules, and staffing plans. Finance managers analyze risks, determine investment strategies, and make pricing decisions. Marketing managers develop advertising plans and make sales force allocation decisions. In manufacturing operations, problems involve the size of daily production runs, individual machine schedules, and worker assignments. Whatever the problem, the first step is to realize that it exists.

How are problems recognized? Problems exist when there is a gap between what is happening and what we think should be happening. For example, a consumer products manager might feel that distribution costs are too high. This recognition might result from comparing performance with a competitor, observing an increasing trend compared to previous years.

Defining the Problem

The second step in the problem-solving process is to clearly define the problem. Finding the real problem and distinguishing it from symptoms that are observed is a critical step. For example, high distribution costs might stem from inefficiencies in routing trucks, poor location of distribution centers, or external factors such as increasing fuel costs. The problem might be defined as improve the routing process, redesign the entire distribution system, or optimally hedge fuel purchases.

Defining problems is not a trivial task. The complexity of a problem increases when the following occur:

- The number of potential courses of action is large.
- The problem belongs to a group rather than to an individual.
- The problem solver has several competing objectives.
- External groups or individuals are affected by the problem.
- The problem solver and the true owner of the problem—the person who experiences the problem and is responsible for getting it solved—are not the same.
- Time limitations are important.

These factors make it difficult to develop meaningful objectives and characterize the range of potential decisions. In defining problems, it is important to involve all people who make the decisions or who may be affected by them.

Structuring the Problem

This usually involves stating goals and objectives, characterizing the possible decisions, and identifying any constraints or restrictions. For example, if the problem is to redesign a distribution system, decisions might involve new locations for manufacturing plants and warehouses (where?), new assignments of products to plants (which ones?), and the amount of each product to ship from different warehouses to customers (how much?). The goal of cost reduction might be measured by the total delivered cost of the product. The manager would probably want to ensure that a specified level of customer service—for instance, being able to deliver orders within 48 hours—is achieved with the redesign. This is an example of a constraint. Structuring a problem often involves developing a formal model.

Analyzing the Problem

Here is where analytics plays a major role. Analysis involves some sort of experimentation or solution process, such as evaluating different scenarios, analyzing risks associated with various decision alternatives, finding a solution that meets certain goals, or determining an optimal solution. Analytics professionals have spent decades developing and refining a variety of approaches to address different types of problems.

Interpreting Results and Making a Decision

Interpreting the results from the analysis phase is crucial in making good decisions. Models cannot capture every detail of the real problem, and managers must understand the limitations of models and their underlying assumptions and often incorporate judgment into making a decision. For example, in locating a facility, we might use an analytical procedure to find a "central" location; however, many other considerations must be included in the decision, such as highway access, labor supply, and facility cost. Thus, the location specified by an analytical solution might not be the exact location the company actually chooses.

Implementing the Solution

This simply means making it work in the organization, or translating the results of a model back to the real world. This generally requires providing adequate resources, motivating employees, eliminating resistance to change, modifying organizational policies, and developing trust. Problems and their solutions affect people: customers, suppliers, and employees. All must be an important part of the problem-solving process. Sensitivity to political and organizational issues is an important skill that managers and analytical professionals alike must possess when solving problems.

Analytics in Practice: Developing Effective Analytical Tools at Hewlett-Packard[26]

Hewlett-Packard (HP) uses analytics extensively. Many applications are used by managers with little knowledge of analytics. These require that analytical tools be easily understood. Based on years of experience, HP analysts compiled some key lessons.

Before creating an analytical decision tool, HP asks three questions:

1. *Will analytics solve the problem?* Will the tool enable a better solution? Should other non-analytical solutions be used? Are there organizational or other issues that must be resolved? Often, what may appear to be an analytical problem may actually be rooted in problems of incentive misalignment, unclear ownership and accountability, or business strategy.
2. *Can we leverage an existing solution?* Before "reinventing the wheel," can existing solutions address the problem? What are the costs and benefits?
3. *Is a decision model really needed?* Can simple decision guidelines be used instead of a formal decision tool?

Jirsak/Shutterstock.com

Once a decision is made to develop an analytical tool, they use several guidelines to increase the chances of successful implementation:

- *Use prototyping*– a quick working version of the tool designed to test its features and gather feedback;
- *Build insight, not black boxes.* A "black box" tool is one that generates an answer, but may not provide confidence to the user. Interactive tools that create insights to support a decision provide better information.
- *Remove unneeded complexity.* Simpler is better. A good tool can be used without expert support.
- *Partner with end users in discovery and design.* Decision makers who will actually use the tool should be involved in its development.
- *Develop an analytic champion.* Someone (ideally, the actual decision maker) who is knowledgeable about the solution and close to it must champion the process.

---

[26]Based on Thomas Olavson and Chris Fry, "Spreadsheet Decision-Support Tools: Lessons Learned at Hewlett-Packard," *Interfaces*, 38, 4, July–August 2008, 300–310.

Key Terms

Algorithm
Business analytics (analytics)
Business intelligence
Categorical (nominal) data
Constraint
Continuous metric
Data set
Database
Decision model
Decision support systems (DSS)
Descriptive analytics
Deterministic model
Discrete metric
Entities
Fields (attributes)
Influence diagram
Interval data
Management science (MS)

Measure
Measurement
Metric
Model
Objective function
Operations research (OR)
Optimal solution
Optimization
Ordinal data
Predictive analytics
Prescriptive analytics
Problem solving
Ratio data
Risk
Search algorithm
Stochastic model
Uncertainty

Fun with Analytics

Mr. John Toczek, an analytics manager at ARAMARK Corporation, maintains a Web site called the PuzzlOR (OR being "Operations Research") at www.puzzlor.com. Each month he posts a new puzzle. If you cannot develop a formal model, the puzzles can be fun and competitive challenges for students. We encourage you to explore these. A good one to start with is "SurvivOR" from June 2010. Have fun!

Problems and Exercises

1. A supermarket has been experiencing long lines during peak periods of the day. The problem is noticeably worse on certain days of the week, and the peak periods sometimes differ according to the day of the week. There are usually enough workers on the job to open all cash registers. The problem is knowing when to call some of the workers who are stocking shelves up to the front to work the checkout counters. How might business analytics help the supermarket? What data would be needed to facilitate good decisions?

2. Suggest some metrics that a hotel might want to collect about their guests. How might these metrics be used with business analytics to support decisions at the hotel?

3. Suggest some metrics that a manager of a fast-food restaurant, such as McDonald's or Chipotle, might want to collect. Describe how the manager might use the data to facilitate better decisions.

4. Classify each of the data elements in the *Sales Transactions* database (Figure 1) as categorical, ordinal, interval, or ratio data.

5. Identify each of the variables in the Excel file *Credit Approval Decisions* as categorical, ordinal, interval, or ratio.

6. A survey handed out to individuals at a major shopping mall in a small Florida city in July asked the following:

   - gender
   - age
   - ethnicity
   - length of residency
   - overall satisfaction with city services (using a scale of 1–5, going from poor to excellent)
   - quality of schools (using a scale of 1–5, going from poor to excellent)

   What types of data would each of the survey items represent?

7. A bank developed a model for predicting the average checking and savings account balance as balance $= -17,732 + 367 \times$ age $+ 1300 \times$ years education $+ 0.116 \times$ household wealth.

   a. Explain how to interpret the numbers in this model.

   b. Suppose that a customer is 36 years old, is a college graduate (so that years education $= 16$), and has a household wealth of $175,000. What is the predicted bank balance?

8. Four key marketing decision variables are price (P), advertising (A), transportation (T), and product quality (Q). Consumer demand (D) is influenced by these variables. The simplest model for describing demand in terms of these variables is

$$D = k - pP + aA + tT + qQ$$

   where k, p, a, t, and q are positive constants.

   a. How does a change in each variable affect demand?

   b. How do the variables influence each other?

   c. What limitations might this model have? Can you think of how this model might be made more realistic?

9. Suppose that a manufacturer can produce a part for $9.00 with a fixed cost of $4,000. The manufacturer can contract with a supplier in Asia to purchase the part at a cost of $12.00, which includes transportation.

   a. If the anticipated production volume is 1,000 units, compute the total cost of manufacturing and the total cost of outsourcing. What is the best decision?

   b. Find the break-even volume and characterize the range of volumes for which it is more economical to produce or to outsource.

10. Return on investment (ROI) is computed in the following manner: ROI is equal to turnover multiplied by earnings as a percent of sales. Turnover is sales divided by total investment. Total investment is current assets (inventories, accounts receivable, and cash) plus fixed assets. Earnings equal sales minus the cost of sales. The cost of sales consists of mill cost of sales, selling expenses, freight and delivery, and administrative costs.

   a. Construct an influence diagram that relates these variables.

   b. Define symbols and develop a mathematical model.

11. Total marketing effort is a term used to describe the critical decision factors that affect demand: price, advertising, distribution, and product quality. Let the variable x represent total marketing effort. A typical model that is used to predict demand as a function of total marketing effort is

$$D = ax^b$$

Suppose that a is a positive number. Different model forms result from varying the constant b. Sketch the graphs of this model for $b = 0$, $b = 1$, $0 < b < 1$, $b < 0$, and $b > 1$. What does each model tell you about the relationship between demand and marketing effort? What assumptions are implied? Are they reasonable? How would you go about selecting the appropriate model?

12. Automobiles have different fuel economies (mpg), and commuters drive different distances to work or school. Suppose that a state Department of Transportation (DOT) is interested in measuring the average monthly fuel consumption of commuters in a certain city. The DOT might sample a group of commuters and collect information on the number of miles driven per day, number of driving days per month, and the fuel economy of their cars. Develop a predictive model for calculating the amount of gasoline consumed, using the following symbols for the data.

$G =$ gallons of fuel consumed per month
$m =$ miles driven per day to and from work or school
$d =$ number of driving days per month
$f =$ fuel economy in miles per gallon

Suppose that a commuter drives 24 miles back and forth to work 20 days each month and achieves a fuel economy of 30 mpg. How many gallons of gasoline are used?

13. A manufacturer of mp3 players is preparing to set the price on a new model. Demand is thought to depend on the price and is represented by the model

$$D = 2{,}000 - 3P$$

The accounting department estimates that the total costs can be represented by

$$C = 5{,}000 + 4D$$

Develop a model for the total profit.

14. The demand for airline travel is quite sensitive to price. Typically, there is an inverse relationship between demand and price; when price decreases, demand increases and vice versa. One major airline has found that when the price (P) for a round trip between Chicago and Los Angeles is $600, the demand ($D$) is 500 passengers per day. When the price is reduced to $300, demand is 1,200 passengers per day.

   a. Plot these points on a coordinate system and develop a linear model that relates demand to price.

   b. Develop a prescriptive model that will determine what price to charge in order to maximize the total revenue.

   c. By trial and error, can you find the optimal solution that maximizes total revenue?

Case: Performance Lawn Equipment

Here, we use the database of a fictitious company, Performance Lawn Equipment (PLE),[27] so that the applications of the worksheets discussed in this text will be more meaningful.

PLE, headquartered in St. Louis, Missouri, is a privately owned designer and producer of traditional lawn mowers used by homeowners. In the past 10 years PLE has added another key product, a medium-size diesel power lawn tractor with front and rear power takeoffs, Class I three-point hitches, four-wheel drive, power steering, and full hydraulics. This equipment is built primarily for a niche market consisting of large estates, including golf and country clubs, resorts, private estates, city parks, large commercial complexes, lawn care service providers, private homeowners with five or more acres, and government (federal, state, and local) parks, building complexes, and military bases. PLE provides most of the products to dealerships, which, in turn, sell directly to end users.

In the United States, the focus of sales is on the eastern seaboard, California, the Southeast, and the south central states, which have the greatest concentration of customers. Outside the United States, PLE's sales include a European market, a growing South American market, and developing markets in the Pacific Rim and China. The market is cyclical, but the different products and regions balance some of this, with just less than 30% of total sales in the spring and summer (in the United States), about 25% in the fall, and about 20% in the winter. Annual sales are approximately $180 million.

PLE employs 1,660 people worldwide. About half the workforce is based in St. Louis; the remainder is split among their manufacturing plants.

Both end users and dealers have been established as important customers for PLE. Collection and analysis of end-user data showed that satisfaction with the products depends on high quality, easy attachment/dismount of implements, low maintenance, price value, and service. For dealers, key requirements are high quality, parts and feature availability, rapid restock, discounts, and timeliness of support.

PLE has several key suppliers: Mitsitsiu, Inc., the sole source of all diesel engines; LANTO Axles, Inc., which provides tractor axles; Schorst Fabrication, which provides subassemblies; Cuberillo, Inc., supplier of transmissions; and Specialty Machining, Inc., a supplier of precision machine parts.

To help manage the company, PLE managers have developed a "balanced scorecard" of measures. These data, which are summarized shortly, are stored in the form of a Microsoft Excel workbook (*Performance Lawn Equipment*) available at www.pearsonhighered.com/evans. The database contains various measures captured on a monthly or quarterly basis and used by various managers to evaluate business performance. Data for each of the key measures are stored in a separate worksheet. A summary of these worksheets is given next:

- *Dealer Satisfaction*, measured on a scale of 1–5 (1 = poor, 2 = less than average, 3 = average, 4 = above average, and 5 = excellent). Each year, dealers in each region are surveyed about their overall satisfaction with PLE. The worksheet contains summary data from surveys for the past 5 years.

---

[27]A case scenario based on *Gateway Estate Lawn Equipment Co. Case Study*, used for the 1997 Malcolm Baldrige National Quality Award Examiner Training course, is available in the public domain.

- *End-User Satisfaction*, measured on the same scale as dealers. Each year, 100 users from each region are surveyed. The worksheet contains summary data for the past 5 years.
- *2012 Customer Survey*, results from a survey for customer ratings of specific attributes of PLE tractors: quality, ease of use, price, and service on the same 1–5 scale. This sheet contains 200 observations of customer ratings.
- *Complaints*, which shows the number of complaints registered by all customers each month in each of PLE's five regions (North America, South America, Europe, the Pacific, and China).
- *Mower Unit Sales* and *Tractor Unit Sales*, which provide sales by product by region on a monthly basis. Unit sales for each region are aggregated to obtain world sales figures.
- *Industry Mower Total Sales* and *Industry Tractor Total Sales*, which list the number of units sold by all producers by region.
- *Unit Production Costs*, which provides monthly accounting estimates of the variable cost per unit for manufacturing tractors and mowers over the past 5 years.
- *Operating and Interest Expenses*, which provides monthly administrative, depreciation, and interest expenses at the corporate level.
- *On-Time Delivery*, which provides the number of deliveries made each month from each of PLE's major suppliers, number on time, and the percent on time.
- *Defects After Delivery*, which shows the number of defects in supplier-provided material found in all shipments received from suppliers.
- *Time To Pay Suppliers*, which provides measurements in days from the time rhe invoice is received until payment is sent.
- *Response Time*, which gives samples of the times taken by PLE customer-service personnel to respond to service calls by quarter over the past 2 years.
- *Employee Satisfaction*, which provides data for the past 4 years of internal surveys of employees to determine their overall satisfaction with their jobs, using the same scale used for customers. Employees are surveyed quarterly, and results are stratified by employee category: design and production, managerial, and sales/administrative support.

In addition to these business measures, the PLE database contains worksheets with data from special studies:

- *Engines*, which lists 50 samples of the time required to produce a lawn-mower blade using a new technology.
- *Transmission Costs*, which provides the results of 30 samples each for the current process used to produce Tracway tractor transmissions and two proposed new processes.
- *Blade Weight*, which provides samples of mower-blade weights to evaluate the consistency of the production process.
- *Mower Test*, which lists test results of mower functional performance after assembly for 30 samples of 100 units each.
- *Employee Retention*, data from a study of employee duration (length of hire) with PLE. The 40 subjects were identified by reviewing hires from 10 years prior and identifying those who were involved in managerial positions (either hired into management or promoted into management) at some time in this 10-year period.

- *Shipping Cost,* which gives the unit shipping cost for mowers and tractors from existing and proposed plants for a supply-chain-design study.
- *Fixed Cost,* which lists the fixed cost to expand existing plants or build new facilities, also as part of the supply-chain-design study.
- *Purchasing Survey*, which provides data obtained from a third-party survey of purchasing managers of customers of Performance Lawn Care.

Elizabeth Burke has recently joined the PLE management team to oversee production operations. She has reviewed the types of data that the company collects and has assigned you the responsibility to be her chief analyst in the coming weeks. To prepare for this task, you have decided to review each worksheet and determine whether the data were gathered from internal sources or external sources or generated. Also, you need to know whether the measures are categorical, ordinal, interval, or ratio. Prepare a report summarizing the characteristics of the metrics used in each worksheet.

Glossary

Algorithm A systematic procedure that finds a solution to a problem.

Business analytics (analytics) The use of data, information technology, statistical analysis, quantitative methods, and mathematical or computer-based models to help managers gain improved insight about their business operations and make better, fact-based decisions.

Business intelligence A term coined in 1958 by an IBM researcher to describe the collection, management, analysis, and reporting of data.

Categorical (nominal) data Data sorted into categories according to specified characteristics.

Constraint A limitation, requirement, or other restriction imposed on any solution.

Continuous metric A metric based on a continuous scale of measurement.

Data set A collection of data.

Database A collection of related files containing records on people, places, or things.

Decision model A logical or mathematical representation of a problem or business situation that can be used to understand, analyze, or facilitate making a decision.

Decision support systems (DSS) Analytical-based computer systems that support decision making.

Descriptive analytics The use of data to understand past and current business performance and make informed decisions.

Deterministic model A model in which all model input information is either known or assumed to be known with certainty.

Discrete metric A metric derived from counting something.

Entities The people, places, or things for which we store and maintain information.

Fields (attributes) Individual elements of data in a database file.

Influence diagram A visual representation of a descriptive model.

Interval data Ordinal data that have constant differences between observations and that have no natural zero.

Management science (MS) An alternative name for *operations research.*

Measure A numerical value associated with a metric.

Measurement The act of obtaining data associated with a metric.

Metric A unit of measurement that provides a way to objectively quantify performance.

Model An abstraction or representation of a real system, idea, or object.

Objective function The quantity of interest in optimization that is to be minimized or maximized.

Operations research (OR) The analysis and solution of complex decision problems using mathematical or computer-based models. Also known as management science.

Optimal solution Any set of decision variables that optimizes the objective function.

Optimization The process of finding a set of values for decision variables that minimize or maximize some quantity of interest.

Ordinal data Data that are ordered or ranked according to some relationship to one another.

Predictive analytics Analysis of past performance in an effort to predict the future by examining historical data, detecting patterns or relationships in these data, and then extrapolating these relationships forward in time.

Prescriptive analytics Using optimization to identify the best alternatives to minimize or maximize some objective.

Problem solving The activity associated with defining, analyzing, and solving a problem and selecting an appropriate solution that solves a problem.

Ratio data Continuous data that have a natural zero.

Risk The probability of occurrence of an undesirable outcome.

Search algorithm A solution procedure that generally finds good solutions without guarantees of finding the best one.

Stochastic model A model in which some of the model input information is uncertain.

Uncertainty Imperfect knowledge of what will happen in the future.

S. Dashkevych/Shutterstock.com

Analytics on Spreadsheets

Learning Objectives

After studying this chapter, you will be able to:

- Find buttons and menus in the Excel 2010 ribbon.
- Write correct formulas in an Excel worksheet.
- Apply relative and absolute addressing in Excel formulas.
- Copy formulas from one cell to another or to a range of cells.
- Use Excel features such as split screen, paste special, show formulas, and displaying grid lines and headers in your applications.

- Use basic and advanced Excel functions.
- Apply principles of spreadsheet engineering to designing and implementing spreadsheet models.
- Use Excel features and spreadsheet engineering to ensure the quality of your spreadsheets.

From Chapter 2 of *Business Analytics: Methods, Models, and Decisions*, First Edition. James R. Evans.

Many commercial software packages are available to facilitate the application of business analytics. Although they often have unique features and capabilities, they can be expensive, generally require advanced training to understand and apply, and may work only on specific computer platforms. Spreadsheet software, on the other hand, is widely used across all areas of business and is standard on nearly every employee's computer. Spreadsheets are an effective platform for manipulating data and developing and solving models; they support powerful commercial add-ins and facilitate communication of results. Spreadsheets provide a flexible modeling environment and are particularly useful when the end user is not the designer of the model. Teams can easily use spreadsheets and understand the logic upon which they are built. Information in spreadsheets can easily be copied from Excel into other documents and presentations. A recent survey identified more than 180 commercial spreadsheet products that support analytics efforts, including data management and reporting, data- and model-driven analytical techniques, and implementation.[1] Many organizations have used spreadsheets to support decision making in marketing, finance, and operations. Some illustrative applications include the following:[2]

- Analyzing supply chains (Hewlett-Packard)
- Determining optimal inventory levels to meet customer service objectives (Procter and Gamble)
- Selecting internal projects (Lockheed Martin Space Systems Company)
- Planning for emergency clinics in response to a sudden epidemic or bioterrorism attack (Centers for Disease Control)
- Analyzing the default risk of a portfolio of real estate loans (Hypo International)
- Assigning medical residents to on-call and emergency rotations (University of Vermont College of Medicine)
- Performance measurement and evaluation (American Red Cross)

---

[1]Thomas A. Grossman, "Resources for Spreadsheet Analysts," *Analytics* (May/June 2010): 8. Analytics magazine.com
[2]Larry J. LeBlanc and Thomas A. Grossman, "Introduction: The Use of Spreadsheet Software in the Application of Management Science and Operations Research," *Interfaces*, 38, 4 (July–August 2008): 225–227.

The purpose of this chapter is to provide a review of the basic features of Microsoft Excel that you need to know to use spreadsheets for analyzing and solving problems with techniques of business analytics. In this text, we use Microsoft Excel 2010 for Windows to perform spreadsheet calculations and analyses. Excel files for all text examples and data used in problems and exercises are provided at www.pearsonhighered .com/evans. This review is not intended to be a complete tutorial; many good Excel tutorials can be found online, and we also encourage you to use the Excel help capability (by clicking the question mark button at the top right of the screen). Also, for any readers that may be Mac users, we caution you that Mac versions of Excel do not have the full functionality that Windows versions have, particularly statistical features, although most of the basic capabilities are the same.

Basic Excel Skills

To be able to apply relevant procedures and techniques, it is necessary for you to know many of the basic capabilities of Excel. We assume that you are familiar with the most elementary spreadsheet concepts and procedures, such as

- opening, saving, and printing files,
- using workbooks and worksheets,
- moving around a spreadsheet,
- selecting cells and ranges,
- inserting/deleting rows and columns,
- entering and editing text, numerical data, and formulas in cells,
- formatting data (number, currency, decimal places, etc.),
- working with text strings,
- formatting data and text, and
- modifying the appearance of the spreadsheet using borders, shading, etc.

Menus and commands in Excel 2010 reside in the "ribbon" shown in Figure 1. Menus and commands are arranged in logical *groups* under different *tabs* (*File, Home, Insert,* and so on); small triangles pointing downward indicate *menus* of additional choices. We often refer to certain commands or options and where they may be found in the ribbon.

Figure 1

Excel 2010 Ribbon

Excel Formulas

Formulas in Excel use common mathematical operators:

- addition (+)
- subtraction (−)
- multiplication (*)
- division (/)

Exponents use the ^ symbol; for example, 2^5 is written as 2^5 in an Excel formula.

EXAMPLE 1   Implementing Price-Demand Models in Excel

You will need "Introduction to Business Analytics" in your book to work on this example. In "Introduction to Business Analytics," we describe two models for predicting demand as a function of price:

$$D = a - bP$$

and

$$D = cP^{-d}$$

Figure 2 shows a spreadsheet (Excel file *Demand Prediction Models*) for calculating demand for different prices using each of these models. For example, to calculate the demand in cell B8 for the linear model, we use the formula

$$=B4-B5*A8$$

To calculate the demand in cell E8 for the nonlinear model, we use the formula

$$=E4*D8^-E5$$

Cell references in formulas can be written either with *relative addresses* or *absolute addresses*. A **relative address** uses just the row and column label in the cell reference; an **absolute address** uses a dollar sign ($ sign) before either the row or column label (or both). Which one we choose makes a critical difference if you copy the cell formulas. If only relative addressing is used, then copying a formula to another cell changes the cell references by the number of rows or columns in the direction that the formula is copied. So, for instance, if we copy the formula in cell B8, =B4−B5*A8, to cell C9 (one column to the right and one row down), all the cell references are increased by one and the formula is changed to

$$=C5-C6*B9$$

Figure 2

Excel Models for Demand Prediction

◢	A	B	C	D	E
1	Demand Prediction Models				
2					
3	Linear Model			Nonlinear Model	
4	a	20,000		c	20,000
5	b	10		d	0.03
6					
7	Price	Demand		Price	Demand
8	$80.00	19200		$70.00	$17,606.66
9	$90.00	19100		$80.00	$17,536.27
10	$100.00	19000		$90.00	$17,474.42
11	$110.00	18900		$100.00	$17,419.27
12	$120.00	18800		$110.00	$17,369.54
13				$120.00	$17,324.25
14				$130.00	$17,282.70

Using a $ sign before a row label (for example, B$4) keeps the reference fixed to row 4 but allows the column reference to change if the formula is copied to another cell. Similarly, using a $ sign before a column label (for example, $B4) keeps the reference to column B fixed but allows the row reference to change. Finally, using a $ sign before both the row and column labels (for example, $B$4) keeps the reference to cell B4 fixed no matter where the formula is copied. You should be very careful to use relative and absolute addressing appropriately in your models.

Copying Formulas

Excel provides several ways of copying formulas to different cells. This is extremely useful in building decision models, because many models require replication of formulas for different periods of time, similar products, and so on. One way is to select the cell with the formula to be copied, click the *Copy* button from the *Clipboard* group under the *Home* tab (or simply press Ctrl-C on your keyboard), click on the cell you wish to copy to, and then click the *Paste* button (or press Ctrl-V). You may also enter a formula directly in a range of cells without copying and pasting by selecting the range, typing in the formula, and pressing Ctrl-Enter.

To copy a formula from a single cell or range of cells down a column or across a row, first select the cell or range, click and hold the mouse on the small square in the lower right-hand corner of the cell (the "fill handle"), and drag the formula to the "target" cells to which you wish to copy.

EXAMPLE 2   Copying Excel Formulas by Dragging

To illustrate the technique of dragging cell formulas to copy them, suppose that in developing the demand-prediction spreadsheet, we entered the formula only in cell B8. Here it is critical to use relative and absolute addressing correctly. Because we want to change the cell reference for the price in column A but keep the references to the model inputs *a* and *b* in cells B4 and B5 constant, the formula in cell B8 should be written as

$$=\$B\$4-\$B\$5*\$A8$$

(In this case, it really doesn't matter if we use $A8 or simply A8 because we are not copying to another column, but it is better practice to keep the reference to column A as absolute)

In Figure 3, we have added a column for the difference and entered the formula =C10−B10 in the first row. Highlight cell D4 and then simply drag the handle down the column. Figure 4 shows the results. Figure 5 shows the formulas for both models that result from this process.

Figure 3

Copying Formulas by Dragging

	A	B	C	D	E
1	Demand Prediction Models				
2					
3	Linear Model			Nonlinear Model	
4	a	20,000		c	20,000
5	b	10		d	0.03
6					
7	Price	Demand		Price	Demand
8	$80.00	$19,200		$70.00	$17,606.66
9	$90.00			$80.00	$17,536.27
10	$100.00			$90.00	$17,474.42
11	$110.00		Click here	$100.00	$17,419.27
12	$120.00		and drag	$110.00	$17,369.54
13			down	$120.00	$17,324.25
14				$130.00	$17,282.70

Figure 4

Results of Dragging Formulas

	A	B	C	D	E
1	Demand Prediction Models				
2					
3	Linear Model			Nonlinear Model	
4	a	20,000		c	20,000
5	b	10		d	0.03
6					
7	Price	Demand		Price	Demand
8	$80.00	$19,200		$70.00	$17,606.66
9	$90.00	$19,100		$80.00	$17,536.27
10	$100.00	$19,000		$90.00	$17,474.42
11	$110.00	$18,900		$100.00	$17,419.27
12	$120.00	$18,800		$110.00	$17,369.54
13				$120.00	$17,324.25
14				$130.00	$17,282.70

Figure 5

Formulas for Demand Prediction Models Spreadsheet

	A	B	C	D	E
1	Demand Prediction Models				
2					
3	Linear Model			Nonlinear Model	
4	a	20000		c	20000
5	b	10		d	0.03
6					
7	Price	Demand		Price	Demand
8	80	=$B$4 - $B$5*$A8		70	=$E$4*D8^-$E$5
9	90	=$B$4 - $B$5*$A9		80	=$E$4*D9^-$E$5
10	100	=$B$4 - $B$5*$A10		90	=$E$4*D10^-$E$5
11	110	=$B$4 - $B$5*$A11		100	=$E$4*D11^-$E$5
12	120	=$B$4 - $B$5*$A12		110	=$E$4*D12^-$E$5
13				120	=$E$4*D13^-$E$5
14				130	=$E$4*D14^-$E$5

Other Useful Excel Tips

- **Split Screen.** You may split the worksheet horizontally and/or vertically to view different parts of the worksheet at the same time. The vertical splitter bar is just to the right of the bottom scroll bar, and the horizontal splitter bar is just above the right-hand scroll bar. Position your cursor over one of these until it changes shape, click, and drag the splitter bar to the left or down.

- **Paste Special.** When you normally copy (one or more) cells and paste them in a worksheet, Excel places an exact copy of the formulas or data in the cells (except for relative addressing). Often you simply want the *result* of formulas, so the data will remain constant even if other parameters used in the formulas change. To do this, use the *Paste Special* option found within the *Paste* menu in the *Clipboard* group under the *Home* tab instead of the *Paste* command. Choosing *Paste Values* will paste the result of the formulas from which the data were calculated.

- **Column and Row Widths.** Many times a cell contains a number that is too large to display properly because the column width is too small. You may change the column width to fit the largest value or text string anywhere in the column by positioning the cursor to the right of the column label so that it changes to a cross with horizontal arrows and then double-clicking. You may also move the arrow to the left or right to manually change the column width. You may change the row heights in a similar fashion by moving the cursor below the row number label. This can be especially useful if you have a very long formula to display. To break a formula within a cell, position the cursor at the break point in the formula bar and press Alt-Enter.

- *Displaying Formulas in Worksheets.* Choose *Show Formulas* in the *Formula Auditing* group under the *Formulas* tab. You will probably need to change the column width to display the formulas properly.
- *Displaying Grid Lines and Row and Column Headers for Printing.* Check the *Print* boxes for gridlines and headings in the *Sheet Options* group under the *Page Layout* tab. Note that the *Print* command can be found by clicking on the *Office* button.
- *Filling a Range with a Series of Numbers.* Suppose you want to build a worksheet for entering 100 data values. It would be tedious to have to enter the numbers from 1 to 100 one at a time. Simply fill in the first few values in the series and highlight them. Then click and drag the small square (fill handle) in the lower right-hand corner down (Excel will show a small pop-up window that tells you the last value in the range) until you have filled in the column to 100; then release the mouse.

Excel Functions

Functions are used to perform special calculations in cells and are used extensively in business analytics applications. All Excel functions require an equal sign and a function name followed by parentheses, in which you specify arguments for the function.

Basic Excel Functions

Some of the more common functions that we will use in applications include the following:

MIN(*range*)—finds the smallest value in a range of cells
MAX(*range*)—finds the largest value in a range of cells
SUM(*range*)—finds the sum of values in a range of cells
AVERAGE(*range*)—finds the average of the values in a range of cells
COUNT(*range*)—finds the number of cells in a range that contain numbers
COUNTIF(*range, criteria*)—finds the number of cells within a range that meet a specified criterion.

We illustrate these functions using the *Purchase Orders* data set in Example 3.

EXAMPLE 3 Using Basic Excel Functions

In the *Purchase Orders* data set, we will find the following:

- smallest and largest quantity of any item ordered
- total order costs
- average number of months per order for accounts payable
- number of purchase orders placed
- number of orders placed for O-rings
- number of orders with A/P terms shorter than 30 months

The results are shown in Figure 6. In this figure, we used the split-screen feature in Excel to reduce the number of rows shown in the spreadsheet. To find the smallest and largest quantity of any item ordered, we use the MIN and MAX functions for the data in column F. Thus, the formula in cell B99 is =MIN(F4:F97) and the formula in cell B100 is =MAX(F4:F97). To find the total order costs, we sum the data in column G using the SUM function: =SUM(G4:G97); this is the formula in cell B101. To find the average number of A/P months, we use the AVERAGE function in column H.

(continued)

The formula in cell B102 is =AVERAGE(H4:H97). To find the number of purchase orders placed, use the COUNT function. Note that the COUNT function counts only the number of cells in a range that contain numbers, so we could not use it in columns A, B, or D; however, any other column would be acceptable. Using the item numbers in column C, the formula in cell B103 is =COUNT(C4:C97). To find the number of orders placed for O-rings, we use the COUNTIF function. The COUNTIF function counts the number of cells within a range that meet a criterion that you specify. For example, you can count all the cells that start with a certain letter, or you can count all the cells that contain a number that is larger or smaller than a number you specify. Examples of criteria are: 25, ">25", B4, "apples", or "25". Note that text and logical formulas must be enclosed in quotes. For this example, the formula used in cell B104 is =COUNTIF(D4:D97, "O-Ring"). We could have also used any cell containing the text O-Ring, such as =COUNTIF(D4:D97,D4). Finally, to find the number of orders with A/P terms less than 30 months, use the formula =COUNTIF(H4:H97,"<30") in cell B105.

Functions for Specific Applications

Excel has a wide variety other functions for statistical, financial, and other applications, many of which we introduce and use throughout the text. For instance, some financial models that we develop require the calculation of net present value (NPV). **Net present value** (also called **discounted cash flow**) measures the worth of a stream of cash flows, taking into account the time value of money. That is, a cash flow of F dollars t time periods in the future is worth $F/(1 + i)^t$ dollars today, where i is the **discount rate**. The discount rate reflects the opportunity costs of spending funds now versus achieving a return through another investment, as well as the risks associated with not receiving returns until a later time. The sum of the present values of all cash flows over a stated time horizon is the net present value:

$$\text{NPV} = \sum_{t=0}^{n} \frac{F_t}{(1 + i)^t} \tag{1}$$

where F_t = cash flow in period t. A positive NPV means that the investment will provide added value because the projected return exceeds the discount rate.

The Excel function NPV(*rate, value1, value2,...*) calculates the net present value of an investment by using a discount rate and a series of future payments (negative values) and income (positive values). *Rate* is the rate of discount over the length of one period (i), and *value1, value2,...* are 1 to 29 arguments representing the payments and income. The values must be equally spaced in time and are assumed to occur at the end of each period. The NPV

Figure 6

Application of Excel Functions to *Purchase Orders* Data

	A	B	C	D	E	F	G	H	I	J
1	Purchase Orders									
2										
3	Supplier	Order No.	Item No.	Item Description	Item Cost	Quantity	Cost per order	A/P Terms (Months)	Order Date	Arrival Date
4	Spacetime Technologies	A0111	6489	O-Ring	$ 3.00	900	$ 2,700.00	25	10/10/11	10/18/11
5	Steelpin Inc.	A0115	5319	Shielded Cable/ft.	$ 1.10	17,500	$ 19,250.00	30	08/20/11	08/31/11
6	Steelpin Inc.	A0123	4312	Bolt-nut package	$ 3.75	4,250	$ 15,937.50	30	08/25/11	09/01/11
7	Steelpin Inc.	A0204	5319	Shielded Cable/ft.	$ 1.10	16,500	$ 18,150.00	30	09/15/11	10/05/11
94	Hulkey Fasteners	D1212	5066	Shielded Cable/ft.	$ 0.95	17,500	$ 16,625.00	30	09/15/11	09/22/11
95	Hulkey Fasteners	D2121	1122	Airframe fasteners	$ 4.25	17,500	$ 74,375.00	30	10/25/11	11/03/11
96	Hulkey Fasteners	D3232	1122	Airframe fasteners	$ 4.25	17,000	$ 72,250.00	30	10/11/11	10/19/11
97	Pylon Accessories	D3333	9764	Gasket	$ 3.75	1,750	$ 6,562.50	15	09/20/11	09/25/11
98										
99	Minimum Quantity	90								
100	Maximum Quantity	25,000								
101	Total Order Costs	$ 2,471,760.00								
102	Average Number of A/P Months	30.64								
103	Number of Purchase Orders	94								
104	Number of O-ring Orders	12								
105	Number of A/P Terms < 30	17								

investment begins one period before the date of the *value1* cash flow and ends with the last cash flow in the list. The NPV calculation is based on future cash flows. If the first cash flow (such as an initial investment or fixed cost) occurs at the beginning of the first period, then it must be added to the NPV result and *not* included in the function arguments.

EXAMPLE 4 Using the NPV Function

A company is introducing a new product. The fixed cost for marketing and distribution is $25,000 and is incurred just prior to launch. The forecasted net sales revenues for the first six months are shown in Figure 7. The formula in cell B8 computes the net present value of these cash flows as =NPV(B6,C4:H4)−B5. Note that the fixed cost is not a future cash flow and is not included in the NPV function arguments.

Insert Function

The easiest way to locate a particular function is to select a cell and click on the *Insert function* button $[f_x]$, which can be found under the ribbon next to the formula bar and also in the *Function Library* group in the *Formulas* tab. You may either type in a description in the search field, such as "net present value," or select a category, such as "Financial," from the drop-down box.

This feature is particularly useful if you know what function to use but are not sure of what arguments to enter because it will guide you in entering the appropriate data for the function arguments. Figure 8 shows the dialog from which you may select the function you wish to use, in this case the COUNTIF function. Once this is selected, the dialog in Figure 9 appears. When you click in an input cell, a description of the argument is shown. Thus, if you are not sure what to enter for the range, the explanation in Figure 9 will help you. For further information, you could click on the *Help* button in the lower left-hand corner.

Logical Functions

Logical functions return only one of two values: TRUE or FALSE. Three useful logical functions in business analytics applications are

IF(*condition, value if true, value if false*)—a logical function that returns one value if the condition is true and another if the condition is false,

AND(*condition 1, condition 2…*)—a logical function that returns TRUE if all conditions are true and FALSE if not,

OR(*condition 1, condition 2…*)—a logical function that returns TRUE if any condition is true and FALSE if not.

Figure **7**

Net Present Value Calculation

◢	A	B	C	D	E	F	G	H
1	Net Present Value							
2								
3		Month	January	February	March	April	May	June
4		Sales Revenue Forecast	$2,500	$4,000	$5,000	$8,000	$10,000	$12,500
5	Fixed Cost	$25,000.00						
6	Discount rate	3%						
7								
8	NPV	$11,975.81						

Figure 8

Insert Function Dialog

Figure 9

Function Arguments Dialog
for COUNTIF

The IF function, *IF(condition, value if true, value if false)*, allows you to choose one of two values to enter into a cell. If the specified *condition* is true, value A will be put in the cell. If the condition is false, value B will be entered. For example, if cell C2 contains the function =IF(A8=2,7,12), it states that if the value in cell A8 is 2, and the number 7 will be assigned to cell C2; if the value in cell A8 is not 2, the number 12 will be assigned to cell C2. Conditions may include the following:

= equal to
> greater than
< less than
>= greater than or equal to
<= less than or equal to
<> not equal to

You may "nest" up to seven IF functions by replacing *value-if-true* or *value-if-false* in an IF function with another IF function:

$$=IF(A8=2,(IF(B3=5,``YES",``")),15)$$

This says that if cell A8 equals 2, then check the contents of cell B3. If cell B3 is 5, then the value of the function is the text string YES; if not, it is a blank space (a text string that is blank). However, if cell A8 is not 2, then the value of the function is 15 no matter what cell B3 is. You may use AND and OR functions as the *condition* within an IF function; for example, $=IF(AND(B1=3,C1=5),12,22)$. Here, if cell B1=3 and cell C1=5, then the value of the function is 12; otherwise it is 22.

EXAMPLE 5   Using the IF Function

Suppose that the aircraft-component manufacturer considers any order of 10,000 units or more to be large, whereas any other order size is considered to be small. We may use the IF function to classify the orders. First, create a new column in the spreadsheet for the order size, say, column K. In cell K4, use the formula

$$=IF(F4>=10000,\text{"Large"},\text{"Small"})$$

This function will return the value *Large* in cell K4 if the order size in cell F4 is 10,000 or more; otherwise, it returns the value *Small*. Figure 10 shows a portion of the results.

	A	B	C	D	E	F	G	H	I	J	K
1	Purchase Orders										
2											
3	Supplier	Order No.	Item No.	Item Description	Item Cost	Quantity	Cost per order	A/P Terms (Months)	Order Date	Arrival Date	Order Size
4	Spacetime Technologies	A0111	6489	O-Ring	$ 3.00	900	$ 2,700.00	25	10/10/11	10/18/11	Small
5	Steelpin Inc.	A0115	5319	Shielded Cable/ft.	$ 1.10	17,500	$ 19,250.00	30	08/20/11	08/31/11	Large
6	Steelpin Inc.	A0123	4312	Bolt-nut package	$ 3.75	4,250	$ 15,937.50	30	08/25/11	09/01/11	Small
7	Steelpin Inc.	A0204	5319	Shielded Cable/ft.	$ 1.10	16,500	$ 18,150.00	30	09/15/11	10/05/11	Large
94	Hulkey Fasteners	D1212	5066	Shielded Cable/ft.	$ 0.95	17,500	$ 16,625.00	30	09/15/11	09/22/11	Large
95	Hulkey Fasteners	D2121	1122	Airframe fasteners	$ 4.25	17,500	$ 74,375.00	30	10/25/11	11/03/11	Large
96	Hulkey Fasteners	D3232	1122	Airframe fasteners	$ 4.25	17,000	$ 72,250.00	30	10/11/11	10/19/11	Large
97	Pylon Accessories	D3333	9764	Gasket	$ 3.75	1,750	$ 6,562.50	15	09/20/11	09/25/11	Small

Figure   10

Classifying Order Sizes Using the IF Function

Lookup Functions

Excel provides some useful functions for finding specific data in a spreadsheet. These functions are useful in many applications:

VLOOKUP(*lookup_value, table_array, col_index_num*) looks up a value in the left-most column of a table and returns a value in the same row from a column you specify. The table must be sorted in an ascending order.

HLOOKUP(*lookup_value, table_array, row_index_num*) looks up a value in the top row of a table and returns a value in the same column from a row you specify.

INDEX(*array, row_num, col_num*) Returns a value or reference of the cell at the in-tersection of a particular row and column in a given range.

MATCH(*lookup_value, lookup_array, match_type*) Returns the relative position of an item in an array that matches a specified value in a specified order.

EXAMPLE 6   Using the VLOOKUP Function

Consider a database of sales transactions for a firm that sells instructional fitness books and DVDs (Excel file *Sales Transactions*). The database is sorted by customer ID, and a portion of it is shown in Figure 11. Suppose that a customer calls a repre-sentative about a payment issue. The representative finds the customer ID—for example, 10007—and needs to look up the type of payment and transaction code.

(continued)

We may use the VLOOKUP function to do this. In the function VLOOKUP(*lookup_value, table_array, col_index_num*), *lookup_value* represents the customer ID. The *table_array* is the range of the data in the spreadsheet; in this case, it is the range A4:H475. The value for *col_index_num* represents the column in the table range we wish to retrieve. For the type of payment, this is column 3; for the transaction code, this is column 4. Thus,

$$VLOOKUP(10007,\$A\$4:\$H\$475,3)$$

returns the payment type, *Credit*

$$VLOOKUP(10007,\$A\$4:\$H\$475,4)$$

returns the transaction code, 80103311.

The HLOOKUP function works in a similar fashion. For most spreadsheet databases, we would normally need to use the VLOOKUP function. In some modeling situations, however, the HLOOKUP function can be useful if the data are arranged column by column rather than row by row.

The INDEX function works as a lookup procedure by returning the value in a particular row and column of an array. For example, in the *Sales Transactions* database, INDEX($A$4:$H$475, 7, 4) would retrieve the transaction code, 80103311, as the VLOOKUP function did in Example 6. The difference is that it relies on the row number rather than the actual value of the customer ID.

In the MATCH function, *lookup_value* is value that you want to match in *lookup_array*, which is the range of cells being searched. The *match_type* is either −1, 0, or 1. The default is 1. If *match_type* = 1, then the function finds the largest value that is less than or equal to *lookup_value*. The values in the *lookup_array* must be placed in ascending order. If *match_type* = 0, MATCH finds the first value that is exactly equal to *lookup_value*. The values in the *lookup_array* can be in any order. If *match_type* = −1, then the function finds the smallest value that is greater than or equal to *lookup_value*. The values in the *lookup_array* must be placed in descending order. Example 7 shows how the INDEX and MATCH functions can be used.

One important note: Excel 2010 changed the names of many of its functions and added several new ones. Although this text uses Excel 2010, you can still use Excel 2007 if you have not upgraded; the Appendix at the end of this text provides a summary of the differences in the functions between these two versions.

Figure 11

Portion of *Sales Transactions* Data

▲	A	B	C	D	E	F	G	H
1	Sales Transactions: July 14							
2								
3	Cust ID	Region	Payment	Transaction Code	Source	Amount	Product	Time Of Day
4	10001	East	Paypal	93816545	Web	$20.19	DVD	22:19
5	10002	West	Credit	74083490	Web	$17.85	DVD	13:27
6	10003	North	Credit	64942368	Web	$23.98	DVD	14:27
7	10004	West	Paypal	70560957	Email	$23.51	Book	15:38
8	10005	South	Credit	35208817	Web	$15.33	Book	15:21
9	10006	West	Paypal	20978903	Email	$17.30	DVD	13:11
10	10007	East	Credit	80103311	Web	$177.72	Book	21:59
11	10008	West	Credit	14132683	Web	$21.76	Book	4:04
12	10009	West	Paypal	40128225	Web	$15.92	DVD	19:35
13	10010	South	Paypal	49073721	Web	$23.39	DVD	13:26

EXAMPLE 7   Using the INDEX and MATCH Functions

Figure 12 shows a portion of the *Purchase Order* database, which has been sorted by item number. Suppose that we wish to identify the range of all orders for item number 1369. We may use the MATCH function to find the row number in the data range for the first and last value of 1369 in column C. For the first value, we use *match_type* = 0; for the last value, we use *match_type* = 1, as follows:

$$= \text{MATCH}(1369,\$C\$4:\$C\$475,0) = 12$$
$$= \text{MATCH}(1369,\$C\$4\$C\$475,1) = 14$$

Note that these are not the row labels of the spreadsheet, but the row numbers of the records in the database.

Now suppose we wish to find the order cost associated with the first order for this item, which is in column G. We can nest the MATCH function within the INDEX function to identify the value in row 12 and column 7 of the database as follows:

$$= \text{INDEX}(\$A\$4:\$J\$475, \text{MATCH}(1369,\$C\$4:\$C\$475,0),7)$$
$$= 63,000$$

Here is where these functions can get quite useful. We can also use these functions to calculate the total cost of this particular item by using the INDEX functions as cell references within the SUM function. For example, the total cost of item 1369 is found by summing the values in rows 12 to 14 of column G in the database (that is, cells G15 to G17 in the spreadsheet) and could be found using the function =SUM(G15:G17). However, note that the INDEX function we described before provides the value in the 12th row of the *Cost per order* column (cell G15 in the spreadsheet). Similarly, the function

$$= \text{INDEX}(\$A\$4:\$J\$475, \text{MATCH}(1369,\$C\$4:\$C\$475,1),7)$$
$$= 42,000$$

provides the value in cell G17 of the spreadsheet. By substituting these in the SUM function we have:

$$= \text{SUM}(\text{INDEX}(\$A\$4:\$G\$475,\text{MATCH}(1369,\$C\$4:\\ \$C\$475,0),7):\text{INDEX}(\$A\$4:\$G\$475,\\ \text{MATCH}(1369,\$C\$4:\$C\$475,1),7))$$

which returns the value $163,800—the total cost of this item.

Spreadsheet Add-Ins for Business Analytics

Microsoft Excel will provide most of the computational support required for the material in this text. Excel (Windows only) provides an add-in called the *Analysis Toolpak,* which contains a variety of tools for statistical computation, and *Solver,* which is used for optimization. These add-ins are not included in a standard Excel installation. To install

	A	B	C	D	E	F	G	H	I	J
1	Purchase Orders									
2										
3	Supplier	Order No	Item No.	Item Description	Item Cost	Quantity	Cost per order	A/P Terms (Months	Order Date	Arrival Date
4	Hulkey Fasteners	C1212	1122	Airframe fasteners	$ 4.25	19,500	$ 82,875.00	30	08/05/11	08/13/11
5	Hulkey Fasteners	C2323	1122	Airframe fasteners	$ 4.25	15,500	$ 65,875.00	30	09/04/11	09/12/11
6	Hulkey Fasteners	C3232	1122	Airframe fasteners	$ 4.25	18,000	$ 76,500.00	30	10/01/11	10/08/11
7	Hulkey Fasteners	C3434	1122	Airframe fasteners	$ 4.25	12,500	$ 53,125.00	30	09/05/11	09/11/11
8	Hulkey Fasteners	C4545	1122	Airframe fasteners	$ 4.25	15,000	$ 63,750.00	30	09/08/11	09/15/11
9	Hulkey Fasteners	C5656	1122	Airframe fasteners	$ 4.25	14,500	$ 61,625.00	30	09/28/11	10/03/11
10	Hulkey Fasteners	D2121	1122	Airframe fasteners	$ 4.25	17,500	$ 74,375.00	30	10/25/11	11/03/11
11	Hulkey Fasteners	D3232	1122	Airframe fasteners	$ 4.25	17,000	$ 72,250.00	30	10/11/11	10/19/11
12	Alum Sheeting	A0443	1243	Airframe fasteners	$ 4.25	10,000	$ 42,500.00	30	08/08/11	08/14/11
13	Alum Sheeting	B0247	1243	Airframe fasteners	$ 4.25	9,000	$ 38,250.00	30	09/05/11	09/12/11
14	Alum Sheeting	B0567	1243	Airframe fasteners	$ 4.25	10,500	$ 44,625.00	30	10/10/11	10/17/11
15	Durrable Products	A1567	1369	Airframe fasteners	$ 4.20	15,000	$ 63,000.00	45	09/25/11	09/30/11
16	Durrable Products	B1468	1369	Airframe fasteners	$ 4.20	14,000	$ 58,800.00	45	09/27/11	10/03/11
17	Durrable Products	B1666	1369	Airframe fasteners	$ 4.20	10,000	$ 42,000.00	45	09/29/11	10/04/11
18	Hulkey Fasteners	C1313	3166	Electrical Connector	$ 1.25	5,600	$ 7,000.00	30	08/25/11	08/29/11

Figure   12   Sorted *Purchase Order* Database

them, click the *File* tab and then *Options* in the left column. Choose *Add-Ins* from the left column. At the bottom of the dialog, make sure *Excel Add-ins* is selected in the *Manage:* box and click *Go*. In the *Add-Ins* dialog, if *Analysis Toolpak, Analysis Toolpak VBA,* and *Solver Add-in* are not checked, simply check the boxes and click *OK*. You will not have to repeat this procedure every time you run Excel in the future.

In addition, Frontline Systems' *Risk Solver Platform* offers many other capabilities for both predictive and prescriptive analytics. Please visit www.solver.com, where you will learn more about this software.

Spreadsheet Modeling and Spreadsheet Engineering

Simple decision models may be developed for a break-even analysis situation. Consider a scenario that involves a manufacturer who can produce a part for $125/unit with a fixed cost of $50,000. The alternative is to outsource production to a supplier at a unit cost of $175. Mathematical models for the total manufacturing cost and the total cost of outsourcing as a function of the production volume, Q, would be as follows:

$$TC \text{ (manufacturing)} = \$50,000 + \$125 \times Q$$
$$TC \text{ (outsourcing)} = \$175 \times Q$$

Many decision models are implemented on spreadsheets. In this section we develop a few spreadsheet models and discuss some approaches for **spreadsheet engineering**—the process of developing good, useful, and correct spreadsheet models. These approaches will be very helpful when addressing more complicated situations.

Because decision models characterize the relationships between inputs and outputs, it is useful to separate the data, model calculations, and model outputs clearly in designing a spreadsheet. It is particularly important not to use input data in model formulas, but to *reference* the spreadsheet cells that contain the data. In this way, if the data change or you want to experiment with the model, you need not change any of the formulas, which can easily result in errors.

EXAMPLE 8   A Spreadsheet Model for the Outsourcing Decision

Figure 13 shows a spreadsheet for implementing the outsourcing decision model (Excel file *Outsourcing Decision Model*). The input data consist of the costs associated with manufacturing the product in-house or purchasing it from an outside supplier and the production volume. The model calculates the total cost for manufacturing and outsourcing. The key outputs in the model are the difference in these costs and the decision that results in the lowest cost. The data are clearly separated from the model component of the spreadsheet.

Observe how the IF function is used in cell B20 to identify the best decision. If the cost difference is negative or zero, then the function returns "Manufacture" as the best decision; otherwise it returns "Outsource." Also observe the correspondence between the spreadsheet formulas and the mathematical model:

TC (manufacturing) = $50,000 + $125 × Q = B6 + B7*B12
TC (outsourcing) = $175 × Q = B12*B10

Thus, if you can write a spreadsheet formula, you can develop a mathematical model by substituting symbols or numbers into the Excel formulas.

	A	B
1	Outsourcing Decision Model	
2		
3	Data	
4		
5	Manufactured in-house	
6	Fixed cost	$50,000
7	Unit variable cost	$125
8		
9	Purchased from supplier	
10	Unit cost	$175
11		
12	Production volume	1500
13		
14	Model	
15		
16	Total manufacturing cost	$237,500
17	Total purchased cost	$262,500
18		
19	Cost difference	-$25,000
20	Decision	Manufacture

	A	B
1	Outsourcing Decision Model	
2		
3	Data	
4		
5	Manufactured in-house	
6	Fixed cost	50000
7	Unit variable cost	125
8		
9	Purchased from supplier	
10	Unit cost	175
11		
12	Production volume	1500
13		
14	Model	
15		
16	Total manufacturing cost	=B6+B7*B12
17	Total purchased cost	=B12*B10
18		
19	Cost difference	=B16-B17
20	Decision	=IF(B19<=0, "Manufacture", "Outsource")

Figure 13

Outsourcing Decision Model Spreadsheet

Mathematical models are easy to manipulate. It is more difficult to find the break-even volume using trial and error on the spreadsheet without knowing some advanced tools and approaches. However, spreadsheets have the advantage of allowing you to easily modify the model inputs and calculate the numerical results. We will use both spreadsheets and analytical modeling approaches in our model-building applications—it is important to be able to "speak both languages."

EXAMPLE 9   Pricing Decision Spreadsheet Model

Another model is one in which a firm wishes to determine the best pricing for one of its products to maximize revenue. The model was developed by incorporating an equation for sales into a total revenue calculation:

$$\text{sales} = -2.9485 \times \text{price} + 3{,}240.9$$
$$\text{total revenue} = \text{price} \times \text{sales}$$

$$= \text{price} \times (-2.9485 \times \text{price} + 3{,}240.9)$$
$$= 2.9485 \times \text{price}^2 + 3{,}240.9 \times \text{price}$$

Figure 14 shows a spreadsheet for calculating both sales and revenue as a function of price.

Figure 14

Pricing Decision Spreadsheet Model

	A	B
1	Pricing Decision Model	
2		
3	Data	
4		
5	Price	$500.00
6		
7	Model	
8		
9	Sales	$1,766.65
10		
11	Total Revenue	$883,325.00

	A	B
1	Pricing Decision Model	
2		
3	Data	
4		
5	Price	500
6		
7	Model	
8		
9	Sales	=-2.9485*B5+3240.9
10		
11	Total Revenue	=B5*B9

Spreadsheet Quality

Building spreadsheet models is part art and part science. The quality of a spreadsheet can be assessed both by its logical accuracy and its design. Spreadsheets need to be accurate, understandable, and user friendly.

First and foremost, spreadsheets should be accurate. **Verification** is the process of ensuring that a model is accurate and free from logical errors. Spreadsheet errors can be disastrous. A large investment company once made a $2.6 billion error. They notified holders of one mutual fund to expect a large dividend; fortunately, they caught the error before sending the checks. One research study of 50 spreadsheets found that fewer than 10% were error free.[3] Significant errors in business have resulted from mistakes in copying and pasting, sorting, numerical input, and spreadsheet-formula references. Industry surveys estimate that more than 90% of spreadsheets with more than 150 rows were incorrect by at least 5%.

There are three basic approaches to spreadsheet engineering that can improve spreadsheet quality:

1. *Improve the design and format of the spreadsheet itself.* After the inputs, outputs, and key model relationships are well understood, you should sketch a logical design of the spreadsheet. For example, you might want the spreadsheet to resemble a financial statement to make it easier for managers to read. It is good practice to separate the model inputs from the model itself and to reference the input cells in the model formulas; that way, any changes in the inputs will be automatically reflected in the model. We have done this in the examples.

   Another useful approach is to break complex formulas into smaller pieces. This reduces typographical errors, makes it easier to check your results, and also makes the spreadsheet easier to read for the user. Finally, it is also important to set up the spreadsheet in a form that the end user—who may be a financial manager, for example—can easily interpret and use. Example 10 illustrates this.

2. *Improve the process used to develop a spreadsheet.* If you sketched out a conceptual design of the spreadsheet, work on each part individually before moving on to the others to ensure that each part is correct. As you enter formulas, check the results with simple numbers (such as 1) to determine if they make sense, or use inputs with known results. Be careful in using the *Copy* and *Paste* commands in Excel, particularly with respect to relative and absolute addresses. Use the Excel function wizard (the f_x button on the formula bar) to ensure that you are entering the correct values in the correct fields of the function. Use cell and range names to simplify formulas and make them more user friendly. For example, suppose that the unit price is stored in cell B13 and quantity sold is in cell B14. Suppose you wish to calculate revenue in cell C15. Instead of writing the formula =B13*B14, you could define the name of cell B13 in Excel as "UnitPrice" and the name of cell B14 as "QuantitySold." Then in cell C15, you could simply write the formula =UnitPrice*QuantitySold. (In this text, however, we use cell references so that you can more easily trace formulas in the examples.)

3. *Inspect your results carefully and use appropriate tools available in Excel.* Conditional formatting allows you to highlight certain cells or ranges of cells, emphasize unusual values, and visualize data by using colors or other formatting features. A conditional format changes the appearance of a cell range based on conditions that you specify. For example, in the outsourcing spreadsheet model, you might want to show a negative cost difference in red. If the condition is true,

---

[3]S. Powell, K. Baker, and B. Lawson, "Errors in Operational Spreadsheets," *Journal of End User Computing*, 21 (July–September 2009): 24–36.

EXAMPLE 10   Modeling Net Income on a Spreadsheet

The calculation of net income is based on the following formulas:

- gross profit = sales − cost of goods sold
- operating expenses = administrative expenses + selling expenses + depreciation expenses
- net operating income = gross profit − operating expenses
- earnings before taxes = net operating income − interest expense
- net income = earnings before taxes − taxes

We could develop a simple model to compute net income using these formulas by substitution:

net income = sales − cost of goods sold − administrative expenses − selling expenses − depreciation expenses − interest expense − taxes

We can implement this model on a spreadsheet, as shown in Figure 15. This spreadsheet provides only the end result and, from a financial perspective, provides little information to the end user.

An alternative is to break down the model by writing the preceding formulas in separate cells in the spreadsheet using a data-model format, as shown in Figure 16. This clearly shows the individual calculations and provides better information. However, although both of these models are technically correct, neither is in the form to which most accounting and financial employees are accustomed.

A third alternative is to express the calculations as a **pro forma income statement** using the structure and formatting that accountants are used to, as shown in Figure 17. Although this has the same formulas as in Figure 16, note that the use of negative dollar amounts requires a change in the formulas (that is, addition of negative amounts rather than subtraction of positive amounts). The Excel workbook *Net Income Models* contains each of these examples in separate worksheets.

the cell range is formatted based on that condition; if the conditional is false, the cell range is not formatted based on that condition. The *Data Validation* feature allows you to define restrictions on what data can or should be entered in a cell. For example, it does not make sense to input a quantity produced that is not a whole number. You can prevent users from entering data that are not valid or allow users to enter invalid data but warn them when they try to type it in the cell. You can also provide messages to define what input you expect for the cell, and instructions to help users correct any errors. *Data Validation* can be found in the *Data Tools* group in the *Data* tab in the Excel ribbon. The Excel *Formula Auditing* tools (in the *Formulas* tab) also help you validate the logic of formulas by visually showing the relationships between input data and cell formulas. We encourage you to learn how to use these tools.

Figure 15

Simple Spreadsheet Model for Net Income

	A	B	C
1	Net Income Model		
2			
3	Data		
4			
5	Sales	$ 5,000,000	
6	Cost of Goods Sold	$ 3,200,000	
7	Administrative Expenses	$ 250,000	
8	Selling Expenses	$ 450,000	
9	Depreciation Expenses	$ 325,000	
10	Interest Expense	$ 35,000	
11	Taxes	$ 296,000	
12			
13	Model		
14			
15	Net Income	$ 444,000	=B5-SUM(B6:B11)

Figure 16

Data-Model Format for Net Income

Figure 17

Pro Forma Income Statement Format

Analytics in Practice: Spreadsheet Engineering at Procter & Gamble[4]

In the mid-1980s, Procter & Gamble (P&G) needed an easy and consistent way to manage safety stock inventory. P&G's Western European Business Analysis group created a spreadsheet model that eventually grew into a suite of global inventory models. The model was designed to help supply chain planners better understand inventories in supply chains and to provide a quick method for setting safety stock levels. P&G also developed several spin-off models based on this application that are used around the world.

In designing the model, analysts used many of the principles of spreadsheet engineering. For example, they separated the input sections from the calculation and results sections by grouping the appropriate cells

---

[4]Based on Ingrid Farasyn, Koray Perkoz, Wim Van de Velde, "Spreadsheet Models for Inventory Target Setting at Procter & Gamble," *Interfaces*, 38, 4 (July–August 2008): 241–250.

and using different formatting. This speeded up the data entry process. In addition, the spreadsheet was designed to display all relevant data on one screen so the user does not need to switch between different sections of the model.

Analysts also used a combination of data validation and conditional formatting to highlight errors in the data input. They also provided a list of warnings and errors that a user should resolve before using the results of the model. The list flags obvious mistakes such as negative transit times and input data that may require checking and forecast errors that fall outside the boundaries of the model's statistical validity

At the basic level, all input fields had comments attached; this served as a quick online help function for the planners. For each model, they also provided a user manual that describes every input and result and explains the formulas in detail. The model templates and all documentation were posted on an intranet site that was accessible to all P&G employees. This ensured that all employees had access to the most current versions of the models, supporting material, and training schedules.

ZUMA Archive/ZUMA Press/Newscom

Key Terms

Absolute address

Discount rate

Net present value (discounted cash flow)

Pro forma income statement

Relative address

Spreadsheet engineering

Verification

Problems and Exercises

1. The Excel file *Science and Engineering Jobs* shows the number of jobs in thousands in the year 2000 and projections for 2010 from a government study. Use the Excel file to compute the projected increase from the 2000 baseline and also the percentage increase for each occupational category.

2. The Excel file *Store and Regional Sales Database* provides sales data for computers and peripherals showing the store identification number, sales region, item number, item description, unit price, units sold, and month when the sales were made during the fourth quarter of 2011.[5] Modify the spreadsheet to calculate the total sales revenue for each of the eight stores as well as each of the three sales regions.

3. The Excel file *President's Inn Guest Database* provides a list of customers, rooms they occupied, arrival and departure dates, number of occupants, and daily rate for a small bed-and-breakfast inn during one month.[6] Room rates are the same

---

[5]Based on Kenneth C. Laudon and Jane P. Laudon, *Essentials of Management Information Systems*, 9th ed. (Upper Saddle River, NJ: Prentice Hall, 2011).

[6]Based on Kenneth C. Laudon and Jane P. Laudon, *Essentials of Management Information Systems*.

for one or two guests; however, additional guests must pay an additional $20 per person per day for meals. Guests staying for seven days or more receive a 10% discount. Modify the spreadsheet to calculate the number of days that each party stayed at the inn and the total revenue for the length of stay.

4. The Excel file *Credit Risk Data* provides information about 425 bank customers who had applied for loans. The data include the purpose of the loan, checking and savings account balances, number of months as a customer of the bank, months employed, gender, marital status, age, housing status and number of years at current residence, job type, and credit-risk classification by the bank.[7]

   a. Use the COUNTIF function to determine how many customers applied for new-car, used-car, business, education, small-appliance, and furniture loans and the number of customers with checking account balances less than $500.

   b. Modify the spreadsheet using IF functions to include new columns, classifying the checking and savings account balances as low if the balance is less than $500, medium if between $500 but less than $2000, and high otherwise.

5. A manager needs to identify some information from the *Purchase Orders* Excel file but has only the order number. Modify the Excel file to use the VLOOKUP function to find the item description and cost per order for the following order numbers: A1567, C8854, and A0207.

6. A pharmaceutical manufacturer has projected net profits for a new drug that is being released to the market over the next five years:

Year	Net Profit
1	$(675,000,000)
2	$(445,000,000)
3	$(175,000,000)
4	$125,000,000
5	$530,000,000

Use a spreadsheet to find the net present value of these cash flows for a discount rate of 8%.

Exercises 7 through 10 will require information available in "Introduction to Business Analytics" to solve.

7. Example 4 in "Introduction to Business Analytics" describes a scenario for new product sales that can be characterized by a formula called a Gompertz curve: $S = ae^{be^{ct}}$. Develop a spreadsheet for calculating sales using this formula for $t = 0$ to 160 in increments of 10 when $a = 20000$, $b = -10$, and $c = -0.04$.

8. Example 5 in "Introduction to Business Analytics" provides data from an experiment to identify the relationship between sales and pricing, coupon, and advertising strategies. Enter the data into a spreadsheet and implement the model in the example within your spreadsheet to estimate the sales for each of the weekly experiments. Compute the average sales for the three stores, and find the differences between the averages and the model estimates for each week.

9. Develop a spreadsheet model for Problem 12 in "Introduction to Business Analytics," using the data provided. Apply the principles of spreadsheet engineering in developing your model.

[7]Based on Efraim Turban, Ranesh Sharda, Dursun Delen and David King, *Business Intelligence: A Managerial Approach*, 2nd ed., (Upper Saddle River NJ: Prentice Hall, 2011).

10. Develop a spreadsheet model for Problem 13 in "Introduction to Business Analytics." Apply the principles of spreadsheet engineering in developing your model. Use the spreadsheet to create a table for a range of prices to help you identify the price that results in the maximum revenue.

11. Develop a spreadsheet model to determine how much a person or a couple can afford to spend on a house.[8] Lender guidelines suggest that the allowable monthly housing expenditure should be no more than 28% of monthly gross income. From this, you must subtract total nonmortgage housing expenses, which would include insurance and property taxes and any other additional expenses. This defines the affordable monthly mortgage payment. In addition, guidelines also suggest that total affordable monthly debt payments, including housing expenses, should not exceed 36% of gross monthly income. This is calculated by subtracting total nonmortgage housing expenses and any other installment debt, such as car loans, student loans, credit-card debt, and so on, from 36% of total monthly gross income. The smaller of the affordable monthly mortgage payment and the total affordable monthly debt payments is the affordable monthly mortgage. To calculate the maximum that can be borrowed, find the monthly payment per $1,000 mortgage based on the current interest rate and duration of the loan. Divide the affordable monthly mortgage amount by this monthly payment to find the affordable mortgage. Assuming a 20% down payment, the maximum price of a house would be the affordable mortgage divided by 0.8.

    Use the following data to test your model: total monthly gross income $= \$6,500$; nonmortgage housing expenses $= \$350$; monthly installment debt $= \$500$; monthly payment per $1,000 mortgage $= \$7.25$.

12. MasterTech is a new software company that develops and markets productivity software for municipal government applications. In developing their income statement, the following formulas are used:

$$\text{gross profit} = \text{net sales} - \text{cost of sales}$$
$$\text{net operating profit} = \text{gross profit} - \text{administrative expenses} - \text{selling expenses}$$
$$\text{net income before taxes} = \text{net operating profit} - \text{interest expense}$$
$$\text{net income} = \text{net income before taxes} - \text{taxes}$$

    Net sales are expected to be $900,000. Cost of sales is estimated to be $540,000. Selling expenses have a fixed component that is estimated to be $90,000 and a variable component that is estimated to be 7% of net sales. Administrative expenses are $50,000. Interest expenses are $10,000. The company is taxed at a 50% rate. Develop a spreadsheet model to calculate the net income. Design your spreadsheet using good spreadsheet-engineering principles.

Case: Performance Lawn Equipment

Part 1: Elizabeth Burke has asked you to do some preliminary analysis of the data in the *Performance Lawn Equipment* database. First, she would like you to edit the worksheets *Dealer Satisfaction* and *End-User Satisfaction* to display the total number of responses to each level of the survey scale across all regions for each year. Second, she wants a count

---

[8]Based on Ralph R. Frasca, *Personal Finance,* 8th ed. (Boston: Prentice Hall, 2009).

of the number of failures in the worksheet "Mower Test." Next, Elizabeth has provided you with prices for PLE products for the past 5 years:

Year	Mower Price	Tractor Price
2008	$120	$3,000
2009	$135	$3,100
2010	$150	$3,250
2011	$175	$3,400
2012	$180	$3,600

Create a new worksheet in the database to compute gross revenues by month and region, as well as worldwide totals, for each product using the data in *Mower Unit Sales* and *Tractor Unit Sales*. Finally, she wants to know the market share for each product and region based on the PLE and industry sales data in the database. Create and save these calculations in a new worksheet. Summarize all your findings in a report to Ms. Burke.

Part 2: The Performance Lawn Equipment database contains data needed to develop a pro forma income statement. Dealers selling PLE products all receive 20% of sales revenue for their part of doing business, and this is accounted for as the selling expense. The tax rate is 40%. Develop an Excel worksheet to extract and summarize the data needed to develop the income statement for 2012 and implement an Excel model in the form of a pro forma income statement for the company.

Glossary

Absolute address An address that uses a dollar sign ($) before either the row or the column label (or both).

Discount rate A reflection of the opportunity costs of spending funds now versus achieving a return for another investment, as well as the risks associated with not receiving returns until a later time.

Net present value (discounted cash flow) A measurement of the worth of a stream of cash flows, taking into account the time value of money.

Pro forma income statement A method of expressing calculations of net income.

Relative address An address that uses just the row and column label in the cell reference.

Spreadsheet engineering The process of developing good, useful, and correct spreadsheet models.

Verification The process of ensuring that a model is accurate and free from logical errors.

The Relational Model

Chapter Objectives

- Learn the conceptual foundation of the relational model
- Understand how relations differ from nonrelational tables
- Learn basic relational terminology
- Learn the meaning and importance of keys, foreign keys, and related terminology
- Understand how foreign keys represent relationships
- Learn the purpose and use of surrogate keys
- Learn the meaning of functional dependencies
- Learn to apply a process for normalizing relations

This chapter explains the relational model, the single most important standard in database processing today. This model, which was developed and published in 1970 by Edgar Frank Codd, commonly referred to as E. F. Codd,[1] then an employee at IBM, was founded on the theory of relational algebra. The model has since found widespread practical application, and today it is used for the design and implementation of almost every commercial database worldwide. This chapter describes the conceptual foundation of this model.

---

[1] E. F. Codd, "A Relational Model of Data for Large Shared Databanks," *Communications of the ACM* (June 1970): 377–387.

RELATIONS

Databases help people keep track of things and relational DBMS products store data in the form of tables. In this chapter, we need to clarify and refine these statements. First, the formal name for a "thing" that is being tracked is **entity,** which is defined as something of importance to the user that needs to be represented in the database. Further, it is not entirely correct to say that DBMS products store data in tables. DBMS products store data in the form of relations, which are a special type of table. Specifically, a **relation** is a two-dimensional **table** consisting of **rows** and **columns** that has the following characteristics:

1. Each row of the table holds data that pertain to some entity or a portion of some entity.
2. Each column of the table contains data that represent an attribute of the entity. For example, in an EMPLOYEE relation each row would contain data about a particular employee and each column would contain data that represented an attribute of that employee, such as LastName, Phone, or EmailAddress.
3. The cells of the table must hold a single value, and thus no repeating elements are allowed in a cell.
4. All the entries in any column must be of the same kind. For example, if the third column in the first row of a table contains EmployeeNumber, then the third column in all other rows must contain EmployeeNumber as well.
5. Each column must have a unique name.
6. The order of the columns with the table is unimportant.
7. The order of the rows is unimportant.
8. The set of data values in each row must be unique—no two rows in the table may hold identical sets of data values.

The characteristics of a relation are summarized in Figure 1.

A Sample Relation and Two Nonrelations

Figure 2 shows a sample EMPLOYEE table. Consider this table in light of the characteristics discussed earlier. First, each row is about an EMPLOYEE entity, and each column represents an attribute of employees, so those two conditions are met. Each cell has only one value, and all entries in a column are of the same kind. Column names are unique, and we could change the order of either the columns or the rows and not lose any information. Finally, no two rows are identical—each row holds a different set of data values. Because this table meets all requirements of the definition of *relation*, we can classify it as a relation.

FIGURE 1

Characteristics of a Relation

1. Rows contain data about an entity
2. Columns contain data about attributes of the entity
3. Cells of the table hold a single value
4. All entries in a column are of the same kind
5. Each column has a unique name
6. The order of the columns is unimportant
7. The order of the rows is unimportant
8. No two rows may hold identical sets of data values

FIGURE 2

Sample EMPLOYEE Relation

EmployeeNumber	FirstName	LastName	Department	Email	Phone
100	Jerry	Johnson	Accounting	JJ@somewhere.com	834-1101
200	Mary	Abernathy	Finance	MA@somewhere.com	834-2101
300	Liz	Smathers	Finance	LS@somewhere.com	834-2102
400	Tom	Caruthers	Accounting	TC@somewhere.com	834-1102
500	Tom	Jackson	Production	TJ@somewhere.com	834-4101
600	Eleanore	Caldera	Legal	EC@somewhere.com	834-3101
700	Richard	Bandalone	Legal	RB@somewhere.com	834-3102

FIGURE 3

**Nonrelational Table—
Multiple Entries
per Cell**

EmployeeNumber	FirstName	LastName	Department	Email	Phone
100	Jerry	Johnson	Accounting	JJ@somewhere.com	834-1101
200	Mary	Abernathy	Finance	MA@somewhere.com	834-2101
300	Liz	Smathers	Finance	LS@somewhere.com	834-2102
400	Tom	Caruthers	Accounting	TC@somewhere.com	834-1102, 834-1191, 834-1192
500	Tom	Jackson	Production	TJ@somewhere.com	834-4101
600	Eleanore	Caldera	Legal	EC@somewhere.com	834-3101
700	Richard	Bandalone	Legal	RB@somewhere.com	834-3102, 834-3191

FIGURE 4

**Nonrelational Table—
Order of Rows Matters
and Kind of Column
Entries Differs in Email**

EmployeeNumber	FirstName	LastName	Department	Email	Phone
100	Jerry	Johnson	Accounting	JJ@somewhere.com	834-1101
200	Mary	Abernathy	Finance	MA@somewhere.com	834-2101
300	Liz	Smathers	Finance	LS@somewhere.com	834-2102
400	Tom	Caruthers	Accounting	TC@somewhere.com	834-1102
				Fax:	834-9911
				Home:	723-8765
500	Tom	Jackson	Production	TJ@somewhere.com	834-4101
600	Eleanore	Caldera	Legal	EC@somewhere.com	834-3101
				Fax:	834-9912
				Home:	723-7654
700	Richard	Bandalone	Legal	RB@somewhere.com	834-3102

Now consider the tables shown in Figures 3 and 4. Neither of these tables is a relation. The EMPLOYEE table in Figure 3 is not a relation because the Phone column has cells with multiple entries. For example, Tom Caruthers has three values for phone, and Richard Bandalone has two values. Multiple entries per cell are not permitted in a relation.

The table in Figure 4 is not a relation for two reasons. First, the order of the rows is important. Because the row under Tom Caruthers contains his fax number, we may lose track of the correspondence between his name and his fax number if we rearrange the rows. The second reason this table is not a relation is that not all values in the Email column are of the same kind. Some of the values are email addresses, and others are types of phone numbers.

Although each cell can have only one value, that value can vary in length. Figure 5 shows the table from Figure 2 with an additional variable-length Comment attribute. Even though a comment can be lengthy and varies in length from row to row, there is still only one comment per cell. Thus, the table in Figure 5 is a relation.

A Note on Presenting Relation Structures

When we write out the relation structure of a relation that we are discussing, we use the following format:

RELATION_NAME (Column01, Column02, … , LastColumn)

FIGURE 5

**Relation with Variable-
Length Column Values**

EmployeeNumber	FirstName	LastName	Department	Email	Phone	Comment
100	Jerry	Johnson	Accounting	JJ@somewhere.com	834-1101	Joined the Accounting Department March after completing his MBA. Will take the CPA exam this fall.
200	Mary	Abernathy	Finance	MA@somewhere.com	834-2101	
300	Liz	Smathers	Finance	LS@somewhere.com	834-2102	
400	Tom	Caruthers	Accounting	TC@somewhere.com	834-1102	
500	Tom	Jackson	Production	TJ@somewhere.com	834-4101	
600	Eleanore	Caldera	Legal	EC@somewhere.com	834-3101	
700	Richard	Bandalone	Legal	RB@somewhere.com	834-3102	Is a full-time consultant to legal on a retainer basis.

FIGURE 6

Equivalent Sets of Terms

Table	Row	Column
File	Record	Field
Relation	Tuple	Attribute

The relation name is written first, and it is written in all capital (uppercase) letters (for example, EMPLOYEE), and the name is singular, not plural (EMPLOYEE, not EMPLOYEES). If the relation name is a combination of two or more words, we join the words with an underscore (for example, EMPLOYEE_PROJECT_ASSIGNMENT). Column names are contained in parentheses and are written with an initial capital letter followed by lowercase letters (for example, Department). If the column name is a combination of two or more words, the first letter of each word is capitalized (for example, EmployeeNumber and LastName). Thus, the EMPLOYEE relation shown in Figure 2 would be written as:

EMPLOYEE (EmployeeNumber, FirstName, LastName, Department, Email, Phone)

BTW

Relation structures, such as the one shown earlier, are part of a database schema. A **database schema** is the design on which a database and its associated applications are built.

A Note on Terminology

In the database world, people generally use the terms *table* and *relation* interchangeably. Thus, any time we use the term *table* we mean a table that meets the characteristics required for a relation. Keep in mind, however, that, strictly speaking, some tables are not relations.

Sometimes, especially in traditional data processing, people use the term **file** instead of *table*. When they do so, they use the term **record** for *row* and the term **field** for *column*. To further confound the issue, database theoreticians sometimes use yet another set of terms: Although they do call a table a *relation*, they call a *row* a **tuple** (rhymes with *couple*) and a *column* an **attribute.** These three sets of terminology are summarized in Figure 6.

To make matters even more confusing, people often mix up these sets of terms. It is not unusual to hear someone refer to a relation that has rows and fields. As long as you know what is intended, this mixing of terms is not important.

We should discuss one other source of confusion. According to Figure 1, a table that has duplicate rows is not a relation. However, in practice this condition is often ignored. Particularly when manipulating relations with a DBMS, we may end up with a table that has duplicate rows. To make that table a relation, we should eliminate the duplicates. On a large table, however, checking for duplication can be time-consuming. Therefore, the default behavior for DBMS products is not to check for duplicate rows. Hence, in practice, tables might exist with duplicate (non-unique) rows that are still called relations.

TYPES OF KEYS

A **key** is one or more columns of a relation that is used to identify a row. A key can be **unique** or **nonunique.** For example, for the EMPLOYEE relation in Figure 2 EmployeeNumber is a *unique key* because a value of EmployeeNumber identifies a unique row. Thus, a query to display all employees having an EmployeeNumber of 200 will produce a single row. In contrast, Department is a *nonunique key*. It is a key because it is used to identify a row, but it is nonunique because a value of Department potentially identifies more than one row. Thus, a query to display all rows having a Department value of Accounting will produce several rows.

From the data in Figure 2, it appears that EmployeeNumber, LastName, and Email are all unique identifiers. However, to decide whether this is true database developers must do more than examine sample data. Instead, they must ask the users or other subject-matter experts whether a certain column is unique. The column LastName is an example where this is important. It might turn out that the sample data just happen to have unique values for LastName. The users, however, might say that LastName is not always unique.

Composite Keys

A key that contains two or more attributes is called a **composite key.** For example, suppose that we are looking for a unique key for the EMPLOYEE relation, and the users say that although LastName is not unique, the combination of LastName and Department is unique. Thus, for some reason the users know that two people with the same last name will never work in the same department. Two Johnsons, for example, will never work in accounting. If that is the case, then the combination (LastName, Department) is a unique composite key.

Alternatively, the users may know that the combination (LastName, Department) is not unique but that the combination (FirstName, LastName, Department) is unique. The latter combination, then, is a composite key with three attributes.

BTW

Composite keys, like one-column keys, can be unique or nonunique.

Candidate and Primary Keys

Candidate keys are keys that uniquely identify each row in a relation. Candidate keys can be single-column keys or they can be composite keys. The **primary key** is the candidate key that is chosen as the key that the DBMS will use to uniquely identify each row in a relation. For example, suppose that we have the following EMPLOYEE relation:

EMPLOYEE (EmployeeNumber, FirstName, LastName, Department, Email, Phone)

The users tell us that EmployeeNumber is a unique key, that Email is a unique key, and that the composite key (FirstName, LastName, DepartmentName) is a unique key. Therefore, we have three candidate keys. When designing the database, we choose one of the candidate keys to be the primary key. In this case, for example, we use EmployeeNumber as the primary key.

BTW

It may help you to understand why the unique keys that could be used as the main identifier for the relation are referred to as candidate keys if you think of them as the "candidates" in the running to be elected "primary key"—but remember that only one candidate will win the election.

The primary key is important not only because it can be used to identify unique rows, but also because it can be used to represent rows in relationships.

FIGURE 7

Defining a Primary Key in Microsoft Access 2010

Primary Key button

The **key symbol** indicates which column or columns are being used as the primary key

Many DBMS products use values of the primary key to organize storage for the relation. They also build indexes and other special structures for fast retrieval of rows using primary key values.

We indicate primary keys by underlining them. Because EmployeeNumber is the primary key of EMPLOYEE, we write the EMPLOYEE relation as:

EMPLOYEE (EmployeeNumber, FirstName, LastName, Department, Email, Phone)

Each DBMS program has its own way of creating and indicating a primary key. Figure 7 shows the CUSTOMER table from an Art Course database in the Microsoft Access table Design view. In table Design view, we can spot the primary key of the table by finding the key symbol next to the names of the columns in the primary key. In this case, a key symbol is located next to CustomerNumber, which means that the developer has defined CustomerNumber as the primary key for this table.

BTW

In Figure 8, the table names are often listed with *dbo* preceding the table name, as in dbo.CUSTOMER. The dbo stands for *database owner*, and it occurs frequently in SQL Server.

Figure 8 shows the same CUSTOMER table in Microsoft SQL Server 2012 Express,[2] as it appears in the Microsoft SQL Server Management Studio graphical utility program. This

---

[2]Microsoft has released various versions of SQL Server, and the latest version is SQL Server 2012. SQL Server 2012 Express is the least powerful version, but it is intended for general use and can be downloaded for free from the Microsoft SQL Server 2012 Express homepage at **www.microsoft.com/express/Database/**. For more information, see online Appendix A, "Getting Started with Microsoft SQL Server 2012 Express Edition."

FIGURE 8

Defining a Primary Key in Microsoft SQL Server 2012

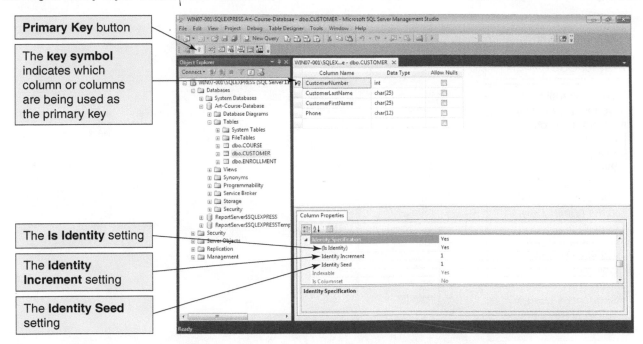

Primary Key button

The **key symbol** indicates which column or columns are being used as the primary key

The **Is Identity** setting

The **Identity Increment** setting

The **Identity Seed** setting

display is more complex, but again we can spot the primary key of the table by finding the key symbol next to the names of the columns in the primary key. Again, there is a key symbol next to CustomerNumber, indicating that CustomerNumber is the primary key for this table.

Figure 9 shows the same CUSTOMER table in Oracle's Oracle Database 11*g* Release 2 Express Edition,[3] as seen in the Oracle SQL Developer graphical utility program. This display is more complex than Microsoft Access, but we can spot the primary key of the table by finding the key symbol next to the name(s) of the primary key column(s) in the Column Name list. Again, there is a key symbol next to CustomerNumber, indicating that CustomerNumber is the primary key for this table.

Figure 10 shows the same CUSTOMER table in Oracle's MySQL 5.5[4] as seen in the MySQL Workbench graphical utility program. This display is more complex than Microsoft Access, but we can spot the primary key of the table by finding the key symbol next to the name(s) of the primary key column(s) in the Column Name list. Again, there is a key symbol next to CustomerNumber, indicating that CustomerNumber is the primary key for this table.

---

[3]Originally just referred to as *Oracle*, the database product is now known as Oracle Database because Oracle Corporation has grown far beyond its database product roots and now owns and sells a large range of products. These can be seen at **www.oracle.com**. As of this writing, Oracle Database 11*g* Release 2 is the latest production version. The freely downloadable Oracle Database Express Edition is available at **www.oracle.com/technetwork/database/express-edition/overview/index.html**. Oracle Database 11*g* Release 2 is an enterprise-class DBMS and, as such, is much more complex than Microsoft Access. It does not include application development tools, such as form and report generators. For more information, see online Appendix B, "Getting Started with Oracle Database 11*g* Release 2 Express Edition."

[4]On February 26, 2008, Sun Microsystems acquired MySQL from MySQL AB. On April 29, 2009, Oracle Corporation made an offer to buy Sun Microsystems, and on January 27, 2010, Oracle acquired Sun Microsystems. For more details, see **www.oracle.com/us/sun/index.htm**. This makes Oracle the owner of both Oracle Database 11*g* Release 2 and the MySQL DBMS. As of this writing, MySQL 5.5 is the latest production version of the popular MySQL DBMS. The free MySQL 5.5 Community Server Edition and the MySQL Workbench can be downloaded from the MySQL Web site at **www.mysql.com/downloads/**. Like SQL Server 2012, MySQL is an enterprise-class DBMS and, as such, is much more complex than Microsoft Access. Also like SQL Server 2012, MySQL does not include application development tools, such as form and report generators. For more information, see online Appendix C, "Getting Started with Oracle MySQL 5.5 Community Server Edition."

FIGURE 9

Defining a Primary Key in Oracle Database 11*g* Release 2

This constraint creates the primary key for CUSTOMER

The constraint type **Primary_Key** indicates which constraints are being used to create the primary key

The columns used in the primary key constraint CUSTOMER_PK are shown in the Columns pane

Sequences used to define primary key values are shown here

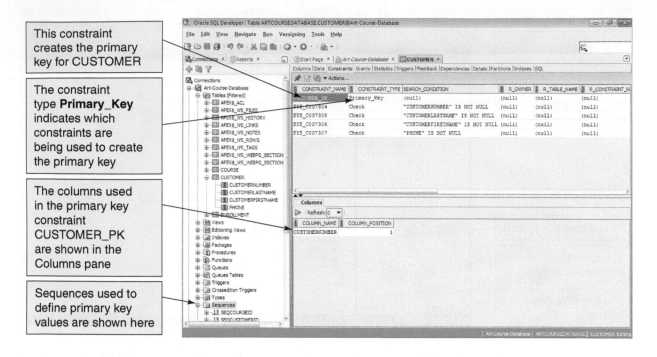

FIGURE 10

Defining a Primary Key in Oracle MySQL 5.5

The **key symbol** indicates which column or columns are being used as the primary key

The **key symbol** indicates which column or columns are being used as the primary key

The **PK check box** selects which column or columns are being used as the primary key

The **AI check box** indicates that AUTO_INCREMENT is being used as the primary key

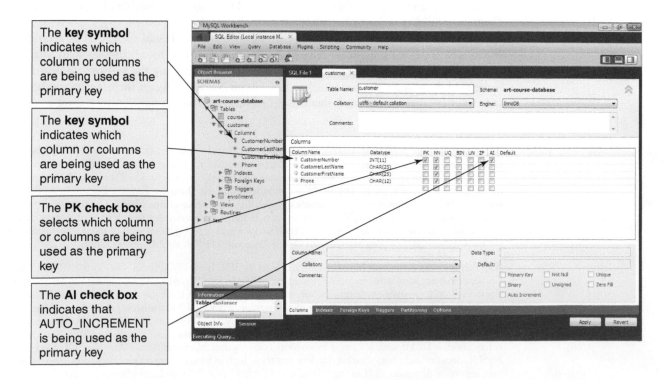

A common method of specifying primary keys is to use SQL.

Surrogate Keys

A **surrogate key** is a column with a unique, DBMS-assigned identifier that has been added to a table to be the primary key. The unique values of the surrogate key are assigned by the DBMS each time a row is created, and the values never change.

An ideal primary key is short, numeric, and never changes. Sometimes one column in a table will meet these requirements or come close to them. For example, EmployeeNumber in the EMPLOYEE relation should work very well as a primary key. But in other tables, the primary key does not come close to being ideal. For example, consider the relation PROPERTY:

PROPERTY (Street, City, State, ZIP, OwnerID)

The primary key of PROPERTY is (Street, City, State, ZIP), which is long and nonnumeric (although it probably will not change). This is not an ideal primary key. In cases like this, the database designer will add a surrogate key, such as PropertyID:

PROPERTY (PropertyID, Street, City, State, ZIP, OwnerID)

Surrogate keys are short, numeric, and never change—they are ideal primary keys. Because the values of the surrogate primary key will have no meaning to users, they are often hidden on forms, query results, and reports.

Most DBMS products have a facility for automatically generating key values. In Figure 7, we can see how surrogate keys are defined with Microsoft Access 2010. In Microsoft Access, Data Type is set to AutoNumber. With this specification, Microsoft Access assigns a value of 1 to CustomerNumber for the first row of CUSTOMER, a value of 2 to CustomerNumber for the second row, and so forth.

Enterprise-class DBMS products, such as Microsoft SQL Server, Oracle MySQL, and Oracle Database offer more capability. For example, with SQL Server, the developer can specify the starting value of the surrogate key as well as the amount by which to increment the key for each new row. Figure 8 shows how this is done for the definition of the surrogate key CustomerNumber for the CUSTOMER table. In the Column Properties window, which is below the dbo.CUSTOMER table column details window, there is a set of **identity** specifications that have been set to indicate to SQL Server that a surrogate key column exists. The **is identity** value for CustomerNumber is set to Yes to make CustomerNumber a surrogate key. The starting value of the surrogate key is called the **identity seed.** For CustomerNumber, it is set to 1. Furthermore, the amount that is added to each key value to create the next key value is called the **identity increment.** In this example, it is set to 1. These settings mean that when the user creates the first row of the CUSTOMER table, SQL Server will give the value 1 to CustomerNumber. When the second row of CUSTOMER is created, SQL Server will give the value 2 to CustomerNumber, and so forth.

Oracle Database uses a **SEQUENCE** function to define automatically increasing sequences of numbers that can be used as surrogate key numbers. When using a SEQUENCE, the starting value can be any value (the default is 1), but the increment will always be 1. Figure 9 shows the existing sequences in the Art Course Database.

MySQL uses the **AUTO_INCREMENT** function to automatically assign surrogate key numbers. In AUTO_INCREMENT, the starting value can be any value (the default is 1), but the increment will always be 1. Figure 10 shows that CustomerNumber is a surrogate key for CUSTOMER that uses AUTO_INCREMENT (AI) to set the value of the column.

Foreign Keys and Referential Integrity

We place values from one relation into a second relation to represent a relationship. The values we use are the primary key values (including composite primary key values, when necessary) of the first relation. When we do this, the attribute in the second relation that holds these values is referred to as a **foreign key.**

Consider the following two relations, where besides the EMPLOYEE relation we now have a DEPARTMENT relation to hold data about departments:

EMPLOYEE (EmployeeNumber, FirstName, LastName, Department, Email, Phone)

and:

DEPARTMENT (DepartmentName, BudgetCode, OfficeNumber, DepartmentPhone)

where EmployeeNumber and DepartmentName are the primary keys of EMPLOYEE and DEPARTMENT, respectively.

Now suppose that Department in EMPLOYEE contains the names of the departments in which employees work and that DepartmentName in DEPARTMENT also contains these names. In this case, Department in EMPLOYEE is said to be a foreign key to DEPARTMENT. We denote foreign keys by displaying them in italics. Thus, we would write these two relation descriptions as follows:

EMPLOYEE (EmployeeNumber, FirstName, LastName, *Department*, Email, Phone)

and:

DEPARTMENT (DepartmentName, BudgetCode, OfficeNumber, DepartmentPhone)

Note that it is not necessary for the primary key and the foreign key to have the same column name. The only requirement is that they have the same set of values.

In most cases, it is important to ensure that every value of a foreign key matches a value of the primary key. In the previous example, the value of Department in every row of EMPLOYEE should match a value of DepartmentName in DEPARTMENT. If this is the case (and it usually is), then we declare the following rule:

Department in EMPLOYEE must exist in DepartmentName in DEPARTMENT

Such a rule is called a **referential integrity constraint.** Whenever you see a foreign key, you should always look for an associated referential integrity constraint.

Consider the Art Course database. The structure of this database is:

CUSTOMER (CustomerNumber, CustomerLastName, CustomerFirstName, Phone)
COURSE (CourseNumber, Course, CourseDate, Fee)
ENROLLMENT (*CustomerNumber*, *CourseNumber*, AmountPaid)

FIGURE 11

Enforcing Referential Integrity in Microsoft Access 2010

The relationship is between CUSTOMER and ENROLLMENT—the foreign key CustomerNumber in ENROLLMENT references the primary key CustomerNumber in CUSTOMER

Use this check box to enforce referential integrity in this relationship

The ENROLLMENT table has a composite primary key of (CustomerNumber, CourseNumber), where CustomerNumber is a foreign key linking to CUSTOMER and CourseNumber is a foreign key linking to COURSE. Therefore, two referential integrity constraints are required:

CustomerNumber in ENROLLMENT must exist in CustomerNumber in CUSTOMER

and:

CourseNumber in ENROLLMENT must exist in CourseNumber in COURSE

Just as DBMS products have a means of specifying primary keys, they also have a way to set up foreign key referential integrity constraints. We discuss the details of setting up referential integrity constraints in this chapter's section of "The Access Workbench." Figure 11 shows the tables from an Art Course database in the Microsoft Access Relationships window and with the Edit Relationships dialog box showing the details of the relationship between CUSTOMER and ENROLLMENT. Notice that the Enforce Referential Integrity check box is checked, so the referential integrity constraint between CustomerNumber in ENROLLMENT (the foreign key) and CustomerNumber in CUSTOMER (the primary key) is being enforced.

Figure 12 shows the same foreign key relationship between CUSTOMER and ENROLLMENT in the Microsoft SQL Server Management Studio program. Again, this display is more complex, but notice that the property Table Designer: Enforce Foreign Key Constraint is set to Yes. This means that the referential integrity constraint between CustomerNumber in ENROLLMENT (the foreign key) and CustomerNumber in CUSTOMER (the primary key) is being enforced.

Figure 13 shows foreign keys in Oracle Database 11*g* Release 2 Express Edition. Here the Foreign Keys tab in the Oracle SQL Developer utility displays the properties of each foreign key.

FIGURE 12

Enforcing Referential Integrity in Microsoft SQL Server 2012

The relationship is between CUSTOMER and ENROLLMENT

We are enforcing the foreign key constraint—which *is* the referential integrity constraint

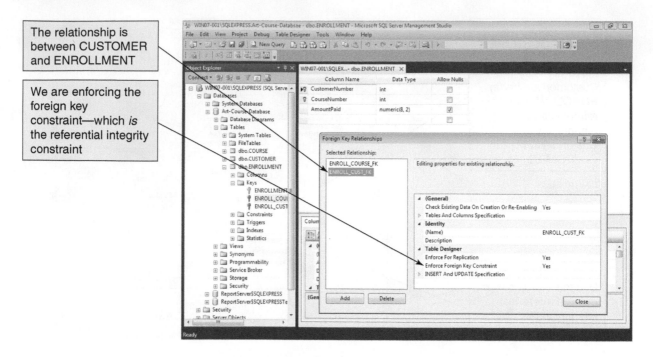

FIGURE 13

Enforcing Referential Integrity in Oracle Database 11*g* Release 2

This constraint creates the foreign key relationship between CUSTOMER and ENROLLMENT

The constraint type **Foreign_Key** indicates which constraints are being used to create the foreign keys

The columns used in the foreign key constraint ENROLL_CUST_FK are shown in the Columns pane

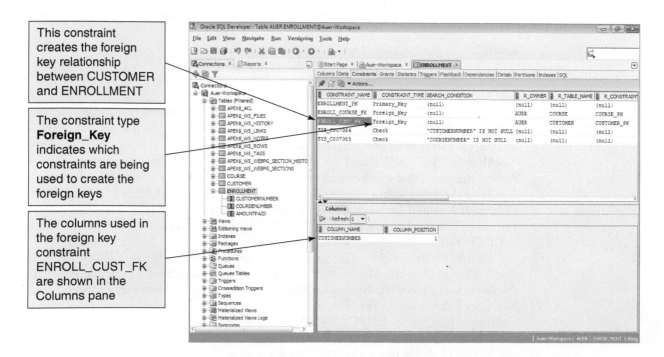

FIGURE 14

Enforcing Referential Integrity in Oracle MySQL 5.5

Figure 14 shows foreign keys in MySQL 5.5. Here the Foreign Keys tab in the MySQL Workbench utility displays the properties of each foreign key.

Just as SQL can be used to specify primary keys, it can also be used to set referential integrity constraints.

THE PROBLEM OF NULL VALUES

Before we leave the discussion of relations and the relationships between them, we need to discuss a subtle but important topic: null values. A **null value** is a missing value in a cell in a relation. Consider the following relation, which is used to track finished goods for an apparel manufacturer:

ITEM (ItemNumber, ItemName, Color, Quantity)

Figure 15 shows sample data for this table. Notice that in the last row of data—the row with ItemNumber 400 and ItemName Spring Hat—there is no value for Color. The problem with null values is that they are ambiguous; we do not know how to interpret them because three possible meanings can be construed. First, it might mean that no value of Color is appropriate; Spring Hats do not come in different colors. Second, it might mean that the value is known to be blank; that is, Spring Hats have a color, but the color has not yet been decided. Maybe the color is established by placing ribbons around the hats, but

FIGURE 15

Sample ITEM Relation and Data

ItemNumber	ItemName	Color	Quantity
110	Small T-Shirt	Red	15
120	Small T-Shirt	Blue	5
150	Small T-Shirt	Green	7
210	Med T-Shirt	Red	8
400	Spring Hat		5

this is not done until an order arrives. Finally, the null value might mean that the hats' color is simply unknown; the hats have a color, but no one has checked yet to see what it is.

You can eliminate null values by requiring an attribute value. DBMS products allow you to specify whether a null value can occur in a column. For Microsoft SQL Server 2012, notice that the column in the dbo.CUSTOMER table column details window labeled Allow Nulls in Figure 8. A check box without a checkmark means that null values are not allowed in this column. Note that in Figure 9, the Oracle Database 11g Release 2 SQL Developer utility is showing the data on the Constraints tab, and this tab does not indicate null values. If, however, we looked at the Columns tab, we would see whether null values are allowed in each column. For MySQL 5.5 note that in Figure 10 the Column Details tab in the MySQL Table Editor shows an NN (NOT NULL) check box that indicates whether null values are allowed in the column. Regardless of the DBMS being used, if nulls are not allowed then some value must be entered for each row in the table. If the attribute is a text value, users can be allowed to enter values such as "not appropriate," "undecided," or "unknown," when necessary. If the attribute is not text, then some other coding system can be developed.

For now, be aware that null values can occur and that they always carry some ambiguity.

FUNCTIONAL DEPENDENCIES AND NORMALIZATION

This section introduces some of the concepts used for relational database design. This chapter presents only the essentials. To learn more, you should consult other, more comprehensive references.[5]

Functional Dependencies

To get started, let us take a short excursion into the world of algebra. Suppose you are buying boxes of cookies, and someone tells you that each box costs $5. Knowing this fact, you can compute the cost of several boxes with the formula:

CookieCost = NumberOfBoxes × $5

A more general way to express the relationship between CookieCost and NumberOfBoxes is to say that CookieCost depends upon NumberOfBoxes. Such a statement tells the character of the relationship between CookieCost and NumberOfBoxes, even though it doesn't give the formula. More formally, we can say that CookieCost is **functionally dependent** on NumberOfBoxes. Such a statement, which is called a **functional dependency,** can be written as follows:

NumberOfBoxes → CookieCost

This expression says that NumberOfBoxes determines CookieCost. The variable on the left, NumberOfBoxes, is called the **determinant.**

Using another example, we can compute the extended price of a part order by multiplying the quantity of the item by its unit price:

ExtendedPrice = Quantity × UnitPrice

In this case, we would say that ExtendedPrice is functionally dependent on Quantity and UnitPrice, or:

(Quantity, UnitPrice) → ExtendedPrice

The composite (Quantity, UnitPrice) is the determinant of ExtendedPrice.

---

[5]See David M. Kroenke and David J. Auer, *Database Processing: Fundamentals, Design, and Implementation*, 12th edition (Upper Saddle River, NJ: Prentice Hall, 2012); and C. J. Date, *An Introduction to Database Systems*, 8th edition (Boston: Addison-Wesley, 2004).

FIGURE 16

ObjectColor	Weight	Shape
Red	5	Ball
Blue	5	Cube
Yellow	7	Cube

Now, let us expand these ideas. Suppose you know that a sack contains either red, blue, or yellow objects. Further suppose you know that the red objects weigh 5 pounds each, the blue objects weigh 5 pounds each, and the yellow objects weigh 7 pounds each. If a friend looks into the sack, sees an object, and tells you the color of the object, you can tell the weight of the object. We can formalize this in the same way as in the previous example:

ObjectColor → Weight

Thus, we can say that Weight is functionally dependent on ObjectColor and that ObjectColor determines Weight. The relationship here does not involve an equation, but this functional dependency is still true. Given a value for ObjectColor, you can determine the object's weight.

In addition, if we know that the red objects are balls, the blue objects are cubes, and the yellow objects are cubes, then:

ObjectColor → Shape

Thus, ObjectColor also determines Shape. We can put these two together and state:

ObjectColor → (Weight, Shape)

Thus, ObjectColor determines Weight and Shape.

Another way to represent these facts is to put them into a table, as shown in Figure 16. Note that this table meets all the conditions in our definition of a relation, as listed in Figure 1, so we can refer to it as a relation. If we call it the OBJECT relation and use ObjectColor as the primary key, we can write this relation as:

OBJECT (ObjectColor, Weight, Shape)

Now, you may be thinking that we have just performed some trick or sleight of hand to arrive at a relation, but one can make the argument that the only reason for having relations is to store instances of functional dependencies. Consider a relation such as the CUSTOMER relation from an Art Course database:

CUSTOMER (CustomerNumber, CustomerLastName, CustomerFirstName, Phone)

Here, we are simply storing facts that express the following functional dependency:

CustomerNumber → (CustomerLastName, CustomerFirstName, Phone)

Primary and Candidate Keys Revisited

Now that we have discussed the concept of functional dependency, we can now define primary and candidate keys more formally. Specifically, a primary key of a relation can be defined as "one or more attributes that functionally determine all the other attributes of the relation." The same definition holds for candidate keys, as well.

Recall the EMPLOYEE relation from Figure 2 (shown without primary or foreign keys indicated):

EMPLOYEE (EmployeeNumber, FirstName, LastName, Department, Email, Phone)

As previously discussed, based on information from users, this relation has three candidate keys: EmployeeNumber, Email, and the composite (FirstName, LastName, Department). Because this is so, we can state the following:

EmployeeNumber → (FirstName, LastName, Department, Email, Phone)

Equivalently, if we are given a value for EmployeeNumber, we can determine FirstName, LastName, Department, Email, and Phone. Similarly, we can state that:

Email → (EmployeeNumber, FirstName, LastName, Department, Phone)

That is, if we are given a value for Email, we can determine EmployeeNumber, FirstName, LastName, Department, and Phone. Finally, we also can state that:

(FirstName, LastName, Department) → (EmployeeNumber, Email, Phone)

This means that if we are given values of FirstName, LastName, and Department, we can determine EmployeeNumber, Email, and Phone.

These three functional dependencies express the reason the three candidate keys are candidate keys. When we choose a primary key from the candidate keys, we are choosing which functional dependency we want to define as the one that is most meaningful or important to us.

Normalization

The concepts of functional dependencies and determinants can be used to help in the design of relations. Recalling the concept that a table or relation should have only one theme, we can define **normalization** as the process of (or set of steps for) breaking a table or relation with more than one theme into a set of tables such that each has only one theme. Normalization is a complex topic, and it consumes one or more chapters of more theoretically oriented database books. Here, we reduce this topic to a few ideas that capture the essence of the process.

The problem that normalization addresses is as follows: A table can meet all the characteristics listed in Figure 1 and still have some modification problems for lists. Specifically, consider the following ADVISER_LIST relation:

ADVISER_LIST (AdviserID, AdviserName, Department, Phone, Office, StudentNumber, StudentName)

What is the primary key of this relation? Given the definitions of candidate key and primary key, it has to be an attribute that determines all the other attributes. The only attribute that has this characteristic is StudentNumber. Given a value of StudentNumber, we can determine the values of all the other attributes:

StudentNumber → (AdviserID, AdviserName, Department, Phone, Office, StudentName)

We can then write this relation as follows:

ADVISER_LIST (AdviserID, AdviserName, Department, Phone, Office, StudentNumber, StudentName)

However, this table has modification problems. Specifically, an adviser's data are repeated many times in the table, once for each advisee. This means that updates to adviser data might need to be made multiple times. If, for example, an adviser changes offices, that change will need to be completed in all the rows for the person's advisees. If an adviser has 20 advisees, that change will need to be entered 20 times.

Another modification problem can occur when we delete a student from this list. If we delete a student who is the only advisee for an adviser, we will delete not only the student's data but also the adviser's data. Thus, we will unintentionally lose facts about two entities while attempting to delete one.

If you look closely at this relation, you will see a functional dependency that involves the adviser's data. Specifically:

AdviserID → (AdviserName, Department, Phone, Office)

Now, we can state the problem with this relation more accurately—in terms of functional dependencies. Specifically, this relation is poorly formed because it has a functional dependency that does not involve the primary key. Stated differently, AdviserID is a determinant of a functional dependency, but it is not a candidate key and thus cannot be the primary key under any circumstances.

Relational Design Principles

From the discussion so far, we can formulate the following design principles for what we can call a **well-formed relation**:

1. For a relation to be considered well formed, every determinant must be a candidate key.
2. Any relation that is not well formed should be broken into two or more relations that are well formed.

These two principles are the heart of normalization—the process of examining relations and modifying them to make them well formed. This process is called *normalization* because you can categorize the problems to which relations are susceptible into different types called *normal forms*.

There are many defined normal forms. Technically, our well-formed relations are those that are said to be in **Boyce-Codd Normal Form (BCNF).** For example, any relation that has the characteristics listed in Figure 1 is called a relation in **first normal form (1NF).** Besides first normal form and Boyce-Codd normal form, other normal forms exist, such as second, third, fourth, fifth, and domain/key normal form.

However, if we simply follow the aforementioned design principles we will avoid almost all the problems associated with non-normalized tables. In some rare instances, these principles do not address the problems that arise (see questions 40 and 41 in the Exercises section), but if you follow these principles, you will be safe most of the time.

The Normalization Process

We can apply the principles just described to formulate the following **normalization process** for normalizing relations:

1. Identify all the candidate keys of the relation.
2. Identify all the functional dependencies in the relation.
3. Examine the determinants of the functional dependencies. If any determinant is not a candidate key, the relation is not well formed. In this case:
   a. Place the columns of the functional dependency in a new relation of their own.
   b. Make the determinant of the functional dependency the primary key of the new relation.
   c. Leave a copy of the determinant as a foreign key in the original relation.
   d. Create a referential integrity constraint between the original relation and the new relation.
4. Repeat step 3 as many times as necessary until every determinant of every relation is a candidate key.

FIGURE 17

Sample PRESCRIPTION Relation and Data

PrescriptionNumber	Date	Drug	Dosage	CustomerName	CustomerPhone	CustomerEmail
P10001	10/17/2013	DrugA	10mg	Smith, Alvin	575-523-2233	ASmith@somewhere.com
P10003	10/17/2013	DrugB	35mg	Rhodes, Jeff	575-645-3455	JRhodes@somewhere.com
P10004	10/17/2013	DrugA	20mg	Smith, Sarah	575-523-2233	SSmith@somewhere.com
P10007	10/18/2013	DrugC	20mg	Frye, Michael	575-645-4566	MFrye@somewhere.com
P10010	10/18/2013	DrugB	30mg	Rhodes, Jeff	575-645-3455	JRhodes@somewhere.com

To understand this process, consider the following relation:

PRESCRIPTION (PrescriptionNumber, Date, Drug, Dosage, CustomerName, CustomerPhone, CustomerEmail)

Sample data for the PRESCRIPTION relation are shown in Figure 17.

Step 1 of the Normalization Process   According to the normalization process, we first identify all candidate keys. PrescriptionNumber clearly determines Date, Drug, and Dosage. If we assume that a prescription is for only one person, then it also determines CustomerName, CustomerPhone, and CustomerEmail. By law, prescriptions must be for only one person, so PrescriptionNumber is a candidate key.

Does this relation have other candidate keys? Date, Drug, and Dosage do not determine PrescriptionNumber, because many prescriptions can be written on a given date, many prescriptions can be written for a given drug, and many prescriptions can be written for a given dosage.

What about customer columns? If a customer had only one prescription, then we could say that some identifying customer column—for example, CustomerEmail—would determine the prescription data. However, people can have more than one prescription, so this assumption is invalid.

Given this analysis, the only candidate key of PRESCRIPTION is PrescriptionNumber.

Step 2 of the Normalization Process   In step 2 of the normalization process, we now identify all functional dependencies. PrescriptionNumber determines all the other attributes, as just described. If a drug had only one dosage, then we could state that:

Drug → Dosage

But this is not true because some drugs have several dosages. Therefore, Drug is not a determinant. Furthermore, Dosage is not a determinant because the same dosage can be given for many different drugs.

However, examining the customer columns, we do find a functional dependency:

CustomerEmail → (CustomerName, CustomerPhone)

To know whether functional dependency is true for a particular application, we need to look beyond the sample data in Figure 17 and ask the users. For example, it is possible that some customers share the same email address, and it is also possible that some customers do not have email. For now, we can assume that the users say that CustomerEmail is a determinant of the customer attributes.

Step 3 of the Normalization Process   In step 3 of the normalization process, we ask whether there is a determinant that is *not* a candidate key. In this example, CustomerEmail is a determinant and not a candidate key. Therefore, PRESCRIPTION has normalization

FIGURE 18

**Normalized
Prescription Customer
Relations and Data**

CustomerName	CustomerPhone	CustomerEmail
Smith, Alvin	575-523-2233	ASmith@somewhere.com
Rhodes, Jeff	575-645-3455	JRhodes@somewhere.com
Frye, Michael	575-645-4566	MFrye@somewhere.com
Smith, Sarah	575-523-2233	SSmith@somewhere.com

PrescriptionNumber	Date	Drug	Dosage	CustomerEmail
P10001	10/17/2013	DrugA	10mg	ASmith@somewhere.com
P10003	10/17/2013	DrugB	35mg	JRhodes@somewhere.com
P10004	10/17/2013	DrugA	20mg	SSmith@somewhere.com
P10007	10/18/2013	DrugC	20mg	MFrye@somewhere.com
P10010	10/18/2013	DrugB	30mg	JRhodes@somewhere.com

problems and is not well formed. According to step 3, we split the functional dependency into a relation of its own:

CUSTOMER (CustomerName, CustomerPhone, <u>CustomerEmail</u>)

We make the determinant of the functional dependency, CustomerEmail, the primary key of the new relation.

We leave a copy of CustomerEmail in the original relation as a foreign key. Thus, PRESCRIPTION is now:

PRESCRIPTION (<u>PrescriptionNumber</u>, Date, Drug, Dosage, *CustomerEmail*)

Finally, we create the referential integrity constraint:

CustomerEmail in PRESCRIPTION must exist in CustomerEmail in CUSTOMER

At this point, if we move through the three steps, we find that neither of these relations has a determinant that is not a candidate key, and we can say that the two relations are now normalized. Figure 18 shows the result for the sample data.

Normalization Examples

We now illustrate the use of the normalization process with four examples.

Normalization Example 1   The relation in Figure 19 shows a table of student residence data named STU_DORM. The first step in normalizing it is to identify all candidate keys. Because StudentNumber determines each of the other columns, it is a candidate key. LastName cannot be a candidate key because two students have the last name Smith. None of the other columns can be an identifier either, so StudentNumber is the only candidate key.

Next, in step 2, we look for the functional dependencies in the relation. Besides those for StudentNumber, a functional dependency appears to exist between DormName and DormCost. Again, we would need to check this out with the users. In this case, assume that the functional dependency:

DormName → DormCost

is true and assume that our interview with the users indicates that no other functional dependencies exist.

FIGURE 19

**Sample STU_DORM
Relation and Data**

StudentNumber	LastName	FirstName	DormName	DormCost
100	Smith	Terry	Stephens	3,500.00
200	Johnson	Jeff	Alexander	3,800.00
300	Abernathy	Susan	Horan	4,000.00
400	Smith	Susan	Alexander	3,800.00
500	Wilcox	John	Stephens	3,500.00
600	Webber	Carl	Horan	4,000.00
700	Simon	Carol	Stephens	3,500.00

In step 3, we now ask if any determinants exist that are not candidate keys. In this example, DormName is a determinant, but it is not a candidate key. Therefore, this relation is not well formed and has normalization problems.

To fix those problems, we place the columns of the functional dependency (DormName, DormCost) into a relation of their own and call that relation DORM. We make the determinant of the functional dependency the primary key. Thus, DormName is the primary key of DORM. We leave the determinant DormName as a foreign key in STU_DORM. Finally, we find the appropriate referential integrity constraint. The result is:

STU_DORM (StudentNumber, LastName, FirstName, *DormName*)

DORM (DormName, DormCost)

with the constraint:

RELATION_NAME (Column01, Column02, … , LastColumn)

DormName in STU_DORM must exist in DormName in DORM. The data for these relations appear as shown in Figure 20.

Normalization Example 2 Now consider the EMPLOYEE table in Figure 21. First, we identify the candidate keys in EMPLOYEE. From the data, it appears that Employee-Number and Email each identify all the other attributes. Hence, they are candidate keys (again, with the proviso that we cannot depend on sample data to show all cases; we must verify this assumption with the users).

In step 2, we identify other functional dependencies. From the data, it appears that the only other functional dependency is:

Department → DeptPhone

Assuming that this is true, then according to step 3 we have a determinant, Department, that is not a candidate key. Thus, EMPLOYEE has normalization problems.

To fix those problems, we place the columns in the functional dependency in a table of their own and make the determinant the primary key of the new table. We leave the determinant as a foreign key in the original table. The result is the two tables:

EMPLOYEE (EmployeeNumber, LastName, Email, *Department*)

DEPARTMENT (Department, DeptPhone)

with the referential integrity constraint:

Department in EMPLOYEE must exist in Department in DEPARTMENT

The result for the sample data is shown in Figure 22.

FIGURE 20

Normalized STU_DORM and DORM Relations and Data

StudentNumber	LastName	FirstName	DormName
100	Smith	Terry	Stephens
200	Johnson	Jeff	Alexander
300	Abernathy	Susan	Horan
400	Smith	Susan	Alexander
500	Wilcox	John	Stephens
600	Webber	Carl	Horan
700	Simon	Carol	Stephens

DormName	DormCost
Alexander	3,800.00
Horan	4,000.00
Stephens	3,500.00

FIGURE 21

Sample EMPLOYEE Relation and Data

EmployeeNumber	LastName	Department	Email	DeptPhone
100	Johnson	Accounting	JJ@somewhere.com	834-1100
200	Abernathy	Finance	MA@somewhere.com	834-2100
300	Smathers	Finance	LS@somewhere.com	834-2100
400	Caruthers	Accounting	TC@somewhere.com	834-1100
500	Jackson	Production	TJ@somewhere.com	834-4100
600	Caldera	Legal	EC@somewhere.com	834-3100
700	Bandalone	Legal	RB@somewhere.com	834-3100

FIGURE 22

EmployeeNumber	LastName	Department	Email
100	Johnson	Accounting	JJ@somewhere.com
200	Abernathy	Finance	MA@somewhere.com
300	Smathers	Finance	LS@somewhere.com
400	Caruthers	Accounting	TC@somewhere.com
500	Jackson	Production	TJ@somewhere.com
600	Caldera	Legal	EC@somewhere.com
700	Bandalone	Legal	RB@somewhere.com

Department	DeptPhone
Accounting	834-1100
Finance	834-2100
Legal	834-3100
Production	834-4100

FIGURE 23

Attorney	ClientNumber	ClientName	MeetingDate	Duration
Boxer	1000	ABC, Inc	11/5/2013	2.00
Boxer	2000	XYZ Partners	11/5/2013	5.50
James	1000	ABC, Inc	11/7/2013	3.00
Boxer	1000	ABC, Inc	11/9/2013	4.00
Wu	3000	Malcomb Zoe	11/11/2013	7.00

Normalization Example 3 Now consider the MEETING table in Figure 23. We begin by looking for candidate keys. No column by itself can be a candidate key. Attorney determines different sets of data, so it cannot be a determinant. The same is true for ClientNumber, ClientName, and MeetingDate. In the sample data, the only column that does not determine different sets of data is Duration, but this uniqueness is accidental. It is easy to imagine that two or more meetings would have the same duration.

The next step is to look for combinations of columns that can be candidate keys. (Attorney, ClientNumber) is one combination, but the values (Boxer, 1000) determine two different sets of data. They cannot be a candidate key. The combination (Attorney, ClientName) fails for the same reason. The only combinations that can be candidate keys of this relation are (Attorney, ClientNumber, MeetingDate) and (Attorney, ClientName, MeetingDate).

Let us consider those possibilities further. The name of the relation is MEETING, and we are asking whether (Attorney, ClientNumber, MeetingDate) or (Attorney, ClientName, MeetingDate) can be a candidate key. Do these combinations make sense as identifiers of a meeting? They do unless more than one meeting of the same attorney and client occurs on the same day. In that case, we need to add a new column, MeetingTime, to the relation and make this new column part of the candidate key. In this example, we assume that this is not the case and that (Attorney, ClientNumber, MeetingDate) and (Attorney, ClientName, MeetingDate) are the candidate keys.

The second step is to identify other functional dependencies. Here, two exist:

ClientNumber → ClientName

and:

ClientName → ClientNumber

Each of these determinants is part of one of the candidate keys. For example, ClientNumber is part of (Attorney, ClientNumber, MeetingDate). However, being part of a candidate key is not enough. The determinant must be the same as the entire candidate key. Thus, the MEETING table is not well formed and has normalization problems.

When you are not certain whether normalization problems exist, consider the three modification operations: insert, update, and delete. Do problems exist with any of them? For example, in Figure 23 if you change ClientName in the first row to ABC, Limited, do inconsistencies arise in the data? The answer is yes, because

ClientNumber 1000 would have two different names in the table. This is sure sign that the table has normalization problems.

To fix the normalization problems, we create a new table, CLIENT, with columns ClientNumber and ClientName. Both of these columns are determinants; thus, either can be the primary key of the new table. However, whichever one is selected as the primary key also should be made the foreign key in MEETING. Thus, two correct designs are possible. First, we can use:

MEETING (<u>Attorney</u>, *ClientNumber*, <u>MeetingDate</u>, Duration)
CLIENT (<u>ClientNumber</u>, ClientName)

with the referential integrity constraint:

ClientNumber in MEETING must exist in ClientNumber in CLIENT

Second, we can use:

MEETING (<u>Attorney</u>, *ClientName*, <u>MeetingDate</u>, Duration)
CLIENT (ClientNumber, <u>ClientName</u>)

with the referential integrity constraint:

ClientName in MEETING must exist in ClientName in CLIENT

Data for the first design are shown in Figure 24.

Notice in these two designs that either the attribute ClientNumber or ClientName is both a foreign key and also part of the primary key of MEETING. This illustrates that foreign keys can be part of a composite primary key.

Note that when two attributes, such as ClientNumber and ClientName, each determine one another they are **synonyms.** They both must appear in a relation to establish their equivalent values. Given that equivalency, the two columns are interchangeable; one can take the place of the other in any other relation. All things being equal, however, the administration of the database will be simpler if one of the two is used consistently as a foreign key. This policy is just a convenience, however, and not a logical requirement for the design.

Normalization Example 4

For our last example, let us consider a relation that involves student data. Specifically:

GRADE (ClassName, Section, Term, Grade, StudentNumber, StudentName, Professor, Department, ProfessorEmail)

Given the confused set of columns in this table, it does not seem well formed, and it appears that the table will have normalization problems. We can use the normalization process to find what they are and to remove them.

FIGURE 24

Normalized MEETING and CLIENT Relations and Data

Attorney	ClientNumber	MeetingDate	Duration
Boxer	1000	11/5/2013	2.00
Boxer	2000	11/5/2013	5.50
James	1000	11/7/2013	3.00
Boxer	1000	11/9/2013	4.00
Wu	3000	11/11/2013	7.00

ClientNumber	ClientName
1000	ABC, Inc
2000	XYZ Partners
3000	Malcomb Zoe

First, what are the candidate keys of this relation? No column by itself is a candidate key. One way to approach this is to realize that a grade is a combination of a class and a student. In this table, which columns identify classes and students? A particular class is identified by (ClassName, Section, Term), and a student is identified by StudentNumber. Possibly, then, a candidate key for this relation is:

(ClassName, Section, Term, StudentNumber)

This statement is equivalent to saying:

(ClassName, Section, Term, StudentNumber) → (Grade, StudentName, Professor, Department, ProfessorEmail)

This is a true statement as long as only one professor teaches a class section. For now, we will make that assumption and consider the alternate case later. If only one professor teaches a section, then (ClassName, Section, Term, StudentNumber) is the one and only candidate key.

Second, what are the additional functional dependencies? One involves student data, and another involves professor data, specifically:

StudentNumber → StudentName

and:

Professor → ProfessorEmail

We also need to ask if Professor determines Department. It will if a professor teaches in only one department. In that case, we have:

Professor → (Department, ProfessorEmail)

Otherwise, Department must remain in the GRADE relation.

We will assume that professors teach in just one department, so we can confirm the following functional dependencies from our discussion above:

StudentNumber → StudentName

and:

Professor → (Department, ProfessorEmail)

If we examine the GRADE relation a bit further, however, we can find one other functional dependency. If only one professor teaches a class section, then:

(ClassName, Section, Term) → Professor

Thus, according to step 3 of the normalization process, GRADE has normalization problems because the determinants StudentNumber, Professor, and (ClassName, Section, Term) are not candidate keys. Therefore, we form a table for each of these functional dependencies. As a result, we have a STUDENT table, a PROFESSOR table, and a CLASS_PROFESSOR table. After forming these tables, we then take the appropriate columns out of GRADE and put them into a new version of the GRADE table, which we will name GRADE_1. We now have the following design:

STUDENT (StudentNumber, StudentName)
PROFESSOR (Professor, Department, ProfessorEmail)
CLASS_PROFESSOR (ClassName, Section, Term, *Professor*)
GRADE_1(*ClassName, Section, Term*, Grade, *StudentNumber*)

with the referential integrity constraints:

StudentNumber in GRADE_1 must exist in StudentNumber in STUDENT
Professor in CLASS_PROFESSOR must exist in Professor in PROFESSOR
(ClassName, Section, Term) in GRADE_1 must exist in (ClassName, Section, Term) in CLASS_PROFESSOR

Next, consider what happens if more than one professor teaches a section of a class. In that case, the only change is to make Professor part of the primary key of CLASS_PROFESSOR. Thus, the new relation is:

CLASS_PROFESSOR_1 (ClassName, Section, Term, *Professor*)

Class sections that have more than one professor will have multiple rows in this table—one row for each of the professors.

This example shows how normalization problems can become more complicated than simple examples might indicate. For large commercial applications that potentially involve hundreds of tables, such problems can sometimes consume days or weeks of design time.

BTW

In the interest of full disclosure, if professors can teach more than one class, then GRADE has what is called a **multivalued dependency.** If you want to learn about dependencies, see one of the more advanced texts mentioned in this chapter and also see exercises 40 and 41.

THE ACCESS WORKBENCH

Working with Multiple Tables in Microsoft Access

In this section, we will:

- See examples of the modification problems discussed in this chapter.
- Work with multiple tables.

Figure AW-1 shows the contacts that have been made with each customer. Note that there is no CustomerID 2—this is because we deleted and reentered the data for Jessica Christman.

Possible Modification Problems in the WMCRM Database

We know from the topics covered in this chapter that we really need a separate table to store the CONTACT data, but in order to illustrate the modification problems

FIGURE AW-1

CONTACT Data

CustomerID	Date	Type	Remarks
1	7/7/2012	Phone	General interest in a Gaea.
1	7/7/2012	Email	Sent general information.
1	7/12/2012	Phone	Set up an appointment.
1	7/14/2012	Meeting	Bought a HiStandard.
3	7/19/2012	Phone	Interested in a SUHi, set up an appointment.
1	7/21/2012	Email	Sent a standard follow-up message.
4	7/27/2012	Phone	Interested in a HiStandard, set up an appointment.
3	7/27/2012	Meeting	Bought a SUHi.
4	8/2/2012	Meeting	Talked up to a HiLuxury. Customer bought one.
3	8/3/2012	Email	Sent a standard follow-up message.
4	8/10/2012	Email	Sent a standard follow-up message.
5	8/15/2012	Phone	General interest in a Gaea.

let us combine it into one table with the data already in CUSTOMER. This table is available in the file WMCRM-Combined-Data.accdb. We will use this database to see modification problems in non-normalized tables and then build the correctly normalized tables in the actual WMCRM database.

We will need to start Microsoft Access 2010, open the WMCRM-Combined-Data .accdb file, and take a look at the WMCRM-Combined-Data database.

Opening an Existing Microsoft Access Database

1. Select **Start | All Programs | Microsoft Office | Microsoft Access 2010**. The Microsoft Access 2010 window appears with the Backstage view displayed, as shown in Figure AW-2.
   - ■ **NOTE:** The menu command or icon location used to start Microsoft Access 2010 may vary, depending on the operating system and how Microsoft Office is installed on the computer you are using.
2. Click the **Open** button to display the Open dialog box, as shown in Figure AW-3.
3. Browse to the **WMCRM-Combined-Data.accdb** file, click the file name to highlight it, and then click the **Open** button.
4. The **Security Warning** bar appears with the database. Click the Security Warning bar's **Enable Content** button to select this option.
5. In the Navigation Pane, double-click the **CUSTOMER_CONTACT** table object to open it.
6. Click the **Shutter Bar Open/Close** button to minimize the Navigation Pane.
7. The CUSTOMER_CONTACT table appears in Datasheet view, as shown in Figure AW-4. Note that there is one line for each contact, which has resulted in the duplication of basic customer data. For example, there are five sets of basic data for Ben Griffey.
8. Close the CUSTOMER_CONTACT table by clicking the document window's **Close** button.
9. Click the **Shutter Bar Open/Close** button to expand the Navigation Pane.

(Continued)

FIGURE AW-2

The Microsoft Access 2010 File Menu

Click the Backstage view **Open** button

FIGURE AW-3

The Open Dialog Box

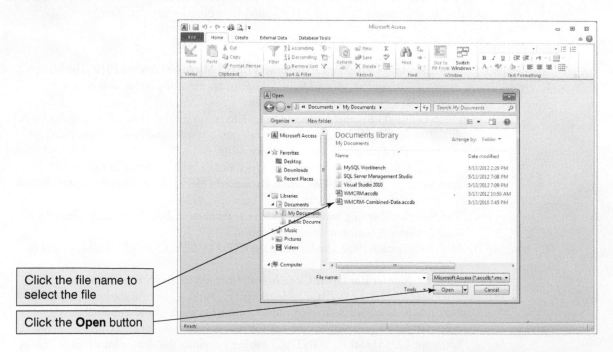

Click the file name to select the file

Click the **Open** button

10. In the Navigation Pane, double-click the **Customer Contact Data Input Form** object to open it. The Customer Contact Data Input Form appears, as shown in Figure AW-5. Note that the form displays all the data for one record in the CUSTOMER_CONTACT table.

11. Close the Customer Contact Data Input Form by clicking the document window's **Close** button.

FIGURE AW-4

The CUSTOMER_CONTACT Table

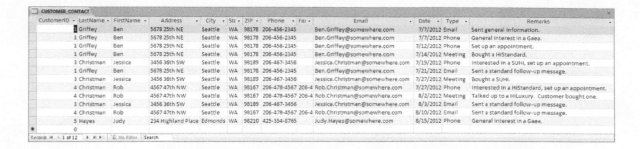

12. In the Navigation Pane, double-click the **Wallingford Motors Customer Contact Report** to open it.
13. Click the **Shutter Bar Open/Close** button to minimize the Navigation Pane.
14. The Wallingford Motors Customer Contact Report appears, as shown in Figure AW-6. Note that the form displays the data for all contacts in the CUSTOMER_CONTACT table, sorted by CustomerNumber and Date. For example, all the contact data for Ben Griffey (who has a CustomerID of 1) is grouped at the beginning of the report.
15. Close the Wallingford Motors Customer Contact Report by clicking the document window's **Close** button.
16. Click the **Shutter Bar Open/Close** button to expand the Navigation Pane.

Now, assume that Ben Griffey has changed his email address from Ben.Griffey@somewhere.com to Ben.Griffey@elsewhere.com. In a well-formed relation, we would have to make this change only once, but a quick examination of Figures AW-4 through AW-6 shows that Ben Griffey's email address appears in multiple records.

FIGURE AW-5

The Customer Contact Data Input Form

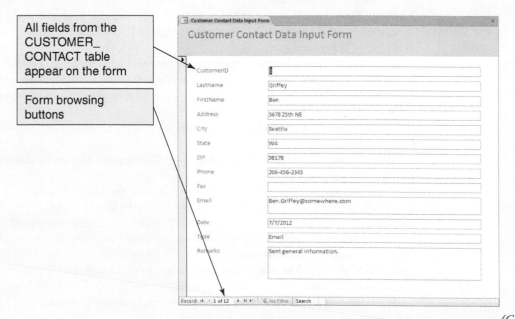

(Continued)

FIGURE AW-6

The Wallingford Motors Customer Contact Report

Contact data for each customer are grouped together and sorted by date

We therefore have to change it in every record to avoid update problems. Unfortunately, it is easy to miss one or more records, especially in large tables.

Updating Ben Griffey's Email Address

1. In the Navigation Pane, double-click the *Customer Contact Data Input Form* object to open it. Because Ben Griffey is the customer in the first record, his data is already in the form.
2. Edit the **Email** address to read *Ben.Griffey@elsewhere.com*, as shown in Figure AW-7.
3. Click the **Next Record** button to move to the next record in the table. Again, the record shows Ben Griffey's data, so again edit the **Email** address to read *Ben.Griffey@ elsewhere.com*.
4. Click the **Next Record** button to move to the next record in the table. For the third time, the record shows Ben Griffey's data, so again edit the **Email** address to read *Ben.Griffey@elsewhere.com*.
5. Click the **Next Record** button to move to the next record in the table. For the fourth time, the record shows Ben Griffey's data, so again edit the **Email** address to read *Ben.Griffey@elsewhere.com*.
6. Click the **Next Record** button to move to the next record in the table. Finally, another customer's data (the data for Jessica Christman's contact on 7/19/2012) appears in the form, so we assume that we have made all the necessary updates to the database records.
7. Close the Customer Contact Data Input form by clicking the document window's **Close** button.
8. In the Navigation Pane, double-click the report **Wallingford Motors Customer Contact Report** to open it.
9. Click the **Shutter Bar Open/Close** button to minimize the Navigation Pane.
10. The Wallingford Motors Customer Contact Report now looks as shown in Figure AW-8. Note that the email addresses shown for Ben Griffey are inconsistent—we missed one record when we updated the table, and now we have inconsistent data. A modification error—in this case an update error—has occurred.
11. Close the Wallingford Motors Customer Contact Report by clicking the document window's **Close** button.
12. Click the **Shutter Bar Open/Close** button to expand the Navigation Pane.

The Customer Contact Data Input Form with the Updated Email Address

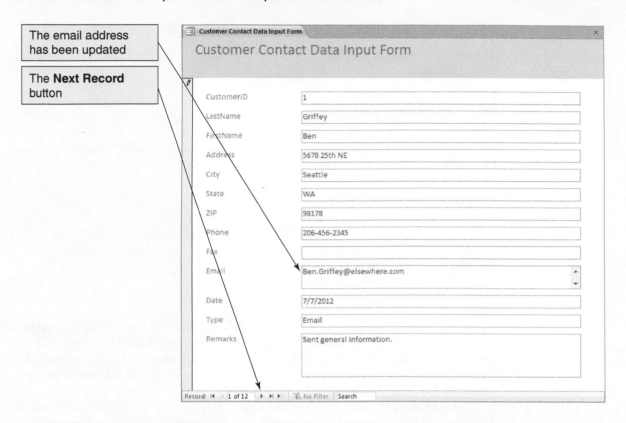

This simple example shows how easily modification problems can occur in tables that are not normalized. With a set of well-formed, normalized tables, this problem would not have occurred.

The Updated Wallingford Motors Customer Contact Report

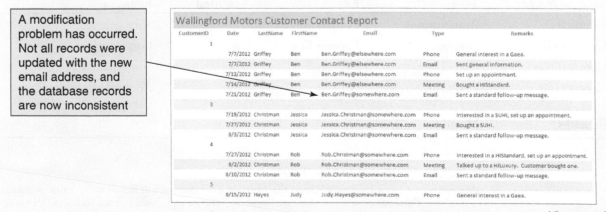

(Continued)

Closing the WMCRM-Combined-Data Database

1. Click the **Close** button to close the database and exit Microsoft Access.

Working with Multiple Tables

The table structure for the CUSTOMER_CONTACT table in the WMCRM-Combined-Data database is:

CUSTOMER_CONTACT (<u>CustomerID</u>, LastName, FirstName, Address, City, State, ZIP, Phone, Fax, Email, <u>Date</u>, <u>Type</u>, <u>Remarks</u>)

Applying the normalization process discussed in this chapter, we will have the following set of tables:

CUSTOMER (<u>CustomerID</u>, LastName, FirstName, Address, City, State, ZIP, Phone, Fax, Email)

CONTACT (<u>ContactID</u>, *CustomerID*, ContactDate, ContactType, Remarks)

with the referential integrity constraint:

CustomerID in CONTACT must exist in CustomerID in CUSTOMER

Note that we have modified a couple of the column names in the CONTACT table—we are using ContactDate instead of Date and ContactType instead of Type. We will discuss the reason for this later in this section. Our task now is to build and populate the CONTACT table and then to establish the relationship and referential integrity constraint between the two tables.

First, we need to create and populate (insert data into) the CONTACT table, which will contain the columns and column characteristics shown in the table in Figure AW-9.[6] The CustomerID column appears again in CONTACT, this time designated as a foreign key. As discussed in this chapter, the term **foreign key** designates this column as the link to the CUSTOMER table. The value in the CustomerID column of CONTACT tells which customer was contacted. All we have to do is look up the value of CustomerID in the CUSTOMER table.

FIGURE AW-9

Database Column Characteristics for the CONTACT Table

Column Name	Type	Key	Required	Remarks
ContactID	AutoNumber	Primary Key	Yes	Surrogate Key
CustomerID	Number	Foreign Key	Yes	Long Integer
ContactDate	Date/Time	No	Yes	Short Date
ContactType	Text (10)	No	Yes	Allowed values are Phone, Fax, Email, and Meeting
Remarks	Memo	No	No	

---

[6]Although we are using it for simplicity in this example, a column, such as Remarks, can cause problems in a database. For a complete discussion, see David M. Kroenke and David J. Auer, *Database Processing: Fundamentals, Design, and Implementation*, 12th edition (Upper Saddle River, NJ: Prentice Hall, 2012).

Note that when we build the CONTACT table there is no "foreign key" setting. We will set up the database relationship between CUSTOMER and CONTACT after we have finished building the CONTACT table.

Note the following:

- Some new data types are being used: Number, Date/Time, and Memo.
- CustomerID must be set as a Number data type and specifically as a Long Integer data type to match the data type Microsoft Access creates for the AutoNumber data type in the CUSTOMER table.
- The Type column has only four allowed values: Phone, Fax, Email, and Meeting. For now, we can simply input only these data values.

Creating the CONTACT Table

1. Select **Start | All Programs | Microsoft Office | Microsoft Access 2010**. The Microsoft Access 2010 window appears.
2. In the quick access list of database files, click **WMCRM.accdb**. The database file opens in Microsoft Access.
3. Click the **Create** command tab.
4. Click the **Table Design** button.
5. The Table1 tabbed document window is displayed in Design view. Note that along with the Table1 window a contextual tab named Table Tools is displayed and that this tab adds a new command tab and ribbon, named Design, to the set of command tabs displayed.
6. Using the steps to create the CUSTOMER table begin to create the CONTACT table. The following steps detail only new information that you need to know to complete the CONTACT table.
   - ■ **NOTE:** When creating the CONTACT table, be sure to enter appropriate comments in the Description column.
7. When creating the CustomerID column, set the data type to **Number**. Note that the default Field Size setting for Number is Long Integer, so no change is necessary. Be sure to set the Required property to **Yes**.
8. After creating the ContactID column, set it as the primary key of the table.
9. When creating the ContactDate column, start by using the column name **Date**. As soon as you enter the column name and try to move to the Data Type column, Microsoft Access displays a dialog box, warning you that Date is a reserved word, as shown in Figure AW-10. Click the **Cancel** button, and change the column name to **ContactDate**.
   - ■ **NOTE:** Normally, you should avoid reserved words such as Date and Time. Generally, column names such as ContactDate are preferred, both to avoid reserved words and to clarify exactly which date you are referring to, and that is why we changed the column names in the CONTACT table.
10. When creating the ContactDate column, set the data type to **Date/Time** and set the format to **Short Date**, as shown in Figure AW-11. Be sure to set the Required property to **Yes**.
11. To name and save the CONTACT table, click the **Save** button in the Quick Access Toolbar.
12. Type the table name **CONTACT** into the Save As dialog box text box, and then click the **OK** button. The table is named and saved, and it now appears with the table name CONTACT.
13. To close the CONTACT table, click the **Close** button in the upper-right corner of the tabbed document window. The CONTACT table now appears as a table object in the Navigation Pane.

(Continued)

The Reserved Word Warning

The column name Date is a reserved word—do **not** use reserved words as column names

Click the **Cancel** button and revise the column name

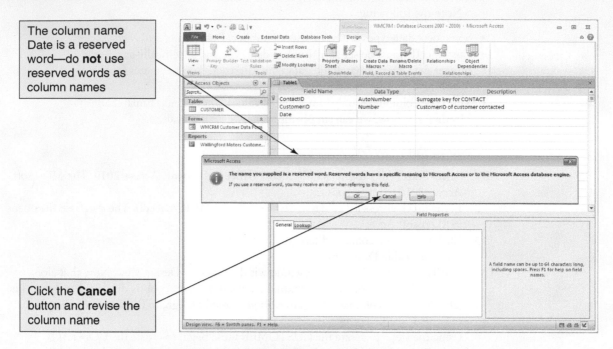

Creating Relationships Between Tables

In Microsoft Access, you build relationships between tables by using the **Relationships window,** which you access by using the **Database Tools | Relationships** command. After a relationship is created in the Relationships window, referential integrity constraints are set in the **Edit Relationships dialog box** within that window by using the **Enforce Referential Integrity check box.**

Setting the Date Format

Select the **Short Date** date format from the drop-down list

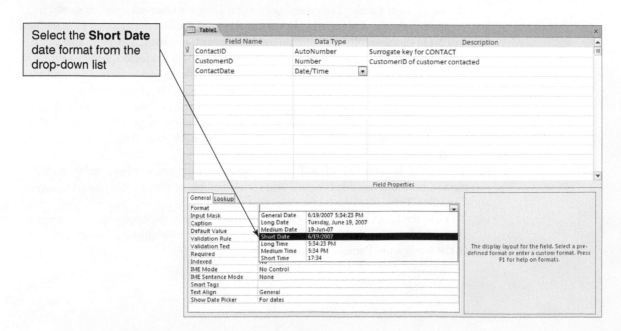

FIGURE AW-12

The Database Tools Command Tab

The **Database Tools** command tab

The **Relationships** button

The **Relationships** command group

Creating the Relationship Between the CUSTOMER and CONTACT Tables

1. Click the **Database Tools** command tab to display the Database Tools command groups, as shown in Figure AW-12.
2. Click the **Relationships** button in the Show/Hide group. As shown in Figure AW-13, the Relationships tabbed document window appears, together with the Show Table dialog box. Note that along with the Relationships window, a contextual tab named Relationship Tools is displayed and that this tab adds a new command tab named Design to the set of command tabs displayed.
3. In the Show Table dialog box, the CONTACT table is already selected. Click the **Add** button to add CONTACT to the Relationships window.
4. In the Show Table dialog box, click the **CUSTOMER** table to select it. Click the **Add** button to add CUSTOMER to the Relationships window.

FIGURE AW-13

The Relationships Window

The **Relationship Tools** contextual command tab

The **Design** command tab

The **Relationships** tabbed document window

The **Show Table** dialog box

Select a table name, then click the **Add** button to add the table to the Relationships window

(Continued)

FIGURE AW-14

The Table Objects in the Relationships Window

The table objects have been enlarged and rearranged into the arrangement shown here

Click, drag, and drop the **CUSTOMER CustomerID field** onto the **CONTACT CustomerID field**

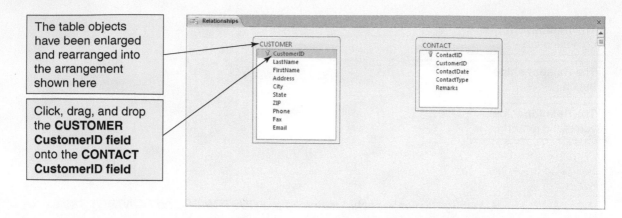

5. In the Show Table dialog box, click the **Close** button to close the dialog box.
6. Rearrange and resize the table objects in the Relationships window using standard Windows drag-and-drop techniques. Rearrange the CUSTOMER and CONTACT table objects until they appear as shown in Figure AW-14. Now we are ready to create the relationship between the tables.
   - **NOTE:** A formal description of how to create a relationship between two tables is "In the Relationships window, drag a primary key column and drop it on top of the corresponding foreign key column." It is easier to understand this after you have actually done it.
7. Click and hold the column name **CustomerID in the CUSTOMER table** and then drag it over the **column name CustomerID in the CONTACT table**. Release the mouse button, and the Edit Relationships dialog box appears, as shown in Figure AW-15.

FIGURE AW-15

The Edit Relationships Dialog Box

The **Edit Relationships** dialog box

Click the **Enforce Referential Integrity** check box and then click the **Create** button to create the relationship

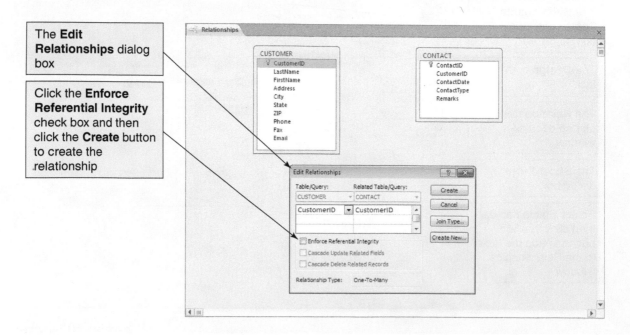

FIGURE AW-16

The Completed Relationship

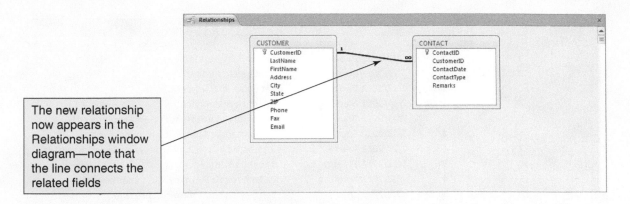

The new relationship now appears in the Relationships window diagram—note that the line connects the related fields

■ **NOTE:** In CUSTOMER, CustomerID is the primary key, and in CONTACT CustomerID is the foreign key.

8. Click the **Enforce Referential Integrity** check box.
9. Click the **Create** button to create the relationship between CUSTOMER and CONTACT. The relationship between the tables now appears in the Relationships window, as shown in Figure AW-16.
10. To close the Relationships window, click the **Close** button in the upper-right corner of the document window. A Microsoft Access warning dialog box appears, asking whether you want to save changes to the layout of relationships. Click the **Yes** button to save the changes and close the window.

At this point, we need to add data on customer contacts to the CONTACT table. Using the CONTACT table in Datasheet view, as discussed earlier, we enter the data shown in Figure AW-1 into the CONTACT table. Again, note that there is *no* customer with CustomerID of 2. Also note that because referential integrity is enabled, we *cannot* enter a CustomerID that does not already exist in the CUSTOMER table. The CONTACT table with the data inserted looks as shown in Figure AW-17. Be sure to close the table after the data have been entered.

Using a Form That Includes Two Tables

Now we will create a Microsoft Access form that will let us work with the combined data from both the CUSTOMER and CONTACT tables.

Creating a Form for Both the CUSTOMER and CONTACT Tables

1. Click the **Create** command tab.
2. Click the **Form Wizard** button in the Forms command group. The Form Wizard appears.
3. Select the **CUSTOMER** table in the Tables/Queries drop-down list. To add all the columns, click the **right-facing double-chevron** button. Do **not** click the **Next** button yet.
4. Select the **CONTACT** table in the Tables/Queries drop-down list. Individually select and add the **ContactDate, ContactType**, and **Remarks** columns to the Selected Fields list by using the **right-facing single-chevron** button. Now click the **Next** button.

(Continued)

Data in the CONTACT Table

ContactID	CustomerID	ContactDate	ContactType	Remarks
1	1	7/7/2012	Phone	General interest in a Gaea.
2	1	7/7/2012	Email	Sent general information.
3	1	7/12/2012	Phone	Set up an appointment.
4	1	7/14/2012	Meeting	Bought a HiStandard.
5	3	7/19/2012	Phone	Interested in a SUHi, set up an appointment.
6	1	7/21/2012	Email	Sent a standard follow-up message.
7	4	7/27/2012	Phone	Interested in a HiStandard, set up an appointment.
8	3	7/27/2012	Meeting	Bought a SUHi.
9	4	8/2/2012	Meeting	Talked up to a HiLuxury. Customer bought one.
10	3	8/3/2012	Email	Sent a standard follow-up message.
11	4	8/10/2012	Email	Sent a standard follow-up message.
12	5	8/15/2012	Phone	General interest in a Gaea.

Record: 13 of 13   No Filter   Search

- **NOTE:** You have just created a set of columns from two tables that you want to appear on one form.

5. When asked "How do you want to view your data?" use the default **by CUSTOMER** selection because we want to see all contacts for each customer. Also use the selected **Forms with subforms** option to treat the CONTACT data as a subform within the CUSTOMER form. Click the **Next** button.

6. When asked "What layout would you like for your subform?" click the **Next** button to use the default Datasheet layout.

7. When asked "What titles do you want for your form?" type the form title **WMCRM Customer Contacts Form** into the Form: text box and the form title **Contact Data** into the Subform: text box. Click the **Finish** button. The completed form appears.

8. Click the **Shutter Bar Open/Close** button to minimize the Navigation Pane. The completed form is displayed as shown in Figure AW-18.

9. Click the **Shutter Bar Open/Close button** to expand the Navigation Pane.

10. Close the form window.

Creating a Report That Includes Data from Two Tables

In this section, we will create a report that includes data from two or more tables. This Microsoft Access report will let us use the combined data from both the CUSTOMER and CONTACT tables.

Creating a Report for Both the CUSTOMER and CONTACT Tables

1. Click the **Create** tab.

2. Click the **Report Wizard** button to display the Report Wizard.

3. Select the **CUSTOMER** table in the Tables/Queries drop-down list. One by one, click **LastName**, **FirstName**, **Phone**, **Fax**, and **Email** to select each one, and then click the **right-facing single-chevron** button to add each column to the Selected Fields list. Do **not** click the Next button yet.

4. Select the **CONTACT** table in the Tables/Queries drop-down list. Individually select and add the **ContactDate**, **ContactType**, and **Remarks** columns to the Selected Fields list by clicking the **right-facing single-chevron** button. Now click the **Next** button.

The Completed Form for CUSTOMER and CONTACT Data

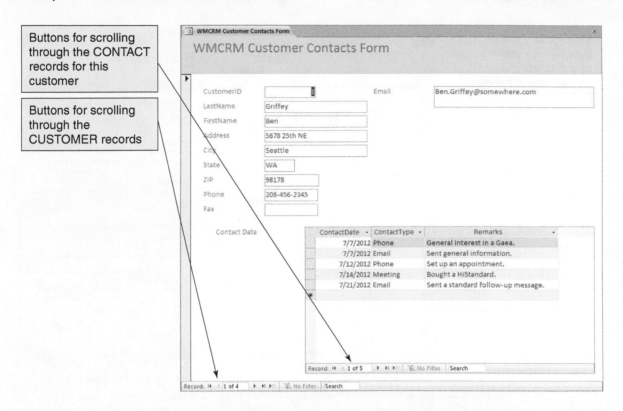

Buttons for scrolling through the CONTACT records for this customer

Buttons for scrolling through the CUSTOMER records

5. When asked "How do you want to view your data?" click the **Next** button to use the default **by CUSTOMER** selection (in order to see all contacts for each customer).

6. When asked "Do you want to add any grouping levels?" click the **Next** button to use the default nongrouped column listing.

7. We are now asked "What sort order do you want for detail records?" This is the sort order for the CONTACT information. The most useful sorting order is by date, in ascending order. Click the **sort field 1** drop-down list arrow and select **ContactDate**. Leave the sort order button set to **Ascending**. Click the **Next** button.

8. We are now asked "How would you like to lay out your report?" We will use the default setting of stepped layout, but click the **Landscape orientation** radio button to change the report orientation to landscape. Then click the **Next** button.

9. When asked "What title do you want for your report?" edit the report title to read **Wallingford Motors Customer Contacts Report**. Leave the **Preview the report** radio button selected. Click the **Finish** button. The completed report is displayed in Print Preview mode.

10. Click the **Close Print Preview** button to close Print Preview.

11. Click the **Home** command tab.

12. Click the **Shutter Bar Open/Close** button to minimize the Navigation Pane. The completed report is displayed as shown in Figure AW-19.

13. Although this may not be the best layout for the report, the Microsoft Access Form Wizard has created a useable report with all columns correctly sized to display the information (if there are any columns that are not correctly displayed use the Layout view in the view gallery to make minor adjustments—this tool can be used to make

(Continued)

FIGURE AW-19

The Wallingford Motors Customer Contact Report

View gallery arrow button—use this button to access Design view if needed

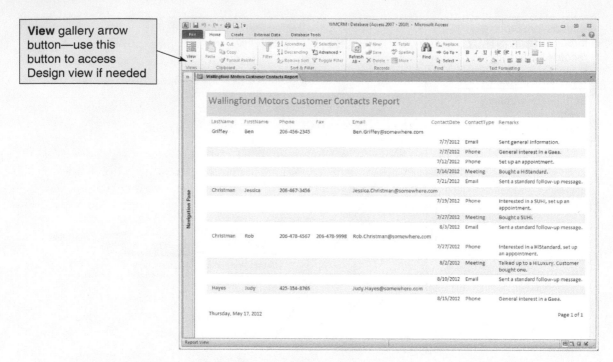

basic adjustments by simply clicking the report section you want to change).

14. Click the **Shutter Bar Open/Close** button to expand the Navigation Pane.
15. Click the document window's **Close** button to close the report window.

Closing the Database and Exiting Microsoft Access

We have finished the work we need to do in this chapter's "The Access Workbench." As usual, we finish by closing the database and Microsoft Access.

Closing the WMCRM Database and Exiting Microsoft Access

1. To close the WMCRM database and exit Microsoft Access 2010, click the **Close** button in the upper-right corner of the Microsoft Access 2010 window.

SUMMARY

The relational model is the most important standard in database processing today. It was first published by E. F. Codd in 1970. Today, it is used for the design and implementation of almost every commercial database.

An entity is something of importance to a user that needs to be represented in a database. A relation is a two-dimensional table that has the characteristics listed in Figure 1. In the database world in general, the term *table* is used synonymously with the term *relation*. Three sets of terminology are used for relational structures. The terms *table, row*, and *column* are used most commonly, but *file, record*, and *field* are sometimes used in traditional data processing. Theorists also use the terms *relation, tuple*, and *attribute* for the same three constructs. Sometimes these terms are mixed and matched. Strictly speaking, a relation may not have duplicate rows; however, sometimes this condition is relaxed because eliminating duplicates can be a time-consuming process.

A key is one or more columns of a relation that is used to identify a row. A unique key identifies a single row; a nonunique key identifies several rows. A composite key is a key that has two or more attributes. A relation has one primary key, which must be a unique key. A relation may also have additional unique keys, called candidate keys. A primary key is used to represent the table in relationships, and many DBMS products use values of the primary key to organize table storage. In addition, an index normally is constructed to provide fast access via primary key values. An ideal primary key is short, numeric, and never changes.

A surrogate key is a unique numeric value that is appended to a relation to serve as the primary key. Surrogate key values have no meaning to the user and are normally hidden on forms, query results, and reports.

A foreign key is an attribute that is placed in a relation to represent a relationship. A foreign key is the primary key of a table that is different from (foreign to) the table in which it is placed. Primary and foreign keys may have different names, but they must use the same data types and sets of values. A referential integrity constraint specifies that the values of a foreign key be present in the primary key.

A null value occurs when no value has been given to an attribute. The problem with a null value is that its meaning is ambiguous. It can mean that no value is appropriate, that a value is appropriate but has not yet been chosen, or that a value is appropriate and has been chosen but is unknown to the user. It is possible to eliminate null values by requiring attribute values.

A functional dependency occurs when the value of one attribute (or set of attributes) determines the value of a second attribute (or set of attributes). The attribute on the left side of a functional dependency is called the determinant. One way to view the purpose of a relation is to say that the relation exists to store instances of functional dependencies. Another way to define a primary (and candidate) key is to say that such a key is an attribute that functionally determines all the other attributes in a relation.

Normalization is the process of evaluating a relation and, when necessary, breaking the relation into two or more relations that are better designed and said to be well formed. According to normalization theory, a relation is poorly structured if it has a functional dependency that does not involve the primary key. Specifically, in a well-formed relation, every determinant is a candidate key.

A process for normalizing relations is shown in this chapter. According to this process, relations that have normalization problems are divided into two or more relations that do not have such problems. Foreign keys are established between the old and new relations, and referential integrity constraints are created.

KEY TERMS

attribute	foreign key	primary key
AUTO_INCREMENT	functional dependency	record
Boyce-Codd Normal Form	functionally dependent	referential integrity
(BCNF)	identity	constraint
candidate key	identity increment	relation
column	identity seed	row
composite key	is identity	SEQUENCE
database schema	key	surrogate key
determinant	multivalued dependency	synonyms
entity	nonunique key	table
field	normalization	tuple
file	normalization process	unique key
first normal form (1NF)	null value	well-formed relation

REVIEW QUESTIONS

1   Why is the relational model important?

2   Define the term *entity* and give an example of an entity (other than the one from this chapter).

3   List the characteristics a table must have to be considered a relation.

4   Give an example of a relation (other than one from this chapter).

5   Give an example of a table that is not a relation (other than one from this chapter).

6   Under what circumstances can an attribute of a relation be of variable length?

7   Explain the use of the terms *file, record,* and *field.*

8   Explain the use of the terms *relation, tuple,* and *attribute.*

9   Under what circumstances can a relation have duplicate rows?

10   Define the term *unique key* and give an example.

11   Define the term *nonunique key* and give an example.

12   Give an example of a relation with a unique composite key.

13   Explain the difference between a primary key and a candidate key.

14   Describe four uses of a primary key.

15   What is a *surrogate key*, and under what circumstances would you use one?

16   How do surrogate keys obtain their values?

17   Why are the values of surrogate keys normally hidden from users on forms, queries, and reports?

18   Explain the term *foreign key* and give an example.

19   Explain how primary keys and foreign keys are denoted.

20   Define the term *referential integrity constraint* and give an example of one.

21   Explain three possible interpretations of a null value.

22   Give an example of a null value (other than one from this chapter) and explain each of the three possible interpretations for that value.

23   Define the terms *functional dependency* and *determinant*, using an example.

24   In the following equation, name the functional dependency and identify the determinant(s):

$$Area = Length \times Width$$

25   Explain the meaning of the following expression:

$$A \rightarrow (B, C)$$

Given this expression, tell if it is also true that:

$$A \rightarrow B$$

and:

$$A \rightarrow C$$

26   Explain the meaning of the following expression:

$$(D, E) \rightarrow F$$

Given this expression, tell if it is also true that:

$$D \rightarrow F$$

and:

$$E \rightarrow F$$

27   Explain the differences in your answers to questions 25 and 26.

28 Define the term *primary key* in terms of functional dependencies.

29 If you assume that a relation has no duplicate data, how do you know there is always at least one primary key?

30 How does your answer to question 29 change if you allow a relation to have duplicate data?

31 In your own words, describe the nature and purpose of the normalization process.

32 This question was intentionally excluded from this edition.

33 This question was intentionally excluded from this edition.

34 This question was intentionally excluded from this edition.

35 This question was intentionally excluded from this edition.

36 This question was intentionally excluded from this edition.

37 This question was intentionally excluded from this edition.

EXERCISES

38 This exercise was intentionally excluded from this edition.

39 This exercise was intentionally excluded from this edition.

40 Consider the following relation:

STUDENT(StudentNumber, StudentName, SiblingName, Major)

Assume that the values of SiblingName are the names of all of a given student's brothers and sisters; also assume that students have at most one major.

A. Show an example of this relation for two students, one of whom has three siblings and the other of whom has only two siblings.

B. List the candidate keys in this relation.

C. State the functional dependencies in this relation.

D. Explain why this relation does not meet the relational design criteria set out in this chapter (that is, why this is not a well-formed relation).

E. Divide this relation into a set of relations that meet the relational design criteria (that is, that are well formed).

41   Alter question 40 to allow students to have multiple majors. In this case, the relational structure is:

STUDENT (<u>StudentNumber</u>, StudentName, <u>SiblingName</u>, <u>Major</u>)

A.   Show an example of this relation for two students, one of whom has three siblings and the other of whom has one sibling. Assume that each student has a single major.

B.   Show the data changes necessary to add a second major for only the first student.

C.   Based on your answer to part B, show the data changes necessary to add a second major for the second student.

D.   Explain the differences in your answers to parts B and C. Comment on the desirability of this situation.

E.   Divide this relation into a set of well-formed relations.

42   The text states that you can argue that "the only reason for having relations is to store instances of functional dependencies." Explain, in your own words, what this means.

ACCESS WORKBENCH KEY TERMS

Edit Relationships dialog box   Relationships window
Enforce Referential Integrity check box

ACCESS WORKBENCH EXERCISES

In this exercise, we will build the some of the tables needed for the database, create the referential integrity constraints between them, and populate them.

The full set of normalized tables for the WPC database is as follows:

DEPARTMENT (<u>DepartmentName</u>, BudgetCode, OfficeNumber, Phone)
EMPLOYEE (<u>EmployeeNumber</u>, FirstName, LastName, *Department*, Phone, Email)
PROJECT (<u>ProjectID</u>, ProjectName, *Department*, MaxHours, StartDate, EndDate)
ASSIGNMENT (<u>ProjectID</u>, *EmployeeNumber*, HoursWorked)

The primary key of DEPARTMENT is DepartmentName, the primary key of EMPLOYEE is EmployeeNumber, and the primary key of PROJECT is ProjectID. Note that the EMPLOYEE table is the same as the table we have created, except that Department is now a foreign key. In EMPLOYEE and PROJECT, Department is a foreign key that references DepartmentName in DEPARTMENT. Note that a foreign key does not need to have the same name as the primary key to which it refers. The primary key of ASSIGNMENT is the composite (ProjectID, EmployeeNumber). ProjectID is also a foreign key that references ProjectID in PROJECT, and EmployeeNumber is a foreign key that references EmployeeNumber in EMPLOYEE.

FIGURE 25

Column Characteristics for the DEPARTMENT Table

Column Name	Type	Key	Required	Remarks
DepartmentName	Text (35)	Primary Key	Yes	
BudgetCode	Text (30)	No	Yes	
OfficeNumber	Text (15)	No	Yes	
Phone	Text (12)	No	Yes	

The referential integrity constraints are:

Department in EMPLOYEE must exist in DepartmentName in DEPARTMENT
Department in PROJECT must exist in DepartmentName in DEPARTMENT
ProjectID in ASSIGNMENT must exist in ProjectID in PROJECT
EmployeeNumber in ASSIGNMENT must exist in EmployeeNumber in EMPLOYEE

A. Figure 25 shows the column characteristics for the WPC DEPARTMENT table. Using the column characteristics, create the DEPARTMENT table in the WPC.accdb database.

B. For the DEPARTMENT table, create a data input form named WPC Department Data Form. Make any necessary adjustments to the form so that all data display properly. Use this form to enter into your DEPARTMENT table the data in the DEPARTMENT table shown in Figure 26.

C. Create the relationship and referential integrity constraint between DEPARTMENT and EMPLOYEE. Enable enforcing of referential integrity and enable cascading of data updates, but do *not* enable cascading of deletions.

D. Figure 27 shows the column characteristics for the WPC PROJECT table. Using the column characteristics, create the PROJECT table in the WPC .accdb database.

FIGURE 26

WPC DEPARTMENT Data

DepartmentName	BudgetCode	OfficeNumber	Phone
Administration	BC-100-10	BLDG01-300	360-285-8100
Legal	BC-200-10	BLDG01-200	360-285-8200
Accounting	BC-300-10	BLDG01-100	360-285-8300
Finance	BC-400-10	BLDG01-140	360-285-8400
Human Resources	BC-500-10	BLDG01-180	360-285-8500
Production	BC-600-10	BLDG02-100	360-287-8600
Marketing	BC-700-10	BLDG02-200	360-287-8700
InfoSystems	BC-800-10	BLDG02-270	360-287-8800

(Continued)

FIGURE 27

Column Characteristics for the PROJECT Table

Column Name	Type	Key	Required	Remarks
ProjectID	Number	Primary Key	Yes	Long Integer
ProjectName	Text (50)	No	Yes	
Department	Text (35)	Foreign Key	Yes	
MaxHours	Number	No	Yes	Double, fixed, 2 decimal places
StartDate	Date/Time	No	No	Medium date
EndDate	Date/Time	No	No	Medium date

E. Create the relationship and referential integrity constraint between DEPARTMENT and PROJECT. Enable enforcing of referential integrity and enable cascading of data updates, but do *not* enable cascading of deletions.

F. For the PROJECT table, create a data input form named WPC Project Data Form. Make any necessary adjustments to the form so that all data display properly. Use this form to enter into your PROJECT table the data in the PROJECT table shown in Figure 28.

G. When creating and populating the DEPARTMENT table, the data were entered into the table before the referential integrity constraint with EMPLOYEE was created, but when creating and populating the PROJECT table the referential integrity constraint was created before the data were entered. Why did the order of the steps differ? Which order is normally the correct order to use?

H. Figure 29 shows the column characteristics for the WPC ASSIGNMENT table. Using the column characteristics, create the ASSIGNMENT table in the WPC. accdb database.

I. Create the relationship and referential integrity constraint between ASSIGNMENT and PROJECT and between ASSIGNMENT and EMPLOYEE. When creating both relations, enable enforcing of referential integrity, but do *not* enable cascading of data updates or cascading of data from deleted records.

J. For the ASSIGNMENT table, create a data input form named WPC Assignment Data Form. Make any necessary adjustments to the form so that all data display

FIGURE 28

WPC PROJECT Data

ProjectID	ProjectName	Department	MaxHours	StartDate	EndDate
1000	2012 Q3 Product Plan	Marketing	135.00	10-MAY-12	15-JUN-12
1100	2012 Q3 Portfolio Analysis	Finance	120.00	05-JUL-12	25-JUL-12
1200	2012 Q3 Tax Preparation	Accounting	145.00	10-AUG-12	15-OCT-12
1300	2012 Q4 Product Plan	Marketing	150.00	10-AUG-12	15-SEP-12
1400	2012 Q4 Portfolio Analysis	Finance	140.00	05-OCT-12	NULL

FIGURE 29

Column Characteristics for the ASSIGNMENT Table

Column Name	Type	Key	Required	Remarks
ProjectID	Number	Primary Key, Foreign Key	Yes	Long Integer
EmployeeNumber	Number	Primary Key, Foreign Key	Yes	Long Integer
HoursWorked	Number	No	No	Double, fixed, 1 decimal places

properly. Use this form to enter into your ASSIGNMENT table the data in the ASSIGNMENT table shown in Figure 30.

K. When creating the relationships between the database tables, we allowed the cascading of data changes between some tables but not between others. (*Cascading* means that changes to data in one table are also made to the other table in the relationship.) The value of a primary key changes in this case, and that change is then made in the values of the matching foreign key. Why did we enable cascading of related field values between (1) DEPARTMENT and EMPLOYEE and (2) DEPARTMENT and PROJECT but not for (3) EMPLOYEE and ASSIGNMENT and (4) PROJECT and ASSIGNMENT?

FIGURE 30

WPC ASSIGNMENT Data

ProjectID	EmployeeNumber	HoursWorked
1000	1	30.0
1000	8	75.0
1000	10	55.0
1100	4	40.0
1100	6	45.0
1200	1	25.0
1200	2	20.0
1200	4	45.0
1200	5	40.0
1300	1	35.0
1300	8	80.0
1300	10	50.0
1400	4	15.0
1400	5	10.0
1400	6	27.5

(Continued)

L. For both the DEPARTMENT and EMPLOYEE tables, create a data input form named WPC Department Employee Data Form. This form should show all the employees in each department.

M. Create a report named Wedgewood Pacific Corporation Department Employee Report that presents the data contained in your DEPARTMENT and EMPLOYEE tables. The report should group employees by department. Print out a copy of this report.

REGIONAL LABS CASE QUESTIONS

Regional Labs is a company that conducts research and development work on a contract basis for other companies and organizations. Figure 31 shows data that Regional Labs collects about projects and the employees assigned to them.

This data is stored in a relation (table) named PROJECT:

PROJECT (ProjectID, EmployeeName, EmployeeSalary)

A. Assuming that all functional dependencies are apparent in this data, which of the following are true?

1. ProjectID → EmployeeName
2. ProjectID → EmployeeSalary
3. (ProjectID, EmployeeName) → EmployeeSalary
4. EmployeeName → EmployeeSalary
5. EmployeeSalary → ProjectID
6. EmployeeSalary → (ProjectID, EmployeeName)

B. What is the primary key of PROJECT?

C. Are all the nonkey attributes (if any) dependent on the primary key?

D. In what normal form is PROJECT?

E. Describe two modification anomalies that affect PROJECT.

F. Is ProjectID a determinant? If so, based on which functional dependencies in part A?

G. Is EmployeeName a determinant? If so, based on which functional dependencies in part A?

FIGURE 31

Sample Data for Regional Labs

ProjectID	EmployeeName	EmployeeSalary
100-A	Eric Jones	64,000.00
100-A	Donna Smith	70,000.00
100-B	Donna Smith	70,000.00
200-A	Eric Jones	64,000.00
200-B	Eric Jones	64,000.00
200-C	Eric Parks	58,000.00
200-C	Donna Smith	70,000.00
200-D	Eric Parks	58,000.00

H. Is (ProjectID, EmployeeName) a determinant? If so, based on which functional dependencies in part A?

I. Is EmployeeSalary a determinant? If so, based on which functional dependencies in part A?

J. Does this relation contain a transitive dependency? If so, what is it?

K. Redesign the relation to eliminate modification anomalies.

GARDEN GLORY PROJECT QUESTIONS

Figure 32 shows data that Garden Glory collects about properties and services.

A. Using these data, state assumptions about functional dependencies among the columns of data. Justify your assumptions on the basis of these sample data and also on the basis of what you know about service businesses.

B. Given your assumptions in part A, comment on the appropriateness of the following designs:

1. PROPERTY (<u>PropertyName</u>, PropertyType, Street, City, Zip, ServiceDate, Description, Amount)

2. PROPERTY (PropertyName, PropertyType, Street, City, Zip, <u>ServiceDate</u>, Description, Amount)

3. PROPERTY (<u>PropertyName</u>, PropertyType, Street, City, Zip, <u>ServiceDate</u>, Description, Amount)

4. PROPERTY (<u>PropertyID</u>, PropertyName, PropertyType, Street, City, Zip, ServiceDate, Description, Amount)

5. PROPERTY (<u>PropertyID</u>, PropertyName, PropertyType, Street, City, Zip, <u>ServiceDate</u>, Description, Amount)

6. PROPERTY (<u>PropertyID</u>, PropertyName, PropertyType, Street, City, Zip, *ServiceDate*)

    and:

    SERVICE (<u>ServiceDate</u>, Description, Amount)

7. PROPERTY (<u>PropertyID</u>, PropertyName, PropertyType, Street, City, Zip, ServiceDate)

    and:

    SERVICE (<u>ServiceID</u>, *ServiceDate*, Description, Amount)

FIGURE 32

Sample Data for Garden Glory

PropertyName	Type	Street	City	ZIP	ServiceDate	Description	Amount
Eastlake Building	Office	123 Eastlake	Seattle	98119	5/5/2012	Lawn Mow	$ 42.50
Elm St Apts	Apartment	4 East Elm	Lynnwood	98223	5/8/2012	Lawn Mow	$ 123.50
Jeferson Hill	Office	42 West 7th St	Bellevue	98040	5/8/2012	Garden Service	$ 53.00
Eastlake Building	Office	123 Eastlake	Seattle	98119	5/10/2012	Lawn Mow	$ 42.50
Eastlake Building	Office	123 Eastlake	Seattle	98119	5/12/2012	Lawn Mow	$ 42.50
Elm St Apts	Apartment	4 East Elm	Lynnwood	98223	5/15/2012	Lawn Mow	$ 123.50
Eastlake Building	Office	123 Eastlake	Seattle	98119	5/19/2012	Lawn Mow	$ 42.50

8. PROPERTY (<u>PropertyID</u>, PropertyName, PropertyType, Street, City, Zip, *Service*)

and:

SERVICE (<u>ServiceID</u>, ServiceDate, Description, Amount, *PropertyID*)

9. PROPERTY (<u>PropertyID</u>, PropertyName, PropertyType, Street, City, Zip)

and:

SERVICE (<u>ServiceID</u>, ServiceDate, Description, Amount, PropertyID)

C. Suppose Garden Glory decides to add the following table:

SERVICE-FEE (PropertyID, ServiceID, Description, Amount)

Add this table to what you consider to be the best design in your answer to part B. Modify the tables from part B as necessary to minimize the amount of data duplication. Will this design work for the data in Figure 31? If not, modify the design so that this data will work. State the assumptions implied by this design.

JAMES RIVER JEWELRY PROJECT QUESTIONS

The James River Jewelry project questions are available in online Appendix D, which can be downloaded from the Web site: **www.pearsonhighered.com/kroenke**.

THE QUEEN ANNE CURIOSITY SHOP PROJECT QUESTIONS

Figure 33 shows typical sales data for the Queen Anne Curiosity Shop, and Figure 34 shows typical purchase data.

A. Using these data, state assumptions about functional dependencies among the columns of data. Justify your assumptions on the basis of these sample data and also on the basis of what you know about retail sales.

B. Given your assumptions in part A, comment on the appropriateness of the following designs:

1. CUSTOMER (<u>LastName</u>, FirstName, Phone, Email, InvoiceDate, InvoiceItem, Price, Tax, Total)

2. CUSTOMER (<u>LastName</u>, <u>FirstName</u>, Phone, Email, InvoiceDate, InvoiceItem, Price, Tax, Total)

3. CUSTOMER (LastName, FirstName, <u>Phone</u>, Email, InvoiceDate, InvoiceItem, Price, Tax, Total)

4. CUSTOMER (<u>LastName</u>, <u>FirstName</u>, Phone, Email, <u>InvoiceDate</u>, InvoiceItem, Price, Tax, Total)

5. CUSTOMER (<u>LastName</u>, <u>FirstName</u>, Phone, Email, InvoiceDate, <u>InvoiceItem</u>, Price, Tax, Total)

6. CUSTOMER (<u>LastName</u>, <u>FirstName</u>, Phone, Email)

and:

SALE (<u>InvoiceDate</u>, InvoiceItem, Price, Tax, Total)

7. CUSTOMER (<u>LastName</u>, <u>FirstName</u>, Phone, Email, *InvoiceDate*)

and:

SALE (<u>InvoiceDate</u>, InvoiceItem, Price, Tax, Total)

8. CUSTOMER (<u>LastName</u>, <u>FirstName</u>, Phone, Email, *InvoiceDate, InvoiceItem*)

and:

SALE (<u>InvoiceDate</u>, <u>Item</u>, Price, Tax, Total)

C. Modify what you consider to be the best design in part B to include surrogate ID columns called CustomerID and SaleID. How does this improve the design?

FIGURE 33

Sample Sales Data for The Queen Anne Curiosity Shop

LastName	FirstName	Phone	InvoiceDate	InvoiceItem	Price	Tax	Total
Shire	Robert	206-524-2433	14-Dec-12	Antique Desk	3,000.00	249.00	3,249.00
Shire	Robert	206-524-2433	14-Dec-12	Antique Desk Chair	500.00	41.50	541.50
Goodyear	Katherine	206-524-3544	15-Dec-12	Dining Table Linens	1,000.00	83.00	1,083.00
Bancroft	Chris	425-635-9788	15-Dec-12	Candles	50.00	4.15	54.15
Griffith	John	206-524-4655	23-Dec-12	Candles	45.00	3.74	48.74
Shire	Robert	206-524-2433	5-Jan-13	Desk Lamp	250.00	20.75	270.75
Tierney	Doris	425-635-8677	10-Jan-13	Dining Table Linens	750.00	62.25	812.25
Anderson	Donna	360-538-7566	12-Jan-13	Book Shelf	250.00	20.75	270.75
Goodyear	Katherine	206-524-3544	15-Jan-13	Antique Chair	1,250.00	103.75	1,353.75
Goodyear	Katherine	206-524-3544	15-Jan-13	Antique Chair	1,750.00	145.25	1,895.25
Tierney	Doris	425-635-8677	25-Jan-13	Antique Candle Holders	350.00	29.05	379.05

FIGURE 34

Sample Purchase Data for The Queen Anne Curiosity Shop

PurchaseItem	PurchasePrice	PurchaseDate	Vendor	Phone
Antique Desk	1,800.00	7-Nov-12	European Specialties	206-325-7866
Antique Desk	1,750.00	7-Nov-12	European Specialties	206-325-7866
Antique Candle Holders	210.00	7-Nov-12	European Specialties	206-325-7866
Antique Candle Holders	200.00	7-Nov-12	European Specialties	206-325-7866
Dining Table Linens	600.00	14-Nov-12	Linens and Things	206-325-6755
Candles	30.00	14-Nov-12	Linens and Things	206-325-6755
Desk Lamp	150.00	14-Nov-12	Lamps and Lighting	206-325-8977
Floor Lamp	300.00	14-Nov-12	Lamps and Lighting	206-325-8977
Dining Table Linens	450.00	21-Nov-12	Linens and Things	206-325-6755
Candles	27.00	21-Nov-12	Linens and Things	206-325-6755
Book Shelf	150.00	21-Nov-12	Harrison, Denise	425-746-4322
Antique Desk	1,000.00	28-Nov-12	Lee, Andrew	425-746-5433
Antique Desk Chair	300.00	28-Nov-12	Lee, Andrew	425-746-5433
Antique Chair	750.00	28-Nov-12	New York Brokerage	206-325-9088
Antique Chair	1,050.00	28-Nov-12	New York Brokerage	206-325-9088

D. Modify the design in part C by breaking SALE into two relations named SALE and SALE_ITEM. Modify columns and add additional columns as you think necessary. How does this improve the design?

E. Given your assumptions, comment on the appropriateness of the following designs:

    1. PURCHASE (<u>PurchaseItem</u>, PurchasePrice, PurchaseDate, Vendor, Phone) .

    2. PURCHASE (<u>PurchaseItem</u>, <u>PurchasePrice</u>, PurchaseDate, Vendor, Phone)

    3. PURCHASE (<u>PurchaseItem</u>, PurchasePrice, <u>PurchaseDate</u>, Vendor, Phone)

    4. PURCHASE (<u>PurchaseItem</u>, PurchasePrice, PurchaseDate, <u>Vendor</u>, Phone)

    5. PURCHASE (<u>PurchaseItem</u>, PurchasePrice, <u>PurchaseDate</u>)

and:

VENDOR (<u>Vendor</u>, Phone)

    6. PURCHASE (<u>PurchaseItem</u>, PurchasePrice, <u>PurchaseDate</u>,Vendor)

and:

VENDOR (<u>Vendor</u>, Phone)

    7. PURCHASE (<u>PurchaseItem</u>, PurchasePrice, <u>PurchaseDate</u>, *Vendor*)

and:

VENDOR (<u>Vendor</u>, Phone)

F. Modify what you consider to be the best design in part E to include surrogate ID columns called PurchaseID and VendorID. How does this improve the design?

G. The relations in your design from part D and part F are not connected. Modify the database design so that sales data and purchase data are related.

GLOSSARY

Attribute: (1) A value that represents a characteristic of an entity. (2) A column of a relation.

Boyce-Codd Normal Form (BCNF): A relation in third normal form in which every determinant is a candidate key.

Candidate key: An attribute or a group of attributes that identifies a unique row in a relation. One of the candidate keys is chosen to be the primary key.

Column: A logical group of bytes in a row of a relation or a table. The meaning of a column is the same for every row of the relation.

Composite key: A key of a relation that consists of two or more columns.

Database schema: A complete logical view of a database.

Determinant: One or more attributes that functionally determine another attribute or attributes. In the functional dependency $(A, B) \rightarrow D, C$, the attributes (A, B) are the determinant.

Entity: Something of importance to a user that needs to be represented in a database. In the entity-relationship model, entities are restricted to things that can be represented by a single table. *See also* **strong entity** and **weak entity**.

Field: (1) A logical group of bytes in a record used with file processing. (2) In the context of the relational model, a synonym for *attribute*.

First normal form (1NF): Any table that fits the definition of a relation.

Foreign key: An attribute that is a key of one or more relations other than the one in which it appears.

Functional dependency: A relationship between attributes in which one attribute or group of attributes determines the value of another. The expressions $X \rightarrow Y$, "X determines Y," and "Y is functionally dependent on X" mean that given a value of X, we can determine the value of Y.

Key: (1) A group of one or more attributes that identify a unique row in a relation. Because relations cannot have duplicate rows, every relation must have at least one key that is the composite of all the attributes in the relation. A key is sometimes called a logical key. (2) With some relational DBMS products, an index on a column used to improve access and sorting speed. It is sometimes called a physical key. *See also* **nonunique key**, **unique key**, and **physical key**.

Multivalued dependency: A condition in a relation with three or more attributes in which independent attributes appear to have relationships they do not have. Formally, in a relation R (A, B, C), having key (A, B, C) where A is matched with multiple values of B (or of C or of both), B does not determine C, and C does not determine B. An example is the relation EMPLOYEE (EmpNumber, EmpSkill, DependentName), where an employee can have multiple values of EmpSkill and DependentName. EmpSkill and DependentName do not have any relationship, but they do appear to in the relation.

Nonunique key: A key that potentially identifies more than one row.

Normalization process: The process of evaluating a relation to determine whether it is in a specified normal form and, if necessary, of converting it to relations in that specified normal form.

Null value: An attribute value that has never been supplied. Such values are ambiguous and can mean the value is unknown, the value is not appropriate, or the value is known to be blank.

Primary key: A candidate key selected to be the key of a relation. Uniquely identifies the records (rows) in a table (relation).

Record: (1) A group of fields pertaining to the same entity; used in file-processing systems. (2) In the relational model, a synonym for row and tuple. *See also* **row**.

Referential integrity constraint: A relationship constraint on foreign key values. A referential integrity constraint specifies that the values of a foreign key must be a proper subset of the values of the primary key to which it refers.

Relation: A two-dimensional array that contains single-value entries and no duplicate rows. The meaning of the columns is the same in every row. The order of the rows and columns is immaterial.

Row: A group of columns in a table. All the columns in a row pertain to the same entity. Also known as tuple or record.

Surrogate key: A unique, system-supplied identifier used as the primary key of a relation. The values of a surrogate key have no meaning to the users and usually are hidden on forms and reports.

Table: A database structure of rows and columns to create cells that hold data values. Also known as a *relation* in a relational database, although strictly only tables that meet specific conditions can be called relations. *See* **relation**.

Tuple: *See* **row**.

Unique key: A key that identifies a unique row.

Index